Do Conventions Matter?

Choosing National Party Leaders in Canada

JOHN C. COURTNEY

McGill-Queen's University Press
Montreal & Kingston • London • Buffalo

© McGill-Queen's University Press 1995
ISBN 0-7735-1357-4 (cloth)
ISBN 0-7735-1358-2 (paper)

Legal deposit fourth quarter 1995
Bibliothèque nationale du Québec

Printed in Canada on acid-free paper

This book has been published with the help of a grant from the Canadian Federation for the Humanities, using funds provided by the Social Sciences and Humanities Research Council of Canada and with support from the University of Saskatchewan Publication Fund.

McGill-Queen's University Press is grateful to the Canada Council for support of its publishing program.

Canadian Cataloguing in Publication Data

Courtney, John C.
Do conventions matter?: choosing national party leaders in Canada
Includes bibliographical references and index.
ISBN 0-7735-1357-4 (bound) –
ISBN 0-7735-1358-2 (pbk.)
1. Political conventions – Canada. 2. Political conventions – Canada – History. 3. Prime ministers – Canada – Selection and appointment.
4. Prime ministers – Canada – Selection and appointment – History. I. Title.
JL196.C68 1995   325.5'6'0971   C95-900650-8

This book was typeset by Typo Litho Composition Inc.
in 10/12 Baskerville.

Do Conventions Matter?
Choosing National Party Leaders in Canada

National leadership conventions in Canada attract widespread public interest but, with growing support for direct democracy and universal voting, may soon become a thing of the past. In *Do Conventions Matter?* John Courtney, a leading authority in the field, explores the party leadership selection process in an age of television-dominated politics and assesses its uncertain future.

Do Conventions Matter? provides a complete overview of national party conventions in Canada. Courtney describes national party conventions from 1919 to 1993, including the selection of Stanfield, Trudeau, Broadbent, Clark, Mulroney, Turner, McLaughlin, Chrétien, Campbell, and Manning. He compares leadership selection practices in Canada with those in the United States, Britain, and Australia, and shows that Canadian conventions remain a distinctive means of choosing party leaders.

Focusing on modern developments in the convention process, Courtney highlights changes in representation over the last thirty years, addresses criticisms about costs and delegate selection practices, and examines the role of the media. He concludes with an examination of the future of conventions in the context of Canadian democracy, given skyrocketing costs, the movement to reform political parties, and the push towards a universal membership vote. He argues convincingly that the objectives of greater representation and greater democracy explain both the emergence of our tradition of conventions to choose the leaders of federal parties and its possible demise in the near future.

JOHN C. COURTNEY is professor of political studies, University of Saskatchewan.

To my parents and to Helen

Contents

Diagrams, Tables, and Appendices

Preface

The Canadian general election of 25 October 1993 confirmed the old adage that nothing is carved in stone. At least not in politics. Canada's national party system was altered dramatically, possibly permanently, that day. The governing Conservatives had been defeated in unprecedented terms; a new majority Liberal government drew its overwhelming support from Ontario and the Atlantic provinces; the Tories and the NDP were both reduced to such small numbers that they lost their official party status in the House of Commons; and the two big winners with almost equal numbers on the opposition benches were regionally, but not nationally, based parties – the Bloc Québécois was drawn exclusively from Quebec, and the Reform party MPs were all, save one, elected in the four western provinces. The regionalized distribution of seats in the House of Commons disguised the more national electoral support that some parties, particularly the Conservatives and NDP, received. But that was scarcely a new feature of the Canadian representational equation. Only its magnitude was.

It was clearly a time to take stock – of parties, elections, the electoral system and, in my view at least, leadership conventions. All three national parties had been led in that election by new leaders (Kim Campbell, Jean Chrétien, and Audrey McLaughlin), all of whom had been selected in large national conventions by their respective parties. That two of them should have fared so badly was seen by some as a reflection of serious inadequacies in the convention system. Not long before, the Reform party had amended its constitution to ensure that Preston Manning's successor would be chosen, whenever that might be, by a direct, universal vote. Reform's electoral success in 1993 implied a measure of public endorsement for the party's commitment to the principle of direct democracy, especially its advocacy of one person, one vote. For their part, the Liberals only a year before the federal election had adopted a combined primary/convention system to select their future leaders. All these events came together at a time and in a way as to cast into doubt the future of national party leadership conventions as Canadians had known them for three-quarters of a century.

This book is my attempt at stock-taking of leadership conventions. Much of what follows had been at the back of my mind or on various scraps of paper for some time before the 1993 election. But it took that event, together with a sabbatical leave and the fortuitous arrival in my office earlier that year of a bright young honours student looking for work as a research assistant, to bring the whole exercise to fruition. Ryan Filson was that student. His dedication, knowledge of Canadian politics, and willingness to help in the collection and analysis of data meant that this book was finished far more expeditiously than it would have been otherwise. Our two-man "think tank North," which lasted for over a year, served as a reminder that a professor and a student sharing a common research interest can also, in the process, become the best of friends. My heartfelt thanks to Ryan for his invaluable assistance on this project.

A number of political scientists and convention and party organizers have generously read portions of this book. I am grateful for the time they have taken to offer suggestions or point the argument or analysis in a different direction. Some of their advice I have followed; some I have not. Nonetheless, the book's shortcomings can scarcely be laid at their feet. Colleagues from the University of Saskatchewan or from other universities or research institutes who have offered suggestions, answered questions or read some section of the book are Keith Archer, Peter Aucoin, Bill Bishopp, Henry Brady, Ken Carty, Darren Filson, Tom Flanagan, Fred Fletcher, Richard Johnston, Larry LeDuc, John Meisel, George Perlin, Ken Shepsle, Leslie Seidle, David Smith, Duff Spafford, David Stewart, Ian Stewart, Patrick Weller, and Alan Whitehorn. I am particularly indebted to Keith Archer of the University of Calgary and to George Perlin and his research associate, Bob Burge, of Queen's University for providing me with the data sets from their delegate surveys of recent national party conventions.

Senior party officials and convention organizers have similarly been very helpful in gathering factual information or in offering suggestions about the book. They are Iona Campagnola, Charles King, and Doug

Richardson of the Liberal party; Fraser Green and Bill Knight of the NDP; and Victor Bursall and Troy Tait of the Reform party. Nancy Jamieson and John Laschinger demonstrated, once again, their profound understanding of convention organizations and of political networking in the Conservative party. Tom Trbovich, former national director of the Progressive Conservative Party of Canada, and Penny Collenette, then acting national director of the Liberal Party of Canada, both granted unrestricted access to their respective party's convention papers in the National Archives of Canada. Those papers, from conventions dating between 1967 and 1990, were a treasure trove of information. Their existence reinforces the inestimable value of archival preservation of party records.

Since the mid-1980s I have received the full support of the University of Saskatchewan to pursue this project. It has come in the form of two sabbatical leaves and a leave-of-absence. For two of those years, one as a Visiting Scholar and one as the Mackenzie King Professor of Canadian Studies, I enjoyed the fellowship of the Government Department and the Center for International Affairs at Harvard University. Another six months was spent at the Hebrew University of Jerusalem where, under the generous sponsorship of the Halbert Centre for Canadian Studies, I served as a Visiting Professor. In all three universities I benefited from the helpful exchanges with professional colleagues and students as well as from departmental seminars where early, tentative versions of some of the chapters in this book were first presented. My department heads at Saskatchewan – first D.J. Heasman, then Hans Michelmann – were totally supportive of this project from the outset.

I was fortunate to have had superb short-term research assistance from graduate and undergraduate students at both Saskatchewan and Harvard: Gerry Baier, Jodi Cockerill, Jon Filson, Joanne Green, Karman Kawchuk, and Kathryn Stoner all worked on various aspects of the research that went into *Do Conventions Matter?* In addition to commenting on the chapter on conventions and the media, Murray Green lined up several CBC-TV contacts for data on audience size and viewership patterns. Ross Howard of the *Globe and Mail* provided me with otherwise unattainable information on convention financing and leadership campaign costs.

I can only express great appreciation to all who have helped to make this book possible. In addition to those named above, I must, of course, thank three institutions for their generous financial support of this project. The Department of the Secretary of State awarded me a Canadian Studies Writing Award which enabled the early stages of the research to get under way in the late 1980s. The Social Sciences and

Humanities Research Council of Canada provided a research grant which ensured that the principal information-gathering and data-analysing tasks could be carried out in the early 1990s. The University of Saskatchewan supplemented these two outside sources of support by awarding me a released-time grant in the early days of the project and by assisting the Department of Political Studies in the preparation of the manuscript in its final days.

One of the pleasures of writing a book in Canada, if one is lucky, is to be able to work with a legend of Canadian publishing, Diane Mew. Her deftness as a copy editor, her perceptive eye for inconsistencies, needless detail, and repetition, and her infectious sense of humour make the final stages of completing a manuscript a joy. I am thankful as well to Philip Cercone and Joan McGilvray who shepherded the book through McGill-Queen's University Press with great care and understanding.

None of this would have been as easily accomplished were it not for the characteristically unselfish support of my family. To them I owe my biggest debt of gratitude. The book may be dedicated to my parents and my wife, but it has in fact been written with my whole family in mind.

I want a hero: an uncommon want,
    When every year and month sends forth a new one,
Till, after cloying the gazettes with cant,
    The age discovers he is not the true one.
                              Byron, *Don Juan*

1 Introduction

Democracy is the recurrent suspicion that more than half of the people are right more than half of the time.

– E.B. White

Two headlines in the *Globe and Mail* in the months leading up to the Conservative leadership convention of 1993 said it all: "Old-fashioned convention expected," and "Tory leadership hopefuls playing old-style politics."[1] As the Tories prepared to meet that June, the process by which they were choosing Brian Mulroney's successor was being popularly described as "old-fashioned," "old-style," and "out-of-date." The picture painted by the media three years earlier when the Liberals chose Jean Chrétien had been much the same. The system used by Canadian parties for virtually the entire twentieth century was described as being outmoded and, by inference, near the end of its time. The cumulative effect of the abuses and excesses of national leadership contests in the previous two decades had taken its toll. Delegate recruitment practices and candidate organization tactics at the constituency level had presented the parties and the leadership hopefuls in a bad public light, and the skyrocketing and essentially uncontrolled costs of winning the leadership of one of the two older parties were widely condemned.

No matter that with each successive modern convention larger numbers of delegates had taken part in the exercise, or that the representational mix of delegates had broadened considerably over what it had been at the early national conventions. No matter that the general public's level of interest in and appetite for convention politics had increased measurably with the arrival in the late 1960s of high drama, multi-candidate, and multi-ballot contests. No matter that the media, and television in particular, treated the events as major political happenings, equivalent in their own way to intensely covered national elections. The day of national leadership conventions was seen as having come and gone; it would be only a matter of time before future leaders would be chosen by different means.

The siren call of direct democracy was beginning to be heard at the same time that party conventions were coming under attack. Indeed the latent, previously undiscovered appeal that direct, unmediated politics held for many was itself one of the reasons that conventions came to fall into disfavour. If conventions were being dismissed as undemocratic and unrepresentative (an irony given the reasons they initially were adopted) and costly, it was because the universal ballot was being seen as the alternative whereby every interested individual could participate directly and inexpensively in the selection of a party leader. Unmediated selections involving hundreds of thousands of individuals would be the ultimate democratic act in choosing leaders.

The possible end of national party conventions for choosing leaders raises a number of interrelated questions. What have Canadian parties done with the leadership convention, an institution they initially imported from the United States in the 1890s?[2] Who has been present to vote on the leadership on the convention floor? How were the participants chosen in the first place, and to whom, if anyone, have they been responsible? Who has run for and won the leadership of Canada's parties? What has it cost them in financial terms, and what kind of organizational networks have they drawn on and established in the process? How have the media handled national leadership conventions, and to what extent has the general public become involved, however vicariously, in the contest itself? What steps have the parties taken to hold their leaders accountable, and how have these altered the relationships among the leader, the parliamentary caucus, and the extra-parliamentary party? Have leadership conventions made a difference to Canadian politics? In fact, do conventions matter? The variety of questions shows how multifaceted an established political institution such as a leadership convention can be.

Great institutions, like great art, have many sides.[3] Accordingly, they are not easily or completely assessed or understood. Different people extract different meanings from them. They examine them with widely varying expectations and interpret them in various ways. At the obvious level this book is about party leadership: selecting, reviewing, and removing leaders by conventions in Canada. But at another level it is about representative politics, for in a curious but completely understandable way, Canadian conventions are also about representation. The centrality of the doctrine of representation helps to explain the origin of leadership conventions at the beginning of this century and the appeal of direct, universal voting on a party's leadership at its end.

To set the stage, the story of how Canadian national parties moved into leadership conventions bears repeating. When the Liberals met in 1919 they did so in the country's first national convention at which a leader would be chosen. Called at Laurier's request in the immediate aftermath of the First World War, the convention was seen by the aging Liberal leader as a way of rejuvenating Liberal spirits and organization. But his death just before the convention led party organizers to add leadership to the meeting's policy and organizational agenda.

Their move was prompted by representational concerns. The parliamentary caucus, which based on past tradition in the party would have selected Laurier's successor, was composed overwhelmingly of French-speaking, Roman Catholic MPs from Quebec. It was seen as "unrepresentative" of the larger Canadian population on the three principal social cleavages of the time region, religion, and language. It was deemed by party officials who wanted to widen the party's support base to be an inappropriate body to select a "national" leader – that is a leader of the whole country. The soon-to-be-held convention, composed of equal numbers of delegates from all federal constituencies, of parliamentarians, and various other federal and provincial party officials was seized upon as the ideal body to compensate for the representational inadequacies of the parliamentary party.

When, eight years later, the Tories met to choose a successor to Arthur Meighen, they followed suit and called their first national leadership convention. Their parliamentary caucus at the time was no less skewed than the Liberal one, but in a different direction. Made up almost exclusively of English-speaking Protestants from Ontario and the western provinces, the Conservative parliamentary group of 1927 was to its party what the Liberal parliamentarians had been to theirs when their party opted for a leadership convention. Legitimating the choice of leader of a national party meant convening a national convention. That both parties followed their respective convention by winning power in the next general election confirmed for party elites and activists the wisdom of having moved to the new, more representative institution for choosing leaders.

The size of the selecting body was larger than anything Canada had known before at the national level. Diagram 1-1 shows that from the early instances of selection of a prime minister (and, consequently, party leader) by a governor general in consultation with a few party notables, to the formal votes taken by opposition parliamentary parties on motions either of the retiring leader or of a caucus committee, no more than one hundred or so MPs, and typically far fewer, had been in-

Diagram 1-1
Growth in Number of Participants in Leadership Selection, 1867–1993:
Liberal and Conservative Parties

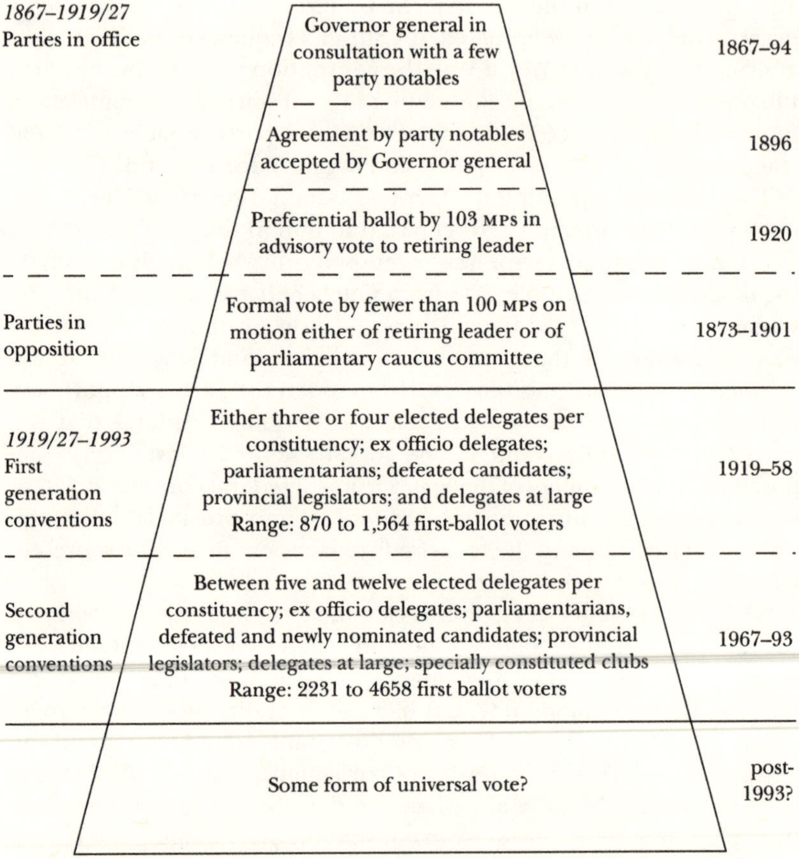

1867–1919/27 Parties in office	Governor general in consultation with a few party notables	1867–94
	Agreement by party notables accepted by Governor general	1896
	Preferential ballot by 103 MPs in advisory vote to retiring leader	1920
Parties in opposition	Formal vote by fewer than 100 MPs on motion either of retiring leader or of parliamentary caucus committee	1873–1901
1919/27–1993 First generation conventions	Either three or four elected delegates per constituency; ex officio delegates; parliamentarians; defeated candidates; provincial legislators; and delegates at large Range: 870 to 1,564 first-ballot voters	1919–58
Second generation conventions	Between five and twelve elected delegates per constituency; ex officio delegates; parliamentarians, defeated and newly nominated candidates; provincial legislators; delegates at large; specially constituted clubs Range: 2231 to 4658 first ballot voters	1967–93
	Some form of universal vote?	post-1993?

volved directly at any one time in the selection of a leader. These practices reflected a close reading in Canada of the nineteenth-century constitutional and political practices of Britain. As Henry Brady and Richard Johnston have noted: "Before 1919, Canada departed hardly at all from conventional British procedure of the time. The party in power left ultimate responsibility for the identification of its leader with the governor-general. The latter would naturally consult with party notables, and the canvassing of party opinion on the matter became more systematic as time passed. Parties in opposition, obviously, could not follow this route. For them, caucus selection became the norm."[4]

The break with those traditions came first on the national political scene in 1919. Following that, the next four decades of conventions saw the number of participants in the leadership selection process jump by up to fifteen times what it had been earlier. The arrival of the first of the modern conventions in 1967 brought with it another substantial increase in the number of participants, and gradually since then parties have brought ever more individuals into the process. The several thousand participants at the Liberal 1990 and Conservative 1993 conventions would have been inconceivable by earlier standards.

Each successive increase has invariably been described by party officials and rank-and-file political activists as a democratizing move. Thus the twin pillars of support on which national conventions were built over the course of the twentieth century have been representational and democratic. Mies van der Rohe's pronouncement about the basic requirement of great modern architecture, to the effect that less is more, has had no application to national party conventions in Canada. More was more, plain and simple. The move from caucus to convention introduced and then nurtured a democratic and representational ethic in Canadian politics from which clearly there could be no turning back. If, in turn, conventions are destined to give way to a yet wider electorate voting directly on party leadership, as seems increasingly likely as the century draws to a close, the cause for the change can be laid at the feet of conventions. They will have been found wanting on democratic and representational grounds – the very reason they were adopted in the first place.

2 Two Generations of Leadership Conventions

Slight causes often have profound effects.

– Wallace Stegner

For the better part of this century, Canadian political leaders have been chosen by their parties in convention. Grounded firmly in representational and democratic theory, this institution has grown and changed from its first to its second generations – from roughly the end of the First World War to the early 1960s, and from the 1960s on. The basic election rules for determining the eventual winner have changed little, but virtually all other aspects of conventions in the late twentieth century would be unrecognizeable to participants in the early contests. The number of candidates and delegates has increased dramatically; so has the number of ballots needed to declare a winner. The influence of parliamentarians over delegates and over the choice made by the convention has diminished, only to be replaced by an enhanced role for experts in modern communications and political organization. Costs of conventions and of conducting serious campaigns have sky-rocketed. But more than any other feature of second generation conventions, television has given an immediacy to leadership selection and has played a dominant role both in shaping the contest and in planning the convention itself.

GETTING UNDER WAY, 1919–61

The Twin Pillars

The year 1919 was a pivotal one in Canadian party politics. It was the first occasion on which a national party held a convention to choose its leader. The Liberals had not planned it that way. Wilfrid Laurier, then in his thirty-second year as leader, was instrumental at the close of the First World War in having a call go out to the rank and file to attend a national convention in Ottawa to plan policy and organization, just as they had at the immensely successful Liberal policy convention held in 1893. It was Laurier's hope that it would heal the wounds (or at least paper over the deep cracks) in the party caused by the conscription issue and the wartime election. But between the time of issuing the call (November 1918) and the meeting itself (August 1919), Laurier unexpectedly died.

From Confederation on, parties in opposition had entrusted the selection of their leader to the members of the parliamentary wing of the party.[1] That would almost certainly have been the case with the Liberals in choosing a successor to Laurier were it not for the deep divisions within the party resulting from the conscription election of 1917 and the absence of any widely acceptable heir apparent in the caucus itself. The Unionists, composed of Liberals who had broken with Laurier in 1917 to join Borden's governing Conservatives, looked destined to remain coalesced in office until at least the time of the next election. The Liberals who had remained loyal to Laurier occupied the opposition benches, but overwhelmingly they were French-speaking Roman Catholics from the province of Quebec.

The Laurier Liberals were mindful of their leader's reflection in 1916 on his own recent, unhappy experiences with religious bigotry, that it had been "a mistake for a French Roman Catholic to take the leadership" of the Liberal party because of the strength of "the forces of prejudice in Ontario."[2] These MPs saw the only hope for future electoral success with a party united around a Protestant leader from a province other than Quebec. Just as Edward Blake had successfully pressed his parliamentary colleagues to choose Laurier as his successor in 1887 in order to widen the party's appeal among Quebeckers, so the party in 1919 shared the view that the man who would succeed Laurier "should be an English-speaking Protestant" from outside Quebec.[3] The Liberal practice of alternating leaders between Quebeckers and non-Quebeckers was taking root. As we will see, much would be said and written about the "alternation principle" in future leadership contests.

There was no obvious successor to Laurier in 1919 in the Liberal caucus. Sixty-two of the eighty-two Laurier Liberals returned to Parliament in the election two years earlier were Quebeckers. W.S. Fielding, Laurier's parliamentary colleague and friend for many years, would doubtless have been acceptable to a number of Liberals. Yet Fielding was *persona non grata* with the Quebec MPs for his abandonment of Laurier over conscription in 1917. As they canvassed the other possibilities (G.P. Graham, W.M. Martin, and William Lyon Mackenzie King), the party's leading organizers recognized that there was a distinct possibility that the new leader would not at the time of selection be an MP, for of the possible leaders mentioned only one, Fielding, had a seat in Parliament.

In the circumstances, what better way of choosing the new leader than by the national convention already called to discuss policy and organization? The Liberal caucus adopted the recommendation of a five-member subcommittee to revise the purposes of the forthcoming convention to include that of choosing the new party leader. For the first time the extra-parliamentary wing of a national political party in Canada, the majority of which would be made up of constituency delegates, was being invited to take part in the selection of the party's new leader. In putting out the official, but modified, call for the August 1919 convention, the caucus indicated that it was willing to abdicate its unquestioned role in choosing Laurier's successor in favour of a large "democratic and representative" convention of the party.

No voices of opposition were raised at the time by Liberals or by the press to transferring the authority for leadership selection from the parliamentary to the extra-parliamentary party. Fielding, knowing he had little support within caucus, had nothing to lose from the change. Nor did other possible leaders, such as Mackenzie King, who lacked a seat in the Commons. Riding associations and provincial Liberal parties, all of whom would be entitled to send delegates to the Ottawa convention, would scarcely reject the opportunity to exercise some influence over the choice of their party's national leader. The fact that a few provincial party leaders had themselves been chosen at conventions could only reinforce the change in process.

From the turn of the century to 1919, conventions of some form or another had been held in every province, except Quebec, by various provincial parties to choose their leaders. No firm pattern had yet been established in the provinces, as caucuses, retiring leaders, party executives, and lieutenant-governors were still often used to choose new leaders. In 1919 provincial leadership conventions were more the exception than the rule, though they had become the accepted means of selecting leaders in the four western provinces, no doubt as a consequence of the more populist-democratic and American influences in that part of the country. (For the Liberal leadership conventions from 1919 to 1958 see tables 2-1 to 2-3.)

For their part, the Conservatives held Canada's second national leadership convention in 1927 under circumstances not dissimilar to those of the Liberals nine years earlier. Out of office at the time, the Conservatives were also leaderless in Parliament. Arthur Meighen, party leader since 1920, had been defeated in the 1926 general election. By the time they held their convention the Conservatives had been in opposition for all but three months of the previous six years, having failed to gain or to retain power in the elections of 1921, 1925, and 1926. Without a single French-speaking Canadian elected from Quebec in the three previous elections, the Conservatives in Parliament were even less representative of the country as a whole than the Liberals had been at the time of Laurier's death. The Tories were mindful of the need to address that problem, but without a credible Quebecker in the national party or in Quebec's undistinguished provincial party, they had no realistic alternative but to chose Meighen's successor from among their English-speaking contingent. The party's parliamentary party met shortly after the 1926 election, and with Meighen's resignation as leader in hand it adopted a resolution calling for a convention to be held at the earliest possible date to chose a new leader.

The Conservatives had, up to 1927, never held a national convention such as the one convened by Laurier in 1893. Without that experience to draw on, they were navigating uncharted waters. Nonetheless, they were able to draw on the recent experience of the provincial Tory parties, a number of which had chosen their leaders by way of a convention. Of these the most significant was in 1920 when the Ontario Liberal-Conservatives (as the party then styled itself) chose their new leader, G. Howard Ferguson, in convention. The party adopted an important resolution at that convention committing the provincial party to select its future leaders by way of a convention summoned specifically for that purpose.

The Tories could not ignore the precedent set by the opposition Liberals in 1919. In Meighen's words, "If the Liberals had formed the Government in 1919 instead of being in Opposition, the Parliamentary group would have chosen the leader. The adoption of the convention by the Liberals for the purpose of selecting a new leader *compelled* the Conservatives to follow the same method when in Opposition."[4]

The Liberals had held their convention at the very time a political party has all of the disadvantages of being out of power. But as frequently happens with intra-party reforms, it is the party in opposition that is more willing to take the risks and to chart the new course than the party in office. So it was in 1919, and again in 1927. That both parties then went on to electoral victory in the subsequent general election (the Liberals in 1921 and the Conservatives in 1930) could only reinforce the virtually unquestioned wisdom of changing the way that national party leaders were chosen. Electoral success was its own reward. (For the Conservative leadership conventions from 1927 to 1956, see tables 2-4 to 2-8.)

What is clear from the 1919 and 1927 experiences is that Canada's two oldest parties embarked on a new course for choosing their leaders at the federal level principally to overcome the representational inadequacies of their respective parliamentary parties. This closely paralleled the experience a century earlier of American parties who replaced the representationally inadequate congressional caucuses with more broadly based national nominating conventions as agents charged with the task of choosing presidential candidates. Had it not been for the unrepresentativeness of the parliamentary party in its regional, linguistic, and religious composition, it is not entirely certain that Canadian national parties would have moved to adopt conventions as vehicles for choosing leaders when they did.

Additionally, the declaration by officials in both parties that a convention was a more democratic way of choosing a party leader than entrusting that task to a small elite in Parliament carried great weight with party organizers anxious to appeal to an expanding electorate, to elected delegates enjoying their newly acquired status within the party, and to the press reporting political events to an increasingly diverse public. It would be no accident in 1993 that Gerry St Germain, president of the Progressive Conservative Party of Canada, chose to refer to his party's leadership contest of that year as the "most open, democratic and representative" in its history.[5] He was the latest in a long line of party officials in both the Conservative and Liberal parties to have invoked those terms. They had become firmly established as part of the Canadian political lexicon decades before the Tories met to choose Brian Mulroney's successor.

Generational Characteristics

Canada's earliest national leadership conventions, beginning after the First World War and ending with those of the late 1950s and early 1960s, shared a number of common features. These derived from the practices and customs of parties coming to grips with a new process for choosing their leaders. In large measure these features now have an historical quality about them, for it cannot be said that they define leadership conventions of the second, or post-1967, generation.

In the early period a party in convention amounted to little more than an extension of the parliamentary party and, at that, of only a relatively small number of influential MPs and senators – the old guard. Working in concert with party notables and organizers, MPs and senators figured prominently in their respective parties' national conventions for the period from 1919 to 1958. They played key roles in planning and organizing conventions, overseeing policy debates, writing policy reports, choosing constituency delegates, and influencing the selection of the new leader. Theirs was a hands-on approach to party affairs, one that matched their status within the caucus or, as the case may be, the cabinet.

The Conservative party failed to win power in all but one of the nine elections between 1921 and 1957. As often happens with parties out of office for prolonged stretches, they took to fighting among themselves over policy, organization, and leadership, thereby worsening any chances they might have had of earning widespread public support and of gaining power. Beginning in 1927 with their first convention, the Tories held no fewer than five national leadership conventions over the next thirty years and selected a sixth leader at a special meeting of the parliamentary caucus and national executive.[6] Nonetheless, little of this denied senior parliamentarians and party officials the principal role in ensuring the selection (and in the case of R.J. Manion in 1940 the abrupt removal) of a favoured candidate as leader. This was true of R.B. Bennett's selection in 1927, billed by party notables as the most obvious way of revitalizing the party in western Canada; of Manion's election in 1938, portrayed as a way of attracting Quebec support because of his Roman Catholicism and his French-speaking wife; of John Bracken's victory in 1942, the result of Arthur Meighen's plan to bring a proven vote-getter from the provincial to the federal arena and to expand the party's support base to include western "Progressives"; and of George Drew's selection in 1948, seen as a way of capitalizing on the Ontario premier's electoral strength in his home province and his warm relations with Maurice Duplessis and the Union Nationale in Quebec.[7]

Only John Diefenbaker's selection in 1956 proved to be the exceptional case in this first generation of leadership conventions. Opposed by virtually all of the party and parliamentary establishment, Diefenbaker combined his overwhelming support among backbench MPs (by one account estimated at roughly 80 per cent) with his widespread populist appeal to party activists in all regions of the country save Quebec. As Diefenbaker himself later acknowledged, the 1956 convention "saw a real and effective determination" by the rank and file to be represented, rather than to have "the leadership determined by a small clique who, having control over the Party machinery and the operation of conventions, had been able, in earlier conventions, to direct or at least to guide the delegates, by various means, to the object of their choice."[8]

Diefenbaker ushered in a new way of gaining a party's leadership, an example emulated successfully in some later leadership campaigns. He effectively bypassed the senior party officials and parliamentarians opposed to his gaining the leadership (a group that included the party's national president, the retiring leader, the acting leader in the Commons, and all but two or three of the Tory frontbenchers in the

House), making his pitch instead to "the little people" and to "average Canadians." By winning the support of delegates at the constituency level, he managed to pressure Tory backbenchers into giving him their convention vote. Support for Diefenbaker among Conservative MPs became a matter of personal political survival: "My people are for John," one of them explained in 1956. "If I were to oppose him I'd probably lose the nomination and I'd certainly lose the election."9 Diefenbaker's first ballot victory carried with it a powerful message for a party's old guard: it was possible to win without them.

For their part, the Liberals chose only half the number of leaders in the first forty years of national conventions as the Tories: Mackenzie King in 1919, Louis St Laurent in 1948, and Lester Pearson in 1958. As the governing party for almost that whole period, the Liberals were able to avoid many of the pitfalls, occasional pratfalls, and damaging quarrels over leadership and policy that became the trademark of their principal opponents. There was certainly little doubt about the extent to which the most influential men of the party, especially the senior ministers in the cabinets of Mackenzie King and St Laurent, controlled the affairs of the party. Even the retiring leader could play a significant role in ensuring a leadership transition to his preferred choice as successor, as was the case with Mackenzie King in 1948. Determined to have St Laurent chosen to succeed him, King intervened on the eve of the convention with a plan to have six prominent Liberals (including C.D. Howe, Douglas Abbott, and Paul Martin) nominated for the leadership then withdraw moments before the balloting began, informally indicating their support for St Laurent. All six dutifully went along with their retiring leader's proposal.10

Confident that the support of the principal figures of the party would translate into votes from delegates at the conventions themselves, the front runners for the Liberal leadership did little to promote their own candidacies. Mackenzie King wrote an acquaintance less than two weeks before his success at the 1919 convention that he had been "most careful to avoid even the appearance of attempting to influence, either directly or indirectly, the choice of Leader of the Liberal Party."11 King's example was later followed by St Laurent who, according to his biographer, "had not lifted a finger in his own behalf" to win the Liberal leadership on the first ballot in 1948.12 For his part, Pearson found his first ballot win in 1958 "an easy one for me. Indeed, it was no contest, in the sense that I made few personal appeals, by canvass, letter, or visit."13 Judged by today's standards of candidate activity in soliciting support on their own behalf, such non-involvement by the leading candidates is as anachronistic as it is surprising.

So far as delegate selection was concerned, constituency executives of both parties were known to have appointed delegates without any semblance of an election when it suited their purposes. Sometimes they even appointed themselves. As recently as 1956, Progressive Conservative provincial executives, with the approval of the convention executive committee, could name riding delegates and alternates in the absence of a local constituency association. MPs and local party executives played a vastly more important role in choosing delegates to attend party conventions and in directing their voting behaviour than is now the case. With or without local elections, the sitting MP could be sufficiently powerful to choose singlehandedly all the constituency delegates. The Liberals' renowned Quebec organizer, Chubby Power, relates in his memoirs how those handpicked delegates would "reflect his [the MP's] views and vote as he direct[ed]."[14] Today's parliamentarians know little of such deferential behaviour on the part of local party activists when it comes to selecting delegates for national conventions, and amendments to party constitutions designed to guarantee constituency elections of delegates are now enforced by the parties themselves.

Exact costs of leadership campaigns of individual candidates have never been easy to obtain regardless of the period of Canadian history. Nonetheless, it is fair to say that the costs of seeking the leadership of a party in the pre-1967 period were barely a fraction of those since. At most, candidates and their organizers from 1919 to the early 1960s would have raised and spent a few thousand dollars. By modern standards campaigns were short, typically a few weeks at most. They did not involve expensive cross-country tours, teams of experts, advisers and organizers, lavish entertainment, expensive floor demonstrations, sophisticated telecommunications and computer networks, and other features of recent conventions. Instead, a few hundred signs, buttons, and hats for the convention floor itself were generally the most that candidates' organizations would have had to buy, and at that only in the later conventions of the 1940s and 1950s.[15]

Walter Gordon, who was instrumental in persuading Lester Pearson to seek the Liberal leadership in 1958, gave an account, astonishing by today's standards, of the absence of political organization and the miniscule funds raised in support of Pearson's campaign. It is worth quoting in full for the picture it paints of campaign preparedness and costs at the end of the first generation of leadership conventions:

I [called Pearson] up *a few days* before [the convention] and [said], "What are you doing? Because while you'll probably win it, you aren't going to win it by all that much unless you do something." He said he wasn't doing anything, so I went down to Ottawa that night and said, "Where are your headquarters?" "Haven't got any." "Who's your manager?" "Haven't got one." "Where's your money?" "Haven't any money." So that was that.

There was Pearson, Mary Macdonald [Pearson's secretary], and myself in this little room, or office, I suppose, and none of us knew anything about politics. Mike [Pearson] had been in government for eight or nine years, but he didn't know much about the political side of it. We got a suite at the Chateau [Laurier]. That was our headquarters. Everybody was coming in from all over. They would rush in and say, "What do you want us to do?" and I would say to them, knowing nothing about it, "What do you think you can do best?" and they would say – and I would say, "Just what we want you to do," and away they would go and do it.

We didn't have any money, apart from only about $3,000.[16]

Such casualness and apparent indifference, whether studied or genuine, might be explained as a luxury an unquestioned front runner could indulge in. (Pearson won easily on the first ballot with 78 per cent of the vote.) But it was no different with his only serious opponent, Paul Martin, who later described the contest as having been "friendly and low-key." In Martin's words, his organization, like Pearson's, was "fairly rudimentary." It began contacting delegates barely three weeks before the convention with Martin's chief organizer admitting that he was "pretty proud" of Pearson and that it was impossible "to say anything bad about him."[17] The Pearson-Martin contest is testimony to the extent to which campaign organization, tactics, and financing have since undergone dramatic changes.

The first generation of leadership conventions drew to a close with the founding convention of the New Democratic Party in 1961. As will be seen, CCF and NDP conventions have been different in a number of significant respects from those of the two older parties, including their frequency and their structural and representational components. In other ways, however, the NDP convention of 1961, at which T.C. Douglas was chosen leader, was similar to those held by the Liberal and Conservative parties between 1919 and 1958. It was smaller than later conventions and its leader was chosen on a single ballot by a three-to-one margin over one other opponent. As had been the case with the other parties, the NDP relied on a leadership convention to approve overwhelmingly the choice of the established, senior figures within the CCF/NDP and the allied trade unions. (For the 1961 NDP convention see table 2-9.)

It was also true of the NDP in 1961 that the man chosen as leader had fewer years of parliamentary experience than his principal opponent. For the older parties, an additional pattern had been established between 1919 and 1958 of favouring as leader a candidate with less cabinet experience (in some cases none at all) than others running in the race. Indeed, five of the nine leaders chosen in the first generation (King, Manion, Bracken, Drew, and Douglas) were not even MPs when selected, all but King and Manion serving as provincial premiers at the time. With rare exceptions (notably David Lewis in 1971 and Jean Chrétien in 1990), these features of leadership selection were to be repeated throughout the second generation of conventions. With conventions, leadership career routes changed markedly from the earlier pre-convention period when parliamentary and cabinet experience at the federal level were judged to be essential qualifications for party leadership.

THE "MORE" GENERATION: 1967–93

Representational Changes

Three features of the first generation of leadership conventions stand out as common to all three of Canada's older parties. Compared to the more recent conventions, the earlier ones had half the delegates, half the candidates, and required far fewer ballots to decide the winner. The nine national conventions held up to 1961 averaged 1,317 delegates, 3.8 candidates, and 1.6 ballots per convention, whereas the ten held since 1967 have averaged 2,722 voting delegates, 7.4 candidates, and 3.4 ballots.[18] Over half of the first generation's conventions were decided on one ballot (five of the nine) and only one (1919) went beyond two ballots. Of the ten conventions since 1967, only one (1990) has been decided on a single ballot. Six of them took four ballots and one went to five ballots before a leader was chosen. (For the Liberal, Progressive Conservative, and New Democratic Party leadership conventions from 1967 to 1993, see tables 2-10 to 2-19.) These data confirm that increased opportunities for intra-party competition lead to increased competition. They may also imply a greater degree of intra-party factionalization in the second than in the first generation of leadership conventions. It would have been inconceivable for the governing Liberals to have had nine candidates seeking the leadership (as they did in 1968 when Pierre Trudeau won with 51 per cent of the vote on the fourth ballot) in one of their earlier conventions when the party leadership effectively controlled the transitions and successfully avoided public confrontations over policies and personalities.

The differences between the first and the second generation of leadership conventions reflect the fundamental representational changes that the Tories and the Liberals have made to their conventions since the mid-1960s. The moves begun in 1919 and 1927 to correct for the regional imbalances by opening up leadership selection to the party's non-parliamentary wing ultimately brought to an end the dominant role of the parliamentary party in the selection of leaders. The change is seen in no more obvious way than in the relative numerical importance of the parliamentary party in the convention itself in each of the two stages of convention development. In 1919 the eighty-five Liberal MPs, who previously would have constituted almost the entire body choosing a new leader, accounted for only 7.5 per cent of that year's convention. But with the passage of time the MPs' share of the total number of delegates continued to diminish, so much so that by 1990 the eighty-two Liberal members made up barely 1.5 per cent of the delegates to that leadership convention.

Gone as well are the days when MPs singlehandedly influenced the selection of and the electoral behaviour of constituency delegates. In their place are candidate organizers whose energy, skills, and resources are suited to that specific task. The world of Chubby Power has been displaced by networks of extra-parliamentary professionals and organizers: experts in media communications and surveys, advisers on local organization, and technicians and managers for constituency delegate selection meetings and convention floor logistics. No serious candidate would stand a chance of winning without them. MPs and constituency delegates who have attended recent national conventions have confirmed that an MP can be incidental to, if not ineffectual in, the local delegate selection process and in "delivering the local vote" to a preferred candidate.[19]

The growth in the numbers of participants in the second generation of leadership conventions is largely a product of the increase in the number of elected constituency delegates and the growth in the number of parliamentary seats. Between 1919 and 1990, when the number of constituencies went from 235 to 295, the size of the riding delegations in the Liberal party, for example, jumped fourfold from three to twelve. As well, new socio-demographic categories of convention delegates have gradually been added by all parties, particularly since the end of the Second World War. Typically these have included provincial and national women's and youth organizations, university clubs, and most recently in the Liberal party, aboriginal clubs. By 1990 in Calgary, when Jean Chrétien was chosen in the party's first leadership convention outside Ottawa, no fewer than twenty different categories of delegates were eligible to attend the convention. At the Tory convention in 1993, at which Kim Campbell was elected leader, the equivalent number was twenty-four.

In admittedly varying degrees, each of these groups has its own responsibilities, membership, interests, and authority structure, which means that the views of its members will not always match those of the parliamentarians or the party establishment. In his analysis of a party's reciprocal deference structure, Samuel Eldersveld has shown that as a party's membership and its sub-coalitional system becomes more heterogeneous, centralized control over the membership becomes "not only difficult but unwise."[20] Modern national leadership conventions in Canada fit Eldersveld's description. The growth in the variety of groups (the heterogeneous sub-coalitions) entitled to delegate status at national conventions has had the effect of dispersing power within the parties, of making the membership less deferential to its parliamentary party, and of lessening the control of the parliamentary wing over the direction of the party's affairs. The struggle within the Conservative party in 1966–7 over John Diefenbaker's leadership, leading directly to a leadership convention against the wishes of the leader and the majority of MPs and eventually to the party's adoption of "leadership review" provisions in its constitution, serves as the classic instance of these altered intra-party relationships that have come to characterize the second generation of conventions.[21]

The Rules of the Game

As we have seen, there were features of the first generation of leadership conventions that are no longer part of the process or that have, as with representation, adapted to changing times. But with respect to the procedural characteristics of choosing the leader, the rules governing the election of the leader have survived largely unchanged in their broad outline from the first to the second generation. On the other hand, rules governing the nomination of candidates have been modified to take into account concerns that all parties have shared from the outset of the second generation of conventions.

Election rules. The basic principles followed in the election of the leader have been in place since 1919. The rules derived from those principles have been simple and straightforward, and as will be seen in chapter 10, they have played the essential role of defining the framework within which convention floor coalition-building has taken place. Although particulars have varied from party to party, it is fair to generalize that for all national leadership conventions, voting is both secret and individual; balloting continues until a winner is declared with a simple majority of the valid votes cast on the final ballot; and the candidate with the lowest number of votes on each ballot is eliminated from the race.

Canadian leadership conventions have never tried any of the systems used in the United States, such as open or declared voting, roll-call voting, a unit rule, or a two-thirds rule. Delegates to Canadian conventions, subject as they are to intense pressure from various quarters to support particular candidates, vote individually and in the privacy of a polling booth. The example was set in 1919 when, for reasons that were never explained, the committee organizing the first national leadership convention decided in favour of the individual secret ballot. It is conceivable that the Liberal convention committee of 1919 rejected a convention floor roll-call vote by province (such as was used in American conventions) for fear of splitting the convention on a pro-Quebec and anti-Quebec basis. It was likely that the entire Quebec delegation would support a candidate who had remained loyal to Laurier in 1917. Given the strong support for Fielding (who had broken with Laurier over conscription) in other parts of the country, the committee might well have felt that a roll-call vote would be too damaging to party unity. Whatever the reason, the decision was made to adopt a secret, individual ballot, something most delegates would be both familiar with and favourably disposed towards as a result of federal and provincial elections.

For the Liberal and Conservative conventions from 1919 to 1958, delegates were issued small booklets of ballots numbered for successive votes. Remaining seated during the voting, the delegates wrote the name of one candidate per ballot when successive votes were called and deposited the ballot in boxes passed to them by the election officials. The NDP has continued to use such a system up to and including the 1989 convention, even though some delegates have commented on the extent to which it effectively denies them a genuinely secret ballot.[22]

Beginning with the Tories in 1967, delegates at conventions of both major parties have voted individually at pre-assigned, numbered voting booths. Organizers of the Liberal convention in 1968 briefly considered requiring delegates to be seated either around their preferred candidate ("to facilitate maximum ease of communication by candidates") or by province. Both possibilities were rejected on the grounds that they "would be extremely difficult to police" and that they implied an unacceptable "regimentation of free Canadian citizens who have come to perform a democratic function."[23]

Electronic voting machines were first used by the Conservatives in 1967, and the Liberals followed suit the next year with an IBM "Votomatic." Because of technical difficulties with the machines and problems experienced by some delegates in using them, there were delays in voting and counting of ballots in 1967. After 1968, both parties reverted to written, hand-counted ballots. Organizers of the 1993 Conservative convention, claiming that it would reduce the time needed to elect the leader, opted to return to machine voting. They used the latest in voting technology, a special voting card similar to a lottery ticket counted by computer scanning. The evidence suggests that the Tories' claim about speeded up voting in 1993 is open to question. The 1967 experiment, in an exceedingly hot and humid Maple Leaf Gardens in Toronto, took the 2,200 voting delegates five ballots to elect Robert Stanfield. In all, it lasted seven hours. By contrast, the 3,500 delegates voting in 1993 at the Tory convention, in Ottawa's equally hot and humid Civic Centre, needed only two ballots to elect Kim Campbell as leader. But from the start of that vote to the final announcement, the whole exercise took five hours.

Voting is not only secret and individual at Canada's party conventions. It is also continuous until one candidate with at least 50 per cent plus one of the valid votes cast is declared the winner. Long adjournments between ballots (possibly lasting overnight) are unknown in Canada. The organizers of the 1976 Tory convention considered, but rejected, a proposal from the chairman of the convention's program and agenda committee to hold the first ballot on a Saturday evening and the second and subsequent ballots on the following afternoon and evening. Supporters of such a split-ballot proposal argued that delegates could review their perceptions of the candidates "in a calmer, more reflective atmosphere and over a longer period of time," instead of making "instant decisions in the chaotic atmosphere of the convention floor." Those opposed to the idea included eleven of the thirteen candidates then in the race and the majority of the convention organizing committee. They rejected it on the grounds that it would lead to "negative media coverage," that the press "would focus on 'machine-type' or 'backroom' politics," and that "the split-ballot would hurt the party by accentuating regional or ideological splits."[24] The claims made on both sides of the issue amounted to a replay of an earlier debate in the political science literature, which suggests, but does not confirm, that debates among academics can occasionally influence political discourse.[25]

The operative principle about convention voting common to all three parties has a Calvinist ring about it. As delegates have been brought together from across the country and charged with the responsibility of choosing a leader, they are expected to stick to the task without unnecessary delays until one has been elected. The 1993 Conservative rule on this aspect of voting, in which thirty minutes was set aside between the announcement of the results of one ballot and the start of the next one, is typical of those adopted by the other parties in recent conventions. The rule was based on the presumption that delegates are able to make rational choices in short order in a highly charged, dynamic atmosphere.

In contrast to American nominating conventions, Canadian parties have all adopted rules whereby low candidates are automatically eliminated from the race. As of 1992, the Liberals placed that requirement in their constitution.[26] In the first generation, practices varied from one convention to another, ranging from elimination of the candidate with the fewest votes after the second ballot to after the fourth ballot.[27] Since the Conservative convention in 1967 all parties have applied the rule that the candidate with the fewest votes on any ballot is eliminated from the race. In more recent conventions all three parties have introduced a further hurdle. Depending on the party, all candidates who did not receive a minimum number of votes per ballot have been automatically eliminated from the race.[28] If all candidates passed that minimum, then the rule of eliminating the low candidate applied.

Nomination rules. Since the beginning of national leadership conventions in Canada one rule governing nominations has remained unchanged: once voting is under way no new candidates can be nominated and previously defeated candidates cannot be renominated. This stands in marked contrast to earlier American national nominating conventions which permitted, even encouraged, that practice as a way of avoiding or breaking voting deadlocks among state delegations on the convention floor.[29] The proverbial smoke-filled rooms were a product of such a system of inter-elite bargaining among state party notables anxious to advance their own interests with blocks of votes to deliver or to withhold. As Canadian leadership conventions were never designed to encourage such practices, it was natural that the early convention organizers gave no serious thought to opting for a nomination system designed to solve a problem they were not about to create. They preferred instead to subscribe to the view that if one wanted to compete for the leadership of a party one had to be in from the start of the voting.

Other regulations governing nominations have been changed in response to the concerns of party organizers to the more open, publicized, and competitive conventions of the second generation. Until the 1980s the two older parties had permitted nominations of candidates to be made either on the day of, or in some cases on the day or two before, the actual vote on the leadership at the convention. This was in keeping with the claim the parties liked to make of being open and free of arbitrary barriers that might discourage potential candidates. From the Liberal convention of 1919 to the Conservative one of 1956, nomination papers needed to be signed by only two delegates.[30] Starting shortly thereafter the number gradually increased, from ten delegates accredited to the Liberal convention of 1958 to one hundred (at least five of whom were from each region of the country) at the Conservative convention of 1993.[31] Amendments adopted to the Liberal constitution in 1992 specified that in future leadership conventions candidates' nomination papers "shall bear the signatures of not less than 300 members of the Liberal Party of Canada, numbering at least one hundred from each of three different provinces or territories."[32] Nomination deadlines have been changed as well. Beginning with the Conservative convention of 1983, and followed by the Liberal ones of 1984 and 1990, the deadline for the nomination of candidates was set at two weeks before the opening of the convention. For the 1993 Tory convention the deadline date was advanced by an additional week.[33]

A financial constraint on nominations was first introduced in 1976 when the Conservatives required a "good faith" deposit of $500 from all nominated candidates.[34] The other two national parties soon followed suit. The amounts have varied from a registration fee of $2,500 for NDP candidates in 1989, to $5,000 and $10,000 good faith deposit for Tory candidates in 1983 and 1993 respectively, to a $25,000 bond for Liberal candidates in both 1984 and 1990. The parties have refunded the deposit to any candidate receiving a minimum number of votes on the first ballot or withdrawing before a specified date. The lowest and highest first ballot hurdles to be overcome for a refund of the deposit have been fifty votes (as in the Conservative convention of 1993) and seventy-five votes (as with the NDP in 1989 and the Liberals in 1990).[35] Between 1976 and 1993 five candidates failed to gain the necessary number of votes needed to have their deposits returned: one Conservative in 1976 and two in 1983, one New Democrat in 1989, and one Liberal in 1990.[36] Brian Mulroney forfeited his deposit in 1976 for not having met the requirement for that convention that a candidate had to file a campaign expense and disclosure form.

Why the changes from the largely unrestricted access to nomination in the earlier conventions to the constraints of the more recent ones? The answer lies in the attempt by party officials to discourage potential nuisance candidates from using a leadership convention as a public forum through which to express their sometimes eccentric and possibly embarrassing views. That, in turn, is a consideration that derives from televised conventions. In the words of a prominent Conservative backroom organizer and fund-raiser active in planning the 1983 Tory convention, "the party would look foolish if [it] had a bunch of losers on TV."[37]

Throughout the first generation of conventions, those who sought their party's leadership were serious candidates.[38] Although the term "serious" lacks great precision, it cannot be so broadly inclusive as to mean that all candidates would have an equal chance of winning or that all would be equally qualified for the job, for that clearly could never be the case. Nevertheless, the term is used here to describe those who, as with H.H. Stevens in the Conservative convention of 1942 and Chubby Power in the Liberal convention of 1948, were established, often distinguished, public figures within their party at the time of being nominated and who were convinced that they have something to say to the assembly about the direction of their party.[39] But such candidates know they have no chance of winning the leadership. That Stevens received only twenty first ballot votes and Power fifty-six was confirmation of their perceived inappropriateness for the position of leader, not as a reflection of their qualifications to speak on matters of importance to the party.[40]

More to the point, "serious candidate" is a term that can most appropriately be applied to those who are the front runners in a contest and those who, as with Paul Martin Jr and Sheila Copps in 1990, or with Jim Edwards in 1993, are somewhere in the next tier of delegate support. This last group includes those men and women who, while in contention for the leadership, have little chance of gaining it without mass defections from the front runners or a series of coalition-building ballots, such as proved decisive for Joe Clark when he won the Tory leadership in 1976. They are credible candidates, often on their way up in the party, who, perhaps with little more than career advancement or an assured cabinet position in mind, have put together an organization with enough financial and personnel resources to attract serious media attention and delegate consideration. In that sense they are contenders with something to offer to the party and, in turn, to gain from their candidacy.

In contrast to the serious candidates are those who terrify party officials because of the possibly offensive views they might express, the media attention they gain, and the precious television time they consume at the convention itself. These are the candidates labelled variously by convention organizers as "frivolous," "marginal," or "nuisance" candidates. They are seen as "opportunists who do not support the goals and objectives" of the party and who seek the leadership "not for reasons of political leadership, but rather to gain political exposure."[41]

Theirs is an almost exclusively second-generation phenomenon. Their initial appearance coincided with the first of the conventions in which television was to play a major part – the Tory leadership contest of 1967 – so no wonder a link has been established in the minds of the planners of modern conventions. With nine serious candidates in the running in 1967 (the largest ever at that point) one of the last things party officials wanted was two extra candidates eating up precious television time and unnecessarily delaying the vote by adding to the number of ballots needed to determine a winner.[42] They had no choice but to place them on the first ballot once the nomination forms had been signed, one form (that of Mary Walker-Sawka) arriving literally moments before the deadline. In the words of the 1968 Liberal convention co-chairman, parties then recognized that they had "to cut these fellows off somehow even if its does run counter to the democratic ethos."[43]

In response to a complaint about the unfairness of the $25,000 bond, the Liberal party president at the time of the 1984 convention noted that the objective had been met: "The purpose of the bond is clear – to ensure the seriousness and good faith of those who state they seek the Party leadership. In that it has kept us free of the more 'esoteric' candidates that previous leadership campaigns (both ours and the PCs) have been plagued with, I feel that it has succeeded in its purpose. To do away with it now would only open the door even wider."[44] Mindful of the need "to balance political democracy with party responsibility,"[45] party officials have chosen to address the issue of minor candidates seeking a platform from which they could air their views through the rules governing candidate nominations. Accordingly, they have not hesitated to impose gradually earlier nomination deadlines, more extensive nomination requirements, and greater financial obligations on individuals who would seek a party's leadership.[46]

Televising Leadership Contests

National television broadcasting arrived at the tail end of the first generation of conventions. The Conservative and Liberal conventions of the 1950s were the first national political conventions to be covered by live television.[47] The parties were aware of the significance of having several hours a day of coverage by CBC television (the lone nationwide broadcaster at the time), but their efforts to accommodate the fledgling electronic media pale in comparison to those of more recent conventions. According to Ruth M. Bell, besides moving the opening ceremonies from the morning to the afternoon to take advantage of television, the 1956 Conservatives "made no major changes in its agenda to accommodate the television cameras."[48] Bell also notes that the members of the electronic media who were present were treated somewhat like intrusive newcomers: "The public relations staff of the party took care to see that the much publicized new medium did not encroach upon the 'working' press, which still was of vital importance. The party was well aware that the printed word and the radio played just as influential a role as the television."[49] For their part, the organizers of the Liberal convention of 1958 struck a special advisory group on television charged with three tasks: to install suitable platforms, towers, and other equipment needed for interviews, news coverage, and panel discussions; to negotiate a television timetable that would best "fit the convention program"; and "to make the appearance of the convention attractive on the screen."[50]

Despite the organizers' efforts, the 1956 and 1958 conventions could not have been great television. There was no sense of drama about the likely outcomes, as both Diefenbaker and Pearson were widely known to be the front runners destined to win handily on the first ballot. The daily sessions of the conventions were devoted almost entirely to delegates discussing and voting on policy resolutions, of which many were parochial and detailed. And the speeches by nominators, seconders, candidates, and several senior retiring parliamentarians were often excessively long and dull. Parties had yet to learn how to adapt their convention-floor proceedings to the realities of television.[51]

The 1960s saw a marked increase in the number of television stations and the size of television viewing audiences in Canada. A second English-language television network (CTV) was created, and the CBC French-language network, Radio-Canada, began its expansion beyond Quebec. In the decade following the Pearson convention, there was a 36 per cent increase in the number of Canadian households with television sets. By 1968, all but 5 per cent of Canadian households had one or more television sets.[52] Beginning with the 1967 Conservative and 1968 Liberal conventions, the parties seized the opportunity offered by live nationwide television coverage to reach a vast audience. Typical of the reasoning that has since gone into planning a modern convention was the agreement reached by the Staging Concepts group of the Conservative party in 1975–6. They noted that one of the underlying principles of their February 1976 convention was that "events would be geared for maximum exposure on TV."[53] In the words of a Conservative national vice-president at the time, "television viewing was the [party's] major priority in convention planning."[54]

The move to capture a sizable television audience, however, came at the cost of discussions of party policy. With the arrival of televised conventions, the Conservatives and Liberals (the NDP has remained something of an exception on this point) abandoned substantive debates and votes on policy resolutions submitted by constituency and other party associations. This had been a feature of the first generation of leadership conventions, with up to two-thirds of a convention's time devoted to consideration of resolutions concerning party policy. Since 1967 parties have opted instead to hold specially convened "policy conferences" for that purpose, effectively separating debates and votes on party policy from leadership selection. In 1968 the committee planning the Liberal April convention specifically rejected holding a policy conference at the same time as the leadership convention because, first, more time than was available at the convention was said to be needed to deal comprehensively with issues of policy; secondly, interest in the leadership question would prevent serious discussion of policy among the delegates; and finally, the new "leadership accountability" provisions of the party's constitution were said to require the party to take a much more responsible attitude towards policy than it had heretofore.[55]

Some policy conferences have been held within a year or so of a new leader's selection, but more typically they have been convened two or three years before or after the selection of a new leader.[56] In the most recent leadership contests, the parties attempted to restore at least some linkage between leadership and policy by holding in the weeks leading up to the convention a number of "forums" or "all-candidate debates" in the various regions of the country. These typically amounted to large meetings with convention delegates, reported by the media and, in some cases, carried on cable television (as with CBC Newsworld's coverage of the five Tory all-candidate debates in 1993) at which the candidates addressed questions of policy.

Scheduling of major events at the conventions themselves has been tightened with an eye to maximizing the prime time exposure of live television broadcasting. In a country spanning six time zones, the task defies both easy and totally satisfactory solution. Convention organizers have established strict time limits (varying from a total of twenty-five to thirty minutes depending upon the party) for candidate speeches and floor demonstrations and, as noted previously, all parties have attempted to minimize the likelihood of nuisance candidates being nominated by constructing a variety of financial and regulatory barriers. What these various moves have amounted to is an organizational attempt to change the convention format, rules, and structure to conform to the realities of television broadcasting. This is the reverse of what the Liberals had intended to negotiate in 1958. In keeping with another 1958 goal, however, there is no question that all parties now clearly aim "to make the appearance of the convention attractive on the screen."[57]

The 1967 and 1968 leadership races in the Tory and Liberal parties set the tone for second-generation conventions. They were arguably the most exciting to that point in Canadian history. Television helped to make them that way. The Conservatives, torn over John Diefenbaker's leadership from the time his government was defeated in the 1963 election, were destined for a series of votes in 1967, given the presence on the first ballot of eleven candidates and the absence of any overwhelmingly obvious front runner or apparent winner. In 1968 the Liberals were looking at a similar dynamic competition over a series of ballots. Trudeau had emerged at the beginning of the convention as the acknowledged first-ballot front runner, but whether he could eventually win the leadership in the face of opposition from eight other candidates remained an open question.

Competition is made for television, whether in politics or in sports. Not surprisingly, media coverage of political events often borrows expressions and metaphors from the language of sports, especially horse racing, as is seen in the use in politics of such familiar terms as front runner, home stretch, dark horse, and starting gate. Beginning with the conventions of 1967 and 1968, the excitement and dynamics of coalition-building among the candidates and delegates made for excellent television. For the first time Canadians could watch from the comfort of their living rooms some of the internal workings of political parties as they sought to resolve the question of their leadership by successive balloting. These early conventions, followed by those of the 1970s and 1980s, had much of the drama and excitement of a competitive sporting event – of a final game of the Stanley Cup playoffs, or the World Series, or the Grey Cup.

There were to be several defining moments of Canadian leadership conventions captured live by television for the audience at home. These ranged from Judy LaMarsh's frantic attempt in the Liberal convention of 1968 to convince Paul Hellyer to withdraw in favour of Robert Winters so as to stop "that bastard" Trudeau; through Flora MacDonald's obvious disappointment with her first ballot showing and Sinclair Stevens's surprise endorsement of Joe Clark in the Conservative contest of 1976; to Simon de Jong's dithering and uncertainty over the best option for him to pursue once he was out of the NDP race in 1989. These and other dramatic episodes helped to create a collective memory that many Canadians were to share of a previously undiscovered thrill and excitement of part of Canada's political process.

To borrow again from the world of horse racing, a televised leadership contest bears similarities to some of the rituals of the race track. A copy of the day's Racing Form is indispensable. It provides the names of the horses listed to run in each race, their age, pedigree, past record, jockey, trainer, weight, and so on. The tote board informs the spectators of the odds on the various entries, and bets are placed accordingly. The analogy should not be forced, but in many ways viewers of televised conventions are like spectators at a horse race, set for the action with their electronic equivalent to a Racing Form. They learn something of the various candidates' records and chances of winning, make their choices and, in some cases, give odds and wager money.

Even when it comes to selecting dates on which conventions are to be held, party officials do so with an eye on the sports calendar. They want to avoid running head-to-head against, or risking the chance of being displaced by, televised coverage of a major sporting event. Before choosing Sunday 22 February 1976 for voting day (the first time a Sunday had been chosen for electing a leader, but with a projected television viewing audience 30 per cent larger than the previous night's Hockey Night in Canada), the Tory organizers ensured that no televised hockey games were scheduled.[58] They had already abandoned plans to hold their convention on two other dates because of conflicts with televised coverage of major sporting events – the Grey Cup weekend in November 1975, and the Winter Olympics from 5 to 15 February 1976.[59] That convention planners sought so diligently to hold their convention when it did not conflict with a major televised sporting event was testimony to the weight that parties had come to attach to television coverage.

Generational Characteristics

With the passage of time the representational feature of conventions had come to assume even greater proportions than it had at the outset. This was seen most graphically in the larger number and the greater mix of delegates attending conventions in the second generation compared with the first. But it was also reflected, though less visibly because they were still formally part of the exercise, in the diminished role that traditional party elites, especially parliamentarians, were expected to play in choosing leaders in the second stage of leadership selection. The new representational arrangements introduced a change in the intra-party power relationships over leadership selection that was soon echoed in the adoption of a leadership review mechanism by the parties. With delegated conventions to choose and to review party leadership, the second generation of conventions made it clear that the authoritative power base had moved away from the parliamentary party and into the hands of the party's self-styled rank and file and grassroot activists.

It was also clear that by intervening increasingly in their own leadership selection contests and governing the races as they did in the second generation, parties had themselves moved into a different stage of development. They were no longer the informal, private, and voluntary associations they had been from their creation around the time of Confederation. In one important respect the national parties had grown more, rather than less, alike. Like countless other organizations in the last half of the twentieth century, they had become institutionalized and complex organizations complete with permanent headquarters, staffs, accountable executive officers, and regular meetings. Their interest was to protect their party's interest. This meant that the logical consequence of their deliberations was the introduction of guidelines, rules, and regulations aimed at ensuring as fair and open a process as possible – justified, of course, in representative and democratic terms – and to ensure maximum coverage for the entire selection process under the watchful eye of television.

The convention-day election rules for balloting on the leadership scarcely changed in the second stage of conventions over those that had been in place throughout the first. But the marked increase in the number of leadership contestants and ballots needed to declare a winner testified to more overtly factionalized parties than Canada had known previously. That change, together with the parties' active encouragement of television as the principal communicative medium for both campaigns and conventions, signalled an end to an earlier, less publicly-engaged period of Canadian politics. In the second generation of conventions, leadership selection became as never before something Canadians talked about, debated, and watched. To acquire the necessary professional help, to win candidate selection races, and to organize national campaigns, serious contestants, at least in the two older parties, needed to raise and to spend vastly larger amounts of money than had ever before. In a word, the second generation could be described as the "more" generation: more delegates, candidates, television, public involvement, and money. The slight representational cause of the early conventions had had profound effects.

3 A Party's Backstop: Leadership Review

What I don't understand is, why was 67 per cent not enough?
– Prince Charles

The Liberal and Conservative parties adopted the convention as the way *to choose* leaders in 1919 and 1927 respectively, but it was not until the mid-1960s that the parties in convention took upon themselves the power *to remove* leaders. Until then, removals were infrequent and, when they occurred, resulted from pressures exerted by members of the parliamentary caucus. No formal procedure was in place for periodic review of the leader. From the time of Confederation the principle had been widely accepted in Canada of allowing a leader who successfully led his party to retain the position subject only to the understanding that he maintain the support of the parliamentary party, particularly its frontbench elite. The parliamentary careers of John A. Macdonald, Wilfrid Laurier, and Mackenzie King come most readily to mind as illustrations of this principle, but numerous other examples from federal as well as provincial politics attest to its general acceptance.

By contrast, leaders who were judged by their frontbench colleagues or by the parliamentary party to be an electoral liability and who did not enjoy a substantial measure of confidence were soon forced out. The replacement of Alexander Mackenzie by Edward Blake as Liberal leader in 1880, the removal of Mackenzie Bowell by Charles Tupper as Tory leader in 1896, and the abrupt departure of Robert Manion following the Conservatives' disastrous showing in the 1940 election illustrate the speed with which parties could dispatch an unsuccessful or unpopular leader.[1] But the idea of having a formal procedure to remove a leader was foreign to Canadian parties and politicians. As Lester Pearson put it in the early 1960s, there was "no institutional way [to dispose of leaders] ... The Leader deposes himself. I don't know what other arrangements there could be."[2] But before long that was to change – for Pearson's Liberal party and also for the Conservative party. The party in convention was to become the authoritative body for deposing leaders, thus completing the shift in intra-party power relationships that came with the adoption of the leadership selection convention in for choosing them.

THE MOTHER OF ALL PARLIAMENTS — AND DOWN UNDER

The general principle of parliamentary parties' granting or withdrawing support for their leaders and of despatching them with speed remains in place in other Westminster-style systems to this day. In Britain it took only two ballots of Conservative MPs, separated by a week of intense intra-party bargaining, for Margaret Thatcher to challenge successfully Edward Heath for the Tory leadership in 1975 and for John Major to replace Thatcher as party leader and prime minister in 1990. In Australia also there were several leadership transitions in the last decade which demonstrated how expeditiously the removal of one leader and the election of another can be handled in a parliamentary system. By examining the election processes and events surrounding recent British Tory and Australian leadership transitions we can appreciate the extent to which the two older Canadian parties have departed from the practices they once shared with other parliamentary democracies and how the NDP leadership selection system resembles, in one sense at least, that of the British Conservative party. We can also better understand the varying degrees of vulnerability of leaders in the three countries to challenges to their leadership from within their respective parties.

Britain's Conservative Party

In 1965 the British Conservative party adopted a process that combined the twin purposes of leadership selection and leadership removal. Modified slightly in 1974, the new system introduced a set of nominating and voting procedures, of which the following are the principal characteristics:

1 The election of a party leader is to take place *annually*, with voting restricted to Conservative MPs.
2 There is a maximum of *three secret ballots*, with a week between the first two and one day between the second and third.

3 *Any number* of candidates may be nominated for the first ballot. Within two days of an inconclusive first ballot new nominations are called for a second ballot, again without restriction as to the number of candidates nominated. Should a third ballot be necessary, only the top-ranked three candidates from the second ballot can be placed on it.

4 To win on the first ballot, a candidate must receive (i) a clear majority of the votes of those *entitled* to vote (that is, of all Conservative MPs); and (ii) at least *15 per cent more* of the votes of those entitled to vote than any other candidate.

5 To win on the second ballot a candidate needs a *clear majority* of the votes of those entitled to vote.

6 For the third ballot, votes are cast *preferentially*. If no candidate receives a clear majority of the first preference votes of those eligible to vote, the lowest-ranked candidate is dropped and that candidate's second choice votes are distributed between the other two in order to determine a winner.[3]

In 1975 Margaret Thatcher challenged Edward Heath for the leadership of the party. Back in opposition after four years in government (1970–4), the Conservatives were deeply divided over Heath's continued leadership. In the words of one respected party insider, it was apparent from the two Tory defeats at the polls in quick succession in 1974 "that the leader of the Party had become an electoral liability."[4] As Heath was not about to resign the leadership, his opponents had no choice under the party's rules but to mount a challenge to him on the occasion of the parliamentary party's annual election of its leader.

At first, Thatcher was not considered to be a serious threat to Heath.[5] Pointing out to the Tory caucus that Heath was widely seen as the likely winner and that Thatcher apparently had little realistic chance of defeating him, her supporters argued that if MPs wanted Heath to make changes in his style of leadership and policies in the years ahead, they had no better opportunity than the leadership vote to indicate their degree of opposition to him. In the circumstances, so the argument went, they could vote against him without risking his defeat. Assured in their own minds of victory, the Heath forces made no policy concessions to wayward supporters and confidently predicted a first-ballot win. In these conditions MPs who preferred Heath to Thatcher, but who nonetheless wished to use the occasion to alert him to the strength of disaffection among his own supporters, could seize the occasion to vote against him.

The first ballot of Tory MPs on 4 February dealt a crippling blow to Heath. Of the 276 caucus members, 130 voted for Thatcher, 119 for Heath, sixteen for Hugh Fraser, and eleven abstained. Heath immedi-

ately announced his resignation as leader. This had the effect of opening up the race on the second ballot to Heath loyalists who previously
had not wanted to challenge his leadership. But it was too late to stop
Thatcher, who on the second ballot one week later obtained 146 votes
– an overall majority – to seventy-nine for William Whitelaw, nineteen
each for James Prior and Geoffrey Howe, eleven for John Peyton, and
two abstentions.

It was subsequently argued that the votes of an unspecified number
of discontented Heath supporters who voted for Thatcher on the first
ballot cost Heath the election. As the argument went, had every Tory
MP in 1975 been asked to cast a tie-breaking vote between Heath and
Thatcher, Heath would have won.[6] If such a claim were true, it adds
weight to the established fact that electoral processes can lead to unintended outcomes.

The system that enabled Thatcher to win the leadership was used
with telling effect against her in 1990.[7] In that year a serious challenge
to Thatcher's prime ministership was undertaken by one of her former
senior ministers, Michael Heseltine. Heseltine stated openly in the
days leading up to the first vote that any MPs who wanted another candidate on the second ballot would have to support him on the first.[8]
He was to discover on the second round of voting how successful that
tactic would be in unseating the incumbent – and in denying him the
leadership. As his aides feared, Heseltine was destined to play the
"stalking horse role – forcing the resignation of Mrs. Thatcher but ultimately losing to a third candidate."[9]

Described variously as "feeble," "overly casual," and "over-confi-
dent," the Thatcher leadership campaign organization badly mis-
judged the mood of the parliamentary party and the strength of the
anti-Thatcher forces. The prime minister was very unpopular and under her leadership the party had sunk to a record low in the public
opinion polls. Much of the opposition to Thatcher and her party was
focused on the introduction of the hated poll tax and on the prime
minister's resistance to European integration. Nevertheless, she had
the backing of almost the entire cabinet. She also had the support of
two-thirds of the Conservative peers and 70 per cent of the party executives at the constituency level. However, the role that these loyalists
could play was limited. They could express opinions through party
channels about the party leadership, but they had no vote on it.
Thatcher noted in her autobiography that "no one would seriously listen to [the members of the extra-parliamentary party] – though they
were formally consulted and pronounced heavily in my favour – when
it came for my fate to be decided."[10] It was among her backbenchers,
particularly the more recently elected MPs, that the prime minister

had fallen out of favour. They simply felt that they could not win again with her as leader.[11]

When the first ballot results were announced on 20 November Thatcher pledged to fight on and stand for the second round. She had won a clear majority of those eligible to vote, but fell four votes short of the necessary 15 per cent lead over Heseltine. Thatcher garnered 204 votes compared to 152 for her opponent, with sixteen abstentions. After consulting individually with the members of her cabinet, however, Thatcher changed her mind. The overwhelming majority of those who had been closest to her and who had felt compelled by loyalty and cabinet solidarity to give her their first ballot support told her that she could not beat Heseltine on the next round. Her continued candidacy would serve only to deny the leadership to one of her closest supporters, none of whom would contest the leadership with her still in the running. Only hours before the nomination deadline for the second ballot Thatcher announced her withdrawal from the race – a dramatic and significant development without recent parallel in British politics. A prime minister "who had won three elections, never been defeated in a Commons censure vote, enjoyed the [first ballot] confidence of a majority of Conservative MPs and was extremely popular with party workers in the country, had been forced to step down."[12] To the departing prime minister it was "treachery with a smile on its face."[13] To one of those closest to her on the first ballot, who then actively campaigned for John Major on the second, it was a matter of pure political survival: "Leaders are not afraid to sacrifice ministers; therefore ministers should not be afraid to sacrifice their leader."[14]

Thatcher loyalists John Major and Douglas Hurd were nominated to stand on the second ballot. The vote on 27 November gave the former a sizable lead, just shy of the required overall majority. He obtained 185 votes to Heseltine's 131 and Hurd's fifty-six. Within minutes of the announcement both Heseltine and Hurd conceded defeat. The next day Major was sworn in as the new prime minister. Thatcher's defeat confirmed, at least in the context of leadership politics, the adage that those who live by the sword also die by it. The process that had enabled her to win the leadership was the process by which she lost it.

Changing Leaders in Australia

All Australian federal party leaders are chosen solely by their colleagues in both houses of Parliament (sitting jointly) and they have to face regular re-election after each general election. In addition, in both major parties (the Australian Labor party and the Liberal party), the leader could be forced to face a challenge at any time. In the Labor party the leader may be removed and another selected by a special meeting of the caucus called for that purpose. In the Liberal party challenges are even easier to mount because no special notice need be given. If an unpopular leader refuses to resign, the caucus may opt either to have a vote of confidence by an open show of hands or to have a "spill" motion, which, if passed by a secret ballot, declares the party leadership to be vacant. No alternative candidates need voice an interest in the leadership until it has been declared vacant.[15]

Between 1985 and mid-1994 five Australian leaders were ousted by their respective parliamentary party and replaced by another MP. In four of these instances – all occurring in opposition parties – the man (Australia has yet to have a female leader federally) walked into a meeting of his parliamentary caucus as leader and emerged hours later as an ordinary MP. On 5 September 1985 Andrew Peacock resigned his position as Liberal party leader after failing to force his deputy from office. Deputy leader John Howard, who stood for the leadership after Peacock abandoned the field, came out on top in the subsequent leadership vote with the support of fifty-seven of his party's seventy MPs and senators. The new leader appeared to be surprised by the turn of events. "I did not believe in my wildest imagination that this might happen today," said Howard. "An extraordinary set of circumstances produced this result."[16]

Extraordinary or not, the Liberals went through the same process less than four years later when, on 9 May 1989, it was Howard's turn to be dumped by his parliamentary party. His successor, by a vote of forty-four to twenty-seven, was none other than Andrew Peacock. Coincidentally, on the exact same day the Australian National party (the smallest of Australia's three major parties and the Liberals' electoral and parliamentary coalition partner) deposed its leader, Ian Sinclair, in favour of Charles Blunt by a secret ballot of its parliamentary caucus.[17] On 23 May 1994 the Liberal leader since 1990, John Hewson, was dumped by the party's caucus in favour of fellow MP Alexander Downer, by a vote of forty-three to thirty-six. The vote had been called by Hewson following months of grumbling by his colleagues about his leadership. By declaring the position vacant and standing for re-election, Hewson hoped to end the uncertainty over the leadership. He did, but not in the way he intended.[18]

The fifth case took place in the governing Australian Labor party in 1991 when the prime minister, Bob Hawke, who had won for his party an unprecedented four straight election victories and who was the longest-serving Labor prime minister ever, joined the ranks of those leaders pushed out by their respective parties when he was replaced by Paul Keating on 19 December 1991. Keating, a former treasury minister and deputy prime minister in the Hawke administration, had resigned from the cabinet the previous June after losing his first bid to replace Hawke. As Australia's economy faltered, Hawke's popularity declined. On the morning of the 19 December, under growing pressure from within the country and his party, Hawke tendered his resignation to the parliamentary party and declared his candidacy in the leadership vote to be held immediately. In that vote he was rejected by his party in favour of Keating by fifty-six votes to fifty-one. Keating was sworn in as prime minister the next day. Hawke became the first Labor prime minister to have been pushed out of office by his own party.[19]

Two points about these recent leadership transitions in British and Australian parties are particularly worthy of emphasis. One concerns the process itself. In each of the cases examined the vote served at one and the same time as a mechanism for granting or withholding approval of the current leader and as a method for choosing a new party leader. In Canada, by contrast, since the mid-1960s the two oldest parties have split these tasks into two stages separated by several months. The other point concerns those eligible to participate in the process. In each of the British and Australian instances discussed, participation in the leadership selection/removal process was restricted to the members of the parliamentary party. Leaders of those parties owe their positions and are responsible solely to their respective colleagues in Parliament, and MPs, in turn, owe their election to the general electorate composed of tens of thousands of voters in each constituency. Thus, British and Australian MPs assert that their place in the leadership selection/removal process is truly "democratic" and "representative," whereas that of delegates chosen to attend national conventions by the members of their local party association is not.

LEADERSHIP REVIEW IN CANADA

From 1919 to the 1960s conventions were used by the Liberal and Conservative parties to select their leaders, but they had no formal say or role in the removal of leaders. From the outset of national leadership conventions there had been an obvious incongruity in the leader's relationship to his party that had never been tackled, let alone resolved. The leader was selected by the extra-parliamentary party, but the "deselection" system was in the hands of the parliamentarians. Removing a leader from office meant employing ill-defined and arbitrary practices that had evolved in response to different methods of selecting leaders. Added confusion came from the games leaders periodically played in defining their own lines of political accountability. Mackenzie King and John Diefenbaker in particular propounded the view that, as they had been selected by a "democratic" convention, they could not be ousted without a similar convention's assent.[20] In King's case, that would have been an impossibility as the Liberals did not meet once in national convention during his thirty years as leader! Ironically, Diefenbaker got caught at his own game when the Tories, in convention, effectively forced him into an unwanted leadership contest and out of office.

The situation throughout the life of the first generation of conventions was far from satisfactory. There existed no mechanism by which a convention could remove a leader; parties rarely met in convention except when there was a leadership vacancy to fill; and ineffective or unpopular leaders could only be pushed to resign by the informal process of persuasion and frontbench or caucus discontent or rebellion.[21] This all changed at the outset of the second generation of conventions when the extra-parliamentary parties, having now more or less regular conventions at which the question of leadership could be raised, successfully asserted their power to conduct a periodic review of the party leadership. As set out in party constitutions, the leadership review mechanism gave convention delegates a formal opportunity to pass judgment on their leader by voting on whether they wished the party to hold a leadership convention. The result of the vote was intended to do one of two things: either give the leader a vote of confidence to carry on, or clear the way for a subsequent leadership convention at which the leader, should he or she so choose, would be a contestant.

From the outset of the debate over leadership review its advocates have argued that the mechanism forms part of the foundation of intra-party democracy. It is said to hold party leaders formally accountable to their members. The Liberal party's national meeting in October 1966 was informed by supporters of a constitutional mechanism for reviewing the party's leadership that the party was not "democratic" if it lacked a system whereby the party faithful would be periodically permitted the opportunity to vote on the desirability of calling a leadership convention. According to one of the proponents of convention-determined leadership review "democracy must be complete. The party must have its checkreins to keep the leader close to the party. Leadership conventions should be a matter of course."[22]

The constitutional provision approved by the Liberals at that meeting in effect granted the party in convention one opportunity between federal elections to force a leadership convention. That process remained unchanged until, as will be seen presently, the party added a different and more complicated wrinkle to it in 1992. The process followed by the Liberals between 1966 and 1992 was set out in the following constitutional terms: "A resolution calling for a leadership convention shall be placed automatically on the agenda of the convention next following a federal general election. If such a resolution is duly adopted by secret ballot, the National Executive shall call a leadership convention to take place within one year of the above-mentioned secret ballot."[23]

At its meeting of November 1966 the Progressive Conservative party handled the issue of leadership review differently and in such a way as to create deep divisions within the party for years to follow. The re-election of Dalton Camp as the party president followed a bitter contest for that post between pro- and anti-Diefenbaker forces. It carried with it a commitment by Camp to hold a national leadership convention before the end of 1967. In effect, the contest in 1966 for the presidency of the Conservative party amounted to Canada's first leadership review by a national party. But the bitter struggle had been so centred on the immediate issue of Diefenbaker's leadership that the more fundamental question of constitutional procedures for reviewing party leadership was left unresolved. Not until three years later did the party adopt a formal amendment to its constitution specifying that a leadership review vote would be held, but only at the first national meeting following an election in which the party failed to form the government and failed to increase its standing in the Commons by at least 20 per cent. Those restrictions were dropped in 1974 when the party approved a motion proposed by its leader, Robert Stanfield, that a formal vote on the desirability of holding a leadership convention be taken at "each general meeting" of the national party. Normally the party held such meetings every two years.[24]

In 1983, at the end of several years of squabbling and three review votes on Clark's leadership, the Tories once again changed their leadership review provisions. They replaced the biennial review with a process that distinguishes between the party in office (when no vote would be taken) and in opposition (when a vote would be held only at the first national convention following a general election). The relevant sections read:

At the first general meeting of the Association after a federal general election in which the Party did not form the government, and only at such meetings, the voting delegates shall be asked by secret ballot:

"Do you wish to have a leadership convention?"

In the event that more than fifty percent (50%) of the votes cast indicate a desire for a leadership convention, the Executive Committee shall call a leadership convention at the earliest convenient date.[25]

The NDP has followed a different path with respect to control over the removal of leaders. Like the system devised by the British Conservative party, the NDP process collapses the two stages (selection and removal) into one. The leader is considered an officer of the party and, like other officers – president, associate president, eleven vice-presidents, and treasurer – is elected for a two-year term at the party's biennial conventions.[26] The party leadership is put to a formal vote only if an alternative candidate emerges to challenge the incumbent or, of course, if the leadership is vacant. Apart from the NDP's founding convention in 1961, and the conventions of 1971, 1975, and 1989, which were genuine leadership contests in that there was a vacancy in the party's leadership and the previous leader was not a candidate, only one leader who has sought re-election has been challenged at a biennial meeting. In 1973 David Lewis defeated Douglas Campbell (a Toronto poet and cab driver) by a vote of 719 to seventy-six. All other NDP leaders have been returned to office unopposed (see table 3–1).

Founded in 1987, the Reform party has been at the forefront of the movement to introduce alternative modes of political participation to Canadians. In particular, the party is a strong advocate of direct democracy. But when it comes to the issue of leadership review, the Reform party has taken a decidedly traditionalist stance. The party had included in its founding constitution (adopted in 1987) a leadership review mechanism that closely resembled the process that the Tories adopted in 1983. At the first party "assembly" (Reform's preferred term for convention has both a religious and a didactic element to it) following a federal election in which Reform either did not form the government or did not enter into a governing coalition, delegates would be asked to vote on the question of calling a leadership assembly. Following the 1988 election, and two years after Preston Manning's selection as the party's first leader, the item was placed on the agenda at the 1989 assembly in Edmonton. Unlike the two older parties who since the outset of leadership review votes have always announced their results, Reform chose not to. According to Manning, the question on the secret ballot was "answered in the negative, thus affirming [him] as leader of the party."[27]

Reform's review process was amended at the 1989 meeting after delegates were asked to choose between the post-election review, then part of the party's constitution, and automatic review at every party assembly. They chose (again in an unannounced vote) the latter. As it now stands, it is a close replica of the process employed by the Progressive Conservative party from 1974 to 1983:

At every Assembly [held biennially], each voting delegate shall be asked "Do you want a Leadership Vote to be called?" Responses shall be by secret ballot ...

If more than 50% of the votes cast are in the affirmative, the Executive Council shall ... announce when a Leadership Vote will be held ... The Leadership Vote must be held not sooner than 3 months and not later than 6 months from the date of the vote held at the Assembly.[28]

It is this procedure that the party used in October 1994 to review Manning's leadership at its first biennial assembly since its electoral success in the 1993 federal election.

THE COSTS OF REVIEW

Party review of a leader's performance has become an accepted part of leadership politics in Canada. From the time that they first adopted the process in the 1960s, the Liberals have held a formal leadership review vote six times and the Conservatives four times (see table 3–2). The Liberals were in government on all occasions save one (1986), whereas the Tories were in opposition each time. Given the absence to date of any attempt by party elites and activists to abandon the leadership review process, it would appear that in some form or another its future has been assured. There is a symmetry in the convention-selection, convention-removal arrangements which distinguishes and commends the second generation of leadership selection over the first. Leadership "accountability," "bear-pit," and "question-and-answer" sessions have entered the Canadian political lexicon and have become regular features of general meetings. Typically held immediately prior to the vote on the leadership convention resolution, such sessions have become one of the standard participatory-democratic institutions that defines modern Canadian parties.

But the change has not been without cost. The parties have discovered that leadership review can exact a heavy toll on their own and on the leader's ability to function effectively. This proved to be particularly so for the Tories throughout the last years of Joe Clark's leadership of the party. The reference in the Conservative constitution to a minimum support level for the calling of a leadership convention of at least 50 per cent is ironic given the difficulties Clark faced in the early 1980s. Under the party's constitution at the time, Clark was obliged to submit himself to a leadership review vote at *each* Conservative national meeting. His failure in January 1983 to win more support than he had received two years previously (fully one-third of the Conservative delegates at both the 1981 and 1983 meetings voted in favour of a leadership convention) prompted Clark to ask the party to hold a leadership convention.[29]

His decision surprised many delegates and observers alike. As Mordecai Richler, covering the leadership review convention for CBC Radio, said at the time, "I didn't anticipate that on Friday night Clark would be traded for a player to be named later and possibly a new team bus."[30] Months later Prince Charles pointedly asked Clark, "Why was 67 per cent not enough?", a question not easy to answer except to note as John Laschinger and Geoffrey Stevens do that "only in politics does one-third beat two-thirds."[31] Clark immediately resigned his party position after his second consecutive two-thirds vote so that he might then campaign freely for the leadership, but in the end it was to no avail. He was defeated by Brian Mulroney on the fourth ballot of the leadership convention held later that year.

Clark's difficulty leading up to his decision to call for a leadership convention stemmed in large measure from the imprecision and uncertainty surrounding the meaning to be attached to the leadership review vote. Fifty per cent support for the incumbent leader, in spite of what a party's constitution might say, was widely judged to be too low for any individual to lead his party. This was the assessment of journalists and politicians alike, even though several Canadian leaders, including Mackenzie King, R.B. Bennett, Pierre Trudeau, and Joe Clark himself, were initially *chosen* by barely more than one-half of the voting delegates. But if a simple majority of delegates voting against a leadership convention was not sufficient, what was? Sixty, 65, or 70 per cent? Or more? This was the question Clark and, in 1986, John Turner had to answer. The record of support registered in previous votes in both parties was of little help, except to suggest that any vote above the 80 per cent level would indicate a virtually unchallengeable level of support for the leader.

Clark himself had received a 93 per cent vote in 1977, some twelve percentage points more than Trudeau had received while *prime minister* two years earlier. Yet Clark's early level of intra-party support (the most impressive in any leadership review vote to date) disappeared after the defeat of his government in 1980. His decision to call a leadership convention was reported to have stemmed from a promise that he had been forced to make to his caucus after the 1981 convention, to the effect that he would call a leadership convention if his support did not increase in 1983 over its previous level.[32] If true, that explanation demonstrates that following several years of intra-party turmoil over its leadership, a parliamentary caucus of the principal opposition party can play a part in driving a leader into an unwanted convention.

The figure on which Clark chose to call the convention will almost certainly now be taken as the floor beyond which no leader will attempt to carry on without risking open party revolt. Turner was clearly mindful of that figure (and fearful of doing no better) in the months leading up to the 1986 Liberal national convention.[33] That he received a 76 per cent endorsement from the Liberal delegates was widely accepted, even by Turner's critics within his party, as a "strong vote of confidence."[34] The Clark and Turner experience with leadership review suggests that there is a grey area between 67 and 76 per cent of the delegates' votes which, if a leader falls within it, will likely lead to debate and uncertainty within the party and the media about whether the leader should carry on. Below the bottom figure, a subsequent leadership convention would be a virtual certainty; above the top one, no convention would likely be necessary. But with a vote between those figures, the leader and the party may have resolved little and may be destined for more in-fighting. The sheer size of the numbers involved sends a contradictory message: there is a considerable measure of support for someone leading a highly divided party.

Difficulties with leadership review are not limited to the uncertainties surrounding the requisite level of support accorded a leader. When two or three thousand delegates to a national meeting are asked if they wish their party to hold a leadership convention and their response is to be registered in a secret, individual vote, the door has been opened to intra-party intrigue and media speculation which have the potential of severely damaging a party's credibility and undermining a leader's authority. The Conservatives were particularly vulnerable on this count because of their constitutional requirement for biennial reviews. Labelled at the time as a "recipe for almost chronic instability within the party,"[35] the requirement calling for a review at each general meeting was abandoned, ironically on the day following the 1983 leadership review vote on Joe Clark. It was replaced by a process in which the party would receive only one opportunity to review the leadership between elections and then only if the party were in opposition. As a result of that change, Brian Mulroney's leadership was never put to the test in a review vote throughout his ten years as head of his party.

Leadership reviews have the potential for drawing any party into dangerous waters. The process is inherently destabilizing given a measure of discontent within a party with its leadership. It invites dissension and it can preoccupy a party, draining its resources and dominating its agenda at the expense of its other public responsibilities. It can be especially disruptive for a party in opposition as the leader lacks the power and patronage of office to cement his or her position and to rein in dissenting voices within the party. The 1986 review of John Turner's leadership is a case in point. The Liberal leader's principal supporters began to organize for the November convention in January of that year. These efforts "would command the attention of a majority of Turner's senior aides in the ensuing eleven months."[36] The whole party was swept up in the leadership issue as the leader's anti-review forces faced off against a patchwork of dump-Turner activists, including many who had backed Jean Chrétien for the leadership in 1984.

The 1986 review included all the trappings of modern leadership conventions with the exception of alternative candidates: ethnic recruiting, packed delegate selection meetings, slates, computerized delegate tracking and polls during the lead-up to the convention, and hospitality suites, placards, buttons, scarves, and planned "spontaneous" demonstrations in support of Turner at the convention itself. The co-chairman of the Friends of John Turner and a principal organizer of the leader's campaign against review said in the fall of 1986, "We had to do a lot of scrounging ... I mean, we did what we had to do to win ... I'm not saying it was pretty. It got nasty, nasty, nasty. It was a dog-fight. Let's face it, what we did was stack the place."[37] The months of insecurity, intra-party turmoil, and messy organizational battles exacted a heavy toll on the leader and the party alike. Two weeks before he passed the review test, Turner commented that from his vantage point "the [leadership review] process is a self-destructive one ... The process itself means open season on the leader."[38]

In theory the review mechanism is intended to permit delegates the opportunity to pass judgment on the performance of their leader. In reality that assessment is carried out in a decidedly artificial context. The leader will undoubtedly be judged against possible, though undeclared, challengers for his job. Joe Clark complained in the months leading up to the 1983 leadership review of having to compete against "ghosts." By his own admission Turner was forced to engage in continuous "shadow boxing" before the 1986 Liberal leadership review.[39] The phantom challengers might include parliamentary colleagues, provincial politicians, or unelected party notables. Like Brian Mulroney in 1983 and Jean Chrétien in 1986, they benefit from being in the public spotlight, from the inevitable media interest and speculation, and from the divisions and discontent that invariably surface in any party. Yet they neither bear the burdens of holding the party leadership nor are subjected to the political risks attendant upon a face-to-face encounter with the existing leader. Although the interests and ambitions of the alternative leaders may be pursued on their behalf by individuals or groups playing the stalking-horse role, the leadership review is a race with only one horse – the incumbent.

The parties have long recognized the many inadequacies and defects of their leadership review processes. In a revealing passage, one constitutional committee struck by the Liberal party reported in 1984 as follows:

There have been no really satisfactory solutions proposed by this or any other party in the area of leadership review. Without question, as demonstrated by the

Conservatives, it is an area fraught with peril, as much for a party as for any incumbent. The efforts required of a leader for a sufficient affirmative vote in any review process, and the interpretation of the media of those efforts and the eventual result, present a "no-win" proposition for all concerned – but clearly this and every party feel the need for some kind of backstop review mechanism.[40]

The recognition that leadership review is dangerous and disruptive for all concerned is counterbalanced by the party's need for a formal mechanism that it can employ in the last resort if an unwanted leader refuses to depart.

If the Liberals and Conservatives are serious about bringing an end to the uncertainties that the current leadership process introduces into both the leader's and the party's affairs, they might put in place a mechanism similar to that employed by the NDP. There are no ghosts or shadow boxers in the NDP process as it requires alternative candidates to declare openly their intentions before it forces a leader seeking re-election to submit to a secret ballot of the delegates at a biennial convention. To remove one leader means voting another in. The adoption of such a system by the older Canadian parties (and by the Reform party for that matter) would have the beneficial effects of sparing the leader the trials of a review vote in the absence of alternative candidates, of forcing potential challengers to declare their intentions, and of enabling both incumbents and delegates to know exactly who was in the running for the leadership. The vote of confidence in an unchallenged leader enhances that leader's credibility and authority – especially when, as in the NDP, it derives from his or her confirmation by acclamation without a recorded vote of the delegates. Weary of the destructive effects of the review process as implemented by their party in 1986 (the logic of which is similar to the German "positive vote on confidence" for choosing a chancellor), several prominent Liberals expressed a preference for the NDP's "put up or shut up" process.[41]

Although different and variable conditions within parties make general principles of leadership review difficult to establish, it is likely that the NDP system has a tendency to discourage challenges to the leadership. This the two older parties may not be prepared to accept. The requirement of an open challenge would generally act as a deterrent to those unwilling to face the charges of disloyalty and ingratitude that would almost certainly accompany any attack on the leadership. Mulroney endorsed Clark weeks before the 1983 Tory review vote, but his endorsement was difficult to accept at face value given the behind-the-scenes organizing that was widely reported to be under way on his behalf.[42] The Tory and Liberal systems lend themselves to that sort of intrigue, whereas a race that would have forced out into the open a challenge to Clark by Mulroney could well have reduced its chances of ever being launched in the first place. As Alberta Liberal leader Nick Taylor commented in 1986, "if a challenger has to stand up and be seen slipping a knife into the toga, chances are he won't do it."[43]

The NDP has demonstrated less proclivity for public disputes over its leadership than the two older parties. This reflects a variety of factors, of course, including an absence of serious challengers in the party at critical junctures and the diverse and dispersed intra-party constituencies whose support they would have to attract in order to wage a successful battle to unseat a leader. As well, the trade union culture of solidarity has no doubt had a significant impact on the NDP. Members do not easily attack leaders, and unions do not easily deal with leadership challenges. But another reason for the absence of public fights over the party's leadership is undoubtedly that any challenge directed against an NDP leader would have to be carefully planned and executed if it were to be something more than token. Serious challengers in any party would have an enormously complex task, given the resources of the incumbent and the scale of modern conventions. In the absence of alternative candidates willing and able to challenge the leader, the NDP has no mechanism for measuring support of its leader and no constitutional provisions by which it can remove an incumbent. Thus their leaders are considerably less vulnerable to removal by their party than are those of the two older parties. In itself that may be sufficient reason for the Liberal and Conservatives *not* to want follow the NDP example, for it would effectively remove the one opportunity the extra-parliamentary party has to force a leader, irrespective of the number of putative candidates, into a leadership contest.

The two older parties have never seriously contemplated adopting the NDP scheme. They have stuck to close variations of the review procedures they adopted in the 1960s. The one departure occurred in 1992 when the Liberal party, enthused by the prospects of giving a greater say to the grassroots membership, opted to extend the review vote to the broader party membership at the constituency level. The arguments in favour of such a scheme were reminiscent of those put forth by the original proponents of leadership review in the 1960s. "The leader should be accountable to all members of the Liberal party," said one Liberal delegate, "and there should be some way that the members ... can say at an appropriate time, 'We think there should be a leadership convention'."[44] The constitutional amendment adopted by the party in 1992 was as follows:

Article 17(4). A resolution calling for a leadership convention shall be placed automatically on the agenda of the convention next following a federal general election. If such a resolution is duly adopted by secret ballot, the National Executive shall call a leadership convention to take place within one year of the above-mentioned secret ballot. During the selection of delegates to the national convention which next follows a general election, all members of the Liberal Party of Canada shall be asked to vote in each constituency association on a resolution calling for a leadership vote. If such resolution is agreed to by a majority of members, voting by secret ballot, the National Executive shall call a leadership vote to take place within one year.[45]

Thus the change adopted by the Liberals in 1992 provided for two ways for party members to lead to the calling of a leadership convention: by a leadership review vote by delegates in a convention, or by members attending constituency meetings called for the purpose of selecting convention delegates.

The party had been warned in advance by the executive vice-president of the Ontario wing of the federal Liberal party that the dual review process "may in fact pose one of the greatest single sources of division and acrimony in [their] Party that one could imagine."[46] Under the new Liberal system, the delegate selection meetings themselves would become opportunities to dethrone the leader and the potential for abuse through special interest group infiltration is great.[47] In addition, the process risks a conflict between the expressed views of the convention delegates and the expressed views of the voting membership on the question of whether or not to hold a leadership convention. It was clear at the party's 1994 convention (at which Chrétien's leadership was reviewed) that the party had come to recognize these and perhaps other dangers and to consider the adoption of the dual review mechanism to have been a mistake. Although the process was not removed from the party's constitution in 1994, it was referred back to committee for further study.[48]

LEADERSHIP REVIEW AND POLITICAL ACCOUNTABILITY

What has the adoption of leadership review votes meant for Canadian parties and leaders? On the face of it, the move to conventions as bodies to remove, as well as to select, leaders has clarified the lines of authority and responsibility within the parties. In reality, however, it has complicated them to the extent that they have given rise to a bifurcated accountability. The practical effect of the change has been to force the leader to account for his or her actions to both the party in convention every few years and to the parliamentary caucus on a continuing basis. Although leaders are formally obliged to defend their actions and policies to convention delegates only, in fact they cannot effectively lead their parliamentary party without keeping it onside. This means accounting for their actions to, and maintaining the support of, those with whom they must work from day to day.

There is, of course, a reverse side to the links between accountability and support. Parliamentarians supportive of their leadership could be openly at odds with the party in convention about who should lead them. The classic instance of intra-party conflict over a party's leadership occurred when Diefenbaker, with the acknowledged support of seventy-one of the party's ninety-five MPs, unsuccessfully fought moves by the party in convention to force him into a leadership convention and out of office.[49] Arguably, it took that episode at the outset of the second generation of conventions to establish where the real control rested when it came to removing a party's leader. Nonetheless, it served to illustrate the possibility, however unlikely it may be, of two wings of the party being divided over its leadership, or of the larger group acting contrary to the expressed preferences of the smaller.

Canadian party leaders of the second generation of conventions have had a dual political responsibility thrust upon them which was unknown to their predecessors or to their counterparts in Britain and Australia. They are accountable to the parliamentary caucus with which they must work and maintain support on a regular basis, and also to the wider party in convention to which they have formal constitutional ties. Such a dual line of accountability has produced uncertainties over the relationships among some leaders (notably Stanfield, Clark, and Turner), their caucus, and their extra-parliamentary party. This is because, as George Perlin has argued, "the difficulties inherent in [such a] situation have been compounded by the fact that the parliamentary party and the party convention represent different institutional and social interests."[50] The tension that review creates may be justified by parties as being politically healthy for all concerned. But equally it may prove to be damaging and destabilizing for a party should the interests of the two groups be divergent and publicly in conflict, for the parliamentary party cannot force an unwanted leader out of office. In Canada, compared to Britain and especially to Australia, "the lack of opportunity for a swift execution makes the task impossible."[51]

The shift from conventions to direct election of leaders, which marked another transition point in leadership selection for many provincial parties in the early 1990s, threatens to complicate intra-party relations even further. If the parties decide to turn the power of leadership *selection* over to the entire membership and yet keep the power of leadership *removal* in the hands of convention delegates, they will have created "a situation in which leaders can be chosen by one group of party members, can be removed by a second and must govern through a third: all composed in different ways and, therefore, representing different interests."[52] The Liberal party's attempt in 1992 (the first by a national party) to reconcile the various interests at play in a leadership review process which included a party membership vote at the local level was not reassuring. When put into practice in 1994 it proved to be a logistical problem for the party, it was not understood by the press, and it led to considerable uncertainty at both the riding and the national levels about the wisdom of a leadership review process that aimed to combine direct democracy locally with a delegated convention nationally. Aggregating the interests of parliamentarians, convention delegates, and local party members in a widened "democratic" review system will be a daunting task for party organizers in the future.

THE VULNERABILITY OF LEADERS

The words of Alderman and Carter about Thatcher's resignation in 1990 are equally apt for all of the leaders and processes, British, Australian and Canadian, discussed in this section. They point out that Thatcher "was not technically brought down by the formal election processes. But ... the procedures played an essential part in producing the circumstances which ultimately rendered her vulnerable to the more informal pressures on her to resign."[53] In other words, institutions such as those by which leaders are chosen or deposed do make a difference to the outcome. But then so does the leader's vulnerability. That, too, is at the heart of any examination of institutional processes by which political leaders can be deposed.

In his comparative study of parties and prime ministers of the older Commonwealth countries, Patrick Weller sets out four criteria for assessing the vulnerability of party leaders to being removed from office. The first is the size of the constituency to which a leader is accountable. Is it large, as in a party convention, or small, as in a parliamentary caucus? "The broader the constituency," Weller argues, "the more difficult it is to call together and the less vulnerable the prime minister is likely to be."[54] The second criterion is the degree of control over the constituency that the leader is able to exert. If the leader successfully dominates the group which does the selecting or de-selecting, he or she is likely to be relatively secure. The larger the constituency (moving in size from a cabinet to a caucus to a convention), the more difficult it is for the incumbent to control it – both its composition and its decisions. Weller contends that a federal system makes it even more difficult for a leader to gain or to retain control of the group, as federalism lends itself to party sub-groupings which can

be quite independent of a leader's influence and yet be constitutionally empowered to have a say over the choice of leader. The third criterion is "the existence of formal occasions on which challenges can
be launched, or at least a set of rules that allow that opportunity to be
created."[55] Leadership elections that could be called at any time, as
well as those that are required annually, provide greater opportunities
to challenge and possibly remove a leader than those held, at most,
every few years. Weller's last criterion for assessing the vulnerability of
a leader is "the need for an alternative." If a leader can be removed
only by a vote in which an alternative candidate is favoured, that
leader is less vulnerable than one who faces a two-staged process
marked by constant "shadow-boxing with unannounced rivals" in the
first phase.[56]

Table 3-3 presents in summary form these four factors in relation to
the parties considered in this chapter. Australian parliamentary caucuses are smaller than those in Britain, and both, in turn, are considerably smaller than Canadian conventions. Because of the small size of
the institution that chooses and may depose them, Australian leaders
are particularly vulnerable. Canadian leaders, on the other hand, are
by far the safest of the three groups of party leaders as their intra-party
constituency is large and broadly based. As Patrick Weller notes,
"There are always logistical and political reasons that make it difficult
for a broad constituency to assert its authority, however unquestioned
that might be."[57]

British Conservative leaders, through their direct control of the
party's central organization and its commanding role in the selection
of parliamentary candidates, have the greatest influence over the
composition of the group that decides the fate of their leadership –
the parliamentary party. The British leader, especially if prime minister at the time, is in a position to assert strong leadership over that
group by promoting and demoting colleagues as well as through wise
distribution of intra-party patronage. By contrast, Canadian leaders
are the least able to influence the composition of the electoral college in which their leadership might be challenged, and convention
delegates are far more remote from the daily cut and thrust of leadership politics and from the leader's patronage power than MPs. A convention is a vast and varied extra-parliamentary organization with a
short shelf-life and an array of competing interests present. As well,
national party leaders in Canada, as in Australia, operate in a federal
system which fosters its own set of complex political relationships.
Powerful and independently minded premiers, such as Alberta's
Peter Lougheed, Quebec's Robert Bourassa, and Saskatchewan's Ross
Thatcher, can quietly convey strong messages of doubt about their

party's national leadership and influence the character and disposition of local delegations attending national conventions.[58]

The opportunities to challenge party leaders vary considerably among the three countries. In Britain, the Tory parliamentary party meets once a year to vote formally on its leadership. Backbenchers in Britain do not, as they do in Australia and Canada, meet in caucus on a regular basis with their party leader to discuss policy and party affairs. Those caucus meetings in Australia are the occasions for the vote on a party's leadership, which means that MPs there have unlimited opportunities to mount an attack on their leader. At the other end of the spectrum of opportunities are the Canadian MPs in caucus who have long since seen the formal power to overthrow their leader taken from their hands and turned over to the party in convention. The frequency of leadership review votes in Canada varies by party. They are held biennially in the NDP and Reform parties, follow each election in the Liberal party, and only come after each election if the party is in opposition in the Conservative party. In comparative terms, the opportunities for challenging a Canadian party leader can best be described as "rare." Even when those opportunities do occur, the meetings are scheduled by the party's national executive in consultation with the leader's office, which effectively means that at least some measure of control over the timing of leadership review votes rests with the leader.

"No leader can be replaced by a vacuum," Weller notes.[59] That is true. But some leaders can be replaced only when their name and that of at least one challenger appears on a ballot. Others can be replaced only when they are forced into contesting two votes, the first with no other contestants, the second open to anyone wishing to seek the leadership. For the NDP and British Tories, the *sine qua non* of a vote to remove a leader from office is a ballot with two or more names on it – the incumbent and at least one challenger. Alternatively, Australian and Canadian parties, with the exception of the NDP, go through a two-stage process with the second vote being the only one in which the names of the candidates are known.

The risks to the challenger in the British Tory and NDP process no doubt serve as disincentives to all but the most intrepid contestants. Nonetheless, although there have been no genuine challenges of the same sort in the NDP, the Heath/Thatcher and Thatcher/Heseltine confrontations in Britain demonstrate that no leader is invincible regardless of the way in which reviews are carried out formally. Given the right conditions and contestants, the "put up or shut up" alternative offers no greater protection to the incumbent than the two-vote system employed by Australian and the majority of Canadian parties.

THE LUCK OF THE IRISH

Brian Mulroney, it must be concluded, was a lucky man, Margaret Thatcher an unlucky woman. He was elected leader of the Conservative party shortly after it changed its leadership review procedure to do away with any review of its leaders while the party was in office. This meant that for his entire period in office Mulroney was never reviewed by his party in convention. Thatcher, according to her party's rules, could have been officially challenged for the leadership once a year. In her fifteen years as Tory leader she was twice, winning the first challenge and losing the second. Although she subscribed to the view that by unwritten convention the procedure by which she had won the leadership was not intended for use when the Tories were in office,[60] her colleagues obviously thought otherwise and forced her out when they became convinced they could no longer win with her.

The Conservatives in the British Parliament can be a bloody-minded lot. When a majority of them senses that the leader has become an electoral liability they do not hesitate to toss him or her out. Their party rules even sanction it, through in Weller's term, an annual "opportunity." Although the leader has influence over its composition, the parliamentary party nonetheless retains a distance from the party leadership. Thatcher was weakest among those with whom she should have had considerable influence, her fellow Conservative parliamentarians, and strongest among those who had no formal vote in the leadership process, the party at the constituency level. As a purely speculative matter and as a reminder that institutions do affect outcomes, it is quite possible that Thatcher, who remained strong among party activists, would have retained her leadership in 1990 had the British Conservatives used a delegated convention system similar to Canada's. But then had a convention system been in place in 1975, she almost certainly would not have won the leadership when she did, for Heath enjoyed far greater popularity in the constituency parties at the time than she did. In any event, in 1990 Heseltine played the role of the stalking horse and the annual contest within the party's narrow leadership selection constituency confirmed her vulnerability.

The Tories in the Canadian Parliament have no equivalent formal role to play in assessing and challenging their party's leadership. As the party's constitutional means of assessing his leadership would have occurred only had the Tories been in opposition, Mulroney had nothing to fear in the way of regular challenges to his leadership in his nine years as prime minister. His popularity in public opinion polls sank lower than Thatcher's. Mulroney had introduced a hated new tax (the GST), as had Thatcher (the poll tax), and he had pushed for closer and highly controversial North American ties via free trade pacts with the United States and Mexico. For her part, Thatcher was at odds with much of her party and public opinion over Britain's relationship with the European Community. From 1990 on, his party's prospects of winning re-election with Mulroney were even more bleak than those of the British Tories under Thatcher. Yet even though such similar conditions held at roughly the same time in the two Conservative parties, Mulroney, unlike Thatcher, had little to fear from his parliamentary caucus because it lacked the constitutionally sanctioned authority to remove him. That authority, of course, lay with the party in convention only.

Why there should be such a difference between the two countries is a complex mix of unique cultural, situational, and intra-party procedural factors. Personalities, issues, political prospects, and the time at which these combine and come before those voting on a party's leadership are vital to understanding such highly-charged political moves as attempting to overthrow a leader. By the same token such moves are undertaken by publicly acknowledged challengers or shadow boxers in full knowledge of the rules of the game. Thatcher suffered the fate she did because the electoral concerns of Tory MPs were able to find expression through the party's institutionalized leadership selection mechanism. For his part, Mulroney benefited from the steps first taken in the late 1960s to end the role that the parliamentary party was to play in assessing and possibly replacing an incumbent leader. Diefenbaker's removal from office symbolized the change that had taken place in the authority structure within Canadian parties. Different from any previous sacking of a party leader, it was the successful culmination of a battle waged by the extra-parliamentary rebels against parliamentary party members loyal to the leader. Fittingly, it helped to mark the end of the first generation and the beginning of the second generation of leadership conventions. It also highlighted what would emerge in the ensuing three decades as one of the differences between the British Tory and Canadian systems. Challenges mounted against the leader were more certain of success when the British leader was prime minister and when the Canadian one was in opposition. The unassailability of Canadian prime ministers had been irrefutable.

4 Mega-Bucks for
Mega-Conventions

It is possible to lose with money; it is impossible to win without it.
– Jeffrey Simpson

Modern conventions have become expensive exercises. The party staging the event wants to capitalize on the opportunity by presenting as colourful and as exciting a media event as possible. As the success of the convention rests on the human organization and financial resources that go into it, hundreds of individuals and millions of dollars (at least in the two older parties) will be needed by the party. Candidates too must be able to raise sizable funds. Without them, they will be in no position to mount a worthy campaign for the leadership. For its part, the public is also involved in the financing of party conventions and leadership campaigns through the federal election expenses legislation. Adopted in 1974, it has provided parties and candidates with the opportunity to use its tax credit provisions to help to finance leadership contests. In all, the total convention costs to the party, candidates, and the public treasury now run into several millions of dollars.

THE COSTS OF CONVENTIONS

Typically within days of the announcement of its leader's resignation, a party begins planning the convention at which a successor will be chosen.[1] How competently those plans are conceived and executed is a direct reflection of the organizational expertise and the human and financial resources of the party. Skilled and knowledgeable organizers, executive officers, paid party officials, and scores of volunteers must be prepared to put in the time and effort to get a convention up and running. Without their contribution, no convention could hope to succeed. But equally, without sufficient funds the party runs the risk of mounting a modestly successful convention at best or of incurring large debts, or both. These are unappealing prospects for any party.

Although every convention is unique and each party has its own history and customs of leadership selection to draw on, national leadership conventions share many organizational and procedural features. At some point early in the planning every party executive or specially constituted convention steering committee will have to decide when and where a convention is to be held. Not only are possible conflicts with major sporting events explored, but other considerations invariably enter into the decision on timing of the convention. Planning for the April 1968 Liberal convention, for example, the executive had to weigh running head-to-head against NHL playoffs (which as it turned out they did) against a number of other considerations brought to their first meeting in December 1967. These included the stated desire of the current leader, Lester Pearson, to step down as quickly as possible and his shock at learning that it would take a minimum of three and a half months to organize the convention; representations from Liberal students opposing an April convention because it would conflict with preparations for final examinations; reminders from Christian Liberals of the dates of the Easter weekend and from Jewish Liberals of the Passover dates; and concerns from politicians about having to give up part of their spring recess from the Commons to stay on in Ottawa.[2]

And Ottawa is now the usual site of large leadership conventions. Since the Tory convention in Toronto in 1967, only one Liberal convention (1990, Calgary) and two NDP (1975 and 1989, Winnipeg) have been held outside Ottawa. The other six have all been staged at Ottawa's Civic Centre. There are two obvious reasons why this should be so: costs and political realities. One of the attractions of Ottawa (even though, in then-Liberal party president Iona Campagnolo's words, the city "is an uncomfortable place for such a big event")[3] is the relative savings, especially in terms of travel costs, that can be achieved because of its location.[4] The Tories estimated in 1976 that by holding their leadership convention in Ottawa rather than in Winnipeg, they saved $106,000, the largest part of which (one-third) came from savings on travel subsidies.[5] This has been of less concern to the NDP because a relatively larger share of delegates attending their national conventions are from Manitoba, Saskatchewan, and British Columbia and far fewer are from Quebec and Atlantic Canada. Choosing Ottawa as the convention site also helps, again in Campagnolo's words, "to protect the political agenda."[6] Although the House of Commons normally agrees not to meet for the three or four days of the convention, the realities of planning a large national convention in the context of parliamentary politics (where governments and ministers may unexpectedly be called on to defend themselves) are such that holding a convention a great distance from the nation's capital could prove to be a political error of considerable magnitude. That the four conventions held in cities other than Ottawa since 1967 have been leadership contests within opposition, not government, parties would tend to confirm this observation.[7]

To organize a convention is an immense task. A range of committees, each responsible for one of a number of tasks critical to a convention's success, needs to be created and staffed by volunteers or paid workers. Provincial, constituency, youth, women's, and campus associations have to be alerted to their obligations under the party's constitution and involved in the critical task of choosing delegates. Rules governing everything from delegate selection to the election of the leader need to be devised and applied. Regular transmission of information from the convention planners to party officials, candidates, delegates, caucus, and the media must be assured. These and countless other tasks all have to be performed under the pressure of time and with a watchful eye on the financial and human resources available. Typical of how parties have arranged their convention planning committees and delegated their organizational responsibilities are the organizations established by the Conservatives in 1976 and the Liberals in 1984. What is apparent from both organization charts is the obligation that a party has to put in place an operational structure attuned to the needs of the party, candidates, delegates, and media (see diagrams 4-1 and 4-2).

The Tories were obviously mindful of these needs as they set about planning the first of the great modern conventions – Toronto in 1967. They held a pre-convention policy conference at Montmorency, Quebec; provided travel subsidies for delegates to the September convention; and budgeted for convention committee meetings, simultaneous translation, equipment rentals, entertainment, travel, telephone, printing, and a variety of other related convention organization costs. Yet the strength of their planning was not matched by fiscal reality. At the end of the exercise they found their total expenditures of $354,000 were $264,000 in excess of their actual revenues, a shortfall equivalent to $1,131,000 in 1993 dollars.[8] Coupled with the debt the party was soon to incur from fighting three federal elections in seven years, the Tories recognized going into the 1976 convention that the spending required to mount large, modern conventions could, if uncontrolled, place unwanted and sizable financial strains on the party.

Accordingly, when the Conservative executive met in the summer of 1975 to begin planning the leadership convention of the following Feb-

Diagram 4-1
Organization Chart: 1976 Progressive Conservative Leadership Convention*

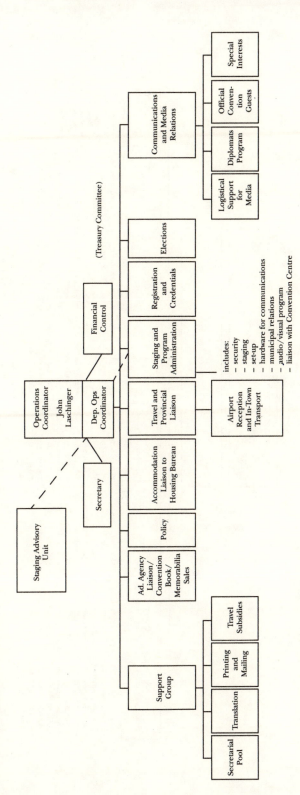

Source: NA, MG28 IV 2, vol. 524, "Convention Budget" file

* An additional committee, the Candidate Liaison Committee, acted as a liaison committee between candidates and the Operations Committee.

Diagram 4-2
Organization Chart: 1984 Liberal Leadership Convention*

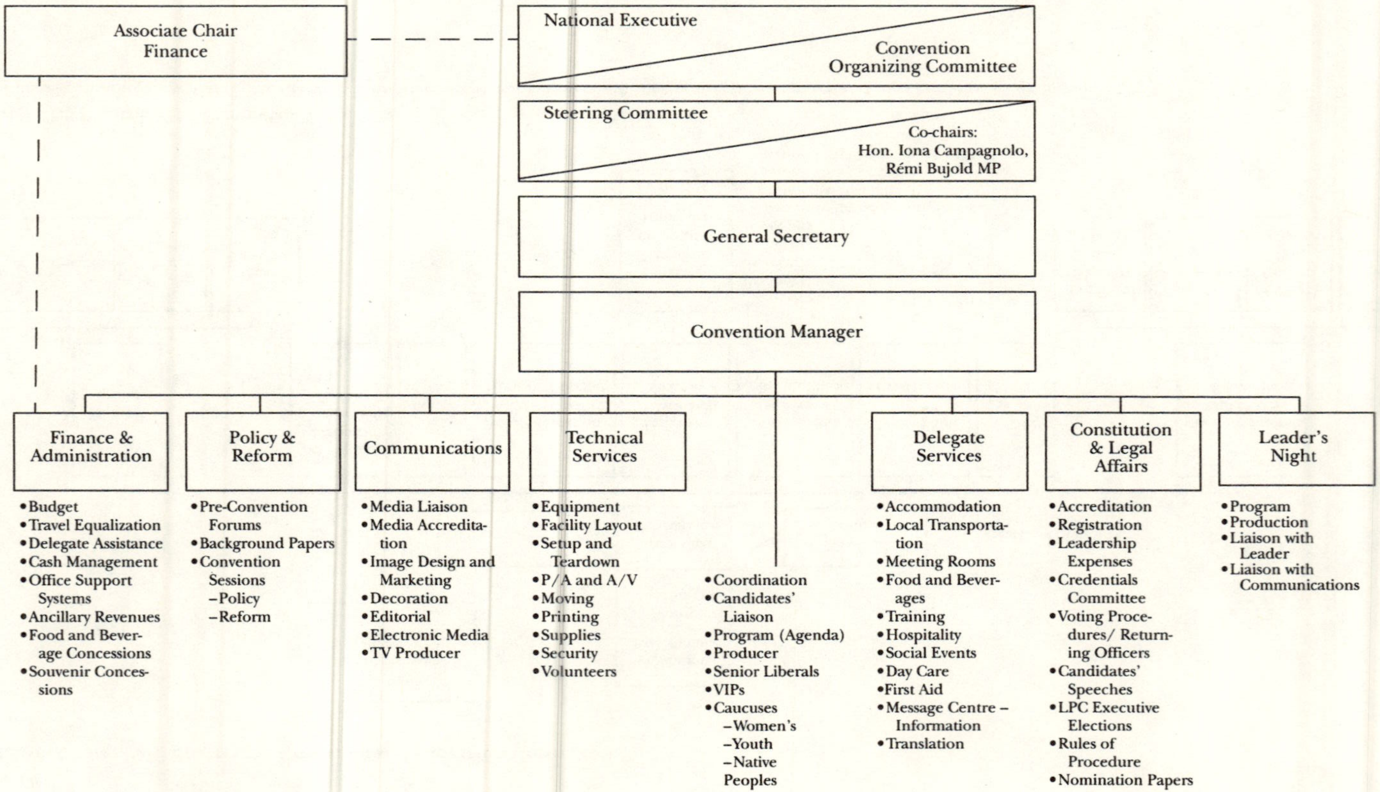

		National Executive		

| | | Convention Organizing Committee | | |

| | | Steering Committee | | |
| | | Co-chairs: Hon. Iona Campagnolo, Rémi Bujold MP |

| | | General Secretary | | |

| | | Convention Manager | | |

Associate Chair Finance

Finance & Administration
- Budget
- Travel Equalization
- Delegate Assistance
- Cash Management
- Office Support Systems
- Ancillary Revenues
- Food and Beverage Concessions
- Souvenir Concessions

Policy & Reform
- Pre-Convention Forums
- Background Papers
- Convention Sessions
  - Policy
  - Reform

Communications
- Media Liaison
- Media Accreditation
- Image Design and Marketing
- Decoration
- Editorial
- Electronic Media
- TV Producer

Technical Services
- Equipment
- Facility Layout
- Setup and Teardown
- P/A and A/V
- Moving
- Printing
- Supplies
- Security
- Volunteers

- Coordination
- Candidates' Liaison
- Program (Agenda)
- Producer
- Senior Liberals
- VIPs
- Caucuses
  - Women's
  - Youth
  - Native Peoples

Delegate Services
- Accommodation
- Local Transportation
- Meeting Rooms
- Food and Beverages
- Training
- Hospitality
- Social Events
- Day Care
- First Aid
- Message Centre – Information
- Translation

Constitution & Legal Affairs
- Accreditation
- Registration
- Leadership Expenses
- Credentials Committee
- Voting Procedures/ Returning Officers
- Candidates' Speeches
- LPC Executive Elections
- Rules of Procedure
- Nomination Papers

Leader's Night
- Program
- Production
- Liaison with Leader
- Liaison with Communications

Source: NA MG28 IV 3, Box 1628, no title.

* An additional committee, the Candidate Liaison Committee, acted as a liaison committee between candidates and the steering committee.

ruary, they adopted a proposal whereby tighter budgetary controls were to be put into effect under the watchful eye and hands-on control of the party's national director and "Operations Coordinator" of the convention planning organization, John Laschinger. This reflected the policy, insisted on by the executive, that the convention was to operate on a break-even basis and that it be self-financing. That the party succeeded, with total expenditures of $612,395 exceeding revenues by only two hundred dollars,[9] was due largely to the timely arrival of amendments to the Income Tax Act contained in the election expenses legislation of 1974 and to the party's ground-breaking use of tax credits to finance the convention. The new tax credit scheme enabled the Conservatives (and subsequently all other registered parties) to charge substantially higher fees for delegates, alternate delegates, and observers without the full brunt of those larger fees being borne by the individuals themselves. For Conservative constituency delegates, for example, fees jumped from $25 in 1967 to $150 in 1976, to $330 in 1983, and to $595 in 1993.

The key to understanding the fee increases lies in a ruling handed down by Revenue Canada early in 1975. The department informed the Tories that "an amount paid to a registered political party as a registration fee for a leadership convention or general meeting of the political party, where such fee merely entitles the contributor to attend and to vote, is a contribution to such a party" and thereby qualified for an official receipt for a tax credit on income tax.[10] The effect of this ruling, based on a provision of the Income Tax Act initially intended to aid registered parties and candidates to raise funds for elections, was to make it considerably easier for parties to raise the money needed to finance large, costly conventions and to run them on a break-even basis.

For delegates, alternates, and observers, the tax credit effectively meant that the net amount they paid to attend a convention would be considerably less than what they were charged on registration as their receipt entitled them to deduct the eligible tax credit directly from tax payable on their income taxes, to a maximum of $500.[11] Parties have now gone well beyond recognizing registration fees as the only type of expense for which tax credits may be claimed. The Liberals in 1990, for example, encouraged delegates and alternates to "do their own fund-raising." The party issued receipts, on the condition the cheques had been made payable to the Liberal Party of Canada, to any individual who had contributed to the registration fee or to the hotel and meal expenses paid by a delegate or alternate attending the convention. Those to whom receipts were issued included "family, friends and businesses."[12]

For both parties and those registering to attend conventions, the tax credit scheme is clearly attractive. For taxpayers, however, it obviously amounts to a transferred cost they assume because of the revenue forfeited from taxes payable. The implications of the tax credit system for the parties, delegates, and the public treasury are seen in the fees and tax credit structure for the most recent Liberal leadership convention. The largest and most expensive national convention to date was held in Calgary in 1990, with 6,400 delegates and alternates eligible to attend at fees set at $675 for youth and $875 for all others, with tax credits of $342 and $408 respectively. The fees for the observers in attendance were set at $500, for which a tax credit of $275 was issued. Had the convention been fully attended, the party would have raised in excess of $5.4 million, of which a maximum of approximately $2.6 million would have been picked up by taxpayers through the tax credit provisions of the Income Tax Act (see table 4-1). In fact, some delegates and alternates failed to register and the party reported collecting approximately $4.2 million in convention fees, of which up to a maximum of about $2 million was paid for out of the pockets of taxpayers.[13]

The post-convention statement of actual income and costs prepared following the 1990 Liberal convention (the most recent complete post-convention revenue and expenditure figures publicly available for either of the older parties) is revealing for the light it sheds on several aspects of convention financing. On the revenue side, the party is almost totally reliant on fees charged delegates and alternates. Observers – ranging from ambassadors and embassy officials to Ottawa lobbyists, academics not otherwise successful in obtaining media passes, and interested members of the general public – also make their contribution towards the self-financing of the convention, though their levies account for only a small proportion of the total revenues. The remainder of the party's revenue is derived from fees collected from those attending the various party-sponsored leadership forums and the leader's night and from other minor sources[14] (see table 4-2).

On the expenditure side of the ledger, the largest single cost of a convention is the travel subsidy program, whereby the party reimburses part of the travel costs of delegates and alternates who have travelled more than a prescribed distance. For the Tories, travel subsidies accounted for roughly 20 per cent of their expenditures in both 1967 and 1976.[15] For the Liberals in 1984, it came to about one-third of their total expenses. No other expenditure that year came close to the travel subsidy, although, at $688,700, finance and administration ($150,00 over the original budget estimate) was a decent second.[16] For the Liberal 1990 convention, travel subsidies accounted for an even larger share of total expenditures given the greater travel costs on a per delegate basis of holding the convention in Calgary rather than Ottawa. Fully $2.2 million – one-half of the party's convention budget – was spent on subsidizing the delegates' travel (see table 4-2). As noted previously, the savings on travel claims is one of the principal reasons why the parties have so rarely held conventions outside of Central Canada, and Ottawa in particular.

One item came in well over budget in the 1984 Liberal convention – the "Leader's Night." Designed as a tribute to retiring leader Pierre Trudeau, the evening was originally allocated a budget of $125,000. At the same time, however, the two co-chairs of the evening gala, Senator Keith Davey and Marc Lalonde, were authorized by the convention steering committee "to find extra funds from other sources, and keep records of all expenses [which] only Herb Metcalfe [would] be authorized to sign for."[17] The amount shown in the "actual" post-convention budget ($278,000) was more than twice the original allocation. But a separate "Absolutely Confidential" budget compiled some time after the convention points to a total cost for the evening of $534,000 (or $695,000 in 1993 dollars), approximately one-half of which would have been raised outside the convention's budgetary framework. Major entertainers and show business personalities (Maureen Forrester, Rich Little, Norman Jewison, Nathalie and René Simard, and Paul Anka) donated their time, but the costs of the film production ($120,000), set design and construction ($60,000), orchestra and musical director ($60,000), gift for the retiring leader ($35,000) and the whole range of other items eventually made for a much more expensive evening than had originally been planned.[18] Nine years later the Tories followed suit with a similarly lavish tribute to Brian Mulroney on his retirement, and although the published reports of the cost of the evening ($300,000) suggest a markedly cheaper tribute than that given Trudeau, the staging, film production, music and entertainment suggest its real figure more likely approximated or exceeded that of the Liberals in 1984.[19]

THE COSTS OF CAMPAIGNS

The cost of mounting a serious campaign for the leadership of either the Liberal or Conservative party has skyrocketed since the advent of modern conventions. The days when a candidate could spend a few thousand dollars, give a good speech, and still receive substantial media attention and delegate votes are long gone. Since 1967 leadership campaigns have become increasingly more highly organized, professionally managed, and technologically sophisticated affairs that carry ever larger price tags. In much the same way that a party strikes and finances an elaborate organizational structure to plan and to operate a convention, so too must a serious leadership candidate bring onside professional expertise to organize a campaign and to arrange for its financing.

The available data on candidates' spending are fragmentary at best. Even for conventions in which candidates were required to disclose their spending, the figures can be incomplete and open to dispute.[20] Spending that one candidate reports, another may not. Although limits on candidate spending have become the norm in national party leadership campaigns, they have varied from party to party and from convention to convention, and they are often exceedingly generous in what they exclude. In the 1993 Conservative leadership campaign, for example, party organizers set a spending limit for candidates of $900,000, but this did not include costs incurred from such big-ticket items as candidate travel, some campaign workers' salaries, and polling. Furthermore, spending limits and disclosure requirements applied only from the time the convention was officially announced by the party to the time the leader was actually chosen. This means that money raised and spent before or after those deadlines was outside the terms of the financial framework set by the convention organizers.

The rising costs of leadership campaigns in the second generation took place in two waves: the first lasted from 1967 to 1976 and the second began in 1983 but had not, as of 1993, ended. (For reported and estimated expenditures of Liberal and Progressive Conservative leadership candidates 1967–1993, see table 4-3.) In the 1967 Conservative leadership race the estimated spending of the winner, Robert Stanfield, was $150,000.[21] This was equivalent to $641,000 in 1993 dollars – or more than Jim Edwards, the third-place Tory candidate in 1993, spent in his run for the leadership. One year after Stanfield's selection, Pierre Trudeau in his successful bid for the Liberal leadership spent an estimated $300,000. This amounted to a hundred-fold increase over Lester Pearson's reported spending only ten years earlier and equalled $1.2 million in 1993 dollars. Second generation conventions were off to an expensive start.

In response to the unquestioned fact that a growing amount of money was needed to finance a leadership campaign, organizers for the 1976 Conservative convention opted to require candidates to disclose the source and amount of the donations to their campaigns as well as their total expenditures. Although Joe Clark's declared spending at approximately $170,000 was below that of six of his eleven rivals, he nonetheless won on the convention's fourth ballot, proving that those spending the greatest amount are not guaranteed victory. Brian Mulroney was widely perceived to be the big-money candidate at that convention. Estimates of his spending ranged from $343,000 to $500,000, or $800,000 to $1.2 million in 1993 dollars. Some delegates on the convention floor actually folded his campaign posters to read "Money" instead of "Mulroney"!

In the 1980s and 1990s, leadership conventions became multimillion dollar affairs. They also varied considerably in their requirements governing spending limits and disclosure and in their definition of what constituted an expense. Arguing that no rules were better than unenforceable ones, organizers of the 1983 Tory convention made no attempt to regulate or to limit candidates' fund-raising and spending. The convention committee meeting at which rules governing campaign financing were discussed concluded that: "(1) financial disclosure would be difficult to enforce; (2) candidate funding was no business of the media or the public; and (3) the delegates were the best built-in safeguard against candidate over-spending."[22] Their decision not to impose spending limits or disclosure requirements no doubt reflected the party's experience in 1976 when it was unable, despite rules all candidates had accepted prior to entering the race, to force compliance with the disclosure regulations it had put in place.[23]

Estimating candidates' spending is an inexact science at the best of times. Bearing that in mind, estimates of candidate spending in 1983 by front runners Joe Clark and Brian Mulroney approached $2 million. In the Liberal race of 1984, John Turner officially reported spending $1,594,941 on his successful leadership bid, with the runner-up Jean Chrétien close behind at $1,528,570. Once again costs escalated with the Liberal leadership race of 1990. As in 1984, several important classes of expenditures were excluded from the spending limit. These included expenses incurred in fund-raising activities, candidate travel and accommodation, volunteer labour, and costs incurred before the leadership campaign was officially launched or after the convention had been held. The exemptions enabled the 1990 front runners Jean Chrétien and Paul Martin Jr to report spending of $2,440,000 and $2,370,000 respectively and still meet the party's $1.7 million per-candidate spending limit set for that race. The Liberals' experience with attempting to administer the spending limit and disclosure requirements in 1990 prompted the co-chairs of the party's expenses supervision committee to acknowledge wryly upon release of the final financial statements that, in exercising its responsibilities, "the Leadership Expenses Committee encountered two different problems: drafting the regulations and implementing them."[24]

No doubt the Tory officials entrusted with enforcing the $900,000 per-candidate spending limit for the party's 1993 campaign felt the same way. Jean Charest, whose total spending approximated $2,300,000, reported spending $842,000 on items included in the limit. But Kim

Campbell's campaign organization, which reportedly spent about $3 million on her leadership bid, acknowledged in its leadership spending reports that it exceeded the limit on unexempt spending by $300,000. In addition, the post-convention decision of the Campbell-appointed board of the party's fund-raising arm to help finance her campaign debts with a $350,000 loan was in violation of the party's own rule that it would not "in any circumstances provide financial assistance" to leadership candidates. In neither case did the party censure Campbell or any members of her campaign organization for these infractions.[25] The party itself was guilty of disregarding its stated requirement of publicly releasing the leadership candidates' financial reports. On the day the reports had been scheduled to be released – six months after the convention – the party did hold a press conference, but its purpose was to announce Kim Campbell's resignation as leader rather than to divulge the financial details of the leadership candidates' campaigns.

The NDP has been relatively unaffected by the trend of rising costs to leadership candidates. As Keith Archer has observed, "For the NDP, money has historically been less plentiful (if not less important) in leadership contests, and the party has been much more inclined to regulate, or at least impose guidelines on, campaign expenditures."[26] In 1971 the NDP became the first Canadian national party to establish spending limits for leadership candidates. Candidates in the race to succeed Tommy Douglas were allowed to spend a total of 3 cents for every member of the party. With membership estimated at the time to be approximately 350,000, the candidates could spend about $10,500 – less than 4 per cent of Trudeau's expenditures three years earlier. This was the equivalent of $38,000 in 1993 dollars.

For the 1975 New Democratic convention, at which Ed Broadbent emerged victorious on the fourth ballot, candidates were allowed to spend a maximum of $15,000, of which $1,000 was reimbursed from the party for travel and mailing costs. The candidates that year also had to disclose all revenue and expenditures, including the names of those contributing sums greater than $10. In 1989 the NDP set a per-candidate spending limit of $150,000. Not one of the candidates was able to raise that much money. Audrey McLaughlin, the biggest spender of the 1989 campaign with $128,575.50, won the leadership on the fourth ballot. Although the reported spending of each of the candidates was less than the value of his or her campaign because such items as volunteer labour from trade unions and party-subsidized candidate travel were not reported as costs, the NDP leadership candidates of 1989 ran far more frugal campaigns than their Liberal and Conservative counterparts in 1990 and 1993 respectively[27] (for expenditures of NDP leadership candidates in 1989 see table 4-4).

For candidates seeking the leadership of one of the two older parties, greater organizational demands, modern campaign techniques, and the cost of new technology combine to make money a major factor in the campaign. There were several features of the Conservative and Liberal conventions of the late 1960s that set them apart from previous conventions and resulted in dramatically higher costs to candidates. At both conventions, more than 2,400 delegates were eligible to attend, a more than 60 per cent increase over the conventions of the 1950s. Coinciding with this growth in numbers was the decline in the ability of the party establishment to control the delegates and to determine the leadership. The greater number of independently-minded delegates, combined with the fact that in both leadership races there were more serious candidates than there had ever been in the past, meant that the contests were more open and competitive and that candidates had to work harder than before to attract delegate support.

The leadership races came to resemble mini-election campaigns as, for the first time, candidates travelled extensively across the country seeking to meet and to convert delegates. One candidate, Davie Fulton, flew a total of 76,000 miles (a record for the time) in the months leading up to the Tory convention in September 1967. Leading candidates such as Stanfield, Roblin, and Fulton in 1967 and Trudeau, Hellyer, and Winters in 1968 established national campaign organizations, headquarters' organizations, and convention week organizations. Nearly every aspect of the conventions of the late 1960s was on a grander scale than had previously been the case.[28] Computerized delegate tracking, although primitive by later standards, was used by leadership candidates for the first time. At the 1967 Tory convention Dalton Camp and Norman Atkins devised for Stanfield a revolutionary convention floor communications system that involved an extensive network of spotters and floor strategists equipped with telephones and walkie-talkies. The following year, various Liberal leadership candidates adopted these techniques.[29]

The second wave of rising campaign costs began with the Conservative and Liberal conventions of the early 1980s. The number of delegate entitled to attend these conventions rose above 3,000 at the Tory convention of 1983 and 3,500 at the Liberal convention the following year. The Liberals went even further for their 1990 leadership convention (the largest gathering to date of delegates to a national leadership convention) as 5,228 voting delegates were eligible to go to Calgary to participate in the selection of John Turner's successor. As a result, leadership campaigns since 1983 have become more professional and more thorough – and therefore more expensive – in their search for delegates than ever before. In 1967 Davie Fulton's campaign organization contacted one-third of the delegates, more than any of his rivals reached. By contrast, sixteen years later Joe Clark's team contacted all but 6 per cent of the voting delegates.[30]

Serious candidates were compelled to establish local organizations in as many constituencies as possible to attempt to influence delegate selection meetings. The need also to sustain media attention over a period of several months meant that extensive national campaign tours became one of the requirements a serious candidate had to meet. Lavish convention-week events staged by candidates to boost the morale of supporters, to create the image of momentum, and to provide an informal setting for last-minute arm-twisting became standard. The advantages that money gave to a candidate in a modern leadership campaign were obvious to John Nunziata, one of the minor candidates of 1990. "Money is dictating this leadership convention," he said. "This is not a battle of ideas. It's a battle of organization and money."[31]

Leadership campaign organizations have come increasingly to rely on polling data to drive the campaign strategy; direct mass mailings and telemarketing to flood the delegates with propaganda and to raise funds; computerized data banks to track delegates' preferences; communications technology such as cellular phones (of which there were an estimated 2,500 to 3,000 at the 1993 Tory convention)[32] to maintain convention floor organization; and other sophisticated electronic gadgets to get the job done. Hats, t-shirts, scarves, buttons, signs, and other paraphernalia to be distributed to delegates and worn or carried by volunteers must be produced in numbers large enough to ensure that no potential supporter is disappointed and no possible worker is improperly attired. All of this costs money, and lots of it.

PUBLIC FINANCING OF
LEADERSHIP CAMPAIGNS

The same tax credit provisions that govern the registration fees paid by delegates to attend party conventions apply to donations made to a leadership candidate. A maximum tax credit of $500 is available for a $1,150 donation to a candidate on condition that the contribution is made payable to the party. The party in turn channels the donation (typically taking a percentage of the donation as its part of a revenue-sharing scheme) to the candidate's official financial agent. This flow-through practice of contributing to candidates by way of a registered party to enable contributions to qualify for tax credits began with the Conservatives in 1976 and has since been adopted by both the Liberals and the NDP for candidate fund-raising in their national leadership contests.[33] It would be hard to quarrel with the conclusion of the Department of National Revenue that the practice of channelling donations to leadership candidates through the party, which is not specifically provided for in the law, "gives the transaction an air of artificiality."[34]

As is the case with candidates generally, those planning campaigns that will cost between several hundred thousand and several millions of dollars rely on a variety of fund-raising techniques.[35] But while undoubtedly helpful to them, the tax credit scheme is of less importance in bringing in the really big donations. At one end of the scale are fund-raising dinners which can raise tens of thousands of dollars in an evening. For events such as these, a tax credit receipt issued for a portion of the ticket cost may be an inducement for at least some of the contributors to attend. At the other end are the large individual or corporate donors who may be persuaded to contribute anything from a few thousand dollars to $20,000 to $25,000, possibly even more.[36] Those big contributions are clearly more attractive than numerous small donations to candidate fund-raisers simply because of the considerably less time and effort needed to raise an equivalent amount of money. From the donor's perspective, however, the tax credit is largely irrelevant.

How often, by whom, and to whom the very large contributions are given is difficult to determine. The lists provided by the parties, months after the election of the leader, often amount to little more than aggregations of names of contributors and amounts donated without matching the two. Contributions may be made before or after the period covered by the party's financial guidelines, in which case they are impossible to trace. As well, big donors may prefer that there be no public disclosure of the amount donated or of the candidate to whom the contribution has been given.[37] The lessons to be drawn from all of this are clear. In Jeffrey Simpson's words: "The more you give, the less valuable the tax deduction, which is limited by law. Thus the largest donors, the very ones who might have a hook into a candidate, will not be known. The smallest donors, who will want the tax receipt, will be known. The system as designed stands the public interest on its head by publicizing those contributions of least importance and hiding those of potentially the greatest."[38]

Revenue-sharing arrangements (through which parties since 1976 have taken anything from 10 to 25 per cent of officially receipted donations raised by the candidates) can actually serve as a disincentive for candidates to use the tax credit system. Candidates seeking to attract large donations are not keen on having to forfeit large amounts of their revenue to the party. Commenting on the preference of campaign organizations for direct contributions to the candidate over the tax credit alternative of revenue-sharing with the party, 1983 Tory leadership candidate Michael Wilson observed that "25 percent is a stiff commission."[39]

The two older parties have addressed some of the concerns raised by candidates about the parties' claim to a portion of creditable contributions. No doubt accepting the point that the revenue-sharing scheme applied in 1976 and 1983 to contributions raised through the tax credit system served neither the candidates nor the party well, the Tories lowered their levy to 10 per cent in 1993. For their part, the Liberals moved in a completely different direction in 1990 to ensure that the party was guaranteed a reasonable take from candidate funds. They switched from requiring a share of a candidate's revenue raised through the tax credit scheme to a tax imposed on candidate expenditures. All candidates were required to make payments to the party equal to 20 per cent of any of their campaign expenditures in excess of $250,000. In all, the party collected $608,151 from the levy. This money went into the party's general revenues and was not used to finance the convention itself.[40]

Given the variations among the parties since tax credits for contributions to candidates were first used in 1976, and the absence of standard accounting procedures by the candidates and parties, it is difficult to draw precise conclusions about the value of tax credits to the financing of leadership campaigns and about their cost to the public purse. As information on candidate fund-raising varies from candidate to candidate, party to party, and convention to convention, and as the parties have yet to establish strictly enforceable guidelines covering all aspects of fund-raising, what is available as part of the public record cannot be considered entirely complete or totally reliable. That said, however, the data available for the 1989 NDP and 1990 Liberal conventions provide little evidence for the claim that the political tax credit is of considerable importance to the financing of campaigns. Instead, the data indicate that it may be of only marginal value to leadership candidates and that the cost to taxpayers has been modest.

It stands to reason that candidates raising relatively small amounts of money from a relatively large number of donors would welcome the tax credit scheme, for it provides contributors to their campaigns with fairly generous tax benefits and it no doubt helps to make the task of fund-raising easier. After the 1989 NDP convention, the winner and the candidate with the highest campaign revenue and expenditures, Audrey McLaughlin, reported receiving $106,051 (excluding the $5,000 that she along with all other candidates were given by the party for candidate travel expenses) from a total of 1,187 individual/union/

association contributors. For his part, Steven Langdon, with mid-range revenues of $52,425, reported that 108 contributors had each donated $100 or more to his campaign. Simon de Jong, whose bank loan of $27,000 made up two-thirds of his total campaign revenue of $42,500, claimed that only $7,835 of his donations had been raised through tax creditable contributions.[41]

None of these is a large amount of money for modern leadership conventions. But then neither were the NDP spending limits of $150,000 or maximum individual contribution limits of $1,000 large by recent standards. The cost to the treasury of the tax credit system is impossible to calculate with any precision given the absence of detail needed to make accurate calculations. But if McLaughlin's and de Jong's revenues are taken as the two most divergent examples of tax creditable contributions, and if the most extreme assumptions are made about the number of contributors eligible for official receipts and the maximum tax credit rate applied to the contributions, the total share of the 1989 NDP contest picked up by the taxpayers for all seven candidates could not have been large – no more than $150,000 in all.[42]

Derived from candidate expenses data publicly released by the Liberal party, table 4-5 shows the approximate dollar value of the tax receipts issued and of the corresponding tax credits for donations to each of the Liberal candidates in 1990. Jean Chrétien, Paul Martin, and Sheila Copps reported spending $2.45 million, $2.37 million, and $806,000, of which approximately $910,000, $400,000, and $450,000 respectively was receipted by the Liberal party. If it were true in each of the calendar years 1989 and 1990 that every amount for which a tax receipt was issued had been claimed in full by a different donor and, secondly, that none of these donors had claimed any other contributions to any registered political party in the period in question, then the absolute maximum possible value of the tax credits obtained by contributors to the campaigns of all the candidates would amount to a total public subsidy of $693,000.[43] In fact, the actual cost to the public purse was probably much less, since some donors gave large sums of money to each of the five candidates, not to mention other parties.[44] Receipts were therefore issued to donors who were not eligible to use them to claim tax credits. It is also likely that many of the donors who were eligible to claim the tax credits did not do so. In his study of party finance for the Royal Commission on Electoral Reform and Party Financing (the Lortie Commission), W.T. Stanbury reveals that throughout the 1980s the proportion of those individuals eligible to claim the political tax credit who actually did so fluctuated between 50 and 65 per cent. For corporations the figure was even less, approximately 30 per cent. That such a large proportion of the eligible contributors did not claim the credit led Stanbury to claim that the tax credit "is not much of an incentive to make a political contribution" and that it may be of "modest significance to parties and candidates in their efforts to obtain contributions" from individuals and corporations.[45]

These data and Stanbury's findings indicate that tax credits may have been of only marginal use to those candidates who ran very expensive campaigns. They were more important for some of those candidates who had difficulty attracting large sums of money to their campaigns. But at the same time the tax credit may be of little help to a candidate who cannot raise sufficient funds in his or her own right.

If the 1989 NDP and 1990 Liberal conventions are taken as representative of other conventions in which the tax credit system was used, then it seems clear that the cost of leadership campaigns to the public purse over the years has not been great. For the 1976 Tory contest it is probable that, as not all candidates used the tax credit system and that the amounts of money raised by candidates in that year were small by more recent standards, the cost to the public treasury was no more than $100,000. Assuming that the value of tax credits issued by the parties for contributions to candidates in 1983, 1984, and 1993 was no more than in 1990, the absolute maximum total cost to the taxpayers for the six leadership campaigns was about $3 million.

The fact that at least some of the funds raised by leadership candidates come from the public purse has contributed to calls for increased accountability and enforceable disclosure rules for leadership candidates' finances. Other concerns frequently raised by concerned citizens, by political scientists, and by some within political parties have created additional pressures for reform. The lack of restrictions on the size of donations, along with the absence of full disclosure of contributions, contributors, and recipients, have given rise to suspicions of undue influence being bought. Uncontrolled or seemingly excessive spending by candidates has encouraged the perception that leadership campaigns are for the rich and that the party leadership, and even the position of prime minister, are available to the highest bidder.

The use of tax credits by parties for donations to leadership candidates has received mixed reviews. The introduction of the practice by some of the Tory candidates in 1976 was seen, in some quarters at least, as something that had to be defended by the party. More recently, it has been called an abuse of the tax system.[46] Others see it in a positive light, as an instrument to encourage a broader segment of the population to participate in party finance and to assist candidates without access to large donations to attract many small contributions and thereby to become able to mount a campaign.[47] But the tax credit has done little to lower the barriers to entry of a leadership race caused by the high costs of the campaign. Some have suggested that the value of the tax credit should be increased. Accepting that the receipting of contributions to leadership candidates "now appears well established," Archer has argued that "in recognition that a party's responsibilities continue, and likely increase, during a leadership contest, contributions to such contests should be tax-creditable over and above the current limits for contributions to parties."[48]

REFORMING THE FINANCING OF LEADERSHIP CAMPAIGNS

Political parties in Canada have characteristically been looked upon as independent, private, and voluntary associations.[49] Only recently have they established guidelines concerning candidate spending limits and disclosure of contributors and amounts of contributions in leadership races, and even then the rules adopted have remained purely internal party matters. But the situation is far from ideal. Parties have found the rules (whatever complexion they may have been given at the time) to be difficult to enforce. Continued failure on the parties' part to enforce complete financial disclosure rules has contributed to the perception that leadership campaign financing is not entirely above board and that undue influence may be for sale to secret benefactors. Lacking the resources to enforce the rules and unwilling to discipline publicly leadership candidates who breaks them, the parties have had to rely on the good will of the candidates.

But in politics, good will cannot always be taken for granted. Two cases in point are Mulroney's refusal to file financial reports with the party in 1976 and Campbell's disregard for the spending limit set by the party in 1993. In neither case was the Conservative party willing or able to take any punitive action against the offending candidate. One of the problems with attempting to control the spending of leadership candidates is that the prize in a leadership race is so valuable that those charged with enforcing the rules face an almost irresistible urge on the part of the candidates' campaign organizations to break them. As the campaign manager of one of the Ontario Tory leadership candidates in 1985 said after the party set a per-candidate spending limit of $500,000, "On the record? It will be tough but you can run a campaign for $500,000. Off the record? Of course you can't, and won't if you want to win."[50]

Those who would like to see reforms introduced into leadership campaign financing have made a strong case for having candidates abide by spending limits and make full financial disclosure of their campaigns. They argue that the amount of money required to mount a competitive campaign should not act as a barrier to entry into the race or determine, or at least appear to determine, the outcome of the process. The high costs of seeking party leadership carry with them certain obvious risks. They may make "some candidates beholden to large private contributors and may deter other qualified candidates from running at all."[51]

But many calling for reform of leadership financing also recognize that the pressure to set a ceiling on the amount that candidates may spend must be balanced against the equally strong pressure that derives from the right of delegates, party members, and the public to be informed. Joe Wearing has warned that criticism of the high levels of candidate spending "can be too puritanical."[52] Candidates must be able to communicate with those chosen to vote on the leadership and with the general public over an extended period of time, all of which requires an organization and activities that cost money. The task, therefore, is to define the public's interest in such terms as to enable sufficient, though not excessive, amounts of money to be raised and spent by candidates, at the same time ensuring that disclosure of sources, restraints on spending, and use of public funds are all done within a framework that is recognized and accepted as legitimate.

Those who favour financial reforms of leadership selection work from the premise that "the choice of leaders is so vital that the process needs to be part of the public domain of politics. It simply is not just the business of a private party."[53] As such, they say, it is in the public interest for the process be open and publicly regulated. The Lortie Commission acknowledged as much. Theirs is by far the most influential voice to have been added in recent years to the call for the state to play a role in defining the terms of campaign financing. The commission rested its case for statutorily-established financial requirements on the fact that parties and candidates have for a number of years used the federal tax credit system as a way of helping to finance their conventions and leadership campaigns. This amounted, in the words of the commission, to acceptance of "a clear public dimension to the process." If candidates are prepared to use the tax system to their advantage, they should be willing to submit to "financial disclosure and accountability rules that match those in the Canada Elections Act on election campaigns and party financing."[54]

Together, the evidence that the parties have failed to establish and enforce appropriate financial regulations, the concerns expressed about the deleterious effects of excessively costly campaigns, and the view that the leadership selection process is part of the public domain, have led to calls for legislation to regulate the financial aspects of leadership campaigns. After hearing the testimony of many experienced party officials, the Lortie Commission concluded that "the value and intent of spending limits can be realised only if they have the sanction of law."[55] The same can be said of disclosure rules. The commission concluded that the principles of fairness and public confidence are undermined in the leadership selection process by the absence of "credible or enforceable spending limits" and "full and complete disclosure, particularly when public monies are used and when there is doubt that the rules are enforced."[56] Seeking to restore public confidence in politics and to promote fairness and the integrity of the electoral system, the commission recommended several changes to the financing of leadership campaigns. In doing so, it was guided by two general objectives:

(1) minimum requirements should be set out in electoral law to ensure that leadership selection in all registered parties is guided by common values and principles that promote the integrity of the electoral process and that affirm the principle of fairness in electoral competition; and

(2) the treatment of the leadership selection process in electoral law should be neither so restrictive nor so intrusive as to impair the capacity of individual parties to establish rules and processes that reflect their own distinct traditions and character.[57]

To give effect to these principles the commission would require parties, as a condition of their registration for electoral and fund-raising purposes, to amend their constitutions to adopt rules requiring leadership candidates to provide full disclosure of financial activities, including size and source of financial contributions of $250 or more; to abide by a spending limit established by electoral law; and to file preliminary financial reports at the leadership convention itself and final reports within three months of the convention. Candidates for the leadership of registered parties would be eligible to use the tax credit system by way of the flow-through mechanism that has already become commonplace, but the practice would be legitimized in electoral law. No limits would be placed on the size of individual donations, but candidates would be required to provide full disclosure and to comply with spending limits for their contributors to be eligible for tax credits.[58]

The commission recommended that a standard formula for a maximum per-leadership candidate spending limit be included in electoral law. The proposed formula would ensure that the spending limit for leadership candidates not exceed 15 per cent of the election expenses permitted the party under the Canada Elections Act for the most recent federal election (which would be 70 cents per eligible voter). As an illustration, for the 1988 federal election there were 17,639,001 names on the voters' list. If the formula had been in place at the time, parties nominating candidates in all 295 constituencies would have been limited to spending $12,347,300 in the election. Thus the maximum spending limit for candidates in the NDP, Liberal, and Conservative leadership conventions of 1989, 1990, and 1993 respectively would have been set at $1,852,095. For any national convention held during the life of the Parliament elected in 1993, the most a party could allow its leadership candidates to spend (based on the 1993 voters' list of 19,471,105) would be $2,044,466. As this mark would be a maximum only, the parties would be free to set and to enforce their own per-candidate spending limits below the 15 per cent if they so chose.

The commission recommended that a few items be exempt from the spending limits. Expenses incurred in holding profitable fund-raising functions and the cost of a candidate's performance deposit are two items that would not be included in the limit. Another is any expenditures incurred either before the party officially announced a leadership convention or after the day the new leader was chosen. Overall, however, the Lortie proposals are much tighter than the recent Liberal and Conservative regulations, as items such as candidate travel and accommodation costs, all staff salaries, and polling costs would be subject to the limit.[59]

The intent of the royal commission was to force the parties to have acceptable and reasonable rules, to establish a framework within which they could operate with different traditions and expectations, and to give them the authority of law to enforce those rules. Indeed, a proposed Canada Elections Commission would ultimately ensure that the leadership candidates and the parties adhered to the regulations.[60] There is no question that, if implemented, the Lortie Commission's recommendations would introduce a measure of state control over leadership selection hitherto unknown to Canadian parties and candidates. Their ultimate effect would be to turn leadership selection into a considerably more institutionalized and publicly regulated process than has been the case in the past. There is no harm in this, however, as the parties have been found wanting in the way they have handled the issue of campaign financing to date, and as the public's interest in how parties chose their leaders is unquestioned.

Those looking to the Lortie Report for answers to all the problems of leadership financing will not find them. Even so, the report's call for a spending limit that would amount to approximately $2 million in 1993 dollars may seem curiously high for a commission concerned with enhancing access to the political process. In fact, the commission did not apply the access objective to party leadership; its objectives were to promote the integrity of party processes and fair competition between leadership candidates. Short of substantial state financial support of leadership candidates (which Lortie wisely did not counsel but which is available to presidential primary contestants in the United States on a matching basis[61]), there seems no acceptable alternative to a spending-limit recommendation based on the clear recognition of the established, but nonetheless costly, organizational and communicative needs of candidates and expectations of delegates. In view of the tasks that serious leadership candidates and their organizations must perform in the course of a few months, the spending limit proposed in the Lortie Report is both sensible and reasonable. But at the same time it should not be expected to reverse what has obviously become a feature of recent leadership conventions in the two older parties – that is, a smaller number of contestants because the high cost of competing has kept some leadership hopefuls out of the race.

The Lortie definition of the leadership campaign period as the time between the official announcement of the date of the convention and the actual date itself does no more to expose campaign contributions and expenses before or after that period than the rules that parties themselves have adopted in the past. As the Liberal 1989–90 experience suggested, the pre-convention announcement period could amount to several months during which individuals who had yet to declare their candidacy could raise money and pay start-up costs. Given the rules that the parties have put in place in the past, it has been impossible for the public to know what has been given to or spent by campaigns outside their official campaign period. In spite of its professed goal of increasing the degree of transparency in the leadership selection process, the commission's recommendation does nothing to address this issue. Though no timetable will ever capture all donations and expenditures, an extended one would lend greater credibility to the system than that contemplated in the Lortie Report. Establishing a financial disclosure period that would run from the date of the current leader's resignation announcement to six months following the convention would allow greater disclosure-controlled time for business transactions to be completed and for candidate campaign debts to be paid off.[62]

Such reservations aside, the Lortie recommendations provide the general framework for reforming leadership campaign financing in Canada. They are based on a reasoned analysis of the situation to date; they address the major problems that have marred the process; and they do so with proposals that wisely accept the financial realities of modern leadership selection.

PUBLIC REGULATION AND
LEADERSHIP CAMPAIGN FINANCE

Seeking the leadership of a national party in Canada has become a costly business. So has organizing and conducting a leadership convention. Candidates and parties alike have had to raise several millions of dollars to cover the expenses they have incurred. Taxpayers, through the parties' use of the political contributions provisions of the Income Tax Act, have indirectly subsidized leadership campaigns and conventions. Not surprisingly, money, which has been one of the hallmarks of the second generation of conventions, has become a central component of the debate about the future of leadership selection in Canada.

Several points have emerged about the parties' role in establishing the parameters of the financing of leadership campaigns. None of the spending, fund-raising, or disclosure rules has been standard among the three parties. The spending limits set by the parties have been established arbitrarily and have had many exemptions and loopholes. The rules have lacked teeth because the parties, who have never chastened publicly any of their own leadership candidates, have had neither the power nor the will to enforce their own regulations. Like the emperor with no clothes, the parties have been found to have engaged in an illusory exercise.

The rules have had little effect on the actual fund-raising and spending activities of the candidates. The opinion that spending limits and disclosure rules for leadership campaigns are important enough to be established and enforced and that the parties are incapable of doing so, along with the fact that the campaign is subsidized by the Canadian public, has led to calls for public regulation of the process. In particular, the Lortie Commission has recommended that a more standardized, transparent, and regulated process be established through federal electoral law.

In his study for the Lortie Commission on the attitudes of 1990 Liberal delegates towards proposed reforms to the leadership selection process, George Perlin reveals that "there was widespread agreement among the delegates on the need to reform the financing of leadership campaigns."[63] Specifically, 90 per cent wanted spending limits on campaigns, 87 per cent wanted candidates to be required to disclose how they spent their campaign funds, and 88 per cent wanted disclosure of sources and amounts of contributions to candidates. Most of the delegates also realized that if such rules were to be enforced it could only be done by the state. Sixty-four per cent and 57 per cent of the delegates indicated that contributions and candidate spending respectively should be regulated by law. And although the vast majority said that contributors to leadership campaigns should be eligible to receive tax credits, 84 per cent thought this should be contingent upon whether or not the recipient candidate met the spending limit and disclosure requirement. Nearly three of every ten delegates (28 per cent) would impose fines of up to $100,000 or more and 2 per cent approved of jail terms as punishment for violations of the spending and disclosure rules.[64]

These opinions of party activists reinforced the concerns previously expressed about the way in which leadership campaigns have been financed in Canada and lend support to the view that the time is propitious for state involvement in setting the terms for financing future contests. Parties have been found wanting in the way they have handled the issue so far. Now their activists (if the Liberal delegates in 1990 can be taken as representative of the larger group of supporters of all parties) want them to yield their carefully guarded prerogative to the state. Political parties have rarely been known to relinquish power freely over matters that affected the regulation of their own affairs unless it was clearly established that the changes were in their own interests. Can there be any doubt of that on this issue?

5 "Mediated" Conventions: From Print to Tube

> I don't know whether [this convention] is good for the party, but it's great television.
>
> – Bob White

All parties agree on one thing – the importance of extensive media coverage of leadership campaigns and conventions. From the time of the first leadership contests of this century, conventions have been planned with the media front and centre. Since 1919 convention officials and serious candidate organizations have struck committees and, in more recent times, appointed paid officials charged with responsibilities for "the press," or "publicity," or "communications." Their titles may have changed, but their fundamental task has remained the same: to get the greatest print, sound, and visual coverage possible for the candidates, the convention, and the party.

As is true generally of any relationship between politics and the media, there is a natural symbiosis at play here. Parties and candidates seek coverage to advance their own goals, just as the media search out stories that fit their views of what the contest is all about. In a curious way, each helps to define the qualities that the other chooses to see in the campaign and at the convention. So, too, do the media, particularly television, help to give shape to the contest – from the importance ascribed by the candidates to gaining media coverage to the information conveyed to delegates and candidates through published public opinion surveys.

MEDIA AND THE EARLY CONVENTIONS

The importance of the media had been recognized in 1919 when, at the Liberal convention that year, acknowledgements of mutual congrat-

ulations were transmitted between the press and the convention participants at the close of the three-day convention. The civility of the
language and the mutual deference to the respective skills of conference organizers and reporters for one another have long since been
replaced by a testier and more sharply defined relationship between
the two. Still, the language of 1919 is suggestive of happier and simpler
times between politicians and the press and, as such, deserves, however
belatedly, some recognition. The official report of the convention
noted that in the convention building itself

There was a press room, with working accommodation for 100 correspondents; a telegraph office, in which the several telegraph companies had their
instruments and operators; and a room for the [party's] official reporters, in
which their work was supplemented by a mimeograph machine, which turned
out hundreds of copies of resolutions, reports of committees, etc., with such
speed that the press correspondents had a constant supply of these copies to
incorporate in their reports and despatches by wire.[1]

What had been done on their behalf clearly pleased the press. As the
convention drew to a close, the Parliamentary Press Gallery and other
correspondents from across the country passed a resolution expressing
their "high appreciation" for the arrangements made for the "facilita-
tion of their work" and for the "admirable" press accommodations and
facilities. For their part, the delegates passed as one of their last orders
of business a "vote of thanks to the press" for "their excellent reports of
the proceedings of this Convention." To complete the evocation of an
earlier era, the party's report noted that that resolution "was adopted
with three cheers for the Press."[2]

From the one hundred or so correspondents present in 1919, the
number of media representatives covering conventions continued to
grow over the years. At the same time there were major changes in the
composition of the press corps, reflecting changes in the media of mass
communications from 1919 on. Of the 287 press representatives accredited to the Liberal convention of 1948, thirty-four were from movie
screen news and photo service organizations, sixty-one from radio, and
the remaining 192 from newspapers and magazines.[3] A decade later,
and less than two years after the Tories had held the first national leadership convention to be carried on television, the number of accredited
press at the Liberal convention reflected the shift away from the print to
the electronic media. Of the approximately two hundred press representatives covering the Pearson convention, 150 were from television and
radio. The CBC English and French-language television networks broadcast a total of six hours of the three-day convention, including two and a

half hours of the final day's election of the leader and an option for an additional half-hour if the network "considered it of special interest."[4]

TELEVISION ARRIVES — AND STAYS

By 1967, when the televised multi-ballot convention (the first to be broadcast in colour) made its dramatic impact on the public's perception of leadership selection, the Tories were able to boast that the more than seven hundred media representatives present at Maple Leaf Gardens constituted the largest number to date for a Canadian political convention. In less than a year the Liberals all but doubled that number with 1,386 media representatives (of whom 35 per cent were from television) accredited to the 1968 convention. Their presence in such large numbers would ensure, according to the newly chosen leader, Pierre Trudeau, that "every yawn will be handed on to a grateful posterity."[5] From the 1970s on, the numbers continued to increase until, in 1993, the Tories issued the largest number of press accreditations – 2,150, or better than one accredited media representative for every two voting delegates.[6]

The arrival of television as a major player in national leadership conventions led to new concerns among convention planners long accustomed to print journalists seated at tables on the periphery of the convention floor. Worried about an overly congested floor at Maple Leaf Gardens, the Tories in 1967 limited access to the floor to five persons per television network at any one time – a restriction that was never to be repeated because of its unpopularity with the networks and its difficulty in administering. The following year the CBC's request to the Liberals to install a "plexiglass studio booth in a prominent position in the Civic Centre so that the operation could be viewed by delegates," while eventually permitted, had been initially turned down "as it would not contribute to, and might constitute a distraction from, the business of the Convention."[7]

Television studios in highly visible booths above the convention floor as well as outdoor compounds (sometimes dubbed "Convention City") for equipment, production trailers, and mobile units have since become standard fare at leadership conventions. Organizers in 1968 voiced concerns about the safety of delegates surrounded by numerous pieces of television equipment, fearing that network demands for floor space and for access for reporters and technicians "would simply suffocate the convention in cameras."[8] If the Liberal organizers sometimes felt that they could not live with the media, at the same time they realized that they could not live without them either. When a question about the availability of meals for media staff was posed to a meeting of convention planners in 1968, party organizer Paul Lafond replied that "arrangements will have to be made. For our own purposes we cannot afford to let them out of Lansdowne Park."9 Sixteen years later the Liberal communications director accepted the unalterable presence of television on the convention floor with a warning against one possible (and ironic) effect of the extreme heat generated by television lights: "heat-induced altercations on the [convention] floor" would be carried across the country by way of live television coverage.[10]

In spite of these concerns, the growth in the number of media accreditations, especially in television, was one indication of the increased currency that both the media and the parties placed in the newsworthiness of the event and in the need to reach a mass audience. The growth took place largely against the backdrop of changes that the parties themselves introduced to accommodate the demands of television and to make their conventions more telephotogenic. Principal among these were the timing of conventions, removing debates on policy resolutions from leadership contests, scheduling of events, and designing decorative and colourful stage sets and hall trappings.

The efforts paid off. The hours that the television networks have devoted to covering the conventions demonstrate the extent to which broadcasters consider the events to be of significant national interest. At a minimum, networks typically transmit live the tributes to the retiring leader, although they are increasingly wary of carrying overly long and excessively adulatory panegyrics without interruption for commercials and editorial disclaimers; the speeches by the candidates, although minor candidates may fare less well than the serious ones in terms of time allotted to covering them; and most if not all of the entire time devoted to the election of the new leader on the final day of the convention. In addition, at least part of the evening national news broadcasts and scheduled public affairs programs throughout the duration of the three- or four-day convention originate from the television booths high above the convention floor.

The size of viewing audiences of the convention election day demonstrates that Canadians have become keen convention watchers. In the three national conventions held between 1989 and 1993, the percentage of adult Canadians watching at least a portion of the election day coverage ranged between 18.6 and 24.1 (CBC-TV), 10 and 18 (CTV) and 5.9 and 8.1 (Radio-Canada) (see table 5-1). For earlier conventions on CBC-TV alone, the figures for the two older parties ranged from a low of 16 per cent in 1967 to a high of 25.3 per cent in 1976 (table 5-2). The data from the two tables show that on most occasions when a new prime minister was chosen, as in 1968 and 1993, or when a multi-candidate and almost certain multi-ballot contest was held, as in

1976 and 1989, the television viewing audience was larger than when the virtually certain outcome of a one- or two-ballot race was widely known in advance.[11]

Even with those differences, however, the fact remains that the television audiences attracted to Canadian conventions on the day the leaders are chosen have been impressive for their size. For recent conventions, they must have been even more impressive than the A.C. Neilsen figures cited in tables 5-1 and 5-2 would suggest, for among the networks not included in those data are Global, CBC Newsworld, and the new kid on the convention block in 1993, MuchMusic.[12] The risk of double-counting the same viewer obviously rules out a cumulative total of all the television networks for any one convention.[13] Nonetheless, it can be reasonably estimated that over one-quarter and, depending upon the convention, possibly between one-third and two-fifths of all adult Canadians watched at least a part of the televised coverage of the major national leadership conventions held since 1967.

The Canadian experience of extensive television coverage of conventions and of capturing sizable viewing audiences contrasts with that of the United States. Starting in 1976 with ABC, and joined four years later by CBS and NBC, the three American commercial networks reduced over the course of a decade the amount of time devoted to covering both the Democratic and Republican conventions by up to 60 per cent of the average coverage from 1956 to 1972.[14] At the same time, the size of the viewing audience slipped from better than one in four (26.1 per cent) in 1952 to little more than one in five (21.3 per cent) in 1984.[15] These changes were the result of a number of social and political factors, principal among them being the widespread adoption since the early 1970s of primaries and caucuses for the selection of delegates to the conventions, and the absence after 1952 of a multi-ballot contest for a party's presidential nomination. Primaries and caucuses effectively shifted the media's and the public's attention to an earlier stage in the selection process. With a majority of the delegates pledged to support one candidate well in advance of the summer convention, the convention increasingly came to function as a "thoroughly choreographed coronation" with attendant loss of public and media interest.[16]

What ends up being carried by television networks in Canada into the living rooms of the nation is not the convention itself. Rather it is the *televised* convention. There is a critical distinction between the two: the one amounts to completely uninterrupted and unembellished coverage from a convention's beginning to its end, the other a shortened, mediated, and interpreted convention. The contest captured by the television camera and interpreted by the principal intermediaries – the news anchors and commentators, themselves often as recognizable to the public as the candidates whose campaigns they are analysing – is defined according to the limits of the medium. With the passage of time these increasingly, and now all but exclusively, have come to mean attractive visuals and terse analyses.

Those who typically are called upon to serve as commentators and analysts on the television programs covering the election of a new party leader are party notables and organizers working for leadership candidates, leading politicians from other parties, and public opinion pollsters. These are the "insiders" in politics whose participation in the coverage is intended to give the television viewers inside information and informed opinion. The right mix of partisan, knowledgeable, and opinionated panelists can make for illuminating discussion and lively television during the long intervals between the announcement of successive ballot results. It is also clear that the process merges observations *of* the convention with participation *in* the convention and could scarcely be expected to produce dispassionate analysis.[17]

The practice of using party insiders and candidate organizers as television commentators reinforces the link between the medium and the event. It also gives a prominence, and possibly an added authority, to the views expressed by party notables who, in their role as television commentators, are called upon to analyse the convention and the candidates. For although the commentators' remarks are heard first by the television audience at home, if significant they are then quickly disseminated to the convention floor by organizers who believe that their candidate stands to gain from them. In 1989, for example, former Ontario NDP leader and United Nations ambassador Stephen Lewis served as a CBC television commentator at the NDP convention. Within minutes of Lewis's dismissal on television of Audrey McLaughlin's speech the night before the leadership vote with the comment that "I would fire her speechwriter," the anti-McLaughlin forces were spreading the word on the convention floor hoping to turn it to their advantage. The phrase uttered by a senior party figure in his role as television commentator became one of the delegates' more repeated and discussed pieces of information going into the vote the next day.[18] By the same token, Hugh Segal's voting-day endorsement of Jean Charest at the Tory convention four years later gave added authority to the pitch offered by the Charest workers on the floor of the convention. The prominence that any prime minister's former chief of staff would enjoy as a senior and respected member of the party was supplemented in this instance by Segal's status throughout the convention as CBC-TV's principal commentator in discussion with news anchor Peter Mansbridge.[19]

Byron Shafer has demonstrated in his study of American nominating conventions that television coverage of the quadrennial Republican and

Democratic contests has contributed significantly to a "'bifurcated convention,' with one version for participants and another for viewers – and a large and growing disjunction between the two."[20] The bifurcated conventions of which he writes are a product of a number of factors unique to American politics. Principal among these are the post-1952 break with the multi-ballot, brokered conventions; the now widespread use of primaries and caucuses to chose delegates, the practical effect of which has been to lock up the nomination well in advance of the convention itself; the increase in the number and importance of single-issue groups represented on the convention floors; and the intra-party divisions over candidate preference often disguised in acrimonious and prolonged debates over procedures, credentials, and party platforms.

None of those conditions has yet had a Canadian equivalent. Although it is true that the Liberal conventions of 1984 and 1990 and the Conservative one of 1993 chose their leaders in fewer ballots than any others of the second generation of conventions, the NDP 1989 convention confirmed that multi-ballot conventions are still possible in Canada. With the exception of the 1990 Liberals, Canadian parties have yet to reach the point of effectively transferring the power of leadership selection from the convention floor to the earlier delegate selection stage. The 1984 Liberal convention marked a shift from the earlier second-generation conventions by the older parties to the extent that there was very little doubt from the outset about its outcome. That was repeated by the Tories in 1993. But it was in 1990 that the successful manipulation of the delegate selection process at the local level took place. Chrétien's campaign organization had the leadership all sewn up before the convention even opened, so much so that some five hundred delegates did not even bother to show up. As will be seen in chapter 11, various provincial parties have gone beyond the American model and have eliminated the delegate selection stage entirely in favour of direct election of leaders by the entire party membership. The trend at the federal level as well is towards some form of the one member, one vote method of leadership selection. With such changes it may be that the role of the media in the early stages of the campaign will become even more significant.

Nor can it be said that single-issue groups have surfaced in Canadian convention politics in anything like the number or with the delegate strength of, say, the National Education Association (the largest interest group of public school teachers in the United States) in the Democratic party, or the Moral Majority (evangelical Protestant fundamentalists) in the Republican party in the 1970s and 1980s.[21] Procedural and credential fights in Canada are extremely rare and, except for the NDP's continued practice of debating and voting on policy resolutions on the floor of the convention, delegate consideration and approval of party policy has been effectively removed from the agenda of leadership conventions. If anything is bifurcated in Canadian convention politics, it is the separation of party policy and leadership selection.[22]

Nonetheless, Shafer's general point about the impact of television on leadership conventions is as valid in Canada as it is in the United States. What the viewers see and hear in their living rooms is what the television producers and editors choose to show and what the anchors, reporters, and commentators choose to say, or not to show or say as the case may be. Of course, it is true that other media of communication are neither preference-free nor complete in their coverage of major political events. Print, magazine, and radio reporters would be (or, at least, should be) the first to acknowledge that the reports they file reflect their own biases, selections, and pre-determined story lines. That will never change. But it is equally true that television now has an immediacy and a comfortable familiarity about it that gives it a special status in the transmission of information.

It is widely accepted that television has become the country's principal and largely unchallenged purveyor of political information. Is there a better illustration of that than the part that the televised convention plays in the information-gathering by the print media at the convention? For much or all of the candidates' speeches, bear-pit and leadership accountability sessions, and the balloting on leadership selection day, newspaper and magazine reporters and commentators are usually found milling about and interviewing less on the floor of the convention than they are conversing with one another and taking in the televised convention proceedings in the (air-conditioned) media room where large-screen television sets broadcast the networks' coverage of the convention. Along with the television viewers at home, they learn about what is taking place at the convention from the reports, analyses, and comments carried on television. As if to complete the media circle, a few of the nationally prominent print columnists occasionally join the politicians as convention analysts on network television.[23]

CANDIDATES, DELEGATES, AND THE MEDIA

The media attach great weight to the coverage of leadership conventions. By the same token candidates and their organizers place top value on gaining media attention for their respective campaigns. The links between the two have long been obvious. From the media's perspective, races for the leadership of a political party receive high priority as essential domestic news. Conventions are, after all, the first stage in ultimately determining who will serve as prime minister of the country. As such, they warrant extensive coverage for the information transmitted to and needed by convention delegates and the general public. The striking parallels between the campaigns for a party's leadership and a general election (extensive tours, media scrums, press conferences, and televised debates) reinforce both the role that the media are expected to play and the importance attached to the activity itself as a critical element in deciding who will govern Canada. Just as the prime minister is news, those who strive to become prime minister are also news.

One of the measures of the deemed worthiness of a party's leadership contest is the number of candidate "mentions" on the evening national television news.[24] Tables 5-3 and 5-4 show that the coverage of the 1990 Liberal and 1993 Conservative races differentiated between parties and among candidates. At 4,336 for the two networks, the total number of television references to the candidates in their capacity as leadership hopefuls, not as ministers dealing with matters of government policy, was distributed unevenly between the two parties. The governing Tories, in the process not only of choosing a new leader but a new prime minister who would soon be engaged in a federal election, received twice as many candidate mentions as the opposition Liberals, even though the Liberal campaign lasted over twice as long. The Tories' edge over the Liberals amounted to 1,911 to 931 mentions on CBC-TV and 959 to 535 on CTV. Clearly, potential prime ministers, and the first female one at that, are considered more newsworthy than potential leaders of the opposition.

Perhaps surprisingly, the number of mentions did not grow incrementally from one month to the next with the approach of the convention. Instead it was erratic. The month in which the candidates declared that they would seek their party's leadership (March 1993 for all the Tories and January 1990 for all the Liberals but Tom Wappel) produced the greatest number of mentions of any save for the month of the conventions themselves. Apart from CTV's reporting of the Tory race, the month before the Tory and Liberal conventions actually produced fewer mentions than the previous month. Coverage of other news stories (in 1990, for example, the dying weeks of the debate over the Meech Lake Accord) undoubtedly helps to explain that fact. But it could also reflect the completion of the competitive delegate selection stage with the interest that it would have engendered in the press. In the case of the Liberals in 1990, there was the knowledge that the contest was over and there was little doubt about who would win in June.

The tables make it clear that there was a sizable differential in the coverage accorded the different candidates. Campbell and Chrétien both greatly outdistanced their nearest competitors by being given half of all news mentions. At the other extreme, the least successful candidates at both conventions received scant mention throughout the campaign. Such data obviously raise the spectre of the media having played an agenda-setting role, first by establishing, then by maintaining, a boundary between presumed major and minor contenders.

Television news coverage of the three principal NDP contenders in the months leading up to the 1989 convention differed from that for the Liberals in 1990 and Conservatives in 1993.[25] At 340 (CBC-TV) and 297 (CTV), the combined number of mentions on the two networks over the nine-month NDP campaign was less than half of those of the Liberals and barely one-fifth of the Conservatives. That gives real meaning to the term "third party" in the context of Canadian politics at the time. Anticipating from the news mentions who the eventual NDP winner would be was problematic. McLaughlin averaged ten percentage points fewer news mentions than Barrett overall and received a majority of mentions only from CBC-TV. Barrett, who announced his candidacy on 29 September, outdistanced his two major opponents by a wide margin in both September and October. Receiving half of all his CBC-TV mentions in the month of October alone, Barrett added to the NDP race an element of excitement. As a former British Columbia premier he quite possibly had greater name recognition with the general public than those already in the race, and as a colourful, outspoken politician he undoubtedly captured the interest of the media. Equally, the attention to Barrett might have arisen from the desire of news organizations to create tension and a more meaningful race, which would mean for them better stories and better television. Liberal party leader John Turner's comment at the time, to the effect that Barrett's entry into the NDP contest would "heat up the race almost to room temperature,"[26] reflected the general lack of interest in the campaign by the media and the public alike (see table 5-5).

From the candidates' perspective, it is obvious from the resources deployed and the arrangements made (including photo-ops, appearances on open line and talk shows, and the use of media specialists and experts on "spin control"[27]) that leadership candidates attach great weight to media coverage. At no point is that coverage more important than in the early stages of a campaign in which it can help to give it a kick-start. In their study of the media and leadership conventions in Canada, Fred Fletcher and Robert Drummond confirmed that "the most important aspect of media influence in the leadership selection process is the identification of viable candidates" and that with the advent of costly, competitive campaigning in the 1960s "candidates unable to demonstrate their viability by gaining media attention in the early stages were out of the game."[28] To be considered viable, a candidate needs media exposure early and often in a campaign – to raise funds, to build an organization, and to drive off potential rivals. If anything, the rush for media attention in the early stages of a campaign reinforces the complex circuity of candidate-media relations, for it comes at the very time that the media themselves are attempting to draw their initial, possibly decisive, portrait of the race. The indicators of candidate viability to which the media are most likely to respond include the very ones that candidates must successfully establish if they are to be taken seriously: support from notables, fund-raisers, and organizers; ability to raise funds; appearance of broad, national appeal; speaking ability; and television performance.[29]

Given the value that candidates and their organizers attach to media exposure, it is important to determine the extent to which the media actually have an impact on the delegates' opinion of the candidates. Surveys of delegates to the 1990 Liberal and 1993 Conservative conventions show that the media were far from being an exclusive source of influence on delegate opinion. Only 16 per cent of the Liberal and 15 per cent of the Conservative delegates said that media news reports had a "great deal" of influence on their opinions of the candidates' strengths and weaknesses. A clear majority in both parties (56 per cent of the Liberal and 54 per cent of the Tory delegates) claimed that media reports had little or no influence on their opinions.[30]

Delegates may have discounted the impact of the media on the formation of their own opinions of candidates, but three-quarters nonetheless held the view that *other* delegates were either profoundly or moderately influenced by the media in forming their opinions. In 1993 (no equivalent question was asked in 1990), 78 per cent of Tory delegates said the media had had either a great deal or some influence on the opinions of their fellow delegates, whereas only 3 per cent believed the media had had no influence on the opinions of other delegates. The 1993 Conservative delegates may have had such a negative, or at least suspect, view of the media as an opinion-shaper that they were unwilling to admit in large numbers that their own views had been shaped by them. But they were markedly less hesitant to ascribe a media influence to the opinions formed by those with whom they had varying degrees of familiarity.[31]

If delegates rely less on the media than candidates like to think they do and to the limited degree to which they themselves admit, where do they turn for their information about the candidates? The answer is, to the candidates themselves. One-third of the delegates to the 1990 and 1993 conventions relied on material furnished by candidates – nearly twice the number of those who got their information from news reports. About half of the delegates reported receiving an equal amount of information on the candidates from news reports and candidates' material: 46 and 51 per cent of the 1990 Liberal and 1993 Conservative delegates respectively.[32]

The 1983 and 1984 surveys of convention delegates had demonstrated that the media played a more important part in the early stages of a campaign than in the later. From the beginning of a campaign through to convention day, the earlier the delegates made up their minds about how they were going to vote the greater the likelihood that they would cite news reports as their principal source of information. That turned out to be true of the 1993 Conservative convention as well. Tory delegates in 1993 who made their choice of candidate before the delegate selection period began were almost two-thirds more likely to cite news reports as their principal source of information than those chosen after the delegate selection process got under way. The 1990 Liberal survey, unlike those of 1983, 1984, and 1993, painted a slightly different picture. News reports were as important a source of information for the 1990 delegates making up their minds during the convention week as they had been for those who decided in the pre-delegate selection period, but between those two stages their significance diminished (see table 5-6).[33]

What is most significant about all four races is that at no point during the campaigns or at the conventions themselves did the media reports ever match or displace candidate materials as the most cited sources of information about the candidates. This underscores the relatively small weight that delegates attach to news reports as a source of information about candidates, preferring instead either candidate material alone or in tandem with news reports. The findings make obvious the need on the candidates' part for effective organizational efforts to produce and to distribute candidate information packages (which now include videotapes, 1–800 and 1–900 telephone numbers, books by candidates, printed biographies, and policy statements) in the knowledge that they are more likely to be valued by delegates as sources of information than media reports.

Of the various media, clearly none is considered the equal of television by the candidates. Seeking his party's leadership in 1983, Brian Mulroney frankly noted the value he attached to national television exposure. Doubtless other candidates for a party's leadership would share his view: "Every night I want to be on the 11 o'clock news. It's fine to shake delegates' hands but you can't win them in five minutes. You've got to reinforce it."[34] It is undoubtedly true that the most effective way to reach thousands of delegates, to reinforce contacts with them, and to speak at the same time to the larger electoral audience of potential party voters is through television. In turn, this helps to explain why a candidate's television image becomes a matter of major interest to convention delegates and party supporters. In the race to succeed Mulroney in 1993, for example, a survey of party activists found that of eleven possible "very important" considerations (including policies) bearing on the choice of the next leader, three of the top four were television-related.[35]

From the 1983 and 1984 convention surveys we learn that part of the explanation for Mulroney's and Turner's victories can be found in the extent to which their television images appealed to the delegates. When rated by delegates according to their television appeal, Mulroney received 53 per cent of the first rankings to Crosbie's 20 per cent and Clark's 11 per cent. Turner, in spite of unfavourable reviews from experts of his overall television performances, nonetheless received more than twice the share of first rankings from Liberal delegates compared with his nearest competitor, 54 per cent to 23 per cent for Chrétien.[36] Although other factors (such as candidates' personal likability, views on policy, and overall ability and competence) entered into the delegates' decisions, the link between television appeal and the candidates' ability to gain power (electability) was present in both conventions. Mulroney's lead in television appeal likely helped him to gain most of the final ballot votes of delegates "who regarded electability as very influential in their choice." For delegates to the Liberal convention the strongest correlation with television appeal was with electability. The 1983 and 1984 findings confirm that television appeal was the single variable positively associated in the minds of delegates with electability.[37]

The views of Conservative and Liberal delegates in the mid-1980s on the importance of their leader's television appeal contrast with those of NDP delegates. Keith Archer's survey of the 1989 NDP convention found that of those delegates who expressed an opinion on the most important characteristics of a leader of the NDP, an "appealing image on TV" was ranked first by only 6 per cent of the delegates. It placed fifth after overall ability and competence (30 per cent), sound views on policy (26 per cent), best able to help the party win the next election (16 per cent) and ability to unite the party (9 per cent). When asked to rank the candidates in respect of their television appeal, delegates placed Dave Barrett, the runner-up, ahead of Audrey McLaughlin, the winner, by 46 per cent to 33 per cent. McLaughlin, however, led Barrett by sizable majorities in terms of her perceived ability to unite the party (68 per cent to 14 per cent) and as the person thought best able to win the next election (57 per cent to 31 per cent). The apparent inconsistency between delegates' preferring a candidate who could help the party win the next election even though she did not have the most appealing television image was interpreted by Archer and Whitehorn in convention-specific terms. The only "candidate with a more positive ranking [than McLaughlin] on TV appeal – Dave Barrett – was perceived as too problematic in other areas (e.g., party unity and soundness on policy). A second possible interpretation is that delegates believed there was sufficient time for McLaughlin to improve her TV image before the next election."[38] It should be added that in more general terms, television appeal of the leader would be expected to be less important than policy to NDP delegates precisely because as an ideologically based party of the left the NDP has prided itself on its emphasis on policy almost, according to one interpretation, "to the point of fetishism."[39]

MEDIA PORTRAITS

The "portraits" of a leadership campaign and convention that the cameras, newspapers, magazines, reporters, television anchors, and commentators paint and interpret are by definition bound to shape the attitudes, and ultimately influence the political behaviour, of the viewing/voting public.[40] And what are the portraits of leadership candidates, campaigns, and conventions that are transmitted? To a considerable extent they tend to be shaped by the media's natural predilection for stories that emphasize conflict over harmony and process over policy. There are, of course, notable exceptions to this tendency. Canada has a number of experienced and responsible reporters and commentators who are known for their detailed, probing, and balanced assessments of policies and personalities. But the fact remains, in the telling words of a CBC news editor, that the media "look for confrontation often to the exclusion of a story. It's overwhelmingly prevalent. It's the nature of journalism to be a storyteller. It needs drama." In the same vein a senior editor of the *Globe and Mail* has admitted that "conflict is news. That's basic."[41]

Thus when conflict surfaces in a leadership contest in the form, let us say, of intense candidate rivalry for delegates, or personal animosity between leading contenders, or splits over policy among government ministers or opposition frontbenchers campaigning for the leadership, a principal demand of the media has been satisfied. This is as it should be, of course, for the media could be said to have failed in one of their tasks if they did *not* report on such differences. Moreover, politics by definition is conflictual, which means that the stories filed about differences and rivalries reflect at least part of the reality of the political world. But the line between objective and incisive reporting of genuine intra-party or inter-candidate conflict on the one hand, and oversimplified, exaggerated, and misrepresented accounts of issues and individuals on the other, is not always observed. Thus, "mediated" politics can sometimes mean trivialized, sensationalized, and distorted reports of politics and politicians.

The inter-candidate rivalry over delegate selection at the constituency level in the 1983 Conservative and 1984 Liberal conventions serves as an illustration. The competition among the organizations of the front-running candidates for slates of delegates was certainly intense. There were several specific episodes of packed delegate selection meetings and of instant party members that were widely and colourfully reported in print and on radio and television. The most celebrated of these contests were the bussing in of derelicts from the Old Brewery Mission in Montreal by Mulroney organizers, voting by nine- and ten-year-olds in Tory meetings, and assiduous recruiting of scores of ethnic Canadians by Liberal organizers working the Sikh, Chinese, Portuguese, and Greek communities of southern Ontario, Calgary, and Vancouver.[42] Overall, the general portrait of delegate selection meetings painted by the media was an unsavoury one. It consisted of slates of hostile delegates competing fiercely with one another at the riding level (dubbed "trench warfare" by Ken Carty[43]) and of candidate organizers using strong-arm tactics (labelled "dirty tricks" by the press[44]) to line up votes from scores of people whose attachment to and knowledge of the party and leadership candidates was open to serious question. Because reports of uncontested and non-conflictual delegate selection elections were not given equal prominence, the impression was created that bitterly fought contests between competing slates of delegates were the norm.

Yet this portrait was inaccurate on two accounts. First, the "Tiny Tories," "Ethnic Liberals," and "Mission Members" of the 1980s may have introduced new twists into the political game of packing meetings, but the practice, though rarer in earlier leadership campaigns, was scarcely new. Since 1967 and 1968 such moves had not been unknown in candidate selection meetings, principally in those constituencies and regions of the country where the party selecting the delegates was particularly weak and was ripe for a takeover by a well-managed operation on behalf of an aspiring candidate. The Tories in Quebec and the Liberals in western Canada fell into that category in the 1960s and 1970s.[45]

Secondly, the 1983–4 reports of fierce inter-candidate organizational rivalry between competing slates of delegates unfairly caricatured delegate selection meetings. Carty has demonstrated in his study of constituency parties in the 1983 and 1984 conventions that the media "accounts of highly mobilized and factionalized grass roots" exaggerated the role played by competing slates of delegates at the local level. Of the constituency delegates attending those two conventions, fewer than two in five ran in the riding election as part of a slate, no more than one-quarter were on an identified slate, and only about one in ten were on an identified slate running against another identified slate.[46] In the Canadian general election of 1988 press reports suggested that of all constituency nominations 66 per cent were contested and 28 per cent produced conflicts over recruitment, whereas in fact the correct numbers were 35 per cent and 9 per cent. In the same way, the popular image of local delegate selection meetings did not match the reality of the situation.[47]

POLLS, CANDIDATES, AND DELEGATES

Nothing better characterizes process-driven coverage of politics than "horse-race journalism." Its principal focus is to report on which candidate is ahead in the race, which ones are behind, and who is gaining or losing to whom. The term characterizes the tendency of many media reports to focus more on the process than on the content of politics. A selection of front-page newspaper headlines during the 1993 Conservative leadership campaign captures the point, beginning with "Contender Campbell has early momentum" from the *Toronto Star* the day following Brian Mulroney's resignation announcement in February, and "Tory horses heading to the post" (*StarPhoenix*, March 9) in the early stages of the campaign. The *Globe and Mail* took its readers from "Tortoise chases the hare" (April 3), through "Segal shies at starting gate" (April 9), "Is Kim Campbell's star beginning to dim?" (April 17) and "Numbers favour a Campbell win" (May 8), to "Campbellmania fizzles" (May 25) and, on the eve of the convention, "Charest has tide, but lacks time" (June 7).

Understandably horse-race journalism is often the subject of critical self-analysis by journalists and editors because of its preoccupation with process over issues, policies or programs.[48] Nonetheless, it clearly persists as one of the marked features of contemporary coverage of politics. A count of the stories carried by the two major television networks on their evening national news broadcasts about the two principal candidates in the Liberal 1990 and Conservative 1993 conventions illustrates the point about horse-race journalism. Table 5-7 shows that process stories (who is winning the battle for delegates? by how much? who is supporting whom? and so on) outnumbered substance or mixed substance/process stories by two to one on CBC-TV and by three to one on CTV.

In fairness, however, the media do not always have many options about what they report. They can do little more than file stories about who is leading, gaining, or losing if the candidates themselves systematically eschew any substantive discussion of issues or carefully craft their campaigns to guard as much as possible against pronouncements (and, therefore, possible slips) on policies. In 1990, for example, Jean Chrétien purposefully downplayed policy. After five months of campaigning for the party's leadership, even within one month of the convention, he had issued only four policy papers. This was part of a larger campaign strategy based on his organization's polls of party members who "like Conservative party delegates who picked Brian Mulroney in 1983, wanted a leader of substantial image, charm and television skills more than one with substance and sombre business acumen."[49]

Public opinion polls are ideally suited to horse-race journalism. For viewers and readers they provide up-to-date information on attitudes and preferences of their fellow citizens; for the media they offer relatively quick and easy copy on one facet of an election or a leadership race. Accordingly, broadcasting networks, major daily newspapers and newsmagazines (sometimes jointly, as with the CTV/*Maclean's* polls, but more typically individually) commission polls of their own, or maintain longstanding contracts with an established survey research firm (as is the case of the *Toronto Star* with Gallup) providing regular polling data. Those who fault the practice allege that the media create news by sponsoring, then reporting prominently on, public opinion polls, and that the dissemination of survey results can influence voting behaviour, an influence the critics consider undesirable. Critics also note that polling encourages horse-race journalism because its results, though "among the least substantive kinds of political journalism," are invariably deemed newsworthy.[50] Defenders of public opinion polling and the publication of survey results during leadership or election campaigns counter that polls provide important collective information which can be factored into individual decision-making. It would enable delegates, for example, to make "inferences about the personal characteristics, policy positions, electability or leadership ability of candidates."[51]

From the early, occasional Gallup poll on party leadership preferences in Canada,[52] surveys of delegates and of the general public have grown in number and frequency and are now a prominent feature of leadership contests. During the four-month campaign in 1993 for the Conservative leadership virtually all major newspapers, newsmagazines, and television networks published at least one poll on either delegate preferences for leader or on the voting intentions of the general public given hypothetical alternative leaders. The principal news outlets and polling firms included The *Globe and Mail* (ComQuest Research Group), the Southam newspaper chain and CTV-*Maclean's* magazine (Angus Reid Group), the *Sun* newspapers and *Financial Post* (COMPAS), *Le Journal de Montréal* (Léger et Léger), the *Toronto Star* (Gallup Poll), *La Presse* (CROP), and CBC (Gallup Poll).

In 1993, as with other recent leadership campaigns, there were basically three kinds of polls or surveys reported by the media. There were surveys of the general public to determine preferences among the leadership candidates and the likely impact on general election voting intentions of the party choosing one candidate over the others. There were polls of convention delegates to determine candidate preferences on the first and subsequent ballots and, in some cases, attitudes on issues of public policy. As well, there were frequent Canadian Press surveys of presidents of Conservative riding associations or other party officials designed to produce a running tally of the results of constituency delegate selection meetings and the known first ballot voting intentions of those chosen. It was also true as well in 1993, as it had been of earlier leadership campaigns, that the coverage by the media of poll and survey results "was more useful to delegates who wanted to learn about the personalities, style, and vote-getting capacities of the candidates and to check their assessments of candidate performance against those of the professional critics than to those concerned about policy directions."[53]

What part do media surveys and polls play in leadership selection? The 1993 Tory leadership race suggests different answers to that question for candidates and for delegates.

Polls and Candidates

For would-be candidates, information gleaned from surveys of the general public and of delegates helps them to assess their electoral chances should they choose to run. In acknowledging early in the race that Kim Campbell had an enormous lead and that there was an "unprecedented consensus" around her, Perrin Beatty, considered a likely contender up to that point, announced that he would not seek his party's leadership but instead would give his support to Campbell.[54] It is difficult to imagine that Beatty's decision, as well as those of other possible candidates who between 5 and 23 March announced that they too would not enter the race (Michael Wilson, Benoit Bouchard, Barbara McDougall, Bernard Valcourt, Otto Jelinek, and Tom Hockin), could have been reached without a careful reading of the polls at that point. Early surveys, beginning with a Gallup poll conducted the night Mulroney announced his resignation and broadcast the following day by CBC radio and television, showed that Campbell was by far the most preferred choice of the electorate to succeed Mulroney and that with her as leader, the Conservative party had the best chance of staying in power.[55] Three other national polls taken between 8 and 18 March (ComQuest, Environics, and Angus Reid) reached identical conclusions: the Tories led by Campbell could beat the Liberals under Jean Chrétien, in one case by a margin of eighteen percentage points.[56]

Potential candidates may rely on more than media polls by commissioning surveys of their own. Such was the case in 1993 with former Conservative leader and prime minister, Joe Clark. After initially announcing that he would neither enter the contest nor run again for Parliament, Clark was persuaded by supporters late in the campaign to reconsider his decision. He did so by commissioning a public opinion poll to determine how he would fare against those already in the race and if he alone could lead the Conservatives to victory in the next general election. With all delegates chosen at that point and all but one-quarter of them committed to other candidates, the results of Clark's poll (which were never announced publicly) could not have shown a great measure of support within the party for him. Accordingly, he confirmed his earlier decision to keep out of the race.[57]

It is equally true that candidates who are doing unexpectedly well in public opinion polls, perhaps even reaching the point of outperforming all other contenders in their preference ratings, will attempt to turn that information to their advantage. By the end of the 1993 Tory race, Campbell's campaign was generally seen to have flattened out, even faltered, whereas that of her principal opponent, Jean Charest, had advanced steadily from its more modest beginnings. The changes in the respective levels of popular support for the two major candidates were stressed by the media in their coverage of the survey results in the final weeks of the campaign. The last published polls of the campaign were seized upon by the Charest organization for the opportunity they presented to give further momentum to his candidacy. From the Angus Reid–Southam News poll released on 22 May to the Gallup poll published on the eve of the convention voting in June, the surveys showed that Charest, not Campbell, stood the greater chance of defeating the Chrétien-led Liberals.[58]

With only days left before the convention balloting, Charest was understandably urging the delegates to heed the poll results.[59] Advising convention delegates to focus their attention on what the public opinion polls were telling them about who should be chosen as the party's new leader, Charest stressed in his convention speech delivered the night before the voting the need for the party to pick a winner. Speaking in a barely disguised political code about his lead in the polls, Charest called on the delegates to ask themselves who could win for them and who their friends and neighbours wanted to lead the Tory party. To reinforce the "winnability" theme of their candidate's speech, Charest workers distributed to delegates and the media copies of the final pre-voting Gallup Poll, along with its accompanying analysis by the polling firm's senior vice-president asserting that the Tories faced "electoral disaster" with a Campbell-led party.[60] For the last three weeks of the campaign, the final media-generated surveys and the coverage devoted to them became an important element of the Charest team's final campaign strategy.[61]

Polls and Delegates

For delegates, media-sponsored polls of the general public and of fellow delegates provide valuable information about rankings and changes over time in the levels of support for candidates and about the party's electoral prospects under alternative leaders. This, in turn, helps to inform their own decision about who to support at the convention. Does this mean that published survey findings will influence delegates to the extent that it leads them to vote differently from the way they would otherwise? Does it mean that convention outcomes will be altered from what they would be otherwise?

These questions are not easily answered, in large measure because as yet there has been no research on the impact, if any, of the publication of public opinion polls on delegate voting behaviour in Canadian conventions. As a minimum, any study of the effects of publishing and broadcasting public opinion polls during leadership campaigns would have to explore such issues as the reliability of polls, the ability of delegates to evaluate poll results, and, for delegates, the appropriateness of allowing media-generated findings to affect their decision-making to the extent of ultimately voting for a candidate other than the one they had initially chosen to support. In the end, it may well be established that the net impact of poll influence on collective voting behaviour in a convention setting is negligible. One assessment of a variety of research into the relationship between polls and voting in the larger context of American elections concluded that there is "little strong evidence" to support one or the other of the contradictory claims that poll publication leads either to increased support for the underdog or to a bandwagon effect for the perceived winner.[62] Alternatively, studies of published polls and delegate voting patterns at Canadian leadership conventions might confirm a finding of the 1988 Canadian election study and of recent research in the United States. In those studies measurable influences on voting behaviour have been detected, including a "modest bandwagon effect" in Canada in 1988 and a "real but limited" effect on American elections.[63]

During the time that the constituency delegates were chosen for the 1993 Tory convention (22 April to 8 May), Kim Campbell was well ahead of the other candidates in polls asking the general public about voting preferences in a general election. The Gallup Poll released ten days before the start of the selection of riding delegates gave a Campbell-led Conservative party 50 per cent of the vote to the Liberals' 29 per cent. The same poll showed a Charest-led party losing to the Liberals by five percentage points. As the preferred successor to Brian Mulroney, Campbell led her next closest rival, Charest, 51 per cent to 15 per cent at the outset of the campaign. For the remainder of the delegate selection period Campbell was never displaced as the front runner, although the gap between the two leading candidates had narrowed to within four percentage points by the end of the seventeen-day stretch.[64]

As the campaign progressed after the delegates were selected, Charest gained on Campbell and eventually overtook her as the public's first choice for Tory leader. By the eve of the convention the Gallup survey showed that only a Charest-led Conservative party could defeat the Liberals.[65] This confirmed other survey findings of the previous three weeks of the campaign that Charest would be the candidate most likely to lead the Tories to victory in the next election. The transposition of the two principal candidates in the polls of the general public over the course of two months had been remarkable, possibly unprecedented, and the media were understandably quick to make that one of their principal stories as the campaign drew to a close. If polls were the only, or even the principal, influence on delegate voting behaviour, Campbell almost certainly would not have won the leadership. At the very least a strong "poll effect" could be expected to have led to a significant number of defections to the newly predicted general election winner, Charest, by initially pro-Campbell delegates.

Tallies and delegate surveys of the 1993 Conservative race help us to understand the role that polls can be inferred to have played in the outcome. Campbell's campaign was quickly off the mark. Her considerable organizational strength was apparent from the results of the earliest constituency delegate selection meetings which, as noted, were held within days of the published polls that showed her enjoying vastly greater general public support than any of her competitors. The first Canadian Press tally of delegates gave Campbell 46 per cent of the delegates chosen by 4 May and 64 per cent of those who had committed their vote to any candidate by that date (table 5-8). At no stage for the remainder of the campaign did Campbell forfeit the lead among Conservative delegates. But the tallies also showed that from 4 May to 4 June Charest's share of decided delegates grew from 19 to 27 per cent while Campbell's remained static at 46 per cent, and that in the last nine days of the campaign Charest's support continued to grow to the point where he received 39 per cent to Campbell's 48 per cent on the first ballot vote.

Perlin's 1993 delegate survey points in a similar direction. It shows that those who decided on their first ballot choice later in the race were less likely to have chosen Campbell and more likely to have selected Charest than those who had made up their minds earlier in the contest. Jim Edwards, along with Charest, benefited with the passage of time. Of the Tory delegates who had decided on their choice of leader before the end of the delegate selection period, 58 per cent supported Campbell, 34 per cent chose Charest and seven per cent Edwards. Of those making up their minds after that point, 41 per cent supported Charest, 35 per cent chose Campbell, and 19 per cent opted for Edwards.[66]

Campbell's victory would appear to be explained by the organizational advantage she enjoyed from the outset of the campaign, together with a sustained and intense level of commitment by delegates supportive of her candidacy. Once onside, in other words, Campbell's supporters tended not to abandon her. At the aggregate level, such slippage as Campbell experienced (highlighted by her drop from 64 per cent of the decideds in early May to 48 per cent on the first ballot six weeks later) appears to have resulted from her failure to maintain her early success in winning the support of previously uncommitted delegates rather than from large-scale defections from among those who previously had given her their support. The available survey data make it impossible to attribute Campbell's reversal in delegate support as the convention approached to her declining support among the general public that was captured in the opinion polls and transmitted through the media to the delegates. But in the absence of survey data showing the opposite, it is difficult to conclude that the polls showing the party would have done better electorally with Charest than Campbell did *not* contribute to her inability to sustain her earlier success in winning over previously uncommitted delegates.

One survey found that 91 per cent of the 1993 Conservative delegates acknowledged following published opinion polls and that 60 per cent said polls played a part in deciding which candidate to support.[67] These findings do not confirm that delegates voted as they did because of the media's polls. Rather they reinforced an obvious truth about political activists. It would be surprising if the overwhelming majority of delegates did *not* follow published polls or take them into account when deciding whom to vote for. Delegates tend to be atypical of the larger population in the degree of their commitment to and interest in politics. The extent to which published poll results might be expected to influence their behaviour and the eventual convention outcome will vary according to a number of factors. These include the variety of sources of information competing for the delegates' attention; the relative weight attached to them by the individual delegates; the degree of scepticism that they would normally be expected to have about surveys accurately predicting hypothetical elections under alternative leaders months, or even years, ahead; and the strength of commitment by delegates to their already-determined first-ballot candidate of choice. Delegates are political junkies, polls being one of the drugs they crave. But other factors influencing delegate behaviour, including, for example, the improved organizational efforts by Charest's team as the 1993 campaign progressed, cannot be discounted.

In explaining the 1993 outcome and the contribution polls may have made to delegate voting behaviour, it is important to note on a more general level that throughout the several weeks or months of any leadership campaign delegates receive information from a variety of sources. In addition to the media reports of the campaign and surveys of delegate and public opinion, delegates are exposed to the literature and other propaganda produced by candidate organizations; meetings with candidates and their organizers; contacts with local, regional, and national party officials and fellow delegates; endorsements by influential members of the party, parliamentarians, and provincial leaders; and cues from other candidates and, possibly, the outgoing leader. Clearly, none of these sources, either in isolation or in combination with others, provides a delegate with wholly dependable or complete information, for rumours, leads, plants, and trial balloons are as much a part of leadership selection processes as they are of politics generally.

Even if the reliability of the information provided to delegates were unquestioned, how that information will be treated by the recipient will vary according to the individual and the situation. Social psychology has demonstrated that the same piece of information can be interpreted differently by different individuals, depending upon their respective biases, predispositions, and moods. Moreover, the likelihood of increasing the amount of misinformation is a function of size: as the number of participants grows, so does the amount of unreliable information. Ideally the group with the greatest amount of accurate information would also be the smallest, two people. Nelson Polsby and Aaron Wildavsky noted in the early editions of their work on American presidential elections that "perceptions (and hence interpretations) of identical indicators may vary widely depending on the delegate's predispositions, or on the amount of reinforcement or counter-interpretation to which he is subjected. Unless a delegate's interpretation of events coincides with those made by others, his predictions and the actions based on them may be invalidated. At best, the delegates swim in a sea of uncertainty."[68] For delegates to Canadian conventions, who too may be swimming in their own sea of uncertainty, polls are only one of several pieces of information to be weighed in the balance as they make their decision about who to support.

THE QUANTUM LEAP FROM PRINT TO TUBE

The dominant medium of mass communication during the seventy-five-year lifetime of leadership conventions in Canada has changed from print to electronic. The quantum leap from the printed page to the living-room tube has brought with it changes to the way in which parties have organized their conventions and candidates have waged their campaigns. It has also led to changes in the character and amount of information the media have transmitted to delegates and to the public. That the general public has become engaged in the process at some point during the campaign, and most obviously in the election day outcome itself, is clear from the size of the television audiences. Canadians have tuned in to national leadership conventions in impressive numbers.

As is also true more generally of the process of electing governments, the months-long process of selecting party leaders has been influenced by the demands and constraints of the media, primarily of television. This is apparent in several ways: in the campaign with its attendant jockeying for early and frequent coverage on the part of candidates and their organizers; in the information transmitted to delegates, candidates, and the public from increasingly frequent media-sponsored polls and surveys as well as from televised all-candidate debates; in the candidate speeches followed by the instant judgments on their influence and merit by commentators, anchors, and spin doctors; in the crowded and colourful convention floor with the demonstrations organized around candidate speeches and on the election day; and finally, in the sense of drama and excitement surrounding the election itself. All of these underscore the extent to which good politics can also be good television.

The larger and more influential role that the media have assumed in leadership selection has not been without consequences. The mass media, television in particular, now plays a bigger part in establishing the viability of candidates than was true of any medium in the past. Journalists, in some cases reflecting their own agendas or interest in preserving the news value of a convention, help to give shape and character to a leadership contest by promoting would-be candidates

(John Turner from 1975 to 1984) and rumoured rivalries (Clark and Mulroney from 1981 to 1983). Attention to the conflictual and horse-race side of the contest comes at the expense of covering substantive issues.

On the other hand, experienced journalists provide delegates with valuable, independent news about candidates and about who, among the candidates, has the "right stuff" to become leader. If a candidate is serious about being named party leader and about leading the party through an election campaign, he or she must be able to withstand the daily rigours of media scrutiny. What better way than a leadership campaign to test a candidate's ability to cope with media stress and to serve as an effective communicator? A party leader's, and especially a prime minister's, ability to communicate effectively is one of the essentials of commanding compliance of parliamentary colleagues and of the party generally, so the media coverage of the candidates' performances during a leadership campaign provides an unmatched opportunity to judge their relative merits.[69]

Late evening television news (the most watched of all newscasts in the country) is national news. Candidates who hope to gain sustained, serious coverage of their bid for the leadership will be those who successfully establish and maintain a national presence. In practical terms this means that if a candidate is to receive national exposure, then assembling a coalition of organizers, fund-raisers, and campaign workers from the various regions and metropolitan centres of the country is the most critical challenge to be met. In this respect, and to a far greater extent than would be true of the typically more local and parochial print media, television has contributed to the development of leadership conventions as national political institutions.

6 Three Conventions in Four Years

> Where Kim Campbell won was in the top three considerations:
> organization, organization, organization – and in that order.
> – John Tory

As we have seen in the previous two chapters, leadership campaigns and conventions have become highly organized, money-centred media events designed to appeal to a growing mass of party members at the delegate selection level. Before we move on to the representational, demographic, and organizational aspects of leadership selection, we must first recall some of the important features of the three national leadership conventions held between the 1988 and 1993 elections. Of the three conventions examined in this chapter – the NDP convention that chose Audrey McLaughlin in 1989, the Liberal convention of 1990 at which Jean Chrétien was selected, and the Conservative one that chose Kim Campbell in 1993 – the Liberal and Conservative conventions fit the description of money- and media-driven conventions well. The NDP convention, like the party itself, differed in several aspects from those of the two older parties.

THE 1989 NDP LEADERSHIP CONVENTION

From the time of his selection in 1975, Ed Broadbent had led his party through four federal elections.[1] Although this was not a party record (Tommy Douglas led the party through four elections, and M.J. Cold-well led the CCF through five), it is remarkable when compared to the other two parties whose leaders have, with the exceptions of Arthur Meighen and Robert Stanfield, never stayed on after two federal election losses. If changing leaders often when a party is on the opposition benches is one of the signs of a party's interest in gaining power, the

NDP history suggests that winning elections is less a consideration for the party than it is for the Liberals and Conservatives. That Broadbent was able to retain a secure hold on the leadership in spite of his inability to lead the party to election victory was probably a reflection of his personal popularity more than anything else. For almost the entire 1980s Broadbent's approval rating in the public opinion polls rarely dipped below 50 per cent.[2] Under his leadership, in the 1988 federal election the NDP won the largest number of seats (forty-three) and attracted the largest percentage of the vote (20.4 per cent) in the party's history.

But the party's showing in that election was weaker than many of the party faithful had expected. After weeks of press speculation that he would step down as party leader, Broadbent announced his resignation on 4 March 1989. That he would resign had been fairly predictable; who his successor would be was not. As journalist Stevie Cameron wrote a few weeks after Broadbent's announcement, "For the first time at a New Democratic Party leadership convention, there will be no prophets, no wise old men of the party like Tommy Douglas, David Lewis and Stanley Knowles, to anoint a new leader. Last time, in 1975, the prophets lined up behind Mr. Broadbent. This time, as one party organizer put it, delegates will have to think for themselves."[3]

At the time of Broadbent's resignation, no obvious successor had emerged from within the party ranks. Prominent New Democrats such as Saskatchewan party leader Roy Romanow and Ontario party leader Bob Rae (then both leaders of the opposition in their respective provinces) preferred to remain in provincial politics and indicated early on that they had little interest in the leadership of the federal party. Citing personal reasons, Stephen Lewis, son of former federal party leader David Lewis and the man most courted of all, refused be a candidate in the race to succeed Broadbent. With the members of the NDP A team declining to run, the leadership of the party was truly up for grabs. It was implicit in Broadbent's resignation announcement that the party's lack of nationally known figures with ability in French who were willing to seek the leadership of the party was a prominent factor in his decision to retire soon after the 1988 election. The long lead-time before the next federal election was intended to give his successor time to prepare for the next contest.

Following Broadbent's resignation, the party moved its upcoming convention from August back to 30 November-2 December so as to allow more time for potential leadership candidates to assess their chances, to establish their platforms, and to organize their campaigns for what promised to be a wide-open race. Keith Archer has noted that "there was nothing in the NDP's formal structure that made the

1989 convention different from the 1987 convention. The difference was that in the interim period, Mr. Broadbent, as the sitting leader, resigned. In a formal sense, all NDP conventions are leadership conventions. In practice, it is a short order of business unless challengers emerge, and to date no serious contender has challenged an incumbent."[4] By moving the date of the convention the party officials indicated that the 1989 convention was different from the 1987 convention; now there was no incumbent and the leadership of the party was at stake. Like their Conservative and Liberal counterparts, New Democratic party officials recognized the value of the free media attention and the dynamic atmosphere that a competitive leadership campaign and convention provide.

The Candidates

With no obvious successor in the parliamentary party, the race attracted several candidates who, although they may have been known within the party circles, were either complete unknowns or, at best, obscure figures in the country. Within a few months of Broadbent's resignation announcement, six candidates had declared their intention to run for the leadership: Roger Lagassé, a British Columbia teacher, Vancouver MP Ian Waddell, Regina MP Simon de Jong, Windsor MPs Steven Langdon and Howard McCurdy, and Yukon MP Audrey McLaughlin. With the exception of Lagassé, a fringe candidate, McLaughlin was the least known and had the least political experience of the group of candidates. Waddell and de Jong had each been in Parliament for over a decade, and Langdon and McCurdy since 1984. By contrast, McLaughlin first won her seat in a by-election in July 1987. When delegates to the 1987 NDP convention were asked who they would like to succeed Broadbent, none of the respondents named McLaughlin.[5] In late September, Victoria MP and former British Columbia premier David Barrett reversed his earlier decision not to enter the race at the urging of some predominantly western MPs and some labour leaders. Having been in the British Columbian legislature for more than twenty-one years, including over three years as premier, before entering the federal Parliament in 1988, Barrett was the closest the party had to a national figure. It soon became apparent that McLaughlin and Barrett were the front runners and the others were left to fight over third place.

There was within the party and among the delegates a large degree of uncertainty over and dissatisfaction with all the declared candidates. Kamloops MP Nelson Riis (who reportedly endorsed McLaughlin because he felt the next leader of the party should be a woman) expressed concerns about his preferred candidate's ability to act as leader because of her lack of experience in Parliament, her limited ability to speak French, and her weak links with the party elites in organized labour and academia.[6] At the same time, many in the party had misgivings about the future of the party, especially in Ontario, if Barrett were to be selected as leader. When the 1989 convention delegates were asked after the convention is there were any candidates for whom they would not have voted under any circumstances, 10 per cent named McLaughlin and fully 38 per cent named Barrett. The latter's unpopularity was exceeded only by Lagassé's, who was named by nearly half (47 per cent) of the delegates. As for the rest of the field, McCurdy was named by 18 per cent of the delegates, de Jong by 14 per cent, Waddell by 9 per cent and Langdon, the least objectionable of all the candidates, by only 7 per cent. Over half (52 per cent) of the delegates reported preferring someone else to all of the declared candidates. Of those, the names most frequently mentioned by these delegates were Stephen Lewis (48 per cent), Bob Rae (18 per cent), Lorne Nystrom (14 per cent) and Bob White (9 per cent).[7]

The Campaign

The 1989 NDP leadership campaign was a much less intensely organized contest than were the Liberal and Conservative campaigns of 1990 and 1993 respectively. Constituency delegates comprised 69 per cent of the total number of delegates, and the leadership candidates made few attempts to recruit new members to influence constituency delegate selection meetings – a practice common to both the Liberal and Conservative parties. Only 6 per cent of the NDP riding associations reported the recruitment of new members in 1989.[8]

Table 6-1 gives information on constituency delegate selection contests from the three older parties that helps our understanding of candidate organizational activity at the local level. By comparing survey results from the five national leadership conventions held between 1983 and 1993 we find that riding delegates chosen by the NDP were more likely to have been selected in uncontested votes than those in the other parties. NDP constituency delegates also tended to be less identified with a particular candidate than those in either the Liberal or Conservative parties. Relatively few NDP delegates (31 per cent in all) had openly identified themselves with one of the leadership candidates. The remainder of the riding delegates had not identified themselves with any of the candidates.[9] In contrast to the prior and subsequent experiences of the other two parties, slates were generally absent from NDP delegate selection meetings, and only 2 per cent of the delegates reported having been chosen after experiencing trench warfare.[10]

The NDP delegate selection process in 1989 was not an organizational battle. Even allowing for the fact that Barrett did better among trade unionists at the convention (who, by definition, were not riding delegates), his joining the race so late and yet garnering so much support at the convention highlighted the different form that grassroots-level candidate organization has assumed in the NDP. In the Liberal and Conservative parties, grassroots organization has been basically about recruiting new party members to take part in the delegate selection process. Characteristically, it has taken a good deal of money to bring the new recruits into the party. In the NDP, by contrast, grassroots organization for leadership conventions has typically been concerned with convincing established, often long-time party members to support one candidate over another. That work, by definition, has been more labour-intensive but less costly than the organizational tactics employed by the Liberals and Conservatives.[11]

The NDP leadership candidates of 1989 made few attempts to manipulate the constituency delegate selection process as a result of a combination of factors. The candidates would have needed sufficient organizational lead-time to meet the requirement in the party's constitution that restricts participation in the delegate selection process to those who joined the party at least 120 days before a convention.[12] Given the scarcity of campaign funds in the NDP (see table 4-4), the leadership candidates simply lacked the resources to conduct extensive organizational forays at the riding level. Perhaps the fact that the prize the candidates sought was worth relatively little might also account for the lack of candidate organization at the delegate selection level. Whereas the two older parties choose prime ministers or at least potential prime ministers, the NDP was choosing the leader of the third-place party. In addition, any leadership candidates making overt efforts to recruit new members and pack meetings ran the risk of alienating a significant segment of the party membership. There is in the party, as Carty notes, a "different orientation toward membership" in that New Democrats view conventions as "the business of an ongoing well-established membership."[13] By not bringing new people into the party during conventions, the NDP has "effectively [forgone] opportunities to expand its organizational base in the interest of maintaining a coherent definition of membership and a stable core of local activists."[14]

Being largely unable or unwilling to manipulate the delegate selection process to ensure that already committed delegates were chosen, the candidates in 1989 had to appeal directly to the party activists who were elected as delegates. The party facilitated their efforts by sponsoring a seven-week, fifteen-city debate circuit in which all of the candidates participated. But the candidates' individual efforts were constrained because of their limited budgets and small organizations. Little contact between candidates and delegates meant that about one-quarter of the delegates went into the convention undecided as to which candidate they would vote for on the first ballot.

Of the seven leadership campaigns, the McLaughlin team was the most effective in personally contacting the delegates: one-third of the delegates said they were approached by McLaughlin herself and most were asked for their support by someone in the McLaughlin organization. At the same time her campaign performance was generally perceived by the delegates and media alike to have been less than scintillating. Said one senior union organizer after the powerful Steelworker's Union, in a move perceived by some to have been a slap in the face for all candidates, declined to endorse any one candidate, "[The union members] all came here to see Audrey McLaughlin and they were ready to endorse her but she was a disappointment."[15] Nevertheless, going into the 1989 convention she had far more committed delegates than any other candidate and a large majority of the delegates believed that McLaughlin would, in fact, be chosen as the successor to Broadbent.[16]

The First Woman Leader

Despite the lacklustre campaign and the delegates' lukewarm enthusiasm for the candidates, voting day at the convention was an exciting exhibition of free-wheeling politics. McLaughlin was ahead on the first ballot although Barrett was closer to her than many had predicted. With fifty-three votes Lagassé was automatically eliminated as the low candidate. He released his delegates and made no move to endorse any other candidate. Langdon was in third place and after the results of the first ballot were announced he gained the endorsement of McCurdy. The two, both searching for a compromise choice and both believing that they were it, had tried to enlist the other minor candidates in a strategy to coalesce around whichever candidate was in third place after the first ballot. Their attempt to build an alternative coalition was not as effective as it might have been because Waddell (who withdrew and threw his support behind second-place Barrett) and de Jong (who stayed on for the second ballot) wanted no part of it. "I'm not going to join any coalition to stop anybody," said de Jong when approached with the deal.

The second ballot saw Barrett, buoyed by the endorsement of Waddell, realize the largest vote gain of all the candidates as he moved to within forty-nine votes of McLaughlin. After much dithering, de Jong moved to support McLaughlin, as did McCurdy.[17] McCurdy was explicit about the motivations for his move, telling Langdon before he left him that "We've got to stop Barrett."[18] Others shared McCurdy's fears that by staying on for the third ballot, Langdon was opening the door for Barrett to overtake McLaughlin and possibly to go on to win on the third ballot. Langdon stayed in the race only to be eliminated on the third ballot. McLaughlin increased her lead over Barrett on the third ballot and went on to win on the fourth with 1,316 votes to 1,072 for Barrett.

The 1989 post-convention survey yielded the following general picture of the demographic, social, and ideological bases of McLaughlin's support on the fourth ballot. Even if it was not very deep, her support spanned a number of socio-demographic variables. It was national in the sense that she received the votes of a majority of delegates from each territory and province save British Columbia, where the vote was split evenly between her and Barrett. Her support was particularly strong in Alberta, Ontario, Quebec, the Maritimes, and the territories.[19] That she was a woman and a fresh face on the political scene certainly helped her candidacy for the leadership of the NDP, a party in which the mood was increasingly in favour of having a woman as leader. She attracted the votes of a majority of both genders although women (72 per cent) were more likely to support her than men (56 per cent). Her support was fairly evenly distributed across the party's ideological spectrum: 67 per cent placed themselves to the left of the party, 59 per cent placed themselves to the right, and 55 per cent thought of themselves as being in the centre. She received majority support from the ex officio delegates (77 per cent) and those elected in the party's youth clubs (69 per cent) and the constituencies (63 per cent). On the other hand she attracted less than two-fifths (37 per cent) of the votes of the trade union delegates. Unlike the party's three previous leadership conventions, in 1989 the union vote was not solidly behind the eventual winner.[20]

The NDP is a small party both in terms of the share of the popular vote and in terms of members elected to Parliament. Of the forty-three New Democrat MPs at the time of the leadership convention, no fewer than six were seeking the leadership. The lack of consensus within the party over its leadership was reflected in the fact that between them the two leading candidates on the first ballot attracted just over half of the vote and that it took the delegates four ballots to choose McLaughlin from a field of seven candidates. The eventual choice was, it seems, a difficult one. There were several reasons for this. McLaughlin was inexperienced politically and had weak ties to the party establishment.

She was generally perceived at the time to be a poor speaker and campaigner. Why then did she win? The major study of the 1989 convention concluded that it was her leadership style, "the perception of her as a winner for the party in federal elections, combined with perceived competence, ability to make tough decisions and to unite the party, that propelled McLaughlin to victory in 1989."[21]

THE 1990 LIBERAL LEADERSHIP CONVENTION

Until the mid-1980s the Liberal party had been free of many of the internecine squabbles over the party leadership that had been so debilitating for the Conservatives. The Turner era and two consecutive election losses brought to the party a divisiveness and a bitterness that the modern party had not seen. Turner's success at the 1984 convention had been at least in part the product of a myth of his invincibility that was soon dispelled by the Mulroney Conservatives in the election later that year. Turner, the shortest-serving prime minister in twentieth century Canada and the shortest-serving party leader in Liberal history, had turned out to be a disappointment for the Liberal party. So when on 3 May 1989 he announced his intention to resign the leadership, few Liberals were sad to see him go.[22] In fact a sizable faction within the party was of the opinion that the Liberals had made the wrong decision in 1984 by choosing Turner over Jean Chrétien and that Turner's resignation offered the party the opportunity to set the situation aright.

The Candidates

Jean Chrétien was the obvious choice to succeed Turner. He had been a member of Parliament from 1963 to 1986, and the strength of his network of supporters and organizers was without rival in the party. Owing largely to his strong second-place showing to John Turner in 1984, Chrétien had solid credentials as the Liberal leader-in-waiting. Party president Iona Campagnolo's tribute to him at that convention, to the effect that although he had finished second on the ballot he was "first in our hearts," reflected his popularity within the party. Whereas the tradition in the Liberal party of alternating between an anglophone and a francophone leader had been a major obstacle to Chrétien's chances of succeeding Trudeau in 1984, it was a boon to his candidacy to succeed Turner. He had strong support from within the party establishment, including many of those who had sided with Turner in 1984. An outspoken patriot and a populist orator (Jeffrey Simpson once described him as the "everyman of Canadian politics"[23]), Chrétien was immensely popular in the country. Polls consistently showed that with him as leader the Liberals could beat the ruling Conservatives. Although these features were key to the establishment of Chrétien as the obvious front runner in the 1990 Liberal leadership race, the success of his leadership bid was assured by his ability to put together a campaign organization capable of raising the funds and attracting the talent required to recruit thousands of new party members and to turn the delegate selection process at the riding level to his advantage.

The party's decision to postpone holding the leadership convention until 20–23 June 1990 was perceived to be a setback for Chrétien, whose supporters had been pushing for an early convention in the belief that it would give tactical advantages to their well-prepared candidate. The perceived practical effect of the party's decision was to give more time for other prospective candidates to raise money, solicit support, and organize their campaigns. In the event, only four Liberals – Hamilton MP Sheila Copps, Montreal MP Paul Martin Jr, and Toronto MPs John Nunziata and Tom Wappel – chose to challenge Chrétien for the leadership. Only Martin was able to put together the financial and organizational resources necessary to mount a competitive campaign and even he remained far behind Chrétien in terms of organization and campaign preparedness.[24] In terms of financing, Chrétien and Martin were in a class by themselves as each had millions of dollars at his disposal throughout the campaign. Although Copps was a serious candidate (polls conducted just prior to the convention showed her to be more popular than Martin across the country and more popular than Chrétien in Quebec[25]), unlike Chrétien and Martin she had not spent years preparing a leadership bid. She attracted neither the money (she spent $800,000) nor the organizational muscle necessary to wage a delegate-by-delegate, riding-by-riding struggle against the Chrétien and Martin organizations. Both Nunziata and Wappel were minor candidates who were unable to attract any significant support, either in terms of funds or workers, from within the party. That the campaigns of Chrétien and Martin were so relatively well funded and well organized ensured that the race for the leadership would be a two-man battle.

Selecting the Delegates

Organization at the constituency level was crucial. An amendment to the party's constitution adopted in 1986 entitled every constituency to elect twelve delegates, making the total elected constituency-level entitlement 3,540 delegates – 68 per cent of the total number of delegates entitled to vote at the 1990 convention. The leadership candidates therefore had a large incentive to establish local organizations to contest delegate selection meetings in every constituency across the country. Those who were unable to do so, as Copps, Nunziata, and Wappel could well attest, soon dropped out of serious contention.

The mobilization of members is central to the delegate selection process. George Perlin has estimated that during the Liberal leadership campaign of 1990, between seventy-five and one hundred thousand people took part in the constituency delegate selection meetings.[26] Nearly three-quarters (73 per cent) of the constituency delegate selection meetings for the 1990 Liberal convention were attended by more than two hundred people (a figure reached by less than 1 per cent of the NDP riding associations in 1989 and by only 17 per cent of the Tory meetings in 1993).[27] The delegate selection process at the constituency level began in Ontario on 15 February 1990 and throughout the rest of the country on 1 March 1990 and continued until 31 May 1990. The length of the period and the fact that recruits became eligible to vote for and to stand for election as delegates after having been a member for merely fourteen days[28] gave the campaign teams of the two main candidates plenty of time to move their key organizers from riding to riding and to recruit instant members to pack delegate selection meetings.

Over four-fifths (81 per cent) of the Liberal riding associations experienced an influx of instant members during the campaign.[29] Many of these instant members were drawn from close-knit and often intensely loyal ethnic communities. Italian, Portuguese, Greek, Chinese, Croatian, and Sikh communities were targeted by organizers of the competing leadership campaigns and were recruited to vote at delegate selection meetings by the thousands. These ethnic Liberals were packed by candidate organizers into many of the key delegate selection meetings in metropolitan areas across the country. The effectiveness of such tactics gave rise to a new generation of powerbrokers in the party – organizers specialized in mobilizing ethnic minorities (sometimes referred to as the "Third Force" in the Liberal party) and herding them en masse to delegate selection meetings.[30]

Every additional body counted in what was, as table 6-1 indicates, the most intensely organized, riding-by-riding battle for delegates between competing campaign organizations in the period from 1983 to 1990. It was particularly fierce between the Chrétien and Martin forces. More than three-quarters (76 per cent) of those who were selected as constituency delegates to the convention had had their selection contested by other party members, about the same as in 1984. But there the similarity between the two Liberal conventions ends. A large majority of these had done so with the organizational support of either one of the leadership campaigns or a special interest or ethnic group. With 83 per cent of riding delegates having been selected after identifying themselves as supporters of a particular candidate, the constituency delegate selection process was "intimately linked with the national leadership decision."[31] That figure was twice what it had been in the Liberal contest six years previously. More than half (56 per cent) of all constituency delegates were identified Chrétien supporters while 15 per cent were openly for Martin, 6 per cent for Copps, 5 per cent for Wappel, and 1 per cent for Nunziata. Only 17 per cent of the delegates were unidentified.[32]

Fully 85 per cent of the constituency delegates were chosen as part of a slate and 76 per cent of them admitted to having been part of an identified slate. These figures were, respectively, more than double and more than triple what they had been in 1984. Of the identified Chrétien and Martin backers, nearly nine out of ten (90 per cent and 88 per cent respectively) also ran as part of an organized slate. Close to half (47 per cent) of all of the riding delegates experienced trench warfare battles featuring one identified slate against another, a vastly higher figure than in any other national leadership contests between 1983 and 1993.[33] Obviously few delegate selection meetings were taken for granted by the leading candidates' campaign organizers. In the midst of the campaign John Rae, Chrétien's national campaign manager, neatly summed up the view of many a backroom and grass-roots organizer of the state of modern-day leadership campaign politics. "This is the day of slate politics," said Rae. "Any campaign now has to be sure that it has the majority of delegates before they go to [the convention]."[34]

The Convention

After the long, gruelling organizational battle at the riding level, the convention itself was anti-climatic. There was no suspense as to what the eventual outcome of the convention would be because of the well-publicized successes of Chrétien's campaign machine. In late May, three weeks before the convention, a Canadian Press tally pegged his support at 2,415 committed delegates while Martin had only 670, Copps 196, Wappel 154, and Nunziata 32.[35] Chrétien easily secured victory on the first ballot with 57 per cent of the vote: the first leader to be chosen on the first ballot of a national leadership convention since Lester Pearson more than thirty years before.

Chrétien got off to a very strong start in his drive for delegates. Approximately two-thirds of the delegates had decided to vote for

Chrétien even before the delegate selection began, and 63 per cent of them went on to vote for him (see table 6-2). On the other hand those who made up their mind in the few weeks before the convention tended to support either Martin or Copps rather than Chrétien. Martin in particular did well in the final stages of the campaign, winning 48 per cent of the delegates who decided how to vote between the end of the delegate selection period and 35 per cent of those who made up their minds after the convention met. Chrétien's share of those who decided in each of the seven campaign stages for whom to vote declined with each successive stage. His juggernaut organization had ensured his victory early enough to make his later losses to his opponents immaterial.

Chrétien's support in the actual balloting was broad and fairly evenly distributed across a variety of socio-demographic variables. He attracted a majority of votes of delegates from every province except Ontario and Saskatchewan and the territories. He was particularly popular among delegates from British Columbia, Alberta, Manitoba, Nova Scotia, and Newfoundland.[36] He was equally preferred by men (56 per cent) and women (54 per cent). By delegate type, his support was concentrated in the constituency (58 per cent) and ex officio (54 per cent) delegations but was weaker among the smaller campus (41 per cent) and women's club (42 per cent) delegations.[37]

Of Chrétien's major rivals, Paul Martin managed only 25 per cent and Sheila Copps 11 per cent of the vote. Territorially, Martin's support was distributed fairly uniformly across the country. The exceptions were his weakness in Newfoundland and his strength in the territories. For her part, Copps received a disproportionate amount of her support from Central Canada, Prince Edward Island, and the Yukon. The delegates' gender was an insignificant factor in the support of the two candidates. As noted, both candidates, and Martin in particular, were more successful at winning over uncommitted delegates later in the campaign than they had been earlier. Martin was much more popular than Copps among the ex officio delegates, winning the votes of 35 per cent of that group compared to her 9 per cent, and he doubled her support among the riding delegates, 22 to 11 per cent. He also matched Chrétien's support among delegates from the party's student (42 per cent) and women's (38 per cent) clubs, while Copps received the support of 17 per cent and 21 per cent of these respective groups.

Of the two remaining candidates, one, John Nunziata, failed to attract enough support to win back his deposit. The other, Tom Wappel, gained 6 per cent of the votes. Although he denied being a single-issue candidate, much of his limited success was due to his ties to the anti-abortion movement. Lawrence Hanson has found that fully 95 per cent of the delegates who went on to vote for Wappel had been elected as part of a slate and that almost three-quarters of his supporters had received assistance from anti-abortion groups. His supporters had, on average, fewer years of experience in the party than the average delegate, as over half of them had joined during the course of the campaign. Where the Liberal presence was relatively weak and the anti-abortion movement was mobilized, Wappel's campaign tactics were particularly effective. This explains his success in Saskatchewan where he received the support of 34 per cent of the delegates.[38] Wappel's tactics contributed to the perception that the Liberal party's delegate selection process was too open and that it left the party vulnerable to penetration by single-issue groups.

The 1990 Liberal leadership convention was in several key respects distinct from other modern Canadian conventions, which were parallel, in their own way, to the post-1968 presidential nominating process of American parties. Four features of the Liberal campaign and delegate selection process are particularly noteworthy in this respect. First, although the amount of money involved was vastly lower than in the United States, the 1990 campaign was dominated by expensive candidate-centred campaigns. Secondly, like the modern American nominating process, the campaign was long (thirteen months from Turner's resignation to Chrétien's selection, including a delegate selection period of three and a half months) and the major candidates had both spent years laying the groundwork for their campaigns. Thirdly, although the early campaign events did not have the significance of the Iowa caucus or the New Hampshire primary, the Liberal delegate selection process was front-loaded in the sense that success early on in the race was more important than the number of delegates involved suggested. Chrétien's formidable lead among decided delegates before the delegate selection process even began, together with his success at the early delegate selection meetings, reportedly induced the Martin campaign to abandon attempts to manipulate many of the later meetings and to switch its emphasis towards wooing already selected Chrétien delegates.[39] Finally, similar to American convention delegates, most of the Liberal delegates had been elected on a slate and were thereby prematurely constrained in terms of their voting options by the organizationally induced commitments they had made. Because of his success at ensuring the election of already committed delegates, Chrétien had for all intents and purposes been chosen as the new leader before the convention even began.

Not surprisingly, the American-style campaign produced a convention that bore many similarities to recent American nominating conventions. The vote was decision-ratifying rather than decision-making in the sense that it was a formality that confirmed the well-publicized results of the delegate selection process. The leader effectively having been chosen in advance, the convention activities were focused primarily on creating a favourable image of the new leader and on adopting constitutionally the principle of one member, one vote for the party's next leadership selection contest. Both of these were done in the hope of increasing the popularity of the party and its chances of returning to power.

Chrétien's overwhelming win, seemingly an indication of party unity and consensus in the party ranks, was at the same time the product of a hard-fought, divisive process tainted by allegations of dirty tricks, instant members, packed delegate selection meetings, and machine politics. As the party rallied around Chrétien, many of the faithful were prepared to adopt reform measures aimed at curbing some of the excesses that the 1990 process had brought to light. Three such reforms that were adopted at the party's 1992 biennial convention are particularly noteworthy: delegates are to be selected by proportional representation rather than by a winner-take-all majority of votes cast; to qualify to vote at a delegate selection meeting a person must (a) have been a member of the party for a period of ninety days immediately preceding the meeting, and (b) have renewed his or her membership at the meeting; and all delegate selection meetings are to be held on the same weekend. Together these reforms promise to make it more difficult for candidates to engage in last-minute mass recruiting, pack delegate selection meetings, shift organizers from riding to riding, and sweep a riding's delegates. It was the hope of party officials that with the reforms they put in place in 1992, delegate selection meetings for the next Liberal leadership contest, whenever it comes, would not be marked by organizational dog fights as in 1990.

THE 1993 PROGRESSIVE CONSERVATIVE LEADERSHIP CONVENTION

Conservatives have fought over their party's leadership for most of this century. The party's extended period on the opposition benches (which gave rise to a mindset George Perlin has dubbed the "Tory Syndrome"[40]) went hand-in-hand with a divisiveness that affected all aspects of its operations. It was particularly damaging to the legitimacy and efficacy of its leadership through the Diefenbaker-Stanfield-Clark years. The selection of Brian Mulroney as leader proved to be a watershed for the party. Unlike his predecessors, Mulroney did not face a serious attempt within his own party to remove him from office throughout his time as leader. Why? Power is both a restorative and a preservative.

Intra-party cohesion derives more from the exercise of the levers of power than from anything else. From Mackenzie King on, the Liberals had learned that lesson well, with smooth transfers of office from one leader, most of them prime ministers at the time, to another. It was implicit in Mulroney's resignation remarks that he wanted the Tories to emulate the Liberal example.

On 24 February 1993 Mulroney announced his intention to resign as leader of the Conservative party and prime minister of Canada. Mired at the mid-teen to low 20 per cent level in the polls for months on end, the Conservative government faced sure electoral defeat under Mulroney's leadership. Clearly the party hoped that a vigorous leadership contest and a fresh face at the top would improve their electoral prospects. In resigning when he did, Mulroney had two wishes for the convention. One was that the convention would be a multi-candidate, dynamic affair in which "delegates only make up their minds after seeing the candidates strut their stuff and choices are only made at the last minute on the floor of the convention."[41] The other was that the Tories would succeed in conducting a leadership transition while in office and that the momentum generated by the convention would sweep the party to victory in the next election. He was to be disappointed on both counts.

The Candidates

By the time Conservative party officials formally announced in early March that the party would hold a leadership convention, defence minister Kim Campbell had already been proclaimed by the media and party insiders alike to be the clear front runner in the race. Female, from Vancouver and billed as bilingual, she had gender, region, and language on her side. She was perceived to be the fresh face the party felt it needed to win a third consecutive election. Attractive, articulate, and intelligent, Campbell was relatively new to federal politics, yet since her election to Parliament in 1988 she had enjoyed a meteoric rise in the Mulroney cabinet. Early public opinion polls showed that she was by far the most preferred choice of Canadians to succeed Mulroney and that with her as leader the Conservative party had the best chance of staying in power.

In early March 1993 columnist Jeffrey Simpson described the Campbell "phenomenon" as follows: "Phenomenon is the right word to describe what's happening. Ms. Campbell has not declared her candidacy. She has said nothing to the party by way of policy direction for the future. She has made no major speeches, released no policy papers, given no extensive interviews. Yet Tories are flocking to her as if to the Second

Coming."[42] By the time of the June convention, she had the support of a plurality of the caucus and of a majority of the cabinet.[43] At the convention itself Campbell received the endorsement of such Tory icons as Robert Stanfield, Davie Fulton, Ellen Fairclough, and Flora MacDonald. The strength of her support among the party notables was matched by her support from party organizers. In Quebec she attracted some former key Mulroney operatives and some of the "nationalist" members of the Tory caucus, which gave her their networks to draw upon. She also attracted many of the heavyweights of the former Big Blue Machine of Ontario and many other prominent strategists, campaigners, and fund-raisers from across the country. There was a degree of consensus within the Tory establishment around Campbell in 1993 that had not been present at the previous three Conservative conventions. This sent a signal to the delegates that despite her lack of roots in the party, Campbell was part of the Tory fold.

Campbell's leadership hopes were greatly enhanced by the lack of competition from other high-profile, well-funded, and well-organized contenders. Jean Charest, the youthful environment minister from Quebec, was her only serious rival in the contest. Charest adopted the "turtle and the hare" metaphor to describe his campaign, which, although Charest had announced his candidacy before Campbell, was much later getting under way. Unlike the ending in the fairy tale, Charest could not overcome Campbell's early lead and organizational strength. That he was relatively young, at thirty-four, and a Quebecker, also hurt his chances of succeeding Mulroney. After meeting with delegates on the campaign trail in eastern Ontario, Charest commented that "the hardest challenge was overcoming views that I was running for next time."[44] Edmonton MP and Conservative whip Jim Edwards was a serious candidate representing the right-wing of the party but, like Sheila Copps three years earlier, he was unable to attract the financial and organizational resources required to contest systematically delegate selection meetings at the constituency level. Toronto-area MPs Patrick Boyer and Garth Turner (both minor candidates yet serious in the sense that each brought a serious message to the dialogue within the party during the campaign) rounded out the small field of candidates.

Why were there so few candidates in the race? The high cost of running a competitive campaign may have been a deterrent for some. Although the Conservative party set a per-candidate spending limit of $900,000 which excluded certain items, to be competitive a candidate would have had to have well over a million dollars at his or her disposal.[45] Perhaps even more important was that Campbell's early strength in terms of media attention, organization, financing, and position in the public opinion polls scared off many of her potential rivals. As one prominent Conservative said after Campbell won the leadership by a much slimmer margin than had appeared likely earlier, "there was no question whatsoever that the early coverage of [Campbell] as front-runner and [of] her virtually as winner before the thing had even started, before a delegate had even been selected, scared a lot of [potential candidates] off. They have a lot of soul searching to do. They got scared off when they should have known better."[46] Even Jean Charest had originally balked at entering the race. Only after being urged to run both for the good of the party and of his own career by many friends and colleagues, including Brian Mulroney, did he decide to declare his candidacy.[47]

Selecting the Delegates

The candidates were well aware that the convention could be either won or lost in the delegate selection process at the constituency level. Each federal riding association was entitled to send six senior and three youth delegates to the leadership convention for a total constituency association entitlement of 2,655 delegates. This accounted for 73 per cent of the total number of delegates eligible to vote at the convention – the highest proportion ever. The two major contenders were able to put together campaign organizations which were, in the words of a Charest organizer, "massive, national and yet decentralized,"[48] and which were well versed in the arts of recruiting instant members, packing meetings, and organizing slates of delegates.

Constituency-level organization was a central component of the principal candidates' campaigns. As table 6-1 shows, about three in five constituency delegates had been challenged for their delegate positions (down from 77 per cent in 1983), and a similar number had identified themselves as supporters of a candidate prior to the meeting (up from 48 per cent in 1983). These figures were respectively lower and higher than in 1983, which suggests that inter-candidate rivalry was not as pronounced as it had been a decade before and that the early attraction focused on Campbell as the all-but certain winner in 1993 translated into an increased share of delegates willing to acknowledge prior identification with a candidate. Campbell's riding-level dominance was confirmed by the fact that 37 per cent of all constituency delegates had openly identified themselves with her prior to their selection, more than double Charest's 17 per cent and well above the 3 per cent who had identified with Edwards and the smattering of delegates with each of Turner and Boyer. The remaining 42 per cent did not identify themselves with any of the candidates. Although the

share of delegates who had run on an identified slate jumped considerably over the earlier Tory contest, it was only half the share in the
1990 Liberal convention. Nearly one of two constituency delegates
were part of a slate and most of these, 37 per cent of the total, were
identified with a leadership candidate as well. It is clear that the candidates' organizers typically did not run slates against one another. Only
12 per cent of the delegates had experienced trench warfare, a share
little different from what it had been a decade before.

In all categories the 1993 Conservatives figures were lower, sometimes dramatically so, than the 1990 Liberal figures. In terms of organizational activity at the riding level, the Tory campaign was somewhere
between the 1989 NDP campaign and the Liberal contest of the following year. Although the number of 1993 delegates experiencing trench
warfare was far lower than in 1990, it was no different from what it had
been in the 1983 Tory campaign and the 1984 Liberal campaign. This
is simply a further demonstration of the uniqueness of the 1990 Liberal constituency organizational competition among second-generation conventions. The Tories' process in 1993 was not marred either by
continuous reports of instant Tories and irregularities at delegate selection meetings, or by the degree of acrimony that had typically characterized Conservative leadership campaigns. This was at least in part a
reflection of the increased civility and discipline that nine years of government had brought to the party.[49]

The lack of organizational activity compared to the 1990 Liberal
process was most likely because the 1993 candidates had had less
time with which to prepare for delegate selection meetings, to recruit
new members, and to move their organizers from riding to riding
than their Liberal counterparts had had three years previously.
Whereas the 1990 Liberal candidates had over eight months from the
time of Turner's resignation to the first delegate selection meeting to
recruit members and to organize slates, the 1993 Conservative candidates had less than two. Furthermore, the Liberal delegate selection
period was spread out over fifteen-weeks but all 295 Conservative
meetings were held between 22 April and 8 May. The short Tory campaign resulted from the departing prime minister's edict against early
organizing, his belated decision to resign, and the party's desire to
hold the convention as soon as possible. It meant that the Tory candidates had to concentrate more on locating supporters within the
already established local associations and then helping them get
elected than on recruiting new members, packing meetings, and running slates. In any event, by the time the delegate selection dust settled, Campbell had about twice as many committed delegates as
Charest (see table 5-8).

The Campaign

Although Campbell never gave up her early lead, her campaign was damaged in the month before the convention by her overly candid performance and the negative media coverage she received because of it. She was generally perceived by the media to have performed poorly in the early all-candidates' debates, whereas Charest exceeded many of their expectations.[50] Campbell subsequently made several gaffes that only served to quicken her campaign's slide. For example, she once referred to those who did not share her view of the need to reduce the deficit as "enemies of Canadians," and she told reporters in response to a question about her past experiences that smoking marijuana was not illegal, something that as a lawyer and former justice minister she must have known to be false. The media had a field day with her stumbles. Statements she had made in an interview before the leadership campaign began, on topics from the political apathetic (she referred to them as "condescending SOBs") to organized religion (she joked about the "evil demons of the papacy") were wrenched out of context and manipulated by several outlets, including the *Toronto Star,* the Canadian Press, and CBC Radio.[51]

The common interpretation at the time was that the media built up Campbell's image to unreasonable proportions and then turned on her when she failed to meet the expectations. Whether that was the case or not, Campbell increasingly came to be portrayed in the media as ambitious, unstable, arrogant; in short, as a "loose cannon." Such words became part of the political code, especially when Campbell was compared to the friendly, stable, and devoted family man, Jean Charest. Campbell's gaffes, the negative media coverage she received because of them, and Charest's campaign performance were almost certainly behind the dramatic shift in public opinion that occurred in mid-May. From that time on, public opinions polls consistently showed that the Conservative party would have the best chance of winning the next election under Charest, not Campbell. This shift in public opinion was reflected in a shift in the delegates' attitudes towards the leading candidates. During the campaign, delegates' opinions of Campbell tended to worsen while their opinions of Charest tended to improve.[52]

At the same time as her media image and position in the polls collapsed, Campbell's campaign organization, originally thought to be formidable, began to come apart at the seams. It had been unwieldy from the very beginning. Jeffrey Simpson described it as resembling "a 15-legged camel: wondrous, strange and going nowhere fast."[53] By mid-April, on the eve of the beginning of the delegate selection period, her campaign was reportedly bogged down by an "extremely slow" decision-making process resulting from a "plethora" of campaign committees and the large number of people on them. At that point her campaign underwent an internal shuffle and Patrick Kinsella, a veteran strategist with whom she had worked previously, was brought in to "toughen up the centre" of the Campbell organization.[54]

Whatever organizational difficulties Campbell experienced in her national campaign, they did not prevent her supporters from engineering the selection of substantial numbers of pro-Campbell delegates at the riding level. Despite Campbell's fall from grace as far as the media and the public were concerned, these delegates tended not to abandon her. But it was true that after the end of the delegate selection period and as the mound of press clippings documenting her gaffes accumulated, Campbell became less successful than Charest at attracting the support of undecided delegates. Notwithstanding that, as the June convention approached, Campbell's lead among decided delegates still remained above 50 per cent (see table 5-8).

Campbell's victory was one almost entirely of organizational superiority in the early stages of the campaign and during the week of the convention itself. Her initial attractiveness and apparent winnability had given her a seemingly insurmountable advantage at the outset of the campaign which, by convention week, had largely evaporated. But it was during that final week that the real differences in campaigns showed. Campbell's delegate tracking, convention-week planning, and floor organization were vastly superior to anything mustered by any other candidate. Charest's troops, on the other hand, were out-hustled on the floor of the "issue sessions" and, most critically, on voting day itself. His organization was weak on delegate tracking and it overestimated his first ballot support. Had they fully understood the size of the ground they had to make up, his strategists, it would have to be assumed, would have been led to design a different convention-week game plan – one that was aimed more directly at Campbell's weaknesses.

Even so, it would have taken a sizable number of Campbell defectors to have brought Charest to within winning distance on the first ballot, and that was not in the works given her organization's ability to keep her supporters on side. Campbell's convention-week organizers were even more successful than Charest's in winning over those who waited until the convention met to decide how they were going to vote (see table 6-2). Charest, unlike Martin and Copps three years earlier, was unable to bring in more of the last-week deciders than his major opponent. For her part Campbell, unlike Chrétien in 1990, was able to reverse her slide in winning over successive waves of new supporters in the last week. That speaks volumes about the strength of her convention-week organization.

The Tories Choose a Prime Minister

The results of the first round of voting left little doubt about who the next leader of the party and the next prime minister would be. With 48 per cent of the vote, Campbell was only seventy-one votes short of a majority. Trailing her by three hundred votes, Charest was too far behind her to have any realistic chance of winning on the second ballot. After the results were announced Boyer quickly moved to the Charest camp and Turner withdrew but did not indicate a preference between the two front runners. Edwards moved to support Campbell, the certain winner at that point. Campbell would have won without Edwards's support, though no doubt by an even slimmer margin. Charest made the larger gain from the first to the second ballot, but Campbell won the leadership on the second ballot with 53 per cent of the vote.

Like McLaughlin's in 1989 and Chrétien's in 1990, Campbell's final ballot support was fairly broad and evenly distributed. The provincial distribution of the final ballot vote shows that Campbell supporters absolutely dominated the delegation from her native British Columbia and that she received more modest majorities among delegates from Saskatchewan, Manitoba, Ontario, New Brunswick, and Newfoundland.[55] According to the delegate survey, she drew the votes of 52 per cent of the male delegates and 61 per cent of the female delegates on the final ballot of the convention. The data indicate that the delegates' length of membership had little impact on Campbell's support. The same was true of delegates according to their ideological self-placement. On the second ballot Campbell received the votes of 57 per cent of those who considered themselves to be on the left wing or at the centre of the party and 52 per cent of those who placed themselves on the party's right wing. According to the distribution of first ballot votes, Campbell's ideological support base was the centre of the party. The same was true of Charest, as the three lesser candidates drew most of their support from the right wing of the party.

In 1993 the Conservative party succeeded in doing what it had not done since 1920 when Arthur Meighen succeeded Robert Borden – carrying out a leadership transition while in office. The party must have hoped that the changeover would spell greater success in 1993 than it did in 1920 when electoral disaster was little more than a year away. But the Tories met with an even worse fate in 1993 than they had in 1921, winning only two seats. The party lost official party status in the House of Commons and was reduced to a marginal position in Canadian national politics. Campbell lost her own seat; less than two months later and exactly six months from her moment of triumph at the convention, she resigned the Conservative leadership. Although possibly nothing (or no one) could have saved the Tories in 1993, it is obvious that the selection of Kim Campbell as leader proved to be disastrous for the party. Upon her resignation Jean Charest, one of the party's two remaining MPs, became interim leader. When the Conservatives gathered at their first post-election national convention (in Hull in April 1995), Charest was confirmed as party leader by 96 per cent of the 1,236 delegates voting on the question of whether to hold a leadership convention. He had become the official leader, though under much different circumstances than he had once hoped.

The Last of the Mega-Conventions?

The 1990 Liberal and 1993 Conservative leadership conventions may well prove to be the last of the mega-conventions that began with the Tory contest of 1967. In the intervening quarter-century leadership conventions had grown in terms of size, costs, organizational demands, and length of campaigns. The toll that those changes had taken on party and candidates alike became apparent by the time the 1990 Liberal contest concluded after a thirteen-month-long marathon of recruiting, organizing, and spending.

The number of candidates contesting the leadership that year had fallen to five from nine in 1968 and seven in 1984. The 1990 "contest" was over on one ballot with the winner, Jean Chrétien, receiving a comfortable 57 per cent of the vote. That contrasted with the 51 per cent win that Pierre Trudeau managed after four ballots in 1968. Following the 1990 meeting, party organizers and delegates speculated openly and enthusiastically about the various electoral reforms (among which were a universal ballot system and a combined direct vote/convention system) that were being considered by the party to be put in place for the next Liberal leadership transition, whenever that might be. For their part, the Tories fared not much differently. Unlike 1967, 1976, and 1983, when either four or five ballots had been needed to choose the leader from among eight to twelve candidates, Kim Campbell won over four opponents on the second ballot.

The multi-ballot races that marked the 1967–83 period of the second generation were effectively over for the two older parties as of the 1984 Liberal contest. The Liberal contest of 1990 in particular bore an unmistakable resemblance to the coronations of Louis St Laurent in 1948 and Lester Pearson in 1958 in the first generation. But there were two obvious differences: the three-fold increase in the number of delegates compared to these earlier Liberal conventions; and the skyrocketing costs of campaigning. The days of Lester Pearson's $3,000 campaign were like pages from another book as the spending of Chrétien and Martin climbed into the millions of dollars. The NDP was different on that score, as on others. In 1989 the seven candidates spent an average of less than $70,000 each. Compared with the two older parties there was an anachronistic and parochial quality about the NDP contest.

The leadership conventions of recent years were often characterized by the media as "old-fashioned" affairs marred by "old-style" politics. The latter included the recruitment of instant members to pack delegate selection meetings, the running of slates, and the type of machine politics that had been particularly prominent during the Liberal and Conservative leadership campaigns from the 1960s on. The Lortie Commission was critical of this type of activity, claiming that it had "undermined the integrity of the leadership selection process."[56] Such a feeling was conveyed by journalist Rosemary Speirs, who wrote during the 1990 Liberal leadership campaign that the result of the party's failure to adopt reform proposals before Turner resigned was "a leadership contest fought on old rules, or lack of rules, that have resulted in unseemly stories in the media about strong-arm tactics, the signing up of 'instant Liberals' and charges of slate packing."[57] Seeking to restore legitimacy to the leadership selection process, the Lortie Commission recommended that the parties reduce the opportunities to recruit instant members and that the state become more involved in the process, particularly in establishing the general terms for strict party-regulated campaign financing.[58] Apart from this, however, the principal reforms would left up to the parties themselves.

The parties have taken up the question of structural reforms to the leadership selection process. A growing number of provincial parties have adopted direct election of the leader by the entire party membership as a seemingly more open, representative, and democratic method of leadership selection, and with the 1993 election the Reform party arrived on the federal scene with a bang and an agenda calling for dramatic changes to the way in which politics is conducted. For its part, in 1992 the Liberal party adopted innovative reforms designed to open up the leadership selection process to more direct involvement by the grassroots of the party and to try to restrict the opportunities for candidate organizational contests at the riding level. After accepting the post-1993 election resignations of Kim Campbell and Audrey McLaughlin, the Conservative party and the NDP both indicated that they were intent on adopting some form of the one member, one vote model to choose their next leaders. Massive changes to the way in which leaders are chosen seemed not far off.

Has the era of the mega-convention come to a close? Features of the most recent leadership conventions, along with the reform movement currently under way, suggest that Canadians may have seen the last of them. The 1993 election could well prove to have been the catalyst needed. Both the Conservative party and the NDP seized upon their rejection by the electorate as an opportunity to begin examining ways of changing their internal procedures, including choosing their leaders, in their struggle to remain politically relevant. Exactly where such a reform process will lead remains an open question. And whether wider participation through a one member, one vote process will enable winning candidates to assemble a broad national coalition of support within their party, as McLaughlin, Chrétien, and Campbell did in their respective conventions, remains an even bigger question.

7 Who's There? Representation and Leadership Selection

I don't care who does the electing, just so I can do the nominating.
— William Marcy "Boss" Tweed of Tammany Hall

Representation has been at the heart of leadership selection by party convention. The abandonment of the parliamentary parties in 1919 and 1927 as the authoritative bodies for choosing party leaders came largely as a consequence of their perceived representational weaknesses. Mindful of Canada's cultural and regional divisions, the parties seized upon national party conventions as ideal assemblies to compensate for the representational inadequacies of their parliamentary caucuses. The presence of an equal number of voting delegates from every constituency imparted to the convention a political legitimacy to select a leader independent of, and possibly even outside of, the parliamentary party.

At one level, the representational theory behind leadership conventions that has marked the two older parties (but not, as will be seen later in this chapter, the NDP) has been an egalitarian one. From the outset, equal voting power was granted territorially-defined political units – the constituency parties – regardless of whether or not the local MP was from that party and irrespective of their size or socio-demographic composition. The two older parties used either the call issued for each convention or their constitution to establish the number of voting and alternate delegates that each constituency would be entitled to send. For a country as socially diverse and as sparsely populated as Canada, there was almost certainly no acceptable alternative to central control within the parties over size of local delegations, but the practical effect of the measure was to reinforce the extent to which the parties were *national*, as opposed to federal, creatures. Although the Liberals insisted for much of the twentieth century that theirs was a federation of provincial parties, they, like the Tories, adhered to a single national standard for determining the number of local representatives to be sent to conventions. This meant that from the outset of conventions the two parties had in place a mechanism which eschewed the American model of using the country's federal structure as units to aggregate and to cast votes.

A second representational principle, like the first an accepted part of leadership conventions from the beginning, has been to grant delegate status to certain individuals because of the positions they have held within the party. Elected or appointed party notables, such as MPs and senators, provincial leaders and legislative members, and executive officers of the various national and provincial branches of a party's organization, have been automatically named delegates. In recent years this type of representation has come under attack from party reformers. To party activists who have supported the call for greater intra-party reforms, an automatic entitlement to delegate status is elitist and anti-democratic. It is seen as a hold-over from the earlier days of a more deferential and less egalitarian society.

Representation at conventions has been justified in one other way as well. To be considered genuinely democratic the convention should have its membership selected so as to guarantee the inclusion of major components of society. The theory behind this concept of representation rests on the premise that delegates who share a characteristic with the group that selects them will best reflect the interests of that group. Such a non-territorial approach to representation draws on an increasingly pervasive view of public institutions. So far, the social interests that parties have accepted as deserving this sort of representational treatment have been defined according to age, gender, and educational affiliation. Race has recently been added to the list by the Liberals.

The two older parties may have differed in some of the particulars, but over the years both have established essentially the same three categories of delegates. These have been constituency-based elected delegates, ex officio delegates, and non-constituency-based elected ones. Broadly defined, each category has been designed to activate one of the three different representational principles – territorial, automatic and group – behind leadership conventions. Throughout the second generation of conventions in particular, a consistent theme that both parties have invoked in adding to the number of participants in all three categories has been one of increasing the number and mix of participants so as to enhance the democratic and representative character of the process by which their leaders have been chosen.

MORE DELEGATES = MORE DEMOCRACY

From the beginning of national conventions the two older parties have stipulated that every constituency association would be entitled to send the same number of delegates to a convention. During the first generation of conventions this usually amounted to three, sometimes four, delegates per riding. In total, constituency delegates normally accounted for 55 to 60 per cent of those voting at a convention, the remainder being made up of various other elected or appointed ex officio delegates. One of the distinguishing features of second generation conventions was the increasing number of delegates each constituency association was entitled to send to successive conventions. Even so, the growth in the size of local delegations did not always translate into a commensurately larger share of the total number of voting delegates. This was because the number of delegates automatically entitled to attend conventions as voting participants and the number of special categories of delegates created to represent newly recognized groups also increased at the same time. Tables 7-1 and 7-2 show the variety of categories of delegates eligible to attend Liberal and Conservative conventions between 1919 to 1993.

The change to the modern conventions in the 1960s brought with it the first of a series of moves to increase the number of constituency delegates. For the most recent conventions this meant constituency delegations three or four times what they had been in the first generation of conventions. The Conservatives started the process in 1967 with five delegates per constituency, then moved to six in both 1976 and 1983, and nine in 1993. The Liberals more than matched the Tories in 1968 with six delegates per riding, then seven in 1984, and twelve in 1990. Combined with a 25 per cent increase in the number of federal constituencies between 1919 and 1990 (from 235 to 295 Commons' seats), the growth in the size of constituency delegations translated into a sizable jump in absolute numbers of riding delegates. The Liberals went from 705 constituency delegates in 1919 to 3,540 in 1990, and the Conservatives from 980 in 1927 to 2,655 in 1993 (see table 7-3). The arguments in favour of both an absolute and a relative increase in the number of constituency delegates were invariably couched in terms of the process of "democratizing" of the party. More participation meant more democracy.

The two parties have long followed the same pattern of granting automatic voting privileges to certain kinds of delegates. These can be grouped into basically three categories: parliamentary (privy councillors, MPs, federal candidates, and senators); provincial and territorial legislative (leaders, members, and candidates); and intra-party organizations elected or appointed by their respective memberships (national and provincial executives and committee members, women's and youth's executives). From the beginning, the number of delegates to which these various groups have been collectively entitled has come close to, but has never constituted, a majority of the voting delegates. In 1990 and 1993 their respective shares dropped to less than one-fifth and one-quarter of all delegates. These relatively low figures were without precedent and reflected the success of the case mounted in the mid-1980s against so-called party elites and in support of greater constituency representation. Tables 7-4 and 7-5 show the total delegate allotment by category and province for the 1990 Liberal and 1993 Conservative conventions.

Some of the differences between the two parties' categories of ex officio delegates were apparent in the 1990 and 1993 conventions. Federal Liberal riding presidents were automatically accredited as voting delegates separate from the twelve to which local associations were entitled, whereas Tory constituency association presidents had to compete for one of the nine local delegate slots if they wished to gain voting accreditation. Liberal provincial legislative members and candidates were, for the first time, no longer entitled to choose a fixed portion of their numbers to become automatic delegates, and provincial Liberal leaders, also for the first time, were no longer automatically entitled to delegate status. All Conservative provincial leaders and legislature members were, as in the past, entitled to attend as voting delegates. The Conservatives accredited members of their national fund-raising organization (PC Canada Fund), their policy advisory committee, and their national campaign committee, but the Liberals did not do the same with their equivalent organizations. The Liberals granted members of their newly created Aboriginal Peoples' Commission ex officio delegate status. There is no equivalent organization in the Conservative party. The Tories have long asserted that their delegates-at-large category allowed provincial and national executives to compensate for obvious representational weaknesses or oversights should they wish to use it for that purpose. These differences in automatic delegate status suggest that the Liberals nationally chose to move further than the Tories to sever their representational links with their elected provincial members and to end convention voting privileges for those who served on important national committees. The Liberal moves promoted the increasingly separate operations of the federal and provincial wings of the party and reflected the mood of much of the party to curtail the influence of the party establishment at national conventions.[1]

In the second generation of conventions the parties, often in response to pressure mounted by women, youth, university-based groups and, most recently in the Liberal party, aboriginals, took steps to allow for the representation at conventions of a greater number of specially constituted clubs. University clubs in both parties have consistently been entitled to select delegates since 1948. In the Liberal party the student delegation grew from fifty-four in 1948 to 488 in 1990.[2] The number in the Tory party went from sixteen in 1948 to 408 in 1983, but fell back to 115 in 1993.[3] Delegates from campus clubs have been joined at the more recent Liberal conventions by those from women's clubs (two per club for 340 potential delegates in 1984 and one per club for 114 potential delegates in 1990) and aboriginal clubs (one per club for 124 potential delegates in 1990). By contrast, in the Conservative party there has been only a sprinkling of delegates from independent clubs (twelve in 1983), women's caucuses (sixteen in 1993), and affiliated associations (twenty-four in 1993). The number of delegates the Conservative party had from specially constituted groups in 1993 was not as large as it had had in 1983 or as the Liberals had in 1990. The shorter campaign in 1993, together with the tighter constitutional provisions introduced in 1986, presented Tory candidates with fewer opportunities to establish new clubs and recruit new members into them. The impact of these changes was most apparent in the markedly smaller number of university delegates eligible to attend the 1993 convention. At 115, that was the smallest student delegation of any second-generation Conservative convention.

The number of club delegates eligible to attend a national leadership convention sometimes bears little relationship to a province's actual share of that social or demographic characteristic in the larger Canadian population. A graphic illustration of this was found in New Brunswick, a province with only ten of the country's nearly three hundred federal constituencies. It was the scene of intense organizational competition by local supporters of the principal candidates prior to both the 1984 and 1990 Liberal conventions. By the time of the 1984 convention the province contained forty-two Liberal women's clubs – a number greater than Ontario's and almost a match for Quebec's forty-four. Two ridings had seven such clubs each. Six years later the number had grown in New Brunswick to forty-six women's clubs. This matched the combined total number of clubs in British Columbia, Alberta, Saskatchewan, Manitoba, Ontario, Quebec, Newfoundland, and the territories. In the lead-up to both conventions the party had placed no limit on the number of women's clubs that could be formed in a riding or province or on the number of clubs to which an individual could have belonged.[4]

REPRESENTATIONAL REFORMS

Women and Youth

Parties have claimed that the increases in the number of elected constituency-level delegates who take part in the exercise of choosing a leader are proof of the parties' commitment to democratic participation at the local level and to an elected assembly that more accurately represents the larger population. Quotas imposed on local associations by the national parties stipulating the share of the local delegations to be made up of youth and women are also justified on the grounds that they help to produce a more representative body. Typical of the kind of claim convention organizers make about the representative complexion of their assembly is that of Michael Meighen, 1976 Conservative convention chairman, when he announced the final delegate accreditation totals for that convention:

The constitutional amendments at the party's March 1974 general meeting helped to ensure that the convention population will be significantly representative of women and young people. In addition, the number of constituency delegates demonstrates the leadership convention will be an open and democratic meeting where the party rank and file have a majority say in the selection of the party's next national leader …

The large number and percentage of constituency delegates clearly underlines that our convention will be broadly representative of our national party. Convention democracy is based to a large degree on the scope of delegate representation. We feel that not only will the party "grassroots" have a predominate voice, but that we have also achieved a healthy and much-needed balance of regional and social interests.[5]

As in the United States, where major party reforms were introduced following the fractious 1968 Democratic convention, Canadian parties moved in the second generation of conventions to bring in *more* delegates and to guarantee delegate positions for certain *types* of delegates in an effort to make national conventions representative of larger numbers of people.[6]

There are no better illustrations of the application of the democratic and representative principles than the changes made by the Liberal party to its constitution in the 1980s to increase the number of constituency delegates, to guarantee gender equality among non-ex officio delegates, and to place a cap on the size of the ex officio delegation. At the national party's biennial convention of November 1982 there had been widespread support for a resolution aimed at bringing about a "fundamental restructuring" of the party. Resolution 40, as it was known, had been proposed and approved initially by the Young Liberals. It denounced the concentration of political power in the hands of "non-accountable, non-legitimate [and] non-elected members of the party." According to the resolution's supporters, the short-term objective was to condemn publicly such close confidants of the prime minister as Senator Keith Davey and then-principal secretary Jim Coutts for having abused, it was claimed, their "informal roles in advising the government" and for having totally bypassed "the democratically accountable executive of the party."[7] One of the long-term objectives was to reduce the number and influence of ex officio and so-called elite delegates to national conventions by placing a ceiling on their numbers and by adding more constituency, women, and youth delegates.

In response to Resolution 40 the party president struck a reform committee with a mandate to design constitutional changes that would give the Liberal party "an organizational leap forward ... into the 21st century."[8] At the end of the exercise, in November 1986, the party adopted several of the proposals of the committee. Central to the reforms was a massive increase in the size of elected local delegations, which resulted in the number of constituency delegates at the Liberals' 1990 leadership convention nearly doubling what it had been in 1984. This measure was complemented by a cap on the automatic ex officio delegation so that it could not exceed 15 per cent of the total number of delegates eligible to attend the convention. According to Iona Campagnolo, the Liberal national president at the time that the changes had been under consideration, the dual purpose of these amendments was "to democratize the party by increasing the power of militants at the expense of the elites" and "to reduce the proportionate number of ex officio delegates because they have tended, in the past, to be white, Anglo-Saxon, male and old."[9]

The president's perception of the unrepresentativeness of the ex officio delegates was widely shared by Liberals attending the two national meetings (Halifax 1985 and Ottawa 1986) at which the reform proposals were debated. At its 1986 convention the party also became the first national party to require constituency, youth, and campus associations to select male and female delegates in equal numbers. With time, these newly added sections of both parties have grown in number, size, and influence. Nowhere has this been truer than of the youth and campus sections, youth being described in their constitution by the Liberals as twenty-five or under and by the Conservatives as under thirty years of age. For the Tory conventions of 1983 and 1993 and the Liberal ones of 1984 and 1990 youth and campus club delegates together made up approximately one-third of all convention delegates in their own right. This was a sizable jump from 1967 and 1968 when they had accounted for 19 and 18 per cent of the Conservative and Liberal conventions respectively.[10]

Unlike senior male party members who enjoyed no reciprocal right, women and youth have been allowed to participate in the selection of delegates in several categories. In the Liberal party, for example, a female aboriginal university student aged twenty-five years or less occupied a privileged position in 1990. She could have voted for five different categories of delegates: constituency youth, constituency senior, and aboriginal, university, and women's club delegates. Given that there was no limit on the number of women's clubs to which she could have belonged, if she lived in New Brunswick she could well have voted many more times than that. An equivalent female in the Tory party in 1993 could have voted in the elections of three classes of delegates: constituency youth, constituency senior, and university club delegates. On the other hand, a non-aboriginal male thirty years of age or older at the time of the 1990 or 1993 selection meetings was entitled to vote in such ridings for one category of delegate only: constituency senior.

The Liberal constitution prior to 1986 guaranteed constituency representation to women and youth, but to no other groups. A practical expression of those guarantees occurred at the time of the intended 1980 Liberal leadership convention (cancelled after the defeat of the Clark government and the calling of the 1980 election), when one of the handful of constituency parties to have elected its seven delegates and seven alternatives chose only four males over the age of twenty-five in its total delegation of fourteen.[11] This admittedly atypical Canadian experience reinforced a larger point about political organizations: the rules, which at some point members of a group have had a hand in establishing, can with the necessary organizational skill and determination be turned to a group's advantage. It is also reminiscent of some of the American experiences in the 1970s with intra-party representational reforms. Implementing the recommendation of its McGovern-Fraser reform commission, the Democratic party in the United States introduced affirmative action rules to encourage representation of women, young people, and minority groups at its convention in 1972. In one state, California, the reform rules were seized upon with such vigour by supporters of presidential candidate George McGovern that traditional political elites were effectively frozen out of his delegation.

Forty-one per cent of the McGovern delegates were minority-group members, from a state in which approximately 18 per cent of the total population was considered part of a minority group. By contrast only 19 per cent were white males over the age of thirty.[12]

Female representation has increased dramatically over the life of leadership conventions in both older parties, especially in the Liberal party. It could scarcely have been otherwise considering its starting point. Fifty-one of the nearly one thousand registered delegates at the 1919 Liberal convention were women.[13] At the first of the modern Liberal conventions in 1968, when the party's constitution called for the election of "at least" one female delegate from among every six-person riding delegation, women accounted for 18 per cent of those in attendance. At the next one in 1984, when constituency associations were required to elect a minimum of two women to the seven-person delegation, the female share of the total number of delegates more than doubled to 40 per cent. In 1990 it reached a record high of 45 per cent.[14] By 1990, at which time they had been constitutionally guaranteed half of all constituency, youth, and campus positions, Liberal women had achieved parity in all save some of the ex officio categories. Even then the ex officio gender imbalance was offset to some extent by the exclusively female category of delegates (Liberal women's clubs have no male counterpart) which brought up to another 114 women to the 1990 convention.

Women were first eligible for election as delegates to a Conservative convention in 1927 at which time they filled 11 per cent of the delegate positions. In 1967 female delegates accounted for 19 per cent of those in attendance. The Conservatives amended their constitution in 1969 to require every constituency association to elect "at least" one woman as part of its five-member delegation. Five years later they added a stipulation that "at least" one man was to be chosen as part of an enlarged six-member local delegation, for without such a change it would have been at least conceivable that women could be elected to all five riding delegate positions and men to none. The attempt to increase the number of female participants through a guaranteed floor eventually met with some success, although its initial impact was marginal. At the party's 1976 and 1983 conventions about one-quarter of the delegates (24 per cent in both cases) were women.[15]

A common, though mistaken, assumption about the way in which the gender rule was to be applied was borne out in elections in many Tory riding associations in 1976 and 1983. Once the one female had been chosen, usually in a special vote, men would then be elected to most of the other positions to be filled. The chairman of the party's constitutional review committee noted in 1986 that the practical effect of the rule was that "the minimum had become the maximum." Claiming that the Tory rules actually worked against women's representational interests, his committee urged removal from the party's constitution of any minimum number of female delegates because "delegate selection should reflect the demographic profile of the constituency."[16] The gender distribution of 1983 Tory delegates by delegate category confirmed the point at issue. Of every hundred non-youth constituency delegates in attendance, seventy-four were men and twenty-six women.[17]

The constitutional review committee's recommendation was turned down, however, by the Tories at their 1986 national meeting. In its place the party approved provisions specifying that of the six senior constituency delegates at least two were to be male and two female, and that three constituency youth delegates were to be chosen without any gender quotas to be met. At the same time they removed a provision in their constitution requiring at-large delegations to be composed equally of men and women. The vigorous debate on the floor of the meeting made it clear that Tories, and Tory women in particular, were less persuaded than their Liberal counterparts of the need to require gender parity at the constituency level. Delegates defeated a proposed constitutional amendment which would have imposed gender equality on constituency delegations. The arguments that carried the day included "affirmative action is a socialist policy and does not belong in the Conservative party" and "you only need to look at [the number of women in] this room to see there is no need for quotas."[18] As the president of the Progressive Conservative Women's Caucus, herself a proponent of a fifty-fifty gender rule for riding association delegations, acknowleged, the majority of women active in the Conservative party disagreed with her and accepted the view that they did not need the "protective element" that total gender equality would provide.[19] That may have been a premature judgment, for although the share of female delegates in attendance at the 1993 convention increased to an all-time party high of 34 per cent, it nonetheless fell short of what the Liberals had accomplished with their parity provisions three years previously.

Aboriginals

What Byron Shafer has described as a party's "wish to reach out to new constituencies"[20] explains the Liberals' move to create a special constitutional category for aboriginal Canadians. At their 1986 meeting the Liberals adopted a resolution endorsing in principle the establishment of an Aboriginal Peoples' Commission within the party's organizational structure, a move without precedent in Canadian party history.

The mandate of the commission was explained in these terms: "To ensure the active participation of Inuit, Indian and Métis Peoples within the Liberal Party of Canada, by providing equitable proportional Aboriginal representation within the Party structure, [and] to create an opportunity to influence the Party's decision and policy-making processes, and [to] seek to redress the current under-representation of Aboriginal Peoples in the Canadian political system."[21]

The commission was subsequently empowered by the party's national executive to issue contingent delegate certificates for the 1990 leadership convention to aboriginal persons selected, one delegate per club, by an aboriginal club. At the outset of that convention, again without precedent, the assembly agreed to set aside the regular constitutional provisions governing establishment of new delegate categories and to grant full delegate status to those holding contingency status. To qualify as a club entitled to send a delegate to the convention, a group of at least twenty-five self-identified Indians, Inuit, and Métis had to have its constitution approved by the party's national executive, another measure of central control over local party affairs.

In all, as many as 124 clubs could have been established for the 1990 convention, the number and interprovincial distribution having been determined by the aboriginal share of the total Canadian population in the 1986 census (3 per cent) in relation to the total number of 1990 convention delegates and by the demographic distribution of aboriginal peoples within a province or territory. Together with the aboriginal commission delegates, the new special categories provided for up to 170 native delegate slots in 1990 (see table 7-4). The actual number in attendance in 1990 was something less than the potential figure, as only 103 clubs were established in time to send delegates to the convention. According to one source, all of the delegates from these clubs were in attendance at the convention as were all of those from the commissions. The party's extraordinary measures to ensure the participation of aboriginals reportedly resulted in at least 149 aboriginal delegates attending the convention.[22]

Can the integration of women and youth into the party serve as a model for native representation? Women and youth started out with separate representation, yet to a considerable degree their representation has now been integrated at the local level. Is this likely to happen with aboriginals? The answer to these questions lies largely in how parties decide to handle native representation – whether they will follow the usual model (usual in the sense that it had been used for women and youth) or whether they will construct a distinctively new model and treat native participation as a special type. The 1990 Liberal experience demonstrated that the party chose to treat native representation differently from representation of any group previously. At that convention Liberal youth and women were guaranteed representation at the constituency and club levels, but by contrast aboriginals were guaranteed representation only via specially constituted, non-constituency-based clubs. The party made no structural attempt to ensure the selection of natives as constituency delegates. As aboriginal Canadians, unlike women and youth, are relatively few in number and are unevenly distributed across the country, it is possible that there is no acceptable alternative to specially constituted clubs short of a party requirement that a minimum number of aboriginal delegates be chosen in ridings "where numbers warrant."

There could be two unintended representational consequences of continuing to handle aboriginal participation the way the Liberals did in 1990. The risk of not requiring constituencies with a significant native population to select a constitutionally stipulated number of aboriginal delegates is that those aboriginals who might choose to seek election as constituency delegates would then be told that their representation at the convention had been taken care of through the specially created clubs. As those clubs reflect with some degree of mathematical precision the number of natives in Canada, the argument in favour of added constituency representation could prove to be neither easily made nor favourably accepted. Equally it could be that, as has been the experience with some minority delegations in the United States, "the concern of these caucuses was with group interests rather than party or candidate interests."[23] In other words, representational reforms aimed at incorporating new groups into broadly based existing ones can produce the opposite effect by creating and reinforcing institutionally based identities separate from those of the larger group.

Representation and Democracy

Why have the various changes in composition and the increases in size of conventions taken place? The answer almost certainly lies in the interpretation that party organizers have given to the principles of representation and democracy. Parties are in the business of competing with one another. It is only natural that when one puts forth a claim to being both more representative and more democratic than its competitors, the others will then strive to match or even to outdo it in their measure of representativeness and democracy. The inter-party rivalry over democracy and representation was captured by the co-chairman of the Liberal party's Standing Committee on Native Affairs when he announced that the Liberals had approved the newly created category of aboriginal delegates for the 1990 convention: "This establishes a benchmark upon which other parties will be judged."[24] Not the Liberal party, but *other* parties! There is a profoundly significant point to be drawn from this sort of competition: the logical culmination of inter-party rivalry over who can out-democratize whom is the universal ballot. Part of the current attraction of the one-member, one-vote ballot to choose party leaders derives from its being grounded in the theory of direct democracy.

To party activists, the media, and many experts on Canadian politics, the leadership convention became an integral part of Canadian democracy. In the words of one authority, it amounted to "the summoning of an unusually large and representative 'parliament' of the party in order to ensure that the leader [was] the choice of the party as a whole."[25] Democracy and representation have become the twin pillars of party conventions, used not only to support increases in the size of local delegations but also to widen the mix of convention participants through the establishment of special, demographically defined categories of delegates.

Women have been included as delegates since the outset of conventions. Their involvement in the workings of the two older parties came first by way of auxiliaries, which were "conceived as forums of political education for newly enfranchised women,"[26] then through constituency parties where, for many years, the part that women played was a largely functional one. They were expected to provide "a ready pool of dedicated volunteers during election campaigns," and little more. Women's more recent and far-reaching participation in all aspects of party life, while not as total or as successfully integrated as that of male activists, has resulted from the reforms introduced by the parties and the active pressure from women's lobby groups within the parties.[27]

Although little is known of the history of party youth organizations, it is likely that the principal purpose of establishing a special category for young Canadians has been to gain a much-needed supply of party volunteers and to socialize them into the party in the hope that they would constitute the party elite of the next generation. From the standpoint of the parties, involving youth in their affairs is a relatively low-cost investment for short-term returns and for potential high-return yields at some point in the future. Thus youth and campus clubs have come to serve as "vehicles for maintaining a continuing flow of new activists to staff the parties' corps of volunteer workers and ... for elite recruitment."[28] The benefits accruing to the youth at the time of their participation as delegates are similarly obvious. There could be returns from making contacts with politicians and their organizations: summer jobs, longer-term employment on "The Hill" with MPs or ministers, and the possibility of eventually launching their own political careers with the support of established party elites.[29] Thus obvious gains for both the parties and the youth lend new meaning to the old expression used of the Jesuits: "Give us a child before he is six, and he will be ours forever."

Studies of final-ballot delegate voting behaviour in the 1983 and 1984 conventions show that neither women nor youth vote as a bloc and that women and youth do not always have the same majoritarian preferences. Had Mulroney and Clark each received the same share of the male vote as they did of the female (50 per cent), the 1983 fourth ballot would have ended in a dead heat. But "the gender gap worked in Mulroney's favour"[30] and he outdistanced Clark among male delegates by winning 57 per cent of their vote. That matched the 58 per cent final-ballot vote that Mulroney was given by delegates in the under-thirty category, which in itself was a reversal for Clark in that the same group seven years earlier had given *him* the majority of its final-ballot support. In 1984 Turner gained a majority of both female and male delegates' votes on the final ballot, 55 and 61 per cent respectively. But the size of his victory "was partly moderated by his relative weakness among younger delegates."[31] He received less than a majority of the youth vote, the rest being split between the two remaining candidates, Chrétien and Donald Johnston.

In the three most recent leadership conventions, the female candidates drew a larger share of the female than of the male vote. Audrey McLaughlin did the best of the three among female delegates, winning 72 per cent of their fourth ballot support. She also did well, although not to the same extent, with male delegates, gaining 56 per cent of their votes. Sheila Copps's support the following year was more evenly divided, 13 per cent of the women delegates' votes to 11 per cent of the mens'. In 1993 Kim Campbell won the votes of 61 per cent of Tory women delegates and 52 per cent of male delegates.[32]

What then, if anything, does the enlarged mix of delegates mean to the party in convention? Does its increased socio-demographic diversity translate into a wider spectrum of political viewpoints? The American experience with specially constituted categories of delegates has demonstrated that "it is much easier to change the processes through which delegates are selected than it is to secure a more 'representative' convention."[33] In her study of delegates attending the 1972 national party conventions in the United States, Jeane Kirkpatrick found that while the Democracts' newly created quotas based on age, gender, and race helped to broaden the demographic mix of delegates to the convention, they did little to widen the party's spectrum of political viewpoints or to represent more accurately the larger and more diverse set of values of ordinary Democratic supporters and of the American pub-

lic generally. In fact Kirkpatrick showed that the 1972 Democratic delegates were actually "less representative of the views and values of
voters than were delegates to the 'unreformed' Republican Convention, and the 'new' political type ... were least representative of all."
This was because the new set of representational rules, like the old,
produced "a convention whose members had much higher incomes,
higher education [and] higher social status" than regular Democrats.
Candidate organizations adapted to the new representational requirements by "filling their 'women' slots with women who shared their
political opinions, and so forth." As a result, there were "no large or reliable relationships between age, sex, race and political perspectives" at
the 1972 Democratic convention. The Democrats' experience failed
to "support the view that the *quality of political representation* is enhanced
by providing quotas for specified groups."[34]

The 1983 Conservative and 1984 Liberal conventions speak to the
issue of female and youth participation in Canadian conventions.
Studies of those conventions lend support to Kirkpatrick's conclusions
about the demographic representativeness of conventions. Female
delegates to the Tory and Liberal conventions "clearly constitute[d] a
socio-economic elite."[35] Nearly one-third of the women delegates in
both parties were employed in professional and senior management
positions; between two-thirds and three-quarters had completed at
least some post-secondary education; and between two-fifths (Liberal)
and three-fifths (Conservative) were from households with annual incomes of $40,000 or more ($58,760 in 1993 dollars). Female delegates, in other words, were more like male delegates than either
group was like the general population. The same was true of the
youth. Between 80 and 90 per cent had either completed or were then
completing a post-secondary degree, and between one-third to two-
fifths were from families with annual incomes of at least $40,000. As
with senior delegates, those in the youth category had "atypical social
backgrounds."[36]

Neither women nor youth at the 1983 and 1984 conventions constituted homogeneous groups with views consistently and widely divergent
from their larger party. Questions dealing specifically with abortion,
daycare, and women's equality elicited statistically significant different
responses from male and female delegates, with the women being more
favourably disposed than the men. Otherwise there was little in the way
of a consistent pattern in gender differences.[37] On some social and
business policy items women were slightly more likely than men to
favour an interventionist and activist role for government; on other social and business items the reverse was the case.[38] In general, male and
female delegates alike tended "to take issue positions which [were] con-

sistent with their party's general policy orientations."[39] Judged in relation to the views held by the larger public, 1983 and 1984 delegates regardless of gender were more "hawkish" on questions of foreign policy, more restrained in support of social welfare programs, more conservative on the question of women's equality, and more liberal on the abortion issue than were men and women in the general population.

Although age affected responses to more issues than the male/female variable, it was not the basis of a major cleavage in either party.[40] In only a few instances (increased spending on post-secondary education being one) did support for an issue in both parties decrease in a linear relationship with age. On a small number of issues there were statistically significant differences between delegates under twenty-five or thirty and all others. These included bilingualism and a foreign policy more independent of the United States. On balance, however, youth delegates tended "to share in the general dispositions of their respective parties rather than in any common age-based set of issue opinions."[41]

On the few issues where the views of specially constituted delegates in both parties diverged a general pattern emerged: "Each party's leadership convention tilted more to the left, [both] in delegates' ideological self-placement and for many specific issues, than it would have done had constituency delegate selection been unconstrained by demographic criteria."[42] Thus in spite of the similarity in demographic composition of women and youth attending their respective party's convention in Canada and the United States, the conclusions reached by Kirkpatrick about the failure of the demographic reforms to have produced different policy perspectives were only partially confirmed in Canada in 1983 and 1984.

The two countries were similar to the extent that on an array of social, business, and economic policy questions convention delegates regardless of gender or age (or race in the Democratic party) held similar views. But Canadian parties differed from American to the extent that issues with a greater resonancy with women than with men (abortion, daycare, and women's equality) and with younger than with older persons (increased support for post-secondary education) were the ones that most divided the delegates on the lines of gender and age respectively. In terms of the larger representational theory, it is important to note that on the issues most salient to women and youth their views more closely corresponded to the opinions of the general public than did those of their fellow delegates. In that respect party-established demographic quotas can be said to have broadened the policy perspectives of convention participants. Otherwise it would be fair to conclude that men and women, youth and older delegates present at the conventions, in spite of their differences, shared largely similar attitudes on most issues of public policy.

To ensure a more socially diverse mix of delegates, and therefore a more heterogeneous mix of policy perspectives, convention organizers presumably would have to ask themselves the Canadian equivalent of a question posed by Austin Ranney, a political scientist and member of the Democrats' McGovern-Fraser commission. Referring to the representational reforms introduced by the Democratic party in time for the 1972 convention, Ranney asked why only women and youth? "Why only these groups? Why not also old people, poor people, union members, Catholics, Jews, or other kinds of people important to the party and the nation?"[43] The inability of conventions to mirror all groups in society is captured in Ranney's question. As with inter-party rivalry over intra-party democracy, the logical conclusion of the impossibility of granting delegate status to all groups is to grant it to none and to allow all party members, regardless of gender, age, or race to participate directly in the election of their leader.

CONVENTION REPRESENTATION IN THE NDP

In no respect has the NDP's organizational structure been more distinctive from that of the two older parties than in its convention representation. The differences derive principally from two longstanding representational practices of the NDP and, before it, of the CCF. One is designed to represent organized labour, the other to award constituency representation according to party membership. Central labour organizations at the district, regional, and national levels as well as head offices of national and international unions are all entitled to send voting delegates to NDP national conventions. So too are affiliated labour unions whose entitlement is fixed at the rate of one delegate for each thousand members of a local union. The size of an NDP constituency association delegation is determined by the size of its membership. It is entitled to one delegate for every fifty party members up to the first two hundred members and to an additional delegate for every hundred members thereafter.[44]

In contrast to the Liberals and Conservatives who had twenty or more different delegate classes at their most recent conventions, the NDP had only six: constituency, affiliated union, youth, central labour, the federal council, and the federal caucus. The members of the latter two classes constitute the party's ex officio delegation. At the NDP's 1989 leadership convention they held only 6 per cent of the potential delegate positions. Affiliated and central labour organizations held 30 per cent of the positions and the constituency associations 62 per cent. The remaining 2 per cent was made up of delegates from the party's youth organization (see table 7-6).

Only three-fifths of the potential affiliated and central labour delegates actually attended the 1989 convention, a rate of participation much lower than for the other delegate categories. This meant that union delegates cast less than one in four votes on the convention floor instead of the nearly one in three to which they were entitled. Although this was an improvement on earlier participation rates (the share of eligible trade union delegates who attended the 1971 and 1975 conventions was 48 and 35 per cent respectively), it nonetheless brings into question the degree of commitment to the NDP on the part of at least some trade unions and the level of interest within the trade union movement generally in the selection of the NDP's leader. Party activists have accounted in various ways for the failure of trade unions to make full use of their entitlement. Reasons they have cited include inadequate trade union funds to send full delegations; delegate status granted by constituency associations to some otherwise likely trade unionist delegates; unfortunate timing of conventions; less likelihood among trade unionists than professionals to be able to attend a convention of several day's duration; and a lack of interest in attending conventions on the part of most union members save for the truly committed elites.[45] Whatever the reasons, the fact remains that the full potential of the trade union delegation has never been realized at an NDP leadership convention.[46]

Over two-thirds of the delegates in attendance at NDP conventions have come from constituency associations. The same has been true, and to about the same degree, of conventions in both the Liberal and Conservative parties. But there the similarity ends. As noted, the two older parties have treated all constituencies the same in that each has been entitled to send the same number of senior and youth delegates to a national convention. The NDP has accepted inherent differences among local associations according to their level of party strength: the larger its membership the greater the number of convention delegates. The differential effect of this rule is obvious in the potential attendance figures for the 1989 convention. Forty-six constituencies were entitled to send delegations of twelve or more. Among them was the Mackenzie riding in northern Saskatchewan with the largest entitlement, forty-two delegates. On the other hand, forty-three ridings could send only one delegate and one Quebec riding (Verchères) was entitled to no representative at all.

At the NDP's 1971 and 1975 national leadership conventions over 85 per cent of the constituency delegates in attendance were from the four provinces in which the party has enjoyed its greatest measure of electoral and organizational strength – British Columbia, Saskatchewan, Manitoba, and Ontario – whose share of the total Canadian population accounted for little more than 50 per cent. In 1989 the share of voting delegates at the convention from those four provinces totalled 80 per cent. In that year Saskatchewan alone, with fourteen federal ridings, was entitled to send 405 riding delegates to the Winnipeg convention. This was in stark contrast to the part of the country east of the Ottawa River in which, in Ken Carty's words, the NDP as a national organization "can hardly be said to exist."[47] With 107 federal seats, Canada's five most easterly provinces were entitled to 288 riding delegates at the 1989 convention. The Quebec constituency delegation, which averaged about one delegate for every two constituencies in the province in 1971 and 1975 and slightly less than one per seat in 1989, has typically accounted for only 3 or 4 per cent of the total number of provincial delegates. The Atlantic provinces have fared even less well. A comparison of the Liberal, Conservative, and NDP constituency delegate totals by province shows how much more equitably the distribution of participants has been in the two older parties than in the NDP and, accordingly, how closely that distribution corresponds to each province's share of the Canadian population (see table 7-7).[48]

The principle of awarding constituency associations with delegate positions according to their membership has had important implications for the NDP and for the political system generally. At the constituency level the formula has rewarded areas of organizational strength, which for the most part have been the areas of the party's electoral strength. But by the same token it has reinforced the party's organizational and electoral weaknesses and has done nothing to impose a valuable political responsibility on the weaker local associations. Were they charged with selecting delegates equal in number to all other associations in the country, local NDP associations would become engaged in an activity from which increased interest in the party's affairs might be generated and important organizational contacts could be established.

By maintaining what amounts to a bonus system of allotting delegate status to organizationally strong constituency associations, by failing to require delegate selection in equal numbers from all federal constituencies, and by guaranteeing a sizable share of the delegate positions for organized labour, the NDP has forfeited an important opportuntity to establish a more national presence in the Canadian political community. In Carty's words, the NDP "remains, in many ways, a profoundly regional party dressed up in national clothing."[49] Weighing the representational interests of trade unions and traditional party supporters as it has, the NDP may have satisfied various established interests within the party. But that has come at a price. It has limited its structural capacity to represent in a more equitable fashion the interests of all regions and provinces. This runs counter to one of the principles of accommodative party democracy established by the older parties in Canada: regionally representative internal party structures. It suggests that in this respect the NDP has yet to achieve the measure of institutional autonomy enjoyed by the two older parties to separate its larger *party* interests from the interests of its major organizational components – powerful provincial parties in three or four provinces, several constituency associations with sizable memberships, and affiliated trade unions.

The party's formal ties with organized labour, combined with its practice of representing areas according to their party membership, are evidence of a different set of representational values in the NDP. A plausible explanation for the difference derives from the view of the labour/farmer movements at the time they created the CCF in the 1930s. Loyalty and service counted heavily in measuring one's commitment to the socialist cause. For the NDP, heir to many of the CCF ideas about political representation, card-carrying membership in the party or in one of its affiliated trade unions has been an obvious way of establishing an individual's credentials as a democratic socialist, even more so if that membership was a longstanding one.

Accordingly, if the party were to base its representational formula at its national conventions on an equal number of delegates from every constituency, that would have the effect of benefiting constituency associations which had done little to establish roots through a sustained local membership and would have disadvantaged those which had worked to establish and to maintain a local presence. There was strong opposition among party activists in 1989 to making such a change. When the delegates to the 1989 convention were asked whether or not the party "should change its system of constituency representation to grant equal numbers of delegate entitlement to all constituencies," 80 per cent opposed the change.[50] Such a high level of opposition among convention delegates to a change in the party's representational system is scarcely surprising given the interests those elected under the current system have to protect in face of a possible massive reallocation of voting power. It is somewhat akin to the response one would expect from Canadian senators if they were asked to vote themselves out of existence.

However, if the NDP is concerned about the inadequacies of its constituency delegate representation formula and yet mindful of the opposition of its members to treating all constituencies equally, it may consider the formula adopted by the Reform party. Like the NDP, the Reform party grants riding delegate representation to its recognized local associations on the basis of membership: one delegate for every forty members up to a total of 240 members and one delegate for every additional hundred members thereafter. But to this the Reform party adds a minimum floor of three delegates per association.[51] This scheme has the dual advantage of rewarding strong local associations with many delegate positions and of ensuring that the membership in the areas in which the party is weak would not be without representation at the party's national meetings.

Neither the NDP nor the CCF before it has ever included in its constitution any guarantee of gender representation among constituency delegates, and its provisions regarding youth representation have been modest compared with those of the other two parties. Why should the NDP be different in not insisting on a certain portion (possibly an equal portion, as with the Liberals) of male and female constituency delegates, and on a sizable representation of younger delegates? Surely such efforts would be in keeping with the NDP's rhetoric about being the party most committed to representing the unempowered. Moreover, as party renewal depends on intergenerational change and on reaching out to new groups of voters, it stands to reason that the party should make the effort to encourage female and young participants to become involved in its affairs.[52]

The answer possibly lies in the party's history of devolving the principal responsibilities for determining the character of convention representation onto its various parts, notably the affiliated trade unions and the local constituency associations. These are the major players in the exercise, and accordingly they have been left to determine for themselves the complexion of their own delegations free of quotas and rules established at the national level. Membership is the critical test, as the party's constitution makes clear, and it is membership in a local association or in an affiliated organization that counts. In this sense, the NDP is much more a "federated" political organization operating at the national level than either of the other two older parties. Its constitution recognizes this in stipulating that it is the provincial parties that advise the federal party "as to the number of individual members in good standing in each federal constituency association within the province."[53] It is not simply, as has been the case with the Tories and Liberals, the central party that has handed down the rules about how many delegates and their gender and age all riding associations shall select. The centrally determined allotment of delegates in the NDP has left room for variations among all associations according to their membership and its gender and age composition. Just as the national party has exhibited little interest in accepting the principle of equal representation from all constituencies, so too has the local party become the accepted guardian of determining the best representational mix for its own delegation.

There may be other reasons why the NDP has evinced less interest than the older parties in constitutional provisions governing the gender and age of convention delegates. As a party the NDP, more so than the trade unions whose male-dominated delegations characteristically lower the overall female ratio at its conventions, has been singled out for its general "openness to increasing the participation of women."[54] This seems apparent from its most recent national conventions. Ranging between 26 and 37 per cent of its convention delegates in 1971 and 1989 respectively, the share of female delegates at NDP conventions, even without minimum gender requirements, was not significantly different from that of the two older parties with gender quotas. The lack of interest in guaranteeing a minimum share of seats to Young New Democrats probably owes much to the party's history. Mindful of the tendency of its "youth section, when it existed, to take a more hard-line Marxist approach" and of its bitter dispute with the youth-dominated Waffle faction between 1969 and 1972, the NDP has been "cautious in fostering youth wings."[55] At no point was this more obvious than in 1975 when the Young New Democrats were allocated just six of the 2,479 delegate positions at its convention that year. For a party ostensibly devoted to equality and a measure of central planning, the NDP's failure to have insisted on gender equality and reasonable numbers of youth at their national conventions reflects an inconsistency between operating ideology and organizational principles.

TINIES, INSTANTS, AND ETHNICS

The two older parties have long prided themselves on their organizational openness. Practising what is in effect an open-door policy, they have maintained a measure of flexibility in recruiting candidates and campaign workers at the constituency level that would be difficult to match if they were more ideologically or structurally constrained. At the same time they have done relatively little to restrict participation in the publicly advertised meetings called for the express purpose of choosing delegates to attend conventions. They have gradually adopted rules governing residency, citizenship, age, and length of membership in the party of those who select the delegates. But the regulations and constitutional provisions have varied from one convention to the next and have been difficult to enforce consistently and with equanimity at the level of the constituency association or club given the variable skills, knowledge, and biases of the myriad executive officers involved. Rules and the way they have been applied have also served as the basis for challenges by candidates' organizers to lists of party members claimed by their opponents to be eligible to vote for delegates. The number of local disputes generated, and the subsequent rulings they have required from national convention officials, prove that open parties can also be vulnerable parties.[56]

The NDP is both less open and less vulnerable to instant memberships than the two older parties. The party has a 120-day cut-off for new members to vote for or stand for election as delegates. Moreover, its leadership candidates have not had the money to put in place high-tech organizations equivalent to their Liberal and Conservative counterparts by which they could conduct mass recruitment campaigns for new members at the constituency level. The NDP also displays a different orientation towards membership. More than the other parties it seems to view conventions as the business of the party's long-time, established activists, which implies that it would rather maintain a smaller yet stable membership than seek a larger but less permanent organizational base.

Openness at the local level invites mischief which, in turn, can have the effect of bringing the party, and beyond it the larger political system, into disrepute. The custom of packing delegate selection meetings with supporters of particular leadership candidates has been one of the distinguishing features of the second generation of Liberal and Conservative leadership conventions. In the most recent delegate selection fights, particularly in the Liberal party's campaigns of 1984 and 1990 in the large metropolitan centres, the process was often dominated by ethnic organizers delivering hundreds or even thousands of voters mobilized from within their respective communities.[57] Unprecedented media coverage of delegate selection meetings, particularly those of 1983 and 1984, painted an unflattering picture of the parties at the local level in the early stages of the leadership contest. The effect of the coverage was to call into question the adequacy of the parties' rules governing the selection of delegates and the establishment of campus and women's clubs.

Reports of nine, ten, and eleven-year-olds ("Tiny Tories") and hostel transients ("Mission Members") voting for constituency delegates marred the Conservative selection process in 1983, just as accounts of last-minute and large-scale recruitment of ethnic supporters sullied the Liberal process in 1984 and 1990.[58] Questionable recruitment practices and delegate selection meetings of campus clubs and women's organizations also received national media attention. Constitutional loopholes enabled shrewd organizers to create additional groups, each with its own delegate entitlement. In the six months between the January 1983 leadership review convention and the June 1983 national convention of the Conservative party, 119 new Tory youth organizations, composed of fifty-three constituency and sixty-six campus clubs, were created.[59] This accounted for more than half the number accredited to the June convention and was clearly a function of the organizational prowess of those in charge of the various contenders' campaigns. Newfoundland, a province with one university, was entitled to send six campus delegates to Winnipeg in January. By June the number had increased to sixty-three campus delegates for the Ottawa convention (almost on a par with Ontario's seventy-two) entirely as a result of the efforts of native-son John Crosbie's provincial organization and his campaign manager, John Laschinger. They succeeded in having delegates named from, among other post-secondary institutions three schools of nursing, a number of district vocational schools and the Newfoundland Flying School.[60]

The numerous media reports of abuses of the delegate selection processes in the early stages of the 1983 leadership campaign prompted several of the leadership candidates to ask party officials to intervene so as to dispel what one of them, Michael Wilson, termed "this cloud of conspiracy that threatens to overshadow the convention."[61] They wanted the situation fully investigated and new rules designed and applied, retroactively if necessary, to put a stop to the "major moral crisis" facing their party.[62] According to another candidate, David Crombie, the selection process had been grabbed "by political bandits" preferring "ten-minute Tories" to longtime Conservatives who had paid their "economic, physical and spiritual dues."[63] Following a meeting of the convention's candidate liaison committee with candidate representatives, a meeting which "did not resolve anything as there was no consensus among the candidates,"[64] the party president's response to the complainants was that nothing could be done to alter the situation. He observed that the Conservatives had established their rules before delegate selection meetings officially got under way and that if some candidates subsequently used them to their advantage by packing meetings with their supporters, "that is our political process – the involvement of people." He was "not about to condemn them for involving more people in our political process."[65]

The debate over the extent and character of the involvement of outsiders in the selection of delegates continued throughout the remainder of the Tory campaign and resumed a year later when the Liberals witnessed many of the same sort of organizational manoeuvres during their leadership campaign. At their first national assemblies following the 1983 and 1984 conventions both parties addressed the issue. They altered their constitutions in the hope of bringing an end to the more unseemly practices of packing delegate selection meetings with exceedingly young or non-resident or non-Canadian participants. In March 1986 the Conservatives approved a set of constitutional amendments restricting the membership of a riding association to citizens or permanent residents of Canada fourteen years of age or older who maintain their principal residence in that riding or are members of the riding executive. The Tories also adopted amendments requiring constituency and affiliated associations to cease issuing new memberships at least one week before the start of delegate selection meetings and to hold all such meetings within a prescribed two- to three-week period. Later that year the Liberals adopted constitutional provisions limiting party membership to those "ordinarily resident" in Canada aged fourteen or over.[66] The Liberals opted not to establish a membership cut-off and delegate selection period, preferring instead to leave these issues for the party's national executive to decide prior to a party convention.

The effectiveness of these rule changes is difficult to determine. The Conservative delegate selection meetings in 1993 were less controversial and acrimonious than they had been a decade earlier. One may surmise that the rule changes imposed in 1986 played some part in this, although other factors were involved, such as the short time in which the candidates had to organize their campaigns. But the 1990 Liberal race was marred by the same sorts of irregularities that had characterized the delegate selection contests of the 1980s. In addition, leadership candidate Tom Wappel's success at marshalling anti-abortion groups and using their members to pack meetings and to run slates in some of the party's weaker riding associations demonstrated the ease with which a well-organized special-interest group could penetrate a local party at the expense of the longstanding membership. The reaction of the party membership to the abuses of the delegate selection process culminated in another series of reforms in the Liberal party aimed at curbing the influx of instant members and the influence of out-of-riding organizers in delegate selection meetings. In 1992 the party did what it had declined to do in 1986 by adding to its constitution a membership cut-off (ninety days before the delegate selection meetings) and a short, prescribed period within which all delegate selection meetings would be held (one weekend).

The new Liberal rules were heralded on the grounds that they would make it more difficult for a candidate's organization to recruit new members and move organizers from riding to riding. But, as the dynamic organizational drives of the 1990 campaign demonstrated, energetic and politically astute organizers will seize every opportunity to turn their party's constitutional provisions and convention rules to their advantage as they set about the task of electing delegates favourably disposed to their particular candidate. The Tory president in 1983 conceded as much when he allowed that if one group makes more of the constitutional opportunities available to it than another, "there is nothing [party officials] can do about it."[67]

A PROFILE OF CONVENTION DELEGATES

Socio-Demographics

Leadership conventions in Canada have often been described by party officials and commentators as representative bodies. In one respect this claim implies that the men and women chosen as delegates have been representative of a larger group, such as the party as a whole or the general population, simply because they have shared certain characteristics in common with its members. Principal among these characteristics in the context of contemporary Canadian politics are region, gender, and language. In another sense the term "representation" suggests that delegates had been charged with a political responsibility – to choose a party leader – and that their selection conferred on them the authority to act for, which is to say to represent the interests of, others. In that respect delegates can be described as agents acting on behalf of a larger population and performing an essential political task. Although both notions of representation – the mirror and the agency – help to explain the development of delegated conventions in Canada, it is in fact the first of these that is invariably cited by the parties themselves as the primary justification for choosing leaders through conventions. Because the agency concept of representation has been the more subtle and less obvious of the two, it has rarely surfaced as a subject of discussion within the parties or in the media. Nonetheless, as will be seen in the final chapter, it rightly forms a part of a normative or evaluative assessment of conventions as institutions for picking political leaders.

How closely have convention delegates mirrored the principal socio-demographic characteristics of society? To answer that question we turn to table 7-8 which presents survey data from studies of delegates attending the 1989 NDP, 1990 Liberal, and 1993 Conservative conventions.

Given the distributional formulas described above, the territorial dimension of convention representation is predictable in all three parties. As was seen in table 7-7, the potential constituency delegates for the Liberal and Conservative conventions reflected more or less equally the distribution of the Canadian population, whereas NDP constituency delegates were drawn overwhelmingly from areas of intra-party and union strength. The same was true of the actual number of delegates from the constituency, club, ex officio and, in the case of the NDP, union categories attending the conventions of the three parties. Table 7-8 confirms that, given its respective share of the total population, each region fared about as expected in the Liberal and Conservative conventions and that the differential treatment of delegate allotment in the NDP distorted the regional composition at its convention. Compared with their share of the total Canadian population, British Columbia and the Prairie provinces were overrepresented and Quebec and the Atlantic provinces were underrepresented at the NDP convention. Ontario received roughly its share of delegates at the NDP convention and it, together with all other regions, were represented in reasonably accurate proportions in the 1990 and 1993 conventions.[68]

The NDP has structured regional representation at its national conventions in such a way that the inequalities among the provinces have assumed dramatic proportions. Quebec in particular has been consistently underrepresented at NDP national conventions. In 1989 only one in fifty NDP delegates attending the convention came from that province, compared with just under one in four delegates at the 1990 Liberal and 1993 Tory conventions. One of the consequences of Quebec's small presence at the NDP convention was apparent in the delegates' responses to the question about the language they spoke at home. Only 2 per cent of NDP delegates acknowledged French as their home language compared to roughly 20 per cent of Liberal and Tory delegates. Such figures brings into question any claim the party might make about having established a truly national presence with organizational support in all regions and from both principal language groups.

The two older parties' affirmative action policies have had important implications for delegate representation at conventions. The efforts of the Liberal party to ensure balanced gender representation at its conventions paid off in 1990 as the survey found that 44 per cent of the delegates were women. The 1993 Conservatives had less stringent gender requirements and at their 1993 convention men outnumbered women by approximately two to one. The two older parties' efforts to guarantee the participation of youth were even more effective. At the 1990 and the 1993 conventions those from fourteen to twenty-nine years of age accounted for approximately one-third of the delegate body, a slightly higher proportion than that of the Canadian public.[69]

The NDP has displayed an openness to increasing the participation of women at the local level without the imposition of quotas. The 1989 convention was relatively well attended by women. Even so, with

37 per cent, of the delegates, women fared worse at that convention than they did at the 1990 Liberal one but better than they did at the 1993 Tory convention.[70] The age distribution of the 1989 NDP delegates distinguished the party from the Liberals and Conservatives. As only 13 per cent of the delegates were under thirty, young people were greatly underrepresented compared to both the other parties and to the Canadian population. This reflects the party's reluctance to promote vigourously its youth wing and its failure to encourage the establishment of youth clubs at the constituency level. In a larger sense it speaks well neither of the party's appeal to the younger generation nor of its ability to recruit new blood into the party.

The NDP delegates were also different from their Liberal and Conservative counterparts in terms of their religious affiliations. In both of the two older parties the overwhelming majority of the delegates indicated a religious affiliation and the religious distribution was comparable to that of the general public, with the plurality (the majority in the case of the Liberals) being Catholic and slightly over one-third being Protestant. For the Conservatives this marked a major transformation since 1967 when 24 per cent of the Conservative delegates were Catholic and 57 per cent were Protestant.[71] As with the Conservative party leadership, the days when being a Tory was practically synonymous with being a Protestant are past. By contrast, only one in every seven NDP delegates was Catholic and less than two in every five were Protestant. Most significant, however, was that compared to those in the two older parties and to society at large, NDP delegates in 1989 were much more likely to be non-believers. Fully 42 per cent of them indicated that they had no religious affiliation.

The areas in which convention delegates of all three parties were most atypical of the general population were education, occupation, and family income. If stratified by these three categories, delegates are clearly an elite group. Approximately half of the delegates in each party possessed university degrees, a level of education attained by just over one-tenth of Canadians. Many more were still in school, as students comprised 6 per cent of the 1989 NDP delegation, 21 per cent of the 1990 Liberal one, and 13 per cent of the 1993 Tory one. In terms of numbers, not to mention likely influence, delegates with professional or managerial backgrounds were preponderate at all three conventions.[72] The price of the dramatic overrepresentation of professionals and managers was the underrepresentation of those in the blue collar/ trade/labour grouping. Even in the NDP, workers and tradesmen were underrepresented, although by less than indicated in table 7-8 because of the low response rate of union delegates to the 1989 survey. To complete this picture, Liberal and Conservative delegates in particular enjoyed a standard of living much higher than that of the average Canadian. Just over half of the delegates of both parties were part of a family making over $60,000 per year and fully 21 per cent of the Liberals and 31 per cent of the Conservatives reported annual family incomes of $100,000 or greater. Incomes of that magnitude were much less common among New Democratic delegates, who collectively had incomes closely commensurate with the income distribution of the Canadian population. Even so, 16 per cent of them indicated that their family income exceeded $80,000 per year.

The composite picture that emerges from this comparative sketch of the socio-demographic characteristics of the three parties' convention delegates reveals that in certain respects the delegates have closely approximated the social and demographic composition of Canadian society, but that in other ways they have been strikingly atypical of it. Although the three parties have differed from one another in the socio-demographic composition of their convention delegates, the Liberals and Conservatives have generally been more alike than either has been like the NDP. The NDP delegates were distinct by virtue of their small proportion of youth, their high degree of English unilingualism, and their regional, religious, and income distribution.

Political Experience

However distinctive they may have been from the Canadian public, delegates to the 1990 Liberal, 1993 Conservative, and 1989 New Democratic conventions had in common a high degree of devotion to and experience in party politics. This point is made clear by table 7-9, which presents a number of categories by which the level of party activity of convention delegates can be gauged.

Based on survey responses, the data show that the delegates in all three parties were usually experienced activists with many years of party membership under their belts. Although Liberal and Conservative leadership candidates recruited thousands of new members to pack delegates selection meetings in the run-up to their respective conventions, few of these newcomers actually made it to the conventions themselves. Less than one-twelfth of the delegates in both parties had signed up in the year of their respective convention.[73] For its part, the NDP had even fewer neophytes selected as delegates, as only 2 per cent of the total had joined the party in 1989. At each convention approximately half the delegates had held a party membership for more than ten years and approximately one-quarter had done so for more than twenty. The most recent conventions were attended typically by delegates who had longstanding party memberships rather than those who had become involved solely because the party was engaged in choosing a new leader. A comparison with the earliest of the modern conventions shows that delegates now have fewer years of party membership than they did previously. Of the delegates attending the Conservative convention of 1967 and the Liberal one of 1968 only 1 and 2 per cent respectively had been party members for less than one year, whereas fully 74 and 64 per cent respectively claimed party memberships of not less than ten years.[74]

The delegates to the conventions of each of the three parties were also remarkably similar in terms of their commitment to and involvement in intra-party affairs. A large proportion either had previously or were currently serving the party in an official capacity at the local, provincial, or national level. More than two-fifths of the NDP delegates were currently serving on the executive of their local federal riding association at the time of the 1989 convention. Three-fifths of the 1990 Liberals and two-thirds of 1993 Tories either were local executive officers when their convention was held or had been previously. Fully 16 per cent of the Conservative delegates either were or had been at one time members of the national executive either of the party or its youth or women's branch, compared with 7 per cent of the Liberals.

Not surprisingly, those attending the most recent Liberal and Conservative conventions were the same individuals who devote their experience and expertise to the party at election time. Only four per cent of the Liberals and 16 per cent of the Tories had never worked for their party in a general election.[75] Fully three in every ten Liberal delegates and one in four of the Tory had worked for their party in at least five federal elections, meaning that their electoral activities stretched back at least to 1974. No doubt the 1989 NDP delegates were similarly experienced but no survey data on this topic are available.

The delegates' intra-party activities were not confined to serving on party executives. They also included attending national meetings of the party. The three parties were similar to each other in that close to a majority or, in the case of the Conservatives, a majority of their delegates had previously attended at least one federal party biennial or leadership convention. The conventions drew so many of the participants from previous conventions that they came close to resembling family reunions.[76] Between just over one-quarter and just over one-third of the delegates had attended their respective party's immediately previous biennial convention. Fifteen per cent of the 1989 NDP delegates had attended the party's 1975 leadership convention and 10 per cent had been delegates at the convention four years prior to that. There were even some 4 per cent who had been present at the party's first leadership convention in 1961. For their part, approximately three-tenths of the delegates to each of the 1990 Liberal and the 1993 Conservative conventions indicated that they had attended their party's immediately previous leadership convention.

The composite picture that emerges from this political profile of convention delegates of all three parties can be captured in one word: experience. The instant memberships and slate activity that marked many local delegates election meetings in some of the most recent leadership races did little to alter the fact that those chosen to attend the conventions were largely longtime activists and party stalwarts who form the backbone of Canadian parties from the local up to the national level.

WHO'S THERE?

In many ways, party convention are about political representation. Who attends? From where? With what qualifications? And with what characteristics? The three older parties have wrestled with these questions since their first leadership conventions. In an apparently never-ending quest to fine-tune the representational balance at conventions, they continue to do so. Quotas to ensure the presence of women and youth have distinguished the Liberal and Conservative formulas. The NDP has eschewed that model in favour of a more *laissez-faire* approach to assembling its local delegations. All three parties have drawn their greatest share of delegates from politically active professional and managerial elites with above-average educations and incomes. That comes as no surprise to observers of Canadian politics who have long noted that the same characteristics dominate the country's larger political class. But in that respect national party conventions do not mirror the larger population from which delegates have been drawn and for which they are said to serve as representatives.

It is on the territorial and regional dimension that noticeable differences exist between the Tories and Liberals on the one hand, and the NDP on the other, and where the two older parties much more closely reflect the regional and linguistic composition of the whole population than the NDP. The two older parties have accepted a representative model based on a presumed equality of all parliamentary seats within an overarching federal structure, whereas the NDP has opted in favour of a system that stresses local autonomy and is designed to reward areas of intra-party strength and union membership.

Both are valid, though necessarily different, expressions of the doctrine of representation. By favouring ridings in which it has an established presence, the NDP has done nothing to encourage the creation of new organizational structures in areas of traditional party weakness or to force the party into establishing local organizations where previously none had existed. The two older parties have handled representational trade-offs differently. Their respective systems have enhanced the importance of constituencies with little measurable interest in the party's well-being while at the same time they have granted no special status to those ridings and sections of the country from which the party regularly drew its greatest support. Thus they have derived their representational model from one of the fundamental premises of parliamentary government – the formal equality of all constituencies regardless of population or political complexion.

8 The Demographics of Leadership

A career in politics is no preparation for government.
— *Yes Minister*

The men and women who serve as party leaders are selected in a cultural, social, and political environment unique to each event. That environment defines both the framework within which the various candidates for the leadership will construct their organization and the terms by which the media, the public, and the delegates will judge the contest and its candidates. Changes in the country's cultural and social composition as well as in its political institutions gradually transform public and party expectations about the qualities needed to lead a party and about the career and political backgrounds of those who are to be chosen as leaders. These changes, in turn, usher in different criteria for judging the appropriateness of leadership hopefuls for the position they seek.

The social and cultural environment from which leadership candidates emerge and within which leaders are chosen is markedly different from what it had been in earlier days of Canadian politics. Canadian society is now more racially, religiously, and linguistically heterogeneous than at any point in its history. These changes have yet to be reflected in the mix of candidates seeking the leadership of either the Liberal or Conservative parties, but they have begun to make their mark on NDP leadership races.

The changing demographic composition of the Canadian population has been captured to the greatest extent in the NDP's recent conventions, particularly in 1989. In 1971 David Lewis became the first Jew to be chosen a national party leader, and four years later Rosemary Brown, the runner-up to Broadbent on the final ballot, was the first female and the first black to seek the leadership of one of the three older parties. The party's growing social diversity was most apparent in its 1989 leadership race when the leading candidate, and eventual winner, was a woman, the runner-up was Jewish, a third candidate was a black, a fourth an Indonesian-born son of Dutch immigrant parents, and a fifth a francophone from British Columbia. The siren call of political correctness prompted one party notable at the time to speculate about who, in socio-demographic terms, would constitute an ideal party leader. According to Ian Waddell, himself a candidate in 1989, the NDP was "looking for a bilingual woman from Western Canada with a Ph.D. in political science married to an Indian chief and whose first cousin is a lesbian."[1]

The selection as leader in 1989 by the NDP of a divorced, female social worker/consultant from the Yukon followed by the Conservatives' choice in 1993 of a twice-divorced, female Vancouverite with a brief history in her party, signalled the extent to which the earlier days of elite domination of leadership succession from within a small circle of male parliamentary notables had ended. Women, whose share of seats in Parliament has never come close to reflecting their numbers in the population as a whole, made a breakthrough on the national political scene with Audrey McLaughlin's win in 1989. The selection of female leaders in two of the three national leadership conventions during the life of the 34th Parliament capped, as it were, an inverted pyramid of female representation. Women, who had won just 13.2 per cent of the 295 Commons seats in the 1988 election, had been named to the slightly higher proportion of 15.4 per cent of the thirty-nine cabinet positions following that election. Whether the success of McLaughlin and Campbell in winning the leadership can be repeated in the near future by female leadership hopefuls in the NDP and Conservative parties remains an open question. The disastrous showings of the NDP and the Conservatives in the 1993 election will not make it any easier for aspiring female leaders in those two parties to argue that McLaughlin's and Campbell's gender had bestowed additional electoral benefits upon them.[2]

There are several variables which, taken together, portray a picture of the social and career backgrounds of the leadership candidates and of the leaders themselves. Principal among these are age, language, occupation, religion, and province. The parliamentary and ministerial experience of the candidates and leaders also help to inform our understanding both of political career routes in Canada and of the part played by the House of Commons and the cabinet as institutions from which candidates and leaders will be drawn. In some respects the characteristics of candidates and leaders have changed little since the early post-Confederation selections. (The demographic characteristics of

Conservative and Liberal leaders chosen between 1867 and 1920 can be seen in tables 8-1 and 8-2.) In other respects they have been modified, initially by the introduction of leadership conventions, and later by the shift from the first to the second generation of conventions.[3]

But first, a question of numbers. How many have run for the leadership of the two oldest parties and the NDP since conventions were introduced? A total of 101 candidates contested the nineteen national leadership conventions between 1919 and 1993, an average of 5.3 for each convention.[4] This was made up of nearly twice as many Tory candidates as Liberal (fifty-four to twenty-nine) in nine conventions as opposed to six. In its four conventions between 1961 and 1989 the NDP had a total of eighteen candidates. The total figures disguise the number of *individual* candidates, however, as thirteen men have run at least twice for their party's leadership. With six of those thirteen winning on their second or third try, the odds suggest that a first-time loser has an almost fifty-fifty chance of making it by standing again[5] (see tables 8-3 to 8-5).

THE CHANGING DEMOGRAPHICS OF LEADERSHIP SELECTION

Age

The average age of all leaders chosen since Confederation by the Conservatives has been 54.5 years and by the Liberals 52.3 years. Compared with party leaders in the pre-convention period, the ages of convention-era leaders at the time of their selection has declined for Conservatives from an average 58 to 51.8 years but moved in the opposite direction for the Liberals by increasing from 47.3 to 54.8 years. The differences between the ages of convention candidates and leaders of the two parties are not statistically significant (see tables 8-6 and 8-7).

As these periods roughly approximate the two parties' respective eras of long-time governing and long-time opposition status, the figures imply that parties in office tend to choose older leaders than those in opposition. A comparison of average age of leaders of governing and of opposition parties confirms this. Prior to Campbell's selection in 1993 at the age of forty-six, the only Tories to have been chosen while the party was in office (or, in the case of Macdonald in 1867, about to be in office) were the five named between 1867 and 1896 and Meighen in 1920. Three of those were in their seventies, and the overall average age for that group of six was sixty years. With Campbell added, the Tory prime ministerial average amounts to fifty-eight years. That compares with an average of 51.8 years for all other Tory leaders who were, of course, taking over a party in opposition. The spread between the age of leaders selected in office and in opposition within the Liberal party shows the Liberals have also had a tendency to select older leaders as prime ministers and younger leaders when the party is in opposition. The average age of the three Liberals chosen while the party was in office (St Laurent, Trudeau, and Turner) was 56.3, which compared with fifty years for the six chosen when the party was out of office. By demonstrating that prime ministers are succeeded as party leaders by individuals who are older than those who replace leaders of the opposition, these figures confirm that for both parties the average age of successors is a function of whether or not the party is in office. There is no surprise here, for leaders of parties in opposition are nearly three times more likely to be replaced than prime ministers (eleven opposition to four governing party conventions from 1919 to 1993). The average age of possible successors would normally be expected to be higher where the leader's period in office is longer than when it is not.

What do the ages of Conservative, Liberal, and NDP candidates and leaders during the convention period show? They make it clear that there were no substantial differences among the three parties either in the average age of their leaders at the time of selection or in the spread between the youngest and oldest leaders of the parties. Tory, Liberal, and NDP leaders were, on average, 51.8, 54.8 and 52.3 years respectively, and the spread between the youngest and oldest leaders was twenty-two years for both the NDP and the Liberals and twenty-five years for the Conservatives. Part way through their respective convention period history, all three parties chose leaders in their sixties: 1948 and 1958 for the Liberals, 1956 for the Conservatives, and 1971 for the NDP. Those relatively advanced ages suggest that Canadian parties had to make do without an entire generation of political recruits during and immediately after the Second World War. They were also the result of the Liberals' long string of electoral victories after 1935, which were accomplished with few changes in their senior ranks; the Conservatives' consistently poor showing in federal elections matched by their inability to attract any significant amount of new blood into their parliamentary party between 1935 and 1957; and the determination of the majority of those attending the 1971 NDP convention to award the party's leadership to David Lewis, the man who had dominated the "socialist elite, as he [had] the whole party" for the previous three decades and whose entire political career had been headed in the direction of the party's leadership.[6]

On the face of it, it would seem that in the three parties collectively there was no trend toward selecting younger or older leaders with the passage of time. Clark, Mulroney, and Campbell were among the youngest chosen, but then so were King at the other end of the convention period in 1919 and Broadbent in the middle of his party's convention history. Turner and Chrétien were only a year or two different from Bennett and Manion, and McLaughlin was only three years younger than Douglas had been in 1961.

But on closer examination it is apparent that changes in both candidates' and in leaders' ages have in fact taken place. The average age of candidates running in the most recent leadership conventions has been considerably lower than before. In only three of the ten conventions since 1967 have the candidates averaged more than fifty years of age. By contrast, in all but two of the earlier nine conventions the average candidate age surpassed fifty years. In the earlier set of conventions, leaders averaged fifty-seven years of age, but since 1967 they have been forty-nine years of age. Thus in yet another respect the second generation of leadership conventions was different from the first: candidates in the post-1967 era became younger by six years and leaders younger by eight years than those who ran and were chosen before. Regardless of party, candidates have tended to be grouped according to roughly the same generation in each of the conventions, the groupings having varied from one convention to another (see tables 8-3, 8-4, and 8-5). The occasional shifts from older to younger groupings demonstrates one dimension of an established party's ability to renew itself. All three parties have passed that test from the time they first used leadership conventions.

Occasionally there have been single candidates well out of the age bracket of those they were running against. This was the case with King at forty-four in 1919, Martin at sixty-four in 1968, Diefenbaker at seventy-two in 1967, and Lewis at sixty-one in 1971. Their age was bound to become an object of discussion among delegates, for it is usually the ages of the majority of a group's members that become the reference point against which individual members of that group will be judged. King's three opponents were between sixty and seventy years of age, five of Martin's seven fellow candidates were either in their thirties or forties, six of Diefenbaker's eight opponents were in their fifties, and the four other candidates against whom Lewis ran averaged thirty-seven years of age. In contrast to both Martin and Diefenbaker, Lewis was able successfully to deflect criticisms of his age, at least in part because, unlike the other two, he was a first-time candidate. King was able to turn his age to his advantage, a lesson not lost on subsequent candidates who strove to do the same with their relative youth.

An individual candidate relatively younger or older than others in the contest may find that he or she will either be charged with "running for the next time" (as was Turner in 1968 and Charest in 1993) or be dismissed as being too old for the party and the country (as happened to Diefenbaker in 1967 and Martin in 1968). In other contests with different dynamics and with different age reference points, the same criticisms could scarcely be made with any telling effect. Turner at thirty-eight lost in 1968 as did Charest at thirty-four in 1993, yet Broadbent won at thirty-nine in 1975 and Clark at thirty-six in 1976. Martin at sixty-four was defeated in 1968, yet St Laurent at sixty-six won some twenty years earlier. Age, it would seem, enjoys a status not unlike that of beauty's: its value may be established in the beholder's eye, but its critical importance will more likely be determined by the larger, sometimes relevant, but undoubtedly relative, question of whose it is being compared with.

Language

Part of the political environment at the federal level has been shaped by the bilingual character of its parliamentary institutions. At no stage in Canadian history has that been truer than in the period since 1969 when the Official Languages Act was passed. Bilingualism has become so pervasive among Canada's governing elites since the beginning of the second generation of leadership conventions that selecting a totally unilingual leader would now be almost entirely out of the question for any party making a serious claim to being truly national and to representing Canadians from all regions and of both official language groups. It is doubtful that the custom dating from John A. Macdonald's time of unilingual English-speaking prime ministers relying on strong Quebec lieutenants to compensate for their inability to speak French and to maintain their party's presence in the province of Quebec (a practice last resorted to by Lester Pearson) would now find widespread acceptance.[7]

This is not to say that the most proficiently bilingual candidates will always win. If that were so, either Roblin or Fulton would have defeated Stanfield in 1967, Harney would have won against Broadbent in 1975, Wagner would have defeated Clark in 1976, Chrétien would have beaten Turner in 1984, and Charest would have won against Campbell in 1993. Rather it is to acknowledge that an acceptable measure of bilingualism is now a basic requirement for the leadership of a national party in Canada.

The efforts made by unilingual politicians to learn a second language either after they have become leader (as in the case of Stanfield, Broadbent, and McLaughlin) or in the years in federal politics leading up to their successful run at the leadership (as with Clark and

Chrétien) attest to the strength of commitment by parliamentary elites of the older parties to the principles embodied in the Official Languages Act. But even more tellingly, they implicitly acknowledge the move to television broadcasting. Previously, print journalism had granted unilingual leaders the protection of having their words translated without visual, instant reminders of their inability to converse in the other language. But with the ubiquitous news coverage, televised debates, and public affairs programming viewers can see, and therefore judge, firsthand their politicians' capacities to speak directly to them in either French or English.

That candidates are expected to have attained an obvious competence in the two official languages was apparent from the 1990 Liberal and 1993 Conservative leadership races. The principal candidates in both contests were fluent, in admittedly varying degrees, in both languages, a facility they were able to display on the media and in intraparty debates during the course of their campaigns. This was a first for the Conservatives who had a pre-1976 history of picking unilingual anglophone leaders from a pool that only intermittently included bilingual candidates.[8] The degrees of competence in 1993 varied from the totally bilingual Jean Charest (described by Graham Fraser as "probably the most effortlessly bilingual speaker of French in the House of Commons"[9]) to the haltingly competent Kim Campbell. No possible candidate in either contest could be unmindful of the political capital made by John Crosbie's bilingual opponents and the unfavourable media response to his outburst during the 1983 Tory campaign. In attempting to answer questions about his inability to speak to Quebeckers in French, he allowed that he could not "talk to the Chinese people in their own language either" and added that "the 3.7 million people in this country who are bilingual should not think they are an aristocracy and that our leaders can no longer come from anyone but them."[10] There might have been widespread public support for such an opinion, but among political and media elites in the 1980s the view had taken firm hold that some capacity to converse and to conduct public affairs in Canada in both official languages ought to be expected of national party leaders and of prime ministers.

It is less certain that an acceptable measure of bilingualism is a basic requirement of national leadership in the NDP and that a truly unilingual anglophone would have little chance of being chosen as leader of that party. In 1989 Barrett's inability to speak French, while an issue with some of the press, by all accounts carried little weight with the delegates. Nor did McLaughlin's very limited French apparently cost her support. If anything, the fact that at least three years would elapse before the next federal election (at which time a leader's knowledge of

French would be put to its greatest test), muted the issue in the expectation that the new leader would have sufficient time to improve his or her ability to speak an acceptable level of French.

This seemingly casual attitude about a candidate's capacity to speak French may be a uniquely NDP phenomenon because of the party's failure to sustain an organizational presence in Quebec and the corresponding absence of any sizable Quebec delegation at their national conventions. An equally plausible explanation, at least in terms of the 1989 convention, may well be the party's consistently dismal showing in federal elections in Quebec. Broadbent had made great efforts during his fourteen years as leader to become proficient in French and to give the NDP a presence in Quebec. Delegates must have wondered in 1989 what the party had to show for it, given their failure to win any seats in the province in the 1988 election. For a brief interval part way through the leadership campaign there were reports of interest from some party elites in recruiting Ontario NDP leader Bob Rae to run for the federal leadership because of his facility in French.[11] This soon gave way to a more widely shared opinion that the party had paid too much attention to Quebec and that the time had come to shift its emphasis elsewhere. Thus NDP candidates with little or no ability to speak French did not, as had been the case with John Crosbie in the Tory contest six years earlier, encounter any serious intra-party concern on that front.[12]

In Laurier, St Laurent, Trudeau, and Chrétien, the Liberal party chose four bilingual, but principally French-speaking, Quebeckers as its leaders – more than all other parties combined and half of the Liberal leaders selected over a 110-year period. As important as bilingualism has been for the Liberals, the party has also a tradition of choosing leaders with an additional socio-linguistic-provincial dimension in mind. To accommodate the two principal language groups and to further their own party's electoral interests, the Liberals have reified Canada's bicultural social variable into a practice of alternating the party's leadership between Quebeckers and non-Quebeckers. In practical terms this tradition (to some Liberals it approaches an inviolable principle) has effectively meant that the party's leadership has rotated regularly between Quebec and Ontario since Edward Blake's selection in 1880. No national Liberal leader has ever come from any other province.[13] In alternating its leadership between the country's two largest provinces, the party has at the same time managed to rotate regularly between English-speaking Protestants and French-speaking Roman Catholics.[14] Unlike any other party, the Liberals have succeeded in addressing three of the country's traditional cleavages – province, language, and religion – in one established practice.

The party did not set out in any conscious or deliberate fashion to put in place a policy of alternating leaders. Indeed, Blake had followed another anglophone Protestant from Ontario, the party's first prime minister, Alexander Mackenzie. But the origins of the practice can be traced to Blake's resignation as leader in 1887 and to his insistence with his parliamentary colleagues that he be succeeded by Laurier, a young, bilingual, Roman Catholic MP from Quebec in whom Blake saw great promise. For Blake, Laurier represented the best chance for the Liberals to succeed where they so far had failed – in Quebec.[15]

The tradition took hold when, after three decades, Laurier was succeeded by an English-speaking Protestant from Ontario, Mackenzie King, and he in turn, after another three decades, by a francophone Catholic from Quebec, Louis St Laurent. Had neither Laurier nor King been leader for so long – had either or both died or resigned soon after taking office, for example – it is questionable whether the practice would have evolved so firmly. Based on the Liberals' experience, candidates with the appropriate mix of socio-linguistic-regional characteristics take time to locate, to encourage, and to promote through the ranks to the point where they are ready to run for the leadership at the appropriate time. From the Conservatives' standpoint, it is conceivable that they too might have chosen leaders on the same principle had there been, in the late nineteenth century, a politically attractive Roman Catholic Quebecker to succeed Macdonald and had the party been prepared to accept such a person as leader. As neither of those conditions was met, the question is academic at best.[16]

At the Liberal convention in 1919, when Laurier's successor was to be chosen, delegates and party notables were mindful of the need to do for the party what Blake had done in 1887. Laurier was known to have agonized over the political fallout of the conscription election of 1917 and the deep schism that the election had created in his party. His view that, in his own words, his successor "must be a Protestant. I'd ask no Catholic to go through what I have suffered!"[17] had been widely reported. According to one of the leading periodicals of the time, "It is understood that the common feeling among Liberals is that Laurier's successor should be an English-speaking Protestant, not because a Frenchman or a Roman Catholic is objectionable, but in recognition of the Protestant element which for more than thirty years gave loyal support to a French and Catholic leader."[18]

With the heir apparent to Mackenzie King upon his retirement in 1948 present in the person of a popular, bilingual Quebecker, St Laurent, the tradition of rotating leaders had become firmly established. That fact was recognized by Pearson a decade later when, in running against fellow Ontarian Paul Martin for the leadership of his party, he acknowledged that Martin's "claim to the leadership by virtue of long service to the party, great experience in government, and shrewd political judgment was strong."[19] But, as Pearson went on to say in his memoirs, Martin had been "handicapped, however much one might deplore it, by the fact that he was a Catholic and half French Canadian, while the tradition of our party was that an English-speaking Protestant succeeded a French-speaking Catholic."[20]

Martin, in his own words, bore a "deep resentment" that there was "such a thing as the principle of alternation" in the Liberal party and that the country would "not favour as successor to St Laurent someone who was French or part French, and Catholic."[21] He was bitter about what he called the "rule" of alternating leaders and about the role that he ascribed to it in determining his own political fate. The tradition amounted to nothing more than a "foolish precept" that was "contrary to the fundamental tenets of liberalism."[22] Twice defeated for the Liberal leadership, Martin was convinced that he had paid the ultimate political price for being considered too French and Catholic in 1958 when it was the turn of an English Protestant to be leader and for not being of the right province and sufficiently French a decade later when Trudeau was chosen.[23]

Chrétien's two runs at his party's leadership illustrate both the positive and negative aspects of the practice for leadership hopefuls. In late 1979, following Trudeau's announced resignation as Liberal leader, Chrétien had been inclined to let his name stand for the leadership of his party. As it turned out he was not given the chance because with the unexpected defeat of the Clark government Trudeau was persuaded to stay on as Liberal leader. In Chrétien's judgment, the major barrier he would have faced had he opted to run "was the Liberal tradition of alternating between anglophone and francophone leaders."[24]

His experience in 1984 when he did become a candidate in the race to succeed Trudeau confirmed his earlier fear. Senior cabinet ministers from Quebec, such as Marc Lalonde, whose support Chrétien had hoped to garner, declared that "it wasn't the time for a francophone leader"; other MPs admitted to Chrétien that they were "for an anglophone this time."[25] Apparently moved to intervene on Chrétien's behalf, Trudeau seized the opportunity to deliver to caucus a message denouncing the alternation tradition and asserting that he thought he had been selected "because [he] was good, not because [he] was French."[26] For his part Chrétien lashed out publicly, in an impolitic phrase claimed by the opposition to represent a slur on Ukrainian women, against the practice of alternating leaders on the grounds that what he called a quota system might mean that the party could at some future time be led only by a "Ukrainian woman."[27]

Turner forces countered Chrétien's objections with approving references to the alternation tradition and the need to chose a leader from outside Quebec. In the event Turner, who had been widely seen as the "prime minister in waiting,"[28] defeated Chrétien by five hundred votes on the 1984 convention's second ballot.

The alternation tradition meant that, with Turner's departure in 1990, it was "Quebec's turn" to have a Liberal leader. Chrétien's principal challenge on that front was to convince delegates that he, rather than Martin, should be the Quebecker they chose. This he managed with the endorsements of many, including Trudeau's one-time right-hand man in Quebec, Marc Lalonde, who had not supported him six years before. One of Chrétien's perceived liabilities in 1984 had been turned into an asset in 1990.

Occupation

Little can be said about the occupational backgrounds of political leaders of the two older parties apart from one word – law. Since Confederation those who have been elected to Parliament and named to the cabinet have been drawn disproportionately from the legal profession. In the Parliament elected in 1988 one-fifth of all MPs and one-third of all cabinet ministers were lawyers.[29] Two of the three national party leaders chosen during the life of that Parliament were lawyers, following in the tradition of law being the overwhelmingly dominant occupational background of Canadian political leaders. Of the twenty prime ministers since 1867, fourteen were lawyers by training before they entered politics, with Tory prime ministers somewhat more likely than Liberal ones to be drawn from law. Nine of the Twelve Conservative prime ministers were lawyers compared with five of the eight Liberals. Of the prime ministers without a background in law, three had been journalists (Mackenzie in the Liberal party, and Bowell and Clark in the Conservative party), and one each came from medicine (Tupper), industrial relations (King), and the public service (Pearson).

Four of the six Liberal leaders since 1919 and six of the nine Conservative leaders since 1927 have been lawyers by training. Both parties have drawn from pools of candidates in which legal backgrounds dominated. Of the twenty-nine candidates to have run in Liberal conventions since 1919, seventeen have been lawyers. For the Conservative party the equivalent numbers have been thirty out of fifty-four. Although the second generation of leadership conventions has seen each of the two older parties move in different directions from their respective occupational mix of the first generation, law nonetheless has remained the occupation of choice for a majority of candidates in both parties (see tables 8-3 and 8-4).

The NDP is truly different from the other two parties in the occupational mix of its leaders and candidates. Only one of its four leaders has been a lawyer, the others having been a clergyman, a professor, and a consultant (see table 8-5). The mixed occupational history of NDP leaders is in keeping with the record of its predecessor, the CCF. J.S. Woodsworth, the party's first leader, was a clergyman. His successor was M.J. Coldwell, a teacher, who in turn was followed by the party's last leader before the creation of the NDP, Hazen Argue, a farmer. The larger pool of candidates from which NDP leaders were chosen between 1961 and 1989 was made up of several times as many professors and teachers as lawyers. Of the eighteen NDP candidates since 1961 as many social workers sought the leadership as lawyers, and in two of the party's four conventions not a single lawyer sought the nomination. These are facts neither of the other two parties (which have yet to have a lawyer-less campaign) could match.

How can this difference between the two older parties and the NDP be explained? The answer is no doubt a complex mix of social, political, and personal variables, including the views of prospective parliamentary candidates of the issues of the day and of the electoral prospects of the various parties. At least part of the answer derives from the occupational socialization of politicians in Canada and some of the unique qualities of the NDP itself.

Law school, followed by some time practising law, followed in turn by running for public office, has been a career route followed by countless federal and provincial politicians since Confederation. Why? Legal training and the practice of law are good preparation for politicians. By definition law is adversarial and concerned with the content and the implications of regulations and statutes. So is government. Thus for a young person interested in eventually entering elected office, law school makes a good deal of sense. What this amounts to is obvious: a measure of occupational pre-selection goes into the decision about what at some time may turn into a political career. If one is sufficiently interested in politics and in trying to play some part in defining public policy, almost certainly one does not choose to become a concert violinist, or a biochemist, or a police officer – which is why so few violinists, biochemists and police officers stand for and are elected to parliament. Whereas if one is interested in the possibility of taking part in the process of governing, choosing the legal profession as the occupational entry point makes a good deal of sense. Economic considerations also favour law as a professional precondition for politics. It is clearly easier for a lawyer than for an hourly-wage employee to devote time to politics. As well, we cannot forget the role that patronage has always played in Canadian politics and the extent to which it helps to account for political choices individuals make, often relatively early in life.

Any individual planning to enter politics has a range of options to consider in attempting to balance political and public policy objectives with career advancement. The most fundamental of these require decisions about both the party and the level of government to enter. For those who have in the past chosen to go into federal politics in the hope of sitting with the governing or principal opposition party and, possibly, of making it into the cabinet, the choice has basically amounted to deciding between the Liberals and the Conservatives. Realistically the NDP has not been able to match the other two older parties at the federal level in holding out the promise of power for aspiring politicians.

But the NDP, like the CCF before it, has occupied a special place for Canada's intellectual left, social gospelites, and social and political activists. It has become the political home for many who otherwise would have had little interest in the more conventional, mainline politics practised by the two older parties. Teachers, members of the clergy, and social workers have been far more likely to be found in the ranks of those nominated and elected by the NDP at both the federal and provincial levels than in the other political parties. The forty-three-member NDP caucus elected in the 1988 general election had over twice as many educators (professors, teachers, and instructors) in it as lawyers. Unconventional by the standards of the other two parties, the NDP's occupational mix has emerged over the years as one of the party's truly distinctive features.[30]

Religion

Two developments have marked recent religious trends in Canada: society has become increasingly secularized, and the number of different religions claiming some level of support has grown. The combined effect has meant that the Christian religion no longer plays the part that it once did in defining the institutions, elite practices, and electoral behaviour of the Canadian political environment. Dual-member ridings persisted at the federal level from Confederation until 1968 in two areas, Halifax and Prince Edward Island, for the very explicit reason of seeking religious accommodation through equal Commons representation for local Protestant and Catholic voters. An informal but strongly entrenched custom adhered to by prime ministers of both parties, one that can be traced back to Macdonald's decision to include in his first cabinet both an Ultramontanist Catholic from Quebec and the leader of the Loyal Orange Order Protestants from Ontario, had been to ensure adequate and balanced religious representation at the cabinet table. Only recently have prime ministers felt less obliged to ensure that particular religious affiliations were recognized by way of appointments to a variety of institutions, including the Senate. The representational questions now raised about prime ministerial appointments to the cabinet, the Senate, and other federal agencies and councils derive more from their linguistic, racial, gender, and regional character than from the religious affiliations of the institution's members. It is equally true that electoral behaviour, which often in the past closely reflected the views espoused by church hierarchies, is now less associated with religious affiliations.[31]

In earlier times, a potential leader's religious attachment was one of the factors that entered into whether or not he was selected. Religion was obviously in Blake's mind when he pushed the Liberals to accept Laurier in 1887, in Laurier's when he contemplated retirement at the end of the First World War, and in Pearson's when he accounted for his success over Martin in 1958. The Conservatives chose Manion as leader in 1938 at least in part because they hoped his Roman Catholicism would translate into political gains in Quebec.

No party leader has been more mindful of the critical importance that religion played in determining political fortune than John Thompson. A convert to the Roman Catholic church from the Methodist, Thompson paid a heavy price both for his Catholicism and for his conversion. On Macdonald's death, Thompson would have brought to the prime ministership and to the Conservative party much that was badly needed as it entered its battle with Manitoba over the School Question: political experience in both provincial and federal politics, support of many valued colleagues and, at forty-six, relative youth. But several in the Conservative party in the Commons, particularly the strongly Protestant Orange element from Ontario, made it clear they would not support a government he led. Thompson declined the governor general's invitation to form a government, bowing instead, according to one of the historians of the period, "to the 'sectarian climate' of the time."[32]

A seventy-year old English-speaking Protestant senator from Quebec, J.J.C. Abbott, was named prime minister. But after a year and a half of Abbott's uninspired leadership, the Conservative government was ready for Thompson. Thompson's new-found support came from the Ontario Protestant wing of the party which had so opposed his earlier candidacy. Part of a letter from Sam Hughes, an Ontario MP and Orangeman, pledging support to Thompson is revealing for its frank admission of the religious barrier Thompson had faced on

Macdonald's death. The "boys" had changed their minds: "What? the pervert? the ultra-montane? the roman catholic? the defender of Mercier's Jesuit Estates Act? *Yes*, all say yes."[33] Thompson's prime ministership ended barely two years later when, within minutes of being knighted by Queen Victoria at Windsor Castle, he died suddenly of a heart attack. The Tories' first experiment with a Catholic leader had ended. Not until Manion's equally brief leadership over fifty years later did the party accept another one.

The Conservatives' history of rarely selecting Roman Catholic leaders stands in marked contrast to the Liberals' habit of alternating leaders according to their religion. Of the sixteen Conservative leaders between 1867 and 1993 all but four were Protestant, whereas of the nine Liberal leaders from 1870 to 1990 fewer were Protestant (four) than Roman Catholic (five). More than three-quarters of those who have sought the Tory leadership since 1927 have been Protestant, whereas three-fifths of those seeking the Liberal leadership have been Roman Catholic.[34] These inter-party differences are statistically significant among convention candidates since 1919, but not among party leaders since 1867 (see table 8-7).

The two parties share one feature on the religious dimension: since 1967–8 in both parties there has been an increase in the number of Roman Catholics who have contested the leadership. For the Tories the numbers have jumped from three in the first generation to eight in the second, with the number of Protestants increasingly only from nineteen to twenty-one. The Liberal increase was even more dramatic, from six Protestant and three Catholic candidates between 1919 and 1958 to five Protestant and fourteen Catholics from 1968 to 1990 (see table 8-8).

Leadership contests from the 1970s on demonstrate that stereotyping of parties by the presumed religious affiliation of their leaders is no longer appropriate. The Conservatives can no longer be said to be a party led almost without exception by a Protestant, nor can the Liberals' alternation tradition correctly predict all their leaders' religious affiliations. The top three candidates in the 1976 Conservative race, two of whom ran again in 1983, were Roman Catholics. These contests amounted to a clear break with the party's decidedly Protestant past. With the exception of Campbell's six-month leadership in 1993, the Tories have not been led by a Protestant since Stanfield. Had the Liberal alternation tradition been rigidly applied in 1984, Turner, a Roman Catholic, would not have succeeded Trudeau.

The religious affiliations of NDP leaders and candidates mark them as being at the same time both more religiously diverse and more non-religious than either of the other two parties. The first leader of the NDP, T.C. Douglas, was a Protestant minister, as was the founding leader of the CCF, J.S. Woodsworth. Unlike the Tories and Liberals, neither of whom has ever had a non-Christian leadership candidate, the NDP has twice (1971 and 1989) had Jews run for its leadership. One of them, David Lewis, was elected leader in one contest, and the other, Dave Barrett, ran second in another. Other NDP leaders and candidates have been less likely than those of the two older parties to have indicated any religious affiliation publicly. This suggests that NDP elites are composed either of a larger number of non-believers or of more individuals who believe public acknowledgment of religious affiliation is irrelevant to politics (see table 8–5). Either or both explanations would be in keeping with the larger party as revealed through survey data. As table 7-8 shows, fully 42 per cent of NDP convention delegates in 1989 admitted to no religious affiliation, compared to 8 per cent of 1990 Liberal delegates and 6 per cent of 1983 Tory delegates.[35]

Province

If the NDP has been unlike the other two parties in the occupational backgrounds and religious affiliations of its leaders and candidates, it is the Liberals who have differed from the other two in the provinces from which their leaders and candidates have been been drawn (see table 8–4). All nine of their leaders have come from either Ontario or Quebec. At the 1958 convention delegates had only two Ontario candidates to choose between, and in 1984 and 1990 all candidates were either from Ontario or Quebec. In the remaining conventions, only five of the twenty-two candidates were from a province other than Ontario and Quebec. Since Confederation no Liberal currently serving as a provincial premier has ever run for the national leadership. The Tories and the NDP, on the other hand, have found their greatest number of candidates and leaders in provinces other than Ontario and Quebec. Between 1867 and 1993 as many Conservative leaders were from Nova Scotia as from Ontario (four each), and as many from Manitoba and Alberta as from Quebec (two for each province). With their remaining leaders from Saskatchewan and British Columbia, the Conservatives since Confederation have chosen someone to lead their party from every province except New Brunswick, Prince Edward Island, and Newfoundland (see table 8-3).

Those who have run for the Tory leadership have included four men who were serving at the time as provincial premiers. Three of them, Bracken, Drew, and Stanfield, were chosen to lead the party and one, Roblin, was defeated on the final 1967 ballot against Stanfield. To recruit provincial premiers for their national leaders was apparently attractive to the Tories because of the prospect it offered the party of gaining office with a proven winner. At the national level the Tories have been plagued by problems often faced by out-of-office parties. Their parliamentary caucus has tended to be small for much of this century (though never reduced to two members before 1993!), and of uneven quality. Although the Tories share the Liberals' preoccupation with winning power, they have not been able to match them in either coopting prospective leaders from extra-political circles (as was the case with St Laurent, Pearson, and Trudeau) or in replenishing the parliamentary party with more-or-less continuous electoral victories. Thus when they wanted proven electoral winners, the Tories had little alternative but to recruit from the one source in which the party had had some measure of electoral success – provincial politics.

The fifty-four Tory candidates from 1927 to 1993 were drawn from eight provinces. The largest number (twenty-three) came from Ontario, but only two of those were elected leader, Manion and Drew. No Ontarian has served as a Tory prime minister since Mackenzie Bowell in the 1890s. More Conservative leadership candidates have been from Saskatchewan (seven) than Quebec (six), and British Columbia and Alberta have each produced as many Tory leadership candidates as Quebec (see table 8-7).

The home provinces of NDP leaders and candidates have more closely resembled those of the Conservative than the Liberal party. Although two of the NDP's four leaders between 1961 and 1989 were from Ontario, one was from Saskatchewan and one, the first for any party from either of the territories, was from the Yukon. No Quebecker has either led or been nominated to lead the NDP. The provinces of the party's greatest national and provincial strength have provided all the candidates. Eight have come from Ontario, five from British Columbia, and four from Saskatchewan. No candidate from any other province has ever been nominated for the national leadership. Like the Conservative party, the NDP has chosen a popular provincial premier to become its national leader. At the time of his election as the first NDP leader in 1961, Tommy Douglas had served for seventeen years as premier of Saskatchewan and had led his party to five successive electoral victories. But, as was the case with the provincial premiers recruited as national Tory leaders, Douglas was not able to translate provincial strength into national success (see table 8-5).

PARLIAMENTARY AND MINISTERIAL CAREERS

In the pre-convention period of Canadian history, leaders were invariably selected from the parliamentary party. Those who played a part at some time or another in naming a new leader for a party included retiring leaders, parliamentary elites, backbench MPs and, if the prime ministership was at issue, even the governor general. Following the British model of leadership selection in a parliamentary system, a model with which Canada's governing elites were closely familiar, it was naturally assumed that the person chosen to lead a party would himself be in Parliament. From Macdonald to Meighen in the Conservative party and from Mackenzie to Laurier in the Liberal party, the men chosen as leaders were either MPs or senators at the time they were selected. As a rule they had several years' experience in the federal cabinet, and many had served as well in provincial legislatures and cabinets.[36]

The likelihood of leaders having already established parliamentary and ministerial careers at the time of their selection changed with the introduction of leadership conventions. It could no longer be taken as a virtual certainty of leadership selection that the person chosen would have come from the ranks of the parliamentary party, or have spent some time on the back, then the front benches, or have served as a minister. Conventions increased vastly the number of participants in the leadership selection process, and opened the door to candidates winning the leadership who had little, or even no, experience as an MP or a cabinet minister.

The environment within which prospective leaders in the convention period honed their political skills and staked out their claim to their party's leadership has been different from what it was in the pre-convention period. It has become an extra-parliamentary environment, one in which leadership candidates have fashioned organizations and established contacts to launch their campaigns and in which delegates have judged alternative leadership hopefuls according to their reading of the public's and the media's reactions to them. None of these changes necessarily depended on a candidate's first-hand knowledge of Parliament or the cabinet or a ministry. Indeed, the reverse may have been true. Many of those who have followed the more conventional career path of advancing through the parliamentary ranks have since the introduction of conventions lost to a candidate with less parliamentary and ministerial experience or without current membership in Parliament. The extent to which a parliamentary career has been discounted as a natural springboard to party leadership testifies to the capacity of large delegated conventions to open up the process to high-profile contestants who, often with carefully-executed career moves and considerable media attention, pursue their ultimate goal of winning their party's leadership from outside their parliamentary party (see tables 8-9 to 8-12).

National party leaders before 1919 in the Liberal party and 1927 in the Conservative party had, respectively, averages of 10.1 and 13.5 years of parliamentary experience when they were chosen. At the time of their selection all were either MPs or, in two cases, senators with many years of previous service in the Commons. Reflecting their party's dominant position for much of the pre-convention period, Conservative leaders brought to the job an average of seven years' ministerial experience. At 1.3 years, the average ministerial experience of three pre-1919 Liberal leaders fell far behind that of the Tories. Leaders of both parties typically had served some time in provincial legislatures and, in small numbers, in provincial cabinets.

The convention period tells a very different story. In the Tory party, a majority of its post-1927 leaders (five of nine) were not members of Parliament when they were selected. The time that Conservative leaders had served previously in Parliament dropped from the pre-convention stage to 5.6 years, a figure that is as high as it is only because of the lengthy pre-leadership parliamentary careers of two Tory leaders, Manion and Diefenbaker.[37] The average disguises the fact that four leaders (Bracken, Drew, Stanfield, and Mulroney) had had no prior parliamentary experience whatsoever when they were selected. At 1.6 years, the Conservative leaders' ministerial experience approximated that of the Liberals in the pre-convention period and reflected the fact that since 1927 the party has, with rare exceptions, been in opposition. Two-thirds of its leaders had had no national ministerial experience when they were chosen by convention. With her selection, Campbell became the first Tory leader since Manion to have served in a federal cabinet. As one-third of all Conservative leaders from 1927 to 1993 were provincial premiers at the time they were chosen, it is not surprising that the Tories' provincial legislative and ministerial experiences exceeded those at the national level.

In one respect, the political backgrounds of Liberal leaders picked since 1919 have been much closer to those of pre-convention Conservatives than Liberals. The average of 7.7 years national ministerial experience of Liberal leaders chosen by convention exceeds only slightly the earlier Conservative figure of seven years. Taken together, these figures suggest that long stretches of one-party dominance invariably give a decided edge to that party's leaders over all others in terms of prior ministerial experience.

Liberal leaders chosen since 1919 have served previously for a considerably longer time in cabinet than their opponents' leaders. Consistent with that is the finding that the parliamentary careers of Liberal leaders (9.7 years) have been longer than those of either Tory or NDP leaders (5.6 and 6.1 respectively). The Liberal's post-1919 figure of

9.7 years in Parliament of new leaders closely approximated that of the pre-convention period. But there the similarity ends. The party in convention has been very different from the earlier one and much more like the convention-period Tories in that half of its leaders have not had a seat in Parliament at the time they were chosen. Regardless of the period of leadership selection, the Liberals have distinguished themselves from the two other older parties: they have never chosen a provincial premier as their national leader, or, indeed, anyone who had served in a provincial legislature or cabinet.

The NDP's relatively short history is obvious from the small number of leaders it has chosen to date. At 6.1 years, their parliamentary experience has more closely approximated that of Conservative than Liberal leaders. But as the NDP has never formed the government nationally it differs from both the other parties in that none of its leaders had any prior federal ministerial experience. Like the Conservatives, the NDP also has recruited directly from provincial politics with the selection of Saskatchewan premier T.C. Douglas in 1961 as the party's first national leader.

The political career routes followed by the nineteen national party leaders chosen by convention are given in diagram 8-1. It shows that the largest single group of leaders has come directly from opposition members of Parliament and that only two of those seven had at some point been in a federal cabinet. Three MPs who were serving as cabinet ministers were chosen as leaders by their parties in convention, but no backbencher on the government side of the House has ever been elected a party leader.

From the career patterns shown in the diagram, it is obvious that the cabinet has not served as the principal pool from which leaders have been drawn. But this is scarcely surprising given the fact that only four of the these leaders were elected by parties in office: the Liberals in 1948, 1968, and 1984, and the Conservatives in 1993. The overwhelming majority of Canada's national leaders have been selected by parties in opposition. In turn, the majority of those chosen to lead a party in opposition have been drawn from outside Parliament. These facts help to inform our understanding both of parliamentary parties as sources of leaders at the time of leadership transitions and of Parliament as an institution within which politicians with leadership aspirations choose to establish and to maintain political careers.

The party usually in opposition in Ottawa throughout this century, the Conservatives, as well as the NDP since it was formed in 1961, have had much greater electoral successes at the provincial than at the national level. Understandably these parties have turned to some of their proven vote-getters to try to do nationally what they have

Diagram 8-1
Prior Elected Public Offices of Party Leaders

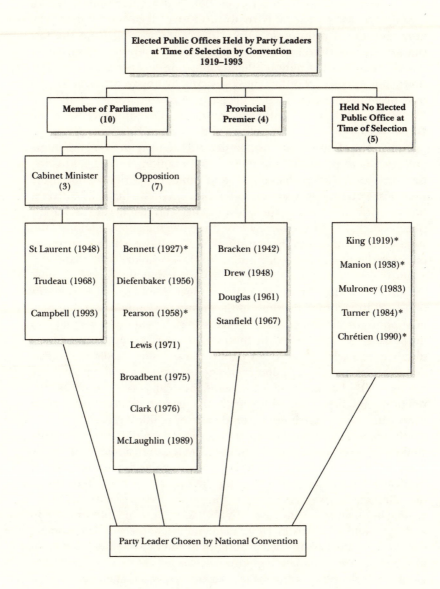

* Prior Cabinet Experience

done provincially. Bracken, Drew, Stanfield, and Douglas brought with them to their national parties a record of having defeated Liberal governments, of having formed and led a government, and of having directed a political party to successive electoral victories. The attractiveness of proven electoral winners is apparent from the fact that on every occasion in which a provincial premier has been nominated for his party's national leadership one has been chosen. The down side of such cooptive moves is equally apparent: none of the four premiers was able to take his party to national office. This reinforces the inherent difficulties of translating electoral success in the "small worlds" of Canadian politics to the "large."[38]

Parties out of office have not limited their choice of non-parliamentary leaders to provincial premiers. King, Manion, Turner, and Chrétien had both prior parliamentary and cabinet experience, but at the time of selection they held no elected office. When selected, Mulroney had no parliamentary or cabinet experience and had never run for any public office. In its own way, each of these five selections demonstrates some of the advantages that outsiders, that is those who are currently out of Parliament, have over insiders, or those who are in Parliament.

Outsiders are unencumbered by the constraints that apply to those within parliamentary parties, notably a measure of collective solidarity on policy, in recorded divisions in the House of Commons, and in public support for the leader. They are freer to stake out positions that may differ from those advanced by the parliamentary group, and they can distance themselves more easily than can leadership candidates in Parliament from possibly unpopular positions advanced by the parliamentary party. By being out of Parliament they can avoid the occasional political minefields buried beneath the government or opposition frontbenches that can, if not defused, destroy political careers.

Outsiders may unshackle themselves at some point from the constraints imposed on MPs and ministers by leaving cabinet and Parliament, as did Turner who was serving at the time as finance minister in Trudeau's government, or by leaving the opposition front benches, as did Chrétien who was serving at the time as the Liberals' external affairs critic. They may, as was the case with both Mulroney and Turner in 1979 and 1980 and Chrétien in 1988, deliberately choose not to become a candidate on their party's behalf and not to enter or re-enter Parliament in a general election. The high-profile outsider enjoys the freedom to employ a "risk-averse" strategy that in some respects is analogous to that of an exiled king awaiting the call to return home. Only when the conditions are right will the individual who has taken steps while abroad to enhance his reputation as the leader-in-waiting heed the call.[39]

Outsiders enjoy a measure of media attention not necessarily greater than, but at least different from, that accorded intra-parliamentary party leadership contenders. As former leadership candidates or some-time MPs and cabinet ministers they are blessed with what many report-ers and politicians seem to favour in covering political leadership – instant name recognition combined with a conjectural story line. Media reports about possible leadership candidates from outside Parliament can play an important part in keeping public and party interest alive in an individual's political future, and they have been known to have gone on over a period of several years. Mulroney, Turner, and Chrétien in the years leading up to their ultimately successful run at the leadership, were featured prominently in countless print and broadcast reports about their political future. The conjectural stories ranged from who would likely run to succeed the current leader and how the various can-didates might be expected to fare, to what sort of a leader the non-par-liamentary party candidate could be expected to be. Such stories have the potential to dominate, and therefore to shape, the early stages of a leadership campaign. Chrétien was to discover that in 1984 when he participated in a televised panel discussion on the CBC's influential public affairs show "The Journal" about Trudeau's resignation that had been announced earlier that day. The program, to Chrétien's dismay, "was accompanied by a lengthy documentary on John Turner."[40]

By definition, MPs who are current or former cabinet ministers and who stand as leadership candidates are insiders. But in the oftentimes Orwellian world of politics not all insiders are equal. The evidence from the early conventions to the most recent ones demonstrates that the candidate who is able to project himself or herself as "new," as hav-ing a "fresh face" or a "fresh approach," and who is described accord-ingly by the media, stands a markedly better chance of winning the leadership than those who have spent longer periods of time in Parlia-ment and, possibly, in cabinet. McLaughlin and Campbell were both described by the media, their organizers, and supporters as the fresh candidates – only the latest in a long history of such descriptions dating back to King's candidacy in 1919. King parlayed his relative youth and his extra-parliamentary career as a labour specialist into an impressive, and ultimately successful, convention performance.[41] There is possibly no better example of the claims of "freshness" and "newness" than Trudeau's 1968 leadership campaign, or of the media's description and the public's perception of the candidate in those terms. The man who had been in Parliament for less than three years, and who had served as minister of justice for only one year at the time that he was chosen Liberal leader, was later described by the retiring leader, Pear-son, as "the man to match the times, the new image for a new era. *His non-involvement in politics became his greatest asset*, along with his personal appeal, his charisma ... Trudeau [was] a man for this season, uncontaminated and uninhibited."[42] This was then a widely held view of Trudeau, one that was shared by the new leader himself. The day following his selection Trudeau admitted to feeling an outsider and a newcomer to the party of which he had just been elected leader.[43]

Trudeau's victory in 1968 reinforced one of the longstanding features of leadership selection through conventions. With the exceptions of Manion, Diefenbaker, Broadbent, and Chrétien, the winner of every national party convention has had less party and cabinet experience than the principal losers. All four provincial premiers to have sought their party's leadership have defeated MPs, and in some cases former cabinet ministers, who were senior, established figures in their respective parliamentary party. The same has been true of all three cabinet ministers to have been elected leader, of four of the seven winners of conventions held by parties in opposition, and of three of the five successful candidates not in Parliament at the time of their election. Two complementary conclusions are obvious. To win a leadership convention at the national level requires little or no experience in Parliament or in cabinet, which in turn means that those who run for the leadership having first established a political career in Parliament and then maintained it through years of parliamentary and cabinet service stand little chance of becoming party leader. As a consequence, until Chrétien's selection in 1990, parliamentary service had become far less essential a component of a prospective candidate's resumé under conventions than was ever previously the case.

WHO WINS? WHO LOSES?

What is the composite picture that emerges of the winners and losers of national leadership conventions? In gender, age, language, and value of parliamentary and ministerial experience, there has been little to distinguish among the three parties. Leaders and candidates have been overwhelmingly male. The historic exceptions have been recent, as it was not until 1975 that the first woman was nominated to contest her party's leadership and not until 1989 that one was elected.[44] Leaders picked since the beginning of conventions have, on average, been between fifty-two and fifty-five years of age, a figure slightly above the age of the total pool of candidates from which they were chosen. The second generation of leadership conventions brought with it candidates and leaders who were younger than those chosen in the first generation, and a measure of fluency in both official languages has become one of the distinguishing marks of party leadership. In both generations of leadership conventions a candidate's long parliamentary and ministerial experience has done little to ensure victory against a politically attractive outsider or a relatively fresh face in Parliament or in cabinet. Thus on gender, age, language, and relative political experience leaders of the three parties have shared much in common.

In other respects, however, the parties have differed. Law has been the dominant occupation of candidates and leaders of the two older parties, whereas those who have sought and been elected to the NDP leadership have come from a considerably greater variety of occupational backgrounds. The NDP and the Conservatives have distinguished themselves from the Liberals by having chosen provincial premiers as national leaders. They also have turned to the non-central Canadian provinces for a much greater proportion of their candidates, with the result that half of the NDP leaders and two-thirds of the Conservative leaders since conventions were first introduced have come from provinces other than Ontario and Quebec. For its part, the Liberal party has been alone in having followed for almost its entire history a tradition of rotating its leadership between the two central Canadian provinces, between Catholic francophones and Protestant anglophones. The Tories have moved a considerable distance from their early history of largely choosing Protestant leaders and have seen an increase in their number of Catholic candidates and leaders. Drawing its leaders and candidates from a greater variety of religions and having a greater share of them admitting of no religious beliefs has been characteristic of the NDP.

The nineteen leaders chosen by conventions between 1919 to 1993 can be described in the following general terms. In the Liberal party the leader has always been a male from either Ontario or Quebec. He has typically been a middle-aged, anglophone Protestant or a francophone Catholic lawyer with less parliamentary and cabinet experience than his major convention opponents. The usual Conservative leader has been a male, middle-aged lawyer from outside central Canada whose background has generally been unilingual anglophone and Protestant. He or she has had an almost fifty-fifty chance of never having run for Parliament before being chosen, has probably had more legislative and ministerial experience at the provincial than at the national level, and has almost certainly served fewer years in Parliament and cabinet than the unsuccessful principal leadership opponents. The NDP leader has usually been a middle-aged, unilingual anglophone male from either a province or territory of NDP strength, but never from Quebec or the Maritimes. He or she has had as much chance of being a clergyman, professor, or consultant as a lawyer, and may have been Jewish or Protestant, but not Catholic. As with the other two parties, the person chosen to lead the NDP nationally has typically served fewer years in Parliament than many of those seeking the leadership at the same convention.

In spite of their particular differences, the socio-demographic and political characteristics of candidates and leaders of the three older parties have had much in common. Overwhelmingly, party leadership has been sought by and awarded to white, professional, university-educated, middle-class males. Most, though by no means all, of the leaders had had some parliamentary experience at the time of their selection. A few, but far from a majority, had had prior federal cabinet experience. Clearly neither the failure to have had long-established roots in the parliamentary party nor the absence of an extended apprenticeship in the cabinet disqualified potential party leaders under the delegates convention system of selecting leaders. By including thousands of non-parliamentary-based partisans in the leadership selection process, parties effectively opened the door to candidates and leaders drawn from outside the relatively small circles of parliamentarians.

9 From Announcement Day to Acceptance Day: The Net Worth of Networks

People – needing other people.

– Jule Styne

Several are called (and others think they deserve to be called), but only one is chosen to lead a party. The man or woman victorious in a national leadership convention gains the job because a majority of the delegates voting on the final ballot find that person preferable to any of the alternatives. Behind that simple and obvious truth are other factors that in combination help to explain why one individual, and not another, has made it to the top. The previous chapter has examined the complex mix of a candidate's socio-demographic-political background and the regional-linguistic considerations that come into play at the time a leader is chosen. No less important are the networks and contacts that a leadership candidate must be able to draw on and the organization a candidate must assemble if he or she seriously hopes to get from one podium to another – from announcement day to acceptance day.

In many ways, networks are at the heart of politics. Creating, nurturing, and using them to good effect can spell the difference between success and failure for a politician. Without established contacts, who in turn can help to locate organizers, advisers, workers, supporters, and funds, no candidate could realistically expect to go far in a campaign. This is at least part of the explanation for the failure of such candidates as John Nunziata and Tom Wappel in 1990 or Patrick Boyer and Garth Turner in 1993 to gain national attention and to earn sizable first-ballot support. In the early stages of the campaign they lacked the contacts needed to make inroads with the delegates, and as the convention approached they were without the organization staffed by volunteers and professional personnel needed to establish and to sustain their credibility as serious candidates.

CANDIDATE NETWORKS

Although details of their size, duration, and composition are often shrouded in mystery, candidate networks provide a promising way to think about leadership campaigns. In contrast to more formal, structured bureaucracies with lines of command and authority structures, networks are informal, interconnected, and non-institutional linkages among persons. They vary in size and resemble a communications circuit in the manner in which they are constructed. Some in the network are in close and direct contact with a candidate, whereas others who are neither in direct nor immediate contact with the candidate are activated on his or her behalf through their friendship with those closer to the candidate. Some are a part of a network because of a longstanding personal friendship with the candidate. Others are a part of it for shorter periods of time and often for largely selfish reasons, including protection of policy interests, advancement of career, or ensuring future access to a possible political leader. As Diagram 9-1 illustrates, the interconnected relationships of a network radiate from the candidate, starting with the primary order of friends and moving on through the second and subsequent orders of friends-of-friends.[1]

A personal network acts as a "reservoir of social relations" from and through which a candidate recruits and mobilizes support. It is also a two-way communications network for transmitting messages between a candidate and his or her supporters. It can serve as a means whereby reciprocal exchange transactions, such as promises and commitments or sale and purchase of political services, can be negotiated privately between its members. Those who are a part of a network are mobilized for basically compatible reasons. Candidates need advice, guidance, and help; those who provide it do so from some mixture of altruistic and self-interested motives that varies from one individual to another.

Details of political networks in Canada are sketchy at best. The membership of a network, even at the level closest to the candidate, is not always fully known, and knowledge about what transpires between candidates and their friends, confidants, and advisers is often incomplete or non-existent. Still, information gleaned from biographies and media accounts of recently successful candidates at least enables us to appreciate the variety of networks that have been assembled by some leadership hopefuls. Some, such as John Turner's in 1984 and Jean Chrétien's in 1990, were composed largely of Liberal notables and activists, many with years behind them in the party who, particularly in

Diagram 9-1
Candidate Networks

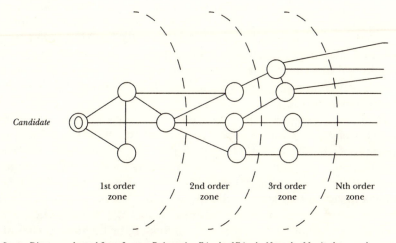

Source: Diagram adapted from Jeremy Boissevain, *Friends of Friends: Networks, Manipulators and Coalitions* (New York: St. Martin's Press, 1974), chap. 2. Reprinted with permission.

Chrétien's case, had been in place waiting for a leadership vacancy to occur at an indefinite point in the future. By contrast, Brian Mulroney's 1983 primary order network was composed of a mixture of close personal friends, some party notables, and an assortment of Conservatives disaffected with Joe Clark's leadership. Others, notably Kim Campbell's, had been created on much shorter notice and drew principally on existing sub-networks of immediate parliamentary and party contacts.

Turner's two runs at the Liberal leadership were separated by the longest stretch between conventions of any twice-nominated candidate – sixteen years. During the interval from 1968 to 1984, Turner had reportedly kept in close touch with the network of supporters and organizers who had been part of his first leadership campaign team.[2] A number of these, such as Jerry Grafstein, Lloyd Axworthy, and David Smith, had become senior figures in the party by 1984: cabinet ministers, senators, and the like. Understandably they emerged as high-profile members of the network in the primary zone closest to the candidate.[3]

By the time Turner took a second run at the leadership his total network of friends, casual acquaintances, and potential workers had grown in size and prestige. In addition to the holdovers from 1968 it included many who, if they were present in 1968 at all, had supported other candidates for leader; others who had become friendly with, or admirers of, Turner in the years leading up to the 1984 convention; and members of the Liberal establishment whose instincts for the party's eventual electoral success prompted them to work on Turner's behalf. The presumed inevitability of Turner's winning the leadership could only help those in the network to get their message out. Not surprisingly, when Turner announced his candidacy in 1984 he was greeted by a rush of Liberal caucus members and cabinet ministers offering their loyalty and support. Within days the network of supporters and workers mushroomed as more than two thousand volunteers offered their services to his campaign.[4]

With the passage of time during intervening years reports of the alleged strength of Turner's organization assumed almost legendary proportions. "Part of the mythology [in 1984]," wrote Greg Weston, "was the existence of some slick, well-oiled campaign machine that was going to carry Turner straight to the Grit throne, that it even included the old Club 195, those faithful followers who had backed him to the final ballot during the 1968 leadership race against Trudeau."[5] The myth had so successfully entered the political folklore by the time Turner officially launched his campaign in 1984 that the media quickly seized on it as "evidence" that he had had the organization and the contacts in place from the time of his earlier defeat to contest the upcoming leadership race.

In reality, the picture proved quite different. There was no doubt that Turner had numerous contacts and friends on his side, but fashioning that network into an organization proved to be problematic. The initial efforts were so marked by confusion that they belied the existence of an experienced organization waiting in the wings. One senior participant labelled it a "messy operation" that barely got off to "a standing start."[6] For help, Turner turned to Bill Lee to take on the job of campaign manager. Described as "possibly the most astute political organizer in the country," Lee had served as Paul Hellyer's campaign manager sixteen years earlier.[7] Turner brought him in to take charge of his campaign for the obvious reason that his network of contacts had not translated into an effective campaign organization with the speed and operational skills necessary to launch and to sustain a three-month drive for the leadership. Turner turned to someone billed as having the organizational expertise of a political pro, though in fact he, like Turner, proved to be somewhat "rusty."[8]

Like Turner, Chrétien tried twice for his party's leadership. By the time he took his first run at the leadership in 1984, some twenty-one years after entering the House of Commons, he had built up an impressive network of supporters and organizers within the Liberal party. It was said at the time to have "been operating quietly and efficiently behind the scenes for almost two years."[9] But the Liberals' adherence

to the French-English alternation tradition and the overwhelming support of Turner by party elites and much of the rank and file effectively
ended Chrétien's chances of becoming leader in 1984.[10]

Resigning his parliamentary seat two years later, Chrétien spent
much of the Turner period strengthening his connections within the
party and building up his store of IOUs. By May 1989 when Turner announced his intention to resign, Chrétien had pieced together a "large,
country-wide network that [had] never really stopped campaigning for
him since his second-place, 'first-in-the-hearts' showing in 1984."[11] It
consisted of the same core group of primary contacts that had been
part of his 1984 team, such as John Rae, Edward Goldenberg, Mitchell
Sharp, and Penny and David Collenette. But to it were added many
Trudeau-era party heavyweights, of whom Keith Davey, Marc Lalonde,
and Jim Coutts were the most prominent, who had either backed
Turner last time around or ostensibly remained neutral. In addition,
several influential provincial politicians, including Robert Nixon of Ontario and Sharon Carstairs of Manitoba, were brought on side. Chrétien
had claimed that he would run in 1990 only "if he had the support of
the majority of the Liberal caucus." He found that it did not take long
to get it. "Most of the MPs were quick to jump in the boat," he later
wrote, noting that he was the strong front runner from the moment he
entered the contest.[12] As had been true of Turner in 1984, Chrétien's
primary network of personal and party contacts had enlarged considerably by the time he launched his second run at the Liberal leadership.

In some respects Chrétien and Turner shared similar experiences after they had been defeated in their first run at their party's leadership.
Both men eventually resigned their seats in the Commons to join
large, established law firms. This assured them of a distance from the
daily grind of parliamentary life and offered them the opportunity to
consolidate friendships, make new political contacts, and enhance
their primary and subsidiary networks. In neither case did the media
lose interest in them, a fact both men understood well with their timing of speeches and participation at important political events. These
served to keep alive speculation about them as possible candidates in
future leadership contests and to create expectations about the state of
their networks' organizational preparedness. By the time they took
their second run at the leadership, both men had become the favourites of the party establishment and were widely seen as the odds-on
favourites to win. Each had successfully managed to establish a power
base within the party from which to derive the authority and leverage
needed to persuade others to join his increasingly larger network.

In spite of these similarities, the circumstances within which each
man had continued to develop his network after his initial defeat were

different. Those differences, in turn, help to inform our understanding of candidates and their networks. The practical effect of a six as opposed to a sixteen-year interval between two conventions was obvious in the two campaigns. With a shorter interval there is less time for the original network to disperse or become out of touch with political organizing and a greater likelihood of sustaining interest in a possible second run at the leadership. Reports of a "rusty" candidate[13] and of numerous organizational faults in 1984 confirmed one of the differences between Turner's second candidacy and Chrétien's.

But it is no less true that a longer interval enables the first-time loser to construct a wider and deeper network in preparation for the second run at the leadership. This helps to account for Turner's win in 1984. In 1968 he had run a poor third on the fourth ballot and had a much greater distance to make up than Chrétien, who had run a respectable second in 1984. With the passage of time Turner had emerged as a principal player in the Trudeau government prior to his surprise resignation as finance minister in 1975. He left a caucus and cabinet still strongly supportive of their leader, but divisions within the party outside Parliament became more apparent with his departure and created an opportunity for him to convert dissatisfied Liberals to his side.[14] Turner's network of friends and acquaintances grew accordingly, and by the time of the convention in 1984 a significant portion of the party's establishment was onside. The expanded network that had grown around Turner confirmed Senator Davey's point that "John Turner returning to active politics was an extremely attractive proposition for the party."[15]

In spite of the longer interval between conventions, Turner had far less time than Chrétien to convert his primary network into an effective campaign instrument once the convention was called. From Trudeau's sudden, though not totally unexpected, resignation announcement to convention election day in 1984 was three and a half months; from Turner's widely expected resignation in 1989 to the 1990 convention was thirteen months. The differences that extra time can make to candidates' abilities to convert networks into campaign organizations became obvious soon after the two candidates entered their second races. Chrétien was afforded the luxury of getting his organization in place well before he declared his candidacy in January 1990. Part of his 1990 primary network had been in his original group only six years previously and had then been active in the party's leadership review fight in 1986. This proved to be an added bonus as he set about mobilizing his larger network for his second run at the leadership.[16] Turner had failed to have his network in a similar state of preparedness. This was a reflection not only of the different individuals involved in the networks but also of the the different circumstances of each transition. Turner's decision in 1979 not to contest the Liberal leadership when Trudeau announced his (abortive) resignation as party leader no doubt eventually cost him some support amongst his personal contacts and organizational network. Clearly, having a large network is no guarantee that it will be converted quickly into an effective political organization.

The opportunities presented to a first-time losing candidate who is part of an opposition party quarrelling over its leadership are necessarily different from those presented to a losing candidate in a governing party relatively united behind its leader. When Chrétien resigned his parliamentary seat in 1986 his party was in opposition and was deeply divided over Turner's leadership. He did not have to wait long for Turner to resign. The announcement came less than five years from the previous leadership convention and only three years after Chrétien had left the Commons. Chrétien's network had stayed alive and well during the interval and was ready to swing into action.

Indeed, it seemed to many in the party that it had never seriously ceased being in action since the 1984 convention. As the Liberals had been in opposition since their defeat in the 1984 general election, the Chrétien network capitalized on an opportunity generally denied to losing candidates' teams when their party forms the government: they can themselves become centres of opposition to the leader, attempting to destabilize the incumbent as the occasion presents itself. For a number in the party during the Turner years the leader-in-waiting became a sort of leader of the Liberal opposition. From 1984 on, Chrétien's team was said to have defined itself "as an alternative to the Turner team. Individually they all had a powerful interest in challenging Turner's leadership; together they had the organizational machinery to do it... When the leadership again came vacant in 1990, this well-practised organization quickly ran over its new opponents and won the leadership long before the convention ever met."[17] Their institutional location gave Chrétien's supporters and contacts within the parliamentary caucus greater degrees of freedom to express their discontent and to mount attacks against Turner's leadership than would have been the case had they been part of a governing party.

Where does a candidate's network come from? Typically, it is made up of a mix of political colleagues whose networks and contacts within the party extend well beyond the candidate himself. As well, it may include some business, personal, and professional acquaintances. The balance among these groups obviously varies from one candidate to another. From Turner's and Chrétien's many years in Parliament and their long involvement in party affairs, it was natural that both candidates would draw their primary political networks from among their numerous caucus, ministerial, and party contacts – from junior political staff and present and former executive assistants, to chiefs of staff and senior cabinet colleagues. For both men their network also included some friends from the business, corporate, and professional circles within which they moved, though for neither candidate were the numbers in this group large in comparison with their parliamentary and party contacts. No notable members of their primary networks traced their friendship with the candidates back to university and pre-parliamentary days.

By contrast, the nucleus of Brian Mulroney's networks in 1983 was drawn more from a circle of close personal friends than from the ranks of the parliamentary and extra-parliamentary parties. Mulroney may never have held public office to that point, but that did not mean he was without roots in the Conservative party from which he was able to craft a political network. His early entry points into the party had all been university-related, which in itself is not unusual for a budding politician.[18] But apart from a short stint as an executive assistant to the federal minister of agriculture in 1962, he had held no job on Parliament Hill. Instead, Mulroney fashioned his political network outside the formal structures and elected offices of the party and of Parliament, developing it among his personal friends and contacts.

His key group of operatives (collectively dubbed the Mulroney Mafia) was composed mainly of buddies from his time at university. His 1983 leadership campaign was "founded largely on the network of old pals who ha[d] been close to him since [his] days at St Francis Xavier, Laval, or his early years among the Tories."[19] It included several former classmates: Michel Cogger as campaign manager, Michael Meighen and Peter White as senior figures in Mulroney's Ontario campaign, and Bernard Roy as head of the Montreal-based Friends of Brian Mulroney. Other college chums part of the 1983 network were Jean Bazin, Fred Doucet, and Sam Wakim. Meighen was a notable exception in that group. Having served as Conservative national president in the 1970s, he was the only one of the seven to have been elected to a party position. He was also the only one to have ever run for Parliament or a provincial legislature.[20]

Mulroney's heavy reliance on longstanding friendships can best be explained by his being a Conservative in Quebec during the 1960s and 1970s – a time when the party was without any serious or effective organization in that province – and by the fact that he had never run for elected public office at any level before seeking the leadership of the party. With his party of choice a largely non-existent organization and elected public office a route he opted not to pursue, Mulroney forfeited the opportunities to create an intra-party network similar to that built by both Turner and Chrétien. Mulroney's personal friendships largely compensated for those lacunae.

After the defeat of the Clark government, the media began to speculate about Mulroney running for the Tory leadership should Clark be forced to call a convention. Rumours of the state of preparedness and the considerable organizational strength of Mulroney's network also began to circulate.[21] It was later said that Mulroney "never stopped massaging his network, keeping it in shape. Every day he called some of its members, the gang from St Francis Xavier, the group from Laval, his workers from '76, and the ones he continued to court."[22]

When Mulroney got his chance to run for the leadership in 1983 his organization, like Turner's the following year, did not perform well for much of the campaign. With less than a month to go to the convention it was described as having "collapsed into chaos," as being marked by feuding and in-fighting among longstanding friends, and as lacking strong direction and control.[23] Mulroney turned late in the Tory race to a veteran organizer, John Thompson, to reassemble his campaign and convention-floor pieces. Experienced in Ontario campaigns and at national party headquarters, Thompson was said to possess "all the qualifications of an organizer, rolled up in an attractive, personable and unambitious package." His ability to take charge of "the chaotic convention organization" proved to be "a stroke of genius" for the Mulroney campaign.[24] As was the case with Turner, Mulroney's extensive network had been mistaken for an effective campaign organization.

To win, a candidate need not have taken years to cultivate and to establish an extensive network of supporters in preparation for a leadership contest. Kim Campbell's run for the Tory leadership in 1993 is a case in point. Campbell was in many ways an outsider. A woman and a British Columbian, she was also relatively new to Parliament and to the Conservative party. Only seven years before she was chosen to lead the federal Conservatives she had run for the leadership of the Social Credit party of British Columbia. With fourteen votes, she had placed last of twelve candidates on the first ballot.

In spite of her brief history in the Conservative party, Campbell nonetheless attracted to her leadership campaign a large group of capable and experienced party activists, people with connections in the Tory party that went far beyond her own. She was able to do this largely because she was seen at the beginning of the race as the all-but-certain successor to Mulroney. As we have seen, the early polls confirmed that with Campbell as leader the Tories would be returned to power. That kind of information is difficult for experienced party handlers to ignore, and accordingly many were drawn or coopted into her campaign even before she had declared her candidacy. Thus Campbell, not having a large, established network that she could call her own, was fortunate to have drawn into her circle of contacts a number of Tories who either as elected officials or as experienced political organizers had networks of their own.

Prior to Campbell's arrival in Ottawa in 1988 her closest group of political confidants had understandably been confined to the west coast. Dating principally from her time in politics and law in British Columbia, it included such provincial Socred and federal Tory operatives as Patrick Kinsella, David Camp, and Brian Smith.[25] As early as the summer of 1992 Campbell had made her first moves to enlarge her points of contact in the federal party and to create a network of organizers and fund-raisers for a possible run at the leadership. Through private dinners in Toronto and Montreal arranged by members of the party establishment she was introduced to potential donors, organizers, and workers. By the end of the year she had succeeded in bringing into her network a number of other influential Tories, seasoned organizers, and fund-raisers from many parts of the country.[26]

By the early stages of the leadership campaign there were indications that Campbell had already won the support, organization, and funds of a good part of the old Mulroney establishment, including some of the more nationalist members of the party's Quebec caucus and many of the central figures of the party's old Big Blue Machine in Ontario.[27] Her Quebec network was drawn principally from fellow cabinet ministers and MPs, Marcel Masse, Gilles Loiselle, Pierre Blais, and Monique Landry to name four – and from heavyweight organizers identified with Mulroney in the province, of whom Jean-Yves Lortie was possibly the best known. Her Ontario network, composed of cabinet colleagues and other parliamentarians, party notables, and veteran organizers, was more representative of the party as a whole. Chief among her early Ontario supporters was Senator Norman Atkins, an organizational force in the party for many years "who had orchestrated Mulroney's 1984 and 1988 electoral victories as well as several successful campaigns for Bill Davis." He was later joined by Paul Curley, a former national director of the party, who was assigned the task of assembling "a skilled team of handlers for the convention."[28]

Given her strength as the unquestioned front runner, Campbell had been able to expand her circle of primary contacts and influential players in Tory politics in a remarkably short time. As the convention ended, it was clear that it had been drawn principally from three sources. The oldest and smallest part of Campbell's network was her west coast circle of political friends that pre-dated her entry into federal politics. They would constitute, in Boissevain's terms, Campbell's primary order of friends. Next in numbers, but probably the most important in terms of public profile and name recognition among rank-and-file delegates, were her parliamentary colleagues. Several of that group, including cabinet ministers Michael Wilson, Tom Hockin, Perrin Beatty, and Bernard Valcourt, had decided against running for the leadership and were eventually drawn into her campaign organization. The largest group in numerical terms were those who as part of Campbell's expanded friends-of-friends network served as strategists and organizers forging the necessary links with the delegates. In Campbell's case a network that was more politically than personally based had grown out of the mobilization of a variety of pre-existing organizational sub-networks.

By sheer dint of numbers and profile of the people involved, Campbell had pieced together the largest and arguably the most impressive network of any 1993 candidate. In terms of structure, it had little to hold it together. Practically none of it was her own, a fact which led to a number of problems within the leadership campaign itself. It was soon apparent that many of those who were drawn to it were there only because her candidacy seemed the surest way of keeping the Tories in office. It is likely that the breadth and depth of Campbell's network and her lack of familiarity with its members created the huge communications lapses and confused messaging that plagued her campaign from beginning to end. This left it with no consistent set of advisers and policies, and no constant set of messages beyond "winnability" and "doing politics differently." It also presaged the sorts of difficulties the new leader would soon encounter in the 1993 general election campaign. That Campbell's network was not a personally-based one, with long-standing personal loyalties to the candidate herself, eventually proved to be part of her undoing in the post-leadership convention and 1993 election campaign period. In Laschinger's words, "Her network came apart. It had no glue."[29]

CANDIDATE ORGANIZATIONS

However they may come to support the candidate, the individuals who comprise the backbone of a candidate's organization are of three broadly defined types: political notables, organizers, and professionals. These are by no means tidy, self-contained categories, for an individual active on a candidate's campaign might properly be included in two, or possibly all three, categories. Candidates attempting to run a campaign with little support from party notables, with few seasoned organizers and only a modicum of professional advice stand little no chance of winning their party's leadership. This helps to account for the fate of such Tories as Michael Starr in 1967, Jim Gillies in 1976, Peter Pocklington in 1983, and Garth Turner and Patrick Boyer in 1993, and such Liberals as Eric Kierans in 1968, John Munro and Eugene Whelan in 1984, and John Nunziata and Tom Wappel in 1990. Their names may be familiar to the party rank and file, possibly even to public at large. With little ultimately to show for it, they may, as did Pocklington in 1983, try to compensate for the absence of a longstanding intra-party network of contacts by spending large sums of money to assemble an instant campaign organization. But even that scarcely makes up for what they lack in organizational depth, professional advice, and exploitable intra-party contacts.[30]

The record suggests that it is possible, though rare, for a candidate going into the balloting with strength in all three groups to lose to an opponent who has far fewer endorsements from party elites and much less organizational strength and professional support. Claude Wagner was to discover this in 1976 when he lost to Joe Clark. Clark, whose support from the parliamentary caucus and party notables at the outset of the voting was only a fraction of Wagner's, and whose campaign organization was the smaller and less professional of the two, eventually beat Wagner after four ballots. As will be seen in the following chapter, Clark owed his victory more to the coalitions built on the floor of the convention through successive ballots than to his pre-convention networks and organization.

Political Notables

By actively seeking the support and endorsements of their cabinet and backbench colleagues in Parliament, candidates hope that once obtained, testimonials will translate into increased voting support from convention delegates. Endorsements and active support from provincial premiers and leaders, MPs, MLAs, mayors, and past party leaders are all pursued with that goal in mind. Associating a candidate's name with that of a political notable is seen as a way to enhance a candidate's campaign, to provide it with a measure of credibility and legitimacy, and to help to attract media and public attention. The theory seems to be that delegates will respect the judgment and will follow the lead of party figures who have passed electoral tests in their own right, who have networks of their own and who may, as with provincial premiers, for example, be thought to be in a position to influence the voting behaviour of large numbers of delegates.

Such, at least, is the theory. In reality, the value to candidates of endorsements by and support from party notables has yet to be confirmed in empirical studies of delegate behaviour. It seems likely that the returns realized from endorsements were greater during the first generation of conventions when choices of party elites carried more weight with delegates and when fewer delegates were selected as part of committed slates. For modern conventions the value of endorsements undoubtedly depends on the degree to which delegates remain impervious to the blandishments of party notables and on the timing of the endorsements. Since as many as three-fifths (1993) to three-quarters (1990) of all delegates acknowledged that they had decided which candidate they were going to support *before* the delegate selection period began, it could be argued that there is a greater premium on endorsements from party notables in the earlier than in the latter part of the campaign.[31] On the other hand, endorsements made late in a campaign, especially if they are staggered over the final week or two, could be used to create an impression of momentum going into the voting in the hopes of winning over the remaining undecided delegates and of attracting second choice support from previously committed delegates in the event of a multi-ballot convention.

An endorsement by a notable, however arguable its actual impact might be, is part of the ritual of leadership politics. As symbolism is no less important in politics than in any other ritualized activity, this "laying on of hands" is a largely symbolic act intended to convey a sense of legitimacy to a candidate. An endorsement could range from an early public pronouncement of support in a widely publicized speech or a letter to delegates during the campaign, to a handshake, an embrace, or the donning of a hat or scarf on the convention floor. Whatever its form, the act means the same thing: public approval by one politician of another.

Two recent Conservative conventions, in 1976 and 1983, illustrate some of the variety of forms that endorsements have taken in Canada. Flora MacDonald's candidacy in 1976 earned widespread media and public attention because she was the first female to seek the national leadership of one of the two older parties.[32] Her gender became an issue in itself and provoked lively debates in the media and among delegates about whether or not the party and the country were "ready" for a female leader.[33] MacDonald was also hurt by the widely held perception in the party that her views on social policies and the role of government in promoting economic growth were far more left-of-centre and "Red Tory" than either the party or the country would accept. According to one of her key supporters, she was portrayed by her opponents as "practically sitting at the feet of Lenin and Mao Tse-tung."[34] To counter these criticisms, the tougher than expected economic and social policies that she championed during the leadership campaign were presented by her workers and organizers as evidence that she in fact held "traditional Tory beliefs" and was not too left-wing for the party.[35]

What helped to bring attention to her avowedly populist candidacy were the strong endorsements of two well-known figures in the party – Richard Hatfield, premier of New Brunswick, and David Crombie, mayor of Toronto. Neither man had an extensive network of contacts in the federal party, but both were electoral successes whose value to MacDonald's campaign derived primarily from their being on the party's left-of-centre wing. What really counted was that they had chosen MacDonald over fellow Red Tories seeking the leadership, Joe Clark and John Fraser. With additional support from Eddie Goodman, longtime Conservative backroom operative and member of Ontario's legendary Big Blue Machine who acted as her principal fund-raiser, MacDonald's campaign gained a measure of attention and credibility it almost certainly would not otherwise have had. Support from three prominent men of the party gave something akin to a political Good Housekeeping seal of approval to a candidate who otherwise might have been able to mount little more than a populist and marginal campaign.

Whether in the final analysis their support made any difference to MacDonald's first ballot vote is a moot point. A post-convention survey of the 1976 convention gives no data for sampling units as small as either Metropolitan Toronto or New Brunswick. But it does show that MacDonald did better than any of her ten opponents in Atlantic Canada, getting first ballot support from 21 per cent of the delegates from that region. Her strength there could be a measure of the influence that Hatfield, as a major force in the Conservative party in Atlantic Canada, had on the area's delegates. An equally plausible explanation is that in addition to whatever the benefit may have been from Hatfield's endorsement, MacDonald's first ballot vote reflected her popularity in the region as a native Nova Scotian and her close ties with many of the party activists throughout Atlantic Canada.[36]

In the event, MacDonald placed poorly on the first ballot (sixth of twelve) and withdrew after the second. Her candidacy is perhaps best remembered on another account. Estimates of supporters and opponents alike at the outset of the voting had shown MacDonald likely to get more votes (between 283 and 328) than she in fact received on the first ballot (214). It appeared that some delegates had lied to the candidate and her organizers about how they intended to vote in the secrecy of the ballot booth, which gave birth to a new term in the lexicon of Canadian politics: the "Flora Factor."[37] The endorsements and support that were given MacDonald by three established figures in the Tory party may have helped little in the voting booth. On the other hand, they undoubtedly raised her profile in the party and conveyed a measure of establishment approbation for her candidacy.

The contrast in Conservative caucus support for Brian Mulroney on the two occasions when he ran for the leadership was remarkable. In 1976 one of the reasons Mulroney's candidacy lacked a sense of legitimacy was because he had neither run for, nor served in, public office.[38] To some extent, at least, that would have been compensated for by a decent measure of support from the parliamentary caucus. That was not to be the case in 1976 when only three of the ninety-five Conservative MPs endorsed him. Seven years later Mulroney still had not sought elected office when he took his successful run at the national leadership. But this deficiency was made less glaring then by virtue of his having been endorsed by roughly one-quarter of the hundred-member parliamentary party, including the dean of the Tory caucus, George Hees, and the candidate whose withdrawal in Joe Clark's favour had created such a sensation at the 1976 convention, Sinclair Stevens. One of the stigmas of Mulroney's 1976 campaign had been that his lack of parliamentary experience was not offset by support from the very people with whom he would have had to work as leader, the Tory MPs. In 1983 the reasonable measure of parliamentary support Mulroney was able to generate effectively curtailed the obvious criticism that would otherwise have been levelled at him. In the words of a Mulroney biographer, the candidate in 1983 had secured "enough bodies from caucus to take the heat off."[39]

In the two conventions in which he sought the leadership, Joe Clark demonstrated that caucus support in and of itself is not critical, nor does it necessarily determine who will win the race. Like Mulroney, Clark had only a corporal's guard of supporters in the Tory caucus in 1976 going into the convention – just three MPs. Caucus endorsements for both Mulroney and Clark compared poorly with those for Claude Wagner and Paul Hellyer.[40] By contrast, Clark's position in 1983 was actually better than either Wagner's or Hellyer's had been in 1976. With fifty-three MPs and senators on his side, Clark had over twice the support in the Tory caucus that Mulroney had at the time. In addition to receiving endorsements from four of those he had defeated in the 1976 contest (Gillies, MacDonald, Fraser, and Grafftey) and two of the three parliamentarians who had supported Mulroney in 1976 (McGrath and Macquarrie), Clark also had the support of the three top candidates from the 1967 race (Stanfield, Roblin, and Fulton). It was an impressive array of notables, but in the event it counted for little as Mulroney, with a smaller and less distinguished array of parliamentarians on his side, captured the leadership.[41] Clark's victory in 1976 testifies to the fact that endorsements from more than a handful of parliamentarians at the outset of voting is not a necessary condition for a successful run at the leadership; his loss in 1983 demonstrates that strong caucus support is not a sufficient condition to win the leadership.

Parliamentarians may have lost much of the influence they once wielded over the leadership decision. Even so, their endorsements are much sought after by the candidates. Its principal value almost certainly resides in its capacity to give at least a measure of legitimacy to a candidate. If it is appropriately timed, as most of them are intended to be, an endorsement can help to keep a candidate's name in the news and, possibly, to sustain a degree of momentum. But in terms of gaining delegate votes, parliamentary notables have been surpassed in importance to leadership candidates by organizers and professionals skilled in the modern techniques of convention politics.

Organizers

To paraphrase Roberto Michels, "he who says modern leadership conventions, says organization." As recently as Lester Pearson's successful run at the Liberal leadership in 1958, candidates could win with little in the way of an organization. That has not been the case in the two older parties since they initiated the latest phase of conventions in the 1960s. No serious candidate could now mount a successful campaign without the men and women who, either as volunteers or as paid workers, bring to the campaign the organizational and managerial skills needed to create and to operate a large, dynamic, and relatively short-term political enterprise. Organizers usually do not have the professional training or expertise of the pollster, or the speech writer, or the policy adviser hired to perform specialized tasks for the candidate. But a seasoned political organizer has the experience and the practical knowledge to know who to recruit to do the polling, the speech writing, and the policy advising. A good organizer's skill is almost exclusively tactical, not strategic. Campaigns can flounder – Campbell's being a case in point – when those best suited to tactics start practising strategy. To put it another way, "the guy who makes the bus run on time doesn't always know where it should go next or why it should go there at all."[42]

For at least some organizers, including those with a strong sense of loyalty to the party, working for one candidate as opposed to another may be as much a business matter as it is a statement of preference. John Laschinger, billed as "Canada's only full-time professional political campaign manager," is one such person.[43] Known in Tory circles from the early 1970s when he became the party's national director, Laschinger has managed a total of thirteen federal and provincial Conservative leadership campaigns. His skills in planning and organizing campaigns, his practical knowledge of Canadian politics, and his network of Tory contacts combine to make him a top-notch organizer and to give his clients the assurance of a well-run campaign as well as an added measure of credibility with the delegates, the party, and the media. Martin, Gregg, and Perlin go so far as to suggest that Laschinger, then manager of John Crosbie's campaign, made as much as any other factor the difference between Crosbie's 639 votes and Wilson's 144 votes on the first ballot of the 1983 Tory convention.[44] For the majority, however, organizing is more of an avocation than a business. Jean-Yves Lortie, the legendary Quebec Tory organizer, falls into this category. "Some people collect stamps or hockey cards," said Lortie in an interview a few days before the 1993 convention, "I'm an organizer. I never took a cent from anyone or lobbied for a job or an honour. I'm in it for the fun. I just enjoy organizing, whether it's federal or municipal [political campaigns] or raising money for Christmas baskets for the needy."[45]

However their allegiance might be acquired, the importance to prospective leadership candidates of attracting the services of well-connected, experienced organizers can hardly be understated. Organizing a modern leadership campaign is an immense undertaking; they need to be built from scratch and up and running on very short notice. Thousands of decisions must be made. The candidate's tour must be organized; the activities of hundreds, if not thousands, of volunteers need to be managed; headquarters and provincial organizations need to be established; financing must be put in place; liaisons with the party, the media, and rival candidates must be maintained; delegate selection meetings must be contested; and the convention week delegate wooing sessions must be conducted in as effective a manner as possible. It takes a special talent to accomplish these tasks and a multitude of other, less visible ones as well. Turner and Mulroney acknowledged as much when they turned, respectively, to Bill Lee and John Thompson to bring needed experience and political savvy to their organization. With few exceptions, conventions are won through organization. Laschinger and Stevens define the role of a political organization as one of making "the big things achievable by getting the small things right."[46]

Recent conventions have shown the delegate selection stage to be the most important part of the leadership campaign. It is here more than at any other point that the race is won or lost. Organizers at the constituency or provincial level have two principal tasks: to ensure that supporters of their candidate are selected as delegates and, if they fail at this, to track, to contact, and to persuade delegates who are either undecided or who back another candidate to support their candidate if not on the first ballot, then on the second and subsequent ballots.

Organizers able to deliver delegate votes are, for obvious reasons, prized commodities much in demand by prospective leadership candidates. Such a person is Jean-Yves Lortie, who has been credited with delivering hundreds of delegates to his preferred candidate in each of the last three Tory conventions.

In 1976 Lortie was chief Quebec organizer for Claude Wagner. In the run-up to that convention Lortie reportedly "more than doubled the number of functioning riding associations [in Quebec], bringing it up to the full complement of 74. He also saw to it that the grassroots he was watering so abundantly were all of strong Wagner stock."[47] In those ridings in which he could not gain control of the executive he recruited new members to try to swamp the delegate selection meetings. Challenged by Brian Mulroney's candidacy in Quebec, Lortie's activity paid off. He was said to have delivered an estimated two-thirds of Quebec delegates to Wagner.[48]

Lortie made similar efforts in 1983, this time on behalf of Brian Mulroney when he took his second run at his party's leadership. Along with Roderique Pageau, Lortie spearheaded the Mulroney campaign in Quebec. In addition to engineering the selection of scores of pro-Mulroney riding delegates, the two were successful in gaining control of the Quebec provincial executive, the body that had the authority to recognize delegate selection meetings, to rule on the validity of delegates' credentials, and to appoint thirty-eight delegates-at-large. Ten years later Lortie was a key player in Kim Campbell's successful campaign. Responsible for the Campbell campaign in fifty of Quebec's seventy-five ridings, Lortie boasted a few days before the convention that he and another Quebec organizer controlled between two hundred and 250 delegates.[49]

Although most political organizers are local party apparatchiks who are quietly efficient and faceless to the general public, some of them are public figures who, by virtue of their prominence in the party or in their private careers, are political notables in their own right. Such individuals are ideally suited to serve leadership candidates as spin doctors or as "connectors" at the convention itself. On the convention floor, connectors are assigned to a particular candidate or candidates. Their job is to keep the lines of communication between the two campaigns open and, in the event their charge drops off the ballot, to deliver the candidate and as many of his or her delegates as possible. Former Newfoundland premier Frank Moores, one of Mulroney's key connectors with the Crosbie campaign in 1983, neatly summed up his responsibilities as to "shift bodies from one camp to the next."[50] It is also often the case that some of the best organizers in a party become, by virtue of their success at getting their candidate elected and of the subsequent largesse of a grateful prime minister, political notables as well. It is a measure of their value to leadership candidates that more than a few Tory and Liberal organizers and fund-raisers have found their way into the Senate or other patronage posts.

Professionals

If organizers can be said to be a part of a candidate's larger network because of their tactical skills, then professionals are brought in because of their understanding and knowledge of political strategies. In the campaign organization of every serious candidate seeking his or her party's leadership there must be several key workers whose experience, skills, and training qualify them for specialized tasks or for strategic planning. Drawn principally from the universities, media, lobbying, advertising, consulting, and polling firms, these are the professionals of a campaign. They are of basically two types. The first provides the tactical or operational assistance to the campaign, such as delegate tracking, polling, image consulting, and media training. The second offers the strategic advice for the larger game plan. Made up of political professionals, or "pols," the second group is expected to design the strategic framework for an effective campaign. Consisting of party insiders, that group might draw heavily on a candidate's personal network. Unlike the first group, it is composed overwhelmingly of unpaid volunteers – of friends and friends-of-friends – whose goal is to win the leadership for their candidate or, at a minimum, advance his or her career within the party.

Professionals with technical or tactical expertise to sell are for the most part hired contractually on a fee-for-service basis or loaned by their company for the duration of a leadership campaign. They may have no known prior connection with either the party or the candidate, but because their expertise is needed they are taken on by the organization for, in some cases at least, "handsome amounts" of money.[51] They may on occasion be active members of the party who are found to be attractive by the candidate because of some special skills or abilities they possess. Such was clearly the case, for instance, with Brian Mulroney's reliance on York University economics professor Charles McMillan as his policy and polling adviser in both 1976 and 1983. Described as "Mulroney's kind of intellectual," McMillan "did not shrink from the hardball of electoral politics, the kind of egghead who was not shocked by Mulroney's profanities."[52]

These professionals are the hired guns of politics. Their work obviously will vary in quality, and its impact on the campaign will relate directly to the weight attached to it by the strategic advisers surrounding the candidate. Media trainers, for example, can tell a candidate how to say something; they cannot tell him or her what to say. When they are allowed to, as was the case in Campbell's 1993 campaign, the result is a lack of focus and of consistent strategic planning. If there is any lesson to be learned from the plethora of conflicting advice, the inappropriate advisers, and the lack of internal discipline that marked the Campbell campaign, it is of the need to establish a strategic frame for a candidacy. Ensuring consistency in both strategy and messages remains one of the principal, but at the same time one of the most difficult, tasks of those at the top of any serious candidate's organization.

Professionals, particularly those with narrow or specialized interests, are part of a new breed of political participants. Once described by Tory backroom veteran and media consultant Nancy McLean as "mercenaries in a sea of missionaries," their expertise has been in increasing demand since the 1967 Conservative convention revolutionized leadership politics in Canada.[53] Each of the three principal candidates in that early contest (Stanfield, Roblin, and Fulton) had assembled as part of his organization a small group of experts in communications and polling. Although by more recent standards much of their work was amateurish and unsophisticated, its impact both at the convention itself and on future candidate organizations was immense. It showed what could be accomplished in everything from careful and intensive analysis and monitoring of delegates during the pre-convention campaign and on the convention floor to coordinated media and public relation campaigns similar to those of election campaigns.

One professional to have observed the innovative organizational structures put together by a number of the Conservative candidates for their 1967 leadership convention was T.J. Scanlon of the School of Journalism, Carleton University. As a communications expert, he advised the campaign team assembled by John Turner for his run at the Liberal leadership in 1968 about the important organizational and communications lessons to be learned from the successful Stanfield campaign of the previous year. Set out in a four-page, single-spaced confidential memo, the advice he offered to the Turner organization was simple: "It would be worth considering adapting Mr Stanfield's procedures to the forthcoming Liberal convention."

Scanlon's views are notable for the light they shed on the earliest example of a successful convention week and floor organization in the era of modern conventions. Fittingly, that organization was found to be based on the equally modern "media and environment" theory of Marshall McLuhan. As they gathered in Toronto in 1967 Tory delegates were seen by the Stanfield team as becoming a "part of a new convention environment." Accordingly, the Stanfield organization was designed to consist "almost entirely of delegates" and to give "an invalid but nonetheless impressive demonstration of growing Stanfield support" among delegates in the days leading up to the convention. For his part, Stanfield concentrated on appearances on the local news media so as to influence the information flowing to the delegates – an approach to information transferral that was supported by "sociological studies." For individual delegates voting at the convention itself, a number of "non-regional" delegate contacts were assigned to give "the impression that Stanfield support was strong" in various parts of the country. Reasoning that last-minute arrangements among candidates "would be far too hectic" to orchestrate once the voting began, the "Stanfield group made all arrangements with other candidates well in advance" of voting day.[54] (See Appendix 9-1 for the complete Memorandum.)

Such a document is no doubt similar to countless others written since 1967 by trained experts whose advice has been sought and whose services have been bought by candidates' organizations on matters within their professional competence. Campaign organizations now call on extra-party professionals to serve as policy advisers, image consultants, computer and communications experts, speech writers, layout and design consultants, pollsters, and the ubiquitous spin doctors. They may be employed in a campaign for only a short time, in order to deal with a specific issue or problem within their professional expertise. Occasionally they may even be assigned expensive and time-consuming, but basically pointless, tasks for no reason other than their professional expertise was thought to be needed by the campaign organization.[55] As the tools of the leadership convention trade have become more technologically sophisticated and as leadership campaigns have come to resemble election campaigns in scale and in expense, the professional's skills have come into demand. As Bradley F. O'Leary, then president of the American Association of Political Consultants, commented in 1987, "more money and more complication mean more consultants."[56]

Occasionally a consultant's influence on a candidate and on a campaign can be considerable, as was acknowledged to be the case with Mulroney and the man dubbed his "intellectual bodyguard," Charles McMillan.[57] To the extent that professional involvement in campaigns (whether leadership or election) amounts to a recognition that certain specialized skills are undoubtedly needed by candidates, the Conservative federal election campaign of 1993 serves as notice of the potential for disaster if professionals try to do too much in a campaign. In that campaign, Allan Gregg, the party's pollster and public opinion guru for over a decade, reportedly "crossed the line from pollster and became top strategist, ad designer, debates coach, and policy chief for Kim Campbell." Arguing that pollsters have become too powerful and too prominent, Gregg agreed that he had gone too far. "I've helped create a monster," he said in a post-election interview. "[Pollsters] are supposed to be cartographers, not drivers."[58]

Candidates in Canadian leadership races naturally attach considerable importance to their performance on the dominant communications medium, television. Some, at least, have employed professionals to help them to sharpen their delivery, to improve their performance, and to change their style. In 1993, for example, the Kim Campbell team turned to a professional image-maker for help after their candidate was judged to have performed poorly in the first two of five televised all-candidates' debates. A specialist in "training politicians and business leaders to appear more natural and intelligent in the media, especially on television" was hired. He supplied Campbell with advice on her debate performance, content, and style, as well as how to fit what she wanted to say into a "45-second groove."[59] No doubt many, if not all, of the major candidates in recent leadership campaigns were given some measure of professional help as they prepared to meet the television cameras.[60]

The role that experts have come to play in the politics of leadership selection, together with the money that it takes to hire many of them, has contributed to a leadership selection process that is "less party-centred and people-centred, more money-centred and professional." The words are Dalton Camp's, the man who more than any other was instrumental in launching the new, more technologically sophisticated and professional leadership convention system in 1967.[61] If the professionalization continues to define Canadian politics in the same way as it has American, Canada is in store for increasingly narrow aspects of election campaigns and leadership races being carved off by political consultants with their own sub-field of specialization. "Political consultantcy" has emerged as a growth industry in the United States in recent years, leading to the creation of a national association of consultants, a trade magazine, an annual conference, and other attributes of an established and institutionalized profession. The services now sold as a straight business proposition to American parties, candidates, and nominees regardless of political stripe or persuasion have become increasingly narrow and focused. The "Complete Guide to Political Products and Services" includes dozens of areas of professional expertise, ranging from law and financial accounting to narrowly defined media and polling specializations.[62]

There is a sense in which hired professionals are easier for leadership candidates to attract to their campaigns than party notables and organizers: all it takes is money. Merely by leafing through the yellow pages a candidate can find the professional expertise needed to join his or her team, although admittedly the number of political professionals in Canada is small and they are not always willing, or able, to work for a candidate. And if there is little team for them to join in the first instance, the money would be wasted. Experts help to round out a campaign organization; they do not make it. The other two structural elements of a solid campaign – networks and strategic planners – are equally critical to securing a party's leadership.

NETWORKS, ORGANIZATIONS, AND MODERN LEADERSHIP CAMPAIGNS

To mount a campaign for office, leadership candidates in pre-1967 contests relied on small networks of intra-party contacts, their own popularity and oratorical skills, a measure of favourable newspaper coverage, and pressure from supportive MPs on local delegates. That is no longer sufficient. Since the conventions of the 1960s, any candidate seriously attempting to win his or her party's leadership has had to put together an experienced and effective team of campaign and convention organizers. This meant relying on primary networks of close and trusted advisers as well as more distant friends-of-friends contacts. The endorsements of respected party notables were still widely sought by leadership hopefuls, but in isolation their value was not what it once was. Instead, as conventions became more expensive, more complicated, and more organizationally demanding, the need for paid organizers and professionals grew.

For basically the same reasons that the balance of power in leadership campaigns has shifted away from party notables and towards organizers and professionals, leadership campaign organizations have increasingly taken the form of hastily created bureaucracies. The scale of the enterprise and the large number of people involved require a formal and structured organization to be put in place. No two organizations will be identical, obviously, as each has different financial and human realities to deal with, different strengths to try to play to, and different networks to draw on. As certain functions must be performed by all serious campaigns with the necessary resources and professional support to create an elaborate campaign organization, it is possible to conceive of something approaching a standard "organization chart." A hypothetical organizational arrangement for a leadership campaign is given in Diagram 9-2.

The chart shows at its pinnacle a manager responsible directly to the candidate for the overall direction and management of the campaign.

Diagram 9-2
Leadership Campaign and Convention Organization Chart

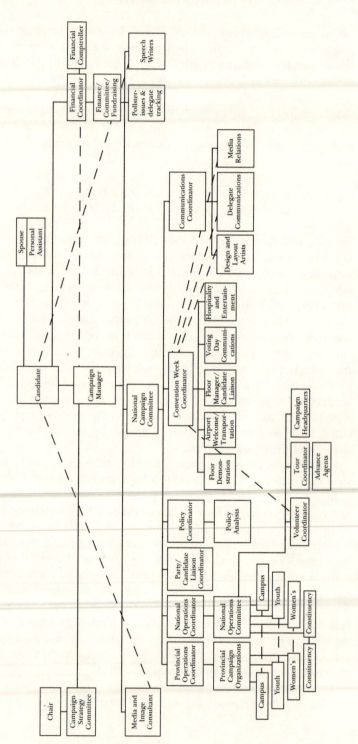

He or she is central to the planning and execution of the whole operation and is often part of the candidate's closest network of advisers and friends. One of the tasks of the campaign manager is to guard the candidate's time and to protect the candidate from the well-meaning people working on his or her behalf. This means ensuring that relatively few people have direct and unrestricted access to the candidate.

In a sense that task can be visualized (as in network theory) as ensuring that workers in the second, third or nth order are restricted in their access to the candidate by those in the first order. Another of the manager's principal responsibilities is to make certain that the total campaign effort is as effectively coordinated as possible. Without coordination, even the best volunteers and professionals could end up working at cross-purposes. A strategy committee, charged with planning the broad outline of the campaign, and expected to make the major decisions about the conduct of the campaign, is composed of the manager, a strategy chairman, and a small group of key strategists and advisers. The strategy committee reports to and advises the candidate through the manager. Fund-raising and financial control are under the direction of a financial coordinator, assisted by a small committee. They report directly to the candidate, for it is "ultimately the candidate who will have to arrange to pick up the tabs and pay the bills, and he or she needs to know what is happening financially."[63] The candidate's pollster, responsible for determining salient issues in the campaign and for tracking delegates, reports to the campaign manager. So do the media consultant and the speech writers, but naturally they have to be given access to the candidate.

At the operations level, the federal basis of the country is captured in a decentralized campaign structure designed to try to ensure the election of delegates favourably disposed to the candidate in the riding associations and in the campus, women's, and youth clubs. This is to be done through a provincial operations coordinator and campaign organizations in each of the provinces and territories.

For candidates with long-established contacts in the party (such as Chrétien as opposed to Campbell) that undoubtedly translates into converting personal networks into organizational ones at the provincial and local levels. A national operations coordinator, possibly the most important official on the operational side, chairs an operations committee and oversees the coordination of several essential activities. These range from maintaining active contacts with delegates, to ensuring that those brought into the organization to arrange the candidate's tour, to line up volunteers, to operate the campaign headquarters, and to coordinate the convention week and election day activities are doing what is expected of them.

The remaining operational responsibilities, like those handled by the provincial and national operations coordinators, are assigned to paid professional experts or skilled and knowledgeable volunteers seasoned with several years experience in the party. Principal among their tasks are policy coordination, liaison with the party over convention planning, budgeting and financial control, communications coordination, and media relations. Together with the campaign manager and the national and provincial operations coordinators, those responsible for the principal operational tasks make up the national campaign committee, the body charged with coordinating all campaign activities. When the leadership race moves from the campaign to the convention stage, the operations wing of the organization is folded into the convention week coordinator who, under the direction of the campaign manager, supervises the implementation of the last week's strategic and operational plans.

That, at least, is the theory. Practice is a very different story. In simple truth, "there is a wide divergence among candidate organizations. They range from the comprehensive, integrated and superbly effective to the fragmented, uncoordinated, and virtually nonexistent."[64] No one familiar with human behaviour in the context of an operational setting would expect an organization to run as smoothly and as rationally as a paper chart implies. According to John Laschinger, a wise candidate is one who accepts "that a certain amount of chaos is inevitable in a ramshackle organization, spread thinly from coast to coast, which by the end will encompass 500 to 1,500 individuals, the vast majority of them untrained volunteers who may be bursting with enthusiasm but who have everyday jobs and everyday lives to distract them."[65]

A sound organizational structure does not ignore the reality of human frailties. It tries to allow for them by channelling energies and expertise where they best belong and where individuals can do the most good. But that is a tall order in a leadership campaign, which understandably is assembled on short notice, works under constraints and pressures of time that have few parallels in the modern world outside politics, and tries to match professionals and volunteers with short-term jobs that are often ill-defined. Unless detected and dealt with in time, power struggles, personality conflicts, and plain incompetence can damage the whole effort irredeemably. Even a candidate's personal network of friends and party acquaintances is not immune to infighting and bickering.

We have seen that even candidates who have eventually gone on to win their leadership race have turned at some point during their campaign to seasoned organizational veterans to bring some measure of order out of chaos. Designed to accomplish a "single unambiguous goal" (which is to say, winning the party leadership), organizations appear on paper to be rational, goal-directed, and hierarchical. But in fact they are "often beset by major internal struggles."[66] It is at the stage of organizational chaos and of internal struggles that a candidate's personal network can prove invaluable. If it is vast and marked by a sense of deep loyalty to the candidate, it can make the difference between getting the organization into fighting shape and not. Like endorsements from notables, networks by themselves are not enough to win a leadership race. But neither are organizations if the operational chemistry is wrong. When both are strong and effectively mobilized, however, the candidate has passed one of the critical hurdles on the road to victory.

10 Who Wins?
Convention Coalitions

> Well, I did it. I voted for that son-of-a-bitch Mulroney – just to defeat Clark.
>
> — Disgruntled Crosbie delegate at the conclusion of the 1983 Tory Convention

One of the established facts of political science is that electoral outcomes are shaped by the institutional context within which voting takes place and the electoral system employed to choose the winner.[1] That has certainly been true of leadership conventions whose six basic rules have defined the institutional framework within which balloting has been conducted in Canada. The rules, essentially the same since 1919, are as follows:

- the ballot is secret and individual;
- the winner must have a clear majority of the valid votes cast;
- the low candidate(s) are eliminated if there is no winner on a ballot and any candidate may withdraw from the race between ballots;
- no new nominations are permitted between ballots;
- the candidates are not permitted to address the delegates once the balloting gets under way, but announcements declaring their elimination or withdrawal are read from the podium; and
- there is continuous voting with non-preferential ballots until a winner is declared.

The cumulative effect of these rules has been both to permit and encourage the formation of convention floor coalitions. Learning how and why voting coalitions have been formed in Canadian conventions helps us to understand better how a leadership contestant emerges as the winner on the final ballot of a multi-ballot convention.[2]

CANDIDATES, BALLOTS, AND
WINNER'S SHARE OF THE VOTE

It stands to reason that as the number of candidates seeking a party's leadership increases so too will the number of ballots. Races with more than two candidates will be over on one ballot, whereas those with several candidates will likely take more than one ballot to select a winner. It is reasonable as well to anticipate that as the number of ballots increases so too will the opportunities for creating two competing coalitions – both aimed at winning and at blocking the other. Thus it could be expected that the greater opportunities available to form competing coalitions in multi-candidate conventions will make for smaller winning margins on the final ballot than would be the case if the contest were settled on one or two ballots.

To examine these questions table 10-1 presents the number of ballots, number of first and final ballot candidates, and the eventual winner's share of the first and of the final ballot vote for the nineteen national leadership conventions held by the three older parties since 1919. Grouped according to the number of ballots needed to declare a winner, the table shows that an average of 3.2 candidates per convention contested the six single-ballot races and that the winner received an average vote of 68.3 per cent on the one and only ballot. The six conventions settled on two or three ballots averaged 5.3 candidates on the first ballot and 3.3 on the final one. In that set of contests the winner received an average of 43.7 per cent of the first ballot vote and 54 per cent of the final vote. For the seven conventions going either four or five ballots, an average of 8.1 candidates were nominated and 2.1 were on the final ballot. In that group of conventions the winner averaged 27.9 per cent of the first ballot vote and 55.3 per cent of the final vote.

These figures lend support to some of our expectations about the relationships among the number of candidates, number of ballots, and percentage of vote going to the winning candidate. Grouped by total number of ballots, the figures expressed in averages confirm that as the number of candidates increases so does the number of ballots needed to elect a majority winner. In addition, the winner's share of the first ballot vote varies inversely to the number of candidates on that ballot. The winner's share of the final ballot vote drops with the increase in the number of ballots from one to two or three ballots but changes marginally in the opposite direction once four or more ballots are needed to elect a leader. Looking at the data in table 10-1 in another way, at the twelve conventions with five or fewer candidates the eventual winners received an average of 62.7 per cent of the vote on the final ballot, whereas the winners of the seven conventions having more than five candidates garnered an average final ballot vote of only 52.7 per cent. Although the relationship is not a linear one, it is clear from these data that additional candidates tend to reduce the winner's share of the vote on the final ballot of the convention.

Table 10-2 shows the probability distribution of the number of ballots that a convention will last, given the initial number of candidates. It confirms a direct relationship between number of candidates and length of balloting. The data show that it is more likely that a convention with four candidates or less will be over on the first than on the second or third ballot. The probability of that happening is gradually reduced from a one-hundred-per-cent certainty with two candidates as each additional candidate enters the race. With three candidates, for example, a one-ballot contest is very likely (93 per cent) and with four candidates it is most likely (57 per cent), but it would not be surprising if a four-candidate race went to either two or three ballots (43 per cent). At the other extreme, once seven or more candidates are on the ballot there is not a chance of a one-ballot victory; instead there is a two-thirds probability that the convention will last at least four ballots. With nine or more candidates there is a 90 per cent or better chance of four or more ballots being needed to declare a winner.[3]

Multi-candidate conventions lasted longer and were marked by tighter finishes on the final ballot than those with only two or three candidates. This was almost certainly a result of the effect that additional candidates had on the initial ballot vote and on the gradual aggregation of votes over the remaining ballots. Additional candidates increase the likelihood of splitting the vote and of denying any candidate a majority vote at the outset. Evidence for this is found in the strong inverse relationship that exists between the number of candidates on the first ballot and the eventual winner's percentage of the vote on that ballot; every additional candidate on the first ballot decreased the eventual winner's share of votes on the first ballot by nearly 6 per cent on average.[4]

It is not surprising that more candidates translate into smaller initial votes for the eventual winner and that greater time is needed to declare a majority winner. A larger number of candidates suggests a party divided over its leadership, whereas fewer candidates indicate, if not the presence of a consensus choice or undisputed front runner for the leadership, at least a party less fragmented over its leadership transition and future direction. In a multi-candidate convention the increased number of ballots needed to dispose of the least acceptable candidates allows the delegates and the remaining candidates valuable time to form competing coalitions. Winning coalitions in multi-candidate and multi-ballot conventions as a rule gain little more than bare majorities on the final ballot. This is a measure of the difficulty in successfully parlaying a modest level of support on the first ballot into a majority of votes on the final ballot.

The coalitions formed around the Conservative candidates in 1976 will be examined more fully later, but at this point that convention serves as an illustration of the time and effort needed to construct a winning coalition. One would not have expected Joe Clark to have won easily or by a wide margin, since on the first ballot he trailed two other candidates and received the support of only 12 per cent of the delegates. The number of ballots needed to declare Clark the majority winner and the small margin of his victory reflected the party's divisiveness over its leadership and the time required to form major competing coalitions through successive ballots. Such evidence suggests a general observation: anything short of a clear front runner and consensus winner is likely to produce competing convention floor coalitions which are at once aimed at winning and at blocking one another and whose effect will be to prolong the voting and to make for a tighter finish.[5]

COALITION THEORY AND CANADIAN CONVENTIONS

Leadership conventions marked by several candidates and several ballots lend themselves to analysis by coalition theory. As each ballot has at least one less candidate than the previous one, and as successive votes are required until a majority winner is declared, the context within which the voting takes place is dynamic and new coalitions are formed around the candidates remaining on each ballot. For the purpose of this analysis, a convention coalition is defined as a discrete, loosely knit aggregate of individual delegates temporarily united through their common electoral support of a candidate. It describes a collection of individual delegates who with possibly different preferred outcomes at the beginning of the voting nonetheless for at least one ballot support the same candidate in an attempt either to maximize what they want out of the election or to minimize what they do not want.[6]

There is a vast literature on coalition formation in electoral and legislative politics which helps to inform an analysis of convention-floor voting in Canada.[7] From the theory of conflict of interest we learn that certain coalitions stand a greater chance of being formed than others. In a leadership contest all candidates and delegates differ from one another. No two are strictly alike in terms, let us say, of social and economic policy preferences. But it is equally true that some candidates and delegates have more in common with one another than with other candidates and delegates and "that members who vote together share common attitudes and interests."[8] Potential coalitions of individuals with compatible goals and preferences based on private benefits and ideological, strategic, and personal considerations are more likely to form and to last than other potential coalitions with greater conflict of interest among their members.

Robert Axelrod has explained the conflict of interest of a coalition as a product of its dispersion, connectedness, and size:

Suppose that the [candidates and their respective delegate supporters] are labeled A, B, C, D, E, F, and G in order of their positions from left to right on the policy dimension. In an ordinal policy dimension, the dispersion of the coalition consisting of ... A, B, and C cannot be compared to the dispersion of the coalition consisting of B, C, and D. However, the coalition consisting of ... A, B, and C is certain to be less dispersed that the coalition consisting of A, B, and D. For this reason, a coalition consisting of adjacent [candidates and their supporters], or a *connected coalition* as it can be called, tends to have relatively low dispersion and thus low conflict of interest for its size.

Of course, the property of a coalition's being connected does not take into account its total spread or dispersion. The coalition ABC has less dispersion than the coalition ABCD. Therefore ABC has less conflict of interest than ABCD, even though both coalitions are connected. Thus the size as well as the connectedness of a coalition affects its conflict of interest.[9]

The theory of conflict of interest is helpful in establishing the framework within which coalition formation in multi-ballot leadership conventions can be explained. So too are several other assumptions and terms common to social choice theory. Delegates and leadership contestants, like voters and candidates and parties competing for public office, are taken to be rational actors capable of ordering their preferences, voting transitively, and acting either sincerely or strategically to further their own interests. The convention floor decisions that delegates make about who to vote for on successive ballots, and that candidates make about whether to stay in the race or to pull out in someone else's favour, are made without either total or reliable information about how others will act. A measure of uncertainty characterizes a multi-ballot convention, particularly in the early ballots. As information gradually becomes more complete and more accurate with each successive ballot, explicable patterns of behaviour by delegates and candidates begin to emerge.

Delegates and candidates alike are knowledgeable people who are capable of making decisions in rapidly moving, dynamic situations.

They need not have contemplated appropriate actions for every particular combination of possibilities they might face following the first ballot. But they are sufficiently well informed and politically aware by the time the convention balloting begins to have established preference orderings of the various candidates and to know what their most preferred through to their least preferred outcome of the convention would be. This assumes that if they were asked to formulate their ordinal preference ordering of all the contestants, they could. But it is not to say that they necessarily follow them at all times. As voting proceeds in a multi-ballot convention, delegates may not cast a sincere vote and candidates may not try to construct an obvious coalition but chose instead to abandon their most preferred options by voting or coalescing strategically to try to block a less desired outcome.

The first piece of totally reliable, unfiltered, and unembellished information that delegates and candidates have to inform their decision-making on the convention floor comes with the announcement of the first ballot results. Polls, rumours, and speculation about who is ahead of whom and by how much now become a thing of the past. For all contests without a first ballot winner, the wheels of convention floor coalition formation are set in motion. In some cases, the process may last a sufficient number of ballots to enable the contenders to make a series of moves designed to construct a winning coalition. In all cases, delegates and candidates must consider their options based on what they have learned from the first round of voting. For the delegates, decisions must be made about staying with their initial choice (which obviously is an option only if the candidate remains in the race) or moving to another candidate. For candidates no longer in the running, decisions must be made about supporting another candidate or remaining uncommitted. For candidates still on the ballot, winning the support of delegates who had initially supported other candidates becomes an organizational imperative, as does consideration of the options about the course of action to follow after the next and subsequent ballots.

Since their four-ballot convention in 1968,[10] the Liberals have not had a convention suited to progressive coalition formation over several ballots. One leader was chosen on two ballots (1984) and another on a single ballot (1990). In 1984 John Turner was just a few percentage points short of a majority and was clearly heading to victory on the second ballot. The 1984 convention, described by Richard Johnston as "not given to high drama,"[11] was remarkable in one respect, however. It is the only recorded instance in a national convention at which three of the four first ballot candidates not on the second ballot (John Roberts, John Munro, and Eugene Whelan) openly supported a candidate on the second ballot (Jean Chrétien) who was obviously going to lose.

Of the four, only Mark MacGuigan backed the certain winner. The post-first ballot choices of the three candidates were clearly not risk-averse strategies. They were an early hint of the intra-party difficulties that Turner would later encounter during his time as Liberal leader. They also suggested that the intensity of their preference for Chrétien over Turner outweighed the incentive to support the obvious winner for whatever gains might have come their way.[12] Equally, Turner may have had little incentive to encourage them to join his coalition because he was virtually certain to win without their support. In Riker's terms, this can be explained as wanting to minimize the size of the winning coalition so as to maximize the benefits for the existing coalition members.[13]

The same is true of the hundreds of delegates at nearly every convention who voted on the final ballot for a candidate who was obviously going to lose, as was Clark in 1983, Chrétien in 1984, and Barrett in 1989. In addition to what has already been suggested, namely that some delegates would rather lose with a more-preferred candidate than win with a less-preferred one, the support by delegates of patently losing candidates can also be partly explained by the prior commitments delegates make and the intensity of those commitments. A majority of the delegates to recent conventions (81 per cent of Conservative delegates in 1983, 78 per cent of Liberal delegates in 1984, and 61 per cent of NDP delegates in 1989) reported making a commitment to vote for the candidate they supported on the first ballot.[14] Although there is no guarantee that all of the delegates honoured their commitments and voted accordingly, the evidence suggests that the majority did so. When the 1983 Conservative delegates were asked how committed they felt to their first choice, 89 per cent of Clark's supporters said "very," compared with 85 per cent of Mulroney's, 82 per cent of Crombie's, 80 per cent of Crosbie's, and 69 per cent of Wilson's.[15] Part of the reason why Clark's support did not evaporate on the fourth ballot in 1983 was the high degree of loyalty he commanded from his supporters. Of those 1989 NDP delegates who had made a commitment to a candidate, 83 per cent said they were committed for as long as the candidate was still in the race.[16] The evidence suggests that commitments and their intensity and duration help to account for the failure of all delegates to flock to the obvious winner on the final ballot. It also helps to explain why final-ballot coalitions of obvious winners are smaller than might otherwise be the case.

Let us see how coalition and social choice theories help to explain the outcome of two of the most recent national leadership conventions to have gone beyond two ballots – the Conservative conventions of 1976 and 1983.

The 1976 Conservative Convention

The 1976 candidates have been placed on a "Left-Right" socio-economic scale as follows: [17]

MacDonald Clark Fraser Grafftey Gillies Mulroney Nowlan Stevens Wagner Hellyer Horner

Within minutes of the announcement of the first ballot results (see table 2-11) Grafftey (who was eliminated from the vote) and Gillies (who withdrew) declared their support for Clark. Their choice of the third over the second-place contender could not have been predicted in terms of sincere preferences, given the points on the spectrum that the candidates occupied. Instead, their endorsement of Clark combined policy preferences with strategic calculations. Although Grafftey was closest to Fraser and Gillies nearest to Mulroney, both clearly chose to help to create a centre-left proto-coalition around the candidate they felt had the greatest chance of beating the centre-right. Stevens, to the surprise of the party's right-of-centre faction, joined the camp assembling around Clark. He explained his move solely on non-ideological grounds: "I like Joe's style. I think we can win with him."[18] All three candidates joining forces around Clark could be said to have moved when they did and where they did to create early momentum for Clark and to demonstrate that he was the candidate with the greatest potential to defeat the party's right-of-centre.

The end of the second ballot saw the candidates who had been eliminated or who had withdrawn move in the following directions: Flora MacDonald and Fraser to the alliance forming around Clark, and Horner, Hellyer, and Nowlan to the right-of-centre candidate still in the lead after two ballots, Wagner. Mulroney, located more or less at the centre of the all-candidate spectrum, gained no coalition partners and benefited little from the delegates' votes freed with the progressive elimination or withdrawal of other candidates. Overtaken as the second-placed candidate by Clark on the second ballot, Mulroney chose to keep his name in despite overtures from both wings of the party seeking his withdrawal and endorsement. Eliminated on the third ballot, Mulroney issued no instructions to his supporters and endorsed neither of the two remaining candidates. The fourth ballot brought the multi-ballot race down to a contest between two more-or-less evenly supported and centrifugally created coalitions. Clark won with 1,187 votes to Wagner's 1,122.

How do delegates deal with the various changes taking place and alliances being formed in such a highly charged and dynamic situation? Let us try to answer that by looking at one hypothetical delegate with the following preference ordering of the candidates based on a composite of ideological, strategic, private benefits, and personal considerations:

Candidates and Ranking of Individual Delegate	First Ballot Vote and Ranking of all Candidates	
1 Gillies	87	(9)
2 Stevens	182	(7)
3 Hellyer	231	(5)
4 Mulroney	357	(2)
5 Clark	277	(3)
6 Horner	235	(4)
7 Wagner	531	(1)
8 MacDonald	214	(6)
9 Fraser	127	(8)
10 Nowlan	86	(10)
11 Grafftey	33	(11)

Learning after the first ballot that Gillies and Stevens have both withdrawn in Clark's favour, the delegate must decide whether it is preferable on the second ballot to vote for his or her next ranked candidate, Hellyer, or to shift to someone else. A vote for Hellyer would be a *sincere* vote in the sense that that would be the delegate's next highest-ranked preference. To vote for another candidate at that point would violate the delegate's preference ordering. But that could nonetheless be justified by the delegate on *strategic* grounds if it was seen as a way of making it more difficult for those even lower on the preference scale to win. The delegate's actions, whether sincere or strategic, would be determined largely by the *intensity* of the delegate's feelings in relation to his or her ranked preferences.[19]

Let us assume the delegate chooses on the second round to support either Hellyer (a sincere choice) or Mulroney (a strategic one) then learns following the announcement of the second ballot results that Hellyer has lost half of his supporters and that Mulroney's growth of sixty-two votes fell well behind Clark's of 255. Having overtaken Mulroney as the second-place candidate, Clark is clearly the candidate around whom the anti-Wagner coalition is forming. With that information, the delegate would almost certainly chose to support his fifth preference over his seventh on the subsequent ballots and stick with Clark for the remainder of the balloting.

Uncertainty about how others are going to vote makes the individual delegate's job of deciding how to vote more difficult than it would be otherwise. In McGregor's terms, "the convention itself produces the dilemma of uncertainty affecting leaders and followers alike: *discovering who everyone else thinks the winner will be.*"[20] But the magnitude of the problem diminishes as the results of successive ballots become known. Our imaginary delegate can learn valuable information from the shifts that have taken place in the ranking and in support of the candidates *between* the first and the second ballot in 1976. For all intents and purposes, Mulroney was out of the race going into the third ballot. Clark's gains from the first to the second ballot had ensured that. That piece of valuable information provides a clue as to how delegates will act subsequent to the second ballot. Multi-ballot contests with a large number of candidates give delegates the opportunity to become part of a coalition constructed between ballots and to employ strategies aimed at maximizing the likelihood of a preferred outcome and at blocking a less desired outcome. Delegates take the information provided by successive ballots and assess the prospects of one candidate defeating another in relation to their own ordered preferences.

The 1983 Conservative Convention

After the first ballot of the 1983 Conservative convention (see table 2-12) two candidates, Brian Mulroney and to a lesser extent John Crosbie, were poised to benefit from the anti-Joe Clark sentiments that permeated the convention. Those party to the "Anybody But Clark" (ABC) movement were strong, vocal, hostile and determined to back either of the other two major front runners in the hope of beating the man they regarded as no longer fit for the job. Clark did not have a chance against such determined opponents, particularly as they had three ballots to agree, so to speak, on the candidate most capable of defeating him.

For the purposes of this analysis the relative positioning of the eight candidates in 1983 on a left-right spectrum has been established as follows:

Crombie   Clark   Crosbie   Mulroney   Wilson   Fraser   Gamble   Pocklington

The interval between the first and the second ballot witnessed the early stages of the stop-Clark movement as those candidates who were eliminated from the race or who withdrew voluntarily moved to create a right-of-Clark coalition. John Gamble and Neil Fraser (both fringe candidates who were automatically eliminated from the race) quickly moved to support third-place candidate John Crosbie.[21] The moves of Michael Wilson and Peter Pocklington, both of whom withdrew from the race in favour of the second-place candidate Brian Mulroney, can be explained as ideologically sincere, given the options available to them and their location on the spectrum. But for both candidates strategic considerations were every bit as important in determining their actions.

Both Wilson and Pocklington were anxious to create a stop-Clark coalition. Their strategy was to use the information provided by the first ballot results to determine which candidate, Mulroney or Crosbie, had the better chance of overtaking Clark and then to yield in his favour. The choice, made as it was in the dynamic atmosphere of the convention and with the knowledge of polls which indicated that Crosbie was the more popular second choice of the delegates, was for Wilson and Pocklington "based on simple arithmetic."[22] "It was simply the numbers," said Michael Perik, Wilson's campaign manager. "[Patrick] Kinsella and I looked at the numbers and came to the conclusion that we had to move quickly to stop Joe Clark. The way to do that was to go to Brian Mulroney."[23] For his part, Pocklington made the same calculation and came to the same conclusion. "We have no preference between Mulroney and Crosbie," said his campaign manager Skip Willis two days before voting day. "We will go to the clear leader. My guess is with the numbers, that will be with Brian."[24] Martin, Gregg, and Perlin relate that "because of Crosbie's greater growth potential, Pocklington was prepared to spot him a number of votes ... Pocklington and his advisors agreed that 200 would be the cut-off point. If Mulroney's vote exceeded Crosbie's by more than 200, then they would consider the Newfoundlander out of contention."[25]

To the ideological left of the other candidates, David Crombie elected to stay on after the first ballot despite his poorer than expected showing.[26] The most significant consequence of Crombie's decision was that Crosbie, who would then have been the lowest of three remaining candidates, avoided elimination on the second ballot. Although it is unclear whether Crombie deliberately stayed on for the second ballot in order to ensure Crosbie's remaining a contender on the third, that was the effect of his decision. He may have been convinced that the greater the number of ballots, the greater the likelihood of defeating Clark and the greater the likelihood of the anti-Clark coalition being formed around Crosbie. In any case, Crombie did in fact endorse Crosbie after the second ballot results were announced. His choice cannot be explained on ideological grounds, for Crombie was widely seen in the party to be to the left of Clark. Nor can it be explained by an overriding desire to participate in the creation of the winning anti-Clark coalition, for the second ballot results confirmed that that was forming around Mulroney not Crosbie. Instead his moves must be seen as reflecting strategic and personal preferences together with a greater ideological affinity with Crosbie than Mulroney.[27]

Mulroney's second-place showing on the first ballot, 217 votes behind Clark and 235 ahead of Crosbie, put him in an excellent position to become the focus of a coalition formed to Clark's right. On the second ballot, Mulroney rose to within sixty-four votes of Clark (whose support actually declined by six votes) and increased marginally the spread between himself and Crosbie to 240 votes. Mulroney's strong showing on the first ballot and his subsequent gains from the first to the second ballot led to the primary anti-Clark coalition forming around his candidacy. It was evident from the second ballot results that Clark's support had foundered and that he was unlikely to win. The third ballot eliminated Crosbie from the race and saw Mulroney edge to within twenty-two votes of Clark. Although, like Mulroney in 1976, Crosbie did not endorse either of the two candidates remaining on the final ballot, his supporters sided with Mulroney over Clark by a margin of approximately two to one, thereby completing the anti-Clark coalition and delivering the leadership to the Quebecker.

What choices faced the Conservative delegate who had ordered his or her preferences in the following way and how might they be explained? And in light of these preferences, how might that delegate have responded to the valuable information provided in the form of results of the successive ballots?

Candidates and Ranking of Individual Delegate	First Ballot Vote and Ranking of all Candidates	
1 Wilson	144	(4)
2 Crosbie	639	(2)
3 Mulroney	874	(3)
4 Crombie	116	(4)
5 Clark	1,091	(1)
6 Pocklington	102	(6)
7 Gamble	17	(7)
8 Fraser	5	(8)

Once again, the delegate's decision whether to vote sincerely according to his or her preference ordering or to violate the ordering and to vote strategically depends primarily on the intensity of the preferences and on the information provided by the first ballot results. Two conditions must be satisfied before the delegate would violate the preference ordering. Taking the top three candidates in order of the delegate's preferences – Crosbie, Mulroney, then Clark – the delegate would vote for Mulroney only if: (a) Clark had some prospect of winning; and (b) Mulroney's prospects of defeating Clark were better than Crosbie's. The information provided by the first ballot was crucial in this determination. Clark *was* leading by a sizable margin and Mulroney *was* in the best position to defeat Clark, a position that was enhanced further by Wilson's and Pocklington's endorsements of him after the first ballot. For a delegate determined to stop Clark, the best and safest course of action would be to "go with the numbers" and vote for Mulroney. Equally, if the delegate's antipathy to Clark was less intense, then opting to stick to the original preference ranking by supporting Crosbie would make sense.

Whichever of these choices the delegate makes on the second ballot, the information provided by the second ballot results would, from one perspective, likely have done little to cause the delegate to sway from that choice. Clark's support had peaked and he appeared to have little chance of winning. At the same time, the contest seemed certain to last two more ballots. Those anti-Clark delegates who had voted for Crosbie on the second round had no need to rush to Mulroney on the third ballot in order to ensure Clark's defeat. On the other hand, Crosbie had failed to make any gains on Mulroney and seemed destined for elimination on the third ballot. A benefit-maximizing delegate would likely seize this opportunity to jump on the Mulroney bandwagon in order to be on the winning side as early as possible. Regardless of the delegate's choice on the third ballot, he or she would almost certainly arrive in the Mulroney camp on the fourth and deciding ballot.[28]

The winning coalition that formed around Brian Mulroney in 1983 shared several characteristics with the winning coalition that formed around Joe Clark in 1976. Both were, to an extent, ideological coalitions. In 1976 the left-of-centre coalition won. In 1983 a centre-right coalition won. Both coalitions could also be considered to be "stop" campaigns. A large part of the reason Clark won in 1976 was that a sizable proportion of the delegates were determined to stop Claude Wagner. An even larger part of the reason Mulroney won in 1983 was that many delegates were determined to defeat Joe Clark. In Perlin's 1983 pre-convention survey, the delegates were asked to name any and all candidates for whom they would *not* vote under any circumstances at the convention. The data reveal that Mulroney was found objectionable by as many delegates as was Clark. Fully 21 and 20 per cent of the delegates declared that they would never vote for Mulroney and Clark respectively. How then was Mulroney able to capitalize on the anti-Clark sentiment throughout the successive ballots while Clark failed to realize any increase in support from the first to the third ballot?

As Martin, Gregg and Perlin point out and as the data in table 10-3 confirm, "the Anyone But Mulroney sentiment [in 1983] was as real and large as the Anyone But Clark feelings, the major difference was that the Anyone But Mulroney camp was housed almost exclusively in the Clark delegation, while the ABC movement was spread throughout the convention."[29] Nearly four out of every five delegates (79 per cent) who wanted someone other than Mulroney as leader suggested Clark on the first ballot. Mulroney enjoyed the first ballot support of slightly more than half of those who wanted someone other than Clark – twice the figure of the next strongest candidate, Crosbie. Clearly, Clark had little opportunity to grow on the "Anyone But" dimension, whereas Mulroney could only benefit from the general elimination or withdrawal of candidates whose first ballot supporters did not want Clark as leader.

All of Clark's challengers were motivated, albeit to varying degrees, by a desire to defeat the former leader. The survey data show that the ABC movement was most significant in the vote shifts from the first to the second ballot. When the delegates who changed their vote after the first ballot were asked what reasons were most influential in their new choice, the most frequently cited reason was a desire to defeat Clark. This was given by fully 47 per cent of the respondents. In comparison, only 6 per cent cited the ABM coalition. Neither factor was very significant from the second to the third ballot. The ABC movement re-emerged on the fourth ballot as 16 per cent of those who changed their vote after the third ballot (overwhelmingly former Crosbie supporters) indicated a desire to defeat Clark as the most influential reason for their new choice.[30] The moves of candidates and delegates over the course of the four ballots demonstrated the overt execution of deliberate, but opposing, blocking strategies aimed at awarding or denying the leadership to one of two competing camps.

WHAT DO CANDIDATE ENDORSEMENTS MEAN?

Professors Krause and LeDuc have observed that "the convention behaviour of candidates themselves strongly suggests that they believe combinations of candidate support to be important ... Each convention seems to offer at least some surface evidence to support this contention."[31] Unlike earlier multi-ballot American nominating conventions in which blocs of delegate votes were under the control of factional leaders and candidates, the institutional context within which Canadian delegates have voted has been largely defined by the substantial degree of freedom that delegates enjoy. Once a delegate's prior commitments (as part of a local slate, for example) have been fulfilled or disregarded, that individual becomes a free agent, well-placed to exercise independent judgment about the best option to pursue. In that context the coalition theory assumption of rational delegates who vote either sincerely or strategically according to their preferences and the intensity of their preferences is particularly apt.

Such a potentially fluid and relatively unorchestrated setting as a Canadian convention gives rise to the obvious question about the ability of candidates to deliver their votes to the candidates of their choice and the related question about the post-endorsement behaviour of a candidate's supporters. Can a retiring candidate who chooses to indicate a preference for another candidate legitimately claim or expect to be able to deliver his or her supporters en masse to that person? To what extent do delegates follow the lead of those for whom they have voted? In other words, what do candidate endorsements mean?

From coalition theory we know that we can expect studies of convention delegate voting behaviour to demonstrate that some candidate liaisons are more likely to form than others. Certain combinations of support are more natural than others, "particularly where they reflect pre-existing ideological, regional or intra-party cleavages."[32] Natural combinations have less inherent conflict of interest than unnatural ones. Survey research data from two multi-ballot conventions (1976 and 1983) demonstrate that natural coalitions have translated into larger shifts of delegates from endorsing to endorsed candidates than those which have cut across cleavages. They have also shown that successful unnatural ones have occasionally been formed and that several attempts at forming natural alliances have not succeeded. For purposes of this analysis, an arbitrary, but not unreasonable, threshold level has been established to judge the success of a transfer of support: at least 70 per cent of an endorsing candidate's first ballot voters must support the endorsed candidate on the final ballot for the transaction to be considered successful.

Table 10-4 reveals how the first ballot supporters of the various candidates in 1976 voted on the fourth ballot. Some of the endorsements, such as those by MacDonald and Gillies of Clark, were ideologically natural and were accompanied by massive shifts of support from the retiring to the recipient candidate. Ninety-three per cent of MacDonald's and 85 per cent of Gillies' first ballot voters ended up with Clark on the fourth ballot. Other attempts at transferring support to natural allies, notably those by Grafftey and Fraser to Clark or by Hellyer and Nowlan to Wagner, were less successful. Their first to final ballot transfers to their endorsed candidate ranged from between 43 and 60 per cent of their first ballot voters. Stevens's surprise endorsement of Clark created an "unnatural alliance"[33] in that Stevens was considered to be on the right and Clark on the left of the party. Nonetheless, with an eventual transfer of 70 per cent of Stevens voters to Clark it was clear that Stevens's choice had the approval of a substantial number of his early supporters. It ranked as the third most successful candidate linkage in that convention.

Table 10-5 shows the shifts in delegate support across the four ballots of the 1983 Conservative convention. Fully half of Wilson's and Pocklington's first ballot supporters went to Mulroney on the second ballot, and by the final ballot 90 per cent of Pocklington's first ballot supporters and 73 per cent of Wilson's were voting for Mulroney.[34] On the second ballot Crosbie too had been a major beneficiary of their withdrawal, gaining as many Pocklington supporters as Mulroney and winning seven Wilson voters for every ten who went to Mulroney. Coming, as it did, in the face of the endorsements of Mulroney by the two retired candidates, Crosbie's impressive second ballot gains from Wilson and Pocklington call into question the ability of candidates to convince a majority of their supporters to accept their preferred candidate at an early stage of the balloting when their delegates are presented with two attractive possible alternatives.

As with Stevens's endorsement of Clark in 1976, Crombie's selection of Crosbie in 1983 constituted a unnatural alliance. He by-passed endorsing the front runner at that point and the man with whom he shared the greatest ideological affinity, Clark, in order to support the second-ranked of the two principal Clark challengers. Fifty-five per cent of Crombie's second ballot supporters agreed with his choice and voted for Crosbie on the third ballot. Thirty per cent favoured Clark, but only 15 per cent chose Mulroney. Given the strategic context within which third ballot votes were cast and the wide dispersion of Crombie defectors following the first ballot, these are remarkable figures. The considerable slippage Crombie experienced from the first to the second ballots had been more or less evenly distributed among the other three candidates, but Clark had received the largest share of it. Over half of Crombie's second ballot supporters voted for his recommended choice, which suggests that Crombie's endorsement carried considerable weight with those who had continued to support him. Still, at 55 per cent it cannot be judged to have been a successful linkage.

The coalitions formed in the multi-ballot conventions of 1976 and 1983 highlight some of the lessons to be drawn from candidate endorsements. They also underscore the importance of avoiding a simple causal explanation between candidate endorsement and delegate behaviour. MacDonald's choice of Clark over all other remaining candidates after the second ballot was ideologically natural. Both candidates shared similar views of economic and social affairs and each was widely known to have preferred the other over any other candidates in the event of defeat or withdrawal. That such an overwhelming share of MacDonald's first ballot supporters chose her preferred candidate on the final ballot suggests the presence of at least three conditions in the MacDonald camp, from which a more general proposition about transferability of support from one candidate to another might be derived. Endorsements will meet with their greatest measurable success when there is an intense loyalty to the departing candidate, a shared preference ordering between that candidate and his or her supporters, and an ideological affinity between the endorsing and the recipient candidates. Pocklington's endorsement of Mulroney in 1983 falls into this category. Although it had an additional ballot in which to be completed and was more complicated at the outset by the presence of two different beneficiaries of Pocklington's withdrawal, it was eventually as successful as MacDonald's endorsement of Clark in 1976.

Though natural, the Fraser, Grafftey, Hellyer, Horner, and Nowlan endorsements were not successful. In contrast to those of MacDonald, Gillies, Wilson, and Pocklington they signified weaker delegate loyalties to their first ballot choice, more diverse preference orderings by their delegates, and less ideological affinity between the candidates and their first ballot supporters. For many candidates in this group the first ballot vote they had received was less an indication of delegate true preferences than of support for a regional "favourite son," or an expression of thanks for "service to the party," or acknowledgment of a strong "convention performance."[35]

The sizable transfer figure among supporters of Stevens on the first ballot to Clark on the fourth implies sufficient supporter loyalty to the departing candidate and agreement between the strategic considerations of the candidate and his first ballot supporters to discount the ideological distance between the two candidates. Crombie's move to Crosbie in 1983 did not match the level of success of Stevens's move to Clark in 1976. The timing and direction of Crombie's endorsement of Crosbie no doubt helped to account for its lower success rate. It came one ballot later than Stevens's and was given to a candidate who at that point had little realistic chance of making it onto the final ballot.

Some endorsed alliances are natural and ultimately successful in bringing together substantial numbers of voters from previously competing camps. Others are not. This was confirmed by the 1976 and 1983 cases when the level of success of an endorsement-produced alliance undoubtedly rested on the the degree of delegate loyalty to a retiring candidate, the extent to which preferences were shared, and the ideological fit between endorsing and endorsed candidates and their supporters. But none of this proves that endorsements make a difference. As Krause and LeDuc conclude, "the hypothesis that candidate endorsements are a significant factor in convention political behaviour can never be conclusively 'proven,' but the evidence makes rejection of it impossible."[36]

A candidate's endorsement may be of little consequence.[37] It may do little more than reinforce the obvious – that the vast majority of a retired candidate's supporters intend to move to a particular candi-

date regardless of the retiring candidate's views. In such a case the retired candidate may have few credible options short of adopting the
opinion of the nineteenth century French politician, Ledru-Rollin:
"There go my people and I must follow them for I am their leader." In
other instances a candidate's endorsement carries little weight with his
previous supporters because of the poor fit between their respective
preference orderings. In still other cases the closeness of fit makes the
candidate's endorsement redundant.

Whatever the situation, it would be wrong to conclude that retiring
or defeated candidates can deliver voters to whomever they choose. So
much depends on the timing of the declaration, the organizational
abilities of the endorsing and endorsed candidate's workers, the delegates' reasons for supporting or not supporting particular candidates,
the loyalty of delegates to a candidate, and the weight they accord to
his expressed views in relation to all the other considerations they must
take into account. To candidates and delegates alike, candidate endorsements are prima facie a sign of momentum. The real test of momentum lies in the results of the subsequent ballots as the delegates act
on the options available to them in light of their preferences. As alternatives are ranked by individuals, not by groups or leaders, the extent
to which preferences of individual supporters of a retiring candidate
coincide is the most significant determinant of the electoral cohesive-
ness of that group on subsequent ballots.

CONVENTIONS AND
SOCIAL CHOICE THEORY

The optimal outcome of a convention is the selection as leader of the
most-preferred candidate of the delegates. Yet the logic of social
choice theory has established that in a multi-candidate race there exists no voting rule that will ensure that the most-preferred candidate is
elected. The selection of a winner may be influenced as much by the
manner in which the preferences are aggregated as by the preferences
themselves.[38] There is always the chance that the voting rules and the
voters' preferences will interact to produce a winner who is considered by a majority of voters to be inferior to another alternative. In
the aftermath of Mulroney's victory at the 1983 Conservative convention there ensued a debate among political scientists over the role
played by the rules in place for that convention in shaping the outcome of the contest.

Without empirical data, but using not unreasonable assumptions of
the delegates' preferences, Terrence Levesque suggested that the convention rules, in particular the rule that required the elimination of the

candidate receiving the lowest number of votes on a ballot, "probably" resulted in the selection of a winner (Mulroney) who was considered by a majority of voters to be inferior to another alternative (Crosbie). Going largely on the basis of Crosbie's apparently strong second preference support, Levesque maintained that had Crosbie been on the final ballot he would have won whether his opponent had been Mulroney or Clark. To Levesque, the delegates' preferences were prevented from taking effect in Crosbie's selection as leader because, as the low man on the third ballot, he was eliminated from the race.[39]

In response to Levesque, Peter Woolstencroft argued that "the retroactive application of various choice rules is a form of abstracted empiricism that neglects the linkages between institutional contexts and behaviour." Clearly, every election requires one decision rule or another and the candidates and the voters must be aware of them. This being so, both the candidates and the voters will premise their strategies and tactics on the rules in place. According to this line of reasoning, any attempt to apply retroactively a different set of rules to the exhibited behaviour of the candidates and voters is a flawed exercise because their behaviour may well have been different had different rules been in place. To Woolstencroft, therefore, the rules of the convention played an integral, determinative role in the behaviour of the candidates and the delegates as they selected the leader.[40]

George Perlin refuted Levesque's contention that Crosbie was the most preferred candidate in 1983. Perlin found that although Crosbie was widely acceptable to delegates as a second choice, he "was not as widely acceptable to Clark delegates as to Mulroney delegates." In the post-convention survey, Tory delegates were asked for whom they would have voted had Crosbie been on the final ballot. The delegates' responses to this hypothetical situation confirmed that although Crosbie would have prevailed against Clark (by a margin of 52 to 45 per cent), he would have been defeated by Mulroney by a margin of 54 to 40 per cent. One could speculate that the reasons behind the Clark delegates' preference for Mulroney over Crosbie derived from Mulroney's bilingualism and his presumed appeal to Quebec. Perlin concluded that, given the delegates' preferences, the rules in place in 1983 produced an optimal winner in Brian Mulroney. They did, however, alter the standings of the second and third most preferred candidates on the third ballot and prevented the second most preferred candidate (Crosbie) from reaching the final ballot.[41]

Keith Archer reached a similar conclusion in his examination of the 1989 NDP convention. Relying on delegate survey data, he found that McLaughlin would have easily defeated every other candidate in a series of two-person contests. He also found that Langdon, who was eliminated after the third ballot, would have defeated Barrett in a two-person contest. He concluded from this that, "contrary to the results of the third ballot, which placed McLaughlin first, Barrett second and Langdon third, in fact the delegates' preference ordering placed Langdon ahead of Barrett." The delegates' preference ordering was prevented from being accurately reflected in the results of the third ballot because of the distribution of second preferences. Just as Crosbie had more second preference support among the Mulroney delegates than among the Clark delegates in 1983, in 1989 Langdon had more second preference support among the McLaughlin delegates than among those supporting Barrett. And since McLaughlin was in a better position to win than Langdon, these delegates had no reason to shift their support to him.[42]

POSTDICTING COALITION WINNERS

Until 1976 it was a truism of Canadian national leadership conventions that the candidate who led on the first ballot of a multi-ballot race went on to win on the final ballot[43] (see table 10-6). In the Tory convention of that year the third-placed candidate on the first ballot became the eventual winner on the fourth. Clark was undoubtedly helped by the large number of candidates in the race (twelve) and by the large number of candidates who went his way after the first ballot (three). But equally important was the momentum created by his sizable gains from the first to the second ballot and the impression this was bound to make on delegates that his was the only candidacy of the centre-left with a chance of defeating the centre-right. His support had all but doubled and he had gained the largest share of votes of any candidate between the first two ballots. To delegates whose preference ordering placed Clark ahead of Wagner, Clark would be the obvious candidate to support. Equally, the reverse would hold for those who preferred Wagner to Clark. For them, stopping Clark meant voting for Wagner. By the end of the second ballot the coalitions had begun to form around the almost certain protagonists of the final ballot.

Clark's experience in 1976 suggests a testable hypothesis: the candidate who gains the largest share of the votes from the first to the second ballot will become the eventual winner.[44] This is confirmed in seven of the eight conventions that have lasted three or more ballots. Only in the NDP convention of 1989 did the candidate who had gained the largest share of the vote from the first to the second ballot fail to go on to eventual victory. Barrett, the 1989 predicted winner on that measure, had increased his first to second ballot tally by 214 votes to McLaughlin's 183.[45] The alternative hypothesis – that the candidate who leads on the first ballot eventually wins on the final one – is satisfied in eleven of the thirteen instances of conventions going to two or more ballots. The only exceptions came from Clark's two runs at the Tory leadership.

Between them, the two alternative explanations capture all thirteen national conventions of two or more ballots. For each of the five conventions that were over on the second ballot, whoever led on the first one went on to win. But only in 1927 and 1942 did the winner also get the greatest increase from the first to the second ballot. In five of the eight multi-ballot conventions, the final ballot winner combined a first ballot lead with the greatest growth in first to second ballot support. Only in the 1976 and 1983 Tory and 1989 NDP conventions was a leader chosen who met only one of the alternate tests.

Both explanations capture two key components of coalition multi-ballot conventions. One is the capacity of candidates and delegates to create a coalition either going into the convention or between the early ballots which has the demonstrated potential of becoming a major, possibly the winning, one. The other is the information that is conveyed to convention participants by successive ballot results about who among the candidates has a realistic chance either of winning or of stopping an apparent winner. On both counts the first-place candidate on the first ballot enjoys a unique advantage. As front runner, he or she becomes the focus of the election floor coalition-building in the attempt to turn early strength into eventual victory. The front runner will be seen at one and the same time as the likeliest eventual winner and as the person to beat. For the candidate with the largest percentage increase between the first two ballots in contests destined to go beyond two votes, the gains signify serious potential for continued growth as the balloting progresses and as the field of contestants narrows. First or second ballot results may not be sufficient to predict final ballot outcomes. Nonetheless, the knowledge that is gained after two ballots about candidate rankings, distances between the principal contenders, and potential for sustained growth should be sufficient to enable participants and observers alike to appreciate who among the candidates are best placed to face off against one another on the final ballot.

11 Mail Order Leadership: One Member, One Vote

And now for something completely different.

– Monty Python

National parties in Canada have arrived at a crossroads. Either they can continue to choose their leaders in some form of a delegated convention or they can adopt some variant of a universal ballot. There is no turning back to the earlier (a few romantics might say halcyon) days of selection by the parliamentary caucus or a group of party notables. The choice that parties are facing has surfaced as part of the larger political agenda because of the changes that a number of provincial parties have made to the way in which they choose their leaders and because of the appeal that direct democracy now holds for many party elites and activists. Since the beginning of the 1990s there has been a noticeable shift away from delegated conventions at the provincial level in favour of some form of universal suffrage. By enabling all party members to participate directly in the process of choosing their leader, the provincial parties have carried the twin supports of leadership selection – representation and democracy – to their logical conclusion. Large-scale, direct participation is justified by political parties as a profoundly democratic act.

A unique confluence of events in the early 1990s produced the right conditions for a switch to a universal membership ballot system. The growth in support for direct, unmediated public participation in politics coincided with the arrival of technological advances that made such participation possible. As yet, however, there has been no widespread consensus on a preferred model of universal balloting, nor has there been any clear agreement on the risks and benefits of adopting such a system in preference to a leadership convention. Nonetheless, federal parties have shown an interest in exploring alternative models of direct democracy leadership selection systems. Serious discussion of a one member, one vote leadership selection system got under way in both the Conservative party and the NDP within months of their disastrous showings in the 1993 federal election. This followed on the heels of constitutional changes adopted first by the Liberal then by the Reform parties designed to give party members a more direct say in their future leadership selections.

WHY NOW?

The public's increased interest in direct, unmediated democracy came at the end of a series of controversial national leadership contests. The conventions of 1976, 1983, 1984, and 1990 had gained widespread attention for their often bitter organizational rivalries, stacked delegate selection meetings, and dirty tricks at the riding level. At the provincial level there were conventions, as with the Alberta Tories in 1985, in which the delegate recruitment practices had been found by many observers and participants to be "objectionable" and from which important lessons could be drawn "for all Canadian parties on how *not* to select leaders."[1] By the end of the 1980s traditional leadership conventions had been cast in an odious light, and media commentators, opinion leaders, and party activists began exploring alternative forms of choosing leaders. These developments coincided roughly with the arrival of the Reform party on the national scene. Its message of direct and universal participation in political decision-making was given an added legitimacy by the party's electoral success in 1993.[2]

Two other more or less simultaneous developments, the first attitudinal, the second practical, also help to account for the the fall from grace of leadership conventions. Alan Cairns has argued persuasively that the adoption of the Charter of Rights and Freedoms in 1982 brought with it a "rights discourse" which has now escaped the confines of the legal and constitutional processes and "is insinuating itself into everyday political activity."[3] This has led Canadians to want to participate more directly in decisions affecting their own interests. The appeal of direct, unmediated participation in a party's leadership selection process is consistent with the cognitive mobilization implied by Cairns's analysis. The logic of the attitudinal change is simple and understandably attractive: as an individual's interests are understood to be directly affected by the leader who is chosen by a party, it is only fitting that the individual be empowered to act on his or her own behalf in the selection process.

What has enabled the shift to take place at the practical level of leadership selection from a delegated convention to an individually based process has been the widespread availability of modern technology, specifically communicative devices. One member, one vote becomes a feasible alternative to party conventions when, in the most advanced form of at-home, armchair political participation, party members have touch-tone phones by which to vote and cable television with a specialty channel from which to be informed of the vote. Direct democracy assumes a concrete relevance when the means are readily available to make it possible. The commercial analogue of teledemocracy for choosing party leaders is the telephone purchase/mail order delivery channel widely available to viewers receiving cable or satellite television signals. If it is possible to order jewellery, books, and CDs through television/telephone technology, why not elect party leaders that way?

PROVINCIAL VARIANTS OF A UNIVERSAL MEMBERSHIP VOTE

Provincial parties have played an important early role in developing universal suffrage leadership selection schemes. Accordingly, their experience helps us to appreciate the variety of models available for direct, universal voting. There is also an historic parallel here. Just as several parties at the provincial level held leadership conventions in the years leading up to the first federal one in 1919, so too have a number of provincial parties experimented with universal membership balloting before any federal party has used it. The older federal parties are clearly mindful of the provincial experiments with direct, universal voting: from the late 1980s they increasingly have looked over their shoulders, as it were, at the Reform party. Whatever choices they will eventually make, Reform has made its. In 1991 it amended its constitution to ensure that its next leader will be chosen by an all-membership vote of the party. So far the Liberals and Conservatives have been the only federal parties to have copied their a new leadership selection system from a provincial party. The Liberals put in place in 1992 a process identical to that used by the Ontario Liberal party earlier the same year, and the Tories in April 1995 accepted a scheme first employed by the Ontario Conservative party in 1990. Neither is as pure a one member, one vote process as has been used by some provincial parties.

One feature of the Canadian party system of the 1990s not present in the period immediately after the First World War is the extensive degree of separateness of the parties now operating in the federal and provincial spheres of politics. Parties, even those bearing the same names and drawing on the same historical roots, often have severed official constitutional links with one another and are now increasingly independent of one another. For its part, the Reform party has consciously chosen not to establish parties at the provincial level but to concentrate on the national scene. A consequence for leadership selection of the increasing independence of parties from one another has been obvious in the variety of universal voting systems employed to date and in the absence of any one generally agreed upon model of universal voting.

Even so, in what may well be a first for Canadian parties, many of the devotees of one member, one vote leadership selection have drawn on the experience of other parties, either in their own or other jurisdictions. As they have embarked on previously uncharted waters, party organizers have taken to exchanging information and offering advice and suggestions to one another. "After picking up the idea from the Parti Québécois," a Winnipeg Tory and proponent of universal balloting, Vaughan Baird, assisted the Manitoba Liberals with their scheme in the early 1990s.[4] The Ontario Conservatives "were very forthcoming in the sharing of information" about their universal vote with the Manitoba Liberals, and the new Manitoba Liberal leader, in turn, was called upon to "assist the national wing of the NDP [to] establish universal suffrage."[5] For their part, the Liberal parties of British Columbia and Alberta and the Tories in Saskatchewan adopted the telephone voting process developed and marketed by Maritime Telephone and Telegraph (M T and T). First used by the Liberals in Nova Scotia in 1992, the "teledemocratic system" has also been chosen by the Conservatives in that province as the means for selecting their new leader in 1995. As more provincial and federal parties adopt some form of universal membership vote in the years ahead, the corpus of information about the alternative schemes and the number of advocates who can explain its workings will have increased significantly. At the moment the method of choice among provincial parties is clearly M T and T's touchtone telephone system.

In September 1984 the Parti Québécois became the first major provincial party to adopt a method of leadership selection in which a new leader would be chosen by a direct vote of the entire membership.[6] Table 11-1 shows that the PQ system was first used in 1985 when Pierre-Marc Johnson beat out five rivals on the first ballot with 58 per cent of the vote to win the race to succeed René Lévesque. Party members voted by secret ballot in the polling and electoral districts as established for Quebec provincial elections. If no candidate received a majority of the vote on the first ballot, the winner was to be decided in a run-off election one week later.[7] Although the experiment failed to revive the party's fortunes among the general electorate (the party was bounced out of office two months after Johnson became premier), it evidently was deemed by

the party to have been a success, for the principal rules were left unchanged when the PQ chose Johnson's successor, Jacques Parizeau in
1988.[8] (see table 11-1 for a list of the various universal membership
schemes employed by provincial parties from 1985 to 1994).

It was to be a few years, however, before other provincial parties followed suit and discarded the delegated convention method of leadership selection in favour of what has since been labelled a universal
membership vote, or UMV.[9] From 1990 to the end of 1994 nine different provincial parties chose their leaders by some variant of the UMV:
the Conservatives in Ontario and Prince Edward Island in 1990; the
Liberals in Nova Scotia and the Conservatives in Alberta in 1992; and
the Liberals in Manitoba and the Liberals and Social Credit in British
Columbia in 1993; and the Liberals in Alberta and the Conservatives
in Saskatchewan in 1994. Others, including the Conservative party of
Manitoba, have adopted the principle of one member, one vote, to select their next leader, whenever that may be. (The results of the provincial contests to the end of 1994 are given in appendix 11-1.)[10]

Except for the Ontario Conservatives and Manitoba Liberals, all of
these parties followed the lead of the Parti Québécois and established
systems incorporating the two basic principles of universal suffrage: all
members participate directly in the selection, and the votes of all members be accorded equal weight. Some, such as the Alberta Conservatives and Quebec's PQ, devised similar systems for casting votes and
rules for determining the winner. In both those cases votes were cast by
party members in provincial constituencies and aggregated in those
units as well. If no candidate won on the first vote, a run-off election
was to be held with preferential votes cast among the top three candidates from the first vote and the winner determined according to the
single transferable vote (STV) system.

Every provincial party has added its own wrinkle to the universal
franchise system. The Tories in Prince Edward Island established one
voting site, in Charlottetown, to which party members travelled from
across the province to cast their vote. The Liberal party of Manitoba,
following the PQ lead, gave its members the option of deciding where
to cast their ballots. Three regional "satellite" polling centres were established, as was a central convention site in Winnipeg. Members also
had the option of sending their ballot through the mail.

The ultimate in decentralized voting came with M T and T's telephone balloting system to select their leaders. Using a touchtone telephone, Liberal party members in Nova Scotia, British Columbia, and
Alberta were to call (for a nominal charge) the 1–900 number of the
candidate of their choice, enter their vote, and punch in their Personal Identification Number to complete the process. Members of

the Saskatchewan Conservative party called a toll-free 1–800 number and followed the voice-recorded instructions in order to cast their vote. As voters could call from anywhere in the province or, for the Saskatchewan Tories at least, anywhere in North America – their home, office, car phone, telephone booth, or one of several regional voting centres – constituencies were irrelevant to the exercise.

The selection process devised by the Ontario Conservative party in 1989 did not go as far as did most later schemes to honour the principles of one member, one vote. It allowed all party members to vote directly in their home riding for their choice of leader. But their votes were not weighted equally. Each riding was assigned one hundred points which were awarded to the candidates in the same proportion as the results of the vote in each riding, the winner being decided by a majority of points, not of votes. As Peter Woolstencroft stated "the logic of democracy did not go beyond the equal standing of constituency associations to individual party members *qua* individuals."[11] The Manitoba Liberals altered the Ontario Tory scheme for their 1993 race by assigning candidates their proportion of a riding's vote out of one hundred if more than one hundred votes were cast. If fewer than one hundred votes were cast (as in fact was the case in all fifty-seven constituencies) no adjustments were made to the actual totals to express them as a share of one hundred. This change was made to the Ontario Tory process to avoid the system substantially overcompensating for ridings with small memberships. Cochrane North, for example, with twenty-three Tory members, had had exactly the same electoral weight in the contest as Nipissing, with 961 party members. The Ontario Conservatives subsequently adopted the weighted-vote changes introduced by the Manitoba Liberals in 1993.

In a majority of the parties, members were charged a fee to register to vote. This came on top of their party membership fees (which were generally in the $5 to $20 range), the registration amount varying from $10 to $45. The Nova Scotia Liberals charged differing amounts to register, depending upon where an individual voted by telephone: $45 if attending the Halifax convention, $25 elsewhere. The Saskatchewan Conservatives, responding to protests from party members who objected to being levied registration charges and telephone costs, dropped the $20 per family registration fee and introduced a toll-free telephone system. Most parties established cut-off dates by which individuals had to have purchased or renewed their memberships, but in two Conservative parties (Prince Edward Island and Alberta) memberships could be purchased up to and including the day of the vote itself. In Alberta thousands of new memberships to vote on the second Tory ballot were sold in the week between the first and the second vote.

Regardless of the process used to cast and to count votes, the various leadership campaigns relied on features that had become common in leadership conventions. During the campaigns themselves, candidates delivered speeches and held meetings with members in various parts of their province in an attempt to woo their support. Organizers and workers recruited members, produced and distributed literature, and solicited support on their behalf. In some races all-candidate television debates were staged. On election day itself interested party supporters and members of the general public were invited to assemble in one of a number of centres to hear the results being posted or to watch them on television. Party organizers clearly hoped to replicate a convention-like atmosphere for the television cameras. Once the winner's name was known, the new leader addressed one of the party gatherings. If the proceedings were televised, as they often were, members who had taken part in the process by mail, in a constituency polling booth, or by telephone were able to watch the wrap-up to the contest in which they had participated earlier in the day much as they would after the polls closed in a provincial or federal election – from the comfort of their own living room. At that point the participant had become the observer.

The provincial experience to date suggests that there are few practical limitations on a Universal Membership Vote scheme. The voting and the counting of votes can be as centralized or as decentralized as party officials wish. The "ballot" can be paper or push-button. The transmission of the vote can be through the postal service or over the telephone. Presumably with properly designed controls for validating them, votes could be cast by way of a fax machine or e-mail. Imagination and availability of technology on the information highway are likely the only real constraints on alternative forms of electing leaders through a direct, universal vote.

JUSTIFYING THE CHANGE

The gradual evolution of leadership selection processes in Canada from the pre-convention era to the first and then to the second generation of conventions has been championed as a move towards a more open, more representative, and more democratic way to choose party leaders. Universal suffrage, whereby all party members are eligible to participate directly in the selection of their leader, verges on the horizon as the next stage of leadership selection precisely because it is seen as a manifestly democratic move. The logic behind the change is claimed to be profoundly progressive: the more participants in a decision, the greater its legitimacy. The description by the Alberta Tories' president of his party's first experience with a UMV typifies the excitement felt by many party elites about the democratizing impact of the leadership reform. He described their 1992 one member, one vote system as "the greatest exercise in democracy ever seen in [this] province."[12]

Proponents of the universal suffrage process accept as fundamental the premise that it is "an incontestably democratic procedure for a political party" to use to select its leader.[13] Effective, widespread participation is advanced by the one member, one vote method of leadership selection. Upon payment of a small membership fee and perhaps an additional registration fee, any individual meeting a party's membership criteria becomes eligible to participate directly in the selection of its leader. At the end of the exercise, leaders chosen by universal suffrage can then claim that they have passed a greater test of party democracy and have achieved office in a more legitimate fashion than those leaders chosen by a convention. Such was Pierre-Marc Johnson's boast after winning the leadership of the PQ: "Robert Bourassa was made leader of the Quebec Liberals by a few thousand people on an arena floor – I was elected by thousands and thousands more."[14] The sentiment was echoed by the first Manitoba party leader chosen under a universal ballot system, Paul Edwards, who "was quick to point out that the leadership contest that he won [in 1993] had had the highest number of total voters of any party" in the province.[15] For the Saskatchewan Conservative's executive director, the party's goal in opting for the telephone system was "to have more people than at any time in the history of this province electing a leader of a political party."[16]

In recent years conventions have become the object of a host of complaints. Among these are concerns that unelected ex officio delegations are too numerous and wield too much influence; that the high cost of convention attendance acts as a deterrent to participation; and that the delegate selection processes are prone to abuse by large, well-funded political machines. The movement to discard the old-style convention system has ultimately been driven by the growing perception among party activists that it is elitist, that it restricts participation in the election of leaders, and that it is not the most democratic way to choose political leaders. Universal suffrage is seen as a way to overcome the more distasteful aspects of the convention system.

The longer list of specific issues that has led party officials to adopt the UMV has a now familiar look to it. With the winner-take-all principle offering a real incentive to candidate organizers to capture as many ridings as possible, delegate selection meetings are often described as little more than head-to-head contests between competing slates of delegates. Critics note that such a practice distorts the reality of the representational equation by denying delegate slots, regardless of the size of the vote cast in their favour, to candidates on the losing side of a local contest. The unfairness of the system is said to manifest itself as well on the floor of the convention when a candidate whom a slate supports drops out of the race. In that situation "the delegate *exercises her/his own discretion* and the individual member *has no control* over the delegate."[17]

The universal ballot is favoured over conventions because it is more accessible to the general population, and as a consequence it is said to be more likely to be representative of a population's socio-demographic characteristics. To some, this amounts to constructing a "level playing field" where, among others, "disabled individuals, people who live in remote rural communities, and those from lower economic groups," will be better able to participate in the leadership selection process.[18] The emphasis on the individual party member and on the opportunity for broader direct participation also amounts to a redistribution of power within the party. As characterized by one of its designers, the PQ system puts "all the power in the hands of the people rather than in the hands of the kingmakers."[19] The same view was expressed by Nova Scotia Liberals, who saw the universal vote as a chance to wrest "control of the party away from downtown Halifax"[20] and by one of the country's leading UMV advocates who maintains that "it is better to have the leader beholden to the many than to the few."[21]

Party officials are also attracted to the idea of a universal vote because of the possibilities it presents for recruiting new supporters and organizers and for substantially expanding the party's membership lists. One of the arguments advanced by advocates of universal suffrage is that the party would reap electoral and organizational advantages by maximizing the opportunities for participation of new members in the leadership selection process. Such, according to Woolstencroft, was the thinking of many of the activists in the Ontario Conservative party who believed that the party had grown out of touch with the population and "that the new system, by mobilizing members, would be the party's vehicle to return to office."[22]

Participation costs are unquestionably lower under a UMV than in a delegated convention. To be able to join a party for as little as $5 and to take part in its leadership selection process either without charge or for a modest fee has an obvious appeal, especially when contrasted with the several hundreds or even thousands of dollars the majority of delegates must spend to attend a convention lasting several days in an often distant city. Party financial assistance, in the form of subsidized hotel and travel arrangements and registration tax credits, still leaves convention delegates a great deal more out of pocket than the token fees charged for participation in a universal ballot.

These are all powerful claims presented on behalf of a reformed leadership selection process. All attempt, in one way or another, to enhance the level of participation in politics and to relate democratic theory more completely to an institutional process with which people can easily identify. Many of them also, however obliquely, are derived from a party's natural motivation for improving its electoral fortunes and possibly taking it into or retaining elected office. The attraction of the reformed process is captured in many ways. This is acknowledged best in the almost certain irreversibility of the decision once it has been made because of the idea's popularity with the wider public. In the words of the president of the Nova Scotia Liberal party: "Once you give people the right to vote this way, you can't take it away from them."[23]

Although, as will be seen, the universal suffrage method of leadership selection has not always lived up to the expectations of its proponents, it nevertheless has been well received by many in the parties that have used it to date and who see it as a model for the future. The Alberta Tories attributed their subsequent electoral victory to the fact that they had effectively drawn such a large number of new members into the party in the lead-up to the election. Asked how he accounted for his party winning another majority government, the Alberta Tory president responded: "The way we elected Ralph Klein really touched a chord. Eighty thousand people took part in the exercise."[24] Even in those parties for which the experiment produced, at best, mixed results in terms of providing an exciting race and attracting new members, the system has received laudatory reviews.

After having identified many of the flaws in the system used by the Ontario Tories in 1990, the party's chief electoral officer commented in his official report that the system was "a tangible and legitimate contribution to the advance of party democracy in Canada" and that "all party members can be justly proud of the system that has been created and implemented."[25] Ontario Tory leader Michael Harris was more assertive: "It is a democratic process I support ... I would encourage all federal and provincial parties to adopt this system."[26] Among British Columbia Liberals who had taken part in that party's first UMV, 71 per cent indicated that the televoting system should be used to select their next party leader and 75 per cent recommended that the national Liberal party adopt the system.[27] Even the 1992 Nova Scotia Liberals – who suffered much embarrassment when the party's first attempt to select a leader failed when the phone balloting network crashed and the vote had to be delayed by two weeks – overwhelmingly endorsed the new system. Over 90 per cent of the participants in that election "felt that the tele-democratic convention system was the best method for selecting future leaders."[28]

The case made in favour of a UMV system, however, has not gone unchallenged in the parties or by media commentators or political scientists. Nor has the experience of all the provincial parties who have used some variant of the new system always lived up to its advance billing. The Alberta Liberals' experience late in 1994 with M T and T's telephone system could scarcely have been worse. Termed a fiasco and a debâcle by party officials, the televote system, together with the party's regulations governing the vote itself, turned the process into a political organization's nightmare. Unable to handle the initial rush of incoming calls, the system crashed soon after voting began and led to an unannounced suspension of voting for forty minutes during which many irate callers were put "on hold" at their own expense. Not all fee-paying registrants had received the PIN codes needed to vote, and some others who had received theirs were informed by the telephone-computer that their code had already been used. Not all proxy ballots may have been valid and, even if they were, not all had been cast or counted on either or both of the two ballots. Other technical and regulatory problems plagued the vote throughout the day and brought into question the ability of the system and of party organizers to run what should have been a model high-tech operation. Undaunted, M T and T promised no repeats of the Alberta experience in the future.[29]

Judging by the experiences of the provinces, the record of the universal suffrage system is decidedly mixed as to whether it invariably mobilizes members in greater numbers than the convention system and whether it is the key to electoral victory. It may be the case that members are not so much attracted to a party by its leadership selection process as they are recruited into it by candidates' campaign organizations during the race. Accordingly, whether or not a party is successful at expanding its membership during a leadership contest is more a function of the candidates and their organizations, of financing, and of the rules and cut-off dates established by the party than of the structure of the selection process itself. It was mainly owing to their poor electoral standings, their less than exciting candidates, and their restrictive rules and cut-off dates that parties such as the Ontario Conservatives and the Manitoba Liberals failed to realize a sizable increase in their memberships during their leadership campaigns. The Saskatchewan Tories issued only just over nine thousand PIN numbers (one free to every party member) for their 1994 contest, which clearly reflected a party in decline; only four years earlier it had held office and had claimed a membership of thirty thousand.

The two parties to have experienced the greatest increase in their memberships – the PQ in 1985 and the Alberta Tories in 1992 – were also the only two between 1985 and 1993 to have conducted a leadership election while in government. In addition, both of these races had a relatively large number of candidates: six and nine respectively. The membership rolls of the PQ increased during the campaign from about 100,000 to over 150,000. For their part, the Alberta Conservatives reportedly had 11,400 members when the campaign was officially launched. Less than three months later the membership had climbed to 105,000 and nearly 80,000 votes were cast on the second and final ballot that elected Ralph Klein as leader.[30] But in that case, unlike all others, the wide-open rules established for the Alberta Conservative race permitted leadership candidates to purchase vast quantities of memberships and to distribute them to recruits free of charge. As well, memberships could be purchased at any time up the close of polls on the two voting days.

As table 11-2 shows, granting all members the right to vote does not necessarily mean that they will exercise it. In the five leadership elections between 1985 and 1993 for which membership data could be obtained, the participation rate varied from a high of 75 per cent in the Alberta Conservative election of 1985 to a low of 24 per cent for the Manitoba Liberals in 1993. In the most extreme case to date, the number of voters in the PEI Conservative leadership election of 1990 (887 voters) was actually smaller than the number of delegates to the party's most recent leadership convention in 1988 (1,171 delegates). In addition to the novelty of the system itself,[31] factors undoubtedly affecting voter turnout in a UMV system would have to include the status of the party at the time; its proximity to power; the intensity of the inter-candidate rivalry; the state of candidate organizations; and the number of candidates. As Blake and Carty conclude, "it is the character and mandate of the party, and the flavour of the policies of the party system that dictate the range and extent of the members involvement in leadership choice."[32]

If the use of the universal suffrage system has not always translated into massive membership drives and high levels of participation, so too has it not always been the ticket to send a party to victory in the subsequent election. Of the ten parties (eleven if the unopposed victory of Parizeau is included) to have used some form of the universal suffrage model since 1985, six had run in a subsequent provincial election by the end of 1994, four had yet to face the general electorate, and the leader of one had resigned. Of the six, only two – the Alberta Conservatives and the Nova Scotia Liberals – went on to win the next election. Although the small number of cases lends itself to few general observations, it is certain that the new system cannot be counted upon to pull a party out of electoral oblivion and into power.

In spite of the considerable support within many provincial parties for the UMV, there are party activists and elites who argue that there are several positive aspects of conventions that a party would sorely miss and several potential pitfalls involved with systems of universal suffrage. To them, the trade-offs that would be required in a shift to a universal, direct vote bring into question the wisdom of making the change.

Some of the obvious trade-offs involve various issues of representation. First, unlike conventions, systems of universal suffrage do not allow for the affirmative action quotas that the parties have developed to ensure that youth and women are adequately represented at their conventions. The change could mean, as it did in the Nova Scotia Liberal party, a marked shift away from younger voters or, as it did in the British Columbia Liberal party, little change over recent conventions in the share of female participants in the leadership leadership selection process.[33] Perlin speculates that the socio-demographic mix of those involved in leadership selection will change with the move to direct election of leaders. In his view, higher-status, higher-income professionals will be relatively less predominant in the exercise, women will be more equally represented, and young people will be relatively less numerous than has been the case with conventions.[34] With the passage of time Perlin may well be right, but it is simply too early in the UMV exercise to be able to demonstrate conclusively the impact, if any, that the change will have on the socio-demographic composition of the electorate.

Second, again unlike conventions, systems of pure universal suffrage do not ensure equitable regional representation. The potential exists for one or more regions or cities to dominate the selection of the leader. The adoption by the British Columbia Liberals of the universal suffrage system in 1993 was a boon for the candidacy of Vancouver mayor Gordon Campbell (who joined the party only a few months before he was elected leader) as it gave additional weight to the large membership in Vancouver. And third, because the votes of all members are counted equally, parties both forfeit and fail to reward the wisdom, experience, and political savvy of their most established and dedicated activists with respect to one of their most important functions, that of choosing a leader. After observing the PQ experiment in 1985, Dalton Camp commented that the main problem with the system was that a "member who signed up yesterday has as much influence and clout as a Cabinet minister. And that is not necessarily a good thing. Party politics are essentially elitist."[35] Nearly a decade later Camp saw no reason to change his view. Based on the experience of the provincial parties to late 1994, he was convinced that the new system amounted to "mobocracy in the disguise of the new, electronic-democracy."[36]

Universal suffrage systems of leadership selection forfeit the personal contact that is such an important part of conventions. As Woolstencroft points out, "the decline of conventions will mean that parties will have lost one of the few opportunities for members from across a province or the country at large to meet as party members and [to] engage in the work of parties."[37] Conventions provide party activists with a forum at which to meet and to work out accommodations concerning the party, its policies and, of course, its leadership. Brady and Johnston have concluded that

a convention, at least to the extent that party regulars dominate it, would look to the long-term interests of the party. The long-term orientation would militate against the choice of an extremist candidate. It would also lead party notables to minimize the overt divisiveness surrounding the choice. Regulars would have relatively complete information about the alternative candidates and thus would be less susceptible than mass primary electorates to "viability" considerations. Choice in convention would serve not just the party's interests but also the country's interests.[38]

Second-generation party conventions of the two older parties have been marked by the extent to which they have attempted to accommodate the country's linguistic, cultural, and regional divisions through a combination of mixed representational categories and equal voting power to all federal constituency associations. How many of those gains would be forfeited by the change remains unclear, but based on the experience to date at the provincial level it is clear that universal democracy has diluted "the strength of party officials who [would otherwise] carry more weight at traditional party conventions."[39] Studies have also confirmed that "party neophytes were definitely empowered by the new process" at the expense of longstanding party members.[40]

Leadership conventions provide several valuable services to a party, not least of which is extensive media coverage, especially on television. Conventions have become major media events that have drawn large television audiences. In contrast to the generally vibrant and lively conventions, where delegates are seen to participate and to be a part of the coalition-building exercise on the convention floor, leadership elections in their most extreme form are decentralized, stay-at-home affairs that have been described as "the yawn of a new era."[41] The process of party members going to polling stations in their home ridings or voting over the phone from the comfort of their living rooms simply "lacks the kind of intensity and drama which the voting process at a convention holds."[42] To party officials understandably keen to maximize television exposure, the UMV must haunt them as the political equivalent to watching paint dry. It has been known to lead, as it did in Manitoba in 1993, to anything but "spellbinding television."[43] The loss of the concentrated promotional opportunities offered by media exposure with the attendant (or at least hoped-for) improvement in the public opinion polls that comes from a three- or four-day convention remains a major concern of party activists and organizers sceptical about a change to a universal, direct ballot.

COMBINED PRIMARY / CONVENTION APPROACH: THE ONTARIO LIBERALS

Conscious of these considerations about the possible gains and losses from a UMV, the Liberal Party of Ontario moved in a different direction when it reformed its leadership selection system in the early 1990s. Preferring to keep the traditional delegated convention format as the way in which its leader would be elected, the party was mindful of the need to make allowance for "direct input [into the process] which democracy requires." But at the same time it was fearful that without the excitement and drama that a convention can produce the selection would prove to be "a media non-event."[44] Thus it adopted a plan which at the riding level would enable party members to choose delegates to attend the leadership convention and at the same time to instruct them on how to cast their first ballot vote at the convention itself. The party was satisfied that although the change introduced a more direct, riding-level vote for delegate selection and permitted constituency members to express their preferences among the candidates, it nonetheless retained the leadership convention as the principal institution in the selection process. This amounted to a hybrid, a plan one of its principal proponents labelled a "Combined Primary/Convention Approach."[45]

There are two significant differences, one at the riding-level delegate selection meetings and the other at the convention itself, between the new Ontario Liberal system and the older convention method of choosing leaders. At meetings held at the constituency level, members vote twice – once for their choice for party leader and once for their choices for delegates. Delegates are selected to support candidates in direct proportion to the share of votes cast in the riding association meeting and are then bound to support on the first ballot at the convention the candidates for whom they had declared at the constituency meeting. Ex officio and independent delegates are free to vote for whomever they wish, as are declared candidates once the first convention ballot is out of the way. The second principal difference from previous leadership selections comes at the convention itself. There the party issues committed riding delegates "a ballot bearing only the name of the candidate for whom they declared."[46] Committed delegates then have the option of dropping it in the ballot box or not. On that ballot they are not permitted to vote for a candidate other than the one to whom they had publicly pledged their support.[47]

These changes were justified on the grounds that winner-take-all delegate allotments made at riding delegate selection meetings in the past did not accurately reflect the variety of candidate choices expressed by the members in attendance. Proportionality was seen as a way of correcting the problem by ensuring that a candidate who received, let us say, 25 per cent of the preferential vote on the first of the two constituency ballots would be guaranteed 25 per cent of the riding delegates elected on the other ballot. According to proponents of the new scheme, had the party taken no steps to ensure that delegates at the convention voted on the first ballot for the candidates whom they were elected to support, then the system would pay "only lip service to the universality aspect of the grass roots vote, since, realistically the 'committed' delegates are free to do as they choose."[48]

The party hoped that the newly designed system, the first in Canada to move explicitly in the direction of an American preferential primary, would generate widespread interest in the media. Its first opportunity to test the new system came in February 1992 when it met to select a successor to David Peterson. The hope of party officials for an exciting day of freewheeling convention politics was realized. With six candidates, the race went a full five ballots (and more than eleven hours) as delegates eventually selected the second-place candidate on the first ballot, Lyn McLeod, by a margin of only nine out of the 2,315 votes (see appendix 11-1). The new leader, not surprisingly a booster of the new system, told the federal party as it began its consideration of alternate forms of leadership selection two weeks later that the Ontario Liberals had "had the benefit of the direct vote and every member feeling as though they [*sic*] had an involvement in selecting the leader." But at the same time they "still had all the dynamics of a convention, which is certainly healthy for the party."[49] Persuaded of the merits of the Ontario system, the federal Liberals adopted it as their own. It will be used when the party chooses a successor to Jean Chrétien.

IMPLICATIONS OF THE
UNIVERSAL SUFFRAGE SYSTEM

Based on the experiences of the provinces, the adoption by a major national party of a direct, universal suffrage method of leadership selection would inevitably introduce changes to the leadership contest itself. Delegate selection meetings would disappear. So would the dynamic convention atmosphere. The new system would also have the potential to affect the type of person chosen as leader and some of the organizational structures and patterns within the parties themselves.

The enlarged electorate and the very structure of a national contest most likely would make for more expensive, though differently organized, leadership campaigns. It is true that a direct, universal election would dramatically lower the participation costs for individual voters compared with those assumed by convention delegates – costs that in the recent past have been at least partially underwritten by the party and by the taxpayer. It would also eliminate some of the heavy costs associated with convention-week and convention-floor organizing for the candidates.

But the larger electorate would mean that candidates would rely even more than they have in the past upon such techniques of mass mobilization as polling, mass mailings, and, increasingly, television advertising and the media generally. The candidates would need more media specialists and organizers well versed in the arts of recruiting new members and in getting out the vote as they aimed their appeals directly at tens, if not hundreds, of thousands of voting members. This would almost certainly ensure that the costs of leadership campaigns would continue to escalate as serious candidates would need well-financed and well-organized political machines which would be capable of operating nationally and of employing the latest and most sophisticated means of reaching a mass electorate. In other words, UMV would bring with it increased incentives for candidate organizations to embrace mass mobilization techniques and to make far greater use of the mass media than has been the case in the past. What this means, in Perlin's words, is that "money is likely to become even more important in leadership politics" under a one person, one vote system than it has been so far.[50]

The structure of the contest and the wider interests represented in the broadened electorate would almost certainly affect the style of leadership campaigns and possibly even the type of candidates and leaders chosen. Assured of at least some public support, individuals with few established roots in the party but with a mass following and an arresting public appeal that worked well on television could be drawn into the race. Equally, advocates of special interests based on narrowly focused policy concerns (such as Tom Wappel's anti-abortion campaign, which received little serious attention in the 1990 Liberal race) could gain wanted attention and a greater measure of support for their cause by appealing to otherwise non-politically mobilized sympathizers.

It may even be true that the vastly larger, but less party-based, electorate would be more likely than a delegated convention to choose as leader a populist outsider (or a populist who claimed to be an outsider) than a more mainstream party insider. The logical strategy for at least some candidates, regardless of their background and power base within the party and the fact that they too enjoyed a healthy measure of caucus support, would be to wrap themselves in a populist cloak and to portray themselves as an anti-establishment candidate. Such seems to have been Ralph Klein's successful strategy in the 1992 Alberta Conservative leadership race. After finishing second on the first ballot by a single vote, Klein, who was supported by a overwhelming majority of the party's legislative members, was described as spending the week before the second ballot "in a news media blitz painting himself as the non-establishment candidate, the representative of the Tory grassroots and the 'unsung heroes' in the party's rural caucus."[51]

The one member, one vote system would lessen the importance of the constituency as an organizational unit critical to the success of a leadership selection exercise. At the formal, constitutional level this would be obvious in the elimination of constituency associations as the political units responsible for the selection of the majority of convention delegates. At the political and organizational level candidates and their organizers, in trying to reach a vast, highly individual and dispersed electorate, would no longer find the constituency – its executive, its membership and, most important, its delegates – the fertile organizational unit it was with conventions. As they would no longer need to attempt to win slates of delegates, riding by riding, through local organizers and contacts, candidates could be expected to turn their organizational efforts instead to winning over a vastly larger but unevenly distributed electorate.[52]

The constituency has long been a party's principal organizational and aggregative unit for leadership politics. Throughout the history of conventions the riding has remained the essential building block from which each serious candidate's organization sought to construct, block by block across the country, a winning coalition. The convention leadership selection process has been effectively structured so as to stress the importance of the local district, and it is from those districts that the networks among party activists and candidate organizers have been established that proved invaluable to a party in future elections and, if the party was successful, in government. The lesson is obvious: myriad local networks built during a delegated convention campaign can prove their worth later when parliamentary candidates need to be recruited and when riding organizers need to be found to run the party's election at the constituency level. To the extent that they would lead to the establishment of more candidate-centred and less constituency-centred organizations, universal vote systems would be less likely than conventions to nurture a party's local organizational and electoral networks.[53]

A direct, universal vote would reduce even further the role that MPs and provincial legislators play in the selection of their leader. The theory implicit in the move to direct democracy is to place them in an electoral context in which their votes carried no more weight in the selection of their leader than the newest and greenest recruit brought in at the last minute. That might be said to be no different from delegated conventions were it not for the fact that delegates chosen to attend national conventions are vastly fewer in number than those who vote on a universal ballot, elected at the constituency level in the majority of cases, and far less likely to be made up of last-minute recruits. The reduced voting power accorded elected members in the universal vote system extends the symbolic message first conveyed in the switch from caucus to convention: no special weight need be attached to the preferences and opinions, in many cases derived after years of legislative experience, of the party's elected members.

Yet it is the men and women of Parliament or of a legislature who have to co-exist most immediately, and then on a continuing basis, with the leader who has been chosen. Parliament carries on; conventions and universal ballots do not. The day following the selection of a leader it is the parliamentarians who have to begin the job of working for the months and years ahead with the new leader. Caucus unrest and dissatisfaction with the convention's choice may make this difficult and may serve to undermine the credibility and authority of the leader and party, as Stanfield, Clark and Turner were to find out with disaffected MPs rebelling openly against their leadership from time to time. No leadership selection system is immune to continued grumbling after the event and no caucus is free of malcontents. But MPs, who share no less an interest in winning the next election than the party rank and file, also have an interest in leadership that is different from that of party delegates. Based on their continuing, daily obligations in politics *and* government or opposition, theirs draws on their reading of the parliamentary, managerial, and organizational skills of their leader and of the possible challengers or candidates for that position. Their experience should count for something when it comes time to choose a leader.[54]

The views of MPs or MLAs need not prevail in the selection of their leader – indeed, it would be idle dreaming to think that, given this century's moves to increase the number of participants in the decision, they would. But the potential value of their contribution ought not to be lightly dismissed. It is instructive to note that the Democratic party in the United States, having removed elected office-holders from the presidential nominating process in its sweeping reforms of the 1970s, reincorporated them into the process in the 1980s through the creation of a "super-delegate" category. It was believed by many Democrats that in its rush to reform its nominating process the party had overlooked the experience and knowledge that its legislative members (state governors, large-city mayors, members of Congress, and the like) could bring to the decision. They were found to provide an element of "peer review" whereby candidates for the presidency would be "screened by politicians who [had] dealt with them personally, instead of just observing them on television."[55]

If it is true that universal suffrage would increase the chances of extra-parliamentary outsiders (or at least those painting themselves as outsiders) winning a party's leadership and of weakening the influence of caucus in the selection of its leader, then it is reasonable to conclude along with Perlin that "direct election would add to the complexity of the relationships between leaders and their parties. There is already instability in these relationships because, whereas leaders are chosen, and may be removed, by party conventions, they must exercise their authority through, and are accountable to, their colleagues in the party in Parliament."[56]

Universal suffrage adds a third collection of interests to these relationships. It is not at all clear how the claims of greater legitimacy of those leaders selected by universal suffrage would stand up to the demands and expectations of the parliamentary party and to the party in convention should the latter continue to meet from time to time. Almost certainly selection by a universal vote would give an added degree of independence to a leader from his or her parliamentary colleagues and open up yet another avenue of responsibility – to a vast, dispersed, and unorganized electorate temporarily and briefly brought into the act of choosing a party leader. It is not clear at this early point in the change to a wider participation system how those responsibilities will be defined and how they will play out within the parties themselves. But it is difficult to disagree with the view expressed by the president of the Saskatchewan Conservative party about the impact of the UMV on intra-party relationships: the change, in his words, "really redefines responsible democracy."[57]

Universal, direct suffrage has become increasingly popular among parties at the provincial level. The appeal of greater democratization is strong. Conscious of the common perception that the universal suffrage system is more democratic than the convention system, national parties will come under increasing pressure to adopt some variant of the new system. The impact of the institutionalization of the universal suffrage system would then be felt on the political system as a whole, and with the wider electorate, leadership politics in Canada would become even more presidentialized in tone and character than it now is. As Woolstencroft has suggested, "institutionalization of the system of direct election will likely cause political parties to look to the state to organize and fund the selection, more or less in the way that US states handle primary elections."[58]

If the pressure for a more participatory process continues to build, the path of the politics of leadership selection in Canada could lead to some variant of American-style primaries. The system devised by the Ontario Liberal party and since adopted by the federal Liberal party closely resembles the type of primary characterized, in the words of V.O. Key, by the "separation of preference vote and delegate election" in which voters would mark their ballots twice – once for the candidate and once for convention delegates.[59] The major difference between the two voting systems is, of course, that in the Liberal system only those who are party members in good standing can vote, whereas in American primaries the vote is open to all of those in a state who self-identify with the party. At a leadership selection workshop at the federal Liberal party's Reform Conference in Halifax in 1985, one participant suggested that "known Liberals" be registered as such, similar to the American system, and that they all be given a vote for the leader. He was not taken seriously.[60] Nonetheless, the 1985 Halifax delegate may have been ahead of his time. The logic of recent changes in leadership selection at the provincial level may compel some parties to assert that their province has a vested interest in overseeing a fair and reasonable selection process. If such a case were found sufficiently compelling, it would be left to the province to establish guidelines and procedures for the race and to assume responsibility for operating it. An American-style primary would then have arrived in Canada.

12 Federal Leadership Selection Reforms: The Wave of the Future?

Yesterday's reform often is today's problem.

– Bert A. Rockman

The movement to reform the leadership selection processes in favour of some form of direct, universal vote has been felt at the federal as well as at the provincial level. Both the Conservative and New Democratic parties have recently adopted alternatives to their previous leadership selection processes, following the lead of the Liberals who, in 1992, put in place a modified convention system for their next leadership race. Of the three older parties, the Liberals have studied the issue most extensively, although when it came down to making a decision about the path the party would follow, it baulked at adopting a radically new process for electing its leaders. The Reform party has gone the furthest of any party and has accepted, in as yet an unspecified form, one member, one vote as the fundamental principle governing its leadership selection process.

STIRRINGS OF CHANGE: THE CONSERVATIVES, THE NDP, AND THE REFORM PARTY

Compared to the Liberal party, both the Conservative and New Democratic parties had given the universal suffrage reforms little more than cursory examination prior to their massive losses in the 1993 federal election. The Tories had first addressed the issue at their 1989 national meeting when a proposal advocating universal suffrage was tabled and the party's executive was given the task of investigating various means by which the process could be implemented.[1] The five-member committee whose report on the one member, one vote scheme had been presented in 1989 was unanimous in its view that delegated conventions had been "abused," that the party members and the public had felt "excluded by the convention process," and that the PQ universal suffrage system offered "the only alternative" to traditional conventions.[2]

By the time Brian Mulroney resigned as party leader four years later, the Tories had made no measurable progress towards changing their convention system. Rumblings were heard from a variety of sources throughout the 1993 Conservative leadership campaign that the time had come for the party to abandon the leadership convention in favour of universal suffrage. Leadership candidate Patrick Boyer, who ran last of the five contestants, was one of those sources. Proposing that all party members should be allowed to participate in the selection of the leader (a system he termed a "hands-on democracy-selection process"), Boyer said at the convention that if he had his way, it "would be the last delegated [leadership] convention in the history of the Conservative Party."[3]

It seems likely that Boyer will get his way, although not under the circumstances that he might have hoped. There can be little doubt that 1993 will prove to be a watershed year for the Conservative party. In completing its first leadership transition while in government since Meighen was selected in 1920, the party then went on the suffer its worst defeat in history. It was this electoral disaster that forced the new leader to resign her past six months after her victory at the Ottawa convention. Jean Charest, runner-up to Kim Campbell at the convention, took over as interim party leader and quickly pushed the party's national executive to examine reforms to the leadership selection process.

In preparation for the April 1995 national meeting of the Conservative party (at which Charest was confirmed as leader), a "restructuring committee" met with party activists across the country to gauge support for internal reforms on a number of issues, including leadership selection. The committee was charged with studying the various systems of direct democracy previously used in the provinces and of choosing from among them or of devising a process of its own that best suited the party's needs and resources.[4] Charest made it clear where he stood on the issue of leadership selection by giving strong endorsement to a universal vote scheme. In a letter to one of the proponents of universal voting he reiterated what he had stated publicly, that "at the federal level the battle is just beginning." He urged supporters of the UMV to "join us" in seeking the plan's adoption and implementation.[5]

Through a series of votes on alternative forms of choosing their future leaders, the Tory delegates at their April 1995 meeting narrowed the final choice to either a pure one member, one vote scheme or a

UMV that would be weighted so as to give all constituencies equal voting power. They chose the latter. The system they adopted, which was first designed by the Ontario Tories for the selection of their leader in 1990, amounts to an all-member, direct vote with equal weight to all ridings irrespective of the number of party members voting. It also means that no delegates will be selected and that a national convention is optional. With the selection of Jean Charest's successor, whenever that might be, leadership conventions in the Conservative party will have become a thing of the past.

The issue of reforming the leadership selection process in the NDP was formally raised for the first time within the party at its 1989 convention. At that time, the party passed without debate a resolution calling for a study of universal suffrage. The matter was referred to a special committee, the purpose of which was to "advise what constitutional and procedural reforms [were] necessary to implement a process of leadership selection by all party members in good standing."[6] In his post-convention survey of the 1989 delegates, Archer found that slightly more than half (52 per cent) said that they were in favour of a change to a one member, one vote system to choose party leaders.[7] Regardless the level of support within the party in 1989 for reforming the method of leadership selection, "the issue did not appear urgent two years later at the 1991 convention, when NDP delegates seemed more concerned with policy matters such as the constitution and free trade."[8]

Compared with the other parties, the NDP's leadership selection process could prove to be the most difficult to change to a universal suffrage system because of its practice of formally electing the leader every two years and its institutionalized relationship with organized labour. It would be difficult, costly, and time-consuming for the party to poll directly its entire membership (estimated by the party's federal secretary at roughly 330,000 early in 1995)[9] for the purpose of reviewing and electing its leader. The NDP would also have to agree on the weight to be assigned to organized labour whose individual members, were they all to vote, would outnumber constituency members by more than two to one in a direct, universal process. That could prove problematic should organized labour not agree to go along with a new system. Under the NDP's constitution a two-thirds vote of approval would be needed to change the leadership selection arrangements, and labour, were it to unite in opposition to a change, could come close to controlling a blocking vote.[10]

Unlike the Liberal, Conservative, and Reform parties, the NDP has two types of members: those who belong to riding associations and members of unions affiliated with the party. Clearly, if every NDP member were granted an equal vote the affiliated members, many of whom do not support the NDP and some of whom belong to other parties, would gain an inordinate share of direct electoral power within the party. Archer has noted that if the NDP were to choose to adopt the direct election system, it would likely have to adopt a formula akin to that devised by the Ontario Conservatives in which "a proportion of electoral votes could be allocated to constituencies, with others being awarded to affiliated unions, central labour, the [New Democrat Youth], federal council and caucus."[11]

The 1993 election results shocked the NDP and its supporters and left many in the party wondering how, if at all, to refashion the party's internal procedural arrangements. Six months after the federal election Audrey McLaughlin announced her intention to resign as leader at the time of the next NDP national convention. That meeting, scheduled for Ottawa in October 1995, would be the occasion for the selection of McLaughlin's successor. There had been no serious suggestion following the 1993 election that the NDP would abandon its biennial convention in favour of a universal vote on its leadership, although it was known that some within the party who were basically opposed to labour's affiliated status might seize the idea of a universal vote weighted in favour of the constituency membership as a way of trying to reduce labour's influence.

The party's constitution effectively ruled out any possibility of *not* holding a biennial constitution in 1995 at which the next NDP leader would be selected. But, given the post-1993 election divisions within the party over the direction and extent that intra-party procedures should be reformed, it remained unclear whether there was a level of active and sustained support for changes in the party's leadership selection process that would be sufficient to lead to the eventual adoption of a one member, one vote system. As none of the provincial New Democratic parties had at that stage yet adopted a universal suffrage method of leadership selection, there were no handy party reference points to which federal NDPers interested in leadership selection reform could allude. Besides, it could be argued that there was a less compelling reason for the NDP to reject their convention system: their local contests have never been tarnished to the same degree as those of the Tories and Liberals by inter-candidate organizational rivalry and competing slates of delegates.

But given time, the change may come in any event. Despite his scepticism of some of the claims made by advocates of universal suffrage, Archer, a close observer of the party, concedes that "the New Democrats may nevertheless find the appeal of greater democratization too difficult to resist."[12] The scheme adopted by the party's executive and governing council early in 1995 to elect McLaughlin's successor later that year proved Archer right. It took the party as far as it could go in the direction of a UMV without requiring a formal constitutional amendment. The plan left the party's traditional delegated convention untouched. But it added what basically amounted to a number of preferential primaries at the constituency and affiliated trade union levels.

In the weeks immediately preceding the party's October 1995 convention a series of "nominating ballots" (one within each of Canada's five regions and one within the trade union affiliates) would be open to participation by any party member. The preferred method for carrying out the all-membership vote, if "operations and finances" allowed, would be a telephone vote. Failing that, a postal vote would be taken of all members. Candidates would have their names placed on the convention ballot either by winning one of the five regional or trade union votes or by gaining at least 15 per cent of the pooled national vote of all members voting. Votes cast by party members at the constituency level would be weighted to count for 75 per cent of the total national vote; those cast by party member trade unionists through their affiliated union would be weighted to count for 25 per cent of the national vote. Justified as a system that would give "the membership more direct involvement in the process" and generate "media and public interest in the period leading up to the convention," the nomination ballot was seen by its defenders as a "party-building opportunity."[13]

The unprecedented collapse of support for the Tories and the marginalization of the NDP in the 1993 federal election can be traced in part to the hugely successful campaign of the Reform party in western Canada and in parts of rural Ontario. Going overnight from one seat in the House of Commons to fifty-two and coming to within three seats of forming the official opposition, Reform's electoral success carried with it a clear message. Its populist roots drew their nourishment from the theory of direct democracy – from the idea that through referendums, plebiscites, and initiatives voters could become directly involved in the act of governing. Included in the ideas and processes that distinguished what the party called the "new politics" from the old was the notion of mass participation in the selection of a party's leader. According to the Reform party constitution amended in 1991, its party leader "shall be elected by the members of the Party by secret vote."[14]

Reform's first constitution, adopted at the party's founding assembly in Winnipeg in October 1987, had stated that its leader would be chosen by delegates in assembly – that is, through the traditional leadership convention system that Canadians were accustomed to up to that point. In Winnipeg Preston Manning had been "acclaimed" leader without opposition and without a recorded vote.[15] More mindful of its populist and participatory rhetoric at its assembly four years later, the party abandoned the delegated assembly as the means of choosing its leader in favour of a universal vote by party members. In the words of the party's chairman of its task force on direct democracy, Reform was prompted to make the move in 1991 from a delegated convention to an all-member vote because the federal Liberals had just the year before gone through a "messy" and "tainted" delegate selection process with considerable "back-stabbing." Reform wanted to choose its leader in "a better way" and in a manner consistent with its "grass roots and populist" philosophy.[16]

The leadership selection provisions it put in place made no reference to how the system was to operate. Like older parties faced with a similar organizational decision, Reform delegated the power to determine the procedure and mechanisms for an all-member leadership vote to the party's executive council. As the Reform party to date has had only one leader it is impossible to know what all-member process will be used to select future leaders. According to a former senior party official, the process may involve "a telephone vote, a paper ballot or even numerous drop-in centres" through which all members could participate in the selection of a new leader. Whatever system is adopted, only one thing is certain: it "would be something other than a leadership convention."[17] The significance of Reform's early switch away from delegated conventions stems from its message of expanded participation in political decision-making. This has struck a responsive chord with many Canadians and has contributed to the attention that other parties, both federal and provincial, have come to pay to the way in which they choose their leaders.

NEITHER FISH NOR FOWL: THE LIBERAL ALTERNATIVE

The Liberal party has pioneered most of the major reforms to the leadership selection process at the federal level. In the early 1980s it became the first to consider adopting a universal suffrage system of leadership selection. Caught up in the mood of change after having spent the better part of a decade discussing alternative forms of choosing leaders, the Liberals in 1990 became the first national party to amend their constitution to ensure that their future leaders would be elected by a "direct vote all of members."[18] But at their 1992 meeting they opted instead for an ambitious, though clearly less radical route of reform. They adopted the Ontario Liberal party's combined primary/convention system. The change amounted neither to a total rejection of the familiar convention format nor to a total acceptance of the one member, one vote principle for choosing leaders. It was neither fish nor fowl.

Discussions aimed at reforming the party's leadership selection process had their origins in Resolution 40 of the party's 1982 policy convention which, as we have seen, condemned manipulative backroom politics and called for a more accountable and more democratic party. From the debate surrounding that issue emerged a President's Committee for Reform with a mandate to "study and [to] recommend long-term structural and organizational reforms."[19] In a preliminary discussion paper released in January 1984, the commission commented that to "a perhaps surprising degree" there was "little debate within the party as to the means employed to select a leader" and that the "convention mechanism ... seem[ed] to be generally accepted."[20]

Over the next several years, however, the idea of reforming the party's national conventions gained momentum. No doubt the media's attention to the often bitter organizational rivalries over competing slates of delegates in some ridings, and the party's subsequent loss of power in the election later that year contributed to this change of mind. In early 1985 party president Iona Campagnolo expressed the sentiments of a growing number of Liberals when she proclaimed that "there is a desire for change in the realm of national conventions."[21] The party, in her view, was determined to move to a universal membership vote: "We don't yet know how we're going to do it, but within a decade, whether it's by a primary system, or a version of the Parti Québécois method used recently, we'll have direct election of our leadership."[22]

It remained for the party to devise the method by which the leadership election would be carried out. Accordingly, the party re-created its Reform Commission and included in it a Universal Suffrage Task Force with a mandate to "consider the alternative means of implementing leadership elections conducted by universal suffrage, and to make recommendations to the Party on how best to accomplish such implementation" (see appendix 12-1).

The frustrations of those Liberals who had supported reform in 1982 had been directed not at the convention system of leadership selection per se but at the lack of intra-party democracy in the Liberal party in general. By 1990, however, the leadership selection system had become the object of criticism within the party. A large proportion of Liberal party activists wanted to discard conventions in favour of a "more open and democratic" method of leadership selection. This much is borne out by Perlin's post-convention survey of delegates to the 1990 Liberal leadership convention. When asked how they thought the leader should be chosen, less than one in five (18 per cent) said by convention similar to the 1990 convention system, whereas a clear majority (55 per cent) said by a direct vote of all party members.[23] Furthermore, when asked for their preference between various schemes of direct election, a majority of the respondents (53 per cent) chose the pure one member, one vote system in which the vote of every member would be counted equally over a system in which the ridings would be weighted equally (supported by 28 per cent) or a system in which the provinces would be weighted proportionate to their population (supported by 14 per cent).[24]

Delegates were asked to assess the relative strengths of the convention system and the universal suffrage system. Their responses indicate that many of the concerns expressed by opponents of universal voting carried little weight with the majority of Liberals present at the party's convention in 1990. Table 12-1 shows that universal suffrage was rated by half of the respondents to be the better system at representing regional interests and in selecting the most competent leader. A majority felt a direct vote would be better at limiting the influence of extremist groups, and roughly two-thirds thought it would be better at keeping down the costs of leadership campaigns and in promoting confidence in the integrity of the process. Most of the delegates rejected some of the most common arguments made in favour of conventions. Less than one-third thought that the convention would be better at representing regional interests, selecting the most competent leader, and reconciling and accommodating conflicting interests.[25] The convention system was rated by a majority of respondents to be the better system only in terms of getting favourable publicity for the party and in recruiting young people into the party.[26] For the Liberals in 1990 the attraction of greater participation by party members in leadership selection clearly outweighed whatever concerns they may have had about the publicity and recruitment difficulties the party would encounter with a universal, direct vote system (see table 12-1).

Through Insight Canada Research, the Liberal party's Task Force on Universal Suffrage also conducted a poll of party members in March 1991. As with Perlin's study, the task force survey found substantially more support for a universal membership vote than for a delegated convention. When asked which system they thought was the best option to use to select the next leader, 45 per cent of those polled favoured a strict universal suffrage system, 26 per cent favoured a combination universal suffrage/delegated convention system, 13 per cent preferred the universal suffrage option provided it would cost less than the convention system, 13 per cent wanted to retain the convention method and 2 per cent favoured the American primary system.[27]

It seems probable that much of this shift in opinion within the party towards support for universal suffrage was the result of the members' first-hand experiences with the convention system as it had operated in the 1984 and 1990 leadership campaigns. Party activists had witnessed two costly campaigns in six years, at a time when the party itself was several millions of dollars in debt. They had seen an influx of instant members; participated in an often much-criticized delegate selection process; and felt the steamroller effect of massive campaign machines. It comes as little surprise that a substantial portion of the delegates at the Calgary convention in 1990 was disillusioned with the process, especially after a thirteen-month-long, slate-ridden, megabuck leadership campaign the outcome of which was known almost from the outset. Yesterday's reform in leadership selection had become today's problem.

Perlin's study shows that to a majority of the 1990 delegates there was a preferable (though nonetheless hypothetical) alternative to choosing a leader by convention. The appeal of greater democratization and of more effective participation in a reformed selection system was undoubtedly attractive to many Liberal party members. To be the first national party to adopt the universal suffrage method of leadership selection and thereby to be able to make the claim that they were at the forefront of intra-party democracy in Canada must have been a tantalizing prospect.

That the Liberals were in opposition at the time also helps to explain their keen interest in reforming their leadership selection process. In opposition, a party's lines of authority are weakened and its degrees of freedom to experiment with new forms of intra-party arrangements are increased. As John Turner, then the party's leader, said at the 1985 Halifax conference: "It is easier to remain open to reform [in the party] when we're in opposition."[28] Time in opposition gives party members an opportunity to search for answers as to why they are not in government and how they can recapture sufficient electoral support to return to office. Given the central role of the party leader in electoral politics and the invariable appeal of the idea of greater democratization in the party, it is not surprising that a party in opposition would seize upon the leadership selection process as an instrument with which it might succeed in recapturing the public imagination.

The contrasting experience of the governing Tories in convention in 1993 and subsequent to their election defeat adds weight to the point that a party in office is less likely than a party in opposition to accept the need for intra-party reforms of its leadership selection processes. Delegates attending the governing Tory party's convention in 1993 were over twice as likely as Liberal delegates had been in 1990 to favour the continuation of a convention system for choosing their leaders. Barely one-third of the Tories, compared to over half of the Liberals, supported the idea of leadership selection by a direct vote of all party members. Three times as many Conservatives as Liberals (23 per cent compared to 8 per cent) favoured the idea of a convention made up entirely of elected riding association delegates.[29]

Table 12-2 shows that the Tories thought conventions better suited than a direct vote to selecting the most competent leader and to reconciling and accommodating conflicting interests. In both these respects the Liberals in 1990 had held the opposite view. The Tories were evenly divided in their judgment of conventions or direct vote as better at representing regional interests, unlike the Liberals who, on that issue, favoured the direct vote over conventions by a wide margin. Only as a system better suited to keeping down the costs of leadership campaigns and at promoting confidence in the integrity of the process did a majority of Tory delegates favour a direct vote over a convention (see table 12-2).

The 1990 Liberal convention in Calgary came at a point in the party's history when it was far more prepared to move to an alternative leadership selection process than it had been in the past. That was clearly less the case with the Tories assembled at the Ottawa convention in 1993. The lead-up to the 1990 convention had been messier at the delegate selection level and far more prolonged than before the one in 1993. Moreover, the Liberal party's reform process – to which there was no equivalent in the Conservative party – had been going on for several years at the time the party assembled in 1990. Proponents of the change were much in evidence at the 1990 convention and openly pressed the case for a change to a direct vote system. By the time the delegates filled out their questionnaires in the post-convention survey, the constitutional amendment calling for the election of a leader by all Liberal members in a direct vote had been accepted. Thus they were addressing a hypothetical question about possible alternatives when, in fact, a change had already been officially sanctioned by a majority vote.

It would be surprising if the post-1993 general election Tory rank and file had not become more amenable to the idea of a direct, universal vote than the 1993 Tory convention delegates had been. Although the party lacked the years of analysing the question that had marked a decade of Liberal history, it reached a point soon after the election of seemingly wanting to adopt a realistic, but as yet undefined, alternative that might help to bring it back to a position of some prominence in federal politics. The searing experience of the election had left the party deeply in debt – by as much as $5.5 million by some estimates.[30] Campbell's selection, and more to the point the system by which she was chosen, had no doubt led some Tories, embittered by their possibly irredeemable fall from political grace in the October election, to blame the convention process. The strong and swift endorsement of a one member, one vote system by the new interim leader, Jean Charest, was justified, in his words, as a way of moving the party "from the back rooms into the front rooms" and of reinventing the Conservatives "as the most modern political party in Canada."[31]

Presented in such terms, and following on the heels of the Alberta Conservatives' electoral success with their UMV-selected leader, Ralph Klein, the universal vote alternative found a greater measure of support among federal Conservative activists than would have been the case had the party been returned to power in the 1993 election and had Klein's Conservatives been defeated. Complementing its justification on democratic and electoral grounds, the one member, one vote process also appealed to those concerned about the party's ability to finance another mega-convention in the foreseeable future and to those hopeful about reinvigorating interest in the Conservatives at the expense of the Reform party. That fact that Reform itself is committed to choosing its next leader through a direct, universal vote will add to the case mounted by Tory advocates of change.

Prior to 1990 the debate in the Liberal party over universal suffrage had focused largely on its general attributes and its pros and cons relative to the convention system. It was not until after the convention of that year, at which the party called for the next leader to be chosen by a direct vote of the entire membership, that the federal Liberals began to examine seriously ways in which such a system might be implemented. The move to adopt the universal suffrage method of leadership selection before the structure and the mechanics of the radically new system had been devised and before the party had seriously considered the system's requirements and implications is perhaps best described as an example of leaping before looking. Upon closer examination of the pure universal, direct suffrage system, the party evidently found it unpalatable. At their meeting on the party's constitution in 1992 it soon backtracked from its position on universal suffrage. When the matter came to a vote the delegates specifically rejected that option.

The arguments that the delegates in 1985, 1990, and 1992 made in favour of or in opposition to variants of the universal suffrage system had a familiar ring to them. They were essentially the same as those that had been commonly heard at the provincial level. These included on the plus side the markedly lower per participant costs; the possibility of recruiting, then subsequently mobilizing in an election, large numbers of new party supporters; and the need to complete the task of wresting the party away from elites. But principal among the claims made on behalf of the change was the assertion that the party's democratic reputation was at stake. At the party conference in Halifax in 1985, those who favoured any one of a number of proposals modelled on the recent PQ experiment with direct election invoked the democratic principle and emphasized the merits of an open contest that would encourage increased participation.[32] The opinion of Armand Bannister, co-chairman of the Reform Commission, was representative of this view. "Choosing delegates is, in effect, not entirely democratic," said Bannister two months before the reform conference. "It [has] been as democratic as we could get, but certainly having the 300,000 Liberals across the country choose a leader directly is the way we want to go."[33] More than five years later, the members of the party's Task Force on Universal Suffrage expressed a similar opinion. Two of their starting assumptions were that "the long-standing method of selecting the National Leader by delegated convention is both antiquated and deleterious to the interests of the Party," and that the universal suffrage system was "fundamentally democratic."[34]

Those who were sceptical of the universal franchise system argued that by abandoning conventions, the party would forfeit the opportunity to boost its public visibility and impart to its supporters an enthusiasm that conventions were known to have delivered. There were fears that a genuinely open process could be easily infiltrated by Conservatives and New Democrats wishing the Liberal party harm. Liberals were also cautioned against adopting any scheme that would replace the equal allotment of delegates from all federal constituencies, irrespective of their party membership, with one that, as with the Liberals whose membership was drawn overwhelmingly from metropolitan central Canada, would favour urban centres in Ontario and Quebec. As well, concerns were expressed about the negative impact that a wide-open vote would have on the participation of women and youth, the two principal groups to have benefited from the party's insistence on the application of a quota system in the selection of delegates.

By the 1990 convention, the Liberals had still not decided how they were going to change their leadership selection process. The mandate of the task force was to come up with the means for implementing a universal suffrage system. In doing so, the party had to address the question of whether or not such a system would be viable for a national party in Canada. Such systems had been designed so far to work in smaller political systems – provincial ones. Would they successfully make the move to the national arena, in which there is a pan-Canadian party system?

The party discovered that from an organizational and financial perspective the direct election of leaders would involve an extensive logistical effort that could very well put it beyond the party's means. If the election went beyond a single ballot that would mean moving from the familiar multi-ballot, majority winner contest with its gradual elimination of candidates to one preferential ballot with the winner decided by single transferable vote. Of this the 1983–5 Reform Commission of the Liberal party was certainly aware. "Whether taken by mail or at central polling stations," the final report of the commission read, "it would not be practical to take a series of run-off votes. Therefore, one transferable ballot in rank-order choice would have to be employed."[35] But even managing a decentralized all-member vote would be more than the party could manage. The volunteers needed to staff polling stations in all federal ridings, if constituency-based voting were adopted, would be beyond the capacity of the party, particularly as it would come at the very time that so many experienced party activists would be working on candidates' campaigns.

The issue of regional representation was raised repeatedly throughout the debate over universal suffrage in the Liberal party. More than any other issue, this one possibly goes to the heart of the question of whether or not national parties in Canada will adopt a true UMV. In a country as diverse as Canada, accommodative national parties have shown that to succeed they must seek to appeal to, to represent, and to articulate diverse interests – regional, linguistic, ethnic, and economic. One of the virtues of delegated conventions in the two older parties is that they have ensured equal constituency representation irrespective of membership size, which has meant that regions in which a party is weak electorally are nonetheless represented in the choice of its leader. That the NDP has never had adequate representation at its conventions from Quebec and the Maritimes has in the past thrown into question its claim to be as truly national a party as the Liberals and Conservatives. The same objection could be levelled at any party, including the two oldest ones, using the universal suffrage method of leadership selection whose membership was not distributed evenly across the country. The system would overrepresent those regions with large party memberships and effectively freeze out those parts of the country with small ones.

In the end, the Liberal's Reform Commission, after considering these various questions, put forth a model of universal suffrage in which all members would be entitled to vote directly for their choice for leader and in which every riding would be weighted equally. The commission proposed that members would cast their ballots at an advance poll, a national leadership meeting, or in their home ridings. There would be a maximum of two ballots. If no candidate won an outright majority on the first ballot, the winner would be decided on a second and preferential ballot held on the same occasion.[36]

However, this proposal was shunted aside at the 1992 party convention in Hull as the delegates called "overwhelmingly" for the next leader of the party "to be elected at a Leadership Convention, with the delegates to that convention being elected in proportion to the popular direct vote received by each Leadership candidate."[37] (For the text of the constitutional amendments adopted see appendix 12-2.) The system adopted by the federal party is identical in its essential respects to the process that had been devised and implemented only weeks before by the Ontario Liberal party.

The scheme that was adopted by the federal Liberals envisaged delegate selection meetings at which party members would vote twice. By having the members present vote for their choice of leader, the first vote would allocate the number of delegate positions to leadership candidates according to their share of the popular vote. (An illustration is given in appendix 12-3 of how the delegate positions would be allocated among the candidates in a riding in which leadership candidate White, for example, received approximately 42 per cent of the vote and was therefore entitled to 42 per cent, or five of the twelve delegate positions.)[38] The second vote would determine which individuals would fill the delegate positions. As White had five positions available, the top five delegates who ran as declared White supporters would be chosen to fill these spots. The remainder of the delegate positions would be allocated among the candidates and to independent delegates in the same manner according to their share of the total first ballot vote. Thus delegates would be selected according to the party's longstanding socio-demographic quotas: of the twelve delegate positions in each riding one-half and one-third respectively would be alloted according to the party's gender and youth requirements.

On the first ballot of the leadership convention itself, those delegates "elected in support of Leadership candidates, shall, if they vote on the first ballot, do so in favour of the candidate they have been elected to support." Thus the five White supporters would have two options: to vote for White or to abstain. They would not be entitled to vote for any other candidate on the first ballot. The justification for this requirement was that the rules should seek to ensure that, on the first ballot at least, the opinions of the riding membership would be reflected as equitably as possible in the initial vote on the leadership. Throughout the convention, independent and ex officio delegates would be free to vote for whichever candidate they wished. Previously declared delegates would be able to do the same after the first ballot.

Proposals for such a combined primary/convention, proportional representation system of leadership selection had been around the Liberal party for a number of years before the system was adopted in 1992. A similar system had been submitted for consideration to the party's 1985 Reform Conference and again at its 1986 convention. Consideration was deferred each time. Sponsored by the party's national executive, the system found favour with the party president, Iona Campagnolo. Arguing that the party members would have an enhanced voice in choosing the leader while at the same time the party would benefit from the drama and the dynamics of a leadership convention, she said in September 1985 that the system would allow the party "to have the best of both worlds."[39]

The record shows, however, that in the years leading up to the 1992 decision to adopt the combined primary/convention approach the party gave that option little serious attention. The reports of the Universal Suffrage Task Force and the Reform Commission focused almost exclusively on the question of the universal, direct vote. The two-vote, proportional delegate allocation system that was finally adopted received only one mention in each of the interim reports of these two bodies. In fact in the first of these reports, issued 30 March 1991, the system had been rejected out of hand. After examining a report recommending proportional delegate representation prepared by the Leadership Procedures Review Committee of the Ontario Liberal party, the federal party's task force concluded that since it "was not in fact a model of universal suffrage, its interest to the Task Force was limited to" the recommendations of the committee relating to the length of the leadership campaign, the retention of a minimum membership voting age, the forty-five-day cut-off for new members and the need for a central voting list.[40]

In the interim report of the Reform Commission issued on 31 July 1991, the system received more serious consideration: "In our mind, universal suffrage is not proportional representation. We suspect that a persuasive case can and will be made that the model adopted by Liberals in Ontario could be used across the country ... We invite discussion on this. We also welcome discussion on definitions of the terms 'universal suffrage' and 'direct vote'."[41] In other words, if the system did not meet the criteria set out in the party's constitution, the criteria could be changed. Evidently, a persuasive case was made for the proportional representation system, for in the final report of the Reform Commission, issued in December 1991, the process was all set out and ready to be adopted by the party at its 1992 Hull meeting.

What, then, was the case that was made for the proportional representation system? The reports of the Universal Suffrage Task Force and of the Reform Commission of the federal Liberal party yield no clues. The most thorough argument in favour of the system had been made by the Leadership Procedures Review Committee of the Ontario Liberal party. The federal party had followed the debate in its Ontario counterpart closely and instead of preparing its own study of the proportional representation system it merely circulated the report of the

Ontario party's Review Committee – the same report that the task force had earlier dismissed out of hand.[42]

Like those of many other parties, the members of the Ontario Liberal party had come to the conclusion that the traditional, delegated convention should be abandoned. However, they also decided that the weaknesses and inadequacies of universal suffrage were too great to merit its adoption. Among these weaknesses and inadequacies of the system that the party identified were: (1) that it could lead to domination of the process by a small number of ridings; (2) that if ridings were weighted equally, that would not amount to one member, one vote; (3) that it would be extremely expensive for candidates; (4) that it would be a departure from having the riding as the basis for Canadian democracy; (5) that it would attract little public interest; (6) that long-time commitment by members to the party would count for nothing; and (7) that the party would lose the intimacy and the personal contact of conventions.[43]

The proportional representation method was seen by the Ontario Liberals and later by their federal counterparts as a way of dealing with some of the traditional convention's weaknesses while at the same time preserving that system's strengths and incorporating some of the strengths of the universal suffrage system. Proportional representation removes the winner-take-all aspect of traditional delegate selection meetings by ensuring that minority views are represented as well. The members of the Leadership Procedures Review Committee of the Ontario Liberal party suggested that the elimination of the winner-take-all slate system would make long-time commitment to the party important again; make it easier to be elected as an independent delegate; and "restore primacy to *policies and ideas*."[44] Although this last assertion is open to debate, it is clear that as a package these arguments appealed to the delegates. The proportional representation system was also considered less expensive for the party and less difficult for it to organize than one involving a direct vote of the entire membership.

That the system was less radical a change than a complete switch to a universal suffrage system was also seen as a point in its favour. Local associations would continue to elect delegates as they traditionally had, but with a different ballot and under different rules. Delegates from across the country would still gather at a central convention site to select a leader. The party would retain the positive aspects of the convention, notably the excitement, the media coverage, the anticipated burst in the polls, and the personal contact between delegates and candidates. Add to this the more effective participation of the grassroots membership that the process would involve and the federal Liberal party had a package that it was able to sell to its members.

The timing of the 1992 Hull meeting could scarcely have been better, for the Ontario party had just used its new hybrid system to elect a new leader. The excitement generated by that six-candidate, five-ballot race in Ontario helped it to gain a prominence with the federal party it would not otherwise have had. The end product of the system was thereby displayed only two weeks before the federal Liberal delegates gathered to decide which leadership selection process the party would adopt. The delegates obviously liked what they had seen and heard about the Ontario process. When the matter of adopting a combined primary/convention system came to a vote, 90 per cent of the Hull delegates favoured the switch.[45]

IMPLICATIONS OF THE COMBINED PRIMARY/CONVENTION SYSTEM

What effects might this new process have on leadership campaigns and conventions? The Ontario Liberal experiment yields some clues. Others can be inferred from the system itself.

In addition to granting a direct vote expressly for indicating a leadership preference, one of the most innovative aspects of the two-vote process at the riding level is that the members' votes are translated into delegate positions (and therefore leadership votes) in as equitable a fashion as possible. The new Liberal system removes the winner-take-all, majoritarian aspect of delegate selection meetings in all but the most exceptional circumstances. With the proportional allocation of votes, a candidate winning 50 per cent plus one of the riding ballots would receive six delegate positions rather than the twelve he or she would almost certainly have received (given the presence of slates) under the older system. By the same token a candidate receiving as little as 8.5 per cent of the vote in a riding would succeed in having a supporter selected as a delegate. Previously that candidate in all likelihood would have been entirely shut out. Just as electoral systems of proportional representation encourage the creation and sustenance of political parties, some major others minor, so the system adopted by the Liberal party should tend to encourage (or perhaps more accurately not discourage) individuals to run for the leadership. The first ballot results of the 1992 Ontario Liberal convention lend support to this claim to the extent that there were six candidates on the first ballot with only 21 percentage points between the lowest (9 per cent) and the highest (30 per cent) of them.

Inasmuch as it lends itself to multi-candidate campaigns with a closer fit between membership preference for leader and first ballot delegate support, the primary/convention system also lends itself to multi-ballot conventions. As was established in chapter 10 with respect to the relationship between number of candidates of number of ballots, it is fair to assume that as the number of candidates increases, it becomes more difficult for a candidate to receive an outright majority of votes in each riding and, therefore, a majority of delegate positions. Moreover, as in the older convention system, the uncommitted ex officio and independent delegates present at the convention introduce a measure of unpredictability in the process.[46]

The new Liberal system raises the prospect of electoral contradictions at the delegate selection level. Differences may arise between the results of the first vote (to express a preference for leader) and the second vote (to select delegates). As well, it is conceivable that the system may override expressed preferential leadership rankings on the delegate selection ballot. The gender and youth quotas, as can be seen in the hypothetical example in appendix 12-3, could displace the rank ordering of second-ballot delegate preferences. It is even conceivable, however unlikely this might be, that a would-be delegate could attract a substantial number of votes, but if he or she had supported an unpopular leadership candidate who had failed to attract enough support to be allocated a delegate position, that person would not be elected as a delegate.

The Ontario Liberal experiment with the system yields no indication that the element of direct democracy in the system did much to stimulate the participation of current members or to attract new ones. Of the 18,016 members who were eligible to vote on the leadership and to select delegates for the Ontario Liberal convention, 11,296 actually did so. Although such a turnout rate is on the high end of the range established by the experiences of the provinces with universal suffrage, it is by no means clear that the combination direct vote/convention system, any more than either the universal suffrage system or the traditional convention system, is in and of itself an effective instrument to ensure a high level of participation by a party's membership.

The system seems unlikely to change significantly the basic features of leadership campaigns. As under the traditional convention system, candidates will seek to enlist hundreds and perhaps thousands of new members to pack delegate selection meetings, although in future Liberal leadership races candidates will be restricted by the ninety-day cut-off mark for new members. Candidates will continue to organize slates of delegates. A combined primary/convention system does not eliminate the slate system. Indeed, to some extent it accepts it and incorporates it into the structure of the process. For a leadership candidate, mobilizing members and getting one's own partisans elected as delegates will remain the name of the game. As with traditional conventions, before, during, and after the delegate selection period candidates will attempt to sway independent and ex officio delegates. Similarly, delegates who are committed to support other candidates on the first ballot will be targeted by the various candidates' organizations searching for post-first ballot support. Conceivably some elected at the riding level to support a particular candidate on the first ballot might even be persuaded by a rival candidate's organizers to abstain from voting on the initial ballot. Organization, both at the riding level and on the convention floor, will remain as critical to a candidate's success as ever.

Going into the convention, the candidates and the delegates will have more complete and accurate information about the relative standing of the candidates than they had previously. In the traditional convention system, candidates and delegates had to rely on polls and on delegate tracking for their information. Except for the votes of the ex officio and independent delegates, as well as those declared delegates who may choose not vote on the first ballot, the primary/convention system guarantees that the approximate outcome of the first ballot will be known in advance. The votes in each riding would simply be aggregated on a country-wide basis. This information would help delegates to assess who is ahead and who is behind and thereby assist them to plan in advance their post-first ballot voting strategies. By the same token, the greater available information would help candidates to determine where to concentrate their efforts to sway delegates, to seek endorsements from the more minor candidates, and to firm up support after the first ballot.

The adoption of the reforms by the Liberal party was intended to give the membership a greater say in the choice of the leader. In the first stage of the leadership race at the local level and on the convention floor it does; in the second and subsequent stages of the convention voting it does not. As in the traditional convention system, once party members vote at delegate selection meetings, their influence dwindles away and they no longer have any means to make their views heard in the leadership decision. But in another sense, the party members definitely have more influence than they did under the older system, as delegates will be sent to the convention to vote on the first ballot in direct proportion to how their riding association voted.

This commitment, manifested as it would be through the use of pre-marked ballots by constituency delegates voting on the first ballot at the convention, introduces a new notion of representation at conventions. In theory, if not always in fact, delegates in the past have been relatively independent actors free to make up their own minds and to vote as they wished regardless of the views of the members who elected them. Slates, of course, have altered the representational equation, but not to the extent that the new Liberal system will. Pre-marked ballots represent a shift away from the secret ballot, the freedom and the individuality that have hitherto been present at Canadian conventions. The representatives called for by the system adopted by the Liberal party are truly *delegates* in the sense that they are *mandated* by a group of party members in the riding in which they were elected. On the first ballot at least, these delegates may not stray from their mandates. That is much more in keeping with the democratic model of committed delegates acting on instructions from the larger population than anything seen in federal political parties so far. Theoretically, it amounts to a replacement of one notion of representation with another: of uninstructed representatives collectively reaching the decision they believe in the best interest of the larger population giving way to delegates obliged to act in a certain way on behalf of a particular group.

Pre-marked ballots deny to delegates the opportunity to make free choices. Whether voting in a general election or for a leadership candidate at a convention, the secret ballot and the freedom of choice that has accompanied it have long been fundamental characteristics of Canadian democracy. As a purely speculative matter, one wonders whether a delegate wishing to cast his or her ballot at a convention for a candidate other than the one pre-marked on the ballot might have the recourse of a Charter challenge? The issue is complicated further by the fact that, as in past conventions, ex officio delegates and those elected as independents will continue to vote secretly and freely. Thus on the first ballot of the convention there will be two classes of delegates. One, having made no previous public commitment, will enjoy complete freedom of choice; another, having made a public declaration of support, will have limited first ballot options. If the Liberals in 1992 were concerned with how equal and democratic this arrangement might be, it was a price they were clearly willing to pay in order to give their membership a greater say in the choice of a leader.

The reasons behind the decision of the federal Liberals to reject the pure UMV will no doubt be weighed carefully by other federal parties as they come at their own pace either to examine reforms to their leadership selection processes or to put in place a particular set of procedures to elect their future leaders. Clearly the trend in Canada has been towards a more participatory selection process, one that gives the grassroots member a greater say in the leadership question. At the same time, however, the federal Liberal party seems to have become more aware and appreciative of the virtues of leadership conventions than it was in the earlier stages of considering reforms. The desire to find a compromise between the demands of members for greater democratization on the one hand and the requirements of a national party in Canada on the other led the Liberal party to adopt a compromise system which combines both the direct vote and the leadership convention. It will, they hope, allow them to realize the best of both worlds.

13 Do Conventions Matter?
Parties, Conventions, and
Canadian Democracy

> In a democracy both deep reverence and a sense of the comic are
> requisite.
>
> – Carl Sandburg

Canadians have long been accustomed to having their political leaders chosen in party conventions. The leadership convention, having operated at both the national and provincial levels for most of this century, has emerged as one of the country's most widely and easily identified political institutions. Recent leadership races, distinguished from earlier ones by their larger number of candidates and delegates and their greater costs, media hype, and dramatic excitement, have captured the public's attention as no other political event, with the obvious exception of a general election, has been able to do. Television has turned the nation's living rooms into extensions of convention floors.

Yet symptomatic of a more general and recent malaise with politics and politicians, traditional leadership conventions are now under attack. Critics prefer some form of universal, direct balloting – the touchtone phone or a postal vote – whereby all who wish to join the party for that express purpose could take part in choosing its leader. Support for a more wide-open model of leadership selection and away from the delegated institution brings into question the continued use of conventions as the means for selecting party leaders. It also raises important issues of party democracy in Canada. If Canadians are indeed witnessing the end of an era, what has it meant to have had leadership conventions as one of their central political institutions over the past seventy-five years, and what are the principal implications for their parties and politics of a move away from delegated conventions?

National conventions in Canada can trace their origins to concerns within parties for improved and protected regional representation (the quintessential Canadian representational loadstone) in the leadership selection process. The explicit change in the process of choosing leaders adopted earlier this century carried with it an implicit change in the representational theory underlying leadership selection in this country. From Confederation to the Liberal convention of 1919 and the Conservative one of 1927, a party's members of Parliament had served as a collective body roughly equivalent to an electoral college. MPs had acted as trustees on their constituents' and the nation's behalf. Their election to Parliament was testament to the authority vested in them by the electorate to act according to their best judgment and in the national interest in selecting, from time to time, their party leaders. Eventually MPs would be held accountable for their actions by the electorate, but until then *they* were the *representative* agents responsible for choosing, sustaining, and removing their leaders.

With the process introduced nationally in 1919, however, categories of delegates entitled to take part in the act of choosing a leader were established first because of geographic, and later because of gender, age, organizational, and racial considerations. The new participants in the leadership selection process grew massively in numbers and influence with the passage of time. That growth came at the direct expense of parliamentarians and the parliamentary party and contributed in its way to the diminishing importance of Parliament and of parliamentary career routes to leadership hopefuls. The new participants had been admitted, ostensibly, because they belonged to parts of society deemed sufficiently important in their own right to be present in a national political institution.

That rationale was tempered, however, by the fact that well into the second generation it became apparent that their presence in the convention process was testimony both to the assertiveness and clout of the various sub-groups whenever party constitutional provisions governing participation at conventions were amended, and to the organizational efforts of the principal leadership contenders competing for delegate support at the riding level and within the various clubs and associations. Groups, defined according to age, gender, educational standing, and union affiliation, had been granted a constitutional standing within their respective parties which was destined to be protected and promoted by the influence their members exerted in the leadership selection process. Whatever its causes, such an "essentially microcosmic" view of representation that the delegated convention introduced was necessarily different in kind from the earlier "trusteeship" variety. It redirected the representational focus from an elected peer group charged with a public responsibility to a deliberately constituted, but non-publicly elected, group designed to mirror certain features of society.[1]

What is clear about this change in the theory of representation is that the principal reason for holding conventions in the first place (to compensate for the regional weaknesses of the caucuses) was eventually displaced by the organizational and demographic imperatives of the parties themselves. Once operationalized, these imperatives (invariably justified on democratic grounds) had the effect of undercutting the regional and provincial dimensions of convention organization and voting. Policy concerns and political interests of female or youth or union delegates by definition cut across region. So do those of delegates generally who are primarily motivated by national policy issues or by the understandable political drive to see their party gain or maintain power. In a curious way, party conventions in Canada gave rise to an unanticipated contradiction. An institution had been established whose justification derived from its regional representative character. Yet arguably one of its eventual strengths resulted from its distinctly nationalizing influence on delegate behaviour and, ultimately, Canadian politics. Territorial representation had been wedded to, then superseded by, a measure of social pluralism in the construction of conventions.[2]

Leadership conventions brought Canadian leaders a measure of authoritative independence from their parliamentary caucus unknown to their counterparts in the British Conservative and Australian parties. Among other leaders chosen in the first generation of Canadian conventions, Mackenzie King effectively silenced caucus critics of his leadership by claiming that what the parliamentary group had not created it could not destroy. Leadership review provisions of the second generation gave constitutional standing to King's views about the direction of leadership accountability.

By choosing and reviewing their leaders in delegated conventions, parties accepted the supremacy of the party outside Parliament. As power moved increasingly in the direction of party members, they became less persuaded by, and more independent of, the leadership preferences of parliamentarians. This in turn helped to open the door to organizers with resources to match their skills and to experts in communications who, together with the organizers, assumed the principal responsibility for persuading the general public, party members, and potential or actual delegates of the merits of their particular candidate. The enhanced role played by the media and candidate organizers in this context came at the expense of parliamentarians. The MPs' experience and judgment concerning the qualities and leadership potential of the various candidates had carried greater weight in the preconvention period, and even throughout the relatively more deferential first generation of conventions, than it did following 1967.

The rules for electing a party leader in convention in Canada effectively established an electoral system that was highly individualistic and relatively free of orchestration by party elites. Unlike earlier American national nominating conventions, which were dominated by inter-elite bargaining by state and local leaders, there was no institutionally enhanced place in Canadian leadership conventions for factional or regional leaders whose bargaining power derived from their acknowledged capacity to deliver a solid core of votes. One of the reasons that premiers, leaders of provincial parties, and the like have had comparatively minor influence on the voting in national conventions was precisely because the institution had been structured in a nonfederal way. Its voting system rested on the uniqueness of individual delegates and on the secrecy of their ballot.

When they originally grafted a variant of the turn-of-the-century presidential nominating convention onto Canada's parliamentary system the Liberals and Conservatives chose, as had the American parties several decades earlier, a system designed to overcome their representational inadequacies. In both the United States and Canada the party elites had opted for a more broadly based structure for choosing their presidential nominees and parliamentary leaders. But although the initial reasons for the change were the same in the two countries, when assessed by the degree to which federalism was an explicit component of the two convention systems the results proved to be markedly different.

In the United States the rules, procedures, and voting arrangements used in national conventions for more than a century after the system's adoption in the 1830s sustained and enhanced the power of state politicians. The governors, mayors, and other party notables who selected and controlled delegates used their votes as bargaining chips when they negotiated with the various candidates seeking the nomination. In attempting to advance their own interests, or that of their local party, state-based politicians emerged as the most powerful players in the presidential nominating process. The switch to primaries and caucuses, carried out on such a large scale in the 1970s and 1980s, effectively curtailed the power of state party notables both in the initial stage of selecting convention delegates and subsequently in bargaining their votes at the convention itself. Even so, the states themselves remained no less important. Primaries and caucuses reinforced their significance as the critical electoral units in the nominating process, whether they were small and early (Iowa and New Hampshire), bunched together ("Super Tuesday"), or late and big (New York and California).

Whereas primaries, caucuses, and roll-call voting procedures on the convention floor visibly reinforced American federalism, there have never been any similar institutional arrangements in place in Canada to suggest that Canadian parties operated in a federal system. An outsider introduced to Canadian politics for the first time through attendance at a national leadership convention could mistakenly gain the impression that Canada had a unitary, not a federal, system of government. Secret ballots are cast by individual delegates in Canada, in contrast to the system favoured by the Americans of publicly announcing the votes on the basis of an alphabetic state-by-state roll call. Delegates attending Canadian conventions of the two older parties prefer to be seated with a group of like-minded delegates regardless of province, in close proximity to the candidate of their choice. In this respect the convention-floor organizational imperative derives not from Canadian federalism but from candidate identification and support. Survey data have demonstrated the extent to which delegates exercise a considerable measure of freedom from provincial party officials and have committed their support directly to a candidate. In the 1983 Conservative and 1984 Liberal conventions, for example, only 3 and 4 per cent of the delegates respectively made commitments to their provincial party or to a provincial party official to support a candidate. By contrast over half of the delegates at both conventions gave a commitment of support directly to a candidate.[3]

The non-federalized institutional arrangements for the aggregation of convention votes and the candidate-centred organization of the contests themselves mean that delegates have been provided with the opportunity to remain free, should they so wish, from having to commit their votes to provincial leaders, provincial party organizations, or local MPs. As the 1983 and 1984 survey data show, the overwhelming number of delegates have chosen to do that. On those rare occasions when premiers sought the national leadership, as in 1967, delegates from their home province supported them overwhelmingly.[4] But even that exceptional behaviour may well have been as much, or more, a manifestation of true preferences for the two front-running candidates as of regional chauvinism or strident boosterism in support of a native son.[5]

A delegate's true preference is the product of many influences. Of these, only one is region or province. The responsiveness of candidates to regional concerns was clearly a factor for some, though not a majority, of the delegates attending the 1983 and 1984 conventions. A candidate's perceived responsiveness to regional interests was "very influential" in the first ballot vote decisions of 40 per cent of the Liberal delegates and 45 per cent of the Conservative delegates. But three other reasons were ranked with greater frequency by Liberals and five others by Conservatives. These included, significantly, the belief that opposing candidates would not be as able to give competent leadership to a government and the candidate's views on policy in general. At

74 and 59 per cent, getting the party into power was, respectively, the most frequently mentioned Tory and second-most frequently mentioned Liberal reason for supporting a candidate.[6]

What these findings suggest is that general national policy considerations tend to count for more with delegates than particular regional or parochial ones, and that the power orientation of delegates attending national conventions is an even far more important reason (the principal one for the Tories in 1983) for supporting one candidate over another. It can be inferred that if regional interests and their perceived protection coincided with these and other leading reasons for delegate choice, they would serve to reinforce the delegates' electoral behaviour. But if they conflicted, as in a classic illustration of political cross-pressures, they would tend to be discounted in favour of larger national and office-seeking interests of the party.[7]

At the outset of a convention destined to go several ballots, delegates are afforded an opportunity to set aside temporarily their preference ordering and to vote on the first ballot for another candidate to whom they may have felt some personal or party obligation. Such behaviour was obvious, for example, in the first ballot votes cast at the 1968 Liberal and 1976 Conservative conventions when 25 and 23 per cent of the delegates respectively voted for a candidate other than their first preference on the first ballot. The reasons given by those delegates who ignored their preference ordering on the first (and in some cases the second) ballot ranged from supporting a candidate because of some past political favours, to voting for a favourite son, to honouring a candidate for his or her services to the party. The candidates who benefited most from this type of voting behaviour were the minor and regional ones. It was the major candidates who needed at least two ballots for their electoral support to reach their true preference level.[8]

Looked at another way, these data point to a fundamental problem faced by minor and regional candidates in a convention system. Unlike major candidates, they have no reserve of true preference voters to draw on as successive ballots take place. One would expect that the share of first ballot support that represented true leadership preference would be markedly higher for the major candidates than for minor and regional ones – an expectation confirmed in both 1968 and 1976. For Trudeau and Winters in 1968 the share of their first ballot support that represented true leadership preference was 98 and 92 per cent respectively, whereas for MacEachen and Greene it was 23 and 7 per cent respectively. In 1976 the spread was even more dramatic. In that convention true preference support accounted for 96 per cent of Clark's and Wagner's first ballot vote, but it amounted to only 20 per cent of Nowlan's and zero per cent of Grafftey's first ballot vote.[9]

It stands to reason that the first ballot vote and true leadership preference should be much more closely matched in a convention with a small number of candidates of whom one is widely anticipated to win the leadership on the first ballot. Knowing that they could reasonably expect to have only one opportunity to support their true preferences, delegates would be less likely to "park" their votes with some other candidate than they would be in a convention destined to last several ballots. The only modern convention to have been settled on one ballot (1990) confirms that with the widely expected election of Chrétien on a single ballot 91 per cent of *all* delegates who voted on the first (and only) ballot voted for their true preference. Minor candidates in 1990, unlike those in 1968, gained little from delegates supporting them for other than true preferential reasons.[10]

It is likely, however, that true preference had come to mean something different in 1990 from what it had meant in the earlier multiballot conventions. In 1968 and 1976 delegates were chosen more independently of candidate organizations than they were in 1990. Accordingly they were freer of prior commitments to candidates and their local organizers about how they would vote at the convention. Delegates chosen to attend the earlier modern conventions were, in representational theory, closer to the "trustee" view of elected representation. Those selected in 1990 were more likely to be "instructed" delegates who were expected by those who had chosen them and by the campaign organizations that had engineered their selection to act on the commitment that they had made at the time of their selection.

Thus the higher association between true preferences and first ballot vote in 1990 may only partially be accounted for by the number of anticipated ballots and the likelihood of one candidate winning on the first ballot. More likely it reflected the strikingly different organizational efforts on behalf of candidates that distinguished the later from the earlier periods of the second generation of conventions, for the success of those later efforts effectively constrained first ballot delegate voting options. As in the United States following the widespread adoption of state primaries and caucuses for presidential nominations, candidate organizers in Canada's two older parties in 1990 (with a one-ballot convention) and 1984 and 1993 (with two-ballot contests) effectively changed the second-generation leadership selection process from a decision-making to a decision-ratifying one.

Candidate organizations were not the only cause of this development, of course. The fewer number of candidates seeking the leadership in the last conventions of the two older parties also reflected the power of public opinion polls and the media. The 1993 Conservative race in particular demonstrated how polls and the role played by the media in generating and interpreting them have added further degrees of certainty to a modern leadership contest as it progressed from a previous leader's announced retirement to the choice of the new leader. Polls and polling firms, simply not as numerous at the outset of the second generation of conventions as in the last decade or so, have helped to shape both the reality and the perceptions of leadership contests. They are relied on by delegates, candidates, and putative candidates to provide clues about the race. As 1993 showed when so many possible entries into the Tory contest did not let their names stand, polls had come to play a significant part in helping the leading players reach their own conclusions.

As with so many other aspects of party leadership selection by convention in Canada, the presence and impact of public opinion polls shows an obvious parallel to developments in the United States over the past two or three decades. Polling has helped to convert leadership races in Canada into something like an American contest, especially as it relates to developments in the early primary and caucus stages of presidential nominations. Winning New Hampshire and Iowa has an inordinate impact on the American contests because the front runner is widely judged to be impossible, or next to impossible, to beat. Thus there is a parallel (suggesting, perhaps unfairly, a twenty-five-year time lag between developments in American and Canadian politics) to be drawn between the decisions made by Lyndon Johnson early in 1968 not to contest the Democratic nomination and Michael Wilson, Barbara McDougall, and others in 1993 not to run for the Tory leadership. They may have overreacted, but that can never be proven, for their decision became a self-fulfilling prophecy. They think they cannot win; they do not enter; therefore they do not win.

As a candidate's electability is such an important (indeed, to many delegates the most critical) consideration in choosing a party leader, polls have become indispensable in providing delegates, candidates, and the media with the essential information about who the delegates and the public puts in the front of the race. This does not deny that issues and ideology are immaterial to delegates. On the contrary, surveys have shown that delegates are not indifferent to the ideas and policies presented by candidates and that issues and ideas are a part of the overall decision-making exercise that the vast majority of delegates go through. Issues divide delegates. But so do other important variables such as candidates' personalities and candidates' ability to perform well in the media, especially on television. Electability contains all of these factors. It implies reasoned assessments about ideas, stands on issues, personalities, media performances *and*, given all of these, the likelihood of gaining office under one candidate as opposed to another. In that sense, delegates are strongly disposed to the prospects of power. As Richard Johnston concluded in his study of delegates attending the 1983 Tory and 1984 Liberal conventions, "many rank-and-file delegates appeared to transcend parochial or ideological considerations and to focus on the long-term electoral well-being of the party."[11]

The cost of making a serious bid for the Tory or Liberal leadership in the second generation of conventions jumped dramatically over what it had been previously and was claimed by some would-be candidates to be the reason they chose not to run. In the months leading up to a modern convention, the principal candidates criss-crossed the country and waged organizational battles for delegate support at the constituency level. The organizational structures they established and the media-driven campaigns they waged bore striking parallels to general elections. So did the financial costs. But unlike party and candidate election expenses, leadership candidate expenditures and fundraising were uncontrolled in any serious way by the two older parties. In varying degrees at the end of each leadership selection contest they left more questions unanswered than answered and, together with widely reported delegate selection fights involving dubious practices in many of the races, served to bring second-generation leadership conventions into disrepute. Mindful of the need to balance reasonable expenditure limits and public accountability of candidate financing with a realistic reading of the amounts of money that modern leadership campaigns require, the Lortie commission proposed a series of recommendations which, if acted upon, should introduce the financial integrity needed in leadership contests.

Information gleaned from polls by possible candidates about their chances of winning, the early and intense coverage of presumed front runners by the media, and the costs of seeking the leadership all contributed to the reduced number of candidates seeking the leadership in the two older parties in the most recent conventions. That reduction, in turn, diminished the opportunities for coalition-building by candidates and their organizers on the floor of the conventions. Except for the 1989 NDP convention, which was unlike other recent conventions in its relatively large number of candidates and its low costs and in the variety of candidate liaisons struck or attempted over its four ballots, no national leadership convention has gone beyond two ballots since 1983. Building coalitions on a convention floor emerged early in the second generation of conventions as one of the tests of a successful candidate's skills in the arena of leadership selection politics, although in the case of Clark in 1976 and Stanfield in 1967 it was scarcely an accurate predictor of subsequent ability to deal with rebellious factions within the party.

Clark and Stanfield proved that winning a party's leadership in convention was no guarantee of intra-parliamentary party harmony in the years ahead. For their part, Turner in 1984 and Campbell in 1993 proved that winning a party's leadership shortly before a general election was no guarantee of their party being returned to office. But then the turmoil in the Conservative party in the decade following John A. Macdonald's death in 1891 showed that leaders chosen by their parliamentary colleagues could have a rough ride of it and, even as prime minister, be in office for only short periods of time before being turfed out by their party. And Tupper's selection in 1896 and Meighen's in 1920 make it clear that leaders chosen by their parliamentary colleagues could soon lead their government to electoral defeat.

A leader's ability to maintain the stability and cohesion needed to lead an effective and credible parliamentary party or to take the party back to office in an election is affected by such a complex mix of social, political, and economic factors unique to each situation that the process by which the leader has been chosen seemingly makes little difference to the outcome. What counts is the fit between the personality of the leader and the situation he or she inherits or has a hand in subsequently creating. Sufficiently motivated by the prospects of gaining or retaining power to look for electoral winners, Liberal and Tory convention delegates, like the parliamentarians who did the choosing of leaders before them, have tried to match their reading of the context of the moment with the leadership alternatives from which they had to choose.

From 1919 to 1993, the Liberals had far greater success in meeting that objective than the Conservatives. Four of the six Liberal conventions were followed by victories in the next general election, whereas the same was true of the Tories in only four of their nine conventions. All of the four victorious Liberal leaders won at least their first two consecutive elections after being selected, but only two of the four Tories led their party to at least two election wins in a row. With something akin to an apostolic relationship, at least from Mackenzie King to St Laurent to Pearson and to Trudeau, the Liberals clearly handled their leadership transitions more adroitly than their principal parliamentary opponent. Accordingly, they laid claim to being the country's natural governing party for most of this century.

To establish that claim they passed more often than not, and certainly more often than the Conservatives, the greatest test facing a national party intent on gaining office in Canada. They created and sustained for much of the twentieth century a series of broadly-based coalitions of interests. At their best these became, to paraphrase Gilbert and Sullivan, the very model of a modern coalition. Created anew by each leader at each convention, and then again at election time, they tended to share the attributes of the governing alliances forged by Mackenzie King and Louis St Laurent. They gave meaning to King's view that "Confederation was based on compromise," and that French and English, urban and rural, eastern and western, and Protestant and Catholic Canadians ought to be present around a cabinet table, in a party caucus and as participants in a leadership convention.[12] They were founded on the premise that Canada's political institutions, including its parties and its leadership selection processes, should not exacerbate the social differences already existing in society. This meant accommodating linguistic, ethnic, regional, and religious differences and, when successfully established, producing consensual and accommodative leaders whose mark would be made through the construction of broadly-based coalitions.

Not all Liberal leaders were as successful in following the lead of King and St Laurent, and not all Tory leaders were without coalition-building skills in contesting elections. Although they both formed governments, Pearson never managed a breakthrough in the west and Trudeau was not again able to recreate his nationally-based electoral coalition of 1968. Turner lacked sufficient support from all regions to put a governing alliance together, and Chrétien, reversing Trudeau's fate in 1972, owed his 1993 electoral success far more to Ontario than Quebec. Helped in their convention coalition-building exercise by their party's close adherence to the alternation tradition, Liberal leaders, who have always been either from Quebec or Ontario, have constructed their electoral coalitions from central Canada out. Because of the preponderance of Commons' seats in those two provinces, they have enjoyed an electoral advantage that Tory leaders, who were drawn overwhelmingly from outside central Canada, could not match. The only two Conservative leaders to have successfully emulated the Liberals in building broad, pan-Canadian electoral coalitions were Diefenbaker (briefly at the time of the 1958 election) and Mulroney in his two election victories of 1984 and 1988. They succeeded because they, like the Liberals, got both Quebec and Ontario onside. Others, from Bennett to Campbell, had little or no success in matching the Liberals at the game that the Grits had made largely their own in the twentieth century.[13]

But even though not all were able to forge victorious electoral alliances, second-generation Liberal and Conservative leaders shared one quality critical to winning a Canadian leadership convention: a proven capacity to construct a broadly-based coalition of convention floor support. Achieved after months of organizational effort and of arm-twisting of constituency, club, association, and ex officio delegates, victory in every Liberal and Tory convention from 1967 to 1993 carried with it a message. By the end of the final ballot, the winner had hammered together a coalition composed of a regionally and socially diverse group of delegates within, of course, the relatively limited range of social diversity among convention delegates. With organizational strength and the demonstrated capacity that came from each successive ballot to emerge either as the likely winner or as the best chance of stopping some other likely winner, candidates reached out to other candidates and delegates for their support. The mark of their success in doing this was the breadth – by gender, age, region, and language group – of their winning coalition. In this respect a leadership convention became a tribal ritual, one which facilitated "interactions that would not ordinarily take place."[14]

Networks, it bears repeating, are at the heart of politics. If one accepts that broadly-based, accommodative parties are central to a healthy democracy like Canada's, then coalitions that are the product of inter-network activity should be encouraged, not discouraged, by the institutions through which political leaders are chosen. Among the most important of a party's tasks are the recruitment and nomination of candidates for public office and the mobilization of voters for elections. But given the centrality of leadership to modern government and politics, none of a party's responsibilities is more critical than the selection of its leaders. The link between that act and the creation and sustenance of networks has been obvious since the outset of party conventions. A candidate (and candidate's organization) sufficiently skilled to have assembled a winning convention coalition has in place the nucleus of an electoral and governing coalition. That some convention-created coalitions transfer well to the electoral level and others do not was no better illustrated than in the contrasting fates of Chrétien and Campbell in 1993. If anything, the election that year proved beyond a doubt that politicians intent on seeking a party's leadership should have established roots and organizational contacts within the party in their own right to help to convert a convention win into a general election win.

Coalition-building in the context of convention politics is a product of bargaining among candidates and between candidates and delegates. A candidate who successfully carries out that task in the socially diverse milieu of Canadian politics has passed a critical test of leadership, for bargains will have had to have been struck along the way with partisans from more than one region, age, occupation, and language group. In that respect convention coalition-building has contributed to the development of basically centrist, consensual political parties and leadership in Canada.

The one member, one vote system poses a threat to accommodative, coalition-building leadership politics. The risk stems from the fact that a true universal balloting system is, in a sense, like a lottery: its winner is determined by the right combination of numbers. Winners in traditional leadership conventions are also determined by majoritarian rules, but the numbers that go into the winning convention combination derive from a different operational premise than that governing universal voting. It is an incontestable fact that members and active supporters of any party are more concentrated in some regions, provinces, or language groups than others. Those differentials have been discounted by Canada's two oldest parties since the outset of conventions by their insistence that each constituency send the same number of delegates to a convention as every other constituency, regardless of the size or complexion of its local membership. The effect of this rule has been to establish an incentive for candidates to seek support from a coalition of diverse (at least as diverse as local political activists normally are) and disbursed delegates and interests: endorsements here, supporters there, and so on.

Whatever its virtues, pure universal voting opens the door to the possibility of candidates playing by the opposite rules – that is of accepting the reality of location of party supporters or possible candidate-driven UMV recruits by going after a narrower set of supportive interests and voters. Some UMV systems that have been tried to date (such as the Ontario Conservative and Manitoba Liberal schemes) have experimented with different designs of weighted votes to guard against disproportionate influence from areas of concentrated membership, but with mixed success at best. The experience of others that have not done this (the Nova Scotia and British Columbia Liberal parties, for example) has confirmed the reality of regionally distorted participation patterns. For parties at the national level in Canada intent on constructing or maintaining a pan-Canadian coalition of diverse social interests and support in all regions, the implications of a one member, one vote system could be profound. For them, an unmodified universal ballot would be a less attractive leadership selection system than a traditional convention or than a markedly attenuated universal vote (such as the federal Liberals have put in place for their next leadership contest) because of the possibility that it would lend itself to candidates whose campaigns would heighten inter-regional, linguistic, and cultural tensions. One of the strengths of a convention system dominated by party regulars mindful of the party's long-term interests is that it "militate[s] against the choice of an extremist candidate."[15]

Conventions are one way of nurturing political networks; the universal ballot is not. Because it is based on the sanctity of the individual as the ultimate political participant, the one member, one vote system does nothing to create or to sustain networks. That is not the same thing as saying that there will not be organizers and supporters working on behalf of candidates to try to assure them of as many voters as possible; given the imperatives of political organization in competitive elections, of course, there will be. Rather it is to recognize that the kind of intra-party networks that are forged with the passage of time and the particular candidate-delegate contacts that are made in the course of a leadership campaign and convention would prove all but impossible to establish when an electorate of tens, possibly hundreds, of thousands of voters is involved.

Realistically, those sufficiently motivated to vote in a UMV leadership contest would turn even more to the media for cues about the contest than do delegates to current conventions. For their part, candidates, to compensate for their inability to establish personal and organizational contacts, would be obliged to make even greater use of the media and advertising to reach the voters. If anything, the process would be more likely to resemble a general election campaign than it now does and the role of the media would become even more pronounced than has been the case under conventions. The increased reliance on the media by candidates and voters alike would come at the expense of cross-regional and cross-social coalitions built over the course of a leadership campaign and of personal networks needed for the organizational well-being of a political party.

We have seen that with the understandable exception of youth and students, the vast majority of those who have served as delegates to national leadership conventions overwhelmingly have had several years of experience in the party. Whether ex officio or elected, delegates returning to successive conventions have an unequalled opportunity to share their reading of the party and its prospects under different candidates with others whose acquaintanceship they are either renewing or making for the first time. There is an inter-generational and inter-regional political socialization that takes place, particularly during the delegate selection period and the week of the convention itself, between political pros, seasoned amateurs, and eager novices. With the passage of time, this leads to a club-like atmosphere in the party. Doubtless a well-functioning political party is like a well-functioning club: those who pay their dues regularly, who have sufficient interest to serve on the executive, and who work for it through good times and bad eventually learn from their particular perspective who among them has the potential to lead and who has not.

Would this be the same with a universal ballot system? Almost certainly not. Much of the evidence to date suggests that those who participate in a universal vote on a party's leadership have far less commitment to the party than the regulars who have served as convention delegates.

Among those who took part in the 1992 Nova Scotia Liberal telephone vote on the party's leadership, for example, slightly more than half had not worked for the party in the previous provincial election. This compared with more than four-fifths at the party's leadership convention in 1986 who had worked for the party in the previous provincial election.[16] Compared with delegates who attended the party's 1987 leadership convention, those who voted in the British Columbia Liberal party's 1993 contest were far less likely to have been members of the party for more than five years, considerably more likely to have voted for a party other than the Liberals in the previous federal election, and three times as likely to have been active in another provincial party before joining the Liberals. One-third of the televoters had supported a party other than the Liberals in the provincial election only two years before.[17]

The figures from the governing Alberta Tories at the time of their 1992 UMV confirm the point even more dramatically. In the party's last leadership convention in 1986, 86 per cent of the delegates had belonged to the party for at least one year, 80 per cent had worked for it on a provincial campaign, and 59 per cent had held some sort of party office.[18] By contrast, in 1992 a majority of the participants said they had joined the party simply to vote for the new leader and only 18 per cent had worked for the party in the previous election. Fully one-quarter of the 1992 participants said they did not plan to *work* for the party in the next provincial election and one-quarter claimed they did not intend to *vote* for the party provincially.[19] David Stewart's assessment of Alberta Tory participants as having "very shallow roots" in the party at the time of its universal vote echoed Adamson, Beaton, and Stewart's conclusion that "party neophytes were empowered" by the Nova Scotia process and Blake and Carty's view that in British Columbia many were recruited during the leadership contest who had "only the most tangential connection to the party."[20]

Does it make any difference if in a vastly widened electorate choosing a party leader many, possibly a majority, have little or no attachment to the party and care little about the party's electoral or organizational well-being? Supporters of direct democracy would undoubtedly say that it did not, arguing that it would actually improve matters by wresting control away from long-dominant, often discredited, party elites and empowering citizens to act on their own behalf. To defenders of the universal ballot, mass participation through a direct, unmediated vote could be seen simply as a logical extension of the political involvement that had begun in the second generation of national leadership conventions when thousands of instant party members were recruited to elect slates of local delegates to party conventions.[21]

But the change to universal membership voting should not be considered risk-free. With the passage of time, the gradual abandonment of delegated conventions in favour of direct, universal voting on national party leadership in Canada could adversely affect both citizen involvement in parties and the parties themselves.[22] By placing a premium on the mobilization of vast, candidate-centred electorates created for each contest, the UMV offers no incentive to individuals to become involved in long-term service to a party. In the leadership convention process the principal local pools from which the great majority of constituency delegates have been chosen were for the most part made up of men and women who loyally served their party at the constituency level; who were involved in fund-raising, door-knocking, scrutineering, or serving as poll captains and the like during elections; and who generally helped to maintain their party between elections. Based on the premise that there is an implicit value in sustaining local political organizations, the convention process serves the interests both of activists and of the party. The continuation of such a mutually beneficial reciprocal relationship would be endangered by a system which devalued the assets of local political voluntarism and removed one of the incentives of long-term political involvement.

By having some measurable commitment to their party, local activists who become convention delegates acquire both opinions and information to share with one another. Admittedly, the vast majority have the party's short-term interests at heart, as is clear from their desire to see the party win office. But by the same token they also share an interest in the party's long-term survival. One of the lessons to be learned from the reforms introduced by American parties to their presidential nominating system after 1968 is that much of that could be lost by a party in moving to a vastly wider and less organizationally structured electorate. The interests of parties qua parties and, subsequently, of parties qua governing coalitions have been less assured in the United States under the reformed system than they had been previously.

The American reforms, directed at widening participation in presidential selection at the state level through primaries and caucuses, have encouraged candidates to wage campaigns aimed at winning the approval of mass, stated-based electorates. This has effectively challenged the role of parties and of party regulars in the aggregation and delivery of votes and replaced it with a system that has inspired candidates to seek the support of factions – that is, of groups acting through political parties in pursuit of their own more narrowly defined interests.[23] In the view of many leading students of American parties, candidates, rather than build coalitions, have had to resort to mobilizing factions. This in turn has enhanced the role of the mass media, as prospective nominees have vied with one another to mobilize short-term factional support on their behalf. As a consequence, electoral and governing coalitions have become more difficult to assemble and the parties' previous strength as coalition-building organizations has diminished.[24]

Conventions are not themselves demographically representative of society. But then neither are primaries – the closest American equivalent to the first stage of the new hybrid leadership selection system adopted by the federal and Ontario Liberal parties. Nor can it be said that direct, universal balloting systems guarantee any greater measure of socio-demographic participation than conventions. Studies of American primaries have shown that they do not broaden significantly the socio-demographic base of the participants in the presidential nominating process. They enlarge it to include several million voters, but the basic mix remains largely unchanged. As with delegates attending American national nominating conventions, those who vote in primaries tend to have higher-income, education, and occupation levels than non-voters.[25]

The few studies available of the demographics of participants in the early attempts by provincial parties in Canada to choose their leaders through some form of a universal membership vote show much the same thing. There may be situations peculiar to the party or to the politics of a particular province that account for some differences. In the Nova Scotia Liberal telephone vote of 1992 participation by older or retired people increased at the expense of students. But when the same televote system was used by the British Columbia Liberals the following year the reverse was the case, as younger party members were more likely to participate than the older. Age aside, the income, education, and gender variables of the telephone participants in the two contests remained largely unchanged over previous conventions.[26] Blake and Carty's conclusion about leadership selection by telephone is apt to the larger context of direct, universal voting. Televoting, they find, has not changed "the basic profile of those participating in the internal life of the political parties. Party membership is simply not representative of the wider electorate: it continues to be largely the preserve of the more affluent and better educated elements of the society."[27]

It may, in fact, be too early to judge the capacity of universal membership vote systems to widen significantly the mix of participants in the leadership selection process. It could be that with time, or the right system, or the right issues and candidates, parties will be able to point to a wider social diversity among those participating in a universal ballot. The early signs are not promising, however, as those who to date have participated either as delegates at conventions or among the larger group of universal ballot participants appear to have been drawn from similar socio-economic backgrounds.

Even if a wider socio-demographic mix were to occur among universal vote electors, that would be no assurance that they would be more responsive than convention participants to the variety of views of Canadians generally and to the long-term well-being of the party. Compared with party activists and notables who participate in national leadership conventions, voters in direct, universal elections may, if anything, be less responsive on both counts. Voter responsiveness is not the same as electoral representativeness. As participants in a UMV system can reasonably be expected to be motivated more by short-term goals and narrowly defined interests than convention delegates, it follows that those who serve as delegates are more likely to draw on their experience and political knowledge and, in the end, be more sensitive to the wider complex of interests that mark the general population. This has certainly been the case in the United States since the late 1960s when party reforms were instituted to widen participation in the presidential nominating process through primaries and caucuses.[28]

Who acts for whom? How many take part in the process? These are valid and important questions about any system that purports to be democratic. But democracy is not exclusively about representation and participation. It is also about authority, accountability, deliberation, and persuasion. Who is authorized to act for whom, and who is accountable to whom? By what process or through what institutions have arguments been put, heard, debated, and resolved? These questions too are at the heart of democratic theory.

It is easy to accept the claim that the move from caucus to convention as the means of choosing leaders was "democratic" because it involved more people. Adding more participants to the leadership selection process could be justified on the simple democratic premise that it effectively broadened the composition of the selecting body on the salient Canadian dimensions of region, culture, and language. As a bonus in terms of democratic theory, the additional participants in the leadership selection process were *authorized* in the weeks or months prior to a convention to act on behalf of others by some delegating body – a constituency party, a club, an association, or a union. (The manner in which some of those participants had been elected or appointed as delegates may have been controversial and disagreeable at the time and may have attracted unwanted publicity, but no one has ever successfully challenged the claim that democracy was not messy or riddled with contradictions.)

The authorization that was accorded delegates to participate in the selection of a leader was different and obviously less complete from that accorded MPs in the earlier caucus stage of choosing leaders, for it carried with it no obligation following the convention for delegates to be held electorally accountable to the body that chose them in the first place. Electoral accountability, however well or poorly it may have been understood by voters and parliamentarians at the time, had been one of the distinctions of the early caucus period of leadership selection. But it largely disappeared with the introduction of leadership conventions when the democratic responsibilities of delegates subsequent to the selection of a leader no longer matched their electoral privileges. Still, the benefits of the trade-off between enhanced representativeness on the one hand and absence of formal accountability on the other became apparent to the parties and the public. This was true especially throughout the second generation of conventions when the candidates, media, and general public shared an appetite for and an understanding of leadership conventions. National parties meeting periodically to choose a new leader or to review the current one's performance became one of the accepted fixtures of Canadian politics. From those meetings came a newly defined set of authoritative and accountable relationships among the leader, the parliamentary, and the extra-parliamentary parties which effectively removed the parliamentary caucus as a player in both the selection and the removal exercises.

Should national parties abandon completely their delegated leadership conventions in favour of a direct, universal vote, further democratic trade-offs would almost certainly follow. The direct, universal vote would represent the ultimate act of individualization of Canadian leadership selection politics. As such, it would rule out any need for prior authorization or subsequent accountability for a participant's vote and would devalue the currency of political experience. Service in the political trenches at the constituency, parliamentary, and national party levels has helped to inform the judgments of the vast majority of those who attend national conventions, whether as part of a candidate-organized slate or not. But the change to a universal vote would come at the cost of the acquired value of political experience – whether acquired in caucus or in the party apparatus – of those working most closely with the leader, the prospective leaders, and the party.

Conventions do matter to Canadian democracy. They have not been without problems, as we have seen, especially when the two older parties turned a blind eye to the financing of candidate campaigns and to questionable organizational tactics employed in the selection of delegates. But these are scarcely insurmountable difficulties, given the sort of statutory financial controls and self-disciplinary reforms that could easily be put in place (to popular acclaim) should parties in their own self-interest choose to address them.

In spite of these blemishes on their record, national parties have demonstrated through their conventions that they have a proven capacity to energize politics and to contribute to the general well-being of a political party; to inform and educate the larger public; and to interest voters in arguably the most important task a party performs – choosing its leader. By carrying out these organizational and pedagogic tasks, parties have discharged an institutional civic responsibility. This must, by any standard, be judged to be at the core of a healthy democracy.

A direct, universal vote on a party's leadership has an appealing ring to it. This will remain the case if delegated conventions involving fewer participants is painted, warts and all, as the unattractive alternative. The profoundly democratic attraction of one member, one vote derives quite simply from its direct inclusion, however fleetingly, of a vastly larger number of people in the process of choosing leaders than had been true heretofore. The strength of that appeal could well outweigh the concerns expressed by critics of direct, universal voting, thus bringing an end to conventions as Canadians have come to know them for the better part of this century. Yet the alleged benefits of universal voting may in the long run be more ephemeral than its proponents claim. The switch could ultimately prove problematic for the health of local political organizations and the larger political community in Canada.

Tables

Table 2-1 Liberal Convention, 5–7 August 1919, Ottawa, Ontario
Leadership Balloting: 7 August

Candidates in order of rank on first ballot	First ballot	Second ballot	Fifth ballot[a]	Parliamentary experience		Provincial experience	
				House or Senate	Cabinet	House	Cabinet
W.L. Mackenzie King	344	411	476	3 yrs.	2 yrs. 4 mo.	–	–
William S. Fielding	297	344	438	16 yrs. 7 mo.	15 yrs. 2½ mo.	14 yrs.	13 yrs. 5 mo.
George Graham	153	124		9 yrs. 10 mo.	4 yrs. 1½ mo.	9 yrs.	2½ mo.
D.D. McKenzie	153	60		13 yrs.	–	4 yrs.	–
TOTAL NUMBER VOTING	947	939	914				

[a] The third and fourth ballots were destroyed after being partially taken because of Mr Graham's and Mr McKenzie's withdrawals.

Table 2-2 Liberal Convention, 5–7 August 1948, Ottawa, Ontario
Leadership Balloting: 7 August

Candidates in order of rank on first ballot	First ballot	Parliamentary experience		Provincial experience	
		House or Senate	Cabinet	House	Cabinet
Louis St Laurent	848	6 yrs. 6 mo.	6 yrs. 8 mo.	–	–
James G. Gardiner	323	12 yrs. 7 mo.	12 yrs. 9½ mo.	21 yrs. 4 mo.	8 yrs. 8½ mo.
C.G. Power	56	30 yrs. 7½ mo.	9 yrs. 1 mo.	–	–
TOTAL NUMBER VOTING	1,227				

Table 2-3 Liberal Convention, 14–16 January 1958, Ottawa, Ontario
Leadership Balloting: 16 January

Candidates in order of rank on first ballot	First ballot	Parliamentary experience		Provincial experience	
		House or Senate	Cabinet	House	Cabinet
Lester B. Pearson	1,074	9 yrs. 3 mo.	8 yrs. 9 mo.	–	–
Paul Martin	305	22 yrs. 3 mo.	12 yrs. 2 mo.	–	–
Lloyd Henderson	1	–	–	–	–
TOTAL NUMBER VOTING	1,380				

Table 2-4 Liberal-Conservative Convention, 10–12 October 1927, Winnipeg, Manitoba
Leadership Balloting: 12 October

Candidates in order of rank on first ballot	First ballot	Second ballot	Parliamentary experience		Provincial experience	
			House or Senate	Cabinet	House	Cabinet
R.B. Bennett	594	780	8 yrs. 2 ½ mo.	5 ½ mo.	8 yrs.	–
Hugh Guthrie	345	320	27 yrs.	2 yrs. 9 mo.	–	–
C.H. Cahan	310	266	2 yrs.	–	4 yrs.	–
R.J. Manion	170	148	9 yrs. 10 mo.	6 mo.	–	–
R. Rogers	114	37	7 yrs. 1 mo.	5 yrs. 10 ½ mo.	12 yrs.	11 yrs.
Sir H. Drayton	31	3	8 yrs. 6 mo.	2 yrs. 8 mo.	–	–
TOTAL NUMBER VOTING	1,564	1,554				

Table 2-5 National Conservative Convention, 5–7 July 1938, Ottawa, Ontario
Leadership Balloting: 7 July

Candidates in order of rank on first ballot	First ballot	Second ballot	Parliamentary experience		Provincial experience	
			House or Senate	Cabinet	House	Cabinet
R.J. Manion	726	830	17 yrs. 10 mo.	5 yrs. 2 ½ mo.	–	–
M.A. MacPherson	475	648	–	–	9 yrs. 5 ½ mo.	5 yrs. 2 mo.
Joseph Harris	131	49	16 yrs. 7 mo.	–	–	–
Denton Massey	128	39	2 yrs. 9 mo.	–	–	–
J.E. Lawson	105[a]		9 yrs. 9 mo.	2 mo.	–	–
TOTAL NUMBER VOTING	1,565	1,566				

[a] Withdrew after first ballot

Table 2-6 Progressive Conservative Convention, 9–11 December 1942, Winnipeg, Manitoba
Leadership Balloting: 11 December

Candidates in order of rank on first ballot	First ballot	Second ballot	Parliamentary experience		Provincial experience	
			House or Senate	Cabinet	House	Cabinet
John Bracken	420	538	–	–	20 yrs. 2 mo.	20 yrs. 4 mo.
M.A. MacPherson	222	255	–	–	9 yrs. 5 ½ mo.	5 yrs. 2 mo.
John G. Diefenbaker	120	79	2 yrs. 8 ½ mo.	–	–	–
H.C. Green	88[a]		7 yrs. 2 mo.	–	–	–
H.H. Stevens	20[a]		28 yrs. 5 ½ mo.	4 yrs. 8 ½ mo.	–	–
TOTAL NUMBER VOTING	870	872				

[a] Withdrew after first ballot

Table 2-7 Progressive Conservative Convention, 30 September – 2 October 1948, Ottawa, Ontario
Leadership Balloting: 2 October

Candidates in order of rank on first ballot	First ballot	Parliamentary experience		Provincial experience	
		House or Senate	*Cabinet*	*House*	*Cabinet*
George Drew	827	–	–	9 yrs. 7 ½ mo.	5 yrs. 1 ½ mo.
John G. Diefenbaker	311	8 yrs. 6 mo.	–	–	–
Donald M. Fleming	104	3 yrs. 3 ½ mo.	–	–	–
TOTAL NUMBER VOTING	1,242				

Table 2-8 Progressive Conservative Convention, 12–14 December 1956, Ottawa, Ontario
Leadership Balloting: 14 December

Candidates in order of rank on first ballot	First ballot	Parliamentary experience		Provincial experience	
		House or Senate	*Cabinet*	*House*	*Cabinet*
John G. Diefenbaker	774	16 yrs. 8 ½ mo.	–	–	–
Donald M. Fleming	393	11 yrs. 6 mo.	–	–	–
E. Davie Fulton	117	11 yrs. 6 mo.	–	–	–
TOTAL NUMBER VOTING	1,284				

Table 2-9 New Democrat Convention, 31 July – 4 August 1961, Ottawa, Ontario
Leadership Balloting: 3 August

Candidates in order of rank on first ballot	First ballot	Parliamentary experience		Provincial experience	
		House or Senate	*Cabinet*	*House*	*Cabinet*
Thomas C. Douglas	1,391	8 yrs. 7 mo.	–	17 yrs. 4 mo.	17 yrs. 4 mo.
Hazen Argue	380	16 yrs. 1 mo.	–	–	–
TOTAL NUMBER VOTING	1,771				

Table 2-10 Progressive Conservative Convention, 5–9 September 1967, Toronto, Ontario
Leadership Balloting: 9 September

Candidates in order of rank on first ballot	First ballot	Second ballot	Third ballot	Fourth ballot	Fifth ballot	Parliamentary experience		Provincial experience	
						House or Senate	Cabinet	House	Cabinet
Robert L. Stanfield	519	613	717	865	1150	–	–	18 yrs.	11 yrs.
Duff Roblin	347	430	541	771	969	–	–	17 yrs. 10 mo.	9 yrs. 5 mo.
E. Davie Fulton	343	346	361	357[b]		19 yrs. 8 mo.	5 yrs. 10 mo.	–	–
George Hees	295	299	277[b]			14 yrs. 9 mo.	5 yrs. 8 mo.	–	–
John G. Diefenbaker	271	172	114[b]			27 yrs. 5 ½ mo.	5 yrs. 10 mo.	–	–
Wallace McCutcheon	137	76[b]				5 yrs. 1 mo.	8 mo.	–	–
Alvin Hamilton	136	127	106	167[a]		10 yrs. 3 mo.	5 yrs. 8 mo.	–	–
Donald M. Fleming	126	115	76[a]			17 yrs. 10 mo.	5 yrs. 10 mo.	–	–
Michael Starr	45	34[a]				15 yrs. 3 ½ mo.	5 yrs. 10 mo.	–	–
John MacLean	10[b]							–	–
Mary Walker-Sawka	2[a]							–	–
TOTAL NUMBER VOTING	2,231	2,212	2,192	2,160	2,119				

[a] Eliminated as a result of this ballot.
[b] Withdrew after this ballot.

Table 2-11 Progressive Conservative Convention, 19–22 February 1976, Ottawa, Ontario Leadership Balloting: 22 February

Candidates in order of rank on first ballot	First ballot	Second ballot	Third ballot	Fourth ballot	Parliamentary experience		Provincial experience	
					House or Senate	Cabinet	House	Cabinet
Claude Wagner	531	667	1003	1122	3 yrs. 4 mo.	–	5 yrs. 4 mo.	1 yr. 8 mo.
Brian Mulroney	357	419	369[a]		–	–	–	–
Joe Clark	277	532	969	1187	3 yrs. 4 mo.	–	–	–
Jack Horner	235	286[b]			17 yrs. 11 mo.	–	–	–
Paul Hellyer	231	118[b]			23 yrs. 6 mo.	5 yrs. 3 ½ mo.	–	–
Flora MacDonald	214	239[b]			3 yrs. 4 mo.	–	–	–
Sinclair Stevens	182[b]				3 yrs. 4 mo.	–	–	–
John Fraser	127	34[a]			3 yrs. 4 mo.	–	–	–
Jim Gillies	87[b]				3 yrs. 4 mo.	–	–	–
Patrick Nowlan	86	42[b]			10 yrs. 3 mo.	–	–	–
Heward Grafftey	33[a]				17 yrs. 11 mo.	–	–	–
R.C. Quittenton	0[a]				–	–	–	–
TOTAL NUMBER VOTING	2,360	2,337	2,341	2,309				

[a] Eliminated as a result of this ballot.
[b] Withdrew after this ballot.

Table 2-12 Progressive Conservative Convention, 8–11 June 1983, Ottawa, Ontario
Leadership Balloting: 11 June

Candidates in order of rank on first ballot	First ballot	Second ballot	Third ballot	Fourth ballot	Parliamentary experience		Provincial experience	
					House or Senate	Cabinet	House	Cabinet
Joe Clark	1,091	1,085	1,058	1,325	10 yrs. 7 ½ mo.	9 mo.	–	–
Brian Mulroney	874	1,021	1,036	1,584	–	–	–	–
John Crosbie	639	781	858[a]		6 yrs. 8 mo.	9 mo.	10 yrs.	6 yrs. 6 mo.
Michael Wilson	144[b]				4 yrs. ½ mo.	9 mo.	–	–
David Crombie	116	67[a]			4 yrs. 8 mo.	9 mo.	–	–
Peter Pocklington	102[b]					–	–	–
John Gamble	17[a]					–	–	–
Neil Fraser	5[a]					–	–	–
TOTAL NUMBER VOTING	2,988	2,954	2,952	2,909				

[a] Eliminated as a result of this ballot.
[b] Withdrew after this ballot.

Table 2-13 Progressive Conservative Convention, 11–13 June 1993, Ottawa, Ontario
Leadership Balloting: 13 June

| Candidates in order of rank on first ballot | First ballot | Second ballot | Parliamentary experience | | Provincial experience | |
			House or Senate	Cabinet	House	Cabinet
Kim Campbell	1,664	1,817	4 yrs. 6 mo.	4 yrs. 4 mo.	2 yrs.	–
Jean Charest	1,369	1,630	8 yrs. 9 mo.	6 yrs. 11 mo.	–	–
Jim Edwards	307[b]		8 yrs. 9 mo.	–	–	–
Garth Turner	76[b]		4 yrs. 6 mo.	–	–	–
Patrick Boyer	53[a]		8 yrs. 9 mo.	–	–	–
TOTAL NUMBER VOTING	3,469	3,447				

[a] Eliminated as a result of this ballot.
[b] Withdrew after this ballot.

Table 2-14 Liberal Convention, 4–6 April 1968, Ottawa, Ontario
Leadership Balloting: 6 April

Candidates in order of rank on first ballot	First ballot	Second ballot	Third ballot	Fourth ballot	Parliamentary experience		Provincial experience	
					House or Senate	Cabinet	House	Cabinet
Pierre E. Trudeau	752	964	1,051	1,203	2 yrs. 5 mo.	1 yr.	–	–
Paul Hellyer	330	465	377[b]		17 yrs. 4 mo.	5 yrs. 1 ½ mo.	–	–
Robert Winters	293	473	621	954	14 yrs. 5 mo.	10 yrs. 10 mo.	–	–
John Turner	277	347	279	195	5 yrs. 10 mo.	2 yrs. 4 mo.	–	–
Paul Martin	277[b]				32 yrs. 6 mo.	17 yrs. 2 mo.	–	–
J.J. Greene	169	104	29[a]		5 yrs.	2 yrs. 4 mo.	–	–
A.J. MacEachern	165	11[c]			10 yrs. 7 ½ mo.	9 mo.	–	–
Eric Kierans	103[b]				10 yrs. 5 ½ mo.	5 yrs.	5 yrs.	5 yrs.
Lloyd Henderson	0[a]				–		–	–
TOTAL NUMBER VOTING	2,366	2,364	2,357	2,352				

[a] Eliminated as a result of this ballot.

[b] Withdrew after this ballot.

[c] Withdrew after the first ballot but his name remained on the ballot because formal notification failed to reach the chairman of the convention in time and eleven supporters missed the notification of his withdrawal. Subsequently eliminated as of this ballot.

Table 2-15 Liberal Convention, 14–16 June 1984, Ottawa, Ontario
Leadership Balloting: 16 June

Candidates in order of rank on first ballot	First ballot	Second ballot	Parliamentary experience		Provincial experience	
			House or Senate	Cabinet	House	Cabinet
John Turner	1,593	1,862	13 yrs. 8 mo.	9 yrs. 9 mo.	–	–
Jean Chrétien	1,067	1,368	21 yrs. 2 mo.	16 yrs. 5 ½ mo.	–	–
Don Johnston	278	192	5 yrs. 8 mo.	4 yrs. 3 ½ mo.	–	–
John Roberts	185[b]		13 yrs. 8 ½ mo.	7 yrs.	–	–
Mark MacGuigan		135[b]	16 yrs.	4 yrs. 3 ½ mo.	–	–
John Munro	93[b]		22 yrs.	15 yrs. 5 mo.	–	–
Eugene Whelan	84[a]		22 yrs.	10 yrs. 10 mo.	–	–
TOTAL NUMBER VOTING	3,435	3,422				

[a] Eliminated as a result of this ballot.
[b] Withdrew after this ballot.

Table 2-16 Liberal Convention, 20–23 June 1990, Calgary, Alberta
Leadership Balloting: 23 June

Candidates in order of rank on first ballot	First ballot	Parliamentary experience		Provincial experience	
		House or Senate	Cabinet	House	Cabinet
Jean Chrétien	2,652	22 yrs. 11 mo.	16 yrs. 8 mo.	–	–
Paul Martin Jr.	1,176	1 yr. 7 mo.	–	–	–
Sheila Copps	499	5 yrs. 9 ½ mo.	–	3 yrs. 3 mo.	–
Tom Wappel	267	1 yr. 7 mo.	–	–	–
John Nunziata	64	5 yrs. 9 ½ mo.	–	–	–
TOTAL NUMBER VOTING	4,658				

Table 2-17 New Democrat Convention, 21–24 April 1971, Ottawa, Ontario
Leadership Balloting: 24 April

Candidates in order of rank on first ballot	First ballot	Second ballot	Third ballot	Fourth ballot	Parliamentary experience		Provincial experience	
					House or Senate	Cabinet	House	Cabinet
David Lewis	661	715	742	1,046	6 yrs. 4 mo.	–	–	–
James Laxer	378	407	508	612	–	–	–	–
John Harney	299	347	431[a]		–	–	–	–
Ed Broadbent	236	223[a]			2 yrs. 10 mo.	–	–	–
Frank Howard	124[a]				13 yrs. 11 mo.	–	3 yrs. 7 ½ mo.	–
TOTAL NUMBER VOTING	1,698	1,692	1,681	1,658				

[a] Eliminated as a result of this ballot.

Table 2-18 New Democrat Convention, 4–7 July 1975, Winnipeg, Manitoba
Leadership Balloting: 7 July

Candidates in order of rank on first ballot	First ballot	Second ballot	Third ballot	Fourth ballot	Parliamentary experience		Provincial experience	
					House or Senate	Cabinet	House	Cabinet
Ed Broadbent	536	586	694	948	7 yrs.	–	–	–
Rosemary Brown	413	397	494	658	–	–	2 yrs. 10 mo.	–
Lorne Nystrom	345	342	413[a]		7 yrs.	–	–	–
John Harney	313	299[a]			1 yr. 8 mo.	–	–	–
Douglas Campbell	11[a]				–	–	–	–
TOTAL NUMBER VOTING	1,618	1,624	1,601	1,606				

[a] Eliminated as a result of this ballot.

Table 2-19 New Democrat Convention, 30 November – 2 December 1989, Winnipeg, Manitoba
Leadership Balloting: 2 December

Candidates in order of rank on first ballot	First ballot	Second ballot	Third ballot	Fourth ballot	Parliamentary experience		Provincial experience	
					House or Senate	Cabinet	House	Cabinet
Audrey McLaughlin	646	829	1,072	1,316	2 yrs. 4 mo.	–	–	–
David Barrett	566	780	947	1,072	11 mo.	–	21 yrs. 11 mo.	3 yrs. 3 mo.
Steven Langdon	351	519	393[b]		5 yrs. 3 mo.	–	–	–
Simon de Jong	315	289[b]			10 yrs. 7 mo.	–	–	–
Howard McCurdy	256[a]				5 yrs. 3 mo.	–	–	–
Ian Waddell	213[a]				10 yrs. 7 mo.	–	–	–
Roger Lagassé	53[b]				–	–	–	–
TOTAL NUMBER VOTING	2,400	2,417	2,412	2,388				

[a] Withdrew after this ballot.
[b] Eliminated as a result of this ballot.

Table 3-1 CCF and NDP Leadership Events of Note, 1932–94

	Date	Place	Event
CCF	1932	Calgary	J.S. Woodsworth elected president unanimously without contest
	1940	Winnipeg	Woodsworth named honorary president[1]
	1942	Toronto	M.J. Coldwell elected president unanimously without contest
	1960	Regina	Hazen Argue elected national leader unanimously without contest[2]
NDP	1961	Ottawa	T.C. Douglas elected leader on first ballot
	1971	Ottawa	David Lewis elected leader on fourth ballot
	1973	Vancouver	Lewis re-elected leader on first ballot challenge by Douglas Campbell
	1975	Winnipeg	Ed Broadbent elected leader on fourth ballot
	1989	Winnipeg	Audrey McLaughlin elected leader on fourth ballot

[1] On 6 November 1940 caucus elected Coldwell acting house leader and on 22 April 1942, following Woodsworth's death, house leader.

[2] On 23 April 1958, following Coldwell's defeat, caucus elected Argue house leader. Coldwell remained president and national leader until the 1960 convention when he was elected honorary national leader.

Table 3-2 Share of Delegates Opposed to Calling a Leadership Convention:
Liberal and Conservative Parties, 1970–1995

Liberal			Conservative		
Year	%	Leader	Year	%	Leader
1970	89	Trudeau	1974	86	Stanfield
1973	90	Trudeau	1977	93	Clark
1975	81	Trudeau	1981	66	Clark
1980	87	Trudeau	1983	67	Clark
1986	76	Turner	1995	96	Charest
1994	91	Chrétien			

	Reform	
Year	%	Leader
1994	92	Manning

Sources: Paul Pihichyn, "Trudeau Leads Asper Ovation," *Winnipeg Free Press*, 23 November 1970, 2; Robert Sheppard, "Liberals' attempt to codify policies falls into disarray," *Globe and Mail*, 7 July 1980, 1; Wayne Cheveldayoff, "Liberals give PM show of support," *Globe and Mail*, 17 Sept 1973; *Canadian Annual Review,* 1973–1986; John Saywell, ed., *1974,* 29; Saywell, ed., *1975,* 91; Saywell, ed., *1977,* 46; R.B. Byers, ed., *1981,* 144; Byers, ed., *1983,* 42; Byers, ed., *1986,* 43; all published by University of Toronto Press; "Tough gun law coming, PM promises Liberals," *StarPhoenix,* 16 May 1994, A1; Larry Johnsrude, "Manning, Reformers deliver tough small-c conservative line," *StarPhoenix,* 17 October, 1994, A1; and Susan Delacourt, "Tories feeling tug to the right," *Globe and Mail,* 1 May 1995, A1.

Table 3-3 Vulnerability Factors in Australia, Britain, and Canada

Country	Party	Constituency	Leaders' influence	Opportunity	Need for alternative
Australia	Labor	narrow	low	unlimited	no
	Liberal	narrow	medium	unlimited	no
Britain	Conservative	narrow	high	annual	yes
Canada	Liberal	broad	low	once per parliament	no
	Conservative	broad	low	once per parliament in opposition only	no
	NDP	broad	low	biennial	yes
	Reform	broad	low	biennial	no

Source: Adapted and expanded from Patrick Weller, *First among Equals: Prime Ministers in Westminster Systems* (Sydney: George Allen & Unwin, 1985), 70. Reprinted by permission of the author.

Table 4-1 Maximum Potential Registration Fees and Tax Credits, 1990 Liberal Leadership Convention*

	Fee	Tax credit	Cost to individual	Number	Cost to treasury	Revenue to party
Delegates/Alternates	$875	$408	$467	4,131	$1,685,448	$3,614,625
Youth/Alternates	$675	$342	$335	2,277	$ 778,734	$1,536,975
Observers	$500	$275	$225	580	$ 159,500	$ 290,000
Total	n.a.	n.a.	n.a.	6,988	$2,623,682	$5,441,600

Sources: Liberal Party of Canada, Ottawa. Actual number of observers obtained from Charles King, director of communications, Liberal Party of Canada. King interview, 12 November 1993.

* Assumptions: Maximum potential number of delegates and alternates. Actual number of observers. Each individual paid his or her own registration and was eligible for the maximum tax credit allowable. This establishes the greatest *potential* cost to the treasury. Clearly not everyone would be eligible for the amount this table assigns to them. For example, some may already have contributed to the party in that year, in which case the amount they could claim on their 1991 income tax would be affected. On the other hand, some delegates (how many is impossible to determine) would have taken advantage of the option of raising funds from a number of different persons, businesses, or other organizations who were eligible for an official receipt. As this would typically be more for smaller than for larger amounts, the cost to the treasury would be greater. For example: a youth delegate who raised $600 from six different sources at $100 each would ensure that each donor received a receipt from the party for $100. The cost to the treasury would be 6 x $75, or $450. Had the $600 been paid by one individual, the maximum tax credit would be $317.

Table 4-2 1990 Liberal Leadership Convention Budget

REVENUE	
Delegate/alternate fees	$ 2,871,177
Youth delegate/alternate fees	$ 1,095,595
Observer fees	$ 268,502
Leadership forums	$ 136,450
Leader's night	$ 12,950
Other	$ 17,720
TOTAL REVENUE	$ 4,402,394[a]

EXPENSES	
Travel assistance	$ 2,202,817
Finance and administration	$ 561,115
Leadership forums	$ 203,203
Opening/leader's night	$ 147,936
Delegate services	$ 326,235
Constitution and legal	$ 202,324
Technical services	$ 374,361
Communications	$ 204,460
Special committees	$ 14,242
1989 convention costs	$ 45,982
TOTAL EXPENSES	$ 4,402,392[b]

Source: W.T. Stanbury, *Money in Politics: Financing Federal Parties and Candidates in Canada,* vol. 1 of the research studies for the Royal Commission on Electoral Reform and Party Financing (Toronto: Dundurn Press, 1991), table 5.8, 483. Reproduced by permission of the Minister of Supply and Services of Canada, 1995.

[a] Total revenue from convention fees reported by the Liberal party was $4,391,943. Reform Commission of the Liberal Party of Canada, "Agenda for Reform," interim report, 31 July 1991, 16.

[b] Total expenses reported to the Chief Electoral Officer was $4,585,660.

Table 4-3 Reported/Estimated Expenditures of Selected Leadership Candidates, 1967–93

		Current $[1]	1993 $[2]
1967:	Robert Stanfield	150,000 (est.)	642,000
1968:	Pierre Trudeau	300,000 (est.)	1,240,000
	John Turner	128,000 (est.)	529,000
1976:	Claude Wagner	266,538	621,000
	Brian Mulroney	343–500,000 (est.)	799–1,165,000
	Joe Clark	168,353	392,000
	Jack Horner	278,383	648,000
	Paul Hellyer	287,788	670,000
	Flora MacDonald	152,704	356,000
	Sinclair Stevens	294,106	685,000
	John Fraser	116,107	270,000
	James Gillies	192,847	449,000
	Patrick Nowlan	58,635	137,000
	Heward Grafftey	83,845	195,000
	Richard Quittenton	9,336	22,000
1983:	Brian Mulroney	1,900,000 (est.)	2,550,000
	Joe Clark	1,900,000 (est.)	2,550,000
	John Crosbie	1,800,000 (est.)	2,416,000
	Peter Pocklington	965,000 (est.)	1,295,000
1984:	John Turner	1,594,941	2,077,000
	Jean Chrétien	1,528,570	1,990,000
	Don Johnston	928,010	1,208,000
	John Roberts	735,919	958,000
	Mark MacGuigan	357,267	465,000
	John Munro	625,000 (est.)	814,000
	Eugene Whelan	191,603	249,000

Table 4-3 Reported/Estimated Expenditures of Selected Leadership Candidates,
1967–93 *(Continued)*

		Current $[1]	*1993 $[2]*
1990:	Jean Chrétien	2,446,036	2,556,000
	Paul Martin	2,371,690	2,478,000
	Sheila Copps	806,064	842,000
	Tom Wappel	143,186	150,000
	John Nunziata	166,076	174,000
1993[3]:	Kim Campbell	3,000,000	3,000,000
	Jean Charest	2,300,000	2,300,000
	Jim Edwards	602,000	602,000
	Patrick Boyer	197,000	197,000
	Garth Turner	65,000	65,000

Sources: For 1967, 1968, and estimates for 1983, see John Laschinger and Geoffrey Stevens, *Leaders and Lesser Mortals: Backroom Politics in Canada* (Toronto: Key Porter Books, 1992), 152. For 1976, see PC Party of Canada, "Confidential report of expenditures of leadership candidates, 1976." For Horner in 1976 see the Ontario Commission on Election Contributions and Expenses, *Political Financing: Studies on Election Spending Limits and Party Leadership Campaigns* (1986), 83. For estimates of Mulroney's spending in 1976, see Laschinger and Stevens, *Leaders and Lesser Mortels* 197; and *Maclean's*, 28 June 1976, 17. Laschinger and Stevens suggest that in 1983 Clark's and Mulroney's spending may have approached $3 million (p. 281, n1). For all 1984 candidates except John Munro, see "Final Expenditures Report," Liberal Papers, MG 28 IV 3, vol. 1645, "Leadership Expenses Committee." For Munro, see Ross Howard, "Liberal leadership attempts leave two ministers in debt," *Globe and Mail*, 31 August 1984, 3. For 1990, see Liberal Party of Canada, "1990 Leadership Convention Candidates' Expenses," press release of 7 November 1990. For 1993, see Ross Howard, "Tory leadership contest cost more than $6-million," *Globe and Mail*, 2 March 1994, A1.

[1] With the exception of the 1993 Tory campaign (see note 3) figures are for reported spending of the candidates unless candidates were not required to file a disclosure form or unless disclosure form could not be located, in which case the figures are estimates only.

[2] Index used was the GDP deflator. *Bank of Canada Review,* May 1987, table H4; and Spring 1994, table H3.

[3] Figures are approximations of actual spending based on reports of the candidates' spending reports. For example, Campbell's campaign organization officially reported spending about $1,200,000 on items included in the party-imposed spending limit (the candidates were not required to report their spending in areas exempt from the limit) but raising $2,800,000. It also reported that she had some debts remaining after the convention. In the interests of accuracy, $3,000,000 is a better figure than $1,200,000.

Table 4-4 Reported Expenditures of NDP Leadership Candidates, 1989

	1989 $	1993 $[1]
Audrey McLaughlin	128,575.50	137,000
Dave Barrett	113,986.98	122,000
Steven Langdon	52,461.91	56,000
Simon de Jong	42,516.85	45,000
Howard McCurdy	72,891.54	78,000
Ian Waddell	39,256.00	42,000
Roger Lagassé	11,891.62	13,000

Source: for 1989 data, Keith Archer, "Leadership Selection in the New Democratic Party," in Herman Bakvis, ed., *Canadian Political Parties: Leaders, Candidates and Organization,* vol. 13 of the Research Studies for the Royal Commission on Electoral Reform and Party Financing (Toronto: Dundurn Press, 1991), 42. Reproduced by permission of the Minister of Supply and Services Canada, 1995.

[1] Index used was the GDP deflator. *Bank of Canada Review,* Spring 1994, table H3.

Table 4-5 Value of Tax Credits to Candidates in the 1990 Liberal Campaign

Candidate	Value of tax credits ($)	Tax receipts issued ($)[a]	Reported Expenditures
Chrétien	302,000	910,000	2,446,036
Martin	112,000	400,000	2,371,690
Copps	193,000	450,000	806,064
Wappel	22,000	45,000	143,186
Nunziata	46,000	100,000	166,076
Lincoln[b]	18,000	45,000	n/a

Sources: Computed from candidate expenses data made available by the Liberal Party of Canada. The total receipted contributions to the candidates is given in Reform Commission of the Liberal Party of Canada, "Agenda for Reform," interim report, 31 July 1991, 16.

[a] The Liberal party reported that total receipted revenue for the candidates was $1,954,958. Note that many donors contributed to two or more candidates.

[b] Clifford Lincoln declared his candidacy but he later withdrew from the race and did not file a report of his expenditures with the party.

Table 5-1 Television Audience Size for the 1989, 1990, and 1993 Leadership Conventions

	New Democratic convention, 1989	Liberal convention, 1990	Progressive Conservative convention, 1993
Voting day	December 2	June 23	June 13
Population (18+)[1]	19,924,000	20,112,000	21,227,000
CBC-TV			
Time of live coverage	2:00–8:10 p.m.	4:00–9:50 p.m.	4:00–9:30 p.m.
Reach[2] (18+)	4,021,000	3,732,000	5,125,000
Percentage	20.2	18.6	24.1
CTV			
Time of live coverage	6:00–8:04 p.m.	4:00–9:42 p.m.	5:18–9:00 p.m.
Reach (18+)	2,000,000[3]	3,238,000	3,820,000
Percentage	10.0[4]	16.1	18.0
Radio-Canada			
Time of live coverage	2:00–8:10 p.m.	3:30–9:50 p.m.	4:00–9:15 p.m.
Reach (18+)	1,492,000[5]	1,177,000	1,709,000
Percentage	7.5	5.9	8.1

Sources: Statistics Canada, 1991 Census, *Age, Sex and Marital Status: The Nation* (Ottawa: Minister of Industry, Science and Technology, 1992), 109. Ratings data for CBC-TV and CTV were obtained from CBC Research. Ratings data for Radio-Canada were obtained from CBC (Montreal). Special thanks to Joanne Gooding of CBC Research and Nicole St-Pierre Lavigne of CBC (Montreal) who did the actual work of retrieval.

1 1991 census data adjusted to include only those 18 years and over at the time of each of the three conventions.

2 Ratings by A.C. Nielsen. In every case except for the ratings of Radio-Canada's coverage of the NDP convention of 1989, the Reach data are the total number of different people (aged 18+) who watched at least one minute of the program. For the ratings of Radio-Canada's coverage of the NDP convention of 1989, the Reach figure is the total number of different people (aged 18+) who watched at least one quarter-hour of the program. Reach data based on one-minute audiences are not comparable to Reach data based on quarter-hour audiences.

3 2,000,000 is a reasonable estimate designed to prevent the double-counting of viewers. It is based on the Reach data available for CTV's coverage of the NDP convention of 1989. In 1989, CTV chose to have their data reported in half-hour and hour breaks:

Time	Reach (18 years and over)
6:00–6:30 p.m.	743,000
6:30–7:00 p.m.	772,000
7:00–8:04 p.m.	1,507,000

These half-hourly and hourly figures cannot be averaged.

4 The percentage of adults 18 years and over is particularly low in part because of the small amount of time that CTV devoted to live coverage of the convention on voting day.

5 For the ratings of Radio-Canada's coverage of the NDP convention of 1989, the Reach figure is the total number of different people (aged 18+) who watched at least one quarter-hour of the program. Reach data based on one-minute audiences are not comparable to Reach data based on quarter-hour audiences.

Table 5-2 Television Audience Size for Selected Leadership Conventions, 1967–84, CBC-TV

Convention and voting day[1]	Time of coverage	Population (18+)[2]	Reach (18+)[3]	Percentage
Conservative convention, 9 September 1967	1:00–10:54 p.m.	12,680,000	2,026,000	16.0
Liberal convention, 6 April 1968	1:30–8:30 p.m.	13,050,000	3,209,000	24.6
NDP convention, 24 April 1971	1:00–5:20 p.m.	13,875,000	1,331,000	9.6
Conservative convention, 22 February 1976	11:30 a.m.–9:00 p.m.	15,550,000	3,938,000	25.3
Liberal convention, 16 June 1984	2:00–10:00 p.m.	18,000,000	3,109,000	17.3

Sources: Ratings data were obtained from CBC Research. Special thanks to Joanne Gooding of CBC Research who did the actual work of retrieval. Dominion Bureau of Statistics, 1966 Census, *Population: Single Years of Age* (Ottawa: Minister of Trade and Commerce, 1968), 25–1, 25–2. Statistics Canada, 1971 Census, *Population: Single Years of Age* (Ottawa: Minister of Industry, Trade and Commerce, 1973), 14–1, 14–2. Statistics Canada, 1976 Census, *Population: Demographic Characteristics* (Ottawa: Minister of Supply and Services, 1978), 11–1. Statistics Canada, 1986 Census, *Age, Sex and Marital Status* (Ottawa: Minister of Supply and Services, 1987), 4–1, 4–2.

[1] Ratings data for the NDP convention of 1975 and the Conservative convention of 1983 are not available as those weeks were not surveyed for CBC-TV by A.C. Nielsen.

[2] Figures for 1967 and 1968 are based on 1966 census data adjusted to include only those 18 years and over at the time of each of the two conventions. The figure for 1971 is based on 1971 census data. The figure for 1976 is based on 1976 census data adjusted to include only those 18 years and over at the time of each of the two conventions. The figure for 1984 is based on 1986 census data adjusted to include only those 18 years and over at the time of the convention.

[3] Ratings by A.C. Nielsen. The Reach data available for the period 1967 to 1984 are for the number of different people aged 2+ who watched at least one quarter-hour of the program. The Reach data for the number of different people aged 18+ who watched at least one quarter-hour of the program are based on the reasonable estimate that those aged 18+ comprise 87 per cent of the Reach for all persons aged 2+. This proportion was derived by taking the average of the Reach 18+/Reach 2+ ratios for the conventions (those of 1989, 1990, and 1993) for which both sets of data are available.

Table 5-3 Candidate Mentions on Evening National Television Newscasts, Liberal Leadership Campaign, 3 May 1989–23 June 1990

	May	June	July	Aug	Sept	Oct	Nov	Dec	Jan	Feb	Mar	April	May	June	Total	Percent
CBC-TV																
Jean Chrétien	41	18	0	3	0	2	8	7	52	18	52	63	40	155	459	49.3
Paul Martin Jr.	22	9	0	0	0	5	4	4	83	15	11	21	2	54	230	24.7
Sheila Copps	3	2	0	0	0	0	0	0	41	14	27	12	4	34	137	14.7
Tom Wappel	0	3	0	0	0	0	0	0	12	1	1	2	0	3	22	2.4
John Nunziata	0	0	0	0	0	0	0	0	30	4	0	41	2	6	83	8.9
Total	66	32	0	3	0	7	12	11	218	52	91	139	48	252	931	
CTV																
Jean Chrétien	7	1	0	0	0	0	1	3	65	10	48	19	10	120	284	53.1
Paul Martin Jr.	2	1	0	0	0	2	0	0	24	4	7	6	0	21	67	12.5
Sheila Copps	5	0	0	0	0	0	2	0	25	14	23	9	0	27	105	19.6
Tom Wappel	0	2	0	0	0	0	0	0	5	4	0	0	7	10	28	5.2
John Nunziata	0	0	2	0	0	0	0	0	17	1	0	26	0	5	51	9.5
Total	14	4	2	0	0	2	3	3	136	33	78	60	17	183	535	

Average Total Number of Mentions CBC-TV and CTV (%)

Jean Chrétien	50.7
Paul Martin Jr.	20.3
Sheila Copps	16.5
Tom Wappel	3.4
John Nunziata	9.1

Source: Data compiled by National Media Archive, Vancouver. CBC-TV (1990) was a one-hour news/public affairs package composed of "The National" and "The Journal." CTV National News was a 25-minute news broadcast.

Table 5-4 Candidate Mentions on Evening National Television Newscasts, Progressive Conservative Leadership Campaign, 24 February–13 June 1993

	Feb	March	April	May	June	Total	Percent
CBC-TV							
Kim Campbell	22	274	204	155	327	982	51.4
Jean Charest	14	82	117	100	312	625	32.7
Jim Edwards	2	21	20	14	118	175	9.2
Garth Turner	1	15	12	6	30	64	3.3
Patrick Boyer	2	22	3	8	30	65	3.4
Total	41	414	356	283	817	1911	
CTV							
Kim Campbell	10	109	84	87	183	473	49.3
Jean Charest	5	42	38	70	192	347	36.2
Jim Edwards	0	19	11	34	24	88	9.2
Garth Turner	0	9	4	3	6	22	2.3
Patrick Boyer	0	8	4	4	13	29	3.0
Total	15	187	141	198	418	959	

Average Total Number of Mentions CBC-TV and CTV (%)

Kim Campbell	50.7
Jean Charest	33.9
Jim Edwards	9.2
Garth Turner	3.0
Patrick Boyer	3.3

Source: Data compiled by National Media Archive, Vancouver. CBC-TV (1993) was a one-hour news magazine, "Prime Time News." CTV National News was a 25-minute news broadcast.

Table 5-5 Selected Candidate Mentions on Evening National Television Newscasts, New Democratic Party Leadership Campaign, 4 March–December 1989

	March-August	September	October	November	December	Total	Percent
CBC-TV							
Audrey McLaughlin	28	8	10	19	43	108	31.8
David Barrett	6	47	93	3	38	187	55.0
Steven Langdon	13	3	3	5	21	45	13.2
Total	47	58	106	27	102	340	
CTV							
Audrey McLaughlin	28	11	7	38	58	142	47.8
David Barrett	15	22	30	30	33	130	43.8
Steven Langdon	12	1	4	4	4	25	8.4
Total	55	34	41	72	95	297	
Average Total Number of Mentions CBC-TV and CTV (%)							
Audrey McLaughlin	39.2						
David Barrett	49.8						
Steven Langdon	11.0						

Source: Data compiled by National Media Archive, Vancouver. CBC-TV (1993) was a one-hour news magazine, "Prime Time News." CTV National News was a 25-minute news broadcast.

Table 5-6 Reliance on News Reports and Candidate Materials by Delegates' Time of Vote Decision

	Time of Decision (%)		
Information sources	Pre-delegate selection	Delegate selection to convention	During convention
1990 Liberal			
News reports	19.1	14.2	19.4
Candidates' material	33.7	44.8	29.1
Both	47.3	40.9	51.5
N =	1,075	232	134
1993 Conservative			
News reports	20.4	12.5	12.5
Candidates' material	27.3	33.9	43.8
Both	52.3	53.4	43.8
N =	461	168	144

Sources: 1990 Liberal and 1993 post-convention surveys (principal investigator, George Perlin). Cross-tabulated responses to the following questions: "When did you decide for whom you would vote on the first ballot [at the convention]?" and "During the campaign did you get more of your information about the candidates from the news reports on television, radio and news papers OR from material the candidates sent you.?" Figures may not add up to 100% due to rounding.

Table 5-7 Number and Content of Stories on Major Leadership Candidates, Liberal 1990 and Conservative 1993[1]

	Process	Substance	Mixed	Total
CBC				
Jean Chrétien	32	17	4	53
Paul Martin Jr.	24	10	4	38
Kim Campbell	82	23	10	115
Jean Charest	60	15	9	84
Total	198	65	27	290
CTV				
Jean Chrétien	22	16	1	39
Paul Martin Jr.	15	11	1	27
Kim Campbell	66	11	3	80
Jean Charest	56	8	3	67
Total	159	46	8	213

Source: Data compiled by National Media Archive, Vancouver.

[1] Periods covered: Liberal, 3 May 1989–23 June 1990, and Conservative, 24 February–13 June 1993. The items included are on the leadership race alone, not government policy if unrelated to the leadership contest. For example, "substance stories" about Kim Campbell and the Canadian armed forces in Somalia are not included unless they related specifically to the leadership race. The comparatively high proportion of "substance stories" in the Liberal race resulted from the then ongoing debate on Meech Lake and Jean Chrétien's and Paul Martin's views on that subject.

Table 5-8 Canadian Press Delegate Tallies and First Ballot Vote, Progressive Conservative Leadership Campaign, 1993

Candidates	Distribution of delegate support						First ballot results	
	4 May[1]	%	14 May[1]	%	4 June[1]	%	13 June	%
Kim Campbell	699	46	1,201	43	1,290	46	1,664	48
Jean Charest	295	19	625	23	761	27	1,369	39
Jim Edwards	83	5	107	4	120	4	307	9
Garth Turner	9	1	13	1	31	1	76	2
Patrick Boyer	14	1	18	1	18	1	53	2
Undecided/wouldn't say	429	28	799	29	572	20	–	–
Total	1,529		2,763		2,792		3,469	

Source: Canadian Press data supplied by Robert Russo.

[1] The figures include results from the majority of riding associations, campus clubs, and a sampling of ex officio delegates. Percentages total may not add up to 100% due to rounding.

Table 6-1 Constituency Delegate Selection in the Progressive Conservative, Liberal, and New Democratic Parties (%)

	PC 1983	Lib. 1984	NDP 1989	Lib. 1990	PC 1993
Selection contested	77	75	51	76	61
Prior identification with a candidate	48	41	31	83	58
Ran as part of slate	39	38	10	85	47
Ran on an identified slate	26	24	6	76	37
Trench warfare (identified slate v. identified slate)	10	12	2	47	12

Sources: For 1983 and 1984, R.K. Carty, "Campaigning in the Trenches: The Transformation of Constituency Politics," in George Perlin, ed., *Party Democracy in Canada: The Politics of National Party Conventions* (Scarborough: Prentice-Hall Canada, 1988), table 1, 86; for 1989, Keith Archer, "Leadership Selection in the New Democratic Party," in Herman Bakvis, ed., *Canadian Political Parties: Leaders, Candidates and Organization*, vol. 13 of the research studies for the Royal Commission on Electoral Reform and Party Financing (Toronto: Dundurn Press, 1991), 15; for 1990, Lawrence Hanson, "Contesting the Leadership at the Grassroots: the Liberals in 1990," in R.K. Carty, ed., *Canadian Political Party Systems: A Reader* (Toronto: Broadview Press, 1991), 428; and for 1993, the 1993 Progressive Conservative post-convention survey, principal investigator, George Perlin.

Table 6-2 Liberal (1990) and Progressive Conservative (1993) First Ballot Support for Candidates by Time of Decision (%)

Liberal 1990	Before Turner quit	When Turner quit	Between quit and conv. announce	Before delegate selection	During delegate selection	Between end of del. selec. and conv.	After convention met
Jean Chrétien	79	64	54	53	39	29	28
Paul Martin Jr.	17	19	32	23	31	48	35
Sheila Copps	3	8	10	11	16	18	32
Tom Wappel	0	6	3	10	13	6	2
John Nunziata	0	3	1	3	1	0	2
N	383	72	220	413	115	119	128

Conservative 1993	Before Mulroney quit	When Mulroney quit	Before delegate selection	During delegate selection	Between end of del. selec. and conv.	After convention met
Kim Campbell	63	71	53	42	30	38
Jean Charest	36	18	36	36	51	33
Jim Edwards	0	6	7	17	16	22
Garth Turner	1	5	2	2	2	4
Patrick Boyer	0	0	2	4	1	3
N	100	62	297	53	112	141

Source: 1990 Liberal convention survey and 1993 Conservative survey.

Note: Sums may be greater than 100% due to rounding.

Table 7-1 Categories of Delegates: Liberal Conventions, 1919–90

Category	1919	1948	1958	1968	1984	1990
CONSTITUENCY DELEGATES						
(Number per constituency)	3	3	3	6	7	12
EX-OFFICIO DELEGATES						
Privy councillors	x	x	x	x	x	x
Senators	x	x	x	x	x	x
Members of Parliament	x	x	x	x	x	x
Defeated candidates	x	x	x	x	x	x
Newly nominated candidates	x	x	x	x	x	x
Provincial legislature members & candidates[1]	x	x	x	x	x	
Provincial party leaders	x	x	x	x	x	
Provincial association presidents	x					
National executive officers[2]	x	x	x	x	x	x
Provincial executive officers[3]	x	x	x	x	x	x
Standing committee members				x	x	
Constituency association presidents					x	x
At-large delegates						x
Past leaders						x
CLUB DELEGATES						
University club delegates[4]		x	x	x	x	x
Women's club delegates					x	x
Aboriginal club delegates						x

Sources: Official convention calls or the party constitution.

[1] The number equivalent to one-quarter the size of the provincial legislature.

[2] National executives of the Liberal Federation of Canada and its women's, youth, university (1958 and 1968 only), and aboriginal (1990 only) wings.

[3] Executives of the provincial and territorial Liberal parties and their women's, youth, and university executives. As of 1948 the provincial association presidents are included in this category. As of 1990 members of the provincial aboriginal commissions are included in this category.

[4] In 1968 regional associations were included.

Table 7-2 Categories of Delegates: Conservative Conventions, 1927–93

Category	1927	1938	1942	1948	1956	1967	1976	1983	1993
CONSTITUENCY DELEGATES									
(Number per constituency)	4	4	3	3	3	5	6	6	9
EX-OFFICIO DELEGATES									
Former lieutenant-governors	x	x							
Privy councillors	x	x	x	x	x	x	x	x	x
Senators	x	x	x	x	x	x	x	x	x
Members of Parliament	x	x	x	x	x	x	x	x	x
Defeated candidates	x	x				x	x	x	x
Newly nominated candidates						x	x	x	x
Members of Prov. legislatures	x	x	x	x	x	x	x	x	x
Provincial party leaders	x	x	x	x	x	x	x	x	x
Past national presidents								x	x
National executive officers[1]				x	x	x	x	x	x
Provincial executive officers						x		x	x
Provincial ex-cabinet ministers	x	x							
Newspaper representatives	x	x							
Convention committee members	x	x	x			x			
Montmorency delegates						x			
National committee members[2]							x	x	x
Past leaders/honorary officers								x	
DELEGATES-AT-LARGE									
Provincial	x	x	x	x	x	x	x	x	x
Dominion	x	x	x						
Special		x							
CLUB DELEGATES									
University club delegates	x			x	x	x	x	x	x
Other club delegates[3]								x	x

Sources: Ruth M. Bell, "Conservative Party National Conventions, 1927–1956: Organization and Procedure" (MA thesis, Department of Political Science, Carleton University, 1965), table IV; and party constitutions.

[1] National executives of the Progressive Conservative Association of Canada and its women's, youth, and university wings.

[2] Members of the Treasury Committee (1976 only), the Policy Advisory Committee (1983 and 1993 only), the National Campaign Committee and the chairmen and board of directors of the PCCF (1983 and 1993 only).

[3] Includes independent club delegates in 1983 and women's caucus and affiliated association delegates in 1993.

Table 7-3 Delegate Allotment by Category, Liberal and Conservative Conventions, 1919–93

Liberal	1919	1948	1958	1968	1984	1990
Maximum potential voting delegates	1,135	1,302	1,534	2,472	3,595	5,228
Voting delegates per seat	3	3	3	6	7	12
Number of seats	235	245	265	264	282	295
Share of delegates (%)						
Constituency	62	56	52	64	55	68
Ex officio	38	40	42	31	29	15
Affiliated clubs		4	6	5	15	14
Other[1]					1	3

Conservative	1927	1938	1942	1956	1967	1976	1983	1993
Maximum potential voting delegates	1,620	1,764	1,258	1,472	2,411	2,575	3,137	3,653
Voting delegates per seat	4	4	3	3	5	6	6	9
Number of seats	245	245	245	265	265	264	282	295
Share of delegates (%)								
Constituency	61	56	58	54	55	62	54	73
Ex officio/at large[2]	39	44	42	46	40	31	33	24
Affiliated clubs					5	8	13	4

Sources: *Proceedings* for each of the Liberal conventions in 1919, 1948, and 1958; and lists of potential delegate registration provided by the Liberal party for the 1968, 1984, and 1990 conventions. Ruth M. Bell, "Conservative Party National Conventions, 1927–1956" (MA thesis, Carleton University, 1965), table V; and lists of potential delegate registration provided by the Progressive Conservative party for the 1967, 1976, 1983, and 1993 conventions.

[1] Includes the non-ex officio women's commission (1984 and 1990) and aboriginal commission (1990) delegates and the ten delegates selected by each provincial and territorial executive (1990).

[2] For the Conservative party's 1927, 1948, and 1956 conventions the at-large category includes the delegates appointed from campus clubs.

Table 7-4 Potential Delegate Registration: 1990 Liberal Convention

	TOTAL	BC	AB	SK	MN	ON	QB	NB	NS	PEI	NFLD	NWT	YK
Privy councillors	62	2	1	1	1	26	23	3	1	1	3	–	–
Senators	54	4	4	4	3	14	11	5	4	1	2	1	1
Members of Parliament	82	1	–	–	5	43	11	5	6	4	5	2	–
Defeated candidates	205	31	26	13	9	53	60	5	5	–	2	–	1
Newly nominated candidates	1	–	–	–	–	–	1	–	–	–	–	–	–
National executive, LPC	10	1	–	1	–	5	3	–	–	–	–	–	–
National executive, YLC	19	2	2	2	1	2	2	2	2	1	1	1	1
National executive, NWLC	39	4	3	4	3	4	1	3	3	4	3	4	3
Aboriginal peoples' commission	45[a]	3	6	3	4	5	4	3	3	3	4	4	3
Presidents plus three members prov./terr. executive	45	3	3	4	4	4	3	4	4	4	4	4	4
Five male prov./terr. delegates	60	5	5	5	5	5	5	5	5	5	5	5	5
Five female prov./terr. delegates	60	5	5	5	5	5	5	5	5	5	5	5	5
Campus club delegates	488	28	52	8	16	156	152	20	32	4	20	–	–
Women's club delegates	114	11	7	5	2	21	–	46	15	7	–	–	–
Aboriginal club delegates	124	22	19	13	16	30	15	–	–	–	–	6	3
Constit. assoc. presidents	280	30	25	12	14	94	71	10	11	4	7	1	1
Male constit. assoc. delegates	1,180	128	104	56	56	396	300	40	44	16	28	8	4
Female constit. assoc. delegates	1,180	128	104	56	56	396	300	40	44	16	28	8	4
Male youth constit. delegates	590	64	52	28	28	198	150	20	22	8	14	4	2
Female youth constit. delegates	590	64	52	28	28	198	150	20	22	8	14	4	2
Total potential delegates	5,228	536	470	248	256	1,655	1,267	236	228	91	145	57	39

Source: Liberal Party, Ottawa.

[a] Plus one additional delegate.

Table 7-5 Potential Delegate Registration: 1993 Progressive Conservative Convention

	TOTAL	BC	AB	SK	MN	ON	QB	NB	NS	PEI	NFLD	NWT	YK
Privy councillors	55	4	3	–	3	22	10	2	4	3	3	–	1
Senators	51	1	2	4	3	9	13	5	7	3	4	–	–
Members of Parliament	157	11	22	4	7	46	56	5	4	–	2	–	–
Defeated candidates	98	15	2	7	4	42	13	3	3	3	3	2	1
Newly nominated candidates	25	5	3	–	1	15	–	–	–	–	1	–	–
MLAs/MHAs/MPPs	135	–	55	9	28	20	–	–	8	–	15	–	–
Provincial leaders	8	–	1	1	1	1	–	1	1	1	1	–	–
Past provincial leaders	13	–	1	1	3	4	–	–	1	2	–	1	–
National executive	64	5	6	4	4	13	10	4	4	3	5	3	3
At-large PCCF	15	1	1	–	–	9	2	–	–	1	1	–	–
PCCF fundraising chair	15	–	5	–	2	3	4	–	1	–	–	–	1
At-large policy advisers	10	–	–	–	–	8	2	–	–	–	–	–	–
Prov. assoc. presidents	8	–	1	1	1	1	–	1	1	1	1	–	–
At-large national campaign	15	1	–	1	–	5	4	1	1	1	1	–	–
Delegates-at-large	122	12	10	5	5	40	30	4	4	4	4	2	2
Youth-delegates-at large	34	4	3	2	2	10	8	1	2	1	1	–	–
National executive, PCYF	9	–	1	–	2	4	2	–	–	–	–	–	–
PCYF presidents	11	1	1	1	1	2	1	1	1	1	1	–	–
NPCWF presidents	16	2	1	–	–	5	2	2	1	1	2	–	–
Constit. assoc. delegates	1,770	192	156	84	84	594	450	60	66	24	42	12	6

Table 7-5 Potential Delegate Registration: 1993 Progressive Conservative Convention   *(Continued)*

	TOTAL	BC	AB	SK	MN	ON	QB	NB	NS	PEI	NFLD	NWT	YK
Constit. youth delegates	885	96	78	42	42	297	225	30	33	12	21	6	3
Campus club delegates	115	11	6	6	3	47	20	11	8	–	3	–	–
Women's caucus delegates	16	2	–	–	1	5	–	2	3	–	3	–	–
Affil. assoc. delegates	24	–	–	2	–	22	–	–	–	–	–	–	–
Total potential delegates	3,671	363	358	174	197	1,224	852	133	153	61	114	26	16

Source: Progressive Conservative Party, Ottawa.

Table 7-6 Potential/Actual Delegate Registration, 1989 NDP Convention

Category	Number of delegates		% of Total provinces' registration	
	Potential	Actual	Potential	Actual
Constituency				
British Columbia	363	357	11.4	14.2
Alberta	177	165	5.6	6.6
Saskatchewan	405	348	12.7	13.9
Manitoba	171	168	5.4	6.7
Ontario	545	508	17.1	20.2
Quebec	182	65	5.7	2.6
New Brunswick	35	27	1.1	1.1
Nova Scotia	39	39	1.2	1.6
PEI	4	3	0.1	0.1
Newfoundland	28	13	0.9	0.5
Yukon	13	13	0.4	0.5
NWT	17	16	0.5	0.6
Total Constituency	1,979	1,722	62.1	68.6
Affiliated unions	796	461	25.0	18.4
Central labour	170	116	5.3	4.6
Youth	60	57	1.9	2.3
Federal Council	139	118	4.4	4.7
Federal caucus	43	36	1.3	1.4
Total	3,187	2,510	100.0	100.0

Source: NDP, Ottawa, 11 January 1990.

Table 7-7 Provincial Breakdown, Potential Constituency Delegates, 1989 NDP, 1990 Liberal, and 1993 Progressive Conservative Conventions

	NDP constituency delegates (%)	Liberal constituency delegates (%)	Conservative constituency eelegates (%)	1991 Canadian population (%)
British Columbia	18.3	10.8	10.8	12.0
Alberta	8.9	8.8	8.8	9.3
Saskatchewan	20.5	4.7	4.7	3.6
Manitoba	8.6	4.7	4.7	4.0
Ontario	27.5	33.6	33.6	36.9
Quebec	9.2	25.4	25.4	25.3
New Brunswick	1.8	3.4	3.4	2.7
Nova Scotia	2.0	3.7	3.7	3.3
P.E.I.	0.2	1.4	1.4	0.4
Newfoundland	1.4	2.4	2.4	2.1
N.W.T.	0.9	0.7	0.7	0.2
Yukon	0.7	0.3	0.3	0.1
Total (N)	1,979	3,540	2,655	

Sources: Lists of potential delegate registration provided by the parties. Statistics Canada, 1991 Census.

Percentages may not add up to 100% due to rounding.

Table 7-8 Socio-Demographic Characteristics of Delegates, 1989 NDP, 1990 Liberal, and 1993 Progressive Conservative Conventions

	NDP 1989 (%)	Liberal 1990 (%)	PC 1993 (%)	1991 Census (%)
REGION				
British Columbia (includes territories)	21	13	12	12
Prairies	37	20	22	17
Ontario	34	36	35	37
Quebec	2	18	19	25
Atlantic	6	14	12	9
N	1,053	1,490	776	
GENDER				
Male	63	56	66	49[a]
Female	37	44	34	51[a]
N	1,053	1,483	1,455	
AGE				
14–24	3[b]	26	21	19
25–29	10[c]	9	11	11
30–39	31	15	14	22
40–49	24	20	24	17
50–59	13	16	19	12
60 and over	19	14	12	20
N	1,028	1,383	1,430	
HOME LANGUAGE				
English	94	74	79	69
French	2	19	21	23
Both/Other	5	7	n/a	8
N	1,053	1,479	1,455	
RELIGION				
Roman Catholic	14	52	41	46
Protestant	38	34	35	36
Other	6	6	24[d]	6
None	42	8	n/a	12
N	957	1,385	1,407	

Table 7-8 Socio-Demographic Characteristics of Delegates, 1989 NDP, 1990 Liberal, and
1993 Progressive Conservative Conventions *(Continued)*

	NDP 1989 (%)	Liberal 1990 (%)	PC 1993 (%)	1991 Census (%)
EDUCATION				
High School or less	20	22	21	57
College/Trade/Some university	27	33	27	32
One or more degrees	53	45	52	11
N	1,053	1,413	768	
OCCUPATION				
Professional/manager business proprietor	43	53	46	19
White collar/sales	18	10	25	17
Farmer/fisherman	4	2	4	2
Blue collar/trade/labour	10	3	4	23
Other (homemaker, student, retired, unemployed, etc.)	24	31	22	39
N	1,049	1,393	622	
FAMILY INCOME				
$40,000 or less	37	25	17	43
$40–60,000	29	23	30	26
$60,000 and over	34	52	53	31
N	1,038	1,423	754	

*Sources:*1989, 1990, and 1993 convention surveys. For census data, see the following publications of Statistics Canada, 1991 Census (Ottawa: Minister of Industry, Science and Technology). For region, see *A National Overview,* 1992, table 2. For gender and age, see *Age, Sex and Marital Status,* 1992, table 4. For home language, see *Home Language and Mother Tongue,* 1992, table 1. For religion, see *Religions in Canada,* 1993, table 1. For education, see *Educational Attainment and School Attendance,* 1993, table 2. For occupation, see *Occupation,* 1993, table 1, and *Labour Force Activity,* 1993, table 1. For family income, see *Selected Income Statistics,* 1993, table 6.

[a] 14 years and over.
[b] 21 and under.
[c] 22–29 years.
[d] Other/none.

Percentages may not add up to 100% due to rounding

Table 7-9 Selected Party Activity Characteristics of Delegates, 1989 NDP, 1990 Liberal, and 1993 Progressive Conservative Conventions

	NDP 1989 (%)	Liberal 1990 (%)	PC 1993 (%)
YEAR OF PARTY MEMBERSHIP			
Year of convention	2	8	7
1–5	18	26	20
6–10	22	18	21
11–20	33	19	23
21–30	18	15	18[a]
31–40	3	9	7[b]
more than 40	3	5	4[c]
N	1,039	1,366	777
PREVIOUS/CURRENT PARTY POSITIONS			
Federal riding executive	42[d]	58	66
Prov./terr. riding executive	48	48	47
National executive/federal council	9	7	16
Prov./terr. executive	9	21	24
Student/youth club executive	n/a	23	31
Women's commission executive	n/a	10	n/a
Prov./terr. council	20	n/a	n/a
Prov. women's/student assoc.	n/a	11	n/a
N	1,050	1,507	780
FEDERAL CAMPAIGNS WORKED			
0	n/a	4	16
1		28	18
2		17	20
3		10	11
4		10	9
5		8	7
6		5	4
7		4	4
8 or more		14	10
N		1,401	752

Table 7-9 Selected Party Activity Characteristics of Delegates, 1989 NDP, 1990 Liberal, and 1993 Progressive Conservative Conventions *(Continued)*

	NDP 1989 (%)	Liberal 1990 (%)	PC 1993 (%)
FEDERAL CONVENTIONS PREVIOUSLY ATTENDED			
0	52	58	46
1	14	18	22
2	9	10	13
3	10	7	8
4	5	0.4	4
5	4	2	3
6 or more	7	5	5
N	1,046	1,476	747
ATTENDED IMMEDIATELY PREVIOUS BIENNIAL CONVENTION[e]			
Yes	28	26	36
No	72	74	64
N	1,041	1,396	750
ATTENDED PARTY'S IMMEDIATELY PREVIOUS LEADERSHIP CONVENTION[f]			
Yes	15	28	31
No	85	72	69
N	1,041	1,409	754

Sources: 1989, 1990 and 1993 convention surveys.

[a] 21–35 years.

[b] 36–45 years.

[c] More than 45 years.

[d] Current only.

[e] 1987 for the NDP, 1986 for the Liberals, and 1991 for the Conservatives.

[f] 1975 for the NDP, 1984 for the Liberals, and 1983 for the Conservatives.

Table 8-1 Demographic Characteristics of Conservative Leaders Chosen Prior to Leadership Conventions, 1867–1920

Name	Age	Religion	Occupation	Province
John A. Macdonald	52	Presbyterian	Lawyer	Ontario
J.J.C. Abbott	70	Anglican	Lawyer	Quebec
John S.D. Thompson	48	Roman Catholic	Lawyer	Nova Scotia
Mackenzie Bowell	70	Methodist	Journalist	Ontario
Charles Tupper	74	Anglican	Physician	Nova Scotia
Robert L. Borden	46	Anglican	Lawyer	Nova Scotia
Arthur Meighen	46	Presbyterian	Lawyer	Manitoba

Table 8-2 Demographic Characteristics of Liberal Leaders Chosen Prior to Leadership Conventions, 1873–87

Name	Age	Religion	Occupation	Province
Alexander Mackenzie	51	Baptist	Journalist	Ontario
Edward Blake	46	Anglican	Lawyer	Ontario
Wilfrid Laurier	45	Roman Catholic	Lawyer	Quebec

Table 8-3 Demographic Characteristics of Conservative Leadership Candidates, 1927–93

Year	Candidates in order of rank on first ballot	Age	Religion	Occupation	Province
1927	R.B. Bennett	57	United	Lawyer	Alberta
	Hugh Guthrie	61	Presbyterian	Lawyer	Ontario
	C.H. Cahan	66	Presbyterian	Lawyer	Quebec
	R.J. Manion	46	Roman Catholic	Doctor	Ontario
	R. Rogers	63	Anglican	Merchant	Manitoba
	Sir Henry Drayton	58	Anglican	Lawyer	Ontario
1938	R.J. Manion	56	Roman Catholic	Doctor	Ontario
	M.A. MacPherson	47	Presbyterian	Lawyer	Saskatchewan
	Joseph Harris	49	Presbyterian	Businessman	Ontario
	Denton Massey	38	United	Businessman	Ontario
	J.E. Lawson	46	United	Lawyer	Ontario
1942	John Bracken	59	United	Professor	Manitoba
	M.A. MacPherson	51	Presbyterian	Lawyer	Saskatchewan
	John G. Diefenbaker	47	Baptist	Lawyer	Saskatchewan
	H.C. Green	47	United	Lawyer	British Columbia
	H.H. Stevens	64	United	Businessman	British Columbia
1948	George Drew	54	Anglican	Lawyer	Ontario
	John G. Diefenbaker	53	Baptist	Lawyer	Saskatchewan
	Donald M. Fleming	43	United	Lawyer	Ontario
1956	John G. Diefenbaker	61	Baptist	Lawyer	Saskatchewan
	Donald M. Fleming	51	United	Lawyer	Ontario
	E. Davie Fulton	40	Roman Catholic	Lawyer	British Columbia
1967	Robert L. Stanfield	53	Anglican	Lawyer	Nova Scotia
	Duff Roblin	50	Anglican	Businessman	Manitoba
	E. Davie Fulton	51	Roman Catholic	Lawyer	British Columbia
	George Hees	57	Anglican	Businessman	Ontario
	John G. Diefenbaker	72	Baptist	Lawyer	Saskatchewan
	Wallace McCutcheon	61	United	Businessman	Ontario
	Alvin Hamilton	55	Protestant	Teacher	Saskatchewan
	Donald M. Fleming	62	United	Lawyer	Ontario
	Michael Starr	56	Ukr. Orthodox	Clerk	Ontario
1976	Claude Wagner	50	Roman Catholic	Judge	Quebec
	Brian Mulroney	36	Roman Catholic	Lawyer	Quebec

Table 8-3 Demographic Characteristics of Conservative Leadership Candidates,
1927–93 *(Continued)*

Year	Candidates in order of rank on first ballot	Age	Religion	Occupation	Province
	Joe Clark	36	Roman Catholic	Journalist	Alberta
	Jack Horner	48	United	Rancher	Alberta
	Paul Hellyer	52	United	Businessman	Ontario
	Flora MacDonald	50	United	Administrator	Ontario
	Sinclair Stevens	49	Protestant	Lawyer	Ontario
	John Fraser	44	Anglican	Lawyer	British Columbia
	James Gillies	51	United	Educator	Ontario
	Patrick Nowlan	44	Baptist	Lawyer	Nova Scotia
	Heward Grafftey	47	Anglican	Lawyer	Quebec
1983	Joe Clark	44	Roman Catholic	Journalist	Alberta
	Brian Mulroney	44	Roman Catholic	Lawyer	Quebec
	John Crosbie	52	United	Lawyer	Newfoundland
	David Crombie	46	n/a	Teacher	Ontario
	Michael Wilson	45	Anglican	Businessman	Ontario
	Peter Pocklington	41	n/a	Businessman	Alberta
	John Gamble	49	Presbyterian	Lawyer	Ontario
1993	Kim Campbell	46	Anglican	Lawyer	British Columbia
	Jean Charest	34	Roman Catholic	Lawyer	Quebec
	Jim Edwards	56	Roman Catholic	Broadcaster	Alberta
	Garth Turner	44	Protestant	Journalist	Ontario
	Patrick Boyer	48	United	Lawyer	Ontario

Note: Excludes John MacLean and Mary Walker-Sawka in 1967, R.C. Quittenton in 1976, and Neil Fraser in 1983.

Table 8-4 Demographic Characteristics of Liberal Leadership Candidates, 1919–90

Year	Candidates in order of rank on first ballot	Age	Religion	Occupation	Province
1919	W.L. Mackenzie King	44	Presbyterian	Indust. Rel. Advisor	Ontario
	William S. Fielding	70	Baptist	Journalist	Nova Scotia
	George Graham	60	Methodist	Journalist	Ontario
	D.D. McKenzie	60	Presbyterian	Lawyer	Nova Scotia
1948	Louis St Laurent	66	Roman Catholic	Lawyer	Quebec
	James G. Gardiner	64	United	Teacher	Saskatchewan
	C.G. Power	60	Roman Catholic	Lawyer	Quebec
1958	Lester B. Pearson	60	United	Civil Servant	Ontario
	Paul Martin	54	Roman Catholic	Lawyer	Ontario
1968	Pierre E. Trudeau	48	Roman Catholic	Lawyer	Quebec
	Paul Hellyer	44	United	Businessman	Ontario
	Robert Winters	57	United	Businessman	Ontario
	John Turner	38	Roman Catholic	Lawyer	Quebec
	Paul Martin	64	Roman Catholic	Lawyer	Ontario
	J.J. Greene	47	Anglican	Lawyer	Ontario
	A.J. MacEachen	46	Roman Catholic	Professor	Nova Scotia
	Eric Kierans	54	Roman Catholic	Economist	Quebec
1984	John Turner	55	Roman Catholic	Lawyer	Ontario
	Jean Chrétien	50	Roman Catholic	Lawyer	Quebec
	Donald Johnston	47	Protestant	Lawyer	Quebec
	John Roberts	50	n/a	Civil Servant	Ontario
	Mark MacGuigan	53	Roman Catholic	Lawyer	Ontario
	John Munro	53	Anglican	Lawyer	Ontario
	Eugene Whelan	59	Roman Catholic	Farmer	Ontario
1990	Jean Chrétien	56	Roman Catholic	Lawyer	Quebec
	Paul Martin	51	Roman Catholic	Lawyer	Quebec
	Sheila Copps	37	Roman Catholic	Journalist	Ontario
	Tom Wappel	40	Roman Catholic	Lawyer	Ontario
	John Nunziata	35	Roman Catholic	Lawyer	Ontario

Note: Excludes Lloyd Henderson in 1958 and 1968.

Table 8-5 Demographic Characteristics of New Democratic Party Leadership
Candidates, 1961–89

Year	Candidates in order of rank on first ballot	Age	Religion	Occupation	Province
1961	Thomas C. Douglas	56	Baptist	Clergyman	Saskatchewan
	Hazen Argue	40	United	Farmer	Saskatchewan
1971	David Lewis	61	Jewish	Lawyer	Ontario
	James Laxer	29		Lecturer	Ontario
	John Harney	39	Roman Catholic	Political Scientist	Ontario
	Edward Broadbent	35		Professor	Ontario
	Frank Howard	45		Logger	British Columbia
1975	Edward Broadbent	39		Professor	Ontario
	Rosemary Brown	44		Social Worker	British Columbia
	Lorne Nystrom	29	United	Teacher	Saskatchewan
	John Harney	43	Roman Catholic	Political Scientist	Ontario
1989	Audrey McLaughlin	53		Consultant	Yukon
	Dave Barrett	59	Jewish	Social Worker	British Columbia
	Steven Langdon	43		Economist	Ontario
	Simon de Jong	47		Businessman	Saskatchewan
	Howard McCurdy	57	United	Professor	Ontario
	Ian Waddell	47	Presbyterian	Lawyer	British Columbia
	Roger Lagassé	n/a		Teacher	British Columbia

Note: Excludes Douglas Campbell in 1975.

Table 8-6 Ages of Liberal, Conservative, and NDP Leaders and Candidates, 1867–1993 (averages in years)

	Conservative	Liberal	NDP
All leaders, 1867–1993	54.5 (s.d. = 10.49) (N = 16)	52.3 (s.d. = 7.50) (N = 9)	n/a
All pre-convention leaders	58.0 (s.d. = 12.70) (N = 7)	47.3 (s.d. = 3.21) (N = 3)	n/a
All convention period leaders	51.8 (s.d. = 8.15) (N = 9)	54.8 (s.d. = 7.96) (N = 6)	52.3 (s.d. = 9.43) (N = 4)
All convention period candidates	50.6 (s.d. = 7.96) (N = 54)	52.5 (s.d. = 8.98) (N = 29)	45.1 (s.d. = 9.70) (N = 18)*

Conservative				Liberal				NDP			
Candidates			Leaders	Candidates			Leaders	Candidates			Leaders
Year	Age	N	Age	Year	Age	N	Age	Year	Age	N	Age
1927	58.5	6	57	1919	58.5	4	44	1961	48	2	56
1938	47.3	5	56	1948	63.3	3	66	1971	41.8	5	61
1942	53.6	5	59	1958	57.0	2	60	1975	38.8	4	39
1948	50.0	3	54	1968	49.7	8	48	1989*	51	7	53
1956	50.6	3	61	1984	52.4	7	55				
1967	57.4	9	53	1990	43.8	5	56				
1976	46.1	11	36								
1983	45.9	7	44								
1993	45.6	5	46								

* No reliable source could be found for the age of Roger Lagassé. He is included in the number of candidates but not in the average age figures.

Table 8-7 Significant Difference Between the Liberal and Conservative Parties at 5%
Level of Confidence

	All Convention Candidates (1919 and 1927–)	All Leaders (1867–)
Age (difference between two means)	No (t statistic = 1.01) d.f. = 81	No (t statistic = 0.54) d.f. = 23
Religious Affiliation (Roman Catholics as opposed to all others)	Yes (X^2 = 10.71) d.f. = 1	No (X^2 = 1.20) d.f. = 1
Province (originating from Quebec or Ontario as opposed to all other provinces combined)	Yes (X^2 = 8.21) d.f. = 1	Yes (X^2 = 6.95) d.f. = 1

Note: Yates' Correction for Continuity used for all X^2.

Table 8-8 Religious Affiliations of Conservative and Liberal Leaders and Candidates, 1867–1993

Party	Years	Number	Protestant	Roman Catholic
CONSERVATIVE				
Leaders	1867–1993	16	12	4
Candidates	1927–93	52	41	11
	1927–56	22	19	3
	1967–93	30	22	8
LIBERAL				
Leaders	1870–1990	9	4	5
Candidates	1919–90	28	11	17
	1919–58	9	6	3
	1968–90	19	5	14

Table 8-9 Parliamentary, Legislative, and Ministerial Experience of Leaders of the Conservative Party, 1867–1993

Name	Term as leader	At the time of selection				
		Parliamentary experience	Parliamentary ministerial experience	Provincial legislative experience	Provincial ministerial experience	MP or senator
John A. Macdonald	1867–91	nil	nil	23 yrs.[a]	12 yrs.[a]	neither
J.J.C. Abbott	1891–92	13 yrs. 3 mo. Commons 4 yrs. Senate	4 yrs.	10 yrs.[a]	1 yr.[a]	Senator
John Thompson	1892–94	7 yrs. 2 mo.	7 yrs. 2 ½ mo.	4 yrs. 7 mo.	3 yrs. 9 mo.	MP
Mackenzie Bowell	1894–96	20 yrs. Commons 2 yrs. Senate	16 yrs. 2 mo.	nil	nil	Senator
Charles Tupper	1896–1901	18 yrs.	10 yrs. 3 mo.	12 yrs.[a]	7 yrs.[a]	Not in Parliament at time of selection
Robert L. Borden	1901–20	5 yrs.	nil	nil	nil	MP
Arthur Meighen	1920–26	12 yrs.	5 yrs.	nil	nil	MP
R.B. Bennett[b]	1926–38	8 yrs. 2 ½ mo.	5 ½ mo.	8 yrs.	nil	MP
R.J. Manion[c]	1938–40	17 yrs. 10 mo.	5 yrs. 2 ½ mo.	nil	nil	Not in Parliament at time of selection
Arthur Meighen[d]	1941–42	17 yrs. Commons 9 yrs. Senate	10 yrs. 4 mo.	nil	nil	Senator
John Bracken[e]	1942–48	nil	nil	20 yrs. 2 mo.	20 yrs. 4 mo.	Not in Parliament at time of selection

Table 8-9 Parliamentary, Legislative, and Ministerial Experience of Leaders of the Conservative Party, 1867–1993 (Continued)

Name	Term as leader	At the time of selection				
		Parliamentary experience	Parliamentary ministerial experience	Provincial legislative experience	Provincial ministerial experience	MP or senator
George Drew	1948–56	nil	nil	9 yrs. 7 ½ mo.	5 yrs. 1 ½ mo.	Not in Parliament at time of selection
John Diefenbaker	1956–67	16 yrs. 8 ½ mo.	nil	nil	nil	MP
Robert Stanfield	1967–76	nil	nil	18 yrs.	11 yrs.	Not in Parliament at time of selection
Joe Clark	1976–83	3 yrs. 4 mo.	nil	nil	nil	MP
Brian Mulroney	1983–93	nil	nil	nil	nil	Not in Parliament at time of selection
Kim Campbell[f]	1993	4 yrs. 6 mo.	4 yrs. 4 ½ mo.	2 yrs.	nil	MP

[a] Prior to 1 July 1867.

[b] From Meighen's resignation in 1926 to Bennet's election as party leader in 1927 Hugh Guthrie served as temporary leader of the party in the House of Commons.

[c] The post of the national party leader was vacant from the time of Manion's resignation in May 1940 to November 1941, when Meighen was chosen to lead the party.

[d] From 1940 to 1943 R.B. Hanson was leader of the party in the House of Commons. Meighen was chosen in 1941 by a meeting of the Dominion Conservative Association executive, MPs, privy councillors, and defeated parliamentary candidates from the 1940 election.

[e] From 1943 to 1945 Gordon Graydon was leader of the party in the House of Commons. Bracken did not enter the House until the general election of 1945.

[f] Following Campbell's resignation in December 1993 Jean Charest served as interim leader of the party.

Table 8-10 Parliamentary, Legislative, and Ministerial Experience of Leaders of the Liberal Party, 1873–1990[a]

Name	Term as Leader	At the time of selection				
		Parliamentary experience	Parliamentary ministerial experience	Provincial legislative experience	Provincial ministerial experience	MP or senator
Alexander Mackenzie	1873–80	5 yrs. 8 mo.[b]	nil	7 yrs.[c]	10 mo.[d]	MP
Edward Blake	1880–87	11 yrs. 7 mo.[e]	2 yrs. 10 mo.	5 yrs. 3 ½ mo.[f]	10 mo.[g]	MP
Wilfrid Laurier	1887–1919	13 yrs.	1 yr.	3 yrs.	nil	MP
W.L. Mackenzie King	1919–48	3 yrs.	2 yrs. 4 mo.	nil	nil	Not in Parliament at time of selection
Louis St Laurent	1948–58	6 yrs. 6 mo.	6 yrs. 8 mo.	nil	nil	MP
Lester B. Pearson	1958–68	9 yrs. 3 mo.	8 yrs. 9 mo.	nil	nil	MP
Pierre E. Trudeau	1968–84	2 yrs. 5 mo.	1 yr.	nil	nil	MP
John Turner	1984–90	14 yrs. 3 ½ mo.	9 yrs. 9 mo.	nil	nil	Not in Parliament at time of selection
Jean Chrétien	1990–	22 yrs. 11 mo.	16 yrs. 8 mo.	nil	nil	Not in Parliament at time of selection

[a] Not until 1873 did those members of the House sitting in opposition to Macdonald's government formally select a leader, although certainly by 1870 Mackenzie had begun to emerge as chief Liberal spokesman.

[b] One year of this period (October 1871 to October 1872) overlapped with membership in the Legislative Assembly of Ontario.

[c] Occurred both before and after Confederation, 1861 to 1867, in the Legislative Assembly of the Province of Canada, and October 1871 to October 1872 in the Legislative Assembly of Ontario. The last term in the Legislative Assembly of Ontario overlapped with service in the House of Commons.

[d] Occurred between 21 December 1871, and October 1872, overlapping with membership in the Legislative Assembly of Ontario.

[e] Five years, three and a half months of this period (July 1867 to October 1872) overlapped with membership in the Legislative Assembly of Ontario.

[f] Overlapped with membership in the House of Commons.

[g] Occurred between 20 December 1871, and 15 October 1872, overlapping with membership in the House of Commons.

Table 8-11 Parliamentary, Legislative, and Ministerial Experience of Leaders of the New Democratic Party, 1961–89

| Name | Term as leader | At the time of selection | | | | |
		Parliamentary experience	Parliamentary ministerial experience	Provincial legislative experience	Provincial ministerial experience	MP or senator
Thomas C. Douglas	1961–71	8 yrs. 7 mo.	nil	17 yrs. 4 mo.	17 yrs. 4 mo.	Not in Parliament at time of selection
David Lewis	1971–75	6 yrs. 4 mo.	nil	nil	nil	MP
Edward Broadbent	1975–89	7 yrs.	nil	nil	nil	MP
Audrey McLaughlin	1989–	2 yrs. 4 ½ mo.	nil	nil	nil	MP

Table 8-12 Mean Parliamentary, Legislative, and Ministerial Experience of Conservative, Liberal, and New Democrat Leaders at Time of Selection (in years)

	Parliamentary experience	Parliamentary ministerial experience	Provincial legislative experience	Provincial ministerial experience
PRE-CONVENTION PERIOD				
Conservative party[a] (N = 6)	13.5	7.0	4.4	2.0
Liberal party[b] (N = 3)	10.1	1.3	5.1	0.6
CONVENTION PERIOD[c]				
Conservative party (N = 9)	5.6	1.6	6.4	4.1
Liberal party (N = 6)	9.7	7.7	0	0
NDP (N = 4)	6.1	0	4.3	4.3

[a] John A. Macdonald is not included, for at the time of his selection as prime minister and party leader (1867) Macdonald's considerable legislative and ministerial experience (23 years and 12 years respectively) had taken place prior to the existence of the Parliament of Canada and within a colonial legislature. To have included Macdonald would have unnecessarily inflated the "Provincial legislative experience" and "Provincial ministerial experience" means and deflated the "Parliamentary experience" and "Parliamentary Ministerial experience" means.

[b] Overlapping membership in the federal parliament and the provincial legislature of Ontario should be noted for Alexander Mackenzie and Edward Blake.

[c] For the Conservatives, the convention period dates from 1927, for the Liberals it dates from 1919, and for the NDP it dates from 1961.

Table 10-1 Convention Ballots, Candidates, and Winner's Share of Votes, 1919–93

Number of ballots	Number of candidates		Winner's % of vote		Party	Year
	on first ballot	on final ballot	on first ballot	on winning ballot		
1	2	2	79	79	NDP	1961
1	3	3	78	78	Liberal	1958
1	3	3	69	69	Liberal	1948
1	3	3	67	67	Conservative	1948
1	3	3	60	60	Conservative	1956
1	5	5	57	57	Liberal	1990
2	5	3	48	62	Conservative	1942
2	5	2	48	53	Conservative	1993
2	5	4	46	53	Conservative	1938
2	6	6	38	50	Conservative	1927
2	7	3	46	54	Liberal	1984
3	4	2	36	52	Liberal	1919
4	5	2	39	63	NDP	1971
4	5	2	33	59	NDP	1975
4	7	2	27	55	NDP	1989
4	8	2	29	54	Conservative	1983
4	9	3	32	51	Liberal	1968
4	12	2	12	51	Conservative	1976
5	11	2	23	54	Conservative	1967

Table 10-2 Probable Number of Ballots Given Number of Candidates on the First Ballot

Number of candidates on first ballot	Probable number of ballots (%)[a]		
	1[b]	2 or 3	4 or more
2	100	0	0
3	93	7	0
4	57	43	0
5	12	62	27
6	1	51	48
7	0	33	67
8	0	19	81
9	0	10	90
10	0	5	95
11	0	2	98
12	0	1	99

[a] Calculated by a sequential response logit model. See Appendix 10–1 for details.
[b] Note that "0" in this column is a rounded number. There is always some possibility, however slight, that a convention with seven or more candidates will last only one ballot.

Table 10-3 ABC and ABM by Reported First Ballot Support, 1983 Progressive Conservative Convention

	Reported first ballot support (%)							
	Clark	Crombie	Crosbie	Gamble	Mulroney	Pocklington	Wilson	N
ABC	1	5	26	2	52	5	8	(191)
ABM	79	3	9	0	0	2	5	(196)

Source: Patrick Martin, Allan Gregg, and George Perlin, *Contenders: The Tory Quest for Power* (Scarborough: Prentice-Hall Canada, 1983), appendix B, table 6, 236. Reproduced by permission of the authors.

Table 10-4 First Ballot to Fourth Ballot, 1976 Progressive Conservative Convention

| | Fourth ballot support (%) | | |
	Clark	Wagner	Non voting
Clark	100		
Wagner	7	93	
Mulroney	71	17	12
MacDonald	93	7	
Hellyer	43	57	
Nowlan	40	60	
Fraser	60	40	
Stevens	70	27	3
Horner	38	63	
Gillies	85	15	
Grafftey	43	57	

Source: Robert Krause and Lawrence LeDuc, "Voting Behaviour and Electoral Strategies in the Progressive Conservative Leadership Convention of 1976," *CJPS* 12 (March 1979), table 6, 113. Reprinted with permission of the authors and the *CJPS*.

Table 10-5 Shifts in Delegate Support Between Ballots,
1983 Conservative Convention (%)

	Ballot 2					
Ballot 1	Clark	Crombie	Crosbie	Mulroney	Did not vote	N
Clark	97	0	2	1	0	(263)
Crombie	13	52	10	10	0	(31)
Crosbie	1	1	92	5	0	(144)
Gamble	0	0	100	0	0	(3)
Mulroney	0	1	1	98	0	(188)
Pocklington	0	0	50	50	0	(20)
Wilson	12	2	35	49	2	(43)

	Ballot 3				
Ballot 2	Clark	Crosbie	Mulroney	Did not vote	N
Clark	95	5	0	0	(267)
Crombie	30	55	15	0	(20)
Crosbie	1	94	6	0	(176)
Mulroney	1	2	97	0	(229)

	Ballot 4			
Ballot 3	Clark	Mulroney	Did not vote	N
Clark	97	3	0	(264)
Crosbie	21	75	4	(192)
Mulroney	1	99	0	(238)

Source: Patrick Martin, Allan Gregg, and George Perlin, *Contenders: The Tory Quest for Power*
(Scarborough: Prentice-Hall Canada, 1983), appendix B, table 3, 235. Reproduced by permission of
the authors.

Table 10-6 Candidate Rankings by Ballots, Liberal, Conservative, and NDP Conventions
Going Beyond One Ballot, 1919–93

Convention	Candidates	Ballots and Rankings				
		First	Second	Third	Fourth	Fifth
Liberal 1919	King	1	1	1		
	Fielding	2	2	2		
	Graham	3	3			
	McKenzie	3	4			
Conservative 1927	Bennett	1	1			
	Guthrie	2	2			
	Cahan	3	3			
	Manion	4	4			
	Rogers	5	5			
	Drayton	6				
Conservative 1938	Manion	1	1			
	MacPherson	2	2			
	Harris	3	3			
	Massey	4	4			
	Lawson	5				
Conservative 1942	Bracken	1	1			
	MacPherson	2	2			
	Diefenbaker	3	3			
	Green	4				
	Stevens	5				
Conservative 1967	Stanfield	1	1	1	1	1
	Roblin	2	2	2	2	2
	Fulton	3	3	3	3	
	Hees	4	4	4		
	Diefenbaker	5	5	5		
	McCutcheon	6	8			
	Hamilton	7	6	6	4	
	Fleming	8	7	7		
	Starr	9	9			
	Maclean	10				
	Walker-Sawka	11				
Liberal 1968	Trudeau	1	1	1	1	
	Hellyer	2	3	3		
	Winters	3	2	2	2	
	Turner	4	4	4	3	
	Martin	4				
	Greene	6	5	5		
	MacEachen	7	6			
	Kierans	8				
	Henderson	9				
NDP 1971	Lewis	1	1	1	1	
	Laxer	2	2	2	2	
	Harney	3	3	3		
	Broadbent	4	4			
	Howard	5				

Table 10-6 Candidate Rankings by Ballots, Liberal, Conservative, and NDP Conventions Going Beyond One Ballot, 1919–93 *(Continued)*

		Ballots and Rankings			
Convention	Candidates	First	Second	Third	Fourth
NDP 1975	Broadbent	1	1	1	1
	Brown	2	2	2	2
	Nystrom	3	3	3	
	Harney	4	4		
	Campbell	5			
Conservative 1976	Clark	3	2	2	1
	Wagner	1	1	1	2
	Mulroney	2	3	3	
	Horner	4	4		
	Hellyer	5	6		
	MacDonald	6	5		
	Stevens	7			
	Fraser	8	8		
	Gillies	9			
	Nowlan	10	7		
	Grafftey	11			
	Quittenton	12			
Conservative 1983	Mulroney	2	2	2	1
	Clark	1	1	1	2
	Crosbie	3	3	3	
	Crombie	5	4		
	Wilson	4			
	Pocklington	6			
	Gamble	7			
	Fraser	8			
Liberal 1984	Turner	1	1		
	Chrétien	2	2		
	Johnston	3	3		
	Roberts	4			
	MacGuigan	5			
	Munro	6			
	Whelan	7			
NDP 1989	McLaughlin	1	1	1	1
	Barrett	2	2	2	2
	Langdon	3	3	3	
	de Jong	4	4		
	McCurdy	5			
	Waddell	6			
	Lagassé	7			
Conservative 1993	Campbell	1	1		
	Charest	2	2		
	Edwards	3			
	Turner	4			
	Boyer	5			

Table 11-1 Provincial Variants of the Universal Membership Vote, 1985–94

Party	Pre-vote membership cut-off date before vote	Voting method	Voting fee	Voting rules	Television coverage
PQ, 1985	45 days	Polls in ridings	No	If no majority of those voting on 1st ballot, a run-off election on 2nd	Yes
Ont PC, 1990	55 days	Polls in ridings	$10	Point system (100 per riding). Majority of points on any ballot	Yes
PEI PC, 1990	7 days	Central voting site	$25	Majority of those voting on any ballot	Yes
NS Lib, 1992	66 days	Telephone	$25/$45	Majority of those voting on any ballot	Yes
Alta PC, 1992	No	Polls in ridings	No	If no majority of those voting on 1st ballot, a run-off election on 2nd	Yes
Man Lib, 1993	10 days	Mail-in ballot, four regional polls	$10	One member, one vote up to one hundred votes in a riding. Prorated if over 100 votes cast	Yes
BC Lib, 1993	46 days	Telephone	$20	Majority of those voting on any ballot	Yes
BC SC, 1993	7 days	Polls in ridings	No	Single transferable vote	Yes
Alta Lib, 1994	7 days[a]	Telephone	$10	If no majority winner on first ballot then STV on second ballot among top three first ballot candidates	Yes
Sask PC, 1994	14 days	Telephone	No	Majority of those voting on any ballot	Yes

Sources: Information derived from Donald E. Blake and R. Kenneth Carty, "Televoting for the Leader of the British Columbia Liberal Party: The Leadership Contest of 1993," paper presented to the Canadian Political Science Association, Calgary, Alberta, 12 June 1994; Bill Cross, "Direct Election of Party Leaders: Provincial Experiences and Lessons Learned," paper presented to the Canadian Political Science Association, Calgary, Alberta, 13 June 1994; "Alberta Liberals to choose new leader in November," StarPhoenix, 2 August 1994, A5; and provided by David A. Milne, University of Prince Edward Island, Ken Azzopardi, executive director PC party of Saskatchewan, C. Shelley Cory, assistant to the deputy leader of the Manitoba Liberal party, and David Stewart, University of Alberta.

[a] Memberships could be purchased and PIN numbers obtained up to and including the day before the vote on the leadership by those who wished to attend and to vote at the convention.

Table 11-2 Member Turnout in Selected Provincial Leadership Elections, 1985–94

Party	Membership	Number of registered voters	Number of first ballot voters	Membership turnout (%)
PQ, 1985	152,000 (est.)	n/a	97,389	64
ON PC, 1990	n/a	33,138	15,858	n/a
NS Lib, 1992	16,687	7,451	6,999	42
Alta PC, 1992	104,894	n/a	78,251	75
Man Lib, 1993	8,104	n/a	1,938	24
BC Lib, 1993	13,446	7,688	6,540	49
BC SC, 1993	46,000 (est.)	n/a	14,833	32
Alta Lib, 1994	56,000 (est.)	19,003	11,004	58
Sask PC, 1994	9,146	9,146	3,298	36

Sources: For the PQ, see Daniel Latouche, "Universal Democracy and Effective Leadership: Lessons from the Parti Quebecois Experience," in R. Kenneth Carty, Lynda Erickson, and Donald E. Blake, *Leaders and Parties in Canadian Politics: Experiences of the Provinces* (Toronto: Harcourt Brace Jovanovich, 1992), 182. For the BC Liberals, see Donald E. Blake and R. Kenneth Carty, "Televoting for the Leader of the British Columbia Liberal Party: The Leadership Contest of 1993," paper presented to the Canadian Political Science Association, Calgary, Alberta, 12 June 1994. For the Ontario PCs, see *Report of the Chief Electoral Officer of the P.C. Party of Ontario Respecting the Leadership Election, May 12, 1990*, Liberal Papers, MG 28 IV 3, vol. 1813, "Reform Conference." For the Nova Scotia Liberals, see Leonard Preyra, "Tele-conventions and Party Democracy: The 1992 Nova Scotia Liberal Leadership Convention," *Canadian Parliamentary Review* (Winter 1993–94), 6. For the Manitoba Liberals, see "Liberal leadership race enlivened by controversy," *Globe and Mail*, 27 May 1993, A4. For the Alberta Tories, see "Conservative 1992 Membership Survey" dated 13 January 1993, provided by David Stewart, Political Science, University of Alberta. For the Alberta Liberals, see Scott Feschuk, "Alberta phone voting crashes," *Globe and Mail*, 14 November 1994, A4. For the Saskatchewan Conservatives, see Mark Wyatt, "Boyd captures Tory leadership," *StarPhoenix*, 21 November 1994, A1.

Table 12-1 Delegate Evaluation of Conventions and Direct Vote
Liberal Convention 1990 (%)

Which system of leadership selection, a convention system or a system in which the
leader is chosen by a direct vote of all the party members, would do the better job in
respect to each of the following?

	Convention	*Direct vote*	*Both the same*
Representing regional interests	29	50	17
Selecting the most competent leader	31	50	17
Recruiting ethnic minorities into the party	35	37	23
Promoting confidence in the integrity of the process	15	68	13
Representing women's interests	32	39	25
Limiting the influence of extremist groups	26	56	13
Getting favourable publicity for the party	55	30	11
Representing Aboriginal people	42	34	20
Recruiting young people into the party	52	30	15
Reconciling and accommodating conflicting interests	33	42	19
Keeping down the costs of leadership campaigns	18	63	15

Source: George Perlin, "Attitudes of Liberal Convention Delegates Toward Proposals for Reform of
the Process of Leadership Selection," in Herman Bakvis, ed., *Canadian Political Parties: Leaders,
Candidates and Organization,* vol. 13 of the research studies for the Royal Commission on Electoral
Reform and Party Financing (Toronto: Dundurn Press, 1991), 71. Reproduced by permission of the
Minister of Supply and Services Canada, 1995.

Rows do not sum to 100 because of "did not answer" and "don't know" responses.

Table 12-2 Delegate Evaluation of Conventions and Direct Vote
Conservative Convention 1993 (%)

Which system of leadership selection, a convention system or a system in which the
leader is chosen by a direct vote of all the party members, would do the better job in
respect to each of the following?

	Convention	Direct vote	Both the same
Representing regional interests	37	37	23
Selecting the most competent leader	47	31	19
Recruiting ethnic minorities into the party	27	41	29
Promoting confidence in the integrity of the process	21	59	18
Representing women's interests	28	35	34
Getting favourable publicity for the party	63	23	11
Recruiting young people into the party	57	23	18
Reconciling and accommodating conflicting interests	44	29	23
Keeping down the costs of leadership campaigns	21	54	22

Source: George Perlin, 1993 post-convention survey.

Rows do not sum to 100 because of "did not answer" and "don't know" responses. "Limiting the
influence of extremist grops" and "representing aboriginal people" questions, both asked of 1990
Liberal delegates, were not asked in 1993.

Appendices

RE: Stanfield Convention

In accordance with a promise I made some time ago I have done an assessment of the convention organization used by the present leader of the opposition, Robert Stanfield, during the Conservative leadership convention. In addition to summarizing the arrangements made by Mr. Stanfield, I have added, where I felt it useful, some comments. It seems to me that it would be well worth considering adapting Mr. Stanfield's procedures to the forthcoming Liberal convention. This seems to me to be of special importance to you because you also hope to win at the convention itself.

It might be noted that the whole Stanfield plan was based on the assumption that the convention is a separate phase of any campaign – a happening of its own. Delegates are no longer part of their home local riding environment but part of a new convention environment. The convention organization used by Mr. Stanfield is completely oriented to Professor Marshall McLuhan's theories of media and environment: the Turner team approach, in my opinion should repeat this same recognition – of the new Ottawa environment.

Since the Stanfield organization was the most successful at the Conservative leadership convention it seems reasonable to assume that it was the best of the Conservative leadership organizations. This assumption is supported by the fact that the Stanfield team worked quite differently from other teams at the convention itself.

First, the Stanfield convention organization – at least as seen in public – consisted almost entirely of convention delegates. The organization made the assumption that delegates are best persuaded by delegates. Therefore, where at all possible, all contacts with delegates at the convention were made by other voting delegates wearing delegate's badges.

Second, the Stanfield convention organization operated on the assumption that conditions change once the convention begins and that organization at the convention itself is different from that required prior to the actual physical start of the convention.

All Stanfield convention workers arrived in Toronto several days ahead of the actual start of the convention. This was designed to have an impact on the press: everywhere they went in the days immediately prior to the convention they should see and talk to Stanfield delegates. They were given an invalid but nonetheless impressive demonstration of growing Stanfield support. Other delegates constantly encountered Stanfield supporters and also found them to be the most numerous. (This organization move ties in directly with McLuhan theories about environmental impact as does some later moves discussed below.)

Once the Stanfield team – over one hundred strong – arrived in Toronto the team was reorganized on the basis of voting polls. For each separate voting machine (called polling station to reduce the strange-sounding names being used) a team of delegate supporters was put together under a polling station captain and assistant. These teams were then given the job of contacting others who were assigned to vote at the same voting station. Thus a worker could contact some other delegates and use the introduction, "I see you're voting at my voting station."

Stanfield delegates were fully briefed on the complications of a voting machine so that [they] could always act helpfully in guiding other delegates who might have voting problems. Since it appears the Liberal party will use a voting device of a completely different type – a data processing or IBM card which will require a delegate to use a pin to push a hole in a card, the Turner team should be fully acquainted with this process. Since each candidate will probably have a number assigned to him for this process the Turner team should consider whether use of this number and continuing attention to the changing form of the ballot (a problem not to my knowledge yet decided) should be a part of the convention campaign.

This meant that every delegate met Stanfield supporters who were voting in his line who were from various parts of the country. This again gave the impression that Stanfield support was strong. Regional contacts are expected because the delegates usually know the commitments of delegates from their own region. The non-regional delegate contact appears less formal and planned and is therefore more impressive: at least that is the assumption that the Stanfield team used.

An attempt was made by every voting poll captain to assess the voting potential of those in his polls. These assessments, of course, could be checked against earlier regional assessments.

(A Turner campaign might face the additional problem of language: Stanfield's Quebec support was almost non-existent so the contact with Quebec delegates was minimal. The Turner campaign with its substantially larger Quebec support and its potential strong Quebec support will face a problem not encountered by Stanfield.)

While the polling teams were working on delegates Mr. Stanfield himself concentrated on working on the local news media and the media feeding the convention city. The team assumed that (and sociological studies support this) information can influence in a two-step process. The delegates would be aware of what is carried on local media either directly or by word of mouth. Thus Mr. Stanfield made as many appearances as possible on Toronto media in the immediate convention and pre-convention period. In Ottawa, this suggests that Mr. Turner should make hot line radio show appearances, guest television appearances and attempt to stimulate interest in local press coverage. He should also use the French language Ottawa media.

This part of the Stanfield campaign to my knowledge has not received attention but it was a vitally important part of creating the atmosphere of potential victory and the awareness of the candidate on the part of the delegates. (Toronto media and Montreal media also reach Ottawa daily.)

When the voting actually started the Stanfield workers were able to use their contacts established with voters in their own voting lines to maintain constant contact. The voting arrangements which acted as a communications handicap to other delegates support groups were right in line with the Stanfield plan of operation.

Stanfield workers stationed themselves at strategic intervals in each voting line and were able to give all delegates the impression of steady sustained Stanfield support. The casual conversation based on the omnipresent Stanfield delegate support was a vital factor in fathering the ultimate votes needed for victory.

To avoid entangling the team with transfer problems during the actual voting the Stanfield group had made all arrangements with other candidates well in advance. These advance arrangements, sawoffs, etc., were negotiated by one person in each case and one liaison contact was established.

Thus the Stanfield group had advance consultations with a McCutcheon worker and an agreed upon method of communication and had an arrangement through one Fulton man for the Fulton move across when his candidate went. The Stanfield team reasoned that last minute arrangements would be far too hectic ... Therefore they carefully planned such agreements in advance. This would suggest you and your supporters should agree in advance which move you should make if in fact you do not win. This can have important future power consequences. It is impossible to deduce from the above – although no specific information was obtained on this point – that Mr. Stanfield had agreed to support Mr. Fulton rather than Mr. Roblin if events had turned out other than they did. Of course, your position may suggest no deals with anyone: the point is an early decision is the only correct one.

T. Joseph Scanlon

SOURCE: NA Liberal Papers, MG 28 IV 3, vol. 1386, "Candidate Liaison Committee" file.

APPENDIX 10-1 A NOTE ON THE SEQUENTIAL RESPONSE LOGIT MODEL

The probabilities in Table 10-2 were arrived at by using a sequential response logit model to the number of candidates on the first ballot and the number of ballots of Canadian conventions. In this case, the number of candidates on the first ballot is the independent variable and the number of ballots is the dependent variable. The 1961 convention was excluded from the analysis because it is 100 per cent certain that any two-candidate convention will be over on the first ballot. Logit models are used for looking at discrete dependent variables like the number of ballots at a convention. (For a description of logit and sequential response models and the statistical procedures and formulae they involve, see G.S. Maddala, *Limited-dependent and qualitative variable in econometrics* [Cambridge: Cambridge University Press, 1983], 22–3 and 49–51.) The purpose of employing such a model was to use the observations of Canadian conventions from 1919 to 1993 to calculate the probable number of ballots that a convention would last given the number of candidates on the first ballot.

The data were grouped into three categories (one ballot, two or three ballots, and four or more ballots) and were analysed in that form. First compared were single ballot conventions and those going two or more ballots. For this estimation there were eighteen observations. The estimated coefficient on the candidates variable is 2.32 and the constant is -9.57. The t-statistics are 2.09 and -1.95 respectively with 16 degrees of freedom. The log likelihood ratio test statistic is 13.43 with one degree of freedom. The McFadden R^2 is 0.63. Conventions lasting two or three ballots were then compared to those lasting four or more ballots. For this test there were twelve observations. The 1919 convention was excluded from the analysis because, given the rule requiring the withdrawal of the low candidate after each ballot, a four-candidate convention cannot go beyond three ballots. Although that rule was first put in place in 1967, it had been effectively honoured before then. The estimated coefficient on the candidates variable is 0.77 and the constant is -4.71. The t-statistics are 1.50 and -1.47 respectively with 10 degrees of freedom. The log likelihood ratio test statistic is 4.34 with one degree of freedom. The McFadden R^2 is 0.27.

APPENDIX 11-1 PROVINCIAL DIRECT ELECTION RESULTS, 1973–94[a]

Parti Créditiste, 23 April 1973

Yvon Dupuis	3,076	2,957
Camil Sampson	1,621	1,809
Fabien Roy	1,178	949
Armand Bois	560	
Total:	6,435	5,715

Parti Québécois, 29 September 1985

Pierre-Marc Johnson	56,925
Pauline Marois	19,471
Jean Garon	15,730
Guy Bertrand	2,733
Francine Lalonde	1,484
Jean Gagnon	1,046
Total:	97,389

Parti Québécois, 19 March 1988
Jacques Parizeau acclaimed

Progressive Conservative Party of Ontario, 12 May 1990

Michael Harris	7,230
Diane Cunningham	5,770
Total:	13,000[b]

Progressive Conservative Party of Prince Edward Island, 19 December 1990

Pat Mella	473
Barry Clark	382
Roger Whittaker	32
Total:	887

Liberal Party of Ontario, 9 February 1992

Murray Elston	740	767	865	988	1,153
Lyn McLeod	667	744	873	1,049	1,162
Greg Sorbara	345	380	402	341	
Charles Beer	247	307	289		
Steve Mahoney	236	213			
David Ramsay	216				

Liberal Party of Nova Scotia, 20 June 1992

John Savage	3,312	3,688
Don Downe	2,832	3,311
Ken MacInnis	755	
John Drish	60	
George Hawkins	39	
Total:	6,998	6,999

Progressive Conservative Party of Alberta, 28 November 1992 and 5 December 1992

Nancy Betkowski	16,393	31,722
Ralph Klein	16,392	46,245
Rick Orman	7,649	284
Doug Main	5,053	
John Oldring	2,789	
Lloyd Quantz	1,488	
Ruben Nelson	1,250	
Elaine McCoy	1,115	
David King	587	
Total:	52,725	78,251

Liberal Party of Manitoba, 5 June 1993

Paul Edwards	1,087
Kevin Lamoureux	851
Total:	1,938

Liberal Party of British Columbia, 11 September 1993

Gordon Campbell	4,141
Gordon Gibson	1,600
Gordon Wilson	531
Linda Reid	166
Wilf Hurd	62
Allan Warnke	36
Charles McKinney	4
Total:	6,540

Social Credit Party of British Columbia, 6 November 1993

Grace McCarthy	7,338	7,357	7,700
Graham Bruce	5,321	5,352	6,245
Claude Richmond	2,083	2,099	
Jim Turner	91		
Total:	14,833	14,808	13,945

Liberal Party of Alberta, 12 November 1994

Grant Mitchell	4,799	4,121
Sine Chadi	3,772	3,587
Adam Germain	1,663	1,357
Gary Dickson	706	
Tom Sindlinger	64	

Progressive Conservative Party of Saskatchewan, 19 November 1994

Bill Boyd	1,985
Grant Schmidt	1,313

SOURCES: For the Créditistes, see John Laschinger and Geoffrey Stevens, *Leaders and Lesser Mortals: Backroom Politics in Canada* (Toronto: Key Porter Books, 1992), 264–5. For the PQ, see Daniel Latouche, "Universal Democracy and Effective Leadership: Lessons from the Parti Québécois Experience," in R.K. Carty, Lynda Erickson, and Donald E. Blake, *Leaders and Parties in Canadian Politics: Experiences of the Provinces* (Toronto: Harcourt Brace Jovanovich, 1992), 183. For the Ontario Conservatives, see *Report of the Chief Election Officer of the P.C. Party of Ontario Respecting the Leadership Election, May 12, 1990*, Liberal Papers, MG 28 IV 3, vol. 1813, no file. For the PEI Tories, see Laschinger and Stevens, *Leaders and Lesser Mortals*, 261. For the Ontario Liberals, see Mike Trickey, "Woman leader a first for Ontario," *Vancouver Sun*, 10 February 1992, A4. For the Nova Scotia Liberals, see Agar Adamson, Bruce Beaton, and Ian Stewart, "Pressing the Right Buttons: The Nova Scotia Liberals and Tele-democracy," a paper presented for the Annual Meeting of the Canadian Political Science Association, June 1993, 11. For the the second ballot results of the Alberta Tories, see *Calgary Herald*, 6 December 1992, A11. For the Manitoba Liberals, see "Edwards new leader of Manitoba Liberals," *Ottawa Citizen*, 6 June 1993, A5. For the BC Liberals see Barbara McLintock and Tom Hawthorn, "Campbell rides new Grit wave," *Province*, 12 September 1993, A4. For the BC Socreds, see Justine Hunter, "McCarthy and Campbell face possible byelection encounter," *Vancouver Sun*, 8 November 1993, A1. For the Alberta Liberals, see Scott Feschuk, "Alberta phone voting crashes," *Globe and Mail*, A4. For the Saskatchewan Conservatives see Mark Wyatt, "Boyd captures Tory leadership," *StarPhoenix*, 21 November 1994, A1.

[a] Though not a direct, universal vote, the Ontario Liberal convention of 1992 has been included as it was a combined riding primary/convention system.

[b] Figures are for points, not votes.

APPENDIX 12-1 THE CONSTITUTION OF THE LIBERAL PARTY OF CANADA (AS AMENDED IN 1990)

Article 16 (9) The leader of the Liberal Party shall be elected by a direct vote of all of the members of the Liberal Party of Canada and said vote shall first take place during the next election of a leader of the Liberal Party of Canada.

(10) The leader of the Liberal Party of Canada shall be elected by direct suffrage of the members of the Liberal Party of Canada. For purposes of such elections, membership shall be as defined in Article 2 of this Constitution.

(11) The National Executive shall, prior to October 30, 1990, establish a Universal Suffrage Task Force.

(a) The mandate of the Task Force shall be to consider the alternative means of implementing leadership elections conducted by universal suffrage, and to make recommendations to the Party on how best to accomplish such implementation.

(b) In considering the alternatives, the Task Force will study various proposals which have been, or will be, offered by Party members and Party organizations regarding alternative universal suffrage methodologies, and related new constitutional provisions or rules. This work may include, but is not limited to: constitutional provisions and/or regulations concerning the weighting of balloting by constituency or region; leadership election expenses; majority or plurality determination of results, and the related issues of subsequent or runoff ballots; and the nature, location and number of voting locations.

(c) By March 30, 1991, the Task Force shall publish an interim report to facilitate discussion among Party members. The Task Force shall publish a final report, with proposed constitutional amendments and additional regulations, no later than October 31, 1991.

(d) The Task Force's final report shall be presented to the National Executive at the first meeting of the National Executive following its completion.

(e) In addition, the Task Force's final report and proposed constitutional amendments and rules shall be placed on the agenda of the Party's next convention for consideration.

(f) In the event that a leadership vacancy occurs prior to the completion of the Task Force's work, the Task Force shall conclude its work promptly and make recommendations to the National Executive on how best to implement universal suffrage for the election of the new leader.

SOURCE: The Liberal Party of Canada, *Constitution*, as amended in 1990.

APPENDIX 12-2 THE CONSTITUTION OF THE LIBERAL PARTY OF CANADA (AS AMENDED IN 1992)

Article 17 (8) The leader of the Liberal Party of Canada shall be elected at a Leadership Convention, with the delegates to that convention being elected in proportion to the popular direct vote received by each Leadership candidate, in accordance with this Constitution and the Rules adopted by the National Executive. The first vote shall take place during the next election of a leader of the Liberal Party of Canada.

(9)(a) At general meetings for the election of delegates to a Leadership Convention called in accordance with this Article 17, each voting member shall be provided with a ballot that permits him or her both to vote directly for the Leadership candidate of his or her choice, and to vote for individual delegates to the Leadership Convention who have either declared their support for a particular leadership candidate, or elected to stand as "undeclared"delegates.

(9)(b) For the purposes of Article 17.(10)(a), the term "voting member" means a person who has been a current member or immediate past member of the Liberal Party of Canada for the period of 90 days immediately preceding the general meeting, and who is either a current member or immediate past member who renews his or her membership at the general meeting.

(9)(c) Delegate selection meetings shall be held on one weekend, with the provincial/territorial association executives determining on which precise day the election will be held in each constituency.

(10) The delegate structure of the Leadership Convention shall be as set out in Article 16.(13).

(11) Delegates elected in support of Leadership candidates, shall, if they vote on the first ballot, do so in favour of the candidate they have been elected to support. Should any leadership candidate fail to win a majority of 50% plus one on any ballot, the leadership candidate who received the fewest votes on that ballot shall retire, and a further ballot shall be held. Successive ballots shall be held in this manner until one candidate receives a majority of 50% plus one vote, and is thereby elected as Leader of the Liberal Party of Canada.

SOURCE: The Liberal Party of Canada, *Constitution*, as amended in 1992.

APPENDIX 12-3 CONSTITUENCY DELEGATE APPORTIONMENT EXAMPLE

Proportion of vote for candidates: White (5/12); Brown (3/12); Green (1/12); Black (1/12); and Independent (2/12)

Rank order of delegates:

1. **Bob A. – male youth Brown**
2. **Sally B. – female Brown**
3. **Steve C. – male Green**
4. Fred D. – male youth Green
5. **Ann E. – female White**
6. **Terry F. – male White**
7. **Sam G. – male White**
8. **Ali H. – male youth White**
9. **Ruth I. – female youth White**
10. Susan J. – female youth White
11. **Jason K. – male youth Brown**
12. Ian L. – male youth White
13. **Ellen M. – female Black**
14. Rick N. – female Black
15. Raza O. – male Green
16. Denny P. – female Brown
17. **Alice Q. – female youth independent**
18. David R. – male White
19. **June S. – female independent**

Bold face indicates elected delegate

Leadership Candidate Checklist

White (5)	Brown (3)	Green (1)	Black (1)	Indep. (2)
Ann E.	Bob A.	Steve C.	Ellen M.	Alice W.
Terry F.	Sally B.			June S.
Sam G.	Jason K.			
Ali H.				
Ruth I.				

Demographic Checklist

Male (4)	Female (4)	Male Youth (2)	Female Youth (2)
Steve C.	Sally B.	Bob A.	Ruth I.
Terry F.	Ann E.	Ali H.	Alice W.
Sam G.	Ellen M.		
Jason K.	June S.		

SOURCE: Derived from Ontario Liberal party, "Rules of Procedure for Meetings of Associations Affiliated with the Ontario Liberal Party," Illustration 3, 46.

Notes

1 The first headline was from an article by Geoffrey York, 25 February 1993, A6, and the second by Ross Howard, 21 April 1993, A3.

2 There was an intermittent pre-Confederation flirtation with conventions, particularly by the Clear Grits and Reformers in the 1850s in Canada West, but it was not until 1893 that a national party, the Liberals, moved to adopt the American model of delegates elected from across the country meeting to plan party and electoral organization and to discuss and adopt party policy. On the early development of conventions in Canada see my *The Selection of National Party Leaders in Canada* (Toronto: Macmillan of Canada, 1973), chaps. 2 and 4.

3 In the world of art, few better accounts of that fact exist than Robert Hughes's *The Shock of the New: Art and the Century of Change*, 2nd ed. (London: Thames and Hudson, 1991).

4 Henry E. Brady and Richard Johnston, "Conventions versus Primaries: A Canadian-American Comparison," in George Perlin, ed., *Party Democracy in Canada: The Politics of National Party Conventions* (Scarborough: Prentice-Hall of Canada, 1988), 245.

CHAPTER 2

1 The details of the selections from 1867 to 1920 are given in my *The Selection of National Party Leaders in Canada* (Toronto: Macmillan of Canada, 1973), chap. 3.

2 O.D. Skelton, *Life and Letters of Sir Wilfrid Laurier,* 2 vols. (Toronto: Oxford University Press, 1921), 2:484.

3 "The Liberal Leadership," *The Round Table* 9 (June 1919), 593–4.

4 John R. Williams, *The Conservative Party in Canada: 1920–1949* (Durham: Duke University Press, 1956), 80.

5 Statement read to the press after the meeting of the party's national executive, a meeting called to set the place and time of the forthcoming convention. CBC Radio News, 7 March 1993.

6 In 1941 Arthur Meighen was chosen party leader for a second time to fill the vacancy created a year earlier by the resignation of R.J. Manion. Largely owing to the party's poor financial situation and the wartime travel constraints, no convention was held in 1941. Instead Meighen was selected at a meeting in Ottawa of the Dominion Conservative Association executive, MPs, privy councillors, and defeated parliamentary candidates from the 1940 election.

7 On this period of Conservative history see, among others, Ruth M. Bell, "Conservative Party National Conventions, 1927–1956" (MA thesis, Carleton University, 1965); J.L. Granatstein, *The Politics of Survival: The Conservative Party of Canada, 1939–1945* (Toronto: University of Toronto Press, 1967); and Williams, *The Conservative Party in Canada.*

8 John G. Diefenbaker, *One Canada: Memoirs of the Right Honourable John G. Diefenbaker: The Crusading Years* (Toronto: Macmillan of Canada, 1975), 281–2.

9 Blair Fraser, "Why the Conservatives are Swinging to Diefenbaker," *Maclean's,* 24 November 1956, 30. For more on Diefenbaker's selection in 1956, see Dalton Camp, *Gentlemen, Players and Politicians* (Toronto: McClelland and Stewart, 1970), 232–55; Diefenbaker, *One Canada: The Crusading Years,* 276–82; and John Meisel, *The Canadian General Election of 1957* (Toronto: University of Toronto Press, 1962), 25–33.

10 Dale C. Thomson, *Louis St. Laurent: Canadian* (Toronto: Macmillan of Canada, 1967), 236–7; and *Report of the Proceedings of the National Liberal Convention, 1948* (Ottawa: National Liberal Federation, n.d.), 199–201.

11 National Archives of Canada (hereinafter NA), *King Papers,* vol. 43, King to W.H.S. Cane, 24 July 1919. To F.A. McGregor, King's secretary at the time, King's lack of interest in actively campaigning for his party's leadership was a product of King's Calvinistic belief in predestination. McGregor, *The Fall and Rise of Mackenzie King: 1911–1919* (Toronto: Macmillan of Canada, 1962), 330–2.

12 Thomson, *Louis St. Laurent,* 236.

13 Lester B. Pearson, *Mike: The Memoirs of the Rt. Hon. Lester B. Pearson,* 3 vols. (Toronto: University of Toronto Press, 1975), 3:28.

14 C.G. Power, *A Party Politician: The Memoirs of Chubby Power,* ed. Norman Ward (Toronto: Macmillan of Canada, 1966), 371. See also my "Norman

Ward and C.G. Power on the 1958 Liberal Leadership Convention," *Queen's Quarterly* 97 (Autumn 1990), 457–73, and *The Selection of National Party Leaders in Canada*, 90–2.

15 Williams compares the American and Canadian conventions of 1948, with campaigns in Canada being less "colorful" and "ingenious" than those in the United States, *The Conservative Party in Canada*, 92.

16 As quoted in Peter Stursberg, *Lester Pearson and the Dream of Unity* (Toronto: Doubleday Canada, 1978), 47–8 (emphasis added).

17 As quoted in Paul Martin, *A Very Public Life*, 2 vols. (Ottawa: Deneau, 1983), 2:313.

18 The number of delegates refers to those voting on the first ballot.

19 Author's interviews with parliamentarians and delegates at Tory, Liberal, and NDP conventions between 1967 and 1993. Data from national convention surveys of the 1970s to 1990s also confirm that parliamentarians had little influence on the selection of delegates and their convention voting choices.

20 Samuel J. Eldersveld, *Political Parties: A Behavioral Analysis* (Chicago: Rand McNally, 1964), 9.

21 This theme is developed more fully in the following chapter and in my "Leadership Conventions and the Development of the National Political Community in Canada," in R. Kenneth Carty and W. Peter Ward, eds., *National Politics and Community in Canada* (Vancouver: University of British Columbia Press, 1986), 94–111. Paragraph reprinted with permission.

22 The problem for some delegates results from the fact that they are seated (usually by the trade union of which they are a delegate or by their constituency) side by side at long tables and mark their ballots in full view of those seated nearby. Delegate interviews with the author, NDP 1989 convention.

23 NA, Liberal Papers, MG 28 IV 3, vol. 1385, "Steering Committee" file, meeting no. 8, 11 March 1968.

24 NA, Conservative Papers, MG 28 IV 2, vol. 527, "Memoranda, General 1975" file, minutes of the Convention Committee of 1–2 November 1975.

25 For my views on a proposal by D.V. Smiley to adjourn convention voting after the first ballot results are known ("to encourage," he claims, "a higher degree of delegate rationality"), see my *The Selection of National Party Leaders in Canada*, 206–8.

26 Liberal Party of Canada, *Constitution*, as amended in 1992, article 17(11).

27 *Report of the Proceedings of the National Liberal Convention, 1948*, 66; *Report of the Proceedings of the National Liberal Convention, 1958* (Ottawa: National Liberal Federation, 1958), 16; and Bell, "Conservative Party National Conventions," 173. The CCF and NDP apparently had no such requirement prior to 1971.

28 The NDP 1989 requirement of seventy-five votes was for the first ballot only. The Liberal rule in 1984 read: "The candidate receiving the lowest num-

ber of votes and all candidates receiving less than 75 votes in any ballot shall be dropped from the list of eligible candidates on subsequent ballots." See NA, Liberal Papers, MG 28 IV 3, vol. 1628, "Constitutional and Legal Affairs." "Rules governing election of leader," 21 May 1984.

29 As recently as 1976 the Tories were requested by one party notable to permit "the fundamental right of nomination from the floor" and "the possibility of an [American-style] draft." The convention organizing committee did not change the rule in place for that convention of closing the official nomination period at 10 a.m. on the Friday before the Sunday vote. No reasons were given for the refusal to change the rules. See Correspondence between Donald J. Matthews (8 August 1975) and the party's national president, Michael Meighen (15 August 1975) in NA, Conservative Papers, MG 28 IV 2, vol. 527, "Memoranda, general 1975" file.

30 Details of the nomination procedures in the Conservative party from 1927 to 1956 are to be found in Bell, "Conservative Party National Conventions," chap. 8, and for the Liberal party for 1919 and 1948 in *The National Liberal Convention, Ottawa, August 5, 6, 7, 1919: The Story of the Convention and the Report of its Proceedings* (Ottawa, n.d., n. p.), 167, and *Report of the Proceedings of the National Liberal Convention, 1948,* 64–5.

31 Starting with their 1976 convention, the Tories established four certification requirements to be met before any individual was considered duly nominated. In addition to the "good faith" deposit and the signatures of delegates and/or party members (both of which have varied according to the convention) they included a double-barrelled certification: by the applicant's constituency executive that the individual was a supporter of the Progressive Conservative party, and by the national convention committee, which came only when all other requirements have been met. See NA, Conservative Papers, MG 28 IV 2, vol. 526, "John Laschinger" file; memo re: PC Candidate Certification Programme.

32 Liberal Party of Canada, *Constitution*, as amended in 1992, s. 17 (5)(b).

33 For their 1989 convention the NDP required that nomination papers be signed by "not less than 50 delegates from at least 8 affiliates or riding associations." Nominations closed 48 hours before the start of the election of the leader. See "Leadership Rules, 1989" and "1989 Convention Agenda," New Democratic Party, Ottawa, 1989.

34 "Resolutions of the Convention Committee of the Progressive Conservative Party of Canada for the 1976 National Leadership Convention." See Progressive Conservative Party, Ottawa, 7 December 1975.

35 Data from convention committee resolutions and rules of Progressive Conservative, Liberal, and New Democratic parties, 1976–93.

36 How many in fact lost their deposits remains unclear. Some parties may have returned the money to the candidates as a gesture of good will, though this could not be confirmed. It is known that on the first ballot of

the 1989 NDP convention Roger Lagassé did not receive the seventy-five votes required by the party for him to qualify to recoup his deposit but that the delegates passed a special motion on the convention floor calling for the rule not to apply in his case. See "NDP members reject rose as floral symbol," *StarPhoenix* (Saskatoon), 4 December 1989, A6.]

37 Staff Barootes, at a meeting of the Regulations Sub-Committee of the Registration Committee. See NA, Conservative Papers, MG 28 IV 2, vol. 532, "Registration Committee" file, meeting of 11 March 1983.

38 Lloyd Henderson, a candidate who received one vote in the Liberal convention in 1958, was an obvious exception. He ran again a decade later, receiving no votes at that time, even though his wife was a voting delegate.

39 Bell, "Conservative Party National Conventions," 35–9 and chap. 9, and Power, *A Party Politician*, chap. 27.

40 Dalton Camp recalls that in his days as a student Liberal he attended the 1948 Liberal convention and voted for Chubby Power. When he informed him of this several years later, Camp remembers Power telling him that he should have asked for a recount as many more delegates to the convention claimed that they voted for him than the number of votes he actually received. See Camp, *Gentlemen, Players and Politicians*, 7–9.

41 NA, Conservative Papers, MG 28, IV 2, vol. 526, "John Laschinger" file; minutes of National Steering Committee of 11 July 1975 and memo re: PC Candidate Certification Programme.

42 That nuisance candidates perform a useful function for candidate organizers and delegates should not be overlooked. With the automatic elimination of bottom candidates from successive ballots, having marginal candidates on the first ballot enables convention participants to learn the ranking and absolute vote totals of the candidates and to plan strategies accordingly. All of this comes at virtually no cost, in that all serious candidates remain on the ballot for the second round.

43 Interview with Senator John Nichol, Ottawa, 9 June 1969. The "cutting off" now apparently works both ways. In 1983 CTV made a prior decision to resume normal programming after five minutes of the twenty-five-minute speech of anti-metric and anti-Quebec Tory candidate Neil Fraser. See Patrick Martin, Allan Gregg, and George Perlin, *Contenders: The Tory Quest for Power* (Scarborough: Prentice-Hall Canada, 1983), 156–7.

44 Letter of Iona Campagnolo to John-Frederick Cameron of 25 April 1984. NA, Liberal Papers, MG 28, IV 3, vol. 1645, "Denise Costello Correspondence" file.

45 Press release, Bill Jarvis, MP, chairman of the PC Candidate Liaison Committee, 9 January 1976. NA, Conservative Papers, MG 28, IV 2, vol. 527, "Memoranda, general 1976" file.

46 These rules apparently worked for the Conservative convention of 1993. John Long, described by the press as an "outsider candidate," withdrew

from the leadership race on the eve of the deadline for candidate nominations so as to recoup the $10,000 he had deposited with the party to enter the nationally televised all-candidate debates. Admitting that he would have liked to have stayed in the race, he noted that "if manna comes from heaven, I'll be there. If it doesn't, I won't." He wasn't. *Globe and Mail,* 13 May 1993, A4.

47 The Lortie Commission errs in claiming that the Progressive Conservative convention of 1967 "was the first to be nationally televised." See Royal Commission on Electoral Reform and Party Financing, *Reforming Electoral Democracy,* 4 vols. (Ottawa, 1991), 1:274.

48 Bell, "Conservative National Party Conventions," 81.

49 Ibid., 84.

50 *Report of the Proceedings of the National Liberal Convention, 1958,* 12.

51 For an illustration of this, see ibid. for the 268-page verbatim report of the entire proceedings of the Liberal leadership convention of 1958. The Liberals planning the 1968 convention heard from committee member, MP, and political scientist Pauline Jewett that there should be no nominating speeches because "every time a nominating speech is made the tv cameras switch somewhere else." See NA, Liberal Papers, MG 28 IV 3, vol. 1385, "Steering Committee" file, meeting of 8 January 1968, 14.

52 Dominion Bureau of Statistics, *Household Facilities and Equipment, May, 1958* (Ottawa, 1959), 18, and Statistics Canada, *Household Facilities and Equipment, May, 1968* (Ottawa, 1978), 22.

53 NA, Conservative Papers, MG 28 IV 2, vol. 524, "Convention Agenda 1976" file marked "Confidential," meeting of 5 August 1975.

54 Del O'Brien, as recorded in the minutes of the executive committee, 1–2 November 1975. Ibid., vol. 527, "Memoranda, General 1975" file.

55 NA, Liberal Papers, MG 28 IV 3, vol, 1386, "Executive Committee," file, meeting of 29 January 1968, and ibid., vol. 1669, "1968 Leadership Convention," Draft Proposed Format for Policy Section of Leadership Convention – 1968, dated 12 February 1968.

56 For an early appeal to end the separation of leadership and policy, see Joseph Wearing, "The Liberal Choice," *Journal of Canadian Studies* 3 (May 1968), 16–17.

57 It was suggested at the time that the Liberal organizers in 1990 delayed announcing the results of the first and only ballot in order to maximize the television coverage of their Calgary convention. Three hours to count a five-candidate, one-ballot vote does seem in inordinately long time. See *StarPhoenix,* 25 June 1990, A1. It was also true that there was considerable national coverage of the simultaneous collapse of the Meech Lake Accord which was competing with the Calgary Liberal convention for television's attention. This raised difficult convention management problems for the Liberals.

58 Memo of 1 October 1975 from Dave Black to John Laschinger *re:* NHL
Schedule February 21, 22, 1976. See NA, Conservative Papers, MG 28 IV 2,
vol. 524, "Convention Agenda" file and ibid., vol. 526, National Steering
Committee meeting of 11 July 1975, in "John Laschinger" file. Planning
for the 1968 Liberal convention, the organizers early in January were
mindful of the possibility of a conflict with the Stanley Cup game on the
Saturday night that the new leader was to be elected. "Has anybody approached Senator Molson to have the game [moved to] Sunday?" one of
the participants asked. See NA, Liberal Papers, MG 28 IV 3, vol. 1385,
"Steering Committee" file, meeting of 8 January 1968, 11.

59 NA, Conservative Papers, MG 28 IV 2, vol. 528, "Convention Report 1976"
file, "Site Report," undated (July 1975?). The Tories had a close call in
June 1993 when it became known that if a sixth game were needed in the
Stanley Cup playoffs between the Montreal Canadiens and the Los Angeles
Kings, it would be scheduled on the same evening as that previously set
aside for the candidates' speeches. CBC-TV and Radio-Canada announced
that in the event of a conflict they would broadcast the game, not the
speeches. This prompted party organizers early in the convention week to
give serious consideration to rescheduling the speeches to an earlier,
though less desirable, time to ensure their full coverage on television. As
Montreal won the series in five games, no changes were needed.

CHAPTER 3

1 On these transitions see my *The Selection of National Party Leaders in Canada*,
37–40, 47–8 and 148–51. The retirement of Kim Campbell seven weeks after the Tories went from the governing party to a rump of only two parliamentary seats in the 1993 election showed that in extraordinary
circumstances Canadian national parties are still capable of swift action
when it comes to deposing unwanted leaders. The prevailing post-election
sentiment in the party was that Campbell must go given her major role in
the Conservatives' humiliating defeat, the fact that she had lost her own
seat and that the party would have extreme difficulty raising money to
maintain a skeleton organization and to pay off its reported $10 million
campaign shortfall with Campbell as leader. For newspaper accounts of
Campbell's exit, see Ross Howard, "Campbell pushed to resign early," *Globe
and Mail*, 8 December 1993, A1 and A2; Hugh Winsor, "Money talks, Tories
listen," ibid., 14 December 1993, A1 and A6; and Giles Gherson, "Her political epitaph should read: Kim, we hardly knew you," ibid., 14 December
1993, A18.

2 As quoted in F.C. Engelmann and M.A. Schwartz, *Canadian Political Parties:
Origin, Character, Impact* (Scarborough: Prentice-Hall Canada, 1975),
243.

3 For the entire procedure see *The Times* (London), 18 December 1974, 4. In 1981 the British Labour party widened its leadership selection process beyond the parliamentary party (PLP) to include trade unions and constituency parties. Each was assigned a fixed share of the total votes needed to elect a leader. The PLP and the constituency Labour associations were each alloted 30 per cent of the total and the trade unions 40 per cent. That system remained in force until September 1993, when it was replaced by a modified one member, one vote process discussed in chapter 11. Three articles by H.M. Drucker give useful background information on the 1981–93 process and its early application: "Leadership Selection in the Labour Party," *Parliamentary Affairs* 29 (Autumn 1976), 378–95; "Intra-Party Democracy in Action: The Election of Leader and Deputy Leader by the Labour Party in 1983," ibid., 37 (Summer 1984), 283–300; and "Changes in the Labour Party Leadership," ibid., 34 (Autumn 1981), 369–91. See also R.M. Punnett, "Selecting a Leader and Deputy Leader of the Labour Party: The Future of the Electoral College," ibid., 43 (April 1990), 179–95; R.M. Punnett, *Selecting the Party Leader: Britain in Comparative Perspective* (London: Harvester Wheatsheaf, 1992), 105–28; and R.K. Alderman and Neil Carter, "The Labour Party Leadership and Deputy Leadership Elections of 1992," *Parliamentary Affairs*, 46 (January 1993), 49–65. Neil Kinnock was the first Labour leader to be chosen under that system (2 October 1983) and John Smith the second (18 July 1992). Both received a clear majority of votes cast by participants in each of the three categories. Smith, who as leader of the opposition died less than two years later, won with more than 90 per cent of the total votes cast by all three groups. His successor, Tony Blair, was elected by an even larger group of participants as a consequence of the reforms Smith had introduced during his brief leadership.

4 Nigel Fisher, *The Tory Leaders: Their Struggle for Power* (London: Weidenfeld and Nicolson, 1977), 147. On Thatcher's selection as leader in 1975, see Hugo Young, *The Iron Lady: A Biography of Margaret Thatcher* (New York: Noonday Press, 1990), 91–9.

5 See "Selling the Tories on Margaret Thatcher," *The Times*, 13 February 1975, 7.

6 Interview with David Wolfson, chief of staff, Political Office Prime Minister's Office, Nuffield College, Oxford, 30 November 1979.

7 Much has been written on the 1990 contest for the Conservative leadership. See, among others, R.K. Alderman and Neil Carter, "A Very Tory Coup: The Ousting of Mrs. Thatcher," *Parliamentary Affairs* 44 (April 1991), 125–39; Bill Coxall, "The Struggle for the Conservative Leadership in 1990," *Talking Politics* 4 (Autumn 1991), 2–9; and *The Economist*, 9 March 1991, 21–4. For the former prime minister's own account of the events of 1990, see her autobiography, *Margaret Thatcher: The Downing Street Years* (New York: HarperCollins Publishers, 1993), 829–62.

In all, Thatcher's leadership was challenged twice. In 1989 Sir Anthony Meyer challenged the prime minister over her leadership style and her opposition to closer integration with Europe. Thatcher was confirmed as leader of her party by a large margin, although by less than had been widely expected. She received 314 out of an eligible 374 votes on the first ballot. Meyer received thirty-three votes, there were twenty-four spoilt ballots and three abstentions. See "Thatcher confirmed as U.K. Tory leader," *Globe and Mail*, 6 December 1989, A3.

8 Interview with William Hague, MP, a Thatcher loyalist on the first ballot who helped to organize John Major's victory on the second. Interview of 11 December 1991, Cambridge, Mass.

9 Alderman and Carter, "A Very Tory Coup," 130.

10 Thatcher, *The Downing Street Years*, 831.

11 Information for the following this section comes from the Hague interview, Alderman and Carter, "A Very Tory Coup," Coxall, "The Struggle for the Conservative Leadership," and *The Economist*, 9 March 1991, 21–4.

12 Coxall, "The Struggle for the Conservative Leadership," 7. Patrick Weller argued five years before Thatcher's removal that the chances were remote of the Tory process ever being used to depose a prime minister. The process required "that some leading figure must be prepared to take on an incumbent prime minister in face-to-face battle. Few people have the prestige or perceived ability; even fewer of those may be willing to face charges of divisiveness and disloyalty. To challenge a prime minister may put one's career at risk; one's reputation might be harmed irreparably. It is one thing to stand without any expectation of winning when the party leadership is vacant, as a means of indicating a future interest; it is quite another to take on an active prime minister. The rules therefore protect a prime minister." Patrick Weller, *First among Equals: Prime Ministers in Westminster Systems* (Sydney: George Allen & Unwin, 1985), 68.

13 Quote taken from the documentary on Margaret Thatcher by the A&E Network entitled "Thatcher: The Downing Street Years," *Biography*, 8 June 1994.

14 Hague interview.

15 Weller, *First among Equals*, 49–52.

16 As quoted in Stephen Taylor, "Peacock's ploy backfires as deputy he sought to oust displaces him," *The Times*, 6 September 1985, 7. For a fuller description of the circumstances that led to Peacock's resignation and Howard's election to the leadership see David Barnett, "The Howard accession: anatomy of an astounding victory," *The Bulletin*, 17 September 1985, 28–33.

17 "Two party leaders ousted," *The Times*, 10 May 1989, 8.

18 I am indebted to Patrick Weller, director of the Centre for Australian Public Sector Management, for information about the Hewson-Downer transition.

19 See Linda Hossie, "Australian PM ousted in Labour Party revolt," *Globe and Mail*, 20 December 1991, A1 and A14; and "Australian Prime Minister Ousted as a Former Ally's Bid Succeeds," *New York Times*, 20 December 1991, A1 and A9.

20 For more on this issue see my *The Selection of National Party Leaders in Canada*, 128–9.

21 For more on this see Donald E. Blake, R.K. Carty, and Lynda Erickson, "Coming and Going: Leadership Selection and Removal in Canada," in Alain G. Gagnon and A. Brian Tanguay, eds., *Canadian Parties in Transition*, 2nd ed. (Toronto: Nelson Canada, 1995), 226. By contrast, in the United States the power of conventions to choose leaders was almost from the outset accompanied by the power to remove leaders: "The convention ... quickly acquired authority over party endorsement. A Whig convention actually deposed a sitting president, John Tyler, in 1844 and then another, Millard Fillmore, in 1853. A Democratic convention then confirmed this ability for both major parties by dumping President Franklin Pierce in 1856." See Byron E. Shafer, *Bifurcated Politics: Evolution and Reform in the National Party Convention* (Cambridge, Mass.: Harvard University Press, 1988), 12.

22 Mark MacGuigan, as quoted in *StarPhoenix*, 11 October 1966, 1. MacGuigan supported a resolution calling for an automatic leadership convention within two years of every federal election.

23 The Liberal Party of Canada, *Constitution*, as amended in 1990, article 16(4).

24 For more on the struggle within the Conservative party that led up to the 1967 convention and the subsequent adoption by the party of formal leadership review procedures see my *The Selection of National Party Leaders in Canada*, 101–4. For the background of the 1974 change see Geoffrey Stevens, "Tory leadership," *Globe and Mail*, 16 March 1974, 6, and Wayne Cheveldayoff, "PC convention gives Stanfield decisive vote of confidence," *Globe and Mail*, 18 March 1974, 1.

25 *Constitution of the Progressive Conservative Association of Canada*, as amended in 1991, articles 12.2 and 12.3.

26 *Constitution of the New Democratic Party*, as amended in 1991, Article VII (1).

27 Preston Manning, *The New Canada* (Toronto: Macmillan Canada, 1992), 221.

28 Reform Party of Canada, *Constitution*, as amended in 1992, articles 6(c) and 6(d). It is no accident that the two leadership review mechanisms the Reform party has had over its seven-year history were essentially reproductions of Tory constitutional provisions. According to the chairman of the party committee that recommended the 1991 constitutional reforms, the committee arrived at its recommendation after examining the other parties' constitutions (Interview with Victor Burstall, 29 June 1994). Some of the information in this paragraph was drawn from the author's interviews

with Reform party insider and political scientist Tom Flanagan, 28 and 29 June 1994.

29 The votes for and against a leadership convention were 714 to 1,409 in 1981, and 795 to 1,607 in 1983.

30 Mordecai Richler, CBC Radio "Sunday Morning," 30 January 1983.

31 John Laschinger and Geoffrey Stevens, *Leaders & Lesser Mortals: Backroom Politics in Canada* (Toronto: Key Porter Books, 1992), 101.

32 Patrick Martin, Allan Gregg, and George Perlin, *Contenders: The Tory Quest for Power* (Scarborough: Prentice-Hall Canada, 1983), 14.

33 An Angus Reid delegate survey conducted in the week before the 1986 Liberal convention found that a majority of the delegates would have been satisfied if Turner received even less than the two-thirds of the vote that Clark had managed in 1983. It found that 34 per cent of the delegates would have accepted Turner's leadership if he received 50 to 59 per cent of the vote. An additional 20 per cent of the delegates indicated that they would stand by Turner if he received 60 per cent of the vote and another 20 per cent said they would support him if he got between 60 and 67 per cent of the vote. Eighteen per cent of the delegates thought Turner needed 67 to 70 per cent of the vote and only 6 per cent indicated that they thought he needed more than that. Peter Maser, "Turner may be safe at 66 per cent," *Ottawa Citizen*, 28 November 1986, A1 and A2. Angus Reid survey of 502 delegates, +/- 5%, 19 in 20.

34 "Turner given strong vote of confidence," *Globe and Mail*, 1 December 1986, 1.

35 John Gray, "The system that haunts Clark," ibid., 13 January 1983, 7.

36 Greg Weston, *Reign of Error: The Inside Story of John Turner's Troubled Leadership* (Toronto: McGraw-Hill Ryerson, 1988), 196.

37 Terry Popowich, as quoted in ibid., 194.

38 As quoted in Graham Fraser, "Turner faces uphill battle," *Globe and Mail*, 15 November 1986, A1.

39 Clark, as quoted in John Gray, "The System that haunts Clark," 13 June 1983, 7; and Turner, as quoted in "Turner given a strong vote of confidence," ibid., 1 December 1986, 1.

40 The Liberal Party of Canada, "Discussion Paper on Reform of the Liberal Party of Canada" (Ottawa, January 1984), 21.

41 John Nunziata as quoted in Iain Hunter, "Battle-weary Liberal on lookout for better way to review party leadership," *Ottawa Citizen*, 1 December 1986, A3.

42 An account of the organizational planning by Mulroney supporters leading up to the 1983 Winnipeg convention is found in L. Ian MacDonald, *Mulroney: The Making of the Prime Minister* (Toronto: McClelland and Stewart, 1984), chap. 9.

43 Taylor, as quoted in Robert Lee, "It was a weekend loaded with mystery," *Ottawa Citizen*, 1 December 1986, A5.

44 As quoted in Joan Bryden, "Opening up the Liberal party," ibid., 22 February 1992, A1.

45 The Liberal Party of Canada, *Constitution*, as amended in 1992.

46 Jack Siegel, "Comments in Response to Reform Commission Draft Amendments," n.d., 12. NAC, Liberal Papers, MG 28 IV 3, vol. 1813, "Constitutional Amendments" file.

47 With sufficient motivation and organizational finesse, special interest groups could attempt to force an unwanted leadership contest by infiltrating the party at the review stage and voting on the review question. The months leading up to the planned one member, one vote (non-delegated) review (the first in Canada) of premier John Savage's leadership of the Liberal party of Nova Scotia in the fall of 1994 witnessed a surge in party memberships. Of the estimated 1,600 new party members (as of mid-July 1994), the overwhelming majority had been purchased by "trade unionists and civil servants angry at government policy and threatening to vote out Savage" See Peter Hays, "Abbass picked to save Savage," The *Daily News* (Halifax), 20 July 1994, 3. In mid-September 1994, with Savage's ability to win the leadership review in doubt, the 130-member party executive approved a change in the party's constitution to delay a leadership vote by an expected nine months. According to the leader, the move was taken because the issue had become one of "how a democratically elected party and government has opened itself unwittingly to attempts of a fair number of people ... who are bent on a course *which is undemocratic.*" (The leadership review "scheme" had been adopted in 1992 when Savage was chosen leader.) "N.S. Liberals cancel Savage leadership review," *Globe and Mail*, 19 September 1994, A5 (emphasis added).

48 According to the Liberal party, 290 of 295 constituency associations voted at their delegate selection meetings on the resolution asking if they favoured calling a leadership convention. In all, 2,021 delegates attended the 1994 convention at which the votes were counted. They too were entitled to vote on the question of calling a leadership convention. Their votes, together with those cast at the riding meetings, totalled 9,400. Of that "meshed" total, 91.2 per cent were opposed to calling a leadership convention. Clearly some double-counting (how much is impossible to know) went on as those delegates elected at the constituency level could have voted at both the riding level and on the floor of the convention. Assuming 7,400 votes were cast at the local meetings, that averages twenty-five voting members per riding in attendance at the delegate selection meetings – a far cry from the thousands involved in local elections of delegates to leadership conventions. This, together with the fact that only 2,021 of 5,200 possible delegates attended the 1994 meeting, confirms the common view that it is often very difficult for local party organizations to fill all their delegate slots and to attract much of a membership crowd to off-year biennial

meetings. Factual information provided by Aurele Gervais, director of communications and organization, Liberal Party of Canada, Ottawa, 7 and 27 July 1994.

49 For a copy of the caucus declaration listing the names of those who supported and those who did not support Diefenbaker see Robert C. Coates, *The Night of the Knives* (Fredericton: Brunswick Press, 1969), 200–3.

50 Perlin, "Attitudes of Liberal Convention Delegates Toward Proposals for Reform of the Leadership Selection Process," in Herman Bakvis, ed., *Canadian Political Parties: Leaders, Candidates and Organization*, vol. 13 of the research studies for the Royal Commission on Electoral Reform and Party Financing (Toronto: Dundurn Press, 1991), 86.

51 Weller, "Party Rules and the Dismissal of Prime Ministers: Comparative Perspectives from Britain, Canada and Australia," *Parliamentary Affairs*, XLVII (January, 1994), 140.

52 Perlin, "Attitudes of Liberal Convention Delegates Toward Proposals for Reform of the Leadership Selection Process," 87.

53 Alderman and Carter, "A Very Tory Coup," 125–6.

54 Weller, *First among Equals*, 63.

55 Ibid., 66.

56 Ibid., 69.

57 Ibid., 64. It is reasonable to append to Weller's conclusions the observation that his argument is undoubtedly more persuausive for government than for opposition party leaders in Canada.

58 Despite the small size of their caucuses, Australian Labor and Liberal party leaders have only "low" and "medium" influence over those constituencies. This is in part because both parties are federations of six state branches which control the selection of the party's parliamentary candidates and the nomination process of these candidates. The leaders therefore have little influence on the careers of their parties' MPs. This is true even when the party is in government, for the prime minister's powers of patronage are more limited than in the British Conservative party. In a Labor government the parliamentary caucus elects the ministers and the prime minister can only distribute the portfolios. Liberal prime ministers control access to the cabinet and promotion within it, but their freedom of choice is restrained by the need to accommodate coalition, state and factional forces. See ibid., 65.

59 Ibid., 67–8.

60 Thatcher, *The Downing Street Years*, 829.

CHAPTER 4

1 Not even days were required in 1968, only minutes. According to the president of the Liberal party at the time: "At the moment of Mr. Pearson's res-

ignation at 12:15 we ha[d] four people go down to all the major hotels and by 20 to 1 they were all booked" for the April convention. NAC, Liberal Papers, MG 28 IV 3, vol. 1385, "Steering Committee" file no. 1, 8 January 1968.

2 Ibid., vol. 1386, "Executive Committee" file, meeting of 17 December 1967.

3 Ibid., vol. 1669, "Candidate Liaison Committee," minutes of 12 April 1984.

4 The 1993 Tory election campaign chairman, John Tory, admitted that economics was a key factor in choosing Ottawa over other cities that had bid for the June meeting, including Halifax, Toronto, Winnipeg, Vancouver, and Edmonton. See Julian Beltrame, "Leadership hopefuls face $900,000 spending limit," *Vancouver Sun*, 8 March 1993, A4.

5 NA, Conservative Papers, MG 28 IV 2, vol. 528, "Convention Report 1976" file, "Site Report," undated (July 1975?).

6 "The P.C. Party has given us full notice that they will defeat the [Liberal] Government at the earliest possible opportunity and, therefore, to protect the political agenda, the convention must be in Ottawa." Statement of party president. NA, Liberal Papers, MG 28 IV 3, vol. 1669, "Candidate Liaison Committee," minutes of 12 April 1984.

7 The realization of the importance of governing parties meeting in Ottawa came early in the life of modern conventions. The Liberal president in 1968 reported to his party's executive that "invitations had been received to hold the Convention in Calgary and in Montreal ... *The fact that we were in office and Parliament could be sitting*, with Ottawa's geographical advantages and accommodation improvements in the Capital City, it appeared preferable to hold it here" (emphasis added). Ibid., vol. 1386, "Executive Committee" file, meeting of the executive committee of 17 December 1967.

8 NA, Conservative Papers, MG 28 IV 2, vol. 524, "1967 Convention Budget." The 1967 Conservative mega-convention was far more expensive than the party's previous conventions had been. The 1927, 1938, 1942, 1948, and 1956 conventions cost the party approximately $20,000, $10,000, $15,000, $52,000 and $76,000 in current dollars respectively. See Ruth M. Bell, "Conservative Party National Conventions 1927–1956, (MA thesis, Carleton University), 1965, 86–7. Conversion of 1967 into 1993 dollars is based on a GDP deflator of 4.28, meaning that items costing $100 in 1967 would have cost $428 in 1993. *Bank of Canada Review*, May 1987, table H4; and Spring 1994, table H3.

9 NA, Conservative Papers, MG 28 IV 2, vol. 524, "Convention Budget" file. The initially forecast expenditure and revenue figures were $403,097 and $450,590 respectively. See the final post-convention "Organization Committee Report" of John Laschinger and Raymond Grenier and the "1976 Leadership Convention Revised Revenue and Expenditure Projections," both

undated. Undocumented suggestions that the Tories actually made sizable surpluses in both 1976 and 1983 are found in Joseph Wearing, "The High Cost of High Tech: Financing the Modern Leadership Campaign," in George Perlin, ed., *Party Democracy in Canada: The Politics of National Party Conventions* (Scarborough: Prentice-Hall Canada, 1988), 78, and Mary Janigan, "The Tories pass the hat," *Maclean's*, 3 October 1983, 16.

10 Letter of E.A. Chater, director, Registration Division, Department of National Revenue to John Laschinger, dated 23 January 1975. NA, Conservative Papers, MG 28 IV 2, vol. 524, "Convention Budget 1976" file.

11 Revenue Canada, *Bulletin 75–2R4*. The actual value of the maximum tax credit has declined in real terms since 1974. A contribution of $100 in 1974 would have been the equivalent of a contribution of $340 in 1993.

12 Liberal Party of Canada, "Memorandum to Provincial and Territorial Presidents from Michael Robinson, Chief Financial Officer, re: Financial Assistance for Delegates/Alternates," dated 18 April 1990.

13 The Liberal party claims to calculate its registration fees according to the revenue "required to pay the Party's budgeted costs of the convention, the travelling expenses of all delegates and alternates to attend the convention and to provide an assistance fund from which some subsidy can be made available to reduce the actual cost to delegates who are truly in need of assistance." It has been the party's practice to assist delegates and alternates with their additional convention expenses by reimbursing them for receipted hotel and meal costs up to a maximum amount per day, provided the individual made an equivalent contribution to the party. See Letter from Denise Costello, assistant comptroller, 1984 leadership convention to John Skelton, Charitable and Non-Profit Organization Section, Revenue Canada, 18 April 1984. NA, Liberal Papers, MG 28 IV 3, vol. 1628, "Costello" file.

14 The original 1984 Liberal convention budget projected a total of 1,500 observers at $400 each, which would have produced a welcome $600,000 for the cash-strapped party. In spite of persistent attempts to meet that objective and periodic prodding from the executive to push observer accreditation more actively, sales never passed the 750 mark. Still, that meant $300,000 to help to finance the convention. Ibid., vol. 1669, "Candidate Liaison Committee," meeting of 17 May 1984.

15 NA, Conservative Papers, MG 28 IV 2, vol. 524, "1967 Convention Budget," and "Convention Budget." No budget or financial figures were found in the 1983 Conservative papers at the National Archives.

16 NA, Liberal Papers, MG 28 IV 3, vol. 1645, "Convention Account" file.

17 Ibid., vol. 1628, "Steering Committee" file, meeting of 4 April 1984.

18 Ibid., vol. 1645, "Convention Account" file.

19 The 1993 spectacle included appearances by Al Waxman, Christopher Plummer, and the stars of CBC Radio's "Double Exposure." The video pre-

sentation included tributes from Ronald Reagan, George Bush, and Margaret Thatcher. See Tim Naumetz, "PM's tribute boasts $300G tab," *Ottawa
Sun*, 11 June 1993, 43. By comparison, the budget approved for the "Robert Stanfield Testimonial" film in 1976 was $23,000. See John Laschinger
memo of 8 January 1976 to Nancy McLean, in NA, Conservative Papers,
MG 28 IV 2, vol. 524, "Convention Budget" file.

20 That is obviously more the case for conventions in which no spending limits were set and no disclosure rules governing contributions were in place,
as was true of the Tories in 1983. According to one defeated candidate,
John Crosbie, "You're not going to get the truth [about campaign costs and
debts] from any of the candidates. They all lie and I'm not going to tell
you" (quoted in "Crosbie left holding $200,000 campaign debt," *StarPhoe-
nix*, 21 September 1983, C8.)

21 It was estimated at the time of the 1967 convention that the total spending
of all of the candidates in that year "must have run into at least a million
dollars." See *Balloons and Ballots* (Toronto: The Telegram, 1967), 53.

22 NA, Conservative Papers, MG 28 IV 2, vol. 532, "Registration Committee"
file, minutes of meeting of Regulations Sub-Committee, 10 March 1983.

23 Brian Mulroney was the only Tory candidate in 1976 to refuse to comply
with the party's regulation that "the name of each campaign contributor
who donates in cash, services or goods, more than $1,000 to the candi-
date's campaign" be disclosed to the Convention Committee within ninety
days of the convention. Mulroney's fund-raisers were said to have promised
that their candidate intended to ignore the party regulation about disclos-
ing names of candidates. His reported reason for not complying was that
he feared political "hard-ball" being played by the Liberals in Quebec
against those who had donated to his campaign. He thereby forfeited his
$500 "good faith" deposit and the post-convention $30,000 sweetener
given by the party from its convention surplus to the candidates. Jack Horner submitted an incomplete account of his finances which included his
expenses but not his sources. It was returned to him for revision. See Progressive Conservative Party, Party President's press release of 16 July 1975,
setting out the agreed upon terms for candidate certification; Graham
Fraser, "PC leadership donors promised tax benefits," *Globe and Mail*, 8
March 1993, A3; Ian Urquhart, "Where money wasn't everything," *Maclean's*, 28 June 1976, 17–8; and Wearing, "The High Cost of High Tech,"
78.

24 Liberal Party of Canada, "Report of the Leadership Expenses Committee,"
co-chaired by Margo Brousseau and Senator Dan Hays, 7 November 1990.

25 After her victory at the June convention, Campbell stacked the PC Canada
Fund with her own supporters. The fund also granted Jim Edwards, who
had moved to support Campbell after the first ballot of the convention, a
loan to cover his campaign shortfall (which was $64,000 according to John

Laschinger, his campaign manager). Citing an unidentified Campbell supporter, Stevie Cameron reported that Campbell spent more than $4 mil-
lion on her campaign. See "Campbell's leadership debt keeps the faithful
hustling," *Globe and Mail,* 4 October 1993, A3. Based on yet to be disclosed
party financial records, the most authoritative report of the leadership candidates' spending is Ross Howard, "Tory leadership contest cost more than
$6-million," ibid., 2 March 1994, A1.

26 Keith Archer, "Leadership Selection in the New Democratic Party," in Herman Bakvis, ed., *Canadian Political Parties: Leaders, Candidates and Organization,* vol. 13 of the research studies for the Royal Commission on Electoral
Reform and Party Financing (Toronto: Dundurn Press, 1991), 41.

27 For more details on leadership campaign financing in the NDP see ibid.,
41–4.

28 For one thing, six tons of liquor were consumed by the approximately ten
thousand conventioneers at the 1967 Conservative convention in Toronto.
See *Balloons and Ballots,* 53.

29 For more details on the use of new communications technology see ibid.,
109–10; Geoffrey Stevens, *Stanfield* (Toronto: McClelland & Stewart,
1973), 192–3; and Joseph Wearing, "The Liberal Choice," *Journal of Canadian Studies* 3 (May 1968), 5.

30 Both figures are from Patrick Martin, Allan Gregg, and George Perlin, *Contenders: The Tory Quest for Power* (Scarborough: Prentice-Hall Canada, 1983),
239.

31 As quoted in Elizabeth Thompson, "The sky's the limit," *Gazette* (Montreal), 31 March 1990, B7.

32 Chris Cobb, "Hold the line: Static expected from glut of cellular phones,"
Ottawa Citizen, 12 June 1993, B3.

33 Several candidates in the 1976 Tory campaign, including Joe Clark, Flora
MacDonald, Sinclair Stevens, and R.C. Quittenton, solicited funds through
the tax credit system by having contributors route their donations to their
campaigns through the PC Canada Fund. The fund issued the receipt to
the donor and returned to the riding associations 75 per cent of everything
raised in a riding, keeping the rest for itself. If a candidate had made the
proper arrangements with the local association, it voted to turn the funds
over to the candidate. See Jonathan Manthorpe, "Use of Election Expenses
Act defended," *Globe and Mail,* 22 January 1976, 8. For his part, at least,
Quittenton had to forfeit to the local association a further 5 per cent of the
total raised in his name for this service, up to a maximum of $500. See Let-
ter of R.C. Quittenton to J.W. O'Kane, 6 January 1976, NA, Conservative
Papers, MG 28 IV 2, vol. 528, "Convention 1976" file.

34 Royal Commission on Electoral Reform and Party Financing, *Reforming Electoral Democracy,* 4 vols. (Ottawa, 1991), 1:279. The first recorded instance of
contributions to a leadership candidate being channelled through a regis-

tered political party is found in NA, Conservative Papers, MG 28 IV 2, vol. 529, "Candidate Liaison Committee" file, 18 March 1983, Bulletin # 4: "An explanation of tax receipting procedures for donations to candidates via PC Canada Fund." See also Wearing, "The High Cost of High Tech," 82. According to Bud Slattery, former director of election financing, Elections Canada, the flow-through practice has never been the subject of any ruling by Elections Canada, contrary to the impression conveyed by the former NDP national secretary in Archer, "Leadership Selection in the New Democratic Party," 42. It is solely a matter for Revenue Canada to decide in its interpretation of the Income Tax Act. (Slattery interview, Ottawa, 1 November 1993.)

35 Some of the information in this paragraph was provided in a confidential interview with a senior Conservative organizer who has served as a candidate fund-raiser and campaign manager.

36 In 1983 and 1984 a $10,000 donation limit was supposedly put in place for the Conservative and Liberal campaigns by some of the candidates themselves. According to Wearing, "Turner's fund-raisers had a rule not to accept $10,000 or more; according to John Rae, only ten Chrétien contributions were over $10,000. Mulroney's financial chairman claimed that none of their contributions was over $10,000." These claims could not be substantiated. See Wearing, "The High Cost of High Tech," 78.

37 That many donors would rather avoid public disclosure seems clear from the candidate expense accounts of some of the candidates in the 1976 Tory race. For example, Jim Gillies reported raising a total of $134,000. Of this, $58,000 had been donated in instalments of exactly $1,000 which, according to rules set by the party for that convention, was the maximum amount a donor could give anonymously. See "Audit indicates $157,897 collected in Clark campaign," *StarPhoenix*, 22 June 1976, 4.

38 "The no-name donations," *Globe and Mail*, 19 January 1990, A6.

39 As quoted in Jeff Sallot, "Tory delegates won't know who's bankrolling candidates," ibid., 2 April 1983, 1.

40 Chrétien turned over $284,354 to the party while Martin paid $277,429, and Copps, $46,368. Both Wappel and Nunziata spent less than a total of $250,000 and therefore paid nothing in levies to the party. See Liberal Party of Canada, press release of 7 November 1990, "Liberal leadership expenses and contributions reports made public." The tax creditable $608,151 was listed by the Liberal party as "not receipted revenue" contributed to the party in 1990. See Reform Commission of the Liberal Party of Canada, "Agenda for Reform" (31 July 1991), 16.

41 Archer, "Leadership Selection in the New Democratic Party," 42, and data kindly provided by Professor Archer, 16 November 1993.

42 Assume that 1,060 of 1,187 McLaughlin contributors gave $100 each; and that 78 individuals contributed $100 each to de Jong. This translates into

$106,000 + $7,800 = $113,800 x .75 = $85,350 maximum tax credits for McLaughlin's and de Jong's contributors combined.

43 The conditions apply for 1989 as well as 1990 because the official campaign period ran from September 1989 to June 1990. A donor could give money in each of these years and be eligible to claim the full value of the tax credits in each year.

44 For example, in 1990 the Bank of Nova Scotia gave $3,000 to each of the five Liberal leadership candidates and $40,000 to the Progressive Conservative party. See "Liberal Party of Canada, 1990 Leadership, Contributions receipted in excess of $100," 7 November 1990, and Elections Canada, *Registered Parties Fiscal Period Returns 1990* (Ottawa: 1991), I:15.

45 W.T. Stanbury, *Money in Politics: Financing Federal Parties and Candidates in Canada,* vol. 1 of the research studies for the Royal Commission on Electoral Reform and Party Financing (Toronto: Dundurn Press, 1991), 229–40, 300.

46 See Jonathan Manthorpe, "Use of Election Expenses Act defended," *Globe and Mail,* 22 February 1976, 8; the Ontario Commission on Election Contributions and Expenses, *Political Financing: Studies on Election Spending Limits and Party Leadership Campaigns* (Toronto, 1986), 80; and Arthur Drache, "Political parties abuse tax system," *Financial Post,* 6 November 1993, 19.

47 See Royal Commission on Electoral Reform and Party Financing, *Reforming Electoral Democracy,* 1:280.

48 Archer, "Leadership Selection in the New Democratic Party," 43. Stanbury presents a case for an increase in the federal tax credit to reflect part of the inflation since 1974 (*Money in Politics,* 416–19).

49 See my "Recognition of Canadian Political Parties in Parliament and in Law," *CJPS* 9 (March 1976), 77–100. As recently as the 1993 Tory campaign, Campbell voiced an opinion common to Canadian politicians. In addressing the issue of legislating spending limits on candidate nominations, she wrote: "The traditions of the Progressive Conservative Party, and those of the party system in Canada, militate against state interference in parties' internal affairs. Thus, wherever possible, worthwhile reforms should be undertaken by parties unilaterally." " 'Doing Politics Differently': Proposals for Democratic Reform" (Ottawa: mimeo, n.d.), 5–6.

50 As quoted in Ross Howard, "Lavish Tory campaigns predicted despite limit," *Globe and Mail,* 14 September 1985, 12.

51 André Blais and Elizabeth Gidengil, *Making Representative Democracy Work: The Views of Canadians,* vol. 17 of the research studies for the Royal Commission on Electoral Reform and Party Financing (Toronto: Dundurn Press, 1991), 75.

52 Wearing, "The High Cost of High Tech," 81. The Lortie Commission accepted the need to weigh controls on expenses with the party and public's demands that "leadership aspirants engage in contestants' debates across

the country and provide frequent opportunities for the critical assessment of their views and policies." *Reforming Electoral Democracy,* 1:279.

53 Douglas Fisher, as quoted in the Ontario Commission on Election Contributions and Expenses, 92.

54 Royal Commission on Electoral Reform and Party Financing, I:280.

55 Ibid., 282.

56 Ibid., 281.

57 Ibid., 283-4.

58 Ibid., 284-5. The floor of $250 on disclosures on contributions is part of a larger package of disclosure recommendations of the commission intended to cover donations to all persons seeking public office: parliamentary candidates, those seeking constituency party nominations, and national party leadership contestants. See ibid., 428-9.

59 The Lortie Commission defined a leadership campaign expense as "the value of any property or services used by a person seeking to be the leader of a registered party during the leadership campaign period if it would be considered to be an election expense if each person seeking to be the leader of a registered party were a candidate" in a federal election. See Section 377 (1) of the proposed legislation in *Reforming Electoral Democracy* 3:142. The expenses that the Lortie Commission recommended be exempt from the spending limit are detailed in sections 371 and 376 of ibid., 139-40 and 142.

60 Ibid., 1:283-5. The proposed structure and responsibilities of the independent multi-member Canada Elections Commission are given at 492-9.

61 Federal contributions towards presidential primary campaigns in the United States are based on the candidate's ability to raise funds in small amounts from several states. On the implications of this process see Nelson W. Polsby and Aaron Wildavsky, *Presidential Elections: Contemporary Strategies of American Electoral Politics,* 8th ed. (New York: Free Press, 1991), 50 ff.

62 Rules governing the financing of NDP 1989 leadership campaigns pointed in this direction. To cover a deficit, candidates could raise money for sixty days after the convention. See Stanbury, *Money in Politics,* 404, and Archer, "Leadership Selection in the New Democratic Party," 41.

63 George Perlin, "Attitudes of Liberal Convention Delegates Toward Proposals for Reform of the Process of Leadership Selection" in Bakvis, ed., *Canadian Political Parties,* 77.

64 These data are analysed more thoroughly in ibid., 77-81. Perlin's findings concerning the attitudes of Liberal convention delegates contrast with R.K. Carty's concerning the opinions of Liberal and other riding executives. In his survey of federal riding executives, Carty found that 80 per cent of the Conservative, 68 per cent of the Liberal, and 57 per cent of the NDP riding presidents surveyed agreed with the statement that "the parties should be left entirely on their own to decide by what standards and principles they

will select their leaders." See Carty, *Canadian Political Parties in the Constituencies*, vol. 23 of the research studies for the Royal Commission on Electoral Reform and Party Financing (Toronto: Dundurn Press, 1991), table 5.9, 133 and 261.

CHAPTER 5

1 *The National Liberal Convention, Ottawa, August 5, 6, 7, 1919: The Story of the Convention and the Report of its Proceedings*, 23–4.

2 Ibid., 24 and 194. The Liberals continued the practice of adopting "resolutions of appreciation" to the press in their 1948 and 1958 conventions: see *Report of the Proceedings of the National Liberal Convention, 1948*, 240; and *Report of the Proceedings of the National Liberal Convention, 1958*, 242. The Tories actually granted voting delegate status to "newspaper representatives" in the 1927 and 1938 conventions. No record could be found of the number of members of the press to have accepted the party's offer.

3 1948 *Report*, 31.

4 1958 *Report*, 241 and 1.25.

5 Trudeau's victory speech, as quoted in Lewis Seale, "Humourous, challenging in victory, Trudeau calls for a just society in Canada," *Globe and Mail* 8 April 1968, 8.

6 Sources: for 1967, *Balloons and Ballots* (Toronto: The Telegram, 1967), 53; for 1968, NA, Liberal Papers, MG 28 IV 3, vol. 1431, "Public Relations re: Leadership Convention 1967–68" file; and for 1993, Randall Pearce, communications director, Progressive Conservative Party of Canada, interview of 23 August 1993.

7 NA, Liberal Papers, MG 28 IV 3, vol. 1431, "Confidential Minutes of Standing Communications Committee," 31 January 1968. The meeting decided that the studio "should be located in a room usually used for storage."

8 Ibid., vol. 1385, "Steering Committee" file, meeting no. 4, 5 February 1968. The Liberals in 1968 were also concerned about losing control of their convention agenda to the demands of television: "We are retreating to the position where the media is [*sic*] taking over our undertaking. They will soon be altering our programme." These are Paul Lafond's words in a memo to fellow convention organizers complaining about television's ever-increasing demands for space, time, and mobility of cameras. See ibid., vol. 1386, "Communications" file, Memo of Paul Lafond of 7 February 1968.

9 Ibid., vol. 1385, "Steering Committee" file, meeting of 8 January 1968.

10 Ibid., vol. 1628, "Steering Committee" file, meeting of 18 April 1984.

11 There are two obvious exceptions: the ten-candidate, five-ballot Tory convention in 1967, and the five-candidate, four-ballot NDP convention of 1971. The relatively smaller CBC-TV audience in 1967 (2 million compared with 3.2 million for the Liberal convention the following year) might

be accounted for by the newness of televised conventions, the time of year (much of Canada was still revelling in a late, end-of-Expo summer), and the fact that the Liberal contest, following three months of unprecedented media attention, was destined to choose a new prime minister, not a leader of the opposition. The NDP contest of 1971 came when the party was at 17 per cent in the Gallup poll, compared with 51 per cent for the governing Liberals, and at a time when the party seemed destined to repeat yet again another poor showing in the next federal election. Additionally, although there were five candidates in the race, David Lewis was widely anticipated to be chosen leader no matter how many ballots it took.

12 Rick Salutin found MuchMusic's offbeat coverage of the Tory convention refreshingly different and appealing. Capturing the "fifties quality of the event," the rock network called its show "Take Me to Your Leader." See Salutin, "Much's unconventional coverage," *Globe and Mail,* 18 June 1992, A11.

13 It would be tempting to conclude that in 1993, for example, over 50 per cent of Canadians eighteen years of age and older (24.% +18.0% +8.1%) watched at least a portion of the Conservative convention on the day the new leader was elected. Unfortunately, channel-switching rules out that possibility, for the same viewer would be double (triple? quadruple?) counted.

14 Byron E. Shafer, *Bifurcated Politics: Evolution and Reform in the National Party Convention* (Cambridge, Mass: Harvard University Press, 1988), 278–9.

15 Ibid., Table 7.1, 229.

16 Ibid., 227.

17 At the Conservative convention of 1976, for example, party insiders who served as television commentators included David Crombie, then mayor of Toronto and prominent Flora MacDonald supporter; John Bassett, broadcaster, publisher, CTV director, party fund-raiser and financial contributor to Claude Wagner's campaign; Eddie Goodman, Tory fund-raiser, operative, and major player in Flora MacDonald's campaign; John Robarts, former Ontario premier and putative candidate for the 1976 race; and Dalton Camp, former party president and prominent backroom Tory operative. See Patrick Brown, Robert Chodos, and Rae Murphy, *Winners, Losers: The 1976 Tory Leadership Convention* (Toronto: Lorimer, 1976), 28.

18 In his television documentary of the NDP convention, Terrence McKenna described Lewis's comment as "a key moment in the convention." (CBC-TV, "Hearts and Heads: Inside the NDP Convention," *The Journal,* 4 December 1989.) Lewis made his voting intentions known the next morning based on his assessment of McLaughlin's "poor speech." He supported Dave Barrett. See *Winnipeg Free Press,* 3 December 1989, 1.

19 In his televised comments on the candidates' speeches the night before the vote on the leadership, Segal had praised Charest's speech and been critical of Campbell's. To some observers, Segal's subsequent endorsement of Char-

est raised questions about the CBC-TV's failure to have guarded against the possibility that the commentator, with his own understandable preferences, would nonetheless not have disclosed them until after the speeches were delivered on the eve of the voting. This begs the question of whether it was the speeches themselves that prompted the final endorsement.

Biases of analysts aside, the link between politics and television was too much for Rick Salutin in 1993: "CTV, not to be out-toried, had three Conservatives with Lloyd Robertson, including *John* Tory, to [Peter] Mansbridge's lone [Hugh] Segal. What's unnerving is how alike all these people seemed. Put them in a lineup and try to pick out the lifetime party hacks from the lifetime journalists. I doubt it's possible without insider knowledge. So you have this fusion and symbiosis between politicians and journalists, and then you put them on the air and *you don't let anyone else on camera all day.* Not even Michael Bliss. It was harrowing." See Salutin, "Take Me to Your Leader" (emphasis in original).

20 Shafer, *Bifurcated Politics*, 261.

21 Endorsing Jimmy Carter for re-election in 1980, the NEA elected 302 delegates to the Democratic convention that year – a group larger than every state delegation except California. "Decision for Christ" and "born again" Christians supportive of the Moral Majority were able to dominate delegate selection in several states, eventually sending over 25 per cent of the delegates in attendance at the Republican convention of 1980. Ibid., 120–4.

22 The Conservative party in 1967 was the last of the two older parties to have wrestled behind the scenes with a highly contentious policy in an attempt to avoid a divisive and possibly catastrophic floor fight. A party policy conference less than a month before the September leadership convention supported the view that Canada was made up of "two founding peoples, or *deux nations.*" This provoked a hostile reaction from John Diefenbaker whose supporters succeeded in having the report embodying the resolution tabled on the convention floor. It was never heard of again. See memo of Gordon Churchill, "*Deux Nations* or One Canada: John Diefenbaker at the 1967 Conservative Convention," *Canadian Historical Review* 64 (December 1983), 597–604, for an account by a Diefenbaker supporter of the crisis and the role he played in defusing it.

23 In their study of the 1976 Conservative convention, Brown, Chodos, et al. claimed that the "the absolute dominance of television" had led to the "virtual elimination of the middlemen – print journalists – who were left with several options, none of them terribly satisfactory: (a) sitting in the press room watching television; (b) tracing all forms of trivia (for colour sidebars); (c) interviewing each other and swapping rumours; and (d) trying to become pundits." *Winners, Losers*, 28–9.

24 It might be argued that "candidate mentions" is not a totally satisfactory variable, since the context and tone are important. Nonetheless, for pur-

poses of this analysis it is judged to have an excellent intuitive fit with "candidate viability."

25 The other candidates for the NDP leadership have not been included in this analysis or in table 5-5 as their total number of mentions was very small. The combined total on the two networks came to ninety-five for the four candidates.

26 "Turner salutes Barrett for joining race," *StarPhoenix*, 30 September 1989, A10.

27 "Spin" in politics has an interesting, though uncertain, etymology. According to William Safire, "spin doctor" is based "on the slang meaning of the verb to *spin*, which in the 1950s meant 'to deceive,' perhaps influenced by 'to spin a yarn.' More recently, as a noun, *spin* has come to mean 'twist,' or 'interpretation'; when a pitcher *puts a spin on* a baseball, he causes it to curve, and when we *put our own spin* on a story, we angle it to suit our predilections or interests." Safire, "Calling Dr. Spin," *New York Times Magazine*, 31 August 1986, 8.

28 Frederick J. Fletcher and Robert J. Drummond, "The Mass Media and the Selection of National Party Leaders: Some Explorations," in George C. Perlin, ed., *Party Democracy in Canada: The Politics of National Party Conventions* (Scarborough; Prentice-Hall of Canada, 1988), 99.

29 These are among the principal indicators listed by Fletcher and Drummond, 99–100.

30 These are up from 7 and 10 per cent in the "great deal of influence" category in 1983 and 1984 respectively, and down from 66 per cent in the 1983 Tory "little or no influence" category. The Liberal 1984 "little or no influence" group was about the same as in 1990 (ibid., table 4, 108). The 1990 and 1993 delegate surveys yielded the following in response to the question: "Would you say that news reports on television and radio and in the newspapers had a great deal of influence, some influence, a little influence, or no influence on your opinions of the strengths and weaknesses of the candidates for the leadership?" (%)

	1990 Liberal	1993 Conservative
Great deal of influence	16	15
Some influence	28	31
A little influence	25	27
No influence	31	27
N=	1,479	777

SOURCE: 1990 Liberal and 1993 Conservative post-convention surveys, principal investigator: George Perlin.

31 The 1993 question was: "What about the other delegates attending the convention, do you think the media had a great deal of influence, some in-

fluence, a little influence or no influence on their opinions of the candidates?"

	1993 Conservative
Great deal of influence	26
Some influence	52
A little influence	19
No influence	3
N=	770

SOURCE: 1993 Conservative post-convention survey.

32 The 1990 delegate survey yielded the following in response to the question: "During the campaign for the leadership in 1990 did you get more of your information about the candidates from the news reports of television, radio, and newspapers OR from material the candidates sent you?"

	1990 Liberal	1993 Conservative
News reports	19	17
Candidate material	35	32
Both equally	46	51
N=	1,463	776

SOURCE: 1990 Liberal and 1993 Conservative post-convention surveys. For the 1983 and 1984 data see Fletcher and Drummond, "The Mass Media," table 3, 108.

33 For the 1983 and 1984 data see Fletcher and Drummond, "The Mass Media," table 7, 110.

34 Patrick Martin, Allan Gregg, and George Perlin, *Contenders: The Tory Quest for Power* (Scarborough: Prentice-Hall of Canada, 1983), 97.

35 With the percentage of respondents saying "yes," the items were: (1) be able to beat Jean Chrétien in debate (90 per cent); (2) have a command of television (86 per cent); and, after favouring less government and lower public spending, (4) be able to beat Audrey McLaughlin in debate (79 per cent). See *Maclean's*/COMPAS poll of 450 delegates attending the 1991 Conservative policy convention; +/-4.7% accuracy range, nineteen times out of twenty. *Maclean's*, 22 March 1993, 16.

36 Fletcher and Drummond, "The Mass Media," 113. Turner entered the 1984 race with a positive television image among Liberals which, as Fletcher and Drummond point out, required "considerable evidence (such as the debates during the 1984 federal election campaign) to shake" (113). A comparable question requiring delegates to choose preferentially from among stated reasons (such as appealing image on television) was not asked in the 1990 and 1993 surveys.

37 Ibid., 113 and 117. In their multivariate analysis of factors in the choices made by delegates of both parties, Brady and Johnston demonstrate that competence was the most consistently important personal criterion and television image the least important in 1983 and 1984. See Brady and Johnston, "Conventions Versus Primaries: A Canadian-American Comparison," in Perlin, ed., *Party Democracy in Canada*, 252, 264 and 265. The apparent contradiction between the Fletcher-Drummond and Brady-Johnston analyses rests on the assumption that assessments of competence are not influenced by media reports. Fletcher and Drummond demonstrated that there was potential for both direct and indirect media influence on delegates.

38 Alan Whitehorn and Keith Archer, "Party Activists and Political Leadership: A Case Study of the NDP," in Maureen Mancuso, Richard G. Price, and Ronald Wagenberg, eds., *Leaders and Leadership in Canada* (Toronto: Oxford University Press, 1994), 47. The data are from the 1989 NDP leadership convention survey, principal investigator: Keith Archer. Non-responses are excluded.

39 Alan Whitehorn, *Canadian Socialism: Essays on the CCF-NDP* (Toronto: Oxford University Press, 1992), 112.

40 Among the general works on the Canadian mass media that bear out these points are E. R. Black, *Politics and the News: The Political Functions of the Mass Media* (Toronto: Butterworths, 1982); Arthur Seigel, *Politics and the Media in Canada* (Toronto: McGraw-Hill Ryerson, 1983); and David Taras, "Prime Ministers and the Media," in Leslie A. Pal and David Taras, eds., *Prime Ministers and Premiers: Political Leadership and Public Policy in Canada* (Scarborough: Prentice-Hall of Canada, 1988), 36–49. Clearly the best, and for our purposes the most appropriate, study of Canadian leadership selection and the mass media is Fletcher and Drummond, "The Mass Media," 97–122. There are also five volumes of the Royal Commission on Electoral Reform and Party Financing research studies edited by Frederick J. Fletcher (in one case with David V.J. Bell) devoted to a study of the media and politics: *Media and Voters in Canadian Election Campaigns; Media, Elections and Democracy; Reaching the Voter: Constituency Campaigning in Canada; Election Broadcasting in Canada;* and *Reporting the Campaign: Election Coverage in Canada* (Toronto: Dundurn Press, 1991), vols. 18–22.

41 Both quotations are from Taras, "Prime Ministers and the Media," 37.

42 See Martin, Gregg, and Perlin, *Contenders*, 40–3; "The Ethnic Factor," a documentary report on the CBC-TV's *The Journal*, 23 May 1984; and Denys Horgan, "Grit Worker Quits Drive for Delegates," *Globe and Mail*, 4 May 1984, 5.

43 R.K. Carty, "Campaigning in the Trenches: The Transformation of Constituency Politics," in Perlin, ed., *Party Democracy in Canada*, 85.

44 Martin, Gregg, and Perlin, *Contenders*, 40.

45 In 1968 one Winnipeg meeting with five hundred people in attendance was described by the press as "solidly packed" by the organizers of Paul Martin Sr and John Turner. Among those in attendance were two busloads of "members," one with sixty students from a local university recruited largely by a professor organizing for one of the candidates and the other with fifty habitués from the Indian-Métis Friendship Centre. See Barry Came, "Five Out of Six Pro-Martin," *Winnipeg Free Press*, 6 February 1968, 3.

46 Carty, "Campaigning in the Trenches," 86 and 92.

47 R.K. Carty and Lynda Erickson, "Candidate Nomination in Canada's National Political Parties," in Herman Bakvis, ed., *Canadian Political Parties: Leaders, Candidates and Organization*, vol. 13 of the research studies for the Royal Commission on Electoral Reform and Party Financing, (Toronto: Dundurn Press, 1991), 129.

48 For an account of this phenomenon at the time of a general election, see R. Jeremy Wilson, "Horserace Journalism and Canadian Election Campaigns," in R.K. Carty, ed., *Canadian Political Party Systems: A Reader* (Toronto: Broadview Press, 1992), 490–507. An analysis of the difficulties the press face in their handling of political news during election campaigns is given by Giles Gherson, "If you're hoping for more than a horse race, don't count on the media," *Globe and Mail*, 8 September 1993, A18.

49 Ross Howard, "Chrétien challengers frustrated by front-runner's campaign style," *Globe and Mail*, 22 May 1990, A3.

50 Michael J. Robinson and Margaret A. Sheehan, *Over the Wire and on TV: CBS and UPI in Campaign '80* (New York: Russell Sage Foundation, 1983), 252. A brief evaluative introduction to public opinion polls is found in Herbert Asher, *Polling and the Public: What Every Citizen Should Know* (Washington, DC: Congressional Quarterly, 1988).

51 Henry E. Brady and Michael G. Hagen, "The 'Horse-Race' or the Issues? What Do Voters Learn from Presidential Primaries?" paper presented to the APSA annual meeting (Washington, DC, 1986), 37.

52 For example, two of the early Gallup surveys on national party leadership in Canada in the 1960s polled on the question of possible successors to the then leaders of the Conservative and Liberal parties: "Paul Martin continues favourite to succeed Pearson as next PM" (23 June 1965) and "Davie Fulton gaining favour as successor to Diefenbaker" (26 June 1965).

53 Fletcher and Drummond, "The Mass Media," 107.

54 As quoted in Peter O'Neil, "Campbell ready to run as Beatty bails out," *Vancouver Sun*, 16 March 1993, A4, and in Graham Fraser, "Scrambling aboard Campbell's bandwagon," *Globe and Mail*, 16 March 1993, A11.

55 The question asked was "If the Progressive Conservative Party had Kim Campbell/Michael Wilson/Perrin Beatty/Jean Charest/Barbara McDougall as its leader, which party's candidate do you think you would vote for?" The findings were as follows (%):

Name	Lib	PC	NDP	Ref.	BQ	Other
Campbell	39	37	14	5	3	2
Wilson	42	31	16	6	4	2
Charest	47	25	16	7	4	2
Beatty	44	26	18	7	4	2
McDougall	43	31	15	6	3	2

The same poll revealed that in the public mind Campbell was the frontrunner in the race to become prime minister: nationally, she had the support of 25 per cent of those polled, Wilson had 17 per cent, McDougall had 14 per cent, Beatty had 7 per cent and Charest was supported by 6 per cent. Thirty-two per cent of those polled either did not know or refused to respond. As public opinion can be highly volatile and possibly unreliable on such hypothetical polls, their results should be treated with caution. What is important for this analysis is the impact that such poll results have on decision-making by potential candidates. See "Kim Campbell threatens Liberal lead," *Gallup Report*, 25 February 1993.

56 The Tory lead over the Liberals with Campbell as leader was 45 per cent to 32 per cent (ComQuest poll taken 8–15 March), 35 per cent to 33 per cent (Environics poll taken 10–25 March), and 43 per cent to 25 per cent (Angus Reid poll taken 15–18 March).

57 Hugh Winsor, "Clark eyes leadership bid," *Globe and Mail*, 14 May 1993, A1; and "Clark won't run," *StarPhoenix*, 15 May 1993, D11.

58 According to the Reid poll, the Tories with Charest as their leader would beat the Liberals 37 per cent to 32 per cent, whereas they would lose under Campbell, 31% to 35% (+/- 2.5% margin of error). The Gallup poll of 12 June gave Charest-led Conservatives 44 per cent to 37 per cent for the Liberals, but Campbell-led Tories would lose to the Liberals 35 per cent to 44 per cent (+/- 3.1% margin of error). See Julian Beltrame, "Poll suggests Charest could beat Campbell or Chrétien," *Ottawa Citizen*, 22 May 1993, A1; and David Vienneau, "Tories need Charest to win election, Gallup finds," *Toronto Star*, 12 June 1993, A1.

59 John Geddes and Jill Vardy, "Charest urges voters to heed poll position," *Financial Post*, 11 June 1993, 5.

60 The survey had been conducted between 1 and 5 June, seven to eleven days before its release. The lateness and the timing of the release as well as the analysis that accompanied it became the subject of some debate in the media "about the ethics and motives of the media and pollsters." See Doug Fisher, "Polling: Gallup survey raises ethical questions," *Ottawa Citizen*, 13 June 1993, C3; and Jeff Sallot, "Beating the bushes for elusive victory," *Globe and Mail*, 14 June 1993, A7.

61 Such a strategy could hardly be faulted given the dramatic increase in Charest's popularity. In response to the question "Who would make the best leader?" the *Globe*/ComQuest Research polls of 8–16 March showed Campbell in the lead with 29 per cent to Charest's 4 per cent. By 1–8 June, Charest had moved to 39 percent to Campbell's second-place 24 per cent. See Hugh Winsor, "Charest favoured in poll," *Globe and Mail*, 10 June 1993, A1.

62 Asher, "Polling and the Public," 115. For a contrary view of bandwagon momentum based on experimental research, see Richard Nadeau, Edouard Cloutier, and J.-H. Guay, "New Evidence about the Existence of a Bandwagon Effect in the Opinion Formation Process," *International Political Science Review* 14 (April 1993), 203–13.

63 Royal Commission on Electoral Reform and Party Financing, *Reforming Electoral Democracy*, 4 vols. (Ottawa, 1991), 1:457–8. For an examination of the link between information provided by polls and voter appreciation of alternative strategies in the 1988 Canadian general election, see Richard Johnston, André Blais, Henry E. Brady, and Jean Crête, *Letting the People Decide: Dynamics of a Canadian Election* (Montreal and Kingston: McGill-Queen's University Press, 1992), chap. 7.

64 "Campbell poses serious threat to Liberal support," *The Gallup Report*, 12 April 1993. The last Gallup survey of the delegate selection period showed Campbell as the preferred successor to Mulroney with 35 per cent to Charest's 31 per cent. The "don't know/refused" were at 24 per cent. See ["Campbell remains in the lead; Charest moves closer," *The Gallup Report*, 14 May 1993, +/- 3.1% margin of error.]

65 "Only Charest would lead Progressive Conservatives to Victory," ibid., 12 June 1993.

66 The 1993 Conservative post-convention survey (total N = 765). For the period ending with the conclusion of the delegate selection period the N = 512; for the second and final period the N = 253.

67 *Financial Post-Sun* poll of 2 June 1993, 10–11, conducted by COMPAS. At 454 respondents, this was one of the smallest polls of delegates in the 1993 campaign (margin of error, +/-4.7%).

68 Nelson Polsby and Aaron Wildavsky, *Presidential Elections: Strategies of American Electoral Politics*, 2nd ed. (New York: Charles Scribner's Sons, 1968), 77.

69 Perlin, *Party Democracy in Canada*, 311. Several of the issues addressed in this paragraph and the preceding one first appeared in *Party Democracy in Canada*. They summarize previous work by Fred Fletcher and George Perlin.

CHAPTER 6

1 For a biography of Ed Broadbent, see Judy Steed, *Ed Broadbent: The Pursuit of Power* (Markham: Penguin, 1988).

2 Gallup public opinion polls from December 1982 to September 1988. The question asked in the polls that is referred to is "Do you approve or disapprove of the way Ed Broadbent is handling his job as leader of the NDP?"

3 Stevie Cameron, "Race for the NDP leader's job is wide open," *Globe and Mail,* 28 March 1989, A5.

4 Keith Archer, "Leadership Selection in the New Democratic Party," in Herman Bakvis, ed., *Canadian Political Parties: Leaders, Candidates and Organization,* vol. 13 of the research studies for the Royal Commission on Electoral Reform and Party Financing (Toronto: Dundurn Press, 1991), 5.

5 Keith Archer and Alan Whitehorn, "Speculation over NDP leadership," *Financial Post,* 7 February 1989, 12.

6 Ross Howard, "Riis says NDP needs a woman as leader," *Globe and Mail,* 2 August 1989, A8.

7 Archer, "Leadership Selection in the New Democratic Party," 46.

8 R.K. Carty, *Canadian Political Parties in the Constituencies,* vol. 23 of the research studies for the Royal Commission on Electoral Reform and Party Financing (Toronto: Dundurn Press, 1991), 123.

9 The 1989 NDP convention survey, principal investigator: Keith Archer.

10 Defined as identified slate versus identified slate, the term was developed and first used by Ken Carty in his "Campaigning in the Trenches: The Transformation of Constituency Politics" in George Perlin, ed., *Party Democracy in Canada: The Politics of National Party Conventions* (Scarborough: Prentice-Hall Canada, 1988), 84–96.

11 I am grateful to Keith Archer for sharing with me several of these insights into NDP constituency organization.

12 *Constitution of the New Democratic Party,* as amended in 1987, Article 6, 3(2).

13 Carty, *Canadian Political Parties in the Constituencies,* 38.

14 Ibid., 240.

15 As quoted in Stevie Cameron, "Steelworkers refuse to endorse candidate for NDP leadership," *Globe and Mail,* 19 September 1989, A9.

16 Sixty-five per cent of the responding delegates said that before the balloting began they believed that McLaughlin would be the likely winner and an additional 11 per cent said that they believed that either McLaughlin or Barrett would be the likely winner. See 1989 NDP convention survey.

17 Only minutes before moving to support McLaughlin, de Jong had met with Barrett and the two seemed to reach a verbal agreement that de Jong would throw his support behind Barrett after the second ballot in exchange for an appointment to the position of caucus whip. Their fifty-seven-second conversation in which the deal was struck was captured on tape by a CBC-TV microphone that de Jong had agreed to wear on his tie. Back on the convention floor and after conversing with his mother, de Jong chose between his "heart and head" and went to McLaughlin. For a transcript of the de Jong-Barrett conversation and a comment on the ensuing

controversy, see Mark Starowicz, "Journal producer defends NDP convention exposé: 'The full, raw, unedited tape,'" *Globe and Mail*, 15 December 1989, A7.

18 Quotes are taken from the documentary on the 1989 convention by CBC-TV entitled "Hearts and Heads: Inside the NDP Convention," *The Journal*, 4 December 1989.

19 The fourth and final ballot distribution of votes by province was as follows (%):

	BC	AB	SK	MN	ON	PQ	NB	NS	PEI	NF	NWT	YK
McLaughlin	50	69	59	57	64	75	80	64	75	90	100	100
Barrett	50	31	41	43	36	25	20	36	25	10	0	0
N=	197	105	170	103	346	20	15	33	4	10	10	9

SOURCE: 1989 NDP convention survey.

20 Data taken from the 1989 NDP convention survey. Note that Archer's survey overestimates McLaughlin's support and underestimates Barrett's support by six percentage points. The survey had a relatively low response rate from union delegates, who were disproportionately supportive of Barrett. This may have affected some of the other variables. For example, the underrepresentation of trade unionists, the vast majority of whom would have been men, may account for McLaughlin's seemingly high level of support among male delegates. See Archer, "Leadership Selection in the New Democratic Party," 52, n8.

21 For a more extensive examination of the voting behaviour of the NDP delegates in 1989 see ibid., 30–9. See also Alan Whitehorn and Keith Archer, "Party Activists and Political Leadership: A Case Study of the NDP," in Maureen Mancuso, Richard G. Price, and Ronald Wagenberg, eds., *Leaders and Leadership in Canada* (Toronto: Oxford University Press, 1994), esp. 44–8.

22 Turner's one-sentence, hand-written note of resignation to the president of the Liberal party stated: "It is my intention to resign as Leader of the Liberal Party of Canada at an appropriate time, after the national executive has chosen a date for a leadership convention." See Susan Delacourt, "Race is on as Turner bows out," *Globe and Mail*, 4 May 1989, A1.

23 Jeffrey Simpson, "Jean Chrétien's comfort zone," ibid., 24 January 1990, A6.

24 This was graphically illustrated in British Columbia. In mid-January Martin supporters placed advertisements in Vancouver's two daily newspapers for recruits willing to join the Liberal party and to vote for pro-Martin delegate slates. By that time, however, Chrétien's supporters had already conducted polls, contacted most Liberal party members in the province at least once, and attracted the support of over two-thirds of the province's riding associ-

ation presidents. See Robert Matas, "Ads seek backers for Martin in B.C.; Chrétien support already organized," ibid., 23 January 1990, A1 and A2.

25 See "Chrétien clear public favorite for Liberal leadership," *The Gallup Report*, 1 June 1990.

26 Perlin, "Attitudes of Liberal Convention Delegates Toward Proposals for Reform of the Process of Leadership Selection," in Bakvis, ed., *Canadian Political Parties*, 59.

27 The 1989 NDP convention survey; 1990 Liberal and 1993 Conservative post-convention surveys, principal investigator: George Perlin.

28 *National Procedures for Election of Delegates and Alternates to Convention: 1990 National Liberal Leadership Convention, Calgary, June 20–23, 1990*, 17 January 1990, section 6.0. The fourteen-day rule was a minimum applied to all Liberal riding associations except those in Newfoundland, where recruits could join the party any time up to the start of the delegate selection meetings. The Ontario wing of the federal Liberal party opted to advance the cut-off dates for new members to twenty-eight days before delegate selection meetings.

29 Carty, *Canadian Political Parties in the Constituencies*, 123–4.

30 Hugh Winsor, "Third Force challenging Liberal elite," *Globe and Mail*, 16 April 1990, A1 and A2.

31 Lawrence Hanson, "Contesting the Leadership at the Grassroots: the Liberals in 1990," in R.K. Carty, ed., *Canadian Political Party Systems: A Reader.* (Toronto: Broadview Press, 1992), 429.

32 The 1990 Liberal convention survey.

33 These data are examined more fully in Hanson, "Contesting the Leadership at the Grassroots," 426–30.

34 As quoted in Rosemary Speirs, "Chrétien camp playing it safe with leadership bid in the bag," *Toronto Star*, 1 April 1990, A1, A2, A12.

35 "2,415 delegates said backing Chrétien," *StarPhoenix*, 30 May 1990, B8.

36 The first and final ballot distribution of votes by province was as follows (%):

	BC	AB	SK	MN	ON	PQ	NB	NS	PEI	NF	NWT	YK
Chrétien	64	76	38	63	44	57	56	68	52	89	30	36
Martin	26	19	26	21	30	28	30	24	24	3	60	45
Copps	10	4	3	12	14	14	13	7	21	8	10	18
Wappel	0	1	34	4	9	0	0	0	0	0	0	0
Nunziata	0	1	0	0	3	0	2	0	3	0	0	0
N=	165	137	80	76	518	257	54	82	29	37	10	11

SOURCE: The 1990 Liberal convention survey

37 The 1990 Liberal convention survey

38 See Hanson, "Contesting the Leadership at the Grassroots," 431–5.

39 Ross Howard, "Lagging Martin switches tactics, plans to woo Chrétien supporters," *Globe and Mail*, 30 April 1990, A10.

40 George Perlin, *The Tory Syndrome: Leadership Politics in the Progressive Conservative Party* (Montreal: McGill-Queen's University Press, 1980).

41 Brian Mulroney, as quoted in Ross Howard, "Mulroney predicts Tory dynasty," *Globe and Mail*, 4 March 1993, A4.

42 Jeffrey Simpson, "By any measure, the Kim Campbell bandwagon is a political phenomenon," *Globe and Mail*, 10 March 1993, A18. For a biography of Kim Campbell, see Robert Fife, *Kim Campbell: The Making of a Politician* (Toronto: HarperCollins Publishers Ltd., 1993); for an insider's account of the 1993 Tory leadership race, see David McLaughlin, *Poisoned Chalice: The Last Campaign of the Progressive Consevative Party?* (Toronto: Dundurn Press, 1994), chap. 4.

43 Campbell was endorsed by eighty-nine of the 211 caucus members and by eighteen of the thirty-five Tory cabinet ministers. For his part, Campbell's principal opponent, Jean Charest, also received plenty of support from his parliamentary colleagues. He was endorsed by sixty-seven caucus members and by twelve cabinet ministers, but his support was disproportionately drawn from retiring MPs and ministers. See "Caucus support rises for Charest, but Campbell holds lead," *The Hill Times* (Ottawa), 13 June 1993, 1; and "Tories take sides," *Toronto Star*, 10 June 1993, A1.

44 As quoted in Ross Howard, "The Turtle picks up momentum," *Globe and Mail*, 10 May 1993, A5.

45 Campbell reportedly spent $3 million whereas Charest reportedly spent $2.3 million. See Ross Howard, "Tory leadership contest cost more than $6-million," ibid., 2 March 1994, A1, A4. Bernard Valcourt was one potential candidate who cited financial difficulties as a reason for not entering the race. See Geoffrey York, "Valcourt lacks money to run," ibid., 16 March 1993, A2.

46 John Tory on "Media," CBC-TV Newsworld, 20 June 1993.

47 Anthony Wilson-Smith, Glen Allen, and Luke Fisher, "Closing the gap," *Maclean's*, 7 June 1993, 18.

48 As quoted in Ross Howard, "PC donor plan just diversion, critics charge," *Globe and Mail*, 29 March 1993, A3.

49 This discipline, however, did not preclude the odd escapade by some of the more creative organizers. Robert Fife relates a story that at one Montreal meeting "a group of Haitian immigrants turned up to vote for a Charest slate because they thought he hailed from Haiti. 'I believe that because [Charest] is a Haitian like us, he'll be better able to help us out in our crisis,'" said one of the clearly and, with little doubt, deliberately misled Haitian recruits. See Fife, *Kim Campbell*, 192.

50 The day after the first debate on 15 April, Hugh Winsor wrote that "Ms. Campbell didn't appear to live up to the public enthusiasm for her campaign." ("Candidates not ready for prime time," *Globe and Mail*, 16 April 1993, A3.) Three days later Ross Howard wrote that Campbell "was judged to have lost lustre for her unspectacular performance." ("Wooing delegates and the public too," ibid., 19 April 1993, A1.) By early May Howard downgraded Campbell's performance in the same debates to "dismal." ("Image-maker drafted to work on Campbell," ibid., 8 May 1993, A6.)

51 The article based on the interview by Peter C. Newman is "Citizen Kim," *Vancouver*, May 1993, 28–38, 51–2. For an examination of how Campbell's remarks were misinterpreted see "Just what was (and wasn't) said," *Globe and Mail*, 19 May 1993, A9.

52 Twenty-three per cent of the delegates reported gaining a higher opinion of Campbell and 41 per cent reported that their opinions of her had worsened during the campaign. For Charest, the comparable figures are 66 per cent and 8 per cent respectively. See 1993 Conservative pre-convention survey, principal investigator: George Perlin.

53 Jeffrey Simpson, "The Campbell image glows but the performances need polishing," *Globe and Mail*, 9 June 1993, A20. According to Robert Fife, Campbell's "organization was top-heavy and slow-moving with nearly 50 directors and countless backroom tacticians who all wanted to exercise their influence" (*Kim Campbell*, 184–5).

54 Ross Howard, "Campbell team shuffles management," *Globe and Mail*, 23 April 1993, A1, A4.

55 The second and final ballot distribution of votes by province was as follows (%):

	BC	AB	SK	MN	ON	PQ	NB	NS	PEI	NF	NWT	YK
Campbell	93	48	57	59	54	42	57	50	20	63	29	25
Charest	7	52	43	41	46	58	43	50	80	37	71	75
N=	81	79	42	46	265	143	30	28	10	24	7	4

SOURCE: 1993 Conservative convention survey.

56 Royal Commission on Electoral Reform and Party Financing *Reforming Electoral Democracy*, 4 vols. (Ottawa, 1991) 1:279.

57 Rosemary Speirs, "Chrétien camp playing it safe with leadership bid in the bag," *Toronto Star*, 1 April 1990, A1, A2, A12.

58 *Reforming Electoral Democracy*, 1:284–5.

CHAPTER 7

1 The Liberals have since reconsidered some of the representational moves taken in the 1980s. In 1992 they amended their constitution to grant the

chair and members of the party's revenue committee and the leaders of all provincial and territorial Liberal parties automatic delegate status. See Liberal Party of Canada, *Constitution*, as amended in 1992, articles 16 (13)(j) and 16(13)(l).

2 The numbers were 54 (1948); 87 (1958); 128 (1968); 201 (1984); and 488 (1990): *Report of the Proceedings of the National Liberal Convention, 1948* (Ottawa: National Liberal Federation, 1948), 25; *Report of the Proceedings of the National Liberal Convention, 1958* (Ottawa: National Liberal Federation, 1958), 16; and lists of potential delegate registration provided by the Liberal party for the 1968, 1984, and 1990 conventions.

3 There were representatives of university clubs at the Conservative party's 1927 convention but no details as to their numbers are available. The numbers for the other years were 16 (1948); 63 (1956); 116 (1967); 198 (1976); 408 (1983); and 115 (1993). In 1938 and 1942 the Conservative party had no campus club delegates. See R.M. Bell, "Conservative Party National Conventions 1927–1956" (MA thesis, Department of Political Science, Carleton University, 1965), table V and 102–3; and lists of potential delegate registration provided by the Progressive Conservative party for the 1967, 1976, 1983, and 1993 conventions.

4 The only restrictions were that the club had to have twenty-five members and to have been recognized by the provincial or territorial women's association one year before the call for the convention was issued. See Ray Guay, "Liberals fail to exploit loophole," *StarPhoenix*, 19 April 1984, B10; and Patrick Martin, "Women will make N.B. delegation fifth largest at Liberal convention," *Globe and Mail*, 7 May 1984, 5.

5 NA, Conservative Papers, MG 28 IV 2, vol. 527, "Memoranda, general 1976" file, press release, 26 January 1976.

6 Among the many studies of the post-1968 representational reforms introduced by American parties, two deal at some length with the nature and impact of the changes: Jeane Kirkpatrick, *The New Presidential Elite: Men and Women in National Politics* (New York: Russell Sage Foundation and The Twentieth Century Fund, 1976); and Byron E. Shafer, *Bifurcated Politics: Evolution and Reform in the National Party Convention* (Cambridge, Mass.: Harvard University Press, 1988). See also Austin Ranney, "Changing the Rules of the Nominating Game," in James David Barber, ed., *Choosing the President* (Englewood Cliffs: Prentice-Hall, 1974), 71–93; and Nelson W. Polsby and Aaron Wildavsky, *Presidential Elections: Contemporary Strategies of American Electoral Politics*, 8th ed. (New York: Free Press, 1991), 140–4.

7 "Discussion Paper on Reform of the Liberal Party of Canada," published by the Liberal Party of Canada (January 1984), Appendix A.

8 Ibid., 9.

9 Campagnolo interview, Halifax, 10 November 1985. In support of their campaign for equal gender representation and a cap on the ex officio dele-

gation, Liberal women at the party's 1985 Halifax meeting circulated a document entitled "Making Gender Equity Work" which claimed that at the 1984 leadership convention the male/female ratio among ex officio delegates was 84/16 per cent.

10 All figures computed from potential delegates lists provided by the parties.

11 Saskatoon-East Liberal Association. Theoretically all Liberal constituency delegates up to the 1986 constitutional amendments could have been women twenty-five years of age or less.

12 William Cavala, "Changing the Rules Changes the Game: Party Reform and the 1972 California Delegation to the Democratic National Convention," *American Political Science Review,* 68 (March 1974), 38–9.

13 Figures compiled from *The National Liberal Convention, Ottawa, August 5, 6, 7, 1919: The Story of the Convention and the Report of its Proceedings* (Ottawa, n.d., n.p.).

14 The sources are the 1968 delegate lists provided the author by the Liberal party; the 1984 figure is from Janine Brodie, "The Gender Factor and National Leadership Conventions in Canada," in George Perlin, ed., *Party Democracy in Canada: The Politics of National Party Conventions* (Scarborough: Prentice-Hall Canada, 1988), 176; and the 1990 figure is from Royal Commission on Electoral Reform and Party Financing *Reforming Electoral Democracy,* 4 vols. (Ottawa, 1991), 1:276. Sylvia Bashevkin gives 47 per cent as the women's share of delegates in 1990 in her "Women's Participation in Political Parties," in Kathy Megyery, ed., *Women in Canadian Politics: Toward Equity in Representation,* vol. 6 of the research studies for the Royal Commission on Electoral Reform and Party Financing (Toronto: Dundurn Press, 1991), table 2.3, 66.

15 Figures for 1927 computed from John R. MacNicol, *The National Liberal-Conservative Convention Held at Winnipeg, Manitoba, October 10 to 12, 1927* (Toronto: Southam Press, 1930) and for 1967 and 1976 from delegate lists provided by the Conservative party. The 1983 figure has been computed from Brodie, "The Gender Factor," and is based on the Perlin survey of delegates. Of the 812 respondents, 193 were female. The party reportedly claimed that 37 per cent of the 1983 delegates were women (176–8).

16 Don Oliver, as quoted in Edison Stewart, "Tories may end quota for women delegates," *Globe and Mail,* 3 December 1985, A8; and PC Party, *Building for the Future: Preliminary Report of the Constitution Review Committee* (November 1985), 4–5.

17 Brodie, "The Gender Factor," 177 and n1, 187.

18 Jeff Sallot and Graham Fraser, " 'Instant' and 'tiny' Tories outlawed as PCs adopt reforms," *Globe and Mail,* 17 March 1986, A4.

19 Kay Stanley, as quoted in Stewart, "Tories may end quota for women delegates."

20 Shafer, *Bifurcated Politics,* 169.

21 NA, Liberal Papers, MG 28 IV 3, vol. 1826, "Leadership Liaising Committee" file, "Backgrounder" attached to memorandum to Executive Board – LPCO enclosing a press release from David C. Nahwegahbow, co-chairman, Standing Committee on Native and Original Peoples' Affairs, 21 September 1989.

22 Interview with Marilyn Buffalo, national director, Aboriginal People's Commission, Liberal Party of Canada, Ottawa, 6 May 1994. In addition to the aboriginals chosen from the clubs or the commissions were those who became delegates either by way of their ex officio status (there were, for example, five aboriginals in the 1990 Liberal caucus) or their success at gaining election at the constituency or youth or women's club level. The party kept no record of the number of aboriginals who gained delegate status in the normal way.

23 Polsby and Wildavsky, *Presidential Elections*, 141.

24 NA, Liberal Papers, MG 28 IV 3, vol. 1826, "Leadership Liaising Committee" file, memorandum to Executive Board – LPCO enclosing a press release from David C. Nahwegahbow, 21 September 1989.

25 J.R. Mallory, *The Structure of Canadian Government* (Toronto: Macmillan of Canada, 1971), 205.

26 Brodie, "The Gender Factor," 174–5.

27 Ibid., 175.

28 George Perlin, Allen Sutherland, Marc Desjardins, "The Impact of Age Cleavage on Convention Politics" in Perlin, ed., *Party Democracy in Canada*, 191.

29 Perlin, Sutherland, and Desjardins note that "careerism" is a strong motive in the voting behaviour of youth delegates and that "loyalites formed in personal networks within the youth wings of the parties and the hope of youth wing members to find roles within their parties appear to be the two most important factors accounting for youth delegate voting preferences" (ibid., 198).

30 Brodie, "The Gender Factor," 186.

31 Perlin, Sutherland and Desjardins, "The Impact of Age Cleavage," 198.

32 Data on youth and women are from the 1983 and 1993 Progressive Conservative, 1984 and 1990 Liberal, and 1989 NDP convention surveys. The surveys overrepresented final support for Mulroney by 2 per cent, Turner by 4 per cent, McLaughlin by 6 per cent, Copps by 1 per cent and Campbell by 2 per cent. The figures given in the text must be considered with these facts in mind.

33 Kirkpatrick, *The New Presidential Elite*, 328.

34 Ibid., 328, 330–1 (emphasis in original).

35 Brodie, "The Gender Factor," 177.

36 Perlin, Sutherland, and Desjardins, "The Impact of Age Cleavage," 192.

37 There were statistically significant gender differences in each party on each of these issues except in one case: Tory women "were slightly, but not signif-

icantly, more likely to advocate increased government funding for day-care." See Brodie, "The Gender Factor," 183.

38 For example, in each party women were more likely to be in favour of increased government spending on job creation than men (56 to 45 per cent in the Conservative party and 58 to 52 per cent in the Liberal party), but they were less likely to favour increased government spending on manpower training (60 to 66 per cent in the Conservative party and 71 to 75 per cent in the Liberal party). Men and women in each party were far less likely to support either of these propositions than the general public. Ibid., 180–1.

39 Ibid., 179 and 182.

40 Perlin, Sutherland, and Desjardins, "The Impact of Age Cleavge," 194; and Richard Johnston, "The Final Choice: Its Social, Organizational, and Ideological Bases," in Perlin, ed., *Party Democracy in Canada*, 212. Johnston performed a multivariate analysis measuring the effects of several factors (including age) on a number of sets of issues. Principal among the questions in which age was a statistically significant variable were post-materialism (including such issues as hawkishness, civil liberties, and moral conservatism), universal social programs, and bilingualism. Older delegates in both parties were more favourably disposed towards the first two of these issues and less favourably disposed towards the last than younger delegates. See Johnston, "The Final Choice," 211–12, 222.

41 Perlin, Sutherland, and Desjardins, "The Impact of Age Cleavage," 194.

42 Johnston, "The Final Choice," 212.

43 Ranney, "Changing the Rules," 78.

44 For more on the NDP delegate allotment system, see Keith Archer, "Leadership Selection in the New Democratic Party," in Herman Bakvis, ed., *Canadian Political Parties: Leaders, Candidates and Organization*, vol. 13 of the Research Studies for the Royal Commission on Electoral Reform and Party Financing, (Toronto: Dundurn Press, 1991), 4–13.

45 Interviews with delegates at NDP conventions in 1971, 1975, and 1989; interview with Clifford A. Scotton, federal secretary, New Democratic Party, Ottawa, 16 May 1969.

46 The higher trade union turnout in 1971 than in 1975 has been explained as a function of the perceived challenge to labour from the left-wing Waffle faction of the party in 1971, the high level of self-interest that was generated within the trade union movement, and the fact that front runner David Lewis was so popular with the union movement. See Archer, "Leadership Selection in the New Democratic Party," 51; Janine Brodie, "From Waffles to Grits: A Decade in the Life of the New Democratic Party," in Hugh G. Thorburn, ed., *Party Politics in Canada*, 5th ed. (Toronto: Prentice-Hall Canada, 1985); and Alan Whitehorn, *Canadian Socialism: Essays on the CCF-NDP* (Toronto: Oxford University Press, 1992), 140, n40. This expla-

nation can be called into question by the fact that in 1989 labour's interests were less threatened by any ideological faction within the party than in either 1971 or 1975, and that none of the candidates was perceived to be particularly pro-union; yet the share of trade union delegates in attendance that year was the highest of any of the three conventions.

47 Carty, *Canadian Political Parties in the Constituencies*, vol. 23 of the research studies for the Royal Commission on Electoral Reform and Party Financing (Toronto: Dundurn Press, 1991), 242. Carty concludes that 95 per cent of NDP constituency-level organization east of the Ottawa River "can best be classified as a paper structure," 243.

48 It has been common knowledge at NDP conventions that some in attendance who would otherwise have been named delegates but who had been unsuccessful because their home ridings had filled their allotments were nonetheless accredited by being named delegates from a constituency with little or no other representation at the convention. Most of the donor ridings were those in areas of the greatest party strength and the recipient ridings were those east of the Ontario border. One reliable estimate of the composition of the thirty-five-member "Quebec delegation" at the 1975 convention was that half of its members were from other provinces, principally Saskatchewan. In an interview with the author at the 1989 convention, one Yukon resident accounted for his presence on the Nova Scotia delegation by noting that the Yukon list was complete and that the McLaughlin organizers had an arrangement with the NDP provincial leader in Nova Scotia, herself a McLaughlin supporter, to add names from outside the province at the convention itself. At times the party has been quite open about this practice. At the 1989 convention the Alberta delegation, for one, openly posted its agenda for Friday, 1 December. The first item on the agenda after the call to order was "Extra Credential Disbursement." In the 1989 delegate survey, 3 per cent of the constituency delegates (approximately fifty delegates at the convention) reported that they had acquired voting status because there were extra credentials or vacancies in the quota of the riding. See 1989 NDP convention survey, principal investigator: Keith Archer. Brief passages of the following paragraphs have appeared in my article "Leadership Conventions and the Development of the National Political Community," in R. Kenneth Carty and W. Peter Ward, eds., *National Politics and Community in Canada* (Vancouver: University of British Columbia Press, 1986), 97–8. Reprinted by permission of the publisher.

49 Carty, *Canadian Political Parties*, 243.

50 Only 12 per cent were in favour of making the change and 8 per cent were undecided or did not answer. See 1989 NDP convention survey.

51 The Reform Party of Canada, *Constitution*, as amended in 1992, article 7(d)(i).

52 Since 1989 the NDP has adopted several constitutional guarantees of representation of women, men, aboriginals, and visible minorities on the party's federal council. Council members are automatically granted voting delegate status at party conventions. See *Constitution of the New Democratic Party*, as amended in 1991, article VIII.

53 Ibid., article VI (3)(2).

54 Carty, *Canadian Politial Parties*, 241.

55 Whitehorn, *Canadian Socialism*, 138.

56 In the Conservative papers on deposit with the National Archives of Canada there are twelve files containing dozens of appeals, objections, letters of protest, and the like submitted for rulings by the Progressive Conservative National Credentials Committee in the months leading up to the 1983 convention. The files contain, among other things, sworn affidavits and legal advice relating to packed and improper meetings and instant members in youth, campus, constituency, and women's clubs. By far the greatest part of the material comes from a relatively small number of clubs and associations, perhaps fifty in all. See NAC, Conservative Papers, MG 28 IV 2, vols. 530 and 531, "Credentials Committee – National President's Correspondence" and "Delegate Selection" files.

57 On 1990, for example, see Hugh Winsor, "Third Force challenging traditional Liberal elite," *Globe and Mail*, 16 April 1990, A1 and A2.

58 The story of a nine-year-old "card-carrying" Tory who had to leave a delegate selection meeting in 1983 before she could cast her vote because it was past her bedtime was good for more copy than a dozen unexceptional delegate selection meetings of the party rank and file. This episode is reported along with others in Jeff Sallot, "Tory brass moves to keep squabbling private," ibid., 31 March 1983, 11.

59 According to the president of the federal Progressive Conservative Youth Federation, at the time the increase reflected "the continuing and growing popularity of the Progressive Conservative Party among young Canadians." See NA, Conservative Papers, MG 28 IV 2, vol. 532, "Youth" file, news release of Randy Dawson, 29 March 1983.

60 The post-secondary institutions, according to Laschinger, were officially recognized with the "complicity of the Tory government of Newfoundland." The flying school was ruled unacceptable by the convention's credentials committee. Laschinger's amusing account of his part in this organizational *putsch* is given in John Laschinger and Geoffrey Stevens, *Leaders and Lesser Mortals: Backroom Politics in Canada* (Toronto: Key Porter Books, 1992), 34–5. It serves as a reminder of how easily political organizations can be cast and manipulated to one's advantage given the right skills and political bravado. Strong exception to the Crosbie organization's success in setting up clubs of dubious status came from St John's Tory MP, James McGrath, who protested, without success, to the party's national

president that creating instant clubs with instant party members and delegates was "unfair to the loyal men and women who worked for the party ... but who will not have an opportunity to be delegates to the leadership convention." See NA, Conservative Papers, MG 28 IV 2, vol. 531, "Credentials Committee – National President's Correspondence (1) and (2)," file, n.d., part of the PC Credentials Committee Committee ruling released on 19 April 1983.

61 Wilson letter of 30 March 1983 to PC national president, Peter Elzinga. See NA, Conservative Papers, MG 28 IV 2, vol. 530, "Correspondence with National President, 1983" file.

62 David Crombie letter of 2 April 1983 to Elzinga, ibid.

63 Ibid.

64 Elzinga letters to Crombie and Wilson of 13 April 1983, ibid.

65 Ibid. Mordecai Richler, covering the January 1983 Tory convention for CBC Radio had this to say about the Clark supporters from Quebec: "Arriving in Winnipeg late on Wednesday night [26 January 1983] I found the air terminal milling with Clark delegates from Quebec. One glance at them and I grasped that it would be difficult to pick up a pool game on the streets of St. Jerome or Chicoutimi this weekend." (CBC Radio "Sunday Morning," 30 January 1993).

66 *Constitution of the Progressive Conservative Association of Canada*, as amended March 15, 1986, Article 13, "Membership and Voting at National Meetings"; and *Constitution of the Liberal Party of Canada*, as amended in 1986, Article 2, "Membership."

67 Elzinga letter to Crombie of 13 April 1983.

68 All three surveys generated a lower response rate from Quebec delegates, although the magnitude of the discrepency in the NDP was much less than in the other two parties. In 1990 23 per cent of those eligible to attend the Liberal convention were from Quebec. The fact that the convention was in Calgary may have resulted in a lower turnout rate for Quebec delegates. No actual attendance figures were available from the Liberal party. See George Perlin, "Attitudes of Liberal Convention Delegates Toward Proposals for Reform of the Process of Leadership Selection" in Bakvis, ed., *Canadian Political Parties*, 67. According to figures released by the Conservative party, in 1993 11 per cent of the registered delegates were from British Columbia or the territories, 18 per cent from the Prairies, 34 per cent from Ontario, 24 per cent from Quebec, and 13 per cent from the Atlantic provinces.

69 In 1990 the largest single one-year age group of survey respondents was twenty-one years (N=70) followed by twenty years (N=56).

70 Although women made up 40 per cent of the non-union delegates in 1989, they comprised only 14 per cent of the union delegation. Given that the 1989 survey met with a relatively low response rate from union delegates it likely overrepresents the proportion of delegates attending the convention

who were women. See Archer, "Leadership Selection in the New Democratic Party," table 1.3, 9 and 52n.8.

71 See my *The Selection of National Party Leaders in Canada*, table 5–1, 106.

72 In the 1990 and 1993 surveys all politicians were classified in the white-collar category.

73 Lawrence Hanson has noted that 16 per cent of the Liberal constituency delegates in 1990 became members of the party during the leadership campaign which officially began in September 1989. See Hanson, "Contesting the Leadership at the Grassroots: the Liberals in 1990," in R.K. Carty, ed., *Canadian Political Party Systems: A Reader* (Toronto: Broadview Press, 1992), 431.

74 See my *The Selection of National Party Leaders*, table 5–10, 124.

75 Note that the 1990 Liberal convention was held nineteen months after the previous election in 1988 but that the 1993 Tory convention was held approximately four and half years after the same election.

76 At the 1989 NDP convention this was true in the literal, as well as the figurative, sense as fully one-quarter of the delegates indicated that they had relatives attending the convention as delegates. See 1989 NDP convention survey.

CHAPTER 8

1 Nick Martin, "Ethnic diversity in race lauded," *Winnipeg Free Press*, 12 December 1989, 35. Forgetting about Ian Waddell's profession, former NDP national secretary Robin Sears quipped, "Thank God, we're free of lawyers" in the 1989 leadership race (ibid.). The likelihood of a lawyer-free leadership convention is very slim given the propensity for political elites to be drawn overwhelmingly from the legal profession. In 1975 the NDP became for the second time (the first being in 1961) the only one of the three older parties to have had no lawyers in its leadership race. That may have been more than compensated for in 1975, however, by the fact that two of the four candidates, including the winner, were political scientists.

2 Ironically, a series of Gallup polls indicated that a woman leader would actually improve the prospects of a national party. The most recent poll in the series (January 1993) found that although for 77 per cent of those surveyed the gender of the leader would make no difference, 17 per cent would be more inclined to support a woman-led party, and only 4 per cent would be less inclined. Since 1975 the proportion of those who would be less inclined to support a party led by a woman has declined. In that year, 73 per cent said the leader's gender would make no difference, 13 per cent would be more inclined to support a woman-led party, and 11 per cent would be less inclined. See "Effects of a woman party leader on electorate remain stable," *The Gallup Report*, released on 14 January 1993. The litera-

ture on the representation of women has grown markedly in the past decade. The research has indicated, among other things, that although the role of women in Canadian politics has increased, there are still a number of barriers to the equitable participation of women. See Janine Brodie with the assistance of Celia Chandler, "Women and the Electoral Process in Canada," and Lisa Young, "Legislative Turnover and the Election of Women to the Canadian House of Commons," in Kathy Megyery, ed., *Women in Canadian Politics: Toward Equity in Representation,* vol. 6 of the research studies for the Royal Commission on Electoral Reform and Party Financing (Toronto: Dundurn Press, 1991).

3 Other socio-demographic variables, such as individual and family income, parents' occupation, rural, small-town or urban background, and ethnic ancestry on both sides of the family have not been included. Reliable and documented evidence could not always be obtained for all candidates. Sources for leaders' and candidates' ages, religions, and occupations include the *Canadian Parliamentary Guide,* Chief Electoral Officer reports, and various newspaper accounts of the conventions and candidates.

4 All demographic tables and analysis in this chapter exclude the following minor candidates seeking their party's leadership: Conservatives Mary Walker-Sawka and John MacLean (1967), Richard Quittenton (1976), and Neil Fraser (1983); Liberals Lloyd Henderson (1958 and 1968); and New Democrat Douglas Campbell (1975). Among them they received a total of twenty-nine first ballot votes, an average of 4.1 per candidate.

5 Those who have stood at two different national conventions were Conservatives' Manion (1927 and 1938), MacPherson (1938 and 1942), Fulton (1956 and 1967), Clark (1976 and 1983), and Mulroney (1976 and 1983); Liberals' Martin (1958 and 1968), Turner (1968 and 1984), and Chrétien (1984 and 1990); and NDPers' Broadbent (1971 and 1975) and Harney (1971 and 1975). Hellyer also ran in two national conventions, but for different parties (Liberal 1968 and Conservative 1976). Fleming sought the Tory leadership at three conventions (1948, 1956, and 1967) and Diefenbaker holds the record at four attempts (1942, 1948, 1956, and 1967). A number of candidates have also sought the leadership of a provincial party. These include Conservatives Bracken, Diefenbaker, Drew, Fulton, Stanfield, Roblin, Hamilton, Wagner, Crosbie, and Campbell; Liberals Fielding, Gardiner, MacGuigan, and Copps; and New Democrats Douglas and Barrett.

6 For an analysis of David Lewis's early career, see Walter D. Young, *The Anatomy of a Party: The National CCF, 1932–61* (Toronto: University of Toronto Press, 1969), 163–7. See also Lewis' autobiography, *The Good Fight: Political Memoirs 1909–1958* (Toronto: Macmillan of Canada, 1981); and Alan Whitehorn, *Canadian Socialism: Essays on the CCF-NDP* (Toronto: Oxford University Press, 1992), 151–76.

7 For more on this onetime common practice see John English, "The 'French Lieutenant' in Ottawa," in R. Kenneth Carty and W. Peter Ward, eds., *National Politics and Community in Canada* (Vancouver: University of British Columbia Press, 1986), 184–200. In the early stages of the 1993 Tory leadership campaign there were widely circulated rumours, which were never taken seriously in the press, of an attempt to draft the finance minister, Don Mazankowski, and the health minister, Benoit Bouchard, to somehow run as a "team" for their party's leadership. See "French not required for PM's job, says Mulroney," *StarPhoenix*, 12 March 1993, B6.

8 To Graham Fraser, 1976 was critical for the Tories: "Since 1976, fluency in French has become one of the dividing points separating serious leadership candidates from those finishing farther down the list. In 1976, Joe Clark used his hard-won ability in French to pull ahead of other candidates, and faced Quebecker Claude Wagner on the last ballot." See "Tory candidates well prepared for French debate," *Globe and Mail*, 21 April 1993, A4.

9 Ibid.

10 As quoted in Graham Fraser, "Question of Quebec has NDP eyeing Rae," ibid., 2 October 1989, A8. See also Patrick Martin, Allan Gregg, and George Perlin, *Contenders: The Tory Quest for Power* (Scarborough: Prentice-Hall Canada, 1983), 121.

11 Fraser, "Question of Quebec has NDP eyeing Rae."

12 I am grateful to Keith Archer of the University of Calgary for his views on bilingualism and the 1989 NDP convention.

13 It might be argued that John Turner was a British Columbian and was therefore an exception to this rule. That is a doubtful proposition. Mackenzie King was never considered to be from Saskatchewan even though he held a federal seat in that province for twenty years. Brian Mulroney was not considered to be a Nova Scotian because he attended university there and was first elected to Parliament from that province. Turner, admittedly more problematic to place in terms of home province, nonetheless has had closer ties with Ontario than any other province. He was born in Britain, spent some of his pre-school years in British Columbia, received his primary education in Ottawa, his university education at UBC, Oxford, and the Sorbonne before moving to Montreal. First elected to Parliament from a Montreal seat in 1962, and re-elected there in 1963 and 1965, he moved from Quebec in the election following Trudeau's selection (an astute move given the alternation tradition) and ran successfully in an Ottawa seat in 1968, 1972, and 1974. Following his resignation from the Trudeau cabinet in 1975 and Parliament in 1976 he joined a Toronto law firm and established residency in that city. During the 1984 leadership campaign he declared he would seek a seat in British Columbia, which he did and from which he was elected in 1984 and 1988. Why had he done this? Almost certainly it was a move calculated to mute criticisms of his being a Bay Street

lawyer with big business connections and to establish bona fide claims to being "of the West" to try to make an electoral breakthrough in that region for the Liberal party. Would he have moved to Vancouver had he lost the Liberal leadership race in 1984? It is highly doubtful. Even winning as he did in 1984, Turner only "moved" to Vancouver in the most nominal fashion. After stepping down as Liberal leader in 1990 (though he stayed on in Parliament for a Vancouver seat until the 1993 election) he re-established residency in Toronto where he once again entered a law firm.

14 Turner, a Roman Catholic, is the exception sandwiched, as it were, between two other Roman Catholics. Perhaps with the reduced salience of religion, such placements are now a thing of the past.

15 On the 1887 change in leaders see Margaret A. Banks, "The Change in Liberal Party Leadership, 1887," *Canadian Historical Review* 38 (June 1957), 109–28; O.D. Skelton, *Life and Letters of Sir Wilfrid Laurier,* 2 vols. (Toronto: Oxford University Press, 1921), 1:341; and Sir John Willison, *Sir Wilfrid Laurier and the Liberal Party: A Political History,* 2 vols. (Toronto: George N. Morang and Company, 1903), 1:34.

16 The French Canadian who might have succeeded Macdonald could not. It had been recognized for some time before Macdonald's death in 1891 that his faithful Quebec colleague, Sir Hector Langevin, would succeed him. An arrangement to that effect, which had been agreed upon some years earlier, had to be abandoned because of scandal charges launched just prior to Macdonald's death against Langevin's department, Public Works. The subsequent inquiry damaged the department's reputation to such an extent that Langevin, although acquitted of personal wrongdoing, resigned from cabinet, his political career ended.

17 W.T.R. Preston, *My Generation of Politics and Politicians* (Toronto: Rose Publishing, 1927), 382.

18 "The Liberal Leadership," *The Round Table* 9 (June 1919), 593–4.

19 Lester B. Pearson, *Mike: The Memoirs of the Rt. Hon. Lester B. Pearson,* 3 vols. (Toronto: University of Toronto Press, 1975), 3:27.

20 For Pearson's views on the need to have a French-speaking candidate do well in the race to succeed him in 1968, see ibid, 3:325–6. Pearson's first choice appears to have been Jean Marchand, but he was convinced by Marchand and others that Trudeau would "make a good leader." Accordingly, Pearson indicated to Trudeau that he was "well-disposed toward him" and that his selection as leader would meet with his "wholehearted approval" (326).

21 Peter Stursberg, *Lester Pearson and the Dream of Unity* (Toronto: Doubleday Canada, 1978), 46 and 47.

22 Paul Martin, *A Very Public Life,* 2 vols. (Ottawa: Deneau, 1983), 2:4 and 310.

23 For Martin's views on the alternating tradition as it played out during his career, see ibid., 2:4–6, 137, 265, 310–17, 487, 612–13, and 617.

24 Jean Chrétien, *Straight from the Heart*, rev. ed. (Toronto: Key Porter Books, 1994), 194. The tradition apparently was a powerful force in leading several of Chrétien's parliamentary colleagues in 1979 to indicate leadership preferences that took him by surprise: "Though a surprising number of English-speaking colleagues said to me, 'Oh, no one gives a damn about that,' an equally surprising number of my French-speaking colleagues did give a damn. They saw the tradition as a positive custom and they were reluctant to break it: one break now could open the way to a series of anglophone leaders later on" (194).

25 Ibid., 198.

26 "If alternation is everything, then I don't belong here as prime minister," Chrétien quoted Trudeau as informing the Liberal caucus (Ibid., 199).

27 "Liberal Leadership Race," in R.B. Byers, ed., *Canadian Annual Review of Politics and Public Affairs 1984* (Toronto: University of Toronto Press, 1987), 15.

28 Ibid., 11.

29 The percentages varied among the parties, with the NDP having the lowest share of lawyers in its caucus and the Liberals the highest: NDP, six of thirty-three (14 per cent); PC, thirty-two of 169 (19 per cent); and Liberal, twenty-two of eighty-two (27 per cent).

30 The post-1988 election NDP caucus contained thirteen educators and six lawyers. Lawyers outnumbered educators in the Conservative caucus by thirty-two to twenty-six, and in the Liberal caucus by twenty-two to seventeen. The leaders of each of the recently successful NDP provincial parties (Bob Rae, Roy Romanow, and Michael Harcourt) were all lawyers. Otherwise the occupational patterns of these provincial parties were similar to those in the federal party as each of the three caucuses contained approximately twice as many educators as lawyers.

31 For more on religion as a variable in voting behaviour, see John Meisel, "Religious Affiliation and Electoral Behaviour: A Case Study," in my *Voting in Canada* (Scarborough: Prentice-Hall Canada, 1967), 144–61; Meisel, *Cleavages, Parties and Values in Canada* (London: Sage Publications, 1974); Harold Clarke, Jane Jenson, Lawrence LeDuc, and Jon H. Pammett, *Political Choice in Canada* (Toronto: McGraw-Hill Ryerson, 1979), 94, 100–3 and 372–3; and Richard Johnston, André Blais, Henry E. Brady, and Jean Crête, *Letting the People Decide: Dynamics of a Canadian Election* (Montreal and Kingston: McGill-Queen's University Press, 1992), 85–6 and 91.

32 Lovell C. Clark, "Macdonald's Conservative Successors, 1891–1896," in John S, Moir, ed., *Character and Circumstance: Essays in Honour of Donald Grant Creighton* (Toronto: Macmillan of Canada, 1970), 62. See also J. Castell Hopkins, *Life and Work of the Rt. Hon. Sir John Thompson* (Toronto: United Publishing Houses, 1895) 190; Steven Muller, "The Canadian Prime Ministers, 1867–1948: An Essay on Democratic Leadership" (Ph.D.

dissertation, Department of Political Science, Cornell University, 1958), 256–7; and P.B. Waite, *The Man from Halifax: Sir John Thompson* (Toronto: University of Toronto Press, 1985).

33 Clark, "Macdonald's Conservative Successors," 146 (emphasis in original). "Pervert" was the expression current at the time to refer to a Roman Catholic convert.

34 No reliable sources could be found for the religions of 1983 Conservative candidates David Crombie and Peter Pocklington and of 1984 Liberal candidate John Roberts. Note also that 1967 Conservative candidate Michael Starr was Ukrainian Orthodox. All four of these candidates have been excluded from the above analysis.

35 The 42 per cent figure is for responding 1989 NDP delegates and includes five responses: agnostic, atheist, non-practising/no formal religion, secular humanist, and none/not applicable. The 8 per cent figure is for responding 1990 Liberal delegates and includes three responses: agnostic, atheist, and none. The data available from the 1993 Conservative survey did not include those who indicated no religion. See 1983 Conservative, 1989 NDP, and 1990 Liberal post-convention surveys.

36 The details of the selections from 1867 to 1920 are given in my *The Selection of National Party Leaders in Canada*, chap. 3. Macdonald, of course, was not in Parliament at the time of his selection as no Parliament existed at the time. He had, at that point, years of legislative and ministerial experience. Tupper, who had had a long parliamentary and ministerial career at the time he was chosen leader in 1896, was not in Parliament when selected. Shortly after being named leader (but not prime minister – Bowell kept that position) he entered the Senate. Upon his subsequent appointment as prime minister some months later he resigned from the Senate to contest a parliamentary seat in the upcoming elections. As Parliament had been dissolved and the election called by the time he had become prime minister, and as his government was defeated at the election itself, Tupper held the distinction, until Turner in 1984, and Campbell in 1993, of being the only prime minister never to have met Parliament in that capacity.

37 Although listed in table 8–9, Meighen's 1941 selection is not included in table 8–12, as that table gives the averages for leaders chosen by party conventions only.

38 The phrase is borrowed from David J. Elkins and Richard Simeon, *Small Worlds: Provinces and Parties in Canadian Political Life* (Toronto: Methuen, 1980).

39 Donald Macdonald, who had resigned from the Trudeau cabinet in September 1977 and as an MP in February 1978, typified the "leader in waiting" in 1979. He had announced following Trudeau's subsequently aborted resignation from the leadership in 1979 that he would be a candi-

date in the upcoming convention. However, with the defeat of the Clark government in the Commons and the calling of the 1980 election Trudeau changed his mind and stayed on as Liberal leader. Macdonald then indicated he would not be a candidate in the 1980 election, just as he had not run in 1979 saying that to accept a "supporting role" such as he had left in 1977 would be a "backward step" in his career. See "Big Mac scorned second-fiddle role," *Toronto Star,* 20 December 1979, A6.

40 Chrétien, *Straight from the Heart,* 199.

41 King, who was first elected to Parliament in 1908, had been defeated in two subsequent attempts to return (1911 and 1917). Having spent much of the time between 1911 and 1919 out of the country working, in particular, on labour relations in the United States, King had been spared direct public involvement in many of the disputes that divided the Liberals during the First World War. Seen by many delegates in 1919 as young and untried, King was said to have turned "the tide to his favour" with a particularly strong and moving convention speech. For an account of King's ultimately successful moves to succeed Laurier, see my *The Selection of National Party Leaders in Canada,* 69–72 and 162–4.

42 Pearson, *Mike,* 3:327 [emphasis added]. For an account of Trudeau's meteoric rise to the Liberal leadership and the situational context within which it took place see my *The Selection of National Party Leaders in Canada,* 164–6. Charisma has a very special meaning which is often overlooked. In Robert Tucker's terms "charismatic leadership is specifically salvationist or messianic in nature." See "The Theory of Charismatic Leadership, *Daedalus* (Summer 1968), 743.

43 Transcript of press conference with Pierre E. Trudeau, National Press Building, Ottawa, 7 April 1968, 7 and 8.

44 Interestingly, these exceptions have occurred only after the proportion of female delegates began to approach the proportion of male delegates.

CHAPTER 9

1 This theory of personal networks is from Jeremy Boissevain, *Friends of Friends: Networks, Manipulators and Coalitions* (New York: St. Martin's Press, 1974), chap. 2. The principal Canadian contribution to the study of political networks is Vincent Lemieux. See his *Les Cheminements de l'influence: Systèmes, stratégies et structures du politique* (Québec: Les Presses de l'Université Laval, 1979) and *Systèmes Partisans et Partis politiques* (Montreal: Presses de l' Université du Québec, 1985). For a review of some of the developments in network models and theory, see Ronald S. Burt, "Models of Network Structure," *Annual Review of Sociology* 6 (1980), 79–141.

2 Christina McCall-Newman, *Grits: An Intimate Portrait of the Liberal Party* (Toronto: Macmillan, 1982), 248.

3 But not without persuasion in some cases. Keith Davey records that Graf-stein, "who had once been John Turner's most effective executive assistant," needed to be "pushed" into Turner's campaign organization by Davey himself. See Keith Davey, *The Rainmaker: A Passion for Politics* (Toronto: Stoddart, 1986), 324.

4 Accounts of Turner's informal contacts and networks in the lead-up to and during the 1984 leadership race are found in Ron Graham, *Promise and Illusion in Canadian Politics: One-Eyed Kings* (Toronto: Collins, 1986), section three, and Jack Cahill, *John Turner: The Long Run* (Toronto: McClelland and Stewart, 1984), esp. chap. 19.

5 Greg Weston, *Reign of Error: The Inside Story of John Turner's Troubled Leadership* (Toronto: McGraw-Hill Ryerson, 1988), 32.

6 John deB. Payne, in Cahill, *John Turner,* 210. According to Payne, "there really was no Club of 195 working in the background to make [Turner] Prime Minister. It might have been there once but now it was a myth. Before March 16, when [Turner] announced he would run, I asked John Swift to come up with the 195 names and he could produce only 23. Then, suddenly, after March 16 there were 695 club members and we didn't know what to do with them all." Doug Richardson, a former principal secretary of Turner's, confirmed Payne's opinion that the Club 195 was largely a creation of the media which "blew it out of proportion." Richardson interview, 6 October 1993; and Mary Trueman, "If there really is a 195 Club, will the members please stand up?," *Globe and Mail,* 13 December 1978, 9.

7 Cahill, *John Turner,* 210. Lee replaced the "politically astute" but inexperienced Heather Peterson, who had served briefly as Turner's first leadership campaign manager (211). In Davey's view, Lee had "come within an ace of making Hellyer prime minister." See Davey, *The Rainmaker,* 325.

8 Compared with the Tories, who had had two national leadership conventions and several major provincial ones over the previous decade, the Liberals had not held a national one since 1968 or a recent major provincial one, apart from Ontario's in 1982. Many of their senior organizers, such as Lee, were unfamiliar with the new, much more advanced convention organization techniques that Conservative organizers had used to great effect in 1976 and 1983. John Laschinger, whose convention organizational skills were legendary in the Conservative party, relates that Lee, while a pro, was nonetheless an "old timer" who was out of touch with modern political organization. Through an intermediary, Lee contacted Laschinger. They had a "three hour dinner together in Ottawa in the sort of restaurant where you'd take your mother on Mother's Day" to plan Turner's floor organization. According to Laschinger, it was non-existent at that time. Laschinger had previously contacted the equally renowned Tory organizer Norman Atkins, to see what he thought of Laschinger passing on organizational advice

to Lee. They agreed it made sense in the political context of the time, as both wanted Mulroney to face Turner, not Chrétien, in the next federal election. They reasoned that Laschinger's organizational experience could possibly help to ensure a Turner win in the Liberal leadership contest. Laschinger interview, 25 July 1994.

9 Cahill, *John Turner,* 211.

10 Forced to run against many in the Liberal establishment, Chrétien embarked on a personalized, populist campaign. It became his trademark style of campaigning ("the little guy from Shawinigan" as he liked to refer to himself) which endeared him to many Canadians and gave him "a surprising amount of strength across the country." See ibid., 71. Chrétien's account of his run for the leadership in 1984 is given in his autobiography, *Straight from the Heart,* rev. ed. (Toronto: Key Porter Books, 1994), chap. 9.

11 Susan Delacourt, "Chrétien is in the driver's seat, but it will not be smooth ride," *Globe and Mail,* 24 January 1990, A8.

12 Chrétien, *Straight from the Heart,* 227.

13 Keith Davey was one of many observers to have used that term to describe Turner's performances on his return to active politics. See *The Rainmaker,* 324.

14 Turner resigned as finance minister in September 1975 and as an MP in February 1976. In November 1975 Trudeau faced his first Liberal party convention since the 1974 election. He received 81 per cent of the leadership review vote, a record low for him. Cahill records that "Turner's resignation from the cabinet split the Liberal Party, creating one of its worst crises. Members were naturally shocked by the angry departure of the heir apparent and its political consequences." See *John Turner,* 182–3.

15 Davey, *The Rainmaker,* 324.

16 Paul Martin's supporters acknowledged at the outset of the 1989–90 campaign that "Chrétien's team ha[d] already had two practice runs – once in 1984 and once in the leadership review vote in 1986." See Susan Delacourt, "Two contenders differ on convention date," *Globe and Mail,* 4 May 1989, A4.

17 Donald E. Blake, R.K. Carty, and Lynda Erickson, "Coming and Going: Leadership Selection and Removal in Canada," in Alain G. Gagnon and A. Brian Tanguay, eds., *Canadian Parties in Transition,* 2nd ed. (Toronto: Nelson Canada, 1995), 231.

18 As a seventeen-year old university student at St Francis Xavier, Mulroney worked as a local volunteer on the provincial Stanfield campaign in 1956. He attended the Tory national convention in Ottawa that year as a campus delegate. He was elected Tory leader on campus the following year and executive vice-president of the Conservative Students' Federation three years later while attending law school at Laval University. See L. Ian MacDonald, *Mulroney; The Making of a Prime Minister* (Toronto: McClelland and Stewart,

1984), 42–3 and 60. Chrétien became president of the Liberal Club at La-val University while a student in the law school there. (*Straight from the Heart*, 12.) Turner recalled having no political leanings as a student at UBC. (Cahill, *John Turner*, 53).

19 John Gray, "'Power' magic word to Mulroney," *Globe and Mail*, 24 October 1983, 10. See also MacDonald, *Mulroney*, chap. 16, appropriately entitled "The Boys"; and Rae Murphy, Robert Chodos, and Nick Auf der Maur, *Brian Mulroney: The Boy from Baie Comeau* (Toronto: Lorimer, 1984), chap. 8.

20 Unsuccessfully, as it turned out, on both occasions. Meighen twice con-tested and lost the federal seat of St-Henri-Westmount in Quebec. Cogger and Bazin may have been friends with Mulroney since college days, but they also had roots of their own in the Tory party. Both were highly re-garded veterans of Tory politics in Quebec and had been part of the Robert Stanfield and Ontario Big Blue Machine networks by the time Mulroney contested the leadership in 1983.

21 An account of Mulroney and his network of close personal contacts in the months leading up to the Winnipeg convention of January 1983 is found in MacDonald, *Mulroney*, chap. 9.

22 Patrick Martin, Allan Gregg, and George Perlin, *Contenders: The Tory Quest for Power* (Scarborough: Prentice-Hall Canada, 1983), 74. It was equally true of Mulroney that he stroked other candidates, their networks and managers. According to Laschinger, "Mulroney did it beautifully" (Lasch-inger interview, 25 July 1994). For an example, see Mulroney's handling of Pocklington, in MacDonald, *Mulroney*, 204.

23 Ibid., 56, and 94–6.

24 Ibid., 99. Thompson's frank assessment of the Mulroney organization was captured in a remarkable memo prepared for the candidate on 22 May 1983. See ibid., Appendix A, 219–26.

25 Kinsella, who styled himself "the best political hack in the country," had been first impressed with Campbell's political abilities when he was an aide to premier Bill Bennett in the mid-1980s. Camp, with whom Campbell "forge[d] a close political alliance," worked with her at the Vancouver law firm Ladner Downs and was president of Campbell's Vancouver Centre PC Association. Smith, to whom Campbell threw her support in the 1986 So-cred leadership convention, was chairman of the board of Canadian Na-tional Railways at the time of the 1993 leadership convention. See Allen Garr, *Tough Guy: Bill Bennett and the Taking of British Columbia* (Toronto: Key Porter Books, 1985), 95, and Robert Fife, *Kim Campbell: The Making of a Pol-itician* (Toronto: HarperCollins, 1993), 61, 70, and 82–3.

26 An account of this period of Campbell's network-building is found in Fife, *Kim Campbell*, 176–8, and David McLaughlin, *Poisoned Chalice: The Last Cam-paign of the Progressive Conservative Party?* (Toronto: Dundurn, 1994), 65–74.

27 However, there were signs that near the end of the campaign Campbell fell out of favour with the Mulroney wing of the party when a number of previously uncommitted notables closely identified with Mulroney, such as Michel Cogger, Frank Moores, Bernard Roy, and Hugh Segal, endorsed Charest (ibid., 199).

28 Ibid., 178 and 198. According to John Laschinger, even though Atkins had been an early proponent of Campbell, he was seen in her organization as being too close to Mulroney and too much a part of the older Tory gang. Thus he was basically "frozen out" and "shunned" by the Campbell people. Asking Curley to join the Campbell team was "a brilliant move." Put in charge of the convention organization, Curley won the race for Campbell "on the floor" (Laschinger interview, 25 July 1994).

29 I am grateful to Nancy Jamieson, one of the high-profile Conservatives working on Campbell's team, and to John Laschinger, campaign manager for Jim Edwards, for their assessments of the Campbell network. See Jamieson letter to the author, 22 June 1994, and Laschinger interview, 25 July 1994. It is Jamieson's view that Charest's network, by contrast, was far more limited (with the exception of a very strong team in Quebec) than Campbell's, but ultimately far more effective in advancing a core message for and about their candidate.

30 It was estimated that Pocklington spent approximately $965,000. Pocklington's organization, in spite of its rapid assembly, was known to have impressed both Mulroney and Crosbie. See Martin, Gregg and Perlin, *Contenders*, 166.

31 1993 Conservative post-convention survey (N=765) and 1990 Liberal post-convention survey (N=1,450). Principal investigator: George Perlin.

32 Mary Walker-Sawka had been a last-minute entry into the Tory race in 1967. She received only two of the 2,231 first ballot votes. Rosemary Brown had unsuccessfully sought the leadership of the NDP in 1975.

33 MacDonald's campaign organization prepared a special memo for its delegate contact workers on how best to deal with delegate objections to voting for MacDonald because she was a woman. See Terry O'Connor, MacDonald campaign manager, "Memo to Campaign Workers", n.p., n.d.

34 Eddie Goodman, *Life of the Party: The Memoirs of Eddie Goodman* (Toronto: Key Porter Books, 1988), 210. James Johnston, former national director of the Progressive Conservatives had this to say of MacDonald in her bid for the leadership in 1976: "Flora will round up all the free libs, all the left-wingers, all the kooks plus a lot of responsible people who don't know her." As quoted in Patrick Brown, Robert Chodos and Rae Murphy, *Winners, Losers: The 1976 Tory Leadership Convention* (Toronto: Lorimer, 1976), 71. A "Red Tory" has been defined as someone "whose sympathy for collectivist public policy associated with state intervention in the economy and society seems to be based, not on liberal notions of progress or the egalitarian val-

ues of social democracy, but on a traditional conservative or Tory value of obligation inherent in a hierarchical society which is necessary for the preservation of the social order." See John McMenemy, *The Language of Canadian Politics* (Toronto: John Wiley and Sons, 1980), 226.

35 Terry O'Connor, "Memorandum to F.M. Delegate Contact People," n.p., n.d.

36 The survey data are from Robert Krause and Lawrence LeDuc, "Voting Behaviour and Electoral Strategies in the Progressive Conservative Leadership Convention of 1976," *CJPS* 12 (March 1979), table 7, 119. They note as well that "MacDonald's Atlantic ties appear to have been an important source of her first-ballot support" (118). For brief accounts of MacDonald's 1976 campaign see Brown, Chodos, and Murphy, *Winners, Losers*, 68–73, and Goodman, *Life of the Party*, 202–19.

37 The low estimate of MacDonald's support, that of her backers, is found in Goodman, 215, and John Laschinger and Geoffrey Stevens, *Leaders and Lesser Mortals: Backroom Politics in Canada* (Toronto: Key Porter, 1992), 196. The higher count was conducted by the Wagner people and is found in *Canadian Annual Review of Politics and Public Affairs, 1976* (Toronto: University of Toronto Press, 1977), 157.

38 Mulroney was criticized for his lack of parliamentary experience at the 1976 convention by no less a parliamentarian than John Diefenbaker, who claimed that "in the British parliamentary tradition, those who have achieved prime ministership must have had years of experience" in Parliament. See John Diefenbaker as quoted in "The young chieftain," *Time*, 1 March 1976, 9.

39 MacDonald, *Mulroney*, 160. Mulroney's 1976 caucus supporters were Heath MacQuarrie, Jim McGrath, and Jack Marshall (105). Although Mulroney's 1983 caucus support was sometimes said to be as high as thirty-one, it more likely was in the mid-twenties. As of early May, he had secured the endorsement of twenty-two MPs and four senators. See Mulroney campaign newsletter of 4 May 1983. MacDonald states that "in the end, some twenty MPs and a few Senators moved onside with Mulroney" (160).

40 Clark's 1976 caucus supporters were Allan McKinnon, Steve Paproski, and Harvie Andre. See David L. Humphreys, *Joe Clark: A Portrait* (Ottawa: Deneau and Greenberg, 1978), 216. By early February Hellyer was estimated to have the support of between twenty-five and thirty MPs. Wagner, whose entry into the 1976 race had been endorsed by ten MPs, likely had twice that many at the beginning of the convention voting. See "Hellyer bemoans decline of old-fashioned virtues," *StarPhoenix*, 14 February 1976, 23; Wagner enters PC race, ibid., 24 November 1975, 5; and "Setback for Wagner second of its kind," ibid., 23 February 1976, 5.

41 Mulroney's caucus support was perceived "as coming from a bunch of mental midgets or right-wing dinosaurs, as compared with the moderate pro-

gressives around Clark," an allegation that clearly bothered Mulroney. See MacDonald, *Mulroney*, 160. Clark's 1983 support from the parliamentary party on the eve of the convention (11 June) was composed of forty-one MPs and twelve senators (information provided by the Clark organization in 1983).

42 Conservative strategist, Nancy Jamieson, letter to the author, 22 June 1994.

43 Laschinger and Stevens, *Leaders and Lesser Mortals*, viii.

44 Martin, Gregg and Perlin, *Contenders*, 127.

45 Jean-Yves Lortie, as quoted in Robert McKenzie, "Campbell to win on first ballot, says key Tory," *Toronto Star*, 8 June 1993, A11.

46 Laschinger and Stevens, *Leaders and Lesser Mortals*, 107.

47 Brown, Chodos, and Murphy, *Winners, Losers*, 88.

48 This was near the mark on the fourth ballot. In a their survey of 1976 delegates, Krause and LeDuc found that on the first ballot Wagner received 49 per cent of the Quebec votes, twice the amount that went to Mulroney. Clark, who had won 9 per cent of Quebec's support on the first ballot, jumped to 38 per cent on the final ballot. Wagner got the remaining 62 per cent. See Krause and LeDuc, "Voting Behavior and Electoral Strategies," 119 and 128.

49 For a description of Lortie's exploits in 1976 see Brown, Chodos, and Murphy, *Winners, Losers*, 89; in 1983 see Martin, Gregg and Perlin, *Contenders*, 12–13; and in 1993 see McKenzie, "Campbell to win," A11.

50 MacDonald, *Mulroney*, 18.

51 Such was reported to have been the case with Pocklington's pollster, Peter Regenstrief. See Martin, Gregg, and Perlin, *Contenders*, 152.

52 MacDonald, *Mulroney*, 13.

53 McLean, as quoted in Graham, *One-Eyed Kings*, 272.

54 NA, Liberal Papers, MG 28 IV 3, "Candidate Liaison Committee," vol. 1386, undated confidential memo from T.J. Scanlon "Re: Stanfield Organization."

55 John Turner's biographer reports that Turner's polling firm, Angus Reid and Associates, was hired at the outset of the 1984 leadership campaign to conduct a "focus research study" into campaign colours. For $12,000 they were to "send people into the streets of all major Canadian cities, holding up colour cards and asking people [for] their reaction to them, a process that would take at least several weeks." The process was cancelled by Bill Lee shortly after he replaced Heather Peterson as Turner's campaign manager. See Cahill, *John Turner*, 211–13.

56 Although Bradley was, of course, speaking of the American political context, there is little doubt that the professionalization of Canadian leadership politics has American roots. The mid-1980s boom in the political consulting industry in the United States prompted one industry insider, James M. Dwinnell, publisher of *Campaigns & Elections*, to declare that "de-

mocracy is a growth business." Dwinnell was echoed by Yvonne Ryzak, a consultant specializing in county supervisor races. "The consulting business is like the mortician business," she said, "someone is always dying and someone is always running for office." See Randall Rothenberg, "The Boom in Political Consulting," *New York Times*, 24 May 1987, Section 3, 1, 6.

57 MacDonald, *Mulroney*, 227.

58 Ross Howard, "The man who fell to earth," *Globe and Mail*, 18 December 1993, D1, D3.

59 Ross Howard, "Expert called in to tune off-key Campbell," ibid., 8 May 1993, A7.

60 In 1990 part of Paul Martin's preparations for the Liberal leadership campaign was his being "'coached' with tips on how to appear in front of the camera." See Susan Delacourt, "Odd mix of attributes, formidable support fuel Martin's chances," ibid., 18 January 1990, A4.

61 Camp, as quoted in Graham, *One-Eyed Kings*, 272. In Kim Campbell's campaign of 1993 it was normal for a chief organizer to receive a weekly fee of $1,750, plus expenses. See Geoffrey York, "Campbell drive takes the high road," *Globe and Mail*, 9 April 1993, A9.

62 For a brief discussion of the variety of services now available to American parties and candidates from political consultants, see Nelson W. Polsby and Aaron Wildavsky, *Presidential Elections: Contemporary Strategies of American Electoral Politics*, 8th ed. (New York: The Free Press, 1991), 209–10.

63 Laschinger interview, 25 July 1994. This does not invalidate the idea that in order to avoid the impression and the possibility that money contributed to a campaign is tied to a candidate's knowledge of the sources and amounts of donations, finances should be handled separately from the candidate through a financial coordinator reporting directly to the campaign manager. It simply recognizes the reality that the campaign's financial responsibility is, in the final analysis, the candidate's.

64 Laschinger and Stevens, *Leaders and Lesser Mortals*, 136.

65 Ibid., 205.

66 F. Christopher Arterton, "Strategies and Tactics of Candidate Organizations," *Political Science Quarterly* 92 (Winter 1977–8), 669.

CHAPTER 10

1 The classic work on this topic remains Douglas Rae, *The Political Consequences of Electoral Laws*, 2nd ed (New Haven: Yale University Press, 1971). See also Bernard Grofman and Arend Lijphart, eds., *Electoral Laws and Their Political Consequences* (New York: Agathon Press, 1986).

2 A superb illustration of the transference of institutional frameworks and election rules from a dominant to a minority culture was exemplified by the way in which the grand chief of the Assembly of First Nations was cho-

sen in July 1994 in Saskatoon. The same six rules as those listed above were used *except that* in addition to receiving a clear majority the winner also had to gain at least 60 per cent of the votes cast. The purpose of the 60 per cent requirement was to ensure that the grand chief had achieved a broad measure of support from the several hundred chiefs voting on the AFN leadership. Prompted by the Assembly's stated goal of selecting a true consensual winner, the rule did little to accomplish that, given the dissension within the Assembly and the strength of the opposition to Ovide Mercredi's candidacy. The AFN ended a contentious leadership race as a bitterly divided organization.

Reminiscent of the blocking strategies that could be employed by presidential contestants in the American Democratic party when its two-thirds rule was in force (the two-thirds majority requirement was dropped by the party in 1936 after one hundred years), the AFN vote very nearly did not produce a winner who met both the majority and the 60 per cent requirements. With the low candidate dropped after each ballot and no new nominations permitted (neither of those two conditions ever applied in the Democratic party), it was conceivable that *no* winner would be selected in the AFN system as the majority winner on a final ballot between two candidates might have fallen short of the needed 60 per cent. It took three ballots to declare Mercredi the winner in a vote that started with five candidates, two of whom dropped off after the first ballot. When eliminated from the race, all challengers (except the one with the smallest number of first ballot votes who described her move as "following the will of her supporters") then openly supported Mecredi's principal opponent. The continuous voting, which did not end until the middle of the night, saw Mercredi win 54 per cent of the first ballot vote, 59.58 per cent of the second ballot vote, and a bare 60 per cent (with three votes to spare of the 432 cast) of the final ballot votes. The "stop Mecredi" coalitions that formed on the floor following each ballot were no different to the kind found in multi-ballot leadership conventions. See Randy Burton, *StarPhoenix*: "Mercredi's future on the line," 6 July 1994, 1; "Mercredi two votes shy of majority: balloting continues into night," 1; "The chiefs are coming, Mercredi warns Ottawa," 1; and Rudi Platiel, "Struggle develops in AFN voting," *Globe and Mail*, 7 July 1994, A1.

3 See Appendix 10–1 for an explanation of the statistical models and procedures used to determine the probabilities.

4 The coefficient is -5.83, the *t*-statistic is -6.81 and the adjusted R^2 is 0.72.

5 The only second-generation leadership contest to have been decided on one ballot was the Liberal 1990 convention. In that race there was little evidence of a stop Chrétien campaign. According to Perlin's 1990 delegate survey, only 0.3 per cent of the delegates (five of 1,507 delegates surveyed)

voted strategically for someone other than their true preference out of a desire to stop Chrétien. In addition, 0.1 per cent of the delegates (two of 1,507) reported having voted strategically out of a desire to stop each of Martin and Wappel. Another 0.3 per cent reported having voted strategically so as to encourage a second ballot. See 1990 Liberal convention survey, principal investigator: George Perlin.

6 Abram de Swaan describes coalitions as political actors *coordinating* their choices into a *common strategy*. Convention-floor coalition differs from this to the extent that while strategic goals may be temporarily shared by delegates, it cannot in any formal sense be said to rely on totally coordinated choices among individual participants. See de Swaan, *Coalition Theories and Cabinet Formations* (Amsterdam: Elsevier Scientific Publishing, 1973), 30.

7 The assumptions underlying coalition and social choice theories are drawn from several sources including, Anthony Downs, *An Economic Theory of Democracy* (New York: Harper and Row, 1957); William Riker, *The Theory of Political Coalitions* (New Haven: Yale University Press, 1962); Steven J. Brams and Michael K. O'Leary, "An Axiomatic Model of Voting Bodies," *APSR* 64 (March 1970), 449–70; Eugene B. McGregor, "Rationality and Uncertainty at National Nominating Conventions," *Journal of Politics* 35 (1973), 459–78; Joseph A. Schlesinger, "The Primary Goal of Political Parties," *APSR*, 69 (September 1975), 840–9; Kenneth Shepsle, "Institutional Arrangements and Equilibrium in Multidimensional Voting Models," *AJPS* 23 (February 1979), 27–59; Shepsle, "The Positive Theory of Legislative Institutions: An Enrichment of Social Choice and Spatial Models," *Public Choice* 50 (1–3, 1986), 135–78; and David Austen-Smith and Jeffrey Banks, "Elections, Coalitions and Legislative Outcomes," *APSR* 82 (June 1988), 405–22. An excellent bibliography on the coalition literature is found in Michael Laver and Norman Schofield, *Multiparty Government: The Politics of Coalitions in Europe* (New York: Oxford University Press, 1991), 291–300.

8 Brams and O'Leary, "An Axiomatic Model," 467.

9 Robert Axelrod, *Conflict of Interest: A Theory of Divergent Goals with Applications to Politics* (Chicago: Markham Publishing, 1970), 169–70 (emphasis in original). Naturally the coalition has to be a winning coalition to get the candidate elected as leader. According to Axelrod, the winning coalition does not have to be large in numbers, for the smaller the coalition the lower its conflict of interest. In those terms, a convention victory of 50 per cent plus one of the delegates' votes would be the ideal size, for it would be "minimal in the sense that it can lose no member ... without ceasing to be connected and winning." Accordingly, the coalition predicted by the theory might best be defined, in Axelrod's terminology, as a *minimum connected winning coalition* (170).

10 Explained together with the 1967 Tory convention through coalition theory in my *The Selection of National Party Leaders in Canada*, Appendix G, 253–9.

11 Richard Johnston, "The Final Choice: Its Social, Organizational, and Ideological Bases," in George Perlin, ed., *Party Democracy in Canada: The Politics of National Party Conventions* (Scarborough: Prentice-Hall Canada, 1988), 220.

12 It was Chrétien and Trudeau, not Turner, who made sure that they were rewarded. Turner, at his first meeting with Whelan after the convention, informed him that he would not be appointed to his cabinet with the comment "Gotta let ya go, big Gene, know what I mean? Sorry, pal, but gotta do it." Chrétien intervened on Whelan's behalf and was instrumental in having Turner appoint him as Canada's ambassador to the Food and Agricultural Organization in Rome, an appointment that was rescinded shortly after by the newly elected Conservative government. A description of the episode is given in Greg Weston, *Reign of Error: The Inside Story of John Turner's Troubled Leadership* (Toronto: McGraw-Hill Ryerson, 1988), 9–10. Munro was appointed to the Canadian Transportation Commission by Trudeau and Roberts ran and was defeated in the 1984 general election. For his part, MacGuigan was named a judge of the Federal Court of Canada by Trudeau.

13 The optimal size of a winning coalition has been a subject of considerable debate in the literature. Downs argues that parties seek to *maximize* their support and to create large winning coalitions. In Riker's theory, *minimum* winning coalitions are preferred to coalitions that are larger than necessary to win because the smaller the coalition the greater the individual coalition member's share of rewards. Schlesinger distinguishes between the goals of benefit-seekers and office-seekers in creating coalitions. He argues that office-seekers want larger than necessary coalitions so as to minimize their dependence on a small number of supporters, whereas benefit-seekers prefer smaller coalitions so as to maximize the policy benefits that will come their way as part of the winning team. See Downs, *An Economic Theory*, chaps. 7–9; Riker, *Political Coalitions*, 32–3; and Schlesinger, 840–9. See also Robert Lyle Butterworth, "A Research Note on the Size of Winning Coalitions," a Comment by Riker and a Reply by Butterworth, *APSR* 65 (September 1971), 741–8; and Kenneth A. Shepsle, "On the Size of Winning Coalitions," a Comment by Butterworth and a Reply by Shepsle, *APSR* 68 (June 1974), 505–24.

14 The 1983 Conservative and 1984 Liberal post-convention surveys, principal investigator: George Perlin; the 1989 NDP convention survey, principal investigator: Keith Archer.

15 Patrick Martin, Allan Gregg, and George Perlin, *Contenders: The Tory Quest for Power* (Scarborough: Prentice-Hall Canada, 1983), 242 n10.

16 Sixteen per cent were committed for the first ballot only and 1 per cent for the first two ballots. See 1989 NDP convention survey.

17 Relative positioning, not distances between the candidates, is the important variable in this analysis of the 1976 and 1983 Tory conventions. The spectra are intuitive approximations of the relative location of the candidates based on the author's interviews and conversations with delegates, candidates, political science colleagues, and journalists at the time of both conventions. It should be recalled that in 1976 Mulroney was considered part of the moderate, progressive, Red Tory wing of the party, whereas in 1983 he was generally seen to be centre to slightly right-of-centre. For a good journalistic assessment of the location of the 1976 candidates, see Geoffrey Stevens, "Search for a leader," *Globe and Mail*, 29 January 1975, 6, and "The moderate wing," ibid., 20 January 1976, 6.

18 As quoted in John Saywell, ed., *Canadian Annual Review of Politics and Public Affairs, 1976* (Toronto: University of Toronto Press, 1977), 157–8.

19 Robin Farquharson in his excellent study of voting logic notes that once an individual has ordered his or her preferences in a systematic fashion that preference ordering remains constant "throughout the course of the voting. It may ... have been modified by earlier arguments or events, but it does not vary after voting has begun." As well, "a voter votes sincerely ... if he chooses the subset with the highest-ranked top." It is not always to a delegate's advantage to act sincerely. "In certain cases he will find that had he chosen a different strategy, the outcome reached would have been different, and in his opinion preferable." See *Theory of Voting* (New Haven: Yale University Press, 1969), 6, 18, and 24.

20 McGregor, "Rationality and Uncertainty," 464 (emphasis in original). Downs expressed the problem this way: "Each voter can make his own voting decision only after estimating what decisions others will make, so a problem of conjectural variation arises to which no solution has been found." See *An Economic Theory*, 163.

21 Their expressed reasons for choosing Crosbie over Mulroney, the second-placed and equally anti-Clark candidate, reflected strategic and personal reasons more than ideological ones. Fraser stated that he moved as he did because he considered Crosbie to be a "straight shooter." Quoted in Alan Cristie, "Fraser loses but his anti-metric cause lives on," *Toronto Star*, 12 June 1983, A13. Gamble reportedly chose Crosbie because he knew him better than Mulroney. see David Vienneau, "Shocked Gamble says his poor showing was disastrous," *Toronto Star*, 12 June 1983, A13.

22 Martin, Gregg and Perlin, *Contenders*, 168.

23 As quoted in Martin Cohen, "Wilson moved quickly to stop Clark," *Toronto Star*, 12 June 1983, A13. There were additional reasons why Wilson did not endorse Crosbie. Martin, Gregg, and Perlin relate that "none of his advisors advocated supporting the Newfoundlander. Said one prominent Wil-

son organizer, 'John made it difficult to go to him.' He was too much 'a one-man show,' 'stubborn,' and with a 'temper.' He added that some of the Wilson people 'saw another Diefenbaker' in Crosbie. All that, plus Crosbie's resistance to learning French, made it next to impossible to recommend endorsing him." See *Contenders*, 169.

24 As quoted in Peter Maser, "Mulroney alliance in works," *Ottawa Citizen*, 10 June 1983, 1. Pocklington's pollster, Peter Regenstreif, confirmed his candidate's strategy. The day before the voting he said that where Pocklington would go in order to stop Clark "all depends on the [first-ballot] numbers. We won't make up our minds until then." See Richard Gwyn, "Stop-Clark movement comes out of the closet," *Ottawa Citizen*, 11 June 1983, 21.

25 Martin, Gregg, and Perlin, *Contenders*, 168.

26 The authors of *Contenders* suggest that among Crombie's reasons for staying on after the first ballot was his desire to stop Clark. Coupled with this was his belief that if he dropped out of the race many of his supports would move to Joe Clark, thereby dashing his hope that he might gain from any slippage in Clark's soft support on the second ballot (165–6).

27 Crombie gave a number of reasons for having chosen Crosbie over Mulroney. These ranged from "he's the man with the experience the party needs," to "he understands political life," to "because you can look him in the eye." Quoted in Kit Collins, "Crombie fails to save Crosbie," *Ottawa Citizen*, 12 June 1983, 25; and in Carol Goar, "The Mulroney challenge," *Maclean's*, 20 June 1983, 12.

28 Not all delegates vote in such a rational manner. John Laschinger, Crosbie's campaign manager in 1983, tells a story that at a dinner party he was seated next to a Mrs Dawson who had been a delegate to the Tory convention earlier that year. Laschinger asked her how she had voted. The following dialogue (as reported by Laschinger) ensued:

MRS DAWSON: I voted for Mike Wilson because he's from Ontario, as I am. Besides, Mulroney was just too slick – I didn't trust him. Clark's such a wimp, and Crosbie couldn't speak French.

LASCHINGER: I see. What did you do on the second ballot?

MRS DAWSON: I voted for Crosbie.

LASCHINGER: Great, but what about his lack of French?

MRS DAWSON: Well, I didn't trust Mulroney at all, and Clark was a wimp.

LASCHINGER: What about the third ballot?

MRS DAWSON: Oh, I voted for Joe Clark.

LASCHINGER: Why? Crosbie was still on the third ballot.

MRS DAWSON: I know, but during the break between the second and third votes, I stood on the floor in front of Clark's seats and I felt so sorry for him and his wife. And besides, Mulroney was so untrustworthy.

LASCHINGER: And you voted for Clark on the fourth ballot?

MRS DAWSON: Oh, no. I voted for Mulroney!

LASCHINGER: What? I thought you said that you couldn't trust him.

MRS DAWSON: That's right. But Clark was such a wimp!

This exchange is found in John Laschinger and Geoffrey Stevens, *Leaders & Lesser Mortals: Backroom Politics in Canada* (Toronto: Key Porter Books, 1992), 195–6. Reprinted with permission.

29 Martin, Gregg, and Perlin, *Contenders*, 195–6.

30 The 47 and 16 per cent figures combined two responses: ABC and Change needed. The ABM movement was not a very influential factor for any of the delegates who changed their vote from the third to the fourth ballot. See 1983 Conservative post-convention survey.

31 Robert Krause and Lawrence LeDuc, "Voting Behaviour and Electoral Strategies in the Progressive Conservative Leadership Convention of 1976," *CJPS* 12 (March 1979), 112.

32 Ibid., 113.

33 Ibid., 114.

34 The latter figures are from Martin, Gregg, and Perlin, *Contenders*, 247.

35 For an analysis of data on 1976 voting strategies and delegate preferences, see Krause and LeDuc, "Voting Behavior and Electoral Strategies," 101–15.

36 Ibid., 114.

37 In 1989, for example, 89 per cent of the NDP delegates who voted for candidates who had dropped out of the race declared that they were not influenced in their fourth ballot vote by the preference of the candidate(s) whom they had supported previously. See 1989 NDP convention survey.

38 Perhaps, as my colleague Duff Spafford has drawn to my attention, the problem ought to be stated another way: social choice theory shows that there is no thoroughly persuasive definition of what makes for the most-preferred candidate.

39 To Terrence Levesque, the pairwise majority winner is the true winner – plausible, but still only one of several possible conclusions to be drawn. See Levesque, "On the Outcome of the 1983 Conservative Leadership Convention: How They Shot Themselves in the Other Foot," *CJPS* 16 (December 1983), 779–84. As if to corroborate Levesque's thesis, an unsubstantiated, but widely circulated, rumour on the convention floor between the second and third ballots in 1983 had it that a number of Mulroney supporters would vote for Clark on the third ballot to ensure that he, not Crosbie, would be Mulroney's opponent on the fourth and final ballot. Perlin's 1983 post-convention study does not confirm this. It shows that twice as many second ballot Mulroney voters switched to Crosbie on the third ballot as to Clark.

40 Peter Woolstencroft, "Social Choice Theory and the Reconstruction of Elections: A Comment on Levesque's Analysis," *CJPS* 16 (December 1983), 785–9.

41 Perlin, "Did the Best Candidate Win? A Comment on Levesque's Analysis," *CJPS* 16 (December 1983), 791–4. In the Crosbie/Clark pairing 3 per cent of the respondents did not express an opinion and 5 per cent did not in the Crosbie/Mulroney pairing.

42 Archer, "Leadership Selection in the New Democratic Party," in Herman Bakvis, ed., *Canadian Political Parties: Leaders, Candidates and Organization,* vol. 13 of the research studies for the Royal Commission on Electoral Reform and Party Financing (Toronto: Dundurn Press, 1991), 25–9.

43 For a statement to that effect, see my *The Selection of National Party Leaders in Canada,* 216, a book that appeared *before* the 1976 convention!

44 In his study of American national nominating conventions, McGregor expressed the hypothesis this way: "Under conditions of certainty, delegates who are anxiously trying to pick a winner find it easier to cast their lot on the third ballot with the candidate who has made the largest gain from the first to the second ballot. If this hypothesis is true, then a corollary is also true: the candidate who gains the largest share of the votes from the first to the second ballot will be the eventual winner no matter how many ballots are needed for nomination." His hypothesis was confirmed in eleven of seventeen multi-ballot conventions between 1872 and 1952, including one (Democratic 1912) that went to forty-six ballots. See McGregor, "Rationality and Uncertainty," 470.

45 Arguing that the number of ballots would act as a counterweight to the linear growth that would otherwise be anticipated by the candidate gaining the largest share of votes between the first two ballots, Raj Chari has developed a model designed to introduce an element of exponential damping to linear growth. His model predicts eight of eight multi-ballot winners in Canadian national leadership conventions, sixteen of twenty provincial conventions since 1961, and seven of fifteen American nominating conventions since 1876. See Raj Chari, "A Leadership Selection Index for Multi-Ballot Party Conventions" (MA thesis, Department of Political Studies, University of Saskatchewan, 1993).

CHAPTER 11

1 Keith Archer and Margaret Hunziker, "Leadership Selection in Alberta: The 1985 Progressive Conservative Leadership Convention," in R. Kenneth Carty, Lynda Erickson, and Donald E. Blake, eds., *Leaders and Parties in Canadian Politics: Experiences of the Provinces* (Toronto: Harcourt Brace Jovanovich, 1992), 81 (emphasis added).

2 Three articles on the Reform party (dealing with its ideas on political representation, its postmodern conservatism, and the ideological orientations and social bases of its assembly delegates) appear in the *CJPS* 27 (June 1994). They are by David Laycock, "Reforming Canadian Democracy? Insti-

tutions and Ideology in the Reform Party Project," 213–47; Richard Sigurdson, "Preston Manning and the Politics of Postmodernism in Canada," 249–
76; and Keith Archer and Faron Ellis, "Opinion Structure of Party Activists:
The Reform Party of Canada," 277–308. See also Tom Flanagan, *Waiting for
the Wave: The Reform Party and Preston Manning* (Toronto: Stoddart, 1995).

3 Alan Cairns, "The Charter and the Constitution Act, 1982," *The Dilemmas of
Constitutional Reform* (Montreal and Kingston: McGill-Queen's Press, 1992),
74. Among Cairn's other essays touching on the theme of citizen empower-
ment are "The Lessons of Meech Lake," ibid., 96–126, and "Passing Judge-
ment on Meech Lake," in Douglas E. Williams, ed., *Disruptions:
Constitutional Struggles, from the Charter to Meech Lake* (Toronto: McClelland
and Stewart, 1991), 223–63.

4 Interview with Vaughan Baird, 25 July 1994. Baird, a keen promoter of the
one member, one vote system, sent Margaret Thatcher a copy of his proposal
for universal ballot while she was British prime minister. "Had she adopted it
then, she'd still be leader today," he claimed in mid-1994. Britain's Labour
party, under John Smith's leadership, adopted electoral reforms aimed at re-
ducing the power of the trade unions in selecting the party leader and at in-
troducing a variant of the one member, one vote system. As noted in chapter
3, Smith's reforms were accepted by the party in 1993 and were employed
for the first time in 1994 to elect Tony Blair as party leader. They reduced the
share of the trade union membership vote from 40 to 33.3 per cent of the total and gave each trade unionist an individual vote. They also raised the share
of votes awarded to Labour's other two "pillars," constituency party members, and MPs and members of the European Parliament (MEPs), from 30 to
33.3 per cent each. In the 1994 one member, one vote party leadership selection, 4.3 million members were entitled to vote in the postal vote; 952,109
voted, for a "turnout" figure of 22 per cent. Voting took place over a three-
week period and no conference or convention was held at the end when the
results were disclosed. From the trade union section, 779,426 voted, or 19.5
per cent of those eligible; from the constituency party membership, 172,356
voted, or 69.1 per cent of the approximately 250,000 eligible; and from the
MPs and MEPs, 327 of 331 voted. Blair won on the first round of a STV ballot
with 60.5 per cent of the MP/MEP votes, 58.2 per cent of the constituency
membership, and 52.3 per cent of the trade union membership. See Jill
Sherman, "Leadership election will test Smith's democratic reforms," *The
Times* (London), 14 May 1994, 8, and Nicholas Wood, "How Labour voters
made their choice," ibid., 22 July 1994, 8.

5 Letter to the author from C. Shelly Cory, assistant to the deputy leader of
the Manitoba Liberal party, 22 July 1994.

6 The first leader actually chosen by an all-member vote was Yvon Dupuis. In
1973 he was elected leader of the third-place Créditistes in Quebec on the
second ballot (see appendix 11–1).

7 For a full description of the rules see Yvon Thériault, "New System for Choosing the Party Leader," *Canadian Parliamentary Review* 8 (Winter 1985–6), 27–8.

8 Parizeau won the leadership unopposed. For an examination of the Parti Québécois' experience with the direct vote system, see Daniel Latouche, "Universal Democracy and Effective Leadership: Lessons from the Parti Québécois Experience," in Carty, Erickson and Blake, eds., *Leaders and Parties in Canadian Politics,* 174–202.

9 The term was coined by Heather MacIvor. It incorporates all the widely varying terms used to describe universal balloting on the leadership selection process, including universal balloting, universal selection, direct democracy, direct election, and one member, one vote. MacIvor, "Explaining the Changes in Canadian Party Leadership Selection," paper presented to the annual meeting of the CPSA, Calgary, Alberta, 14 June 1994.

10 A considerable literature has accumulated in a short time on direct democracy and provincial leadership selection. In addition to Theriault, "New System," and Latouche, "Universal Democracy," on the PQ, there are several other articles and unpublished papers on specific provincial parties' experiences with a direct election method of leadership selection. For the Ontario Conservatives in 1990, see Peter Woolstencroft, " 'Tories Kick Machine to Bits': Leadership Selection and the Ontario Progressive Conservative Party," in Carty, Erickson and Blake, ed., *Leaders and Parties in Canadian Politics,* 203–25; for the Nova Scotia Liberals in 1992, see Agar Adamson, Bruce Beaton, and Ian Stewart, "Pressing the Right Buttons: The Nova Scotia Liberals and Tele-Democracy," paper presented to the annual meeting of the CPSA, Ottawa, June 1993, and Leonard Preyra, "Tele-Conventions and Party Democracy: The 1992 Nova Scotia Liberal Leadership Convention," *Canadian Parliamentary Review* 16 (Winter 1993–4), 2–11; for the Alberta Conservatives in 1992, see David K. Stewart, "Grassroots Democracy and Federal Party Membership: The 1992 Alberta Progressive Conservative Leadership Selection," paper presented to the annual meeting of the Atlantic Provinces Political Science Association, Antigonish, October 1993, and "Electing the Premier: An Examination of the 1992 Alberta Progressive Conservative Leadership Election," paper presented to the annual meeting of the CPSA, Calgary, June 1994; and for the British Columbia Liberals in 1993, see Donald E. Blake and R. Kenneth Carty, "Televoting for the Leader of the British Columbia Liberal Party: The Leadership Contest of 1993," paper presented to the annual meeting of the CPSA, Calgary, June 1994. Two more general papers presented to the CPSA in June 1994 were Heather MacIvor, "Explaining the Changes in Canadian Party Leadership Selection," and Bill Cross, "Direct Election of Party Leaders: Provincial Experiences and Lessons Learned." MacIvor also

presented a paper, "Leadership Selection in Canadian Political Parties: Is Constitutional Government Being Perverted into Democracy?" to the Party Politics in the Year 2000 Conference, Manchester, England, January 1995.

11 Woolstencroft, " 'Tories Kick Machine to Bits'," 212.

12 Ted Carruthers, Alberta Conservative party president, as quoted in Lorne Gunter, "How Premier Ralph Klein fooled the pundits," *Western Report,* 14 December 1992, 6.

13 The words are Jeffrey Simpson's, "A democratic model," *Globe and Mail,* 2 October 1985, A6.

14 Pierre-Marc Johnson, as quoted in "PQ election system 'takes fun out of politics'," *StarPhoenix,* 30 September 1985, A11.

15 Cory letter, 22 July 1994. Edwards won in a contest in which 1,938 votes were cast. Gary Filmon had been chosen leader of the Tories in a convention in 1983 in which 549 first ballot votes were cast. Gary Doer won the NDP leadership in a 1988 convention in which 1,663 first ballot votes were cast.

16 Ken Azzopardi, as quoted in Dave Traynor, "PCs expect 9,000 eligible voters," *StarPhoenix,* 8 November 1994, D5.

17 Cory letter, 22 July 1994 (emphasis added).

18 Tom Regan, "Phoning the future," *Daily News* (Halifax), 31 May 1994, 17.

19 Jules Pascal Venne, as quoted in Francois Shalom, "Johnson makes voting history with universal suffrage format," *Globe and Mail,* 30 September 1985, 3.

20 Regan, "Phoning the Future," 17.

21 Baird interview, 25 July 1994.

22 Woolstencroft, " 'Tories Kick Machine to Bits'," 214.

23 John Young, as quoted in Regan, "Phoning the Future," 17.

24 Ted Carruthers during CBC Newsworld coverage of the 15 June 1993 Alberta provincial election.

25 NA, Liberal Papers, MG 28 IV 3, vol. 1813, no file, *Report of the Chief Electoral Officer of the P.C. Party of Ontario Respecting the Leadership Election, May 12, 1990,* issued 4 July 1990.

26 Letter to the editor, *Globe and Mail,* 12 November 1992, A20.

27 Blake and Carty, "Televoting for the Leadership of the B.C. Liberal Party," 5.

28 The survey was based on the responses of 1,802 of those who voted in the 20 June 1992 leadership election of the Liberal party of Nova Scotia. See Adamson, Beaton and Stewart, "Pressing the Right Buttons," 28.

29 The newspaper headlines said it all: Mark Lisac, "A mess from start to finish," *Sunday Journal* (Edmonton), 13 November 1994, A1; Don Martin, "Horror Show: Liberal leadership experiment fails in every way imaginable," *Calgary Herald,* 13 November 1994, D1; and Scott Feschuk, "Alberta phone voting crashes," *Globe and Mail,* 14 November 1994, A1.

30 Robert Sheppard, "Tory numbers tell the story," *Globe and Mail*, 18 November 1992, A23. The growth in the party's membership was particularly spec-
tacular in ridings in which the party had fallen out of favour. To give but
two examples, in Edmonton-Gold Bar (which contained only eighteen
members before the race began), 923 members voted on the final ballot;
the riding of Cardston contained only six party members before the leadership race, yet 767 people voted in that riding on the final ballot. See *Calgary Herald*, 6 December 1992, A11.

31 Blake and Carty found that 10.3 per cent of those who joined the BC Liberal party in 1993 did so specifically because televoting was used for electing the party leader. Blake and Carty, "Televoting for the Leadership of the
B.C. Liberal Party," 6–7.

32 Ibid., 11.

33 Comparing the 1986 Liberal convention in Nova Scotia with the 1992
UMV, Adamson, Beaton, and Stewart found that 6.7 per cent and 14.5 per
cent of the 1986 delegates were retired and students respectively. In 1992
the numbers were 22.9 per cent and 5.7 per cent. See Adamson, Beaton,
and Stewart, table 2. Blake and Carty found that the female participation in
the BC Liberal party's conventions of 1974 and 1987 was 47 per cent and
33.7 per cent respectively. In the 1993 televote, 42.1 per cent of the participants were female. See Blake and Carty, "Televoting for the Leadership of
the B.C. Liberal Party," 14.

34 George Perlin, "Attitudes of Liberal Convention Delegates Toward Proposals for Reform of the Process of Leadership Selection," in Herman Bakvis,
ed., *Canadian Political Parties: Leaders, Candidates and Organization*, vol. 13 of
the research studies for the Royal Commission on Electoral Reform and
Party Financing (Toronto: Dundurn Press, 1991), 87.

35 Dalton Camp, as quoted in Francois Shalom, "Johnson makes voting
history with universal suffrage format," *Globe and Mail*, 30 September 1985,
3.

36 Camp, "Charest should heed Nova Scotia lesson on perils of reform," *Toronto Star*, 21 September 1994, A25.

37 Woolstencroft, " 'Tories Kick Machine to Bits'," 224.

38 Henry E. Brady and Richard Johnston, "Convention Versus Primaries: A
Canadian-American Comparison," in George Perlin, ed., *Party Democracy in
Canada: The Politics of National Party Conventions* (Scarborough: Prentice-
Hall Canada, 1988), 245.

39 Blake and Carty, "Televoting for the Leadership of the B.C. Liberal Party,"
18.

40 Adamson, Beaton, and Stewart, "Pressing the Right Buttons,"17.

41 This comment was made by an observer of one of the convention week
events staged by the Parti Québécois in 1985. See Dalton Camp, "The yawn
of a new era," *StarPhoenix*, 3 October 1985, A4.

42 David McFadden, "Choosing the Party Leader: Is There a Better Way?," *Canadian Parliamentary Review* 9 (Summer 1986), 23.

43 Interview with Paul Thomas, University of Manitoba, 14 July 1994.

44 The words are those of the Ontario Liberal party's constitutional chairman, Jack Siegel. "Leadership Selection Discussion Paper: Combined Direct Vote/Convention Approach," January 1991, 8.

45 Ibid., 1 ff. The title page of the Siegal discussion paper refers to "combined direct vote/convention approach," whereas the rest of the document uses the term "combined primary/convention approach."

46 Ontario Liberal Party, "Rules of Procedure for the Leadership Convention 1992," article 24.1.

47 According to an Ontario Liberal party official, some of the previously declared delegates to the party's 1992 leadership convention did not vote. The number is unknown. In addition, there were "few or no complaints" from previously declared delegates who had changed their minds and who wanted to vote for a candidate other than the one for whom they had declared. Interview with Hillary Dawson, riding association coordinator of the Ontario Liberal party, 24 November 1993.

48 Siegel, "Leadership Selection Discussion Paper," 6.

49 Joan Bryden, "Opening up the Liberal Party," *Ottawa Citizen*, 22 February 1992, A1.

50 Perlin, "Attitudes of Liberal Convention Delegates," 87.

51 Ashley Geddes, "It's Klein at the helm," *Calgary Herald*, 6 December 1992, A10.

52 This is not to say that UMV candidates (particularly those running in systems in which votes are cast and aggregated by constituency) would not try to appropriate the machines that their caucus supporters possessed in their constituencies and to use them as a means of recruiting and getting voters out on their behalf. It makes good political sense to turn to the established networks to activate support, as Klein proved in Alberta in 1992. But that would be the case regardless of the leadership selection system.

53 Evidently most of the federal riding association presidents were either unfamiliar with or not dissuaded by the implications that the universal suffrage system has for riding executives. Carty's survey of federal riding association presidents found that direct election was supported by 52 per cent of Conservative, 57 per cent of New Democrat, 68 per cent of Liberal riding association presidents. See R.K. Carty, *Canadian Political Parties in the Constituencies*, vol. 23 of the research studies for the Royal Commission on Electoral Reform and Party Financing (Toronto: Dundurn Press, 1991), table 5.8, 133.

54 These points are developed further in my "The Morning After: Delegate Accountability," *Parliamentary Government* 4 (1983), 8 ff.

55 Thomas E. Mann, "Elected Officials and the Politics of Presidential Selection," in Austin Ranney, ed., *The American Elections of 1984* (Durham, NC:

Duke University Press, 1985), 103. By 1984, superdelegates accounted for 22 per cent of the total number of Democratic delegates. Their role in that convention is analysed in Priscilla L. Southwell, "The 1984 Democratic Nomination Process: The Significance of Unpledged Superdelegates," *American Politics Quarterly* 14 (January-April 1986) 75–88.

56 Perlin, "Attitude of Liberal Convention Delegates," 86.

57 Dwight Dunn as quoted in Dave Traynor, "Sask. PCs unfazed by Alta.'s high-tech voting disaster," *StarPhoenix*, 15 November 1994, A5.

58 Woolstencroft, " 'Tories Kick Machine to Bits'," 220.

59 V.O. Key, *Politics, Parties, & Pressure Groups*, 5th ed., (New York: Thomas Y. Crowell Company, 1964), 410.

60 CBC radio tape of the proceedings of the Leadership Selection Workshop of the November 1985 Halifax Liberal Reform Conference provided by Ken McCreath, bureau chief, CBC National Radio News. For a comparison between Canadian conventions and American primaries in which the authors "support conventions and find fault with primaries," see Brady and Johnston, "Convention Versus Primaries," 243–70.

CHAPTER 12

1 Peter Woolstencroft, " 'Tories Kick Machine to Bits': Leadership Selection and the Ontario Conservative Party," in R. Kenneth Carty, Lynda Erickson, and Donald E. Blake, eds. *Leaders and Parties in Canadian Politics: Experiences of the Provinces* (Toronto: Harcourt Brace Jovanovich, 1992), 203–4.

2 PC committee appointed to study the one member, one vote concept. Members were F. Simar (chair), Vaughan Baird, Jean Casselman-Wadds, Heward Grafftey, and Al Fortier. Information provided by Vaughan Baird, 27 July 1994.

3 Patrick Boyer, as quoted in "Clock watching," *Ottawa Sun*, 11 June 1993, 38. See also Stuart McCarthy, "Democracy? Not quite," ibid., 6 June 1993, T5.

4 See Ross Howard, "Charest looks ahead and sees Stanfield," *Globe and Mail*, 28 February 1994, A1; and "Tory leadership convention years away," *StarPhoenix*, 28 February 1994, A9.

5 Charest letter to Vaughan Baird, 8 March 1994. I am indebted to Peter Woolstencroft of the University of Waterloo and Lynne Agnew of the PC Restructuring Committee for information provided in the following paragraph about the April 1995 Hull general meeting of the Conservative party.

6 Resolution T-28 in New Democratic Party, "1989 Convention Resolutions," 171.

7 Thirty-six per cent of the delegates were opposed to the change and 12 per cent were undecided or did not answer the question. See Keith Archer,

"Leadership Selection in the New Democratic Party," in Herman Bakvis, ed., *Canadian Political Parties: Leaders, Candidates and Organization.* vol. 13 of the research studies for the Royal Commission on Electoral Reform and Party Financing (Toronto: Dundurn Press, 1991), 47.

8 Alan Whitehorn, *Canadian Socialism: Essays on the CCF-NDP* (Toronto: Oxford University Press, 1992), 114.

9 Of the 330,000, approximately 100,000 were constituency members and 230,000 were members through affiliated trade unions. An undetermined amount of double-counting occurs as some (possibly "a few at the most") trade union members are also members of an NDP constituency party. Interview with Fraser Green, NDP federal secretary, 26 January 1995.

10 Some of these issues are examined in Suzanne Hayward and Alan Whitehorn, "Leadership Selection: Which Method?," research paper presented to the Douglas Coldwell Foundation, April 1991.

11 Archer, "Leadership Selection in the NDP," 49.

12 Ibid., 49.

13 "Federal NDP Leadership Selection Committee Report to Federal Executive," 15 December 1994, 8–9, and "New Democratic Party Leadership Rules 1995," 20 January 1995.

14 *Reform Party of Canada Constitution* (amended 1992), s. 6(a).

15 The word is Manning's. His account of the almost-contested selection is given in his book *The New Canada* (Toronto: McClelland and Stewart, 1992), 151–3. The only other candidate for the leadership, Stan Roberts, withdrew from the race at the last moment "alleging irregularities in the registration of delegates and the handling of funds" (153). See also Tom Flanagan, *Waiting for the Wave: The Reform Party and Preston Manning* (Toronto: Stoddart, 1995), chap. 4.

16 Interview with Victor Burstall, 29 June 1994.

17 Interview with Tom Flanagan, former director of Reform's policy, strategy and communications department, 28 June 1994.

18 Constitution of the Liberal Party of Canada (amended 1990), Article 16 (9).

19 "Remarks by the Honorable Iona Campagnolo, PC, President, Liberal Party of Canada, to the first meeting of the President's Committee for Reform, June 1983," in Liberal Party of Canada, "Discussion Paper on Reform of the Liberal Party of Canada" (Ottawa, January 1984), 4.

20 Ibid., 21. Why the commission was surprised about the lack of debate within the party over the leadership selection process is unclear. The party had been in government for all but nine months of the previous twenty years. The last leadership convention held by the party, that at which Pierre Trudeau was chosen, had taken place sixteen years previously. Even though the Liberals were aware of the many well-publicized, controversial episodes that took place during the Conservative leadership campaign of 1983, they had not at that point experienced them first-hand.

21 Iona Campagnolo, as quoted in "Grits questioning conventions," *Globe and Mail*, 23 January 1985, 8.

22 Iona Campagnolo, as quoted in Michael O'Connell, "What Iona thinks about Grit reform," *Halifax Daily News*, 9 November 1985, as found in NA, Liberal Papers, MG 28 IV 3, vol. 1813, no file.

23 The remainder of the respondents said the leader should be chosen either by a convention made up entirely of elected riding delegates (8 per cent) or by a convention made up mostly of elected riding delegates but partly of elected delegates from the party's youth, aboriginal, and women's organizations (16 per cent). See Perlin, "Attitudes of Liberal Convention Delegates Toward Proposals for Reform of the Process of Leadership Selection," in Herman Bakvis, ed., *Canadian Political Parties: Leaders, Candidates and Organization*, vol. 13 of the research studies for the Royal Commission on Electoral Reform and Party Financing (Toronto: Dundurn Press, 1991), 70.

24 Ibid., 73.

25 Ibid., 72.

26 Perlin's findings were examined by the Task Force on Universal Suffrage set up after the 1990 convention. In their interim report, the members of the task force gave the actual figures for some of the categories in which a majority of the delegates found universal suffrage to be the better system but they misleadingly claimed that the delegates "were divided on whether or not universal suffrage or a convention was the better way to attract media attention to the party" and to "recruit young people." See The Reform Commission, the Liberal Party of Canada, "Interim Report of the Task Force on Universal Suffrage," 30 March 1991, 23.

27 A summary of a survey conducted by Insight Canada Research for the Liberal Party of Canada, undated (March 1991?), NA, Liberal Papers, MG 28 IV 3, vol. 1813, no file.

28 Press conference at the conclusion of the Halifax meetings, 11 November 1985.

29 One 1990 option, favoured by 16 per cent of the Liberals, was not included in 1993: "By a convention made up entirely of elected delegates mostly from the riding associations but also including delegates elected by youth, aboriginal people, and women's organizations." See 1993 post-convention survey, N=769.

30 David Roberts, "Tiny federal Tory caucus strives to reinvent party," *Globe and Mail*, 2 September 1994, A4.

31 Ibid., and "Tory leadership convention years away," *StarPhoenix*, 28 February 1994, A9, and Progressive Conservative party video, "New Beginnings," (Ottawa, March 1995).

32 The most thorough debate of the issue of a universal franchise took place in the Leadership Selection Workshop of the November 1985 Halifax Liberal Reform Conference.

33 "Liberals eye PQ contest to get ideas," *Globe and Mail*, 11 September 1985, 5.

34 The Reform Commission, the Liberal Party of Canada, "Universal Suffrage," 6 February 1991, 2.

35 President's Committee on Reform, the Liberal Party of Canada, "Final Report of the President's Committee on Reform of the Liberal Party of Canada," 85.

36 The proposed system was set out in the Liberal Party of Canada, "Road Map to Reform: The Draft Constitutional Amendments of the Reform Commission," Article 16.(13–19), released in December 1991.

37 Joan Bryden, "Opening up the Liberal Party," *Ottawa Citizen*, 22 February 1992, A1.

38 This example is derived from a similar example in a paper prepared by Jack Siegal for the Ontario Liberal party entitled "Leadership Selection Discussion Paper: Combined Direct Vote/Convention Approach," dated January 1991.

39 "Liberals eye PQ contest to get ideas," *Globe and Mail*, 11 September 1985, 5.

40 The Reform Commission, "Interim Report of the Task Force on Universal Suffrage," 8.

41 Ibid., "Agenda for Reform," 19–20.

42 Interview with Charles King, director of communications, the Liberal Party of Canada, 12 November 1993.

43 NA, Liberal Papers, MG 28 IV 3, vol. 1813, no file. Ontario Liberal Party, "Leadership Procedures Review Committee Report," issued 20 March 1991, 5–8.

44 "Leadership Procedures Review Committee Report," 10–11 (emphasis in original).

45 King interview, 12 November 1993.

46 According to Article 16.(2) of the Liberal party's constitution, the ex officio delegation may comprise up to 15 per cent of the total number of delegates eligible to attend the convention. One can only speculate about the likely number of independents that will be present at future Liberal conventions. For their part, the Ontario Liberals in 1992 reportedly elected only 160 independent delegates, about 7 per cent of the total number of riding delegates. See Richard Mackie, "Liberals must rebuild, would-be leaders say," *Globe and Mail*, 17 January 1992, A6. It is almost certain that the organizational prowess of candidates' campaign organizations will ensure that very few truly independent members will succeed in getting elected as delegates.

CHAPTER 13

1 The distinctions are to be found in two of the leading works on representation: A.H. Birch, *Representation* (Toronto: Macmillan, 1972), 55, and

Hanna Fenichel Pitkin, *The Concept of Representation* (Berkeley: University of California Press, 1972).

2 In his American Political Science Association presidential address, Samuel Beer drew a similar distinction between competing forces in American federalism. See his "Federalism, Nationalism and Democracy in America," *APSR*, 72 (March 1978), 9–21.

3 Asked "If you did make a commitment to vote for your first ballot choice, to whom did you make that commitment?" the respective Conservative 1983 and Liberal 1984 responses were, in percentages: the candidate himself (58 and 52); the local party organization (17 and 21); campus or other club (5 and 2); provincial party organization (3 and 4); MP (3 and 9); member of a national organization (3 and 3); and other (11 and 9). See Post-Convention Questionnaire for Delegates to the 1983 Progressive Conservative and 1984 Liberal Leadership Conventions," principal investigator: George Perlin. A similar question was not asked of delegates in 1990 and 1993.

4 In 1989 Barrett had good support, but also considerable opposition, in his home province, British Columbia. See Archer, "Leadership Selection in the New Democratic Party" in Herman Bakvis, ed., *Canadian Political Parties: Leaders, Candidates and Organization*, vol. 13 of the research studies for the Royal Commission on Electoral Reform and Party Financing (Toronto: Dundurn Press, 1991), table 1:13.

5 On the first ballot in 1967 Stanfield won 95 per cent of the Nova Scotia delegates' votes and Roblin 82 per cent of the Manitoba votes. See George Perlin, *The Tory Syndrome: Leadership Politics in the Progressive Conservative Party* (Montreal: McGill-Queen's University Press, 1980), 142.

6 John C. Courtney and George Perlin, "The Role of Conventions in the Representation and Accommodation of Regional Cleavages," in Perlin, ed., *Party Democracy in Canada: The Politics of National Party Conventions* (Scarborough: Prentice-Hall of Canada, 1988), 139. Data on reasons for delegate voting preferences were not tabulated in the same categories in the 1990 and 1993 Perlin surveys.

7 Another factor determining the impact of region on voting choice is candidates' organizational networks. Candidates have different success rates in contacting delegates to ask for support, which is a direct consequence of the strength of a candidate's regional or provincial organization. In both the Liberal 1983 and Conservative 1984 conventions there was an association between this factor and first ballot support. Ibid., 124–44.

8 In 1968, for example, the first ballot support for Greene, MacEachen, Kierans, Hellyer, and Martin exceeded (in some cases by a factor of three or four to one) their true preference level, whereas for Trudeau, Turner, and Winters (the three contestants on the fourth and final ballot) it fell short of their true preference level. Trudeau was the candidate with the greatest spread. His first ballot vote trailed his true preference level by close to 15

percentage points. Not until the third ballot were the two levels equal. See Robert Krause and Lawrence LeDuc, "Voting Behaviour and Electoral Strategies in the Progressive Conservative Leadership Convention of 1976," *CJPS* 12 (March 1979), 104–5.

9 Data for 1968 are from Lawrence LeDuc, "Party Decision-Making: Some Empirical Observations on the Leadership Selection Process," *CJPS* 4 (March 1971), 100 and 103, and for 1976 from Krause and LeDuc, "Voting Behaviour and Electoral Strategies," 104 and 105.

10 For the 9 per cent who did not opt for their true preference, the principal reasons given for supporting some other candidate included having changed their mind (21 per cent) and stating that their true first preference was not running (13 per cent). The distribution of true leadership preferences and actual candidate support in 1990 shows that the minor candidates had only slightly larger first ballot support and the two principal candidates had only slightly smaller first ballot support than their respective levels of true preference. The spread ranged from +0.9 per cent for Wappel to -1.3 per cent for Chrétien. See data computed from Perlin survey of 1990 Liberal convention, questions number D19, D20, and D21 (N of 1,300/1,435 responding, or 90.6 per cent). N=91 respondents to question D21 asking why they did not vote for their first preference. The 13 per cent figure combined two responses: Lloyd Axworthy not running and Number One choice not running.

11 Richard Johnston, "The Final Choice: Its Social, Organizational and Ideological Bases," in Perlin, ed., *Party Democracy in Canada*, 220.

12 NA, W.L.M.King Diaries, diary entry for 27 February 1934. For more on King as a conciliator and as an accommodative leader see my "Prime Ministerial Character: An Examination of Mackenzie King's Political Leadership," *CJPS* 9 (March 1976), 77–100.

13 Mulroney's success in fashioning a winning coalition in 1984 is examined in my "Reinventing the Brokerage Wheel: The Tory Success in 1984," in Howard R. Penniman, ed., *Canada at the Polls 1984* (Washington, DC American Enterprise Institute for Public Policy Research, 1988), 190–208.

14 Daniel Latouche, "Universal Democracy and Effective Leadership: Lessons from the Parti Québécois Experience," in R. Kenneth Carty, Lynda Erickson, and Donald E. Blake, eds., *Leaders and Parties in Canadian Politics: Experiences of the Provinces* (Toronto: Harcourt Brace Jovanovich, 1992), 200.

15 Henry E. Brady and Richard Johnston, "Conventions Versus Primaries: A Canadian-American Comparison," in Perlin, ed., *Party Democracy in Canada*, 245.

16 Agar Adamson, Bruce Beaton, and Ian Stewart, "Pressing the Right Buttons: The Nova Scotia Liberals and Tele-Democracy," paper presented to the annual meeting of the CPSA, Ottawa, June 1993, 12.

17 The percentages for 1987 and 1993 respectively are: member for > 5 years
   [> 6 years in 1993 survey] 56.7 and 31.1; voted Liberal federally, 94.3 and
   65.0; and previously active in another provincial party 6.7 and 19.2.
   Donald E. Blake and R. Kenneth Carty, "Televoting for the Leader of the
   British Columbia Liberal Party: The Leadership Contest of 1993," paper
   presented to the annual meeting of the CPSA, Calgary, June 1994, 14–15.
   The BC Liberals may not be the most typical of provincial parties. They had
   hardly existed in any important way for close to forty years at that point.
18 Keith Archer and Margaret Hunziker, "Leadership Selection in Alberta:
   The 1985 Progressive Conservative Leadership Convention," in Carty,
   Erickson, and Blake, eds., *Leaders and Parties in Canadian Politics*, 86–92.
19 David Stewart, "Grassroots Democracy and Federal Party Membership: The
   1992 Alberta Progressive Conservative Leadership Election," paper presented to the annual meeting of the Atlantic Provinces Political Science Association, Antigonish, October 1993, 3–4. Stewart's post-leadership
   selection study of Alberta Conservatives found that several months after
   Klein's selection the share of those who took part in the selection who had
   decided by that point *not* to vote Tory in the next provincial election had
   climbed to one-third. The principal factor that subsequently led the vast
   majority of them to vote Conservative in the election was the Klein government's pre-election decision to end a variety of perks for provincial MLAs.
   (Stewart, information provided the author, 28 August 1994.)
20 Stewart, "Grassroots Democracy," 4; Adamson, Beaton, and Stewart, "Pressing the Right Buttons," 17; and Blake and Carty, "Televoting for the
   Leader," 12.
21 A UMV system, like the traditional convention, would be open to organizational manipulation and abuse. Memberships could still be purchased by
   candidate organizers for "instant" recruits; information could still be with-
   held or distorted for partisan advantage; and other problems that surfaced in the national conventions of the 1970s and 1980s could still
   persist, albeit under a different guise. For an article generally favourable
   to a UMV system and to the proposition that "the 1992 Nova Scotia Liberal
   Leadership Convention represent[ed] both a quantitative and qualitative
   change in the numbers and nature of the participants," see Leonard
   Preyra, "Tele-Conventions and Party Democracy: The 1992 Nova Scotia
   Liberal Leadership Convention," *Canadian Parliamentary Review* 16
   (Winter 1993–4), 6.
22 Could this be true as well at the provincial level? Possibly, although in some
   provinces the scale of the political units themselves and the relatively less
   diverse social mix of their populations would conceivably lessen its likelihood. In the most extreme example, as the results in the Tory leadership
   contests of Prince Edward Island in 1988 and 1990 showed when more
   took part in the convention than in the universal vote, it was no exaggera-

tion to say that to hold a provincial leadership convention was in fact to hold *more than* a universal ballot! When the Nova Scotia Liberals held their leadership televote in 1992, at which party members could, if they had so chosen, attend and vote at the day-long "convention" in Halifax, they were doing so in a province in which the most distant delegates lived a maximum of four hours by car from Halifax. The Manitoba Liberal scheme of 1993 was designed to allow any party members who wished to participate to do so at polling stations no more than a day's return drive from their homes. These are far removed from the distances participants in national party leadership votes would have to travel, and they raise questions about the "non-transferability" of institutions developed for basically micro-systems to the macro-level.

23 Nelson W. Polsby, *Consequences of Party Reform* (Toronto: Oxford University Press, 1983), 65.

24 Of the vast literature on reform of the American presidential nominating process, see James W. Caesar, *Presidential Selection: Theory and Development* (Princeton: Princeton University Press, 1979), esp. 260–303; James W. Davis, *National Conventions in An Age of Party Reform* (Westport, Conn.: Greenwood Press, 1983); James I. Lengle, *Representation and Presidential Primaries: The Democratic Party in the Post-Reform Era* (Westport, Conn.: Greenwood Press, 1981); Polsby, *Consequences of Party Reform*, esp. 64–75; Austin Ranney, "Changing the Rules of the Nominating Game," in James David Barber, ed., *Choosing the President* (Toronto: Prentice-Hall of Canada, 1974), 71–93; and Byron E. Shafer, *Bifurcated Politics: Evolution and Reform in the National Party Convention* (Cambridge, Mass: Harvard University Press, 1988), 290–325.

25 Herb Asher, "The Three Campaigns for President," in Alexander Heard and Michael Nelson, eds., *Presidential Selection* (Durham: Duke University Press, 1987), 216–46, esp. 221–4; Kirkpatrick, 328–9; Lengle, 110; Schafer, 292–3 and 341; and Austen Ranney, "Turnout and Representation in Presidential Primary Elections," *APSR* 66 (March 1972), 21–37.

26 Participation by retired individuals in the Nova Scotia telephone leadership selection system jumped from 6.7 per cent in the 1986 convention to 22.9 per cent in 1992. Students dropped from 14.5 to 5.7 per cent. Female participation increased slightly over the previous convention (from 40 to 42.3 per cent). According to the authors, whatever change there may have been in income levels was small. See Adamson, Beaton, and Stewart, "Pressing the Right Buttons," tables 2 and 16. In British Columbia males and under-55-year-olds made up 60.9 and 46.1 per cent of the party membership and 57.9 and 41 per cent of the televoters respectively. University-educated and high-income respondents made up 48.1 and 33.8 per cent of the party membership and 50.1 and 36.5 per cent of the televoters respectively. In 1987 the percentage figures for participants who were male, under fifty-

five, university-educated and high-income were 66.3, 42.5, 61.4, and 38.7 per cent. See Blake and Carty, "Televoting for the Leader," 14.

27 Ibid., 15.

28 Heard and Nelson, eds., *Presidential Selection*; Lengle, 110–17, and Kirkpatrick, 328–31. It is Lengle's conclusion that "only the illusion of control and responsiveness is present in presidential primaries and participatory conventions, an illusion perpetuated by the beneficiaries of those systems" (113).

Bibliography

ABBREVIATIONS

APSR *American Political Science Review*

AJPS *American Journal of Political Science*

CHR *Canadian Historical Review*

CJEPS *Canadian Journal of Economics and Political Science*

CJPS *Canadian Journal of Political Science*

CPSA Canadian Political Science Association

JCS *Journal of Canadian Studies*

JP *Journal of Politics*

I. POLITICAL LEADERSHIP (GENERAL)

Bunce, Valerie. *Do New Leaders Make a Difference?* Princeton: Princeton University Press, 1981.

Burns, James MacGregor. "A Note on the Study of Political Leadership," *Roosevelt: The Lion and the Fox*. New York: Harcourt, Brace and World, 1956, 481–7.

– *Leadership*. New York: Harper and Row, 1978.

Dion, Leon. "The Concept of Political Leadership: An Analysis," *CJPS* 1 (March 1968), 2–17.

Edinger, Lewis J., ed. *Political Leadership in Industrialized Societies*. New York: John Wiley and Sons, 1967.

– "Political Science and Political Biography: Reflections on the Study of Leadership," *JP* 26 (May and August 1964), 423–39 and 648–76.

– "Approaches to the Comparative Analysis of Political Leadership," *Review of Politics* (Fall 1990), 509–23.

Gibb, Cecil A. "Leadership," *The Handbook of Social Psychology.* Vol. IV, 2nd ed. Edited by Gardner Lindzey and Elliot Aronson. Don Mills: Addison-Wesley Publishing, 1969, 205–82.

Gouldner, Alvin W. *Studies in Leadership.* New York: Harper and Brothers, 1950.

Lasswell, Harold D. *Psychopathology and Politics.* New York: The Viking Press, 1960.

Marvick, Dwaine, ed. *Political Decision-Makers: Recruitment and Performance.* Glencoe, Illinois: Free Press, 1961.

Paige, Glenn D. *The Scientific Study of Political Leadership.* New York: Free Press, 1977.

"Philosophers and Kings: Studies in Leadership," *Daedalus* 97 (Summer 1968), 683–1082.

Prewitt, Kenneth. "Political Socialization and Leadership Selection," *Annals of the American Academy of Political and Social Science* 361 (September 1965), 109–10.

–, and Heinz Eulau. "Social Bias in Leadership Selection, Political Recruitment and Electoral Context," *JP* 32 (May 1971), 293–315.

Punnett, R.M. *Selecting the Party Leader: Britain in Comparative Perspective.* London: Harvester Wheatsheaf, 1992.

Seligman, Lester G. "The Study of Political Leadership," *Political Behavior: A Reader in Theory and Research.* Edited by Heinz Eulau, Samuel J. Eldersveld, and Morris Janowitz. Glencoe: Free Press, 1956, 177–83.

Tucker, Robert C. "The Theory of Charismatic Leadership," *Daedalus* 97 (Summer 1968), 731–56.

Weber, Max. *The Theory of Social and Economic Organization.* Toronto: Collier-Macmillan Canada, 1964.

Weller, Patrick. *First Among Equals: Prime Ministers in Westminster Systems.* Sydney: George Allen & Unwin, 1985.

– "Party Rules and the Dismissal of Prime Ministers: Comparative Perspectives from Britain, Canada and Australia," *Parliamentary Affairs* 47 (January 1994), 133–43.

II. LEADERSHIP SELECTION AND PARTY CONVENTIONS IN CANADA (GENERAL)

Bakvis, Herman, ed. *Canadian Political Parties: Leaders, Candidates and Organization.* Vol. 13 of the research studies for the Royal Commission on Electoral Reform and Party Financing. Toronto: Dundurn Press, 1991.

Bashevkin, Sylvia. "Women's Participation in Political Parties," *Women in Canadian Politics: Toward Equity in Representation.* Vol. 6 of the research studies for the Royal Commission on Electoral Reform and Party Financing. Edited by Kathy Megyery. Toronto: Dundurn Press, 1991, 61–80.

Blais, André, and Elizabeth Gidengil, *Making Representative Democracy Work: The Views of Canadians.* Vol. 17 of the research studies for the Royal Commission on Electoral Reform and Party Financing. Toronto: Dundurn Press, 1991.

Blake, Donald E., R.K. Carty, and Lynda Erickson. "Ratification or Repudiation: Social Credit Leadership Selection in British Columbia," *CJPS* 21 (September 1988), 513–37.

Brodie, Janine. "The Gender Factor and National Leadership Conventions in Canada," *Party Democracy in Canada: The Politics of National Party Conventions.* Edited by George Perlin. Scarborough: Prentice-Hall Canada, 1988, 172–87.

–, and Celia Chandler. "Women and the Electoral Process in Canada," *Women in Canadian Politics: Toward Equity in Representation.* Vol. 6 of the research studies for the Royal Commission on Electoral Reform and Party Financing. Edited by Kathy Megyery. Toronto: Dundurn Press, 1991, 3–60.

Carty, R.K. "Campaigning in the Trenches: The Transformation of Constituency Politics," *Party Democracy in Canada: The Politics of National Party Conventions.* Edited by George Perlin. Scarborough: Prentice-Hall Canada, 1988, 84–96.

– *Canadian Political Parties in the Constituencies.* Vol. 23 of the research studies for the Royal Commission on Electoral Reform and Party Financing. Toronto: Dundurn Press, 1991.

–, ed. *Canadian Political Party Systems: A Reader.* Toronto: Broadview Press, 1992.

– "Choosing New Party Leaders: The Progressive Conservatives in 1983, the Liberals in 1984," *Canada at the Polls, 1984.* Edited by Howard Penniman. Washington: American Enterprise Institute for Public Policy Research, 1988, 55–78.

–, and Lynda Erickson. "Candidate Nomination in Canada's National Political Parties," *Canadian Political Parties: Leaders, Candidates and Organization.* Vol. 13 of the research studies for the Royal Commission on Electoral Reform and Party Financing. Edited by Herman Bakvis. Toronto: Dundurn Press, 1991, 97–190.

–, Lynda Erickson and Donald E. Blake. *Leaders and Parties in Canadian Politics: Experiences of the Provinces.* Toronto: Harcourt Brace Jovanovich, 1992.

Chari, Raj. "A Leadership Selection Index for Multi-Ballot Party Conventions." MA thesis, Department of Political Studies, University of Saskatchewan, 1993.

Clarke, Harold, Jane Jenson, Lawrence LeDuc, and Jon H. Pammett. *Political Choice in Canada.* Toronto: McGraw-Hill Ryerson, 1979.

Courtney, John C. *The Selection of National Party Leaders in Canada.* Toronto: Macmillan, 1973.

– "Has the Canadian Prime Minister Become 'Presidentialized'?" *Presidential Studies Quarterly* 14 (Spring 1984), 238–41.

– "Leadership Conventions in Canada: A Comment," *Presidential Studies Quarterly* 11 (Winter 1981), 44–7.

– "Leadership Conventions and the Development of the National Political Community in Canada," *National Politics and Community in Canada.* Edited by R. Kenneth Carty and W. Peter Ward. Vancouver: University of British Columbia Press, 1986, 94–111.

– "National Leadership Conventions in Canada," *The New Canadian Encyclopedia.* 2nd ed. Edmonton: Hurtig, 1988, 1193.

– "The Defeat of the Clark Government: The Dissolution of Parliament, Leadership Conventions, and the Calling of Elections in Canada," *JCS* 17 (Summer 1982), 82–90.

– "The Morning After: Delegate Accountability," *Parliamentary Government* 4, no. 2 (1983), 8–9, and 15.

–, and George Perlin. "The Role of Conventions in the Representation and Accommodation of Regional Cleavages," *Party Democracy in Canada: The Politics of National Party Conventions.* Edited by George Perlin. Scarborough: Prentice-Hall Canada, 1988, 124–44.

English, John. "The 'French Lieutenant' in Ottawa," *National Politics and Community in Canada.* Edited by R. Kenneth Carty and W. Peter Ward. Vancouver: University of British Columbia Press, 1986, 184–200.

Goldfarb, Martin, and Thomas Axworthy. *Marching to a Different Drummer: An Essay on the Liberals and Conservatives in Convention.* Toronto: Stoddart, 1988.

Hockin, Thomas A. ed. *Apex of Power: The Prime Minister and Political Leadership in Canada.* Toronto: Prentice-Hall Canada, 1971.

Johnston, Richard. "The Final Choice: Its Social, Organizational, and Ideological Bases," *Party Democracy in Canada: The Politics of National Party Conventions.* Edited by George Perlin. Scarborough: Prentice-Hall Canada, 1988, 204–42.

–, André Blais, Henry E. Brady, and Jean Crête. *Letting the People Decide: Dynamics of a Canadian Election.* Montreal: McGill-Queen's University Press, 1992.

Jones, Elwood H. "Ephemeral Compromise: The Great Reform Convention Revisited," *JCS* 3 (February 1968), 21–8.

Laschinger, John, and Geoffrey Stevens. *Leaders and Lesser Mortals: Backroom Politics in Canada.* Toronto: Key Porter, 1992.

Lederle, John W. "National Party Conventions: Canada Shows the Way," *Southwestern Social Science Quarterly* 25 (September 1944), 118–33.

– "The National Organization of the Liberal and Conservative Parties in Canada." Ph.D. dissertation, Department of Political Science, University of Michigan, 1942.

Leduc, Lawrence. "Leaders and Voters: The Public Images of Canadian Po-
litical Leaders," *Leaders and Leadership in Canada.* Edited by Maureen
Mancuso, Richard G. Price, and Ronald Wagenberg. Toronto: Oxford
University Press, 1994, 53–74.

Lele, J., G. Perlin, and H. Thorburn. "Leadership Conventions in Canada: The
Form and Substance of Participatory Politics," *Social Space: Canadian Perspectives.* Edited by D.I. Davies and Kathleen Herman. Toronto: New Press,
1971, 205–13.

MacIvor, Heather. "The Leadership Convention: An Institution under Stress,"
Leaders and Leadership in Canada. Edited by Maureen Mancuso, Richard G.
Price, and Ronald Wagenberg. Toronto: Oxford University Press, 1994, 13–
27.

Mancuso, Maureen, Richard G. Price, and Ronald Wagenberg, eds. *Leaders and
Leadership in Canada.* Toronto: Oxford University Press, 1994.

McFadden, David. "Choosing the Party Leader: Is There a Better Way?" *Canadian Parliamentary Review* 9 (Summer 1986), 22–4.

Muller, Steven. "The Canadian Prime Ministers, 1867–1948: An Essay on
Democratic Leadership." Ph.D. dissertation, Department of Political Science, Cornell University, 1958.

Ontario Commission on Election Contributions and Expenses. *Political Financing: Studies on Election Spending Limits and Party Leadership Campaigns.* Toronto, 1986.

Pal, Leslie A., and David Taras. *Prime Ministers and Premiers: Political Leadership
and Public Policy in Canada.* Scarborough: Prentice-Hall Canada, 1988.

Perlin, George. *Party Democracy in Canada: The Politics of National Party Conventions.* Scarborough: Prentice-Hall Canada, 1988.

– "Leadership Selection in the P.C. and Liberal Parties: Assessing the Need for
Reform," *Party Politics in Canada,* 6th edition. Edited by Hugh G. Thorburn.
Scarborough: Prentice-Hall Canada, 1991, 202–20.

Pickersgill, J.W. *The Liberal Party.* Toronto: McClelland and Stewart, 1962.

Punnett, R.M. "Selection of Party Leaders: A Canadian Example," *Journal of
Commonwealth Political Studies* 8 (March 1970), 54–69.

Royal Commission on Electoral Reform and Party Financing. *Reforming Electoral Democracy.* Vol. I. Ottawa, 1991.

Sandwell, B.K. "The Convention System in Politics," *Queen's Quarterly* 55
(Autumn 1948–49), 343–49.

Smiley, D.V. "The National Party Leadership Convention in Canada: A
Preliminary Analysis," *CJPS* 1 (December 1968), 373–97.

Stanbury, W.T. *Money in Politics: Financing Federal Parties and Candidates in
Canada.* Vol. I of the research studies for the Royal Commssion on Electoral
Reform and Party Financing. Toronto: Dundurn Press, 1991.

Wearing, Joseph. "The High Cost of High Tech: Financing the Modern Leadership Campaign," *Party Democracy in Canada: The Politics of National Party*

Conventions. Edited by George Perlin. Scarborough: Prentice-Hall Canada, 1988, 72–83.

III. LEADERSHIP IN CANADA: BIOGRAPHICAL STUDIES

Beal, John R. *The Pearson Phenomenon.* Toronto: Longmans, 1964.

Borden, Henry. *Robert Laird Borden: His Memoirs.* 2 vols. Toronto: Macmillan, 1938.

Brown, Robert Craig. *Robert Laird Borden: A Biography. Volume I: 1854–1914.* Toronto: Macmillan of Canada, 1975; *Robert Laird Borden: A Biography. Volume II: 1914–1937.* Toronto: Macmillan of Canada, 1980.

Buckingham, William, and Hon. George W. Ross. *The Hon. Alexander Mackenzie: His Life and Times.* Toronto: Rose Publishing Company, 1892.

Cahill, Jack. *John Turner: The Long Run.* Toronto: McClelland and Stewart, 1984.

Chrétien, Jean. *Straight from the Heart.* Rev. ed. Toronto: Key Porter Books, 1994.

Clarkson, Stephen, and Christina McCall. *Trudeau and Our Times. Volume I: The Magnificent Obsession.* Toronto: McClelland and Stewart Inc., 1990.

Courtney, John C. "Prime Ministerial Character: An Examination of Mackenzie King's Political Leadership," *CJPS* 9 (March 1976), 77–100. Reprinted in *Mackenzie King: Widening the Debate.* Edited by John English and J.O. Stubbs. Toronto: Macmillan, 1978, 55–88.

– " 'An Alternative View' of Mackenzie King: A Rejoinder," *CJPS* 9 (June 1976), 308–9.

Creighton, Donald. *John A. Macdonald.* 2 vols. Toronto: Macmillan, 1952 and 1955.

Davey, Keith. *The Rainmaker: A Passion for Politics.* Toronto: Stoddart, 1986.

Dawson, R. MacGregor. *William Lyon Mackenzie King: A Political Biography, 1874–1923.* Toronto: University of Toronto Press, 1958.

Diefenbaker, John G. *One Canada: Memoirs of the Right Honourable John G. Diefenbaker: The Crusading Years.* Toronto: Macmillan, 1975; *One Canada: The Years of Achievement, 1956–62.* Toronto: Macmillan, 1976; and *One Canada: The Tumultuous Years, 1962–67.* Toronto: Macmillan, 1977.

Esberey, Joy E. *Knight of the Holy Spirit: A Study of William Lyon Mackenzie King.* Toronto: University of Toronto Press, 1980.

– "Personality and Politics: A New Look at the King-Byng Dispute," *CJPS* 6 (March 1973), 37–55.

– "Prime Ministerial Character: An Alternative View," *CJPS* 9 (March 1976), 101–6.

Ferns, H.S., and B. Ostry. *The Age of Mackenzie King: The Rise of the Leader.* London: William Heinemann, 1955.

Fife, Robert. *Kim Campbell: The Making of a Politician.* Toronto: HarperCollins Publishers, 1993.

Flanagan, Tom. *Waiting for the Wave: The Reform Party and Preston Manning.* Toronto: Stoddart, 1995.

Goodman, Eddie. *Life of the Party: The Memoirs of Eddie Goodman.* Toronto: Key Porter Books, 1988.

Gordon, Walter. *A Political Memoir.* Toronto: McClelland and Stewart, 1977.

Graham, Roger. *Arthur Meighen.* 3 vols. Toronto: Clarke, Irwin and Company, 1960, 1963, and 1965.

Graham, Ron. *One-Eyed Kings: Promise and Illusion in Canadian Politics.* Toronto: Collins, 1986.

Haaland, J.B. "An Examination of Personality in Canadian Politics: A Study of the Career of Arthur Meighen." MA thesis, Department of Political Studies, University of Saskatchewan, 1977.

Hardy, H. Reginald. *Mackenzie King of Canada.* London: Oxford University Press, 1949.

Harkin, W.A., ed. *Political Reminiscences of the Rt. Hon. Sir Charles Tupper.* London: Constable and Co., 1914.

Hopkins, J. Castell. *Life and Work of the Rt. Hon. Sir John Thompson.* Toronto: United Publishing Houses, 1895.

Humphreys, David L. *Joe Clark: A Portrait.* Ottawa: Deneau and Greenberg, 1978.

Hutchinson, Bruce. *The Incredible Canadian: A Portrait of Mackenzie King.* London: Longmans, Green and Co., 1953.

Lewis, David. *The Good Fight: Political Memoirs 1909–1958.* Toronto: Macmillan, 1981.

Longley, J.W. *Sir Charles Tupper.* Toronto: Makers of Canada, 1916.

MacDonald, L. Ian. *Mulroney: The Making of a Prime Minister.* Toronto: McClelland and Stewart, 1984.

MacLeod, Thomas H., and Ian MacLeod. *Tommy Douglas: The Road to Jerusalem.* Edmonton: Hurtig, 1987.

Manning, Preston. *The New Canada.* Toronto: McClelland and Stewart, 1992.

Martin, Paul. *A Very Public Life.* 2 vols. Ottawa: Deneau, 1983.

McGregor, F.A. *The Fall and Rise of Mackenzie King: 1911–1919.* Toronto: Macmillan, 1962.

McLaughlin, Audrey. *A Woman's Place: My Life and Politics.* Toronto: MacFarlane, Walter & Ross, 1992.

McNaught, Kenneth. *A Prophet in Politics: A Biography of J.S. Woodsworth.* Toronto: University of Toronto Press, 1959.

Murphy, Rae, Robert Chodos, and Nick Auf der Maur. *Brian Mulroney: The Boy from Baie Comeau.* Toronto: Lorimer, 1984.

Neatby, H. Blair. *William Lyon Mackenzie King, 1924–1932: The Lonely Heights.* Toronto: University of Toronto Press, 1963.

Peacock, Donald. *Journey to Power.* Toronto: The Ryerson Press, 1968.

Pearson, Lester B. *Mike: The Memoirs of the Rt. Hon. Lester B. Pearson.* 3 vols. Toronto: University of Toronto Press, 1972, 1973, and 1975.

Pickersgill, J.W. *The Mackenzie King Record, 1939–1944.* Toronto: University of Toronto Press, 1960.

–, and D.F. Forster. *The Mackenzie King Record, 1944–1945, 1945–1946, 1947–1948.* Vols 2–4. Toronto: University of Toronto Press, 1968 and 1970.

Pope, Joseph. *Memoirs of the Right Honourable Sir John Alexander Macdonald.* 2 vols. Ottawa: J. Durie and Son, 1894.

– *Correspondence of Sir John Macdonald.* Toronto: Oxford University Press, n.d.

Radwanski, George. *Trudeau.* Toronto: Macmillan, 1978.

Saunders, E.M. *The Life and Letters of Rt. Hon. Sir Charles Tupper.* London: Cassell and Company, 1916.

Schull, Joseph. *Laurier: The First Canadian.* Toronto: Oxford University Press, 1965.

Sharpe, Sydney, and Don Braid. *Storming Babylon: Preston Manning and the Rise of the Reform Party.* Toronto: Key Porter Books, 1992.

Sigurdson, Richard. "Preston Manning and the Politics of Postmodernism in Canada," *CJPS* 27 (June 1994), 249–76.

Simpson, Jeffrey. "Preston Manning: the Common Sense of the Common People," *Faultlines: Struggling for a Canadian Vision.* Toronto: HarperCollins Publishers, 1993, 107–41.

Skelton, O.D. *Life and Letters of Sir Wilfrid Laurier.* 2 vols. Toronto: Oxford University Press, 1921.

Steed, Judy. *Ed Broadbent: The Pursuit of Power.* Markham: Penguin, 1988.

Stevens, Geoffrey. *Stanfield.* Toronto: McClelland and Stewart, 1973.

Stursberg, Peter. *Diefenbaker: Leadership Gained 1956–62.* Toronto: University of Toronto Press, 1975.

– *Diefenbaker: Leadership Lost 1962–67.* Toronto: University of Toronto Press, 1976.

– *Lester Pearson and the Dream of Unity.* Toronto: Doubleday, 1978.

Thomson, Dale C. *Alexander Mackenzie: Clear Grit.* Toronto: Macmillan, 1960.

– *Louis St. Laurent: Canadian.* Toronto: Macmillan, 1967.

Trudeau, Pierre Elliott. *Memoirs.* Toronto: McClelland and Stewart, 1993.

Van Dusen, Thomas. *The Chief.* New York: McGraw-Hill, 1968.

Waite, P.B. *The Man from Halifax: Sir John Thompson.* Toronto: University of Toronto Press, 1985.

Watkins, Ernest. *R.B. Bennett.* London: Secker and Warburg, 1963.

Weston, Greg. *Reign of Error: The Inside Story of John Turner's Troubled Leadership.* Toronto: McGraw-Hill Ryerson, 1988.

Willison, Sir John S. *Sir Wilfrid Laurier and the Liberal Party: A Political History.* 2 vols. Toronto: George N. Morang and Company, 1903.

IV. LEADERSHIP SELECTION IN THE CONSERVATIVE PARTY

Balloons and Ballots. Toronto: Telegram Publishing, 1967.

Bell, Ruth M. "Conservative Party National Conventions, 1927–1956." MA thesis, Department of Political Science, Carleton University, 1965.

Brown, Patrick, Roger Chodos, and Rae Murphy. *Winners, Losers: The 1976 Tory Leadership Convention.* Toronto: Lorimer, 1976.

Camp, Dalton. *Gentlemen, Players and Politicians.* Toronto: McClelland and Stewart, 1970.

Churchill, Gordon. "*Deux Nations* or One Canada: John Diefenbaker at the 1967 Conservative Convention," *CHR* 64 (December 1983), 597–604.

Clark, Lovell C. "The Conservative Party in the 1890s," *Report of the Canadian Historical Association* (1961), 58–74.

– "Macdonald's Conservative Successors, 1891–1896," *Character and Circumstance: Essays in Honour of Donald Grant Creighton.* Edited by John S. Moir. Toronto: Macmillan, 1970, 143–62.

Courtney, John C, "Reinventing the Brokerage Wheel: The Tory Success of 1984," *Canada at the Polls, 1984.* Edited by Howard Penniman. Washington: American Enterprise Institute for Public Policy Research, 1988, 190–208.

Coates, Robert C. *The Night of the Knives.* Fredericton: Brunswick Press, 1969.

Granatstein, J.L. *The Politics of Survival: The Conservative Party of Canada, 1939–1945.* Toronto: University of Toronto Press, 1967.

Johnston, James. *The Party's Over.* Don Mills: Longmans, 1971.

Krause, Robert, and Lawrence LeDuc. "Voting Behaviour and Electoral Strategies in the Progressive Conservative Leadership Convention of 1976," *CJPS* 12 (March 1979), 97–135.

Lind, Philip B. "Davie Fulton's Campaign for Leadership – 1967." MA thesis, Department of Political Science, University of Rochester, 1968.

MacNicol, John R. *National Liberal-Conservative Convention Held at Winnipeg, Manitoba, October 10 to 12, 1927.* Toronto: Southam Press, 1930.

Martin, Patrick, Allan Gregg, and George Perlin. *Contenders: The Tory Quest for Power.* Toronto: Prentice-Hall, 1983.

McLaughlin, David. *Poisoned Chalice: The Last Campaign of the Progressive Conservative Party?* Toronto: Dundurn, 1994.

Perlin, George C. *The Tory Syndrome: Leadership Politics in the Progressive Conservative Party.* Montreal: McGill-Queen's University Press, 1980.

Punnett, R.W. "Leadership Selection in Opposition: The Progressive Conservative Party in Canada," *Australian Journal of Politics and History* 17 (August 1971), 188–201.

Saywell, John T. "The Crown and the Politicians: The Canadian Succession Question: 1891–1896," *CHR* 37 (September 1967), 273–6.

Vineberg, Michael. "The Progressive Conservative Leadership Convention of 1967." MA thesis, Department of Political Science, McGill University, 1968.

Wearing, Joseph. "A Convention for Professionals: The PCs in Toronto," *JCS* 2 (November 1967), 3–16.

Williams, John R. *The Conservative Party in Canada: 1920–1949*. Durham: Duke University Press, 1956.

V. LEADERSHIP SELECTION IN THE LIBERAL PARTY

Banks, Margaret A. "The Change in Liberal Party Leadership, 1887," *CHR* 38 (June 1957), 109–28.

Brown, George W. "The Grit Party and the Great Reform Convention of 1859," *CHR* 16 (September 1935), 245–65.

Courtney, John C. "Norman Ward and C.G. Power on the 1958 Liberal Leadership Convention," *Queen's Quarterly* 97 (Autumn 1990), 457–73.

Hanson, Lawrence. "Contesting the Leadership at the Grassroots: The Liberals in 1990," *Canadian Political Party Systems: A Reader.* Edited by R.K. Carty. Toronto: Broadview Press, 1992, 426–30.

Iglauer, Elizabeth. "Profiles: Prime Minister/Premier Ministre," *New Yorker,* 5 July, 1969, 36.

Jones, Elwood H. "Ephemeral Compromise: The Great Reform Convention," *JCS* 3 (February 1968), 21–8.

Lederle, John W. "The Liberal Convention of 1893," *CJEPS* 16 (February 1950), 42–52.

– "The Liberal Convention of 1919 and the Selection of Mackenzie King," *Dalhousie Review* 27 (April 1947), 85–92.

Leduc, Lawrence. "Party Decision-Making: Some Empirical Observations on the Leadership Selection Process," *CJPS* 4 (March 1971), 97–118.

– "The Leadership Selection Process in Canadian Political Parties: A Case Study." Ph.D. dissertation, Department of Political Science, University of Michigan, 1970.

"The Liberal Leadership." *The Round Table* 9 (June 1919), 593–4.

McCall-Newman, Christina. *Grits: An Intimate Portrait of the Liberal Party.* Toronto: Macmillan, 1982.

The National Liberal Convention, Ottawa, August 5, 6, 7, 1919: The Story of the Convention and the Report of its Proceedings. Ottawa: n.p., n.d.

Official Report of the Liberal Convention Held in Response to the Call of Hon. Wilfrid Laurier, Leader of the Liberal Party of the Dominion of Canada. Toronto: Budget Printing and Publishing Co., 1893.

Perlin, George. "Attitudes of Liberal Convention Delegates Toward Proposals for Reform of the Process of Leadership Selection," *Canadian Political*

Parties: Leaders, Candidates and Organization. Vol. 13 of the research studies for the Royal Commission on Electoral Reform and Party Financing. Edited by Herman Bakvis. Toronto: Dundurn Press, 1991, 57–96.

Power, C.G. *A Party Politician: The Memoirs of Chubby Power.* Edited by Norman Ward. Toronto: Macmillan, 1966.

Quinn, Herbert F. "The Third National Convention of the Liberal Party," *CJEPS* 17 (May 1951), 228–33.

Regenstreif, Peter. "Note on the 'Alternation' of French and English Leaders in the Liberal Party of Canada," *CJPS* 2 (March 1969), 118–22.

Report of the Proceedings of the National Liberal Convention, 1948. Ottawa: National Liberal Federation of Canada, n.d.

Report of the Proceedings of the National Liberal Convention, 1958. Ottawa: National Liberal Federation of Canada, n.d.

Santos, C.R. "Some Collective Characteristics of the Delegates to the 1968 Liberal Party Leadership Convention," *CJPS* 3 (June 1970), 299–308.

Ward, Norman. "The Liberals in Convention: Revised and Unrepentant," *Queen's Quarterly* 65 (Spring 1958), 1–11.

Wearing, Joseph. "The Liberal Choice," *JCS* 3 (May 1968), 3–20.

VI. LEADERSHIP SELECTION IN THE CCF-NDP

Archer, Keith. "Leadership Selection in the New Democratic Party," *Canadian Political Parties: Leaders, Candidates and Organization.* Vol. 13 of the research studies for the Royal Commission on Electoral Reform and Party Financing. Edited by Herman Bakvis. Toronto: Dundurn Press, 1991, 3–56.

Hayward, Suzanne, and Alan Whitehorn. "Leadership Selection: Which Method?" Research paper presented to the Douglas Coldwell Foundation, April 1991.

Knowles, Stanley. *The New Party.* Toronto: McClelland and Stewart, 1961.

McHenry, Dean E. *The Third Force in Canada: The Cooperative Commonwealth Federation 1932–1948.* Berkeley: University of California Press, 1950.

Thomlinson, Neil. "Intra-party Caucuses and NDP Leadership Selection in 1989." MA thesis, Department of Political Studies, University of Saskatchewan, 1992.

Whitehorn, Alan. *Canadian Socialism: Essays on the CCF-NDP.* Toronto: Oxford University Press, 1992.

–, and Keith Archer. "Party Activists and Political Leadership: A Case Study of the NDP," *Leaders and Leadership in Canadian Politics.* Edited by Maureen Mancuso, Richard G. Price, and Ronald Wagenberg. Toronto: Oxford Press, 1994, 28–52.

Young, Walter D. *The Anatomy of a Party: The National CCF 1932–61.* Toronto: University of Toronto Press, 1969.

VII. POLITICS AND THE MEDIA IN CANADA

Bell, David V.J., and Fredrick J. Fletcher, eds. *Reaching the Voter.* Vol. 20 of the research studies for the Royal Commission on Electoral Reform and Party Financing. Toronto: Dundurn Press, 1991.

Black, E.R. *Politics and the News: The Political Functions of the Mass Media.* Toronto: Butterworths, 1982.

Fletcher, Frederick J., ed. *Media and Voters in Canadian Election Campaigns: Media, Elections and Democracy; Constituency Campaigning in Canada; Election Broadcasting in Canada;* and *Reporting the Campaign: Election Coverage in Canada.* Vols. 18, 19, 21, and 22, of the research studies for the Royal Commission on Electoral Reform and Party Financing. Toronto: Dundurn Press, 1991.

–, and Robert J.Drummond. "The Mass Media and the Selection of National Party Leaders: Some Explorations," *Party Democracy in Canada: The Politics of National Party Conventions.* Edited by George Perlin. Scarborough: Prentice-Hall Canada, 1988, 97–123.

Hackett, Robert A., and Lynne Hissey. "Who Sets the Agenda? Perspectives on Media and Party Politics in Canada," *Party Politics in Canada,* 6th ed. Edited by Hugh G. Thorburn. Scarborough: Prentice-Hall Canada, 1991, 42–52.

Nadeau, Richard, Edouard Cloutier, and J.-H. Guay. "New Evidence about the Existence of a Bandwagon Effect in the Opinion Formation Process," *International Political Science Review* 14 (April 1993), 203–13.

Siegal, Arthur. *Politics and the Media in Canada.* Toronto: McGraw-Hill Ryerson, 1983.

Taras, David. "Prime Ministers and the Media," *Prime Ministers and Premiers: Political Leadership and Public Policy in Canada.* Edited by Leslie A. Pal and David Taras. Scarborough: Prentice- Hall Canada, 1988, 36–49.

Wilson, R. Jeremy. "Horserace Journalism and Canadian Election Campaigns," *Canadian Political Party Systems: A Reader.* Edited by R.K. Carty. Toronto: Broadview Press, 1992, 490–507.

VIII. SOCIAL CHOICE, COALITION, AND NETWORK THEORIES

Arterton, F. Christopher. "Strategies and Tactics of Candidate Organizations," *Political Science Quarterly* 92 (Winter 1977–78), 663–72.

Austen-Smith, David, and Jeffrey Banks. "Elections, Coalitions and Legislative Outcomes," *APSR* 82 (June 1988), 405–22.

Axelrod, Robert. *Conflict of Interest: A Theory of Divergent Goals with Applications to Politics.* Chicago: Markham Publishing, 1970.

Boissevain, Jeremy. *Friends of Friends: Networks, Manipulators and Coalitions.* New York: St Martin's Press, 1974.

Brams, Steven J., and Michael K. O'Leary. "An Axiomatic Model of Voting Bodies," *APSR* 64 (June 1970), 449–70.

Burt, Ronald S. "Models of Network Structure," *Annual Review of Sociology* 6 (1980), 79–141.

Butterworth, Robert Lyle. "A Research Note on the Size of Winning Coalitions." A Comment by William Riker and a Reply by Butterworth, *APSR* 65 (September 1971), 741–8.

Downs, Anthony. *An Economic Theory of Democracy.* New York: Harper and Row, 1957.

Eldersveld, Samuel J. *Political Parties: A Behavioral Analysis.* Chicago: Rand McNally, 1964.

Farquharson, Robin. *Theory of Voting.* New Haven: Yale University Press, 1969.

Grofman, Bernard and Arendt Lijphart, eds. *Electoral Laws and Their Political Consequences.* New York: Agathon Press, 1986.

Laver, Michael, and Norman Schofield. *Multiparty Government: The Politics of Coalitions in Europe.* New York: Oxford University Press, 1991.

Lemieux, Vincent. *Les Cheminements de l'influence: Systèmes, stratégies et structures du politique.* Québec: Les Presses de l'Université Laval, 1979.

– *Systèmes partisans et partis politiqués.* Québec: Les Presses de l'Université du Québec, 1985.

Levesque, Terrence J. "On the Outcome of the 1983 Conservative Leadership Convention: How They Shot Themselves in the Other Foot," *CJPS* 16 (December 1983), 779–84.

McGregor, Eugene B. "Rationality and Uncertainty at National Nominating Conventions," *JP* 35 (May 1973), 459–78.

Perlin, George C. "Did the Best Candidate Win? A Comment on Levesque's Analysis," *CJPS* 16 (December 1983), 791–4.

Rae, Douglas. *The Political Consequences of Electoral Laws.* New Haven: Yale University Press, 1971.

Riker, William. *The Theory of Politial Coalitions.* New Haven: Yale University Press, 1962.

Schlesinger, Joseph. "The Primary Goal of Political Parties," *APSR* 69 (September 1975), 840–9.

Shepsle, Kenneth A. "On the Size of Winning Coalitions," a Comment by Butterworth and a Reply by Shepsle, *APSR* 68 (June 1974), 505–24.

– "Institutional Arrangements and Equilibrium in Multidimensional Voting Models," *AJPS* 33 (February 1979), 27–60.

– "The Positive Theory of Legislative Institutions: An Enrichment of Social Choice and Spatial Models," *Public Choice* (50:1986), 135–78.

de Swaan, Abram. *Coalition Theories and Cabinet Formations.* Amsterdam: Elsevier Scientific Publishing, 1973.

Woolstencroft, Peter. "Social Choice Theory and the Reconstruction of Elections: A Comment on Levesque's Analysis," *CJPS* 16 (December 1983), 785–9.

IX. UNIVERSAL MEMBERSHIP VOTING IN CANADA

Adamson, Agar, Bruce Beaton, and Ian Stewart. "Pressing the Right Buttons: The Nova Scotia Liberals and Tele-Democracy." Paper presented to the annual meeting of the CPSA, Ottawa, 1993.

Blake, Donald E., and Kenneth R. Carty. "Televoting for the Leader of the British Columbia Liberal Party: The Leadership Contest of 1993." Paper presented to the annual meeting of the CPSA, Calgary, June 1994.

Cross, Bill. "Direct Election of Party Leaders: Provincial Experiences and Lessons Learned." Paper presented to the annual meeting of the CPSA, Calgary, June 1994.

Latouche, Daniel. "Universal Democracy and Effective Leadership: Lessons from the Parti Québécois Experience," *Leaders and Parties in Canadian Politics: Experiences of the Provinces*. Edited by R. Kenneth Carty, Lynda Erickson, and Donald E. Blake. Toronto: Harcourt Brace Jovanovich, 1992, 174–202.

MacIvor, Heather. "Explaining the Changes in Canadian Party Leadership Selection." Paper presented to the annual meeting of the CPSA, Calgary, June 1994.

– "Leadership Selection in Canadian Provincial Parties; Is Constitutional Government Being Perverted into Democracy?" Paper presented to the Party Politics in the Year 2000 Conference, Manchester, England, January 1995.

Malcolmson, Patrick. "Two Cheers for the Leadership Convention," *Policy Options* 10 (December 1992), 24–5.

Preyra, Leonard. "Tele-conventions and Party Democracy: The 1992 Nova Scotia Liberal Leadership Convention," *Canadian Parliamentary Review* 16 (Winter 1993–94), 2–11.

Stewart, David K. "Grassroots Democracy and Federal Party Membership: The 1992 Alberta Progressive Conservative Leadership Selection." Paper presented to the annual meeting of the Atlantic Provices Political Science Association, Antigonish, October 1993.

– "Electing the Premier: An Examination of the 1992 Alberta Progressive Conservative Leadership Election." Paper presented to the annual meeting of the CPSA, Calgary, June 1994.

Thériault, Yvon. "New System for Choosing the Party Leader," *Canadian Parliamentary Review* 8 (Winter 1985–86), 27–8.

Woolstencroft, Peter. " 'Tories Kick Machine to Bits': Leadership Selection and the Ontario Progressive Conservative Party." *Leaders and Parties in Canadian Politics: Experiences of the Provinces*. Edited by R. Kenneth Carty, Lynda Erickson, and Donald E. Blake. Toronto: Harcourt Brace Jovanovich, 1992, 203–25.

X. PARTY CONSTITUTIONS

Constitution of the New Democratic Party, as amended in 1991.

Constitution of the Progressive Conservative Association of Canada, as amended in 1991.

Liberal Party of Canada, *Constitution,* as amended in 1992.

Reform Party of Canada Constitution, as amended in 1992.

Index